Visual C++ User's Guide

Microsoft® Visual C++™

Development System for Windows® 95 and Windows NT™
Version 4

Microsoft Corporation

PUBLISHED BY
Microsoft Press
A Division of Microsoft Corporation
One Microsoft Way
Redmond, Washington 98052-6399

Library of Congress Cataloging-in-Publication Data
Microsoft Visual C++ programmer's references / Microsoft Corporation.
   -- 2nd ed.
       p.   cm.
   Includes index.
   v. 1. Microsoft Visual C++ user's guide -- v. 2. Programming with
MFC -- v. 3. Microsoft foundation class library reference, part 1 --
v. 4. Microsoft foundation class library reference, part 2 -- v.
5. Microsoft Visual C++ run-time library reference -- v.
6. Microsoft Visual C/C++ language reference.
   ISBN 1-55615-915-3 (v. 1). -- ISBN 1-55615-921-8 (v. 2). -- ISBN
1-55615-922-6 (v. 3). -- ISBN 1-55615-923-4 (v. 4). -- ISBN
1-55615-924-2 (v. 5). -- ISBN 1-55615-925-0 (v. 6)
   1. C++ (Computer program language) 2. Microsoft Visual C++.
I. Microsoft Corporation.
QA76.73.C153M53   1995
005.13'3--dc20   95-35604
                                                              CIP

Printed and bound in the United States of America.

   3 4 5 6 7 8 9 QMQM   0 9 8 7 6

Distributed to the book trade in Canada by Macmillan of Canada, a division of
Canada Publishing Corporation.

A CIP catalogue record for this book is available from the British Library.

Microsoft Press books are available through booksellers and distributors worldwide. For further
information about international editions, contact your local Microsoft Corporation office. Or
contact Microsoft Press International directly at fax (206) 936-7329.

America Online is a registered trademark of America Online, Inc. Macintosh is a registered trademark of
Apple Computer, Inc. dBASE, dBASE II, dBASE III, dBASE IV, and Paradox are registered trademarks
of Borland International, Inc. Btrieve is a registered trademark of Btrieve Technologies, Inc. CompuServe is
a registered trademark of CompuServe, Inc. GEnie is a trademark of General Electric Corporation. Intel is a
registered trademark of Intel Corporation. FoxPro, Microsoft, Microsoft Press, MS, MS-DOS, Visual Basic,
Win32, Win32s, Windows, and XENIX are registered trademarks and Visual C++, Visual FoxPro, and
Windows NT are trademarks of Microsoft Corporation in the U.S. and/or other countries. MIPS is a regis-
tered trademark of MIPS Computer Systems, Inc. Motorola is a registered trademark of Motorola, Inc.
ORACLE is a registered trademark of Oracle Corporation. Prodigy is a trademark of Prodigy Services
Company. Unicode is a trademark of Unicode, Inc.

Acquisitions Editor: Eric Stroo
Project Editor: Brenda L. Matteson

Contents

Contents

Chapter 3   Using the Text Editor   75

Contents

Chapter 6   Using the Dialog Editor   149

Part 2   Customizing Visual C++

Part 3   Command-Line Tools

Chapter 26   LINK Reference   569

Chapter 28   LIB Reference   607

Chapter 29   BSCMAKE Reference   615

Part 4   Appendices

Appendix A   Decorated Names   653

Figures and Tables

List of Figures

List of Tables

Contents

Introduction

The Microsoft Visual C++™ version 4.0 Development System for Windows® 95 and Windows NT™ is an integrated development environment for C and C++ applications, with support for multiplatform and cross-platform development. It includes a C++ application framework, the Microsoft Foundation Class Library version 4.0, which facilitates the development of applications for Windows as well as the porting of applications to multiple platforms. You can easily develop an application for Windows on one platform using Visual C++ and Microsoft Foundation Class Library (MFC), and then use the same code to build applications for other platforms.

Microsoft Developer Studio

Microsoft Developer Studio is the development environment in which the elements of Visual C++ run. It consists of an integrated set of tools that all run under Windows 95 or Windows NT. Developer Studio gives you the tools to complete, test, and refine your application all in one place. It includes a text editor, resource editors, project build facilities, an optimizing compiler, an incremental linker, a source code browse window, an integrated debugger, and Books Online. You can control the operation of all the tools from a single application. Because these tools run under Windows, they use a variety of familiar methods in their operation. For example, you can select a variable name in an editor window while debugging and drag that name into the Watch window. The debugger then evaluates the variable and displays the result in the Watch window. Or you can select and drop a control from the toolbar in the dialog box editor onto a dialog box under creation. You can then size and position the control as required for your application. Developer Studio also includes toolbars so you can quickly invoke commands by clicking a button. To help you choose the correct button, each one displays a descriptive label if the mouse pointer rests on it. If the default toolbars are not to your liking, you can customize them or create your own toolbars with the toolbar buttons of your choice.

Powerful Wizards

Visual C++ provides some powerful tools that work in conjunction with the MFC application framework:

- AppWizard. AppWizard generates a complete suite of source files and resource files based on classes from the MFC library. By selecting options in AppWizard, you can customize the starter files that AppWizard generates. Once you have completed your selections in AppWizard, Visual C++ builds a functional skeleton application for Windows from those starter files, without any further work on your part.

- OLE ControlWizard. ControlWizard creates a set of starter files for an OLE control. This set includes all the files necessary to build an OLE control, including source and header files, resource files, a module-definition file, a project file, an object description language file, and so on. These starter files are compatible with ClassWizard. You can then use ClassWizard to define your control's events, properties, and methods, some of which have been preimplemented in the MFC library.

- ClassWizard. ClassWizard automates the creation and editing of classes, and creates additional classes based on MFC. It creates the source code for new classes and creates member functions and message maps in those classes, as well as making it easy to bind Windows messages to code. It also maps dialog box data to member variables and validates that data.

- Custom AppWizard. With Custom AppWizard you can create your own project type and add it to the list of types available when you create projects. It creates the starter source files for the new AppWizard type, and allows you to modify or add dialog boxes to your AppWizard. Custom AppWizards are useful for creating generic application project types that can repetitively generate common functionality—application types that can be used over and over again.

When you build an application for Windows with Visual C++, you run AppWizard, a custom AppWizard that you have created, or OLE ControlWizard to create the skeleton of your application. You then run ClassWizard to flesh out the application's classes, message handling and data handling, or a control's events, properties, and methods. Finally, in your classes, you add the functionality required for your application.

Reusable Components

Visual C++ includes Component Gallery. Component Gallery contains a number of reusable components that you can insert into your projects. Some of the components take the form of Wizards, which request information about your project and provide you with choices about the functionality to insert. In additon, you can add your own components or components from other vendors to Component Gallery. Your components can take the form of reusable C++ classes with any associated resources, or your own OLE controls. Components created by vendors can range from reusable code segments to OLE controls to entire tools, such as a code analysis tool.

Developer Studio Projects

Microsoft Developer Studio organizes development in project workspaces. A project workspace contains one or more projects. Each project consists of a set of source files required for an application and one or more configurations for that project. A configuration specifies such things as the platform for which the application is intended, and the tools and settings to use when building. Within a project workspace, one project can be a subproject of another project. This organization creates a dependency relationship used by the build system to automatically keep both the project and the subproject up to date when building the output files. The inclusion of multiple projects with subprojects in a workspace allows you to group, build, and maintain dependencies among related applications. By using multiple configurations, you can extend the scope of a single project but still maintain a consistent source-code base from which to work.

With the Project Settings dialog box, you can quickly set options for any configuration in a project, any file in a configuration, or all the files in a project. If you have file types in your project that the build system does not process by default, you can specify custom commands to process those files.

Developer Studio includes a Project Workspace window, which displays various aspects of the projects. In FileView, you can examine relationships among the files contained in the project, and take the appropriate actions on the files. In ResourceView, you can examine the resources in a project, and open them in the appropriate editors. With Visual C++ installed, you can examine classes and their members in ClassView, and quickly display a class hierarchy, add a member, or open the file containing the class.

Once you have specified the projects in your workspace, the configurations that your project is to build, and the tool settings for those configurations, you can build the project with the commands on the Build menu. If you are creating an application for a platform other than the one on which you are running Visual C++, the development environment can automatically transfer the application to the remote machine after it is built.

Build Error Correction

If your build has errors, Developer Studio can help you fix them more quickly. The Output window displays a list of errors generated during a build. If you press the F4 key, Developer Studio displays an editor window with the source file and marks the line of code associated with the first error in the Output window so you can immediately correct the code. With menu commands and keyboard shortcuts, you can then move quickly to the next or previous error.

Integrated Debugger

After you have corrected all the build errors, you can use the integrated debugger to correct logic errors. The debugger allows you to monitor your program as it runs and to stop it at locations or situations of your choosing. You can set a breakpoint on a particular line of code, for instance, and have your application execute until it reaches that line. You can have your application suspend execution when it receives a specified Windows message or when a specific exception occurs. If you are interested in the values assigned to a variable, you can have the debugger break whenever your application changes the variable's value.

With the integrated debugger, you can debug both client and server applications that use OLE. The debugger can execute a client OLE application line by line, and when the client calls the server OLE application, another instance of Developer Studio starts, with its debugger executing the server application. This method allows you to determine if both the client and server sides of your OLE application are functioning properly.

Developer Studio can also start its integrated debugger for any program that fails while it is running, whether the program has debug information or not, and whether Developer Studio was running beforehand or not. The debugger starts up while the program is still alive, and this "Just-in-Time" debugging allows you to analyze the living program rather than conduct a postmortem examination after it dies. With Just-in-Time debugging, it is possible to find and fix the problem in the program and let it continue running.

The debugger also supports multiplatform and cross-platform development by allowing you to debug an application running on a remote machine.

Source Code Browse Window

As you are developing and debugging your application, you need to see the classes and other symbols that you are using in a variety of contexts. When you build your application, Developer Studio can create a browse information file with information about the symbols in your program. The browse window displays this information and allows you to move readily among instances of the symbols in your source code. You can easily view all the symbols contained in a given file, display the definition of any symbol in the file and all its references in your project, and then open the file containing a particular reference by double-clicking the entry in the window. In the browse window, you can view calling relationships among functions. The ease with which you can examine the relationships among symbols and move among the files containing them facilitates the maintenance, revision, and debugging of your code.

Visual C++ also parses source files after you create them and displays the information in ClassView. You can immediately open a file at a definition of a member function or at a reference to a data member. After you build your project, you can view graphs of inheritance relationships among classes.

User Preferences

With Microsoft Developer Studio you can customize its operation to suit your preferences. You can select fonts, specify colors for particular types of text, and zoom or shrink the text in a window. For example, in text editor windows, you can display language elements, such as comments or keywords, in the color of your choice. When you establish a layout for the windows associated with a particular project workspace, Developer Studio retains that layout of open files and window positions the next time you start the project. When you are debugging an application, you can choose which windows and toolbars to display, and Developer Studio retains your selections for all subsequent debugging sessions.

If you have some preferences for shortcut keys other than the defaults, you can change any of the shortcut keys to your liking, add shortcut keys, set multiple shortcut keys for a command, and specify the windows in which any shortcut is active. You can use the Keyboard command on the Help menu to display a list of the current keyboard shortcuts and print all or part of the list. Developer Studio also provides keyboard emulations for BRIEF® and Epsilon™ text editors. In a text editor window, you can record keystrokes and then play them back to recreate that sequence of commands.

Extensive Information

Developer Studio provides several methods to learn about the development environment or the supporting software. *Tutorials* contains a series of tutorials to familiarize you with Developer Studio, with the methods and processes you need to use within Developer Studio, and with the development of C++ applications using Visual C++ and the Microsoft Foundation Class Library. From your source code in an editor window, you can readily get information about a class from the Microsoft Foundation Class Library, a function name from the C Run-Time Library, or a language element. If you select a name in an editor window, and press F1 or CTRL+F1, Developer Studio displays reference information for that name.

InfoView in the Project Workspace window displays the table of contents for Books Online. Books Online contains the entire Visual C++ documentation set as well as reference information from a number of software development kits (SDKs). New Visual C++ Features refers you to new topics in Books Online, and Key Visual C++ Topics refers you to topics that group information by subject. You can browse through the table of contents and select topics to view. From any topic, you can search through all the text of Books Online for the occurrence of a selected word or combination of words with the Search command on the Help menu. If you need information about an open dialog box, you can choose the Help button to view descriptions of its controls, and methods to access further information, if necessary.

Visual C++ User's Guide

In the *Visual C++ User's Guide*, you will find procedures that show you how to undertake various development tasks with Microsoft Developer Studio. *Visual C++ User's Guide* also includes reference information on underlying command-line tools.

Development Environment

CHAPTER 1

Creating Applications Using AppWizard

AppWizard is the tool you use to create a Windows-based application that is based on the Microsoft Foundation Class Library (MFC). You can use AppWizard to quickly create an executable file (.EXE) or a dynamic-link library (DLL).

AppWizard's interface is simple and easy to understand but also powerful and flexible enough to quickly generate Windows-based applications. Using AppWizard, you can generate applications with the following features:

- Single-document, multiple-document, or dialog-based interfaces

- OLE support and database (ODBC and DAO) support

- Docking toolbars, a status bar, support for context-sensitive help, and a three-dimensional interface

- Immediate built-in functionality such as the Open, Save As, and Print commands on the File menu

- Control over window frame styles

When you have finished defining application and project options, AppWizard generates the starter files necessary to build a Windows-based application. These starter files include source files, header files, resource files, a project file, and so on.

The Visual C++ source files contain skeletal versions of the classes that make up your application. This AppWizard-generated code is based on MFC to provide compatibility with ClassWizard and to simplify your development work. When you build AppWizard-generated code, you get a working, skeleton application with a wealth of built-in functionality.

See Also   Starting an AppWizard Project, Creating an MFC AppWizard EXE Project, Choosing Options for Dialog-Based Applications, Choosing Database Options, Choosing OLE Options, Choosing SDI and MDI Application and Project Options, Creating an MFC AppWizard DLL Project, Understanding AppWizard-Created Files, Creating a Custom AppWizard

Starting an AppWizard Project

You start AppWizard from either the New Project Workspace dialog box or the Insert Project dialog box. These two dialog boxes begin a series of dialog boxes in which you choose options to create your project. You will choose options that determine the basic architecture of your application, such as EXE or DLL, the kind of support it provides, such as OLE Automation or Windows Sockets, the appearance and manipulation of the user interface, such as 3D controls and docking toolbars, and so on. For more information on projects, see Chapter 2, "Working With Projects." For more information on the Insert Project dialog box, see "Inserting and Deleting Projects" on page 52.

Once started, AppWizard displays a series of steps showing options for the features of your application. The series is a forking path. Depending on your application's architecture, some steps may not be displayed. You select options by cycling through the steps, forwards or backwards. You can change the options at any time before you create an AppWizard application.

▶ **To create a new project and application**

1 Start Visual C++.

2 From the File menu, choose New.

 The New dialog box appears.

3 In the New box, select Project Workspace.

4 Choose OK.

 The New Project Workspace dialog box appears.

5 In the Name text box, type a name.

6 From the Type list, select MFC AppWizard (exe) or MFC AppWizard (dll) to create a project based on the MFC library.

 The Type list allows selection of various project types. Of the displayed project types, AppWizard helps you create an MFC AppWizard (exe) Project and an MFC AppWizard (dll) Project. OLE ControlWizard helps you create an OLE control, and Custom AppWizard helps you create a custom AppWizard.

 If you select one of the remaining project types, you can build a project that is not based on the MFC library. You must, however, use the Insert Files Into Project dialog box to specify the files you want added to a project. For more information on the Insert Files Into Project dialog box, see "Adding and Removing Files from Projects" on page 53 in Chapter 2. If you choose to create a non-MFC project, you will have to either write or have access to the considerable amount of code that AppWizard and MFC would otherwise provide.

7 From the Platforms list box, select any of the available target platforms.

   Note   Win32® is the default platform. To select other platforms, the associated cross-development edition of Visual C++ version 4 must be installed.

8 In the Location text box, type a path to the new workspace. A directory will be created if you specify one that does not exist.

   $-$or$-$

   Use the Browse button to select a drive and a directory.

9 Choose Create.

   Microsoft Developer Studio creates a workspace and/or inserts a project into a workspace. With the workspace structure created, AppWizard displays either the AppWizard .EXE file options or the AppWizard DLL options, depending on which project type you choose. For more information on projects and workspaces, see Chapter 2, "Working With Projects." For more information on the MFC AppWizard .EXE file options, see "Creating an MFC AppWizard EXE Project" below. For more information on the MFC DLL options, see "Creating an MFC AppWizard DLL Project" on page 17.

See Also   Creating an MFC AppWizard EXE Project, Choosing Options for Dialog-Based Applications, Choosing Database Options, Choosing OLE Options, Choosing SDI and MDI Application and Project Options, Creating an MFC AppWizard DLL Project, Creating an MFC Form-Based Application With AppWizard, Understanding AppWizard-Created Files, Creating a Custom AppWizard

Creating an MFC AppWizard EXE Project

If you choose MFC AppWizard (exe) from the Type list in the New Project Workspace dialog box or the Insert Project dialog box, AppWizard creates a project that will generate an executable (.EXE) file. For more information on projects, see Chapter 2, "Working With Projects." For more information on the Insert Project dialog box, see "Inserting and Deleting Projects" on page 52 of Chapter 2.

Once you choose Create from either dialog box, Microsoft Developer Studio creates a workspace and/or inserts a project into a workspace. AppWizard then displays the available architecture options as shown in Figure 1.1.

Figure 1.1 AppWizard's Architecture Options

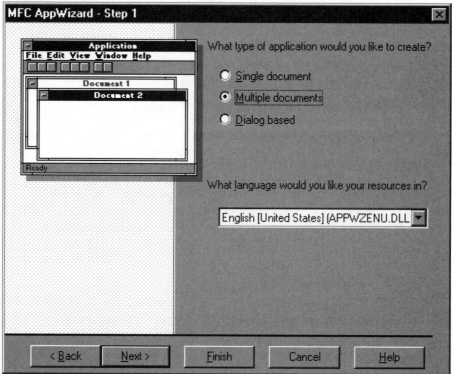

▶ **To select an architecture type and resource language**

1 From MFC AppWizard - Step 1 of 1, select one of the three architecture types:

- *Single document* A single document interface (SDI) architecture allows a user to work with just one document at a time. Windows Notepad is an example of an SDI application.

- *Multiple documents* A multiple document interface (MDI) architecture allows a user to open multiple documents, each with its own window. Windows File Manager is an example of an MDI application.

- *Dialog based* A dialog-based architecture displays a simple dialog box for user input. MFC Trace Options is an example of a dialog-based application.

As you make AppWizard feature selections, the left side of AppWizard's dialog box displays a representation of the selected features. For example, selecting multiple document architecture displays two documents in the "application's" window on the left side of the AppWizard dialog box.

2 Select a language for the resource text.

Note English is the default language for resource text. To select other languages, the language DLL must already be installed on your system. The file-naming convention is

LANGUAGE.DLL, where *LANGUAGE* is of the form APPWZ*.DLL and * is a three-letter language specifier such as "DEU" or "JPN".

3 Choose Next to display MFC AppWizard - Step 2 of 6.

If your application has a single or multiple document interface, the AppWizard database options for single and multiple document interfaces are displayed. If your application has a dialog-based document interface, the AppWizard options for dialog-based interfaces are displayed.

See Also   Creating Applications Using AppWizard, Starting an AppWizard Project, Choosing Options for Dialog-Based Applications, Choosing Database Options, Choosing OLE Options, Choosing SDI and MDI Application and Project Options, Creating an MFC AppWizard DLL Project, Creating an MFC Form-Based Application With AppWizard, Understanding AppWizard-Created Files, Creating a Custom AppWizard

Choosing Options for Dialog-Based Applications

After choosing to create a dialog-based application from MFC AppWizard - Step 1, AppWizard provides three additional steps to help you develop your dialog-based application. The following three procedures describe the features that AppWizard offers.

▶ **To select application options**

1 From MFC AppWizard - Step 2 of 4, you can choose from the basic features that are described below:

• *About box*   Select this option to add an About box to your application's Control-menu box. The About box lists your application's version number and copyright date. You can edit the generated About box so that it also contains brief product- and author-specific information.

• *Context-sensitive help*   Select this option to add a Help button to the dialog box that your project generates. A starter rich-text (.RTF) file, a help project (.HPJ) file, and a batch file are provided to help you write your application's help system. These files are in the HLP directory. For convenience, the .RTF and .HPJ files take the base name of your project. *Project*.RTF contains one or more topics that are hooked to your dialog box's Help button. You can use any rich-text format word processor, such as Microsoft Word for Windows, to add information to this file. The .HPJ file controls compiling *project*.RTF into a WinHelp help file. The batch file, MAKEHELP.BAT, compiles *project*.RTF into a help file. Type MAKEHELP.BAT from the command line to create a help file from *project*.RTF. In order for your help file to respond to your dialog-based application's Help button, both the help file and the application must use the same base filename and must reside in the same directory.

- **3D controls** This option adds a three-dimensional look to your application's user interface.

- **OLE automation** Select this option if you want to expose your application to OLE Automation clients. This option allows your application to be accessed by other Automation clients, such as Microsoft Excel.

- **OLE controls** Select this option if you want your application to use OLE controls. If you do not choose this option and, at a later time, want to insert OLE controls into your project, you must add a call to **AfxEnableControlContainer** in your application's **InitInstance** member function. For additional information about MFC OLE support, see Chapter 5, "Working With OLE," in *Programming with MFC*.

- **Windows sockets** This option allows you to write applications that communicate over TCP/IP networks.

- **Please enter a title for your dialog** This option allows you to override the default name that is added to your dialog box's title bar. The project name is used by default.

2 From MFC AppWizard - Step 2 of 4, choose Next.

MFC AppWizard - Step 3 of 4 is displayed. This step allows you to select the following application options.

- **Would you like to generate source file comments?** AppWizard generates and inserts comments in the source files that guide you in writing your program. Source-file comments indicate where you need to add your own code. A README.TXT file that describes each of the files is also produced. This option is recommended.

- **How would you like to use the MFC library?** The Microsoft Foundation classes can be linked from a static library or a shared DLL. Applications comprised of multiple modules benefit from using the shared DLL because they are more space efficient. By default, applications created from your AppWizard project are linked with the shared MFC DLL.

3 Choose Next.

MFC AppWizard - Step 4 of 4 is displayed. This step displays the classes that AppWizard will create for you. You can use the fields in this step to change the names of the classes and the names of the class's header (.H) and implementation (.CPP) files, as described in the next procedure.

▶ **To change class names and file names**

1 From MFC AppWizard - Step 4 of 4, select a class from the top pane, which is entitled "AppWizard creates the following classes for you."

The associated class name, base class, header file, and implementation file names are displayed in the boxes below the top pane.

2 Change the names as required.

3 Choose Finish.

The New Project Information dialog box is displayed.

▶ **To create your application**

The New Project Information dialog box displays the details of the options you have chosen from the previous AppWizard steps.

1 Choose OK when you are satisfied that the options are correct.

AppWizard will generate the new application's source files according to the options you have selected.

2 If you want to modify any of these options, choose Cancel to close the New Project Information dialog box.

Choosing Cancel lets you access the steps you have used previously to specify your project's options.

See Also   Creating Applications Using AppWizard, Starting an AppWizard Project, Creating an MFC AppWizard EXE Project, Understanding AppWizard-Created Files, Creating a Custom AppWizard

Choosing Database Options

If, in MFC AppWizard - Step 1, you choose to create a project with a user interface that uses either single or multiple documents, Step 2 allows you to choose whether and to what degree you want your project to support open database connectivity (ODBC) or Microsoft Data Access Objects (DAO).

▶ **To select a database support option**

• Select one of the database support options:

  • *None* This option excludes the libraries that support open database connectivity. If the application does not use a database, choosing this option builds a smaller application.

- *Header files only*   This option provides the minimal level of database support by including all the database header files and link libraries. With this option, AppWizard does not create any database-specific classes; you must do it yourself.

- *Database view without file support*   This option includes all the database header files and link libraries and creates a record view and recordset for you. With this option, the application has document support but no serialization support.

- *Database view with file support*   This option includes all the database header files and link libraries and creates a record view and recordset. With this option, the application has document support and also has serialization support.

For additional information about MFC database support, see Chapter 7, "Working With Databases," in *Programming with MFC*.

▶ **To define a data source**

- If your application includes a database view, you must define a data source. Choose the Data Source button.

The Database Options dialog box appears and enables you to select from the following options:

- *ODBC or DAO*   If you are working primarily with an external (ODBC) database file, select ODBC. If you are working primarily with a Microsoft Jet (MDBC) database file, select DAO. For more information on ODBC and DOA, see "Database Overview" in *Programming with MFC*.

- *Snapshot*   A snapshot is the result of a query and is a view into a database at one point in time. A snapshot is static in nature. All records found as a result of the query are cached. Using a snapshot, you will not see any changes that occur to the original records.

- *Dynaset*   A dynaset is the result of a query that provides an indexed view into the data of the queried database. A dynaset caches only a key into the original data and thus offers a performance gain over a snapshot. Because you have a key that points directly to each record that was found as a result of a query, you can tell if a record has changed or was removed. You will also have access to updated information in the queried records.

- *Table*   A table provides you with a means of directly manipulating the data in a base table in a database (DAO only).

- *Detect dirty columns* This option creates a data cache to detect whether data values or NULL status has changed. You may turn this option off for better performance, but you must explicitly call both **SetFieldDirty** and **SetFieldNull**.

- *Bind all columns* This option creates a recordset that has data members for all columns in the selected database.

Use one of the following two procedures to select an ODBC database or a DAO database.

▶ **To select an ODBC data source**

1 In the Database Options dialog box, select ODBC.

2 From the ODBC drop-down list, select a data source.

To be visible from the ODBC drop-down list, a data source must be registered with the ODBC Administrator, which is accessed from the Control Panel. For instructions on registering an ODBC data source, see the article "ODBC Administrator" in *Programming with MFC*.

3 Choose OK.

Some database drivers (SQL Server, for example) present a login dialog box at this point. Fill in the information required to gain access to the data source.

4 Choose OK.

The Select Database Tables dialog box appears.

5 Select the tables for which you want recordsets created.

6 Choose OK.

MFC AppWizard - Step 2 of 6 reappears.

7 Choose Next.

MFC AppWizard - Step 3 of 6 appears.

▶ **To select a DAO data source**

1 In the Database Options dialog box, select DAO.

2 Choose the Browse button — the button with the ellipsis just to the right of the DAO text box.

The Open dialog box appears.

3 Select a database file (.MDB format).

4 Choose OK.

The Database Options dialog box reappears.

5 Choose OK.

The Select Database Tables dialog box appears.

6 Select the tables for which you want recordsets created.

7 Choose OK.

MFC AppWizard - Step 2 of 6 reappears.

8 Choose Next.

MFC AppWizard - Step 3 of 6 appears.

See Also   Creating Applications Using AppWizard, Starting an AppWizard Project, Creating an MFC AppWizard EXE Project, Choosing SDI and MDI Application and Project Options, Creating an MFC AppWizard DLL Project, Creating an MFC Form-Based Application With AppWizard, Understanding AppWizard-Created Files, Creating a Custom AppWizard

Choosing OLE Options

If, in MFC AppWizard - Step 1, you choose to create a project with a user interface that uses either single or multiple documents, Step 3 allows you to choose whether and to what degree you want your project to support OLE.

▶ **To select OLE options**

AppWizard generates application support code for a variety of OLE application types. Selecting any of the OLE options enables the standard OLE resources and adds extra OLE commands to the application's menu bar.

1 Select from the following OLE options:

- *None*   By default, AppWizard does not create an application with OLE support.

- *Container*   This option enables your application to contain linked and embedded objects.

- *Mini-server*   This option allows only the creation of embedded objects.

- *Full-server*   This option enables your application to run in stand-alone mode and to support both linked and embedded items as well as to create objects to be contained in compound documents.

- *Both container and server*   This option enables your application to be both a container and a server.

- *Yes, please*   Select this option to use the OLE compound-file format to serialize your OLE container application's documents. Documents containing one or more OLE objects are saved to one file but access is allowed to the individual OLE objects' files. This option provides load on demand of, and incremental saves to, the individual OLE objects' native data.

- *No, thank you*   Select this option to not use the OLE compound-file format to serialize your OLE container application's documents. This option forces the loading of an entire file containing OLE objects into memory. Incremental saves to individual OLE objects are not available. If one OLE object is changed and subsequently saved, all OLE objects in the files are saved.

- *OLE automation*   Select this option if you want to expose your application to OLE Automation clients. This option allows your application to be accessed by other Automation clients, such as Microsoft Excel.

- *OLE controls*   Select this option if you want your application to use OLE controls. If you do not choose this option and, at a later time, want to insert OLE controls into your project, you must add a call to **AfxEnableControlContainer** in your application's **InitInstance** member function.

For additional information about MFC OLE support, see Chapter 5, "Working With OLE," in *Programming with MFC*.

2 Choose Next.

MFC AppWizard - Step 4 of 6 appears.

See Also   Creating Applications Using AppWizard, Starting an AppWizard Project, Creating an MFC AppWizard EXE Project, Choosing SDI and MDI Application and Project Options, Creating an MFC AppWizard DLL Project, Creating an MFC Form-Based Application With AppWizard, Understanding AppWizard-Created Files, Creating a Custom AppWizard

Choosing SDI and MDI Application and Project Options

If, in MFC AppWizard - Step 1, you choose to create a project with a user interface that uses either single or multiple documents, Step 4 allows you to choose various user-interface options. You can also select MAPI and Windows Sockets support.

▶ **To select application options**

1 Specify the basic features you want your application to have by selecting from the options described below.

- *Docking toolbar*   Select this option to add a toolbar to the application that your project generates. The toolbar contains buttons for creating a new document; opening and saving document files; cutting, copying, pasting, or printing text; displaying the About box; and entering SHIFT+F1 Help mode. Enabling this option also adds menu commands to display or hide the toolbar.

- **Initial status bar**   Select this option to add a status bar to the application that your project generates. The status bar contains automatic indicators for the keyboard's CAPS LOCK, NUM LOCK, and SCROLL LOCK keys and a message line that displays help strings for menu commands and toolbar buttons. Enabling this option also adds menu commands to display or hide the status bar.

- **Printing and print preview**   Select this option to add the code to handle print, print setup, and print preview commands by calling member functions in the **CView** class of the MFC library. It also adds commands for these functions to your application's File menu.

- **Context-sensitive help**   Select this option to add a Help button to the dialog box that your project generates. A starter rich-text (.RTF) file, a help project (.HPJ) file, and a batch file are provided to help you write your application's help system. These files are in the HLP directory. For convenience, the .RTF and .HPJ files take the base name of your project. *Project*.RTF contains one or more topics that are hooked to your dialog box's Help button. You can use any rich-text format word processor, such as Microsoft Word for Windows, to add information to this file. The .HPJ file controls compiling *project*.RTF into a WinHelp help file. The batch file, MAKEHELP.BAT, compiles *project*.RTF into a help file. Type MAKEHELP.BAT from the command line to create a help file from *project*.RTF. In order for your help file to respond to your dialog-based application's Help button, both the help file and the application must use the same base filename and must reside in the same directory.

- **3D controls**   This option adds a three-dimensional look to your application's user interface.

- **MAPI (Messaging API)**   This option allows you to write an application that creates, manipulates, transfers, and stores mail messages.

- **Windows sockets**   This option allows you to write an application that communicates over TCP/IP networks.

- **How many files would you like on your recent file list?**   This option sets the number of files to be remembered on the "most recently used" list.

2 If your application requires adjustment of other advanced options, choose the Advanced button.

The Advanced Options dialog box appears.

3 Select the Document Template Strings tab to modify the filenames and extensions that will identify your application:

- **File extension**   The file extension associated with a document created by your application. Typing a file extension allows the Windows 95 Explorer to print your application's documents, without launching your application, when they are dropped onto a printer icon.

- **File type ID**   This ID is used to label your document type in the system registry.

- *Language*   This selection controls the language in which strings are displayed in the edit boxes of the Localized Strings control group.

- *Main frame caption*   The name displayed in the title bar of your application's main frame window.

- *Doc type name*   The filename associated with the selected class. This option is available only if the selected class is derived from class **CDocument**.

- *Filter name*   The string that appears in the List Files Of Type list box in the Open and Save As dialog boxes. This field does nothing unless you type a file extension in the File Extension edit box.

- *File new name (OLE short name)*   The name that appears in the File New dialog box if there is more than one new document template. If your application is an OLE server, this name is used as *the short name of your OLE object.*

- *File type name (OLE long name)*   If your application is an OLE server, this name is used as the long name of your OLE object. It is also used as the file type name in the system registry.

4 Select the Window Styles tab and choose from the following list for the user-interface frame styles. If your project uses a single document interface, the MDI child frame styles are grayed out.

- *Use split window*   Enables your application's windows to use a split bar. The split bar will split the application's main views. In an MDI application, the MDI child frame's client window is a split window, and in an SDI application, the main frame's client window is a split window. For more information on split windows, see "Adding Splitter Windows" in *Tutorials*.

- *Thick frame*   This option specifies that the main frame window have a sizing border.

- *Minimize box*   This option specifies that the main frame window include a minimize box. This is the default option.

- *Maximize box*   This option specifies that the main frame window include a maximize box. This is the default option.

- *System menu*   This option specifies that the main frame window include a system menu. This is the default option.

- *Minimized*   This option specifies that the main frame window open as an icon.

- *Maximized*   This option specifies that the main frame window open to the full size of the display.

- *Thick frame*   This option specifies that the frames of all MDI child windows have a sizing border.

- *Minimize box*   This option specifies that MDI child windows include a minimize box. This is the default option.

- *Maximize box*   This option specifies that MDI child windows include a maximize box. This is the default option.

- *Minimized*   This option specifies that MDI child windows open as icons.

- *Maximized*   This option specifies that MDI child windows open maximized.

5 From the Advanced Options dialog box, choose Close.

6 Choose Next.

MFC AppWizard - Step 5 of 6 appears.

The AppWizard project options for source code are displayed.

▶ **To select project options**

1 You can select settings for these project options:

- *Would you like to generate source file comments?*   AppWizard generates and inserts comments in the source files that guide you in writing your program. Source-file comments indicate where you need to add your own code. Selecting this option is recommended.

  A README.TXT file that describes each AppWizard-generated file is also produced.

- *How would you like to use the MFC library?*   The Microsoft Foundation classes can be linked from a static library or a dynamic-link library. If your application mixes both MFC and non-MFC code, use MFC as a statically linked library. If your application is comprised of multiple modules that all use only the MFC library, it will use less disk and memory space by using the shared DLL.

2 Choose Next.

MFC AppWizard - Step 6 of 6 is displayed. This step displays the classes that AppWizard will create for you. You can edit the fields in this step to change the names of the classes and the names of the class's header (.H) and implementation (.CPP) files, as described in the next procedure.

▶ **To change class names and file names**

1 Select a class from the top pane, which is entitled "AppWizard creates the following classes for you."

  The associated class name, base name, header file, and implementation file names are displayed in the boxes below the top pane.

  If you choose your application's view class, the Base Class text box becomes a drop-down list from which you can specify a view type.

2 Change the names and select a view type as required.

3 Choose Finish.

  The New Project Information dialog box is displayed.

▶ To create your application

You can modify any of the options displayed in the New Project Information dialog box.

1 If you want to make modifications to any of the options, choose the Cancel button to close the New Project Information dialog box and return to the AppWizard steps.

2 Choose OK when you are satisfied that the options are correct.

AppWizard will generate the new application's source files according to the options you have selected.

See Also   Creating Applications Using AppWizard, Starting an AppWizard Project, Choosing Database Options, Choosing OLE Options, Creating an MFC AppWizard DLL Project, Creating an MFC Form-Based Application With AppWizard, Understanding AppWizard-Created Files, Creating a Custom AppWizard

Creating an MFC AppWizard DLL Project

If you choose MFC AppWizard (dll) from the Type list in the New Project Workspace dialog box or the Insert Project dialog box, AppWizard creates a project that will generate a dynamic-link library (DLL). For more information on projects, see Chapter 2, "Working With Projects." For more information on the Insert Project dialog box, see "Inserting and Deleting Projects" on page 52 in Chapter 2.

Once you choose Create from either dialog box, Microsoft Developer Studio creates a workspace and/or inserts a project into a workspace. AppWizard then displays the available DLL options.

▶ To select MFC DLL project options

1 You can select settings for these project options:

- *What type of DLL would you like to create?*   The two Regular DLLs can be loaded by any Win32 application.

  The MFC Extension DLL can be loaded only by an MFC application. Applications comprised of multiple modules benefit from using a DLL that uses a shared copy of MFC because they use less disk and memory space. Also, a system running multiple MFC applications runs more efficiently if the applications link dynamically to MFC.

- *What features would you like in your DLL?*   OLE automation exposes your DLL's class to OLE Automation clients. This option allows objects of this class to be accessed by Automation clients, such as Microsoft Visual Basic® and Microsoft Excel. With Windows Sockets support you can write applications that communicate over TCP/IP networks.

- ***Would you like to generate source file comments?*** AppWizard generates and inserts comments in the source files that guide you in writing your program. Source-file comments indicate where you need to add your own code. Selecting this option is recommended.

  A README.TXT file that describes each AppWizard-generated file is also produced.

▶ **To create your application**

1 Choose Finish.

  The New Project Information dialog box displays the project options you have selected.

2 If you want to modify any of the options displayed here, choose Cancel to close the New Project Information dialog box and return to the previous AppWizard steps.

3 Choose OK when you are satisfied that the options are correct.

  AppWizard will generate the new application's source files according to the options you have selected.

See Also Creating Applications Using AppWizard, Starting an AppWizard Project, Creating an MFC AppWizard EXE Project, Choosing Database Options, Choosing OLE Options, Choosing SDI and MDI Application and Project Options, Creating an MFC Form-Based Application With AppWizard, Understanding AppWizard-Created Files, Creating a Custom AppWizard

Creating an MFC Form-Based Application With AppWizard

With AppWizard you can create MFC form-based applications that give you access to data in existing databases.

▶ **To create an MFC form-based application**

1 Start Visual C++.

2 From the File menu, choose New.

  The New dialog box appears.

3 In the New box, select Project Workspace.

4 Choose OK.

  The New Project Workspace dialog box appears.

5 Type a name in the Name text box.

6 From the Type list, select MFC AppWizard (exe).

7 From the Platforms list box, select any of the available target platforms.

Note Win32® is the default platform. To select other platforms, the associated cross-development edition of Visual C++ version 4.0 must be installed.

8 Accept the default path to the new project workspace or type a new one in the Location text box. A directory will be created if you specify one that does not exist.

−or−

Use the Browse button to select a drive and a directory.

9 Choose Create.

MFC AppWizard - Step 1 is displayed.

10 Choose either Single Document or Multiple Documents.

11 Select a language for the resource text.

Note English is the default language for resource text. To select other languages, the language DLL must already be installed on your system. The file-naming convention is *LANGUAGE*.DLL, where *LANGUAGE* is of the form APPWZ*.DLL and * is a three-letter language specifier such as "DEU" or "JPN".

12 Choose the Next button.

MFC AppWizard - Step 2 of 6 appears.

13 Select either Database View Without File Support or Database View With File Support.

If you choose Database View Without File Support, AppWizard creates a record view and recordset for you. With this option, the application has document support but no serialization support. If you choose database view with files support, AppWizard creates a record view and recordset. With this option, the application has document support and also has serialization support.

14 Choose the Data Source button.

The Database Options dialog box appears and enables you to select from the following options:

- **ODBC or DAO**   If you are working primarily with an external (ODBC) database file, select ODBC. If you are working primarily with a Microsoft Jet (MDBC) database file, select DAO. For more information on ODBC and DOA, see Database Overview in *Programming with MFC*.

- **Snapshot**   A snapshot is the result of a query and is a view into a database at one point in time. A snapshot is static in nature. All records found as a result of the query are cached. Using a snapshot, you will not see any changes that occur to the original records.

- *Dynaset*   A dynaset is the result of a query that provides an indexed view into the data of the queried database. A dynaset caches only a key into the original data and thus offers a performance gain over a snapshot. Because you have a key that points directly to each record that was found as a result of a query, you can tell if a record has changed or was removed. You will also have access to updated information in the queried records.

- *Table*   A table provides you with a means of directly manipulating the records and data in a base table in a database (DAO only).

- *Detect dirty columns*   This option creates a data cache to detect whether data values or NULL status has changed. You may turn this option off for better performance, but you must explicitly call both **SetFieldDirty** and **SetFieldNull**.

- *Bind all columns*   This option creates a recordset that has data members for all columns in the selected database.

Use one of the following two procedures to select an ODBC database or a DAO database.

▶ **To select an ODBC data source**

1 In the Database Options dialog box, select ODBC.

2 From the ODBC drop-down list, select a data source.

   To be visible from the ODBC drop-down list, a data source must be registered with the ODBC Administrator, which is accessed from the Control Panel. For instructions on registering an ODBC data source, see the article "ODBC Administrator" in *Programming with MFC*.

3 Choose OK.

   Some database drivers (SQL Server, for example) present a login dialog box at this point. Fill in the information required to gain access to the data source.

4 Choose OK.

   The Select Database Tables dialog box appears.

5 Select the tables for which you want recordsets created.

6 Choose OK.

   MFC AppWizard - Step 2 of 6 reappears.

7 Choose Next to display the next AppWizard step.

   The AppWizard OLE options are displayed for your single or multiple document application.

▶ **To select a DAO data source**

1 In the Database Options dialog box, select DAO.

2 Choose the Browse button — the button with the ellipsis just to the right of the DAO text box.

3 Use the Open dialog box that appears to select a database file (.MDB format).

4 Choose OK.

The Database Options dialog box reappears.

5 Choose OK.

The Select Database Tables dialog box appears.

6 Select the tables for which you want recordsets created.

7 Choose OK.

MFC AppWizard Step - 2 of 6 reappears.

8 Choose Next to display the next AppWizard step.

If your application is for single or multiple documents (not dialog-based), the AppWizard OLE options are displayed.

See Also   Creating Applications Using AppWizard, Starting an AppWizard Project, Creating an MFC AppWizard EXE Project, Choosing Database Options, Choosing OLE Options, Choosing SDI and MDI Application and Project Options, Creating an MFC AppWizard DLL Project, Understanding AppWizard-Created Files, Creating a Custom AppWizard

Understanding AppWizard-Created Files

AppWizard always creates a basic list of files, regardless of which options you choose. AppWizard uses the name that you specify in the Name box to derive names for most of its files and classes.

You'll undoubtedly want to examine the source-ode files you create. If you choose to have AppWizard add comments to the files it creates for your project, AppWizard will also create a text file, README.TXT, in your new application directory. This file explains the contents and uses of the other new files created by AppWizard.

For additional information about the files that AppWizard creates, see the article "AppWizard: Files Created" in *Programming with MFC*.

See Also   Creating Applications Using AppWizard, Starting an AppWizard Project, Creating an MFC AppWizard EXE Project, Choosing Database Options, Choosing OLE Options, Choosing SDI and MDI Application and Project Options, Creating an MFC AppWizard DLL Project, Creating an MFC Form-Based Application With AppWizard, Creating a Custom AppWizard

Creating a Custom AppWizard

You can use AppWizard to create custom AppWizards that will generate applications with the specific features you need. For more information on how to create a custom AppWizard, see Chapter 24, "Creating Custom AppWizards."

See Also   Creating Applications Using AppWizard, Starting an AppWizard Project, Creating an MFC AppWizard EXE Project, Choosing Database Options, Choosing OLE Options, Choosing SDI and MDI Application and Project Options, Creating an MFC AppWizard DLL Project, Creating an MFC Form-Based Application With AppWizard, Understanding AppWizard-Created Files

CHAPTER 2

Working with Projects

The project workspace organizes your projects and their elements, and maintains your preferences for the display of information. The project workspace consists of a subdirectory and various files. The files describe the individual projects in the project workspace, and how to display them.

There are three basic scenarios for using project workspaces. Before you create your project workspace, you should determine which scenario for project workspace organization suits your needs best. For further information, see "Using Project Workspaces: Three Basic Scenarios" on page 26. You can modify the three scenarios in a number of ways to fit your specific requirements.

When you create or open a project workspace, Microsoft Developer Studio displays the elements of your Project Workspace in the project workspace window, as shown in Figure 2.1.

Figure 2.1 The Project Workspace Window

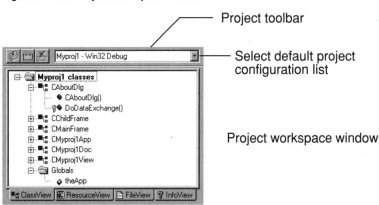

Project toolbar

Select default project configuration list

Project workspace window

Tabs to access panes

When you open a project workspace file, Developer Studio displays the Project Workspace window, along with other windows, in the last locations and states that you chose for them. You can dock or undock, size, move, or hide the Project Workspace window.

In the Project Workspace window, Developer Studio creates panes, which you access from the tabs at the bottom of the window. Certain panes contain a specific view of all the projects in your workspace. Each pane has at least one top-level folder, which contains the elements that make up that view of the project; expanding the folder displays the details of that view. In a project workspace containing Visual C++ projects, for instance, the Project Workspace window contains the following panes by default.

Pane Title	Description
FileView	Displays the projects that you have created. Expanding the top-level folders shows files within the project.
ResourceView	Displays the resource files included in your projects. Expanding the top-level folders shows the resource types.
ClassView	Displays the C++ classes defined in your projects. Expanding the top-level folders shows the classes; expanding a class shows its members.
InfoView	Displays the table of contents for Books Online. Expanding the top-level folders shows books and topics.

Each folder within a view can contain other folders or various kinds of items. The items may consist of subprojects, files, resources, classes, topics, and so on.

It is important to keep in mind that the organization of the items in a folder represents the relationships of the items in the project, not the physical location of items. A project folder, for instance, contains icons representing the files used to build the project. The icons show whether or not the files are used in the build process, as well as the relationship of source files to their dependent files, such as header files. Those files could reside in any directory on any drive accessible from your machine.

The default project configuration is shown in bold type in the panes. If you choose a build command, you build that default project configuration.

You can access information about elements of the project workspace from the views in the Project Workspace window. Selecting any item and pressing ALT+ENTER opens the property page for that item. Double-clicking any item in a pane displays that item in an appropriate way: source files in a text editor, dialog boxes in the dialog editor, information topics in the topic window, and so on.

Pop-up menus take action on selections in the Project Workspace window. When you make a selection, and then press the right mouse button with the mouse pointer over the selection, the pop-up menu appears. It contains commands appropriate for the selection.

See Also Working with Window Types, Customizing the Toolbar, Customizing the Keyboard, Setting Text Editor Options

Project Workspaces

In Microsoft Developer Studio, you organize your work in a project workspace. A project workspace consists of a location — the workspace directory — and some files in that directory, which describe the workspace and its contents. When you first create a project workspace, you create a directory for the project workspace and a project workspace file with the extension .MDP. The project workspace file is what you save when you have completed working in your new project workspace and what you open when you want to resume work in your project workspace.

The project workspace directory is the root directory for the project workspace, and all subsequent projects that you add to this project workspace are added in subdirectories under the project workspace directory. By default, Developer Studio selects the Projects subdirectory under the Developer Studio installation directory as the initial location for all your project workspace directories. You can, however, choose another location. If you do choose another location, Developer Studio retains that location as the initial location for subsequent project workspaces that you create. The project workspace directory contains the following files:

- The project workpace file (.MDP)

- The project workspace makefile (.MAK)

Usually all source files associated with the first top-level project are created in the project workspace directory. You can add source files to the project from any location, however, without copying or moving them to this subdirectory.

Elements of Project Workspaces

Project workspaces have the following elements:

Project
A set of zero or more source files, with one or more configurations. A project also specifies the type of application to build. Your project workspace can contain any number of projects. A project can contain subprojects.

Configuration
Settings for a project that specify a platform on which the output file is to run, and tool settings with which to build the output. You can add any number of configurations to a project. By default, when you create a new project, you create Debug and Release configurations.

Within a project workspace, projects can have the following relations:

Top-level project
A project that is not a dependency of any other project. Not a subproject of any other project. A project workspace has at least one top-level project.

Subproject
A project that has a dependency relationship with another project. The build system determines if it needs to build the subproject before it builds the containing project. Any project can be a subproject of any other project.

Files Associated with Project Workspaces

When you create a project workspace, Developer Studio creates two or more associated files. In the case of Visual C++ projects, for instance, it creates a project makefile (.MAK) and a project workspace file (.MDP) to store information.

The .MAK file stores the following kinds of information required to build the project:

- The names and locations of the source files that are used to build each project.
- The settings for the tools required to build each project, such as compiler and linker options.
- The tools and actions required to build the project.

The .MDP file stores the following kinds of information for your particular workspace:

- The look and organization of Microsoft Developer Studio for the project workspace (choice and locations of windows, for instance).
- Breakpoints that you have set.
- Other information related to your local setup, such as fonts and colors.

If you work in a group, you generally want to share the makefile with other members of your group, so that they can build the projects defined in the project workspace. To do this, see "Maintaining Makefiles Under Source-Code Control" on page 128 in Chapter 4 for more information. You probably should not share the project workspace file, because it contains information about your local organization and appearance.

Developer Studio may also generate a number of other transient files as you use it, depending on the project type and the settings that you choose. Developer Studio manages these files without any explicit intervention on your part.

Using Project Workspaces: Three Basic Scenarios

There are three basic scenarios for using project workspaces. These consist of the following cases:

- A top-level project only
- A top-level project with a single subproject
- An empty top-level project with multiple subprojects, which also may have subprojects

These are very basic, general organizations. You can modify or expand them in innumerable ways to serve your particular development needs.

Top-Level Project

This organization is suitable for the development of a single application without any dependencies on any other applications. Choose this organization if you want to develop, for instance, a single application generated by AppWizard, a single console application, or a static library. Figure 2.2 shows the relationships among the elements of a top-level project.

Figure 2.2   Top-Level Project

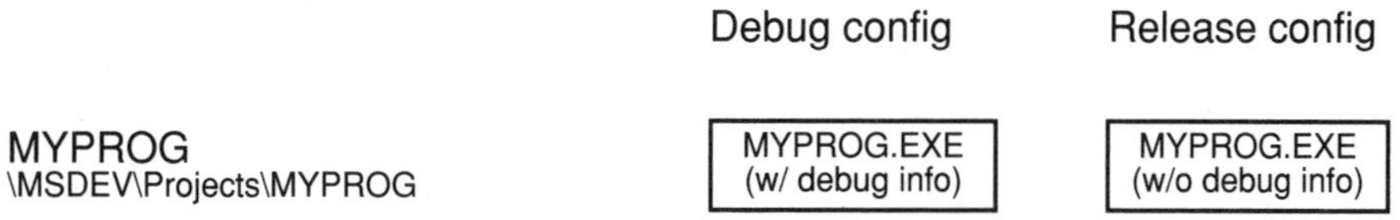

	Debug config	Release config
MYPROG \MSDEV\Projects\MYPROG	MYPROG.EXE (w/ debug info)	MYPROG.EXE (w/o debug info)

▶ **To create a top-level project**

1 From the File menu, choose New.

   The New dialog box appears.

2 From the New list, choose Project Workspace.

   The New Project Workspace dialog box appears.

3 Select the project type from the list of types.

4 In the Name text box, type a name for the project workspace.

   This name is also the name of the initial top-level project.

5 From the Platforms list, select any of the available platforms for which you want to create applications.

   Note   Win32 is the default platform. You must install the Microsoft Visual C++ Cross-Development Edition for Macintosh® before other platforms are available.

6 In the Location text box, type another directory name in which you want to create this project workspace subdirectory if you do not want to use the default directory, PROJECTS.

   If you revise this location, Developer Studio retains the new location as the new default for creating project workspaces.

7 Choose the Create button.

Now you can add files if necessary, modify the source code, add functions to classes or add message-handlers, change the settings for your application, and so on.

Note   If you chose an AppWizard, OLE ControlWizard, or Custom AppWizard type, the wizard created a set of starter files for your application. You can now modify those files to complete your application.

You build a configuration of your application by selecting a configuration to build, using the Default Configuration drop-down list on the Project toolbar, and then choosing the Build command from the Build menu.

Top-Level Project with a Single Subproject

An organization that has a top-level project with a single subproject is suitable for the development of an application that depends on another application. You could choose this organization if you want to develop, for instance, an executable generated by AppWizard that uses a dynamic-link library (DLL) also generated by AppWizard, or a console application that uses a static library that you create. Figure 2.3 shows the relationships among the elements of a top-level project with a single subproject.

Figure 2.3 Top-Level Project with a Single Subproject

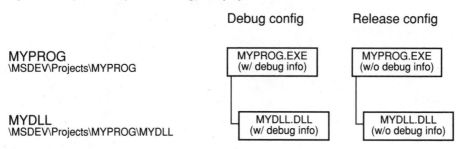

► **To create a top-level project with a subproject**

1 Create a top-level project.

2 From the Build menu, choose Subprojects.

The Subprojects dialog box appears.

3 Choose the New button.

The Insert Project dialog box appears, with the Subproject option selected, and the existing top-level project selected in the drop-down list. Retain these default choices.

4 In the Name text box, type a name for the subproject.

This name is appended to the existing project workspace directory to form the fully qualified path for the new subproject directory.

5 From the Type list, select a project type.

6 Select any of the available platforms for which to create initial Debug and Release configurations.

7 Choose the Create button.

If you have chosen an application type for a type generated by AppWizard, OLE ControlWizard, or Custom AppWizard, the dialog box(es) for that wizard appear.

After you have responded to any wizard dialog boxes, the Subprojects dialog box reappears. Your newly created subproject is selected for inclusion.

8 Choose the Close button.

You have completed creating a top-level project with a single subproject. In FileView, the top-level project displays an icon representing the dependency relation for the subproject. The subproject also has a top-level representation.

Now you can add files if necessary, modify the source code, add functions to classes or add message-handlers, change the settings for the application, and so on.

When you build in this project workspace, you can build either the subproject or both the top-level project and the subproject.

▶ **To build the subproject only**

1 Select the subproject with the configuration you want to build from the Set Default Project Configuration drop-down list on the Project toolbar.

−or−

From the Build menu, choose Set Default Configuration, and choose from the list in the Default Project Configuration dialog box.

2 From the Build menu, choose Build.

▶ **To build both the top-level project and the subproject**

1 Select the top-level project with the configuration you want to build from the Set Default Project Configuration drop-down list on the Project toolbar.

−or−

From the Build menu, choose Set Default Configuration, and choose from the list in the Default Project Configuration dialog box.

2 From the Build menu, choose Build.

If the subproject output file is out of date, the build system first builds it, and then it builds the top-level project. If it is not out of date, the build system builds only the top-level project.

If you want to force the system to rebuild all the output files, choose Rebuild All from the Build menu. This method ensures, for instance, that you are always testing both elements of your project workspace with the most up-to-date changes.

Note If you have an output executable created by a project which calls a DLL created by a subproject, you need to do one of three things in order to run the executable and have it find the DLL. You can add the output directory for the DLL to your path, you can specify the output directory for the DLL to be same as the output directory for the executable, or you can move the DLL after it is built to a directory on the path, using a custom build command. In the case when you're debugging, it is preferable to set the output directories to be the same for the executable and the DLL.

Empty Top-Level Project with Multiple Subprojects

This organization is suitable for the development of a suite of related applications, some of which have other applications on which they depend. Choose this organization if you want to develop, for instance, two executables generated by AppWizard, one of which uses a DLL also generated by AppWizard, or two console applications, one of which uses a static library that you create. Figure 2.4 shows the relationships among the elements of an empty top-level project with multiple subprojects.

Figure 2.4   Empty Top-Level Project with Multiple Subprojects

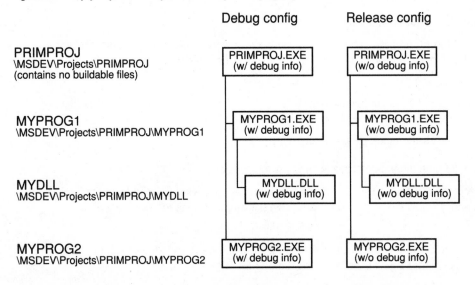

The following procedure assumes that all the applications in your suite are AppWizard applications. The approach is appropriate for other project types, however.

▶ **To create an empty top-level project with multiple subprojects**

1 Create a top-level project.

   Note   In this case, select Application in the Type list. This option creates the project workspace and the top-level project without any source files. You will not add any files to the top-level project in this example.

The directory that you create in this case contains the project workspace files. It also serves as the root for the subdirectories that you create for the rest of the projects in your application suite.

2 From the Build menu, choose Subprojects.

The Subprojects dialog box appears.

3 Choose the New button.

The Insert Project dialog box appears, with the Subproject option selected, and the existing top-level project selected in the drop-down list. Retain these default choices.

4 In the Name text box, type a name for the subproject.

This name is appended to the existing project workspace directory to form the fully qualified path for the new subproject directory.

5 Select the MFC AppWizard (exe) project type.

6 Select any of the available platforms for which to create initial Debug and Release configurations.

7 Choose the Create button, and complete the AppWizard dialog boxes as they appear.

After you have responded to the dialog boxes, the Subprojects dialog box reappears.

8 Repeat steps 3 through 7 for the second subproject. Select the top-level project from the drop-down list of the Insert Project dialog box.

9 Repeat steps 3 through 7 for the subproject contained by the first executable project. In the Insert Project dialog box, select the MFC AppWizard (dll) project type, and select the first AppWizard executable from the drop-down list.

10 Choose the Close button.

When you have completed adding the top-level project and all the subprojects, the FileView pane in your Project Workspace window looks like the one shown in Figure 2.5. The empty top-level project displays only icons representing dependency relations for the AppWizard executable subprojects. Each subproject also has a top-level representation.

Figure 2.5 FileView with Multiple Subprojects

Now you can add files if necessary, modify the source code, add functions to classes or add message-handlers, change the settings for the application, and so on.

When you build in this project workspace, you now have a number of choices. You can build the following combinations:

- The subproject DLL of the subproject AppWizard executable
- The subproject AppWizard executable that contains the subproject DLL, as well as the contained DLL
- The subproject AppWizard executable that does not contain a subproject
- Both AppWizard executables and the DLL

▶ **To build the subproject DLL only**

1 Select the subproject DLL with the configuration you want to build from the Set Default Project Configuration drop-down list on the Project toolbar.

   –or–

   From the Build menu, choose Set Default Configuration, and choose from the list in the Project Default Configuration dialog box.

2 From the Build menu, choose Build.

▶ **To Build the subproject executable and its subproject DLL**

1 Select a configuration of the subproject executable to build from the Set Default Project Configuration drop-down list on the Project toolbar.

   –or–

   From the Build menu, choose Set Default Configuration, and choose from the list in the Project Default Configuration dialog box.

2 From the Build menu, choose Build.

If the subproject DLL is out of date, the build system first builds it, and then it builds the subproject executable. If it is not out of date, the build system builds only the subproject executable.

▶ **To build the second subproject executable only**

1 Select a configuration of the second subproject executable to build from the Set Default Project Configuration drop-down list on the Project toolbar.

−or−

From the Build menu, choose Set Default Configuration, and choose from the list in the Project Default Configuration dialog box.

2 From the Build menu, choose Build.

▶ **To build the entire suite of applications**

1 Select a configuration of the empty top-level project to build from the Set Default Project Configuration drop-down list on the Project toolbar.

−or−

From the Build menu, choose Set Default Configuration, and choose from the list in the Project Default Configuration dialog box.

2 From the Build menu, choose Build.

The build checks the subprojects, working its way down the chain of dependencies, and builds the selected configuration in all the subprojects that are out of date. In this case, the build system takes no action for the top-level project because there is nothing to build.

In this example, the top-level project does not build anything. You could choose to have it build something, however, if the structure of your application suite lent itself to that organization. You could, for example, choose to have it build an online help file by adding the help source files to the top-level project and applying custom build commands to the files to create the online help file as output.

If you want to force the system to rebuild all the output files, choose Rebuild All from the Build menu. This method ensures, for instance, that you are always testing both elements of your project workspace with the most up-to-date changes.

Note If you have an output executable created by a project that calls a DLL created by a subproject, you need to do one of three things in order to run the executable and have it find the DLL. You can add the output directory for the DLL to your path, you can specify the output directory for the DLL to be same as the output directory for the executable, or you can move the DLL after it is built to a directory on the path, using a custom build command. In the case when you're debugging, it is preferable to set the output directories to be the same for the executable and the DLL.

Managing Project Workspaces

Project workspaces contain projects that you can build. A project consists of a single set of files and a set of one or more project configurations. Each project configuration, together with the set of files, determines the binary output file that you create.

When you create a project workspace, by default you always create one project with two configurations for each platform:

- A version with debugging information included and optimizations disabled (Debug)

- A version with no debugging information and optimizations enabled (Release)

After you have created that initial project workspace, you can add:

- New projects to your existing workspace.

- New configurations to an existing project.

- Subprojects to any project.

  A subproject establishes a dependency of one project on another. A project that builds an executable program that depends on a static library is one example. If the static library is a subproject of the project that builds the executable program, then the library will be updated before the executable program is built. Each configuration of a subproject is made a dependency of the corresponding configuration in the containing project. Building a configuration of the executable program also builds the same configuration of the subproject.

Creating a Project Workspace

When you start a software development task with Microsoft Developer Studio, you create a project workspace and an initial project in the workspace. The initial project has Debug and Release configurations for each platform that you choose. Before you create your project workspace, you should determine which of the basic scenarios for project workspace organization suits your needs best. For further information, see "Using Project Workspaces: Three Basic Scenarios" on page 26.

With Visual C++, there are essentially two ways to create a new project workspace and the initial new project in the workspace:

- Choose an AppWizard, OLE ControlWizard, or Custom AppWizard project type. These choices automatically create starter files with the appropriate classes using the Microsoft Foundation Class Library (MFC). For more information on AppWizard, see Chapter 1, "Creating Applications Using AppWizard." For more information on OLE ControlWizard, see "The OLE Control Tutorial" in *Tutorials*. For more information on Custom AppWizard, see Chapter 24, "Creating Custom AppWizards."

- Choose another project type. In this case, you must create all the files, and select the files to add to the project.

When you create a new project workspace for Visual C++, Microsoft Developer Studio always creates the following two files:

- Makefile. This file has the extension .MAK. It contains all commands, macro definitions, options, and so forth to specify how to build all the configurations for all projects in the project workspace.

- Workspace configuration file. This file has the extension .MDP. It contains environment settings for Developer Studio, such as window sizes and positions, insertion point locations, state of project breakpoints, contents of the Watch window, and so on.

You cannot modify these files directly.

When you create a project workspace, you select a root directory in which to create your project workspace directory. By default, Developer Studio selects the PROJECTS directory under your installation directory. You can, however, choose another directory. If you choose another directory, Developer Studio uses that choice for all subsequent project workspaces that you create.

When you create a project workspace, you must specify a name that is used both for the project workspace directory and the initial project in the workspace. Developer Studio creates a subdirectory of this name in the root directory. This subdirectory contains the files for your project workspace and the files for your initial project.

Developer Studio also specifies subdirectories for intermediate and final output files for the various projects that you specify. These subdirectories enable you to build various configurations of a project without overwriting intermediate and final output files with the same names. With the Settings command on the Build menu, you can open the General tab in the Project Settings dialog box and modify these subdirectories, if you choose.

When you create the initial project in a new project workspace, you automatically create two configurations: Debug and Release. The Debug version specifies settings to include debugging information and to disable optimizations during the build. The Release version doesn't specify settings to include debug information, and enables any optimizations that you have chosen.

If you use AppWizard, OLE ControlWizard, or Custom AppWizard to create the initial project for Visual C++, these tools also write the starter files into the project directory and subdirectories. If you use another project type, the files for the project can initially be in the project directory or in any other directory that you want. You can add files from any directory to a project. Adding files to a project does not move the files on your disk drives. The project merely records the name and location of the file and displays an icon in the project window to indicate the file's relationship to other files in the project.

Note If you add files from directories above the project workspace directory, Developer Studio uses absolute paths in the filenames for those files in the project's .MAK file. Because of the absolute paths, it is difficult to share the .MAK file. Other developers in your group may have other drive names or higher-level directory structures. See "Maintaining Makefiles Under Source-Code Control" on page 128 in Chapter 4 for further information about sharing makefiles.

▶ **To create a project workspace**

1 From the File menu, choose New.

The New dialog box appears.

2 Select Project Workspace from the list.

3 Choose OK.

The New Project Workspace dialog box appears.

4 From the Type list, select the type of application that you want to create.

5 In the Name text box, type the name for the project workspace . This name is also used for the initial project in the Project Workspace window.

Developer Studio automatically creates a new subdirectory with this name for your project workspace and for the files for the initial project.

6 Select the platform type or types from the Platforms list.

Note Win32 is the default platform. You must install the Microsoft Visual C++ Cross-Development Edition for Macintosh® before other platforms are available.

7 If you want, type a different location for the root directory for this project workspace in the Location text box, or choose the Browse button and select a location.

8 Choose the Create button.

If you chose a project type that does not generate starter files, you now need to add the files to your projects. See "Adding and Removing Files from Projects" on page 53 for more information.

Project Types

Each project has a project type, which you choose when you create the project. The project type specifies what to generate and specifies some default settings required in order to build that output type. It specifies, for instance, the settings that the compiler uses for the source files, the libraries that the linker uses to build each project configuration, the default locations for output files, defined constants, and so on.

You can select from the following nine project types in Visual C++ version 4.0:

MFC AppWizard (exe)   Applications with a full graphical interface, developed with MFC. Visual C++ automatically creates skeleton files with the appropriate classes and adds the files to the project. The file extension is .EXE.

MFC AppWizard (dll) Function libraries developed with MFC. Visual C++ automatically creates skeleton files with the appropriate classes and adds the files to the project. The file extension is .DLL.

OLE ControlWizard OLE controls, developed with MFC. Visual C++ automatically creates skeleton files with the appropriate classes and adds the files to the project. The file extension is .OCX.

Application Applications with a full graphical interface, developed with Windows NT Win32 API functions or with MFC. The file extension is .EXE.

Dynamic-Link Library Function libraries developed with Windows NT Win32 API functions that are called dynamically at run time by 32-bit Windows-based programs. The file extension is .DLL.

Console Application Applications developed with Console API functions, which provide character-mode support in console windows. The Visual C++ run-time libraries also provide output and input from console windows with standard I/O functions, such as **printf**() and **scanf**(). The file extension is .EXE.

Static Library Standard libraries created directly by the build, using the object files and other library files belonging to the project. The generated library is composed of all the object files in the project, all the object files generated by the project, and all the libraries in the project. The file extension is .LIB.

Makefile Any type of command-line program or any makefile created by an application other than the current version of Developer Studio. With this project type, you can represent the project files, display class information, and view resources in the Project Workspace window, as well as add this project as a subproject to other projects.

Custom AppWizard A custom modification to MFC AppWizard. Visual C++ automatically creates starter files with the appropriate classes and adds the files to the project. You can subsequently add these to the list of types displayed. The file extension is .AWX.

In addition to these project types, you can create custom AppWizards, and add these project types to the list.

Platform Types

The platform type for a project configuration specifies the operating environment. If you have installed the Visual C++ Cross-Development Edition for Macintosh®, for example, you can create project configurations for both Win32 and Macintosh platforms. The platform type specifies default settings required by a given platform, such as settings that the compiler uses for the source files, the libraries that the linker uses to build each project configuration, the default locations for output files, defined constants, and so on. It also specifies the tools required to build the final output files for that platform.

Saving a Project Workspace

You can save the workspace files and all other files that you have modified with the Save All command.

▶ **To save all files in a project workspace**

- From the File menu, choose Save All.

  Microsoft Developer Studio saves all files that you have modified — whether or not they are included in a project — without any further action on your part.

Closing a Project Workspace

You can close the workspace files with the Close Workspace command.

▶ **To close a project workspace**

- From the File menu, choose Close Workspace.

  If necessary, Microsoft Developer Studio prompts for actions concerning the windows that are open and the files that you have modified — whether or not they are included in a project.

Opening an Existing Project Workspace

Opening an existing project workspace loads all project workspace information, and restores all the environment settings to their state when you last saved the project workspace.

▶ **To open an existing project workspace**

1 From the File menu, choose Open Workspace.

The Open Project Workspace dialog box appears.

The default selection in the List Files Of Type drop-down list is Project Workspaces (.MDP).

2 Select the drive and directory containing the project workspace that you want to open.

3 Select the .MDP file for the project workspace from the File Name list and choose OK.

–or–

Double-click the filename in the list.

The Project Workspace window appears, as shown in Figure 2.1, and displays views of the projects in the workspace.

Opening Other File Types

You can open file types other than project workspace files in the Project Workspace window. In particular, you can open makefiles (.MAK), or you can open executable files to debug them or to view their resources.

▶ **To open an existing makefile with the extension .MAK**

1 From the File menu, choose Open Workspace.

The Open Project Workspace dialog box appears.

2 Select Makefiles from the drop-down list to display .MAK files.

3 Select the drive and directory containing the makefile that you want to open.

4 Select the .MAK file from the list and choose OK.

−or−

Double-click the filename in the list.

If you have a project workspace currently open, Developer Studio saves the workspace and asks if you want to close document windows associated with that workspace.

If your makefile has a different extension, or has the name MAKEFILE, you can use the Open command on the FIle menu to open it as a makefile.

▶ **To open an existing makefile without the extension .MAK**

1 From the File menu, choose Open.

The Open dialog box appears.

2 Select All Files from the drop-down list to display all files.

3 From the Open As drop-down list, select Makefile.

4 Select the drive and directory containing the makefile that you want to open.

5 Select the file from the list and choose OK.

−or−

Double-click the filename in the list.

If you have a project workspace currently open, Developer Studio saves the workspace and asks if you want to close document windows associated with that workspace.

The Project Workspace window appears, and Developer Studio takes the appropriate action for the file opened. For instance, if you open a project makefile from any previous version of Visual C++, Developer Studio asks if you want to convert the makefile to the current format. If you choose to convert the file, Developer Studio creates a project workspace and its associated files. It then displays the Save As dialog box so that you can save the new project workspace and its new associated makefile under a new name.

Note The new version of the makefile is incompatible with previous versions of Visual C++. If you want to continue to use the original makefile with the previous version of Visual C++, choose a different name under which to save new project workspace and makefile.

You should set the directories for intermediate and output files as well, so that Developer Studio does not overwrite the files created by the previous version. See "Selecting the Directories for Output Files" on page 59 for more information.

You can also open an executable file and create a project workspace for it in order to debug it.

▶ **To open an executable file for debugging**

1 From the File menu, choose Open Workspace.

   The Open Project Workspace dialog box appears.

2 Select Executable Files from the drop-down list to display .EXE files in the File Name list.

3 Select the drive and directory containing the executable file that you want to open.

4 Select the .EXE file and choose OK.

   –or–

   Double-click the filename in the list.

   If you have a project workspace currently open, Developer Studio saves the workspace and asks if you want to close document windows associated with that workspace.

The Project Workspace window opens and displays the executable as a folder in the FileView pane. You can now choose debugging commands from the Build menu, and debug the executable. When you close the project workspace, Developer Studio asks if you want to save the new project workspace associated with this executable file.

▶ **To open an executable file to view its resources**

1 From the File menu, choose Open.

   The Open dialog box appears.

2 Select Executable Files from the drop-down list to display all files.

3 From the Open As drop-down list, select Resources.

4 Select the drive and directory containing the executable file that you want to open.

5 Select the file and choose OK.

   –or–

   Double-click the filename in the list.

   The resource browser window appears and displays the resources in the selected file.

Specifying Subprojects in a Project Workspace

Subprojects indicate dependency relationships in the project workspace. When you build a project containing a subproject, the subproject is built first if it is out of date, and then the containing project is built. The dependency relationship is established by configuration. That is, if you build the Debug configuration of the containing project, you also build the Debug configuration of the subproject. Subprojects can contain other subprojects. All subprojects also have a top-level representation in the FileView pane.

When you specify a subproject, you can either create a new project and give it a subproject relationship, or you can choose an existing project and give it a subproject relationship.

▶ **To create a new project as a subproject**

1 From the Build menu, choose Subprojects.

The Subprojects dialog box appears.

2 From the Select Project To Modify list, select the project that is to contain the new subproject.

3 Choose the New button.

The Insert Project dialog box appears, with the Subproject option selected, and the selected project displayed in the Subproject Of drop-down list. Retain these default choices.

4 In the Name text box, type a name for the subproject.

This name is appended to the existing project workspace directory to form the fully qualified path for the new subproject directory.

5 From the Type list, select a project type.

6 Select any of the available platforms for which to create initial Debug and Release configurations.

7 Choose the Create button.

If you have chosen an application type for a type generated by AppWizard, OLE ControlWizard, or Custom AppWizard, the dialog box(es) for that wizard appear.

After you have responded to any wizard dialog boxes, the Subprojects dialog box reappears. Your newly created subproject is selected for inclusion.

8 Choose OK.

▶ **To include an existing project as a subproject**

1 From the Build menu, choose Subprojects.

The Subprojects dialog box appears.

2 From the Select Project To Modify list, select the project that is to contain the subproject.

The Select Subprojects To Include list displays the projects that you can include as subprojects of the selected project. Projects that are already subprojects for this project have a check next to them.

3 From the Select Subprojects To Include list, select the project (or projects) that you want to include as a subproject.

4 Choose OK.

If you have included a project in another project as a subproject, you can remove it from the project, and by doing so, remove its dependency relationship. This does not, however, remove the project from the project workspace.

▶ **To remove a subproject from a project**

1 From the Build menu, choose Subprojects.

The Subprojects dialog box appears.

2 From the Select Project To Modify list, select the project that now contains the subproject.

The Select Subprojects To Include list displays projects that are already subprojects with a check next to them.

3 From the Select Subprojects To Include list, select the project (or projects) that you want to remove as a subproject.

4 Choose OK.

Working with Views

In the Project Workspace window, Developer Studio creates panes, which you access from the tabs at the bottom of the window. Certain panes contain a specific view of all the projects in your workspace. Each pane has at least one top-level folder, which contains the elements that make up that view of the project; expanding the folder displays the details of that view. In a project workspace containing Visual C++ projects, for instance, the Project Workspace window contains the following panes by default.

Pane Title	Description
FileView	Displays the projects that you have created. Expanding the top-level folders shows files within the project.
ResourceView	Displays the resource files included in your projects. Expanding the top-level folders shows the resource types.
ClassView	Displays the C++ classes defined in your projects. Expanding the top-level folders shows the classes; expanding a class shows its members.
InfoView	Displays the table of contents for Books Online. Expanding the top-level folders shows books and topics.

You can switch from one pane to another by selecting a tab at the bottom of the
Project Workspace window, as shown in Figure 2.6. You can also switch using
CTRL+PAGE UP and CTRL+PAGE DOWN.

Figure 2.6   Project Workspace Window

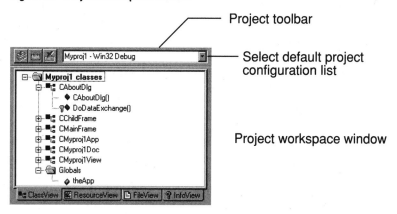

Project toolbar

Select default project
configuration list

Project workspace window

Tabs to access panes

Each pane contains a hierarchical (tree), view consisting of various nodes. You can
expand the nodes in the hierarchy to display their contents, or collapse the nodes to
display the organization. The top-level node (or nodes) in a pane is the *folder*. Each
folder can contain a variety of items. Some items are *container* items, such as
resource scripts, which contain resources used in the program. Container items can
also be expanded. A bottom-level node, which you cannot further expand, represents
an *editable item*. You open the item in an appropriate editor — text editors for
source files or classes, dialog box editor for dialog box resources, and so on — to edit
the resource.

   Tip   While using any pane in the Project Workspace window, you can click the right mouse
button when the mouse pointer is over the selection to display a pop-up menu of frequently
used commands. The available commands depend on the current selection. For example, if
the selection is a source file, the pop-up menu shows the Properties command and several
commands also available on the Build menu, such as Build and Compile.

Using Folders

The top-level node (or nodes) in a pane is the *folder*. Each folder can contain a
variety of items, including other folders. You can open a folder to display the items
that it contains, or you can close a folder to simplify the view in the pane.

The types of panes displayed in the Project Workspace window depend on the type of
project. In Visual C++ projects, for instance, Microsoft Developer Studio displays a
pane that contains the classes in the project.

▶ **To open a folder**

• Double-click the folder.

 –or–

• Click the plus sign (+) to the left of the folder.

▶ **To close a folder**

• Double-click the folder.

 –or–

• Click the minus sign (–) to the left of the folder.

Working with Items

Each folder in a pane can contain a variety of items. Some items are *container* items, such as resource scripts, that contain resources used in the program. Container items can be expanded in the same way folders can be expanded. A bottom-level node that you cannot expand further represents an *editable item*. Rather than expanding these nodes, you open the item in an appropriate editor—text editors for source files or classes, dialog box editor for dialog box resources, and so on—to edit the resource. All items have properties, which you can view and edit on an item's property page(s). Each type of item has a distinct set of properties.

▶ **To open an editable item**

• Double-click the item.

 The appropriate editor for the item opens and displays the item.

▶ **To view or change an item's properties**

• Select the item, and then press ALT+ENTER.

 –or–

• Select the item, click the right mouse button, and from the pop-up menu, choose Properties.

 –or–

• Select the item, and from the Edit menu, choose Properties.

The property page for the item appears. If the item has editable properties, you can edit them on the property page, and those edits take immediate effect.

▶ **To delete resources or files from a folder**

• Select the item, and press the DEL key.

Shortcut Methods for Views

While using any view in the Project Workspace window, you can click the right mouse button when the mouse pointer is over the selection to display a pop-up menu of frequently used commands. The commands available depend on the current selection. For example, if the selection is a source file, the pop-up menu shows the Properties command and several commands also available on the Build menu, such as Build and Compile.

You can use the shortcut methods listed in Table 2.1 to navigate in the various views, to expand and contract nodes, to select items, and so on.

Table 2.1 Shortcut Methods for Views

Method	Result
HOME	Moves to first node in tree
END	Moves to last node in tree
PAGE UP	Moves up one page (number of visible items determines page size)
PAGE DOWN	Moves down one page (number of visible items determines page size)
CTRL+PAGE UP	Activates previous Project Workspace window pane
CTRL+PAGE DOWN	Activates next Project Workspace window pane
UP ARROW	Moves to previous node in list
DOWN ARROW	Moves to next node in list
CTRL+UP ARROW	Moves focus up one item
CTRL+DOWN ARROW	Moves focus down one item
SHIFT+UP ARROW	Extends selection up one item
SHIFT+DOWN ARROW	Extends selection down one item
LEFT ARROW	Collapses current node if possible; otherwise, moves to parent node
RIGHT ARROW	Expands current node if possible; otherwise, moves to first child node
BACKSPACE	Moves to parent node
ENTER	Performs default action on node (opens/closes folder, opens item in the editor, and so on)
PLUS SIGN	Expands current node if expandable
MINUS SIGN	Collapses current node if collapsible
ASTERISK	Fully expands current node, including all child nodes

Table 2.1   Shortcut Methods for Views *(continued)*

Method	Result
Click plus sign	Expands current node if expandable
Click minus sign	Collapses current node if collapsible
Double-click	Performs default action on node (opens/closes folder, opens item in the editor, and so on)
CTRL+click	Selects or deselects item (noncontiguous selection)
SHIFT+click	Selects block from current selection to item (contiguous selection)

Using FileView

The FileView pane shows relationships among the source files and the dependent files used to build all project configurations included in the project workspace. The relationships in FileView are logical relationships, not physical relationships, and do not reflect the organization of files on your hard disk. FileView also shows subprojects within the project workspace, if any exist.

The default project configuration in the workspace is indicated in FileView by bold type. You can select the default configuration either by using the pop-up menu in FileView or by using the Select Default Project Configuration drop-down list on the Project toolbar.

When you expand the top-level folder in FileView, it displays the files included in the project, and the Dependencies folder. If you expand the Dependencies folder, it displays files that the source files in the project depend on, such as .H or .ICO files. Figure 2.7 shows an expanded FileView.

Figure 2.7   The FileView Pane

FileView uses file icons to convey additional information about the files in the project. Table 2.2 shows the icons and their meanings.

Table 2.2   File Icons in FileView

Icon	Meaning
	Developer Studio can use this file in a build, and it is included in the build for this project.
	Developer Studio can use this file in a build, but it is not included in the build for this project.
	Developer Studio uses this file as an explicit dependency in a project.
	Developer Studio cannot build this file using the default tools. Files in this category might include documentation or specifications. You could specify custom tools for these files.
	Developer Studio refers to this project as a subproject of the project that contains it. When Developer Studio builds the containing project, it first builds the output of this subproject if it is out of date with respect to its input files.

If you have installed a source-code control system that conforms to the Microsoft Common Source Code Control Interface, the icons also represent some source-code control states. A grayed icon indicates that a file is under source-code control. A check next to the icon for a file under source-code control indicates that you have the file checked out.

Using ClassView

Visual C++ derives the ClassView pane from the contents of the source files included in the project workspace. It shows all the C++ classes for which definitions are available, and the members of those classes. The relationships in ClassView are logical relationships, not physical relationships.

Note   Visual C++ computes the contents of ClassView as a background process. This may mean that there is some delay from the time you open a project workspace or save a revised file until the view is ready to be displayed. If you are completing other processes that use significant computing resources, the delay may increase.

In ClassView, you can:

- Add member functions to the selected class.
- Add member variables to the selected class.
- Go to the definition of the class or member.
- Go to the references to the class or member.
- Display derived class or base class graphs.
- Set a breakpoint on a member function.

The folder name shown in bold type in ClassView represents the default project configuration. When you expand the top-level folder in ClassView, it displays the classes included in that project. If you expand any class, it displays the members in that class. Figure 2.8 shows an expanded ClassView.

Figure 2.8   ClassView

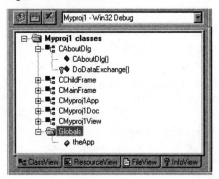

ClassView uses icons to convey additional information about the classes and class members in the project. Table 2.3 shows the icons and their meanings.

Table 2.3   Icons in ClassView

Icon	Meaning
▪▫	Class
♔♦	Protected member function
☎♦	Private member function
♦	Public member function
♔♦	Protected member variable
☎♦	Private member variable
♦	Public member variable

You can group the items in a class either alphabetically by name or alphabetically in access specifier groups— that is, private, protected, or public.

▸ **To group members in a class**

1 Select one or more class nodes.

2 Click the right mouse button to display the pop-up menu.

3 Choose Group By Access to toggle the grouping.

   If the command has a check, the members are already grouped by access specifier; if not, they are grouped alphabetically.

Adding Members from ClassView

From ClassView, you can add a member function or a member variable to the selected class. This mechanism allows you to readily add member functions that do not handle messages or member variables that are not used in a data-exchange and data-validation context.

Note If you want to add a message-handler function for user interface objects or member variables for data exchange and data validation, you should use ClassWizard. ClassWizard is specifically designed to take the relevant information and use it to insert elements in your source files at the appropriate locations.

▶ **To add a member function**

1 Select the class to which you want to add a function.

2 With the mouse pointer over the selected class, click the right mouse button to display the pop-up menu, and choose Add Function.

   The Add Member Function dialog box appears.

3 In the Function Type text box, type the function's return type.

4 In the Function Declaration text box, type the function declaration. The Function Type text box contains the return type for the function, so here you type only the function name, followed by a list of the names and types of formal parameters enclosed in parentheses.

5 Select an access specifier for the function from the Access group of options.

6 If you want a static function, select the Stactic check box.

7 If you want a virtual function, select the Virtual check box.

8 Choose OK.

This procedure adds a declaration to the header file for the class, and a corresponding function body in the implementation file for the class.

▶ **To add a member variable**

1 Select the class to which you want to add a variable.

2 With the mouse pointer over the selected class, click the right mouse button to display the pop-up menu, and select Add Variable.

   The Add Member Variable dialog box appears.

3 In the Variable Type text box, type the Variable type.

4 In the Variable Declaration text box, type the variable name.

5 Select an access specifier for the variable from the Access group of options.

6 Choose OK.

This procedure adds a definition to the header file for the class.

See Also Working with Classes, Adding a New User-Interface Class, Adding a Message Handler, Defining Member Variables, Access Specifiers, Methods, Storage-Class Specifiers, C++ Declarations, C++ Definitions, Controlling Access to Class Members

Browsing Symbols from ClassView

From ClassView, you can get information about the use of the classes, functions, and variable symbols in your application. You can select a symbol, and then automatically open that source file to the definition or declaration of the symbol, or find references to those symbols in your application's source files.

▶ **To find a definition or declaration**

1 Select the symbol for which you want to find the definition or declaration.

2 With the mouse pointer over the selected class, click the right mouse button to display the pop-up menu, and select Go To Definition or Go To Declaration.

−or−

Double-click the name of the symbol.

Visual C++ opens a text editor window and displays the source file containing the definition or declaration, with the insertion point positioned there.

Note Visual C++ computes the contents of ClassView as a background process. This may mean that there is some delay from the time you open a project or save a revised file until the view is computed, and you can find a definition or declaration. If you are completing other processes that use significant computing resources, the delay may increase.

▶ **To find references**

1 Select the symbol for which you want to find references.

2 With the mouse pointer over the selected class, click the right mouse button to display the pop-up menu,and select References.

Note If you have not built your application with the option to build a browse information file, a message box appears, asking if you want to build the browse information file. If you choose Yes, it builds the browse information file, and you can then find references. If you choose No, the references are not available.

The Definitions And References browse information window appears, with the symbol that you chose selected.

See Also Browsing Through Symbols, Finding Definitions and References

Displaying Graphs from ClassView

From ClassView, you can display graphs showing the class derivations and the function-calling order in your application.

Note If you have not built your application with the option to build the browse information file, a message box appears, asking if you want to build the browse information file. If you choose Yes, it builds the browse information file, and you can then find references. If you choose No, the references are not available. Building a browse information file increases your build times.

▶ **To display a class graph**

1 Select the class for which you want to display a graph.

2 With the mouse pointer over the selected class, click the right mouse button to display the pop-up menu, and choose Base Classes to display a graph of the derivation for this class, or Derived Classes to display a graph of classes derived from this class.

   The browse information window appears, with a graph for the class that you chose.

3 Select the function for which you want to display a graph.

4 With the mouse pointer over the selected class, click the right mouse button to display the pop-up menu, and choose Calls to display a graph of the functions that this function calls, or Called By to display a graph of functions that call this function.

   The browse information window appears, with a graph for the function that you chose.

See Also Browsing through Symbols, Displaying Function Information

Setting Breakpoints in ClassView

From ClassView, you can quickly set breakpoints for use in the integrated debugger. You can set breakpoints on the definition of member functions.

▶ **To set a breakpoint**

• Select the member function, click the right mouse button to display the pop-up menu, and choose Set Breakpoint.

The breakpoint is set at the definition, and the breakpoint symbol appears in the source file at the breakpoint location.

Using ResourceView

Microsoft Developer Studio derives the ResourceView pane from the contents of the resource file (or files) included in the project workspace. ResourceView displays all the resource types and all the individual resources of each type. ResourceView is described fully in Chapter 5, "Working with Resources."

Using InfoView

The InfoView pane shows the organization of Books Online. You can display any topic in its hierarchy. InfoView is described fully in the section of Books Online titled Using InfoViewer.

Using Projects

A project consists of a project configuration and a set of files, which together determine the final binary output file that you create. Developer Studio creates the final output file from the following elements:

- Settings for the platform for which you are building, such as the locations and names of libraries

- Settings for the type of binary output file, such as application, static library, dynamic-link library, and so on

- Tools — compiler, linker, and so on — required to build for the specified platform, as well as their settings

- The set of source files

The information for building each individual project is stored in the makefile for the project workspace, along with the information for all other projects in the workspace.

Inserting and Deleting Projects

You can insert new projects into your project workspace. You could, for instance, create an initial project with Debug and Release configurations specifying an application for the Win32 environment, and add source files to the projects. Later, within the project workspace you could create a project specifying a DLL with Debug and Release configurations for the Win32 environment, and add an entirely disjunct set of files to this project.

▶ **To insert a new project into an existing project workspace**

1 From the Insert menu, choose Project.

The Insert Project dialog box appears, with the Top-Level Project option selected.

2 In the Name text box, type a name for the project.

This name is appended to the existing project workspace directory to form the fully qualified path for the new project directory.

3 From the Type list, select the project type.

4 Select any of the available platforms for which you want to create initial Debug and Release configurations.

5 Choose the Create button.

If you have chosen an application type for a type generated by AppWizard, OLE ControlWizard, or Custom AppWizard, the dialog box(es) for that wizard appear.

The new project that you just created becomes the default project in the project workspace. If you chose a type other than AppWizard, Custom AppWizard, or OLE ControlWizard, you must now add files to your project. You can then build your new project by choosing Rebuild All from the Build menu.

▶ **To delete a project from a project workspace**

1 From the Build menu, choose Configurations.

The Configurations dialog box appears.

2 In the Projects And Configurations box, expand the project that you want to delete.

Projects are the leftmost entities in the tree. You can click the plus or minus sign to expand or contract them to show or hide their configurations.

3 Select each configuration in the project you want to delete in turn, and choose the Remove button.

Respond Yes to the message box that appears each time. When you have removed the last configuration, the project is removed as well.

4 Choose the Close button.

Note Deleting a project removes it as a subproject from any other project in the project workspace.

Adding and Removing Files from Projects

When you add a file to a project, you add the file to all project configurations in that project. For instance, if you have a project named MyProject, with Debug and Release configurations, and an additional project configuration named MyShipProj based on the Release configuration, adding a file adds it to all those project configurations.

▶ **To add files to a project**

1 From the Set Default Project Configuration drop-down list on the Project toolbar, select the project to which you want to add files.

If the Project toolbar is not displayed, choose Toolbars from the View menu, and select Project from the list.

2 From the Insert menu, choose Files Into Project.

The Insert Files Into Project dialog box appears.

3 Select the file type to display.

4 If necessary, select the drive and directory to view.

Note If you add files from directories above the project workspace directory, Microsoft Developer Studio uses absolute paths in the filenames for those files in the project's .MAK file. Because of the absolute paths, it is difficult to share the .MAK file. Other developers in your group may have other drive names or higher-level directory structures.

5 Select one or more files from the File Name list. You can use the SHIFT or CTRL key in conjunction with the mouse to make multiple selections.

6 Choose OK.

This procedure adds the files to the selected project.

Repeat the steps for all types of files that you want to add, or to add files from different subdirectories. When you close the Files Into Project dialog box, Visual C++ automatically scans the files for dependencies. It adds all the included files that it finds to the Dependencies folder for each project to which you've added files.

Visual C++ automatically scans the added project files recursively for **#include** directives, both bracketed (*<incl.h>*) and quoted (*"incl.h"*). It scans both source files (.C, .CPP, or .CXX) and resource files (.RC or .R), and adds all the included files that it finds to a Dependencies folder. The files in this folder can have extensions of .H, .HXX, .INC, .FON, .CUR, .BMP, .ICO, .DLG, or .TLB. You cannot directly add or delete the files included in this folder.

Visual C++ also refers to the following two exclusion files:

SYSINCL.DAT   This file, which contains a default list of system include files, is installed by the setup program on your computer in the directory in which you installed Microsoft Developer Studio (MSDEV.EXE).

MSVCINCL.DAT   This is a text file that you can create and put in your Windows directory. You can list in it additional files that you want to exclude, such as headers for external class libraries or some of the include files in a large project. You should use this file for additions because SYSINCL.DAT may be overwritten if you reinstall Visual C++, if you modify your installation with Setup, or if you update your installation. If you use the Developer Studio text editor to create this file, you must exit Developer Studio and then restart it for the file to become effective.

These lists should contain only files that are not likely to change often. Whenever Visual C++ updates dependencies, it excludes the files in these lists from dependency scanning and does not display them in the Dependencies folder. If you change only files in either of these lists, you must choose Rebuild All from the Build menu in order to build your selected project. If you merely choose Build, the dependency folder has no changes in it, and Visual C++ reports that your project is up to date. Alternatively, you could select the source files that include the changed dependencies, and choose Compile from the pop-up menu in order to explicitly build those files.

After those files have been built, choose Build from the Build menu to build the project.

If you create a new source file, or open a source file that is not included in the current default project, you can quickly add it to a project with the pop-up menu.

▶ To add an open source file to a project

1 With the mouse pointer in the source file, click the right mouse button.

2 From the pop-up menu, choose Add To Project, and select the project name from the cascading menu.

▶ To remove files from a project

- Select the file in FileView, and from the Edit menu, choose Delete.

    −or−

- Press the DEL key.

You can hold down the CTRL or SHIFT keys and use the mouse to select multiple files in the Project Workspace window.

 Tip Press CTRL and click a selection to toggle the selection state for the clicked item. You can use this method to quickly remove a file from a multiple selection.

▶ To move or copy files from one project workspace to another

1 In the FileView pane of the Project Workspace window, select the files that you want to move or copy.

   You can hold down the CTRL or SHIFT keys to select multiple files in the Project Workspace window.

2 From the Edit menu, choose Cut if you want to move the files, or Copy if you want to copy the files.

3 Close the current project workspace.

4 Open the destination project workspace.

5 Select the project to receive the files.

6 From the Edit menu, choose Paste.

If you move or copy selections that include files in Dependencies folders, Visual C++ explicitly moves or copies only the source files. Visual C++ automatically updates the dependencies before building the project, however, and they appear in the appropriate Dependencies folders.

Creating and Deleting Configurations in a Project

A project configuration consists of settings that determine the characteristics of the final output file for a project. When you create a new project configuration for a project, it initially has the settings from an existing project configuration. The new project configuration always uses the same set of files as that existing project configuration. You must also specify a platform for the configuration.

A new configuration is a way to make a variation of a project that you are currently building. It could merely specify a different platform, or it could specify different optimization options, for instance.

▶ **To create a project configuration**

1 From the Build menu, choose Configurations.

The Configurations dialog box appears.

2 In the Projects And Configurations box, select the project to which you want to add a configuration.

Projects are the leftmost entities in the tree. You can click the plus or minus sign to expand or contract them to show or hide their configurations.

3 Choose the Add button.

The Add Project Configuration dialog box appears.

4 In the Configuration text box, type a new name.

This name, along with the platform type, will be used to identify the new configuration.

5 From the Copy Settings From drop-down list, select the configuration from which the new configuration copies its initial settings.

6 From the Platform drop-down list, select a platform for the new configuration.

You can select the same platform as the project on which you are basing the new one if you want merely a variation of the existing settings.

7 Choose OK.

The Configurations dialog box reappears.

8 Choose the Close button.

A new project configuration is now available from the Set Default Project Configuration drop-down list on the Project toolbar. You can now choose new settings for this configuration, and those settings will be retained in the project configuration.

Note If you choose settings incompatible with the project type for the project or platform on which you based this configuration, you may not get the result that you expect.

If you add files to the project containing this configuration, those files are also used to build the configuration.

▶ **To prevent a file from being built in a configuration**

1 From the Build menu, choose Settings.

The Settings dialog box appears.

2 Select the General tab.

3 In the Settings For pane, select the file that you want to exclude from the build.

4 Select the Exclude File From Build check box.

5 Choose OK.

▶ **To delete a configuration from a project**

1 From the Build menu, choose Configurations.

The Configurations dialog box appears.

2 In the Projects And Configurations box, expand the project from which you want to delete a configuration.

Projects are the leftmost entities in the tree. You can click the plus or minus sign to expand or contract them to show or hide their configurations.

3 Select the configuration that you want to remove.

4 Choose the Remove button.

Respond Yes to the message box that appears.

5 Choose the Close button.

Updating Dependencies in a Project

After editing one or more source files to add **#include** directives, you can explicitly update the project dependencies to add included files to the appropriate dependency folders.

▶ **To update dependencies in all the files in the workspace**

1 From the Build menu, choose Update All Dependencies.

The Update All Dependencies dialog box appears.

2 In the Projects box, select the project you want to update.

3 Choose OK.

Visual C++ scans the project files recursively for **#include** directives, both bracketed (<*incl.h*>) and quoted ("*incl.h*"). It also refers to the following two exclusion files:

SYSINCL.DAT   This file, which contains a default list of system include files, is installed by the setup program on your computer in the directory in which you installed Microsoft Developer Studio (MSDEV.EXE).

MSVCINCL.DAT   This is a text file that you can create and put in your Windows directory. You can list in it additional files that you want to exclude, such as headers for external class libraries or some of the include files in a large project. You should use this file for additions because SYSINCL.DAT may be overwritten if you reinstall Visual C++, if you modify your installation with Setup, or if you update your installation. If you use the Developer Studio text editor to create this file, you must exit Developer Studio and then restart it for the file to become effective.

These lists should contain only files that are not likely to change often. Whenever Visual C++ updates dependencies, it excludes the files in these lists from dependency scanning and does not display them in the Dependencies folder. If you change only files in either of these lists, you must choose Rebuild All on the Build menu in order to build your selected project. If you merely choose Build, the dependency folder has no changes in it, and Developer Studio reports that your project is up to date.

Specifying Settings for a Project Configuration

Specifying settings at the project configuration level is sufficient for most projects. But if you want, you can specify different settings within a project configuration for various files.

Project configurations have a hierarchical structure of settings. The settings specified at the project configuration level apply to all files within the configuration. However, you can specify settings for individual files if you need to compile files with settings different from the general configuration settings. For instance, if you specify Default optimizations for a configuration, all files contained within the configuration use Default optimizations. You can, however, specify specific optimization settings — or the setting for no optimizations at all — for any individual files in the configuration. The settings that you specify at the file level in the project configuration override options set at the configuration level.

You can specify some types of settings, such as linking, only at the project configuration level.

You can specify settings at the following levels within a project configuration:

- Project configuration level. Settings specified at this level apply to all actions. Any settings specified for the project configuration apply to every file in the project unless overridden at the file level.

- File level. Settings specified at this level apply to file-level actions, such as compiling. Any settings specified for the file apply only to that file and override any settings specified at the project configuration level.

Selecting the Directories for Output Files

You can select the directories in which to put the intermediate and final output files for each project configuration. By putting these files in different directories, you can maintain copies of the same files built in different ways — for instance, the Debug and the Release versions of your project.

▶ **To select output directories**

1 From the Build menu, choose Settings.

The Project Settings dialog box appears, as shown in Figure 2.9.

2 In the Settings For pane, select the node for which you want to set directories.

If you select the project configuration node (highlighted in the left pane of Figure 2.9, below), you can set both intermediate and output directories; if you select a file, you can set only the intermediate directory.

3 Select the General tab.

The General tab is one of several that contain options for the project. This tab specifies how the project uses the Microsoft Foundation Class Library (MFC) and which directories the project uses for intermediate and final output files.

4 In the Intermediate Files text box, type the directory name for the intermediate files (.OBJ files, for instance).

5 If you are setting directories for the project level, type the directory name for the final output files (.EXE files, for instance) in the Output Files text box.

6 Choose OK.

Figure 2.9 Project Settings Dialog Box

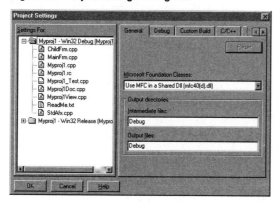

Specifying Project Configuration Settings

You can set options for a project configuration only when it is selected.

▶ **To specify project settings**

1 From the Build menu, choose Settings.

The Project Settings dialog box appears, as shown in Figure 2.9.

2 In the Settings For pane, select the project configuration, such as Win32 Debug shown in Figure 2.9.

You can also select multiple project configurations, and specify settings common to all the configurations.

3 From the tabs at the top of the dialog box, select the type of settings that you want to specify.

4 Specify the settings you want on the selected tab.

On the C/C++ and Link tabs in Visual C++, you can select from the Category list at the top of the tab to set options in various categories, if necessary.

For more information on linker or Visual C++ compiler settings, see option descriptions in Chapter 20, "Setting Compiler Options," and Chapter 21, "Setting Linker Options."

When you have completed specifying the settings on a tab, you can select another and specify additional settings. CTRL+TAB displays the next tab, and CTRL+SHIFT+TAB displays the previous tab.

5 When you have completed setting options, choose OK.

Note If you specify settings incompatible with the project type that you chose when you created your project, you may not get the result that you expect.

Specifying File Settings

A file is built with the settings from a project configuration when you build that configuration. However, for each individual file, you can specify settings that are different from, or in addition to, the project configuration's settings.

▶ **To set file options in a project**

1 From the Build menu, choose Settings.

The Project Settings dialog box appears, as shown in Figure 2.9.

2 In the Settings For pane, expand the project, such as MyProj1 Win32 Debug shown in Figure 2.9, and select the file or files.

3 From the tabs at the top of the dialog box, select the type of options that you want to display.

4 Set the options you want on the selected tab.

On the C/C++ tab in Visual C++, you can select from the Category list at the top of the tab to set options in various categories, if necessary.

For more information on linker or Visual C++ compiler settings, see option descriptions in Chapter 20, "Setting Compiler Options," and Chapter 21, "Setting Linker Options."

When you have completed specifying the settings on a tab, you can select another and specify additional settings. CTRL+TAB displays the next tab, and CTRL+SHIFT+TAB displays the previous tab.

5 When you have completed specifying settings, choose OK.

Note   If you specify settings incompatible with the project type that you chose when you created your project, you may not get the result that you expect.

You can also specify common settings across multiple projects or project configurations. Within the projects in your project workspace, you can select any combination of files.

▶ **To specify file settings in multiple project configurations**

1 From the Build menu, choose Settings.

The Project Settings dialog box appears, as shown in Figure 2.9.

2 In the Settings For pane, expand the project configuration, such as MyProj1 Win32 Debug shown in Figure 2.9, and select the file or files.

Click the plus signs or double-click the node names to expand the graph of project files if necessary, and use the SHIFT and CTRL keys with the mouse to make multiple selections.

3 From the tabs at the top of the dialog box, select the type of settings that you want to display. The visible tabs depend on the files or configurations that you have selected. Only those tabs with settings common to the selections appear.

4 Specify the settings you want on the selected tab. Only the settings common to all the selections are available.

On the C/C++ tab in Visual C++, you can select from the Category list at the top of the tab to specify settings in various categories, if necessary.

For more information on linker or Visual C++ compiler settings, see option descriptions in Chapter 20, "Setting Compiler Options," and Chapter 21, "Setting Linker Options."

When you have completed specifying the settings on a tab, you can select another and specify additional settings. CTRL+TAB displays the next tab, and CTRL+SHIFT+TAB displays the previous tab.

5 When you have completed specifying settings, choose OK.

Note If you specify settings incompatible with the project type that you chose when you created your projects, you may not get the result that you expect.

Specifying Custom Build Tools

You can specify custom build tools for use with any project or with any individual files that do not already have a tool associated with them. These tools then process the files at the appropriate point in the build if the output file is out of date with respect to the input file. For instance, you can add an .L file to your project, specify a lexical analyzer to process the file and produce a .Y output file, and then specify a parser generator to process that file to create a C source-code file for Visual C++. You could also select the output file for a configuration, to copy it to a specific directory for testing, for instance. Microsoft Developer Studio provides a number of macros for use in these commands.

Note By default, a number of file types have tools associated with them, such as .C or .CPP files in Visual C++. You cannot specify a custom tool for these files.

You can specify more than one custom tool for a file or project, and the tools run in the order that you specify them.

The custom tools run on files only in builds of the configurations in which you selected the files. That is, if your file set includes an .L file, and you select it only in one configuration, the tools that you specify run only in that configuration.

▶ **To specify custom build tools**

1 From the Build menu, choose Settings.

The Project Settings dialog box appears.

2 In the Settings For pane, select the source files or output files from project configurations for which you want to specify a custom tool or tools.

Selecting the top-level node specifies the output file for a configuration.

3 Select the Custom Build tab.

If you have made multiple selections, the Input File text specifies multiple selections.

4 In the Description text box, type a description.

This description appears on the Build tab of the Output window when the command runs.

5 In the Build Command(s) list, select the first line, and type the command that you want to run on the input file.

If you type more than one command in the grid, the build process runs them in order, from top to bottom.

Note   The command must include all required options, including the input file name or names and output file name or names. You may want to use a directory macro to specify the location for the output file.

6 In the Output File(s) list, select the first line, and type the name of an output file that is created by the build commands specified in the Build commands grid.

If the commands create more than one output file, type additional names in the subsequent lines of the grid.

7 Choose OK.

For example, assume that you want to include in your project a file named MYLEXINF.L. You first want a lexical analyzer to process MYLEXINF.L to produce a .Y file with the same base name (MYLEXINF.Y). You then want a parser generator to process MYLEXINF.Y to produce a .C file. First, you add MYLEXINF.L and MYLEXINF.C to your project using the Files Into Project command on the Insert menu. (If you have not already created a version of MYLEXINF.C, Microsoft Developer Studio recognizes that and asks if you want to add a reference to the file anyway.) You then choose the Settings command from the Build menu, and select MYLEXINF.L in the appropriate configuration. Next, select the Custom Build tab, and type commands similar to the following in the Build Command(s) list:

```
lexer $(InputPath) $(IntDir)\$(InputName).y
parser $(IntDir)\$(InputName).y $(ProjDir$)\$(InputName).c
```

This puts the intermediate output, MYLEXINF.Y, in the directory used for intermediate files, and generates MYLEXINF.C in the project directory.

In the Output File(s) list, type $(ProjDir)\$(InputName).C. When you build this project, the build system checks the date of MYLEXINF.C. If its date is earlier than MYLEXINF.L, the build system runs these custom commands to rebuild MYLEXINF.C.

Macros for Custom Build Commands

You can use the File and Directory drop-down lists to insert any of the following directory and filename macros in either grid at the current insertion point location. The File and Directory drop-down lists are on the Custom Build tab of the Project Settings dialog box, accessed with the Settings command from the Build menu.

Label	Macro	Description
Intermediate	**$(IntDir)**	Path to the directory specified for intermediate files, relative to the project directory
Output	**$(OutDir)**	Path to the directory specified for output files, relative to the project directory
Target	**$(TargetDir)**	Fully qualified path to the directory specified to output files
Input	**$(InputDir)**	Fully qualified path to the project directory

Label	Macro	Description
Project	$(ProjDir)	Fully qualified path to the project directory
Workspace	$(WkspDir)	Fully qualified path to the project directory
Microsoft Developer	$(MSDevDir)	Fully qualified path to the installation directory for Microsoft Developer Studio
Remote Target	$(RemoteDir)	Fully qualified path to the remote output file
Target Path	$(TargetPath)	Fully qualified name for the project output file
Target Name	$(TargetName)	Base name for the output file
Input Path	$(InputPath)	Fully qualified name for the input file
Input Name	$(InputName)	Base name for the input file
Workspace Name	$(WkspName)	Name of the project workspace
Remote Target Path	$(RemoteTargetPath)	Fully qualified name for the remote output file

If you have made multiple selections, during a build the input macros are set in turn to each file that you have selected for each configuration that you have selected.

Using Precompiled Headers

You can greatly speed compile time by compiling any C or C++ files — including inline code — only once into a precompiled header (.PCH) file and thereafter using the precompiled header for each build. Visual C++ offers two ways to create and use precompiled header files. One method is to use AppWizard and allow it to set default compiler options for your application. The other method is to use the Precompiled Headers category on the C/C++ tab of the Prject Settings dialog box.

The simplest way to use precompiled headers is to generate a new application using AppWizard. It sets default compiler options to create a precompiled header file, STDAFX.PCH, from STDAFX.H for use by all the skeleton files it creates.

If you do not use AppWizard to create your application, you can select the Precompiled Headers category on the C/C++ tab in the Project Settings dialog box and select the Automatic Use Of Precompiled Headers option to create an easy-to-use precompiled header file. For more information, see "Precompiled Headers" on page 407 in Chapter 20 or the "/Yd option" on page 565 in Chapter 25.

Building a Project Configuration

From Microsoft Developer Studio, you can build or rebuild the program or library that a project configuration defines. When you build a project configuration, Developer Studio processes only the files in the project that have changed since the last build. When you rebuild a project configuration, Developer Studio processes all the files in the project. You can either choose to build a single project configuration, or the default project configuration, or you can choose multiple configurations to build in one operation.

When you create a project, Developer Studio sets default options for both Debug and Release configurations. The Debug configuration contains full symbolic debugging information that can be used by the integrated debugger in Developer Studio or by other debuggers that use the Microsoft debug format. Developer Studio also turns off all optimizations in the Debug configuration because they generally make debugging more difficult. The Release configuration does not contain any symbolic debugging information, and it uses any optimizations that you have set after creating the projects. Depending on your installation and the choices you made when you created your project, you may have other default project configurations with other options, or you may have specifically created other project configurations with other options. Each project configuration also specifies the directories in which the intermediate and final files are created.

Setting the Default Project Configuration

When you set the default project configuration, subsequent build commands act on the default configuration and build its output. If the project associated with the default configuration contains subprojects, the same configuration in the subprojects gets built if the output file for the configuration in the subproject is out of date.

▶ **To set the default project configuration**

• From the Set Default Project Configuration drop-down list on the Project toolbar, choose a project configuration.

 −or−

1 From the Build menu, choose Set Default Configuration.

 The Default Project Configuration dialog box appears.

2 In the Project Configurations list, select the default project configuration.

3 Choose OK.

Building the Default Project Configuration

You can choose the project configuration that you want to build by default. This is the project configuration that you build when you choose Build *project* from the Build menu. If this project configuration contains any explicit project dependencies, and those project configurations are out of date, they are built first.

▶ **To select a project configuration**

- From the Set Default Project Configuration drop-down list on the Project toolbar, choose a project configuration.

  −or−

1 From the Build menu, choose Set Default Configuration.

  The Default Project Configuration dialog box appears.

2 In the Project Configurations list, select the default project configuration.

3 Choose OK.

▶ **To build the default project configuration**

- From the Build menu, choose Build *project*, where *project* represents the program or library defined by the project configuration.

If you want to ensure that all files associated with a project configuration get built, whether or not they are out of date, you can choose the Rebuild All command.

Note If you have updated any files that appear in either SYSINCL.DAT or MSCVINCL.DAT, you must choose Rebuild All to ensure that the changes are incorporated in the build. See "Updating Dependencies in a Project" on page 57.

▶ **To rebuild the default project configuration**

- From the Build menu, choose Rebuild All.

Information about the build is displayed in the Output window. The Output window displays information from the build tools and lists any errors or warnings that occur during the build. If no errors are reported, the build completed successfully. If errors are reported, you need to debug them. For information on debugging build errors, see "Debugging Compiler and Linker Errors" on page 323 in Chapter 17.

▶ **To stop a build**

- From the Build menu, choose Stop Build.

Developer Studio stops the currently executing tool if possible; otherwise, it stops the build as soon as the currently executing tool finishes.

Since builds occur in the background, you can continue to use Developer Studio during a build. However, some menu commands and toolbar buttons are disabled during a build. You can use the tabs at the bottom of the Output window to view the previous output from another tool while you are running the current build, and then choose the Build tab to return to the current build output.

An audible message notifies you when the build is complete. Unless you have a sound card installed, all audible events issue a beep. If you have a sound card installed, you can use the Sound application in the Windows Control Panel to assign the three standard system events listed below to different sounds.

System Event	Indicates
Asterisk (*)	Build has completed without errors or warnings.
Question (?)	Build has completed with warnings.
Exclamation (!)	Build has completed with errors.

In some cases, you may need to stop building your project before the process finishes.

Compiling Files

You can select and compile files in any project in your project workspace.

▶ **To compile selected files**

1 Select the files in the FileView pane of the Project Workspace window.

2 With the mouse pointer over the selection, click the right mouse button to display the pop-up menu, and choose Compile.

If you have specified a custom tool (or tools) for a file, when you select Compile, Developer Studio runs that tool with the file as input, and produces the output specified.

Removing Intermediate Files

You can remove all files from the Intermediate directories in any project configuration in your project workspace. Removing the files forces Developer Studio to build these files if you subsequently choose the Build command.

▶ **To remove intermediate files**

1 From the Set Default Project Configuration drop-down list on the Project toolbar, choose a project configuration.

–or–

2 From the Build menu, choose Set Default Configuration.

The Default Project Configuration dialog box appears.

3 In the Project Configurations list, select the default project configuration.

4 Choose OK.

5 Select the project in the FileView pane of the Project Workspace window.

6 With the mouse pointer over the selected project, click the right mouse button to display the pop-up menu, and choose Delete Intermediate Files.

This procedure deletes the intermediate files from the intermediate files directory associated with the selected configuration.

Building Multiple Project Configurations

Any project workspace can have more than one project configuration. Instead of selecting each project configuration in turn and building it as the default configuration using the Build *project* command on the Build menu, you can select multiple project configurations and build them all.

Note You can also build multiple project configurations by using subprojects, and building the appropriate containing project. See "Using Project Workspaces: Three Basic Scenarios" on page 26 for more information.

▶ **To build multiple project configurations**

1 From the Build menu, choose Batch Build.

The Batch Build dialog box appears. By default, all project configurations in the project workspace are selected.

2 If you don't want to build certain project configurations, clear the check boxes in the Project Configurations list.

3 Choose the Build button to build only those intermediate files of each project configuration that are out of date, or the Rebuild All button to build all intermediate files for each project configuration.

The results for each project configuration are separated in the Output window by a line containing the name of the project configuration being built.

▶ **To stop building multiple projects**

• From the Build menu, choose Stop Build.

Developer Studio stops the currently executing tool if possible; otherwise, it stops the build as soon as the currently executing tool finishes. The build of the project configuration currently in progress ends. A message box appears, asking if you wish to continue building the remaining project configurations. If you choose Yes, then the batch build continues from the next configuration in the list. If you choose No, then the entire batch build is stopped.

Using External Projects

In Microsoft Developer Studio you can have two types of external projects:

- Projects that are built using a makefile not created by the current version of Developer Studio.

  You can open an existing makefile in Developer Studio to create external projects. External projects are called that because they originally used external methods to set compiler or linker options, for instance, rather than using the methods available within Developer Studio. Developer Studio uses NMAKE to build the external project, and automatically sets certain internal project options to build the project with NMAKE. You can continue to use external methods to set options, if you choose.

- Projects that are built using methods other than the internal build system in Developer Studio.

  You can specify a new project with the Makefile project type, and then specify tools other than NMAKE which Developer Studio needs to run to build the project, using the Project Settings dialog box.

All external projects use project settings on the General tab of the Project Settings dialog box. If you open an existing makefile, named either explicitly MAKEFILE or *filename*.MAK, Developer Studio uses NMAKE as the command-line tool to build the project. If you create an external project by choosing Makefile from the Type list in the New Project Workspace or Insert Project dialog box, Develper Studio prompts you to open the Project Settings dialog box and explicitly specify the tool that Developer Studio must run to build the project.

Once you create an external project, you can add files to it, or you can add it to other projects as a subproject. Adding the source files comprising the external project to the project workspace enables you to view those files in FileView, to open them from FileView, to add them to your source-code control system from Microsoft Developer Studio, and so on.

If your external project generates an executable file compatible with the Microsoft Developer Studio debugging format, you can debug it from within Developer Studio.

Opening an Existing Makefile

When you open an existing makefile (MAKEFILE or *filename*.MAK) that Developer Studio does not recognize as a makefile that it created, it displays a message box asking if you want to create a project to wrap the makefile. If you choose No, Developer Studio does not open the file. If you choose Yes, Developer Studio creates a project workspace and its associated file for the external makefile. The external makefile becomes a part of the project workspace. (Remember that the command-line tool, NMAKE, creates the resulting project files: executable programs, DLLs, static libraries, and so on.)

▶ **To open an existing makefile with the extension .MAK**

1 From the File menu, choose Open Workspace.

The Open Project Workspace dialog box appears.

2 Select All Files from the drop-down list to display all files.

3 From the Open As drop-down list, select Makefile.

4 Select the drive and directory containing the makefile that you want to open.

5 Select the file from the list and choose OK.

−or−

Double-click the filename in the list.

If you have a project workspace currently open, Developer Studio saves the workspace and asks if you want to close document windows associated with that workspace.

Developer Studio displays a message box asking if you want to convert the external makefile into a project workspace with an external project containing the external makefile.

6 Choose Yes to convert the makefile.

If you choose No, Developer Studio cancels the conversion process.

If you have installed multiple platforms, Developer Studio displays the Platforms dialog box. It displays selections for all the platforms that you have installed.

7 In the Platforms list, select the platforms for which you want to create external projects. By default, Developer Studio selects all installed platforms.

8 Choose OK.

Developer Studio displays the Save As dialog box, with a default name for the Developer Studio project workspace file.

9 Either enter a new name, or accept the default name, and select OK to create the project workspace file. If necessary, choose a drive or directory for the file.

Note You cannot use the name of the existing makefile for the Developer Studio project workspace file. If you used that name, the project workspace file would overwrite the existing makefile, and would then have no file to run.

If your makefile has a different extension, or has the name MAKEFILE, you can use the Open command from the FIle menu to open it as a makefile.

▶ **To open an existing makefile without the extension .MAK**

1 From the File menu, choose Open.

The Open dialog box appears.

2 Select All Files from the drop-down list to display all files.

3 Select Makefile from the Open As drop-down list.

4 Select the drive and directory containing the makefile that you want to open.

5 Select the .MAK file from the File Name list and choose OK.

–or–

Double-click the filename in the list.

If you have a project workspace currently open, Developer Studio saves the workspace and asks if you want to close document windows associated with that workspace.

Developer Studio displays a message box asking if you want to convert the external makefile into a project workspace with an external project containing the external makefile.

6 Choose Yes to convert the makefile.

If you choose No, Developer Studio cancels the conversion process.

If you have installed multiple platforms, Developer Studio displays the Platforms dialog box. It displays selections for all the platforms that you have installed.

7 In the Platforms list, select the platforms for which you want to create external projects. By default, Developer Studio selects all installed platforms.

8 Choose OK.

The Save As dialog box appears, with a default name for the Developer Studio project workspace file.

9 Either enter a new name, or accept the default name, and select OK to create the project workspace file. If necessary, you can choose a drive or directory for the file.

Note You cannot use the name of the existing makefile for the Developer Studio project workspace file. If you used that name, the project workspace file would overwrite the existing makefile, and would then have no file to run.

Developer Studio opens a Project Workspace window for the project and shows FileView with only the external project-level nodes and the external makefile as a source file in each. You can use the menu commands to add or delete files from these projects. You can also use the Settings command on the Build menu to change the settings for external projects.

Creating an External Project

You can create an external project to run external commands, such as batch files or other executables, to build the project.

▶ **To add an external project to an existing project workspace**

1 From the Insert menu, choose Project.

The Insert Project dialog box appears, with the Top-Level Project option selected.

2 In the Name text box, type a name for the project.

This name is appended to the existing project workspace directory to form the fully qualified path for the new project directory.

3 Fom the Type list, select the Makefile.

4 Select any of the available platforms for which you want to create initial Debug and Release configurations.

5 Choose the Create button.

The project appears in the Project Workspace window. You now need to specify the tools used to build the target.

6 From the Build menu, choose Settings.

The Project Settings dialog box appears. It displays the tabs with options for the project.

7 Select the General tab.

8 From the following list, select the options that apply or fill in the appropriate information in the text boxes.

- **Build Command Line** The command line that the operating system executes for this project when you choose Build from the Build menu. By default, the system executes Microsoft NMAKE with the /F option followed by the name of the external makefile. You can, however, add any batch or executable filename along with command-line options and input files.

- **Rebuild All Options** The options added to the command line when you choose Rebuild All from the Build menu. By default, the /A option for Microsoft NMAKE is added.

- **Output File Name** The name of the file that is created when you build the project. This could be an application or static library, for instance.

- **Browse Info File Name** Name of the browse information file to create for this project. It must have the extension .BSC.

9 Select the Debug tab.

10 Select the General category from the Category list, and enter the information required for debugging in the text boxes. Developer Studio uses this information when you choose commands such as Go or Step Into on the Debug menu.

- **Executable For Debug Session** The name of the program that the external makefile builds if you are debugging an executable program, or the name of the executable file that calls a DLL if you are debugging a DLL. If you are debugging an executable file on a remote machine, this executable file on the local machine contains the symbolic debugging information.

- **Working Directory** The working directory that the application uses when it runs. This directory may be different from the output files directory in the project. It could contain test cases, for instance.

- *Program Arguments (for .EXE files)*   Arguments that need to be passed to the executable file when it starts.

- *Remote Executable Rath And File Name*   The name for the executable file that you are debugging on a remote machine. The location for this executable file is specified relative to the remote machine.

11 Select the Additional DLLs category from the Category list on the Debug tab, and specify the information required for debugging. Developer Studio uses this information when you choose commands such as Go or Step Into on the Debug menu.

- *Modules*   Each line in the grid specifies whether or not to preload symbols for the module when you start debugging, the local name of the DLL, and if you are debugging remotely, its remote name. After you type a name, a check box appears at the left of the grid in that line. Selecting the box preloads symbols. If you preload symbols, you can set breakpoints before the module loads. Clearing the box does not preload symbols.

- *Try To Locate Additional DLLs*   If this check box is selected, the debugger asks for additional DLLs when debugging begins.

12 Choose OK.

Developer Studio creates both a makefile and a project workspace file, with the extension .MDP, for the external project. The project workspace file stores information about your local configuration — syntax coloring, editor preferences, key assignments, window layout, and so on. The makefile stores information required to build the project.

Building a Single File Without a Project Workspace

You can create a single source file and then build a console application directly from that source file. This method is generally useful only for relatively simple applications.

▶ **To build a console application from a single source file**

1 Close any open project workspace.

2 Create or open a source file in a text editor window.

3 From the Build menu, choose Build.

Developer Studio displays a message box asking if you would like to create a project workspace.

4 Choose Yes.

The Save As dialog box appears if you have not yet given the source file a name.

5 If necessary, give the source file a new name, with an extension for a file that Developer Studio can build, such as .C, .CXX, or .CPP for Visual C++.

If you don't use one of these file extensions, Developer Studio does not build anything because it cannot find a type of source file in the project to build.

6 Choose OK.

Developer Studio creates a default project workspace using the base name of the source file as the base name for the project. It uses default settings for a console application for the project configuration and builds the application.

Running a Program

When you have completed building a project configuration, you can start the application from Developer Studio. You can also run applications and dynamic-link libraries in the integrated debugger.

▶ **To run an executable program**

- From the Build menu, choose Execute *project*, where *project* represents the program defined by the project configuration.

▶ **To run an application in the integrated debugger**

- From the Build menu, choose Debug, and from the cascading menu, choose Go, Step Into, or if you have a source file open and it has the focus, Run To Cursor.

If you are debugging a DLL, you need to prepare for your debugging session as described in "Debugging DLLs" in Chapter 17 on page 334. For more information on debugging your programs, see Chapter 17, "Using the Debugger."

CHAPTER 3

Using the Text Editor

Microsoft Developer Studio provides an integrated text editor to manage, edit, and print source files. Most of the procedures for using the editor should seem familiar if you have used other Windows-based text editors. With the text editor, you can:

- Use the File menu to create source files, open single files, open multiple files, and save and print source files.

- Use virtual spaces for advanced cursor positioning.

- Identify sections of code by matching group delimiters.

- Find matching conditional statements.

- Move around in a source file with the Go To dialog box.

- Use bookmarks to mark frequently accessed lines in your source file.

- Navigate source files using a wide range of commands.

- Perform advanced find and replace operations in a single file or multiple files.

- Use regular expressions with Developer Studio, BRIEF® emulation, and Epsilon™ emulation.

- Specify text selection for lines, multiple lines, and columns.

- Cut, copy, paste, and delete text with the Edit menu.

- Use drag-and-drop editing.

- Record and play back keystrokes.

- Emulate two popular text editors: BRIEF and Epsilon.

- Customize the text editor with save preferences, virtual spaces, the selection margin, and tabs and indents.

- Modify the font style, size, and color.

- Set syntax coloring for source files and user-defined types.

- Control the source window by switching between windows, opening new windows, splitting window views, and using full-screen mode.

Tip While using the text editor, in many instances you can click the right mouse button to display a pop-up menu of frequently used commands. The commands available depend on what the mouse pointer is pointing to and whether you are in edit or debug mode. For example, if you click while pointing to the name of a file, the pop-up menu shows a command to open that file, as well as other commands including Copy, Insert/Remove Breakpoint, and Properties.

File Management

The text editor File menu has several commands for standard file management. With these commands you can perform the following actions:

- Creating files
- Opening files
- Opening multiple files
- Saving files
- Printing files

Creating Files

The New command creates a new source file. Creating a source file does not affect other open source files.

▶ **To create a new source file**

1 From the File menu, choose New.

   The New dialog box appears.

2 Select Text File, and then choose the OK button.

3 From the File menu, choose Save.

   The Save As dialog box appears.

4 Select a path where you want to store the source file.

5 In the File Name box, type a file name.

   The default extension given to a file is the last extension used when you saved a file. You can type another extension or select one from the Save As Type box.

6 Choose the Save button.

New files are labeled Text*n* until they are saved. The *n* is a sequential number.

Opening Files

When you open a source file, its name is added to the Window menu. You cannot use the Open command on the File menu to open another copy of an open source file.

▶ **To open a file**

1 From the File menu, choose Open.

The Open dialog box appears.

2 Select the drive and directory where the file is stored.

3 If you want read only, select the Open As Read Only check box.

Note You can edit a file even if the Open As Read Only check box is selected. When you save the file, the Save As dialog box appears, allowing you to save the file using a different name.

4 Specify the types of files to display in the Files Of Type box.

Files with the chosen extension are displayed in the list box. For example, Project Workspaces displays all files with the .mdp extension. The Files Of Type drop-down list box initially lists commonly used file extensions. The default shows the .c, .cpp, .cxx, .h, and .rc extensions.

−or−

Specify wildcard patterns in the File Name box to display file types. You can use any combination of wildcard patterns, delimited by semicolons. For example, if you type `*.h;*.cpp`, all files with these extensions are displayed. The wildcard patterns you specify are retained until you close the dialog box.

5 Select a filename, then choose the Open button.

−or−

Double-click the filename.

You can also open a file by double-clicking the file icon in the Project Workspace, or by dragging the icon of a non-project file into the application window.

 Tip The names of the four most recently opened files are displayed at the end of the File menu. To open one of these files, choose its name from the menu.

Note The number of files on the list of most recently opened files is controlled by the FileCount item in the Registry.

The text editor commands that can open or activate a new file are described in the following table.

Command	Description
Bookmark	Edits or navigates bookmarks.
GoTo	Moves to a specified location.
GoToErrorTag	Moves to the line containing the current error or tag.
GoToNextErrorTag	Moves to the line containing the next error or tag.
GoToPrevErrorTag	Moves to the line containing the previous error or tag.
WindowList	Manages the currently open windows.

See Also Viewing and Changing the Shortcut Keys

Opening Multiple Files

You can open multiple files from the Open dialog box by using the mouse to select a file or group of files. Before you can select files, they must be visible in the Directories window.

▶ **To open two or more files in sequence**

1 From the File menu, choose Open.

The Open dialog box appears.

2 Select the drive and directory where the files are stored.

The default is the current drive and directory.

3 Specify the types of files to display in the Files Of Type box.

Files with the chosen extension are displayed in the list box. For example, Project Workspaces displays all files with the .mdp extension. The Files Of Type drop-down list box initially lists commonly used file extensions. The default shows the .c, .cpp, .cxx, .h, and .rc extensions.

−or−

Specify wildcard patterns in the File Name box to display file types. You can use any combination of wildcard patterns, delimited by semicolons. For example, if you type `*.h;*.cpp`, all files with these extensions are displayed. The wildcard patterns you specify are retained until you close the dialog box.

4 Click the first file or directory you want to select.

5 Hold down the SHIFT key while you click the last file or directory in the group, and then choose the Open button.

▶ **To open two or more files out of sequence**

1 From the File menu, choose Open.

The Open dialog box appears.

2 Select the drive and directory where the files are stored.

The default is the current drive and directory.

3 Specify the types of files to display in the Files of Type box.

Files with the chosen extension are displayed in the list box. For example, Project Workspaces displays all files with the .mdp extension. The Files of Type drop-down list box initially lists commonly used file extensions. The default shows the .c, .cpp, .cxx, .h, and .rc extensions.

–or–

Specify wildcard patterns in the File Name box to display file types. You can use any combination of wildcard patterns, delimited by semicolons. For example, if you type `*.h;*.cpp`, all files with these extensions are displayed. The wildcard patterns you specify are retained until you close the dialog box.

4 Hold down the CTRL key while you click each file or directory that you want. Once your selection is complete, choose the Open button.

To cancel a selection, hold down CTRL while you click the selected file or directory.

Saving Files

As you make changes to a source file, an asterisk (*) appears in the title bar to indicate that the file has changed since it was last saved. Each source window associated with a source file can retain its own sizing and other window attributes.

▶ To save a file

1 Switch to the source window.

2 From the File menu, choose Save.

If you already named the file, the Save command saves changes without displaying the Save As dialog box.

If your file is unnamed, the Save As dialog box appears.

3 In the File Name box, type the filename.

4 Select the drive and directory where the you want to save the file.

5 Choose the Save button.

▶ To save all open files

• From the File menu, choose Save All.

▶ To save selected open files

1 From the Window menu, choose Windows.

The Windows dialog box appears.

2 Select one or more files from the file list.

3 Choose the Save button.

4 Choose the Cancel button.

You can also save another copy of an existing file. This procedure is useful for maintaining revised copies of a file while keeping the original unchanged.

▶ **To save a new file or another copy of an existing file**

1 Make the file active by clicking the source window.

2 From the File menu, choose Save As.

The Save As dialog box appears.

3 In the File Name box, type the filename.

4 Select the drive and the directory where you want to save the file.

5 Choose the Save button .

▶ **To set Save options**

1 From the Tools menu, choose Options.

The Options dialog box appears.

2 Select the Editor tab, and then select the desired save option.

- To save open files before running any tool, select the Save Before Running Tools check box.

- To always prompt before saving a file, select the Prompt Before Saving Files check box.

- To automatically reload externally modified files that have been loaded (but not yet changed) by the editor, select the Automatic Reload check box.

3 Choose the OK button.

Printing Files

With the text editor, you can print selected text or a complete file. Text is printed in the default font for the printer if the default editor font is used. Otherwise, the text prints with the selected editor font, if that font is available on the printer.

You can customize your print jobs by adding headers and footers and by adjusting margins.

▶ **To print selected text in a source file**

1 Select the text you want to print.

2 From the File menu, choose Print.

The Print dialog box appears. Under Print Range, the Selection option is automatically selected for you.

3 Choose the OK button.

▶ **To print a complete source file**

1 Move the focus to the source file you want to print.

2 From the File menu, choose Print.

The Print dialog box appears.

3 Under Print Range, select the All option button.

4 Choose the OK button.

▶ **To customize a print job**

1 From the File menu, choose Page Setup.

The Page Setup dialog box appears.

2 In the Header and Footer boxes, type the header or footer text, codes, or both. You can use the drop-list to insert codes into the text box. Only one of the alignment options (left, centered, or right) is available at a time for either header or footer.

To print	Use
Filename	**&f**
Current page number	**&p**
Current system time	**&t**
Current system date	**&d**
Left aligned	**&l**
Centered	**&c**
Right aligned	**&r**

3 Under Margins, type the left, right, top, and bottom measurements.

4 Choose the OK button.

Moving Around in Source Files

The text editor provides a variety of methods to move around in a source file. In addition to using the regular mouse movement and page controls, you can:

- Use virtual space for advanced cursor control.
- Identify sections of source code by matching group delimiters.
- Find matching conditional statements.
- Use the Go To dialog box to navigate your source files.
- Set bookmarks to mark frequently accessed lines in your source files.
- Choose from a wide-range of source file navigation commands.

Using Virtual Space

All editors support moving the cursor by one character position. This feature has been implemented in many ways. The most common difference among text editors is whether or not you can move the cursor into a location that does not currently contain text. For example, if your cursor is on column 20, and there is no text on the line below the current line, moving the cursor down can do one of two things: Either the cursor moves to column 1—because there is no text on the line below—or the cursor remains on column 20. This latter behavior is called virtual space.

With the Developer Studio's text editor, you can treat text selection and space insertion in two ways. When you select the Virtual Spaces option, spaces are inserted between the end of the line and the insertion point before new characters are added to the line. When you clear the Virtual Spaces option, the text editor behaves like Microsoft Word for Windows, and the insertion point is set to the end of the line.

▶ **To enable virtual spaces**

1 From the Tools menu, choose Options.

   The Options dialog box appears.

2 Select the Compatibility tab.

3 In the Recommended Options For list box, select the editor emulation in which you want to have virtual spaces.

4 Select the Enable Virtual Space check box.

5 Choose the OK button.

Many word processors support the idea of moving the cursor one sentence at a time. Developer Studio's text editor supports this as well (SentenceUp and SentenceDown), but most source code doesn't have the spacing and punctuation marks needed for sentence navigation. Instead, you can use LineUp and LineDown to navigate single lines of source code.

Matching Group Delimiters

Source code is often grouped using delimiters such as (), { }, and []. These groupings are called levels. You can navigate these levels using the LevelUp and LevelDown commands. The editor understands nested levels, and matches the correct delimiter even if the level spans several pages and itself contains many levels.

The LevelUp command searches backwards for one of the right-side delimiters, and then positions the cursor before the matching left-side delimiter. The LevelDown command searches forward for a left-side delimiter, and then positions the cursor after the matching right-side delimiter.

▶ **To search forward for a matching level**

● Press the LevelDown key combination.

The command begins searching for one of the left-side delimiters, which are (, {, and [. When the left-side delimiter is found, the cursor is positioned at the matching right-side delimiter. If a matching delimiter cannot be found, the editor beeps.

The editor also provides the command GoToMatchBrace. When the cursor is initially positioned next to a delimiter, the GoToMatchBrace command moves the cursor to the matching delimiter in a block. Since this command works independently of whether the character is a right-side or left-side delimiter, you can quickly jump between the start and end of a level.

▶ **To move to a matching brace**

1 Place the insertion point immediately in front of a brace.

2 Press the GoToMatchBrace key combination.

The insertion point moves forward or backward to the matching brace. Choosing the command again returns the insertion point to its starting place. If a matching brace cannot be found, the editor beeps. This method also works for parentheses, angle brackets, and square brackets.

See Also   The Navigating Commands, Viewing and Changing the Shortcut Keys

Matching Conditional Statements

Another way of grouping source code is between compiler preprocessor statements. The editor will allow you to move from inside a conditional statement to the enclosing preprocessor statement. For example, ConditionalUp will move the cursor to the enclosing **#if**, **#ifdef**, **#else**, **#elif**; while ConditionalDown will move the cursor to the enclosing **#else**, **#elif**, **#endif**. If the cursor is positioned on a preprocessor statement, it is considered to be in the next conditional block while moving down, and in the previous conditional block while moving up.

▶ **To move to the matching preprocessor statement**

• Move the insertion point to the line that is enclosed by preprocessor statements.

  • Press the ConditionalUp key combination to move the insertion point up to the line containing the matching preprocessor statement (such as **#ifdef**).

  • Press the ConditionalDown key combination to move the insertion point down to the line containing the matching preprocessor statement (such as **#endif**).

Note   If you hold down the SHIFT key, you can use the ConditionalUpExtend and ConditionalDownExtend key combinations to select text from the current cursor position to the enclosing **#if, #ifdef, #else, #elif**, or **#endif** preprocessor statement. This key binding of the SHIFT key with ConditionalUpExtend and ConditionalDownExtend is available in the standard configuration after installation. If you have changed shortcut key assignments, this keystroke combination may not be available.

See Also   The Navigating Commands, Viewing and Changing the Shortcut Keys

Using Go To

The Go To dialog box is organized into three areas: a list of Go To What items, additional selection criteria, and navigation buttons. Depending on the Go To What selection, the additional selection criteria format changes to either an edit control or a list box. You can display Help text in all cases. The following table lists the Go To What types and related additional selection criteria.

Go To What	Additional Selection Criteria	Comments
Address	Enter address expression	Type any valid debugger expression.
Bookmark	Enter bookmark name	Type the bookmark name.
Definition	Enter identifier	This requires browse information.
Error/Tag	Enter error/tag	Select one of the listed error/tags.
InfoViewer Annotations	Enter InfoViewer annotated topic	Type the annotated topic.
InfoViewer Bookmarks	Enter InfoViewer bookmark name	Type the bookmark name.
Line	Enter line number	Type the line number.
Offset	Enter offset	Type the decimal or hexadecimal number.
Reference	Enter identifier	Type the browse information.

▶ **To use the Go To dialog box**

1 From the Edit menu, choose Go To.

The Go To dialog box appears.

2 In the Go To What list box, select the type.

3 Enter the additional selection criteria.

4 Choose one of the navigation buttons: Go To, Previous, or Next.

Note If the Go To What item is undefined, the additional selection criteria box is greyed. For example, if you have not defined any bookmarks, the Enter Bookmark Name text box is grayed.

Using Bookmarks

You can set bookmarks to mark frequently accessed lines in your source file. Once a bookmark is set, you can use menu or keyboard commands to move to it. You can remove a bookmark when you no longer need it.

You can use both named and unnamed bookmarks. Named bookmarks are saved between editing sessions. Once you create a named bookmark, you can jump to that location whether or not the file is open. Named bookmarks store both the line number and the column number of the location of the cursor when the bookmark was created. This location is adjusted whenever you edit the file. Even if you delete the characters around the bookmark, the bookmark remains in the correct location.

Unnamed bookmarks are temporary. They are removed when the file containing them is closed or reloaded. Unnamed bookmarks store only the current line, not the column offset of the cursor. When a line containing an unnamed bookmark is deleted, the bookmark is also removed. You can jump to an unnamed bookmark by activating the file and using either the BookmarkNext or BookmarkPrev command. The advantage of unnamed bookmarks is that they are very easy to set (just use BookmarkToggle), and they provide you with visible feedback in the selection margin of your document.

▶ **To set a named bookmark**

1 Move the insertion point to the line and column where you want to set a named bookmark.

2 From the Edit menu, choose Bookmark.

The Bookmark dialog box appears.

3 In the Name box, type the name of the bookmark.

4 Choose the Add button to add the named bookmark to the list of bookmarks.

5 Choose the Close button.

▶ **To remove multiple named bookmarks**

1 From the Edit menu, choose Bookmark.

The Bookmark dialog box appears.

2 In the Name box, select the names of the bookmarks to be removed.

3 Choose the Delete button to remove the selected bookmarks.

4 Choose the Close button.

▶ **To go to a named bookmark**

1 From the Edit menu, choose Bookmark.

The Bookmark dialog box appears.

2 In the Name box, select the name of the bookmark to go to.

3 Choose the Go To button.

▶ **To remove a named bookmark**

1 From the Edit menu, choose Bookmark.

   The Bookmark dialog box appears.

2 In the Name box, select the name of the bookmark to be removed.

3 Choose the Delete button to remove the selected bookmark.

4 Choose the Close button.

▶ **To set an unnamed bookmark**

1 Move the insertion point to the line where you want to set a bookmark.

2 Press the BookmarkToggle key combination.

   The line is selected, or marked in the margin if you have set the selection margin.

▶ **To move to the next bookmark after the insertion point**

• Press the BookmarkNext key combination.

▶ **To move to the previous bookmark before the insertion point**

• Press the BookmarkPrev key combination.

▶ **To remove an unnamed bookmark**

1 Move the insertion point to anywhere on the line containing the unnamed bookmark.

2 Press the BookmarkToggle key combination.

The text editor commands that are associated with bookmarks are described in the following table.

Command	Description
Bookmark	Edits or navigates named bookmarks.
BookmarkClearAll	Clears all unnamed bookmarks in the window.
BookmarkNext	Moves to the line containing the next named or unnamed bookmark.
BookmarkPrev	Moves to the line containing the previous named or unnamed bookmark.
BookmarkToggle	Toggles an unnamed bookmark for the current line.

Note These bookmark commands can open files or activate different files in the open Windows list. These commands are an easy way to move between text in a number of different source files. For more information on opening files, see "Opening Files" earlier in this chapter.

See Also Viewing and Changing the Shortcut Keys

The Navigating Commands

The text editor commands for moving around in a source file are described in the following table.

Command	Description
CharLeft	Moves the cursor one character to the left.
CharRight	Moves the cursor one character to the right.
ConditionalDown	Finds the next matching preprocessor condition.
ConditionalUp	Finds the previous matching preprocessor condition.
DocumentEnd	Moves the cursor to the end of the file.
DocumentStart	Moves the cursor to the beginning of the file.
GoToIndentation	Moves the cursor to the end of the indentation.
GoToMatchBrace	Finds the matching brace.
Home	Moves the cursor alternately between the beginning of the current line and the beginning of the text on that line.
IndentToPrev	Moves the cursor to the position of the next text that is on the previous line.
LevelDown	Searches forward for the end of the next bracketed level.
LevelUp	Searches back for the beginning of the previous bracketed level.
LineDown	Moves the cursor one line downward.
LineEnd	Moves the cursor to the end of the text on the current line.
LineStart	Moves the cursor to the beginning of the current line.
LineUp	Moves the cursor one line upward.
PageDown	Moves the cursor one page downward.
PageUp	Moves the cursor one page upward.
ParaDown	Moves the cursor forward to the beginning of the next paragraph.
ParaUp	Moves the cursor backward to the beginning of the previous paragraph.
SentenceLeft	Moves the cursor back to the previous beginning of a sentence.
SentenceRight	Moves the cursor forward to the next end of a sentence.
WindowEnd	Moves the cursor to the bottom of the text window.
WindowStart	Moves the cursor the the top of the text window.
WordLeft	Moves the cursor backward one word.
WordRight	Moves the cursor forward one word.

Note The command Home is distinct from the LineStart command. LineStart always moves the cursor to the first column in the line, while Home moves the cursor to different locations depending on the cursor's current location. The Home command moves the cursor to the first non-blank character in the line. However, if the cursor is already located on the first non-blank character, Home moves to the first column of the line.

See Also Viewing and Changing the Shortcut Keys

Finding and Replacing Text

The text editor supports two common searching methods: full string searching and incremental searching. With full string searching, the entire search string is specified before the search begins. With incremental searching, the search is performed as the string is typed.

With the advanced find and replace capabilities of the text editor, you can search for text in a single source file or in multiple files. You can search for literal text strings or use regular expressions to find words or characters. You can even use tagged regular expressions for searching and replacing.

With the find and replace commands of the text editor, you can:

- Find text in a single file.
- Find text in multiple files.
- Replace text.
- Use regular expressions with Developer Studio, BRIEF emulation, and Epsilon emulation.

If you use any of the incremental search commands (IncrementalSearch, IncrementalSearchBack, IncrementalSearchRE, IncrementalSearchREBack), you can modify the search by toggling the word mode (CTRL+W), regular expression mode (CTRL+T), and case sensitive mode (CTRL+C). These keystrokes are not bindable and only affect the incremental search command.

Since IncrementalSearch finds the match while you are typing, you rarely need to type the complete search string. If you are looking for a string that occurs multiple times in your file, just repeat the IncrementalSearch command after you have typed enough to specify the string. Incremental search stops when the ESC key is pressed.

The text editor commands for searching in a source file are described in the following table.

Command	Description
Find	Finds the specified text.
FindBack	Finds the previous occurrence of the specified text.
FindForward	Finds the next occurrence of the specified text.

Command	Description
FindNext	Continues the search forward, finding the next occurrence of the specified text.
FindNextWord	Finds the next occurrence of the selected text.
FindPrev	Continues the search backward, finding the previous occurrence of the specified text.
FindPrevWord	Finds the previous occurrence of the selected text.
FindRE	Searches forward for a string using regular expressions.
FindREPrev	Searches backward for a string using regular expressions.
FindRepeat	Continues the previous search.
FindReplace	Replaces specific text with different text.
FindReplaceRE	Replaces specific text with different text found by using regular expressions.
FindTool	Activates the Find combo box tool.
IncrementalSearch	Starts an incremental search forward.
IncrementalSearchBack	Starts an incremental search backward.
IncrementalSearchRE	Starts a regular expression incremental search forward.
IncrementalSearchREBack	Starts a regular expression incremental search backward.

See Also   Viewing and Changing the Shortcut Keys, Using Regular Expressions with Developer Studio, Using Regular Expressions with BRIEF Emulation, Using Regular Expressions with Epsilon Emulation

Finding Text in a Single File

With the Find command, you can search the active window for the following types of text strings:

- **Whole Word Match**   Matches all occurrences of a text string not preceded or followed by an alphanumeric character or the underscore (_).
- **Case Match**   Searches for text that matches the capitalization of the text string.
- **Regular Expressions**   Uses special character sequences—regular expressions — to search for text. If you select the Regular Expression check box in the Find dialog box, you can build the search string using regular expressions from the drop-down list.

You can set bookmarks at every occurance of the text string or expression. You can then use the Next Bookmark command to move to each bookmark in your file.

▶ **To find a text string**

   1 Move the insertion point to where you want to begin your search.

   The editor uses the location of the insertion point to select a default search string.

2 From the Edit menu, choose Find.

The Find dialog box appears.

3 In the Find What text box, type the search text or a regular expression.

–or–

Select the menu button to the right of the combo box to display a list of regular search expressions. When you select an expression from this list, the expression is substituted as the search text in the Find What text box. If you do use regular expressions, be sure the Regular Expression check box is selected.

You can also use the drop-down list to select from a list of up to 16 previous search strings.

4 Select any of the Find options.

5 To begin your search, choose Find Next or Mark All. The Find dialog box disappears when the search begins. To repeat a find operation, use the shortcut keys or toolbar buttons.

6 To continue your search, use the Find Next or Find Previous toolbar buttons.

▶ To begin a find without the Find dialog box

1 Type or select a search string in the Standard toolbar Find box.

2 Press ENTER.

Note   You can use regular expressions with the Standard toolbar Find box if you have previously selected the Regular Expression check box in the Find dialog box.

▶ To find a string using incremental search

1 Press the IncrementalSearch key combination.

The cursor moves to the status bar.

2 Begin typing the search string.

As you type each character, the text editor selects the matching string in your file.

3 If necessary, press the IncrementalSearch key combination to go to the next match in your file.

4 Press the ESC key or use any of the navigational commands to end the search.

Note   If there is no match, the text editor beeps and displays a warning in the status bar.

 Tip   You can assign shortcut keys to three of the options in the Find dialog box: EditToggleCaseSensitivity, EditToggleFindMatchWord, and EditToggleRE. By using the shortcut keys, you can change the search criteria without displaying the Find dialog box.

See Also   Viewing and Changing the Shortcut Keys, Finding and Replacing Text

Finding Text in Multiple Files

With the Find in Files command on the File menu, you can search multiple text files for the following types of text strings:

- **Whole Word Match**   Matches all occurrences of a text string not preceded or followed by an alphanumeric character or an underscore (_).

- **Case Match**   Searches for text that matches the capitalization of the text string.

- **Regular Expressions**   Uses special character sequences—regular expressions—to search for text. If you select the Regular Expression check box in the Find dialog box, you can build the search string using regular expressions from the drop-down list.

▶ **To find a text string in multiple source files**

1 From the File menu, choose Find In Files.

The Find In Files dialog box appears.

2 In the Find What text box, type the search text or a regular expression.

–or–

Select the menu button to the right of the combo box to display a list of regular search expressions. When you select an expression from this list, the expression is substituted as the search text in the Find What text box. If you do use regular expressions, be sure the Regular Expression check box is selected.

You can also use the drop-down list to select from a list of up to 16 previous search strings.

3 In the In Files Of Type box, select the file types you want to search.

You can use the drop-down list to select from common file types or to type text specifying other file types.

4 In the In Folder box, select the primary folder that you want to search. Choose the Browse button (...) to display the Choose Directory dialog box if you want to change drives and directories.

5 If necessary, select one or more of the Find options.

6 To select additional folders to search, choose the Advanced button.

The Look In Additional Folders portion of the dialog box appears.

7 If necessary, select the Look In Folders For Project Source Files check box.

8 If necessary, select the Look In Folders For Project Include Files check box.

Note   These project source and project include file folders are the same as the project's directory paths. For more information on how to view and change these directory paths, see "Setting Directories" in Chapter 22, "Customizing Microsoft Developer Studio."

9 To add a folder to the Look In Additional Folders list, double-click the empty selection. Then type the path and filename, or use the Browse button (...) to display the Choose Directory dialog box to change drives and directories.

To remove a folder from the Look In Additional Folders list, select the folder and press DEL.

Developer Studio retains the contents of the Find In Files list between uses of the Find In Files command in any single session.

10 Choose the Find button to begin the search.

The Output window displays the list of file locations where the text string appears. Each occurrence lists the fully qualified filename, followed by the line number of the occurrence and the line containing the match.

11 To open a file containing a match, double-click the entry in the Output window.

An editor window containing the file opens, with the line containing the match selected. You can jump to other occurrences of the text string by double-clicking the specific entries in the Output window, or you can use the GoToNextErrorTag command.

When you jump to a found string location specified in the Output window, the corresponding source file is loaded if it is not already open in the editor.

Note The Output window is a virtual window that is maintained even when it is not displayed. You can display the output from your last multiple-file search done during your current session by choosing the Output command from the View menu and by choosing the Find In Files tab in the Output window.

See Also Finding and Replacing Text, Using Regular Expressions with Developer Studio, Using Regular Expressions with BRIEF Emulation, Using Regular Expressions with Epsilon Emulation

Replacing Text

With the Replace command, you can search the active window for the following types of text strings, and replace each with another text string:

- **Whole Word Match** Matches all occurrences of a text string not preceded or followed by an alphanumeric character or an underscore (_).

- **Case Match** Searches for text that matches the capitalization of the text string.

- **Regular Expressions** Uses special character sequences—regular expressions— to search for text. If you select the Regular Expression check box in the Find dialog box, you can build the search string using regular expressions from the drop-down list.

▶ **To replace text**

1 Move the insertion point to where you want to begin your search.

The editor uses the location of the insertion point to select a default search string.

2 From the Edit menu, choose Replace.

The Replace dialog box appears.

3 In the Find What text box, type the search text or a regular expression.

 Tip Select the menu button to the right of the combo box to display a list of regular search expressions. When you select an expression from this list, the expression is substituted as the search text in the Find What text box. You can also use the drop-down list to select from a list of up to 16 previous search strings. If you do use regular expressions, be sure the Regular Expression check box is selected.

4 In the Replace With text box, type the replacement text.

Select the menu button to the right of the combo box to display a list of replacement options.

5 Select any of the remaining Find options.

6 To begin the search, choose the Find Next button.

The Replace command selects the first matching text string.

7 Replace the current selection by choosing the Replace button.

−or−

Replace all identical strings by choosing the Replace All button.

−or−

Skip the current selection and find the next selection by choosing the Find Next button.

See Also Using Regular Expressions with Developer Studio, Using Regular Expressions with BRIEF Emulation, Using Regular Expressions with Epsilon Emulation

Using Regular Expressions with Developer Studio

A regular expression is a search string that uses special characters to match a text pattern in a file. You can use regular expressions with both the Find and Replace commands.

▶ **To use a regular expression**

1 From the Edit menu, choose either Find or Replace.

2 In the Find What text box, type a regular expression.

3 In the Replace With text box, type a regular expression if required.

Tip Select the menu button to the right of the combo box to display a list of regular search expressions. When you select an expression from this list, the expression is substituted as the search text in the Find What text box. You can also use the drop-down list to select from a list of up to 16 previous search strings. If you do use regular expressions, be sure the Regular Expression check box is selected.

The following table lists valid regular expressions.

Regular expression	Description
.	Any single character.
[ ]	Any one of the characters contained in the brackets, or any of an ASCII range of characters separated by a hyphen (-). For example, b[aeiou]d matches bad, bed, bid, bod, and bud, and r[eo]+d matches red, rod, reed, and rood, but not reod or roed. x[0-9] matches x0, x1, x2, and so on.
	If the first character in the brackets is a caret (^), then the regular expression matches any characters except those in the brackets.
^	The beginning of a line.
$	The end of a line.
\(\)	Indicates a tagged expression to retain for replacement purposes. If the expression in the Find What text box is \(lpsz\)BigPointer, and the expression in the Replace With box is \1NewPointer, all selected occurrences of lpszBigPointer are replaced with lpszNewPointer.
	Each occurrence of a tagged expression is numbered according to its order in the Find What text box, and its replacement expression is \n, where 1 corresponds to the first tagged expression, 2 to the second, and so on. You can have up to nine tagged expressions.
\~	Not the following character. For example, b\~ad matches bbd, bcd, bdd, and so on, but not bad.
\{c\!c\}	Any one of the characters separated by the alternation symbol (\!). For example, \{j\!u\}+fruit finds jfruit, jjfruit, ufruit, ujfruit, uufruit, and so on.
*	None or more of the preceding characters or expressions. For example, ba*c matches bc, bac, baac, baaac, and so on.
+	At least one or more of the preceding characters or expressions. For example, ba+c matches bac, baac, baaac, but not bc.
\{\}	Any sequence of characters between the escaped braces. For example, \{ju\}+fruit finds jufruit, jujufruit, jujujufruit, and so on. Note that it will not find jfruit, ufruit, or ujfruit, because the sequence ju is not in any of those strings.

Regular expression	Description
[^]	Any character except those following the caret (^) character in the brackets, or any of an ASCII range of characters separated by a hyphen (-). For example, x[^0-9] matches xa, xb, xc, and so on, but not x0, x1, x2, and so on.
\:a	Any single alphanumeric character [a-zA-Z0-9].
\:b	Any white-space character. The \:b finds tabs and spaces. There is no alternate syntax to express :b.
\:c	Any single alphabetic character [a-zA-Z].
\:d	Any decimal digit [0-9].
\:n	Any unsigned number \{[0-9]+\.[0-9]*\![0-9]*\.[0-9]+\![0-9]+\}. For example, \:n should match 123, .45, and 123.45.
\:z	Any unsigned decimal integer [0-9]+.
\:h	Any hexadecimal number [0-9a-fA-F]+.
\:i	Any C/C++ identifier [a-zA-Z_$][a-zA-Z0-9_$]+.
\:w	Any English word (that is, a string of alphabetic characters) [a-zA-Z]+.
\:q	Any quoted string \{"[^"]*"\!'[^']*'\}.
\	Removes the pattern match characteristic in the Find What text box from the special characters listed above. For example, 100$ matches 100 at the end of a line, but 100\$ matches the character string 100$ anywhere on a line.

Note   You can use regular expressions with the Find button on the toolbar if you have previously selected the Regular Expression check box in the Find dialog box or the Replace dialog box.

Using Regular Expressions with BRIEF Emulation

A regular expression is a search string that uses special characters to match a text pattern in a file. You can use regular expressions with both the Find and Replace commands.

▶ **To use a regular expression**

1 From the Edit menu, choose either Find or Replace.

2 In the Find What text box, type a regular expression.

3 In the Replace With text box, type a regular expression if required.

Tip   Select the menu button to the right of the combo box to display a list of regular search expressions. When you select an expression from this list, the expression is substituted as the search text in the Find What text box. You can also use the drop-down list to select from a list of up to 16 previous search strings. If you do use regular expressions, be sure the Regular Expression check box is selected.

The following table lists valid regular expressions for the BRIEF emulation.

Regular expression	Description
?	Any single character.
[ ]	Any one of the characters contained in the brackets, or any of an ASCII range of characters separated by a hyphen (-). For example, b[aeiou]d matches bad, bed, bid, bod and bud, and r[eo]+d matches red, rod, reed and rood, but not reod or roed. x[0-9] matches x0, x1, x2, and so on.
	If the first character in the brackets is a tilde (~), then the regular expression matches any characters except those in the brackets.
%	The beginning of a line.
$	The end of a line.
{ }	Indicates a tagged expression to retain for replacement purposes. If the expression in the Find What text box is {lpsz}BigPointer, and the expression in the Replace With box is \0NewPointer, all selected occurrences of lpszBigPointer are replaced with lpszNewPointer.
	Each occurrence of a tagged expression is numbered according to its order in the Find What text box, and its replacement expression is \n, where 0 corresponds to the first tagged expression, 1 to the second, and so on. You can have up to ten tagged expressions.
~	Not the following character. For example, b~ad matches bbd, bcd, bdd, and so on, but not bad.
{c|c}	Any one of the characters separated by the alternation symbol (|). For example, {j|u}+fruit finds jfruit, jjfruit, ufruit, ujfruit, uufruit, and so on.
@	None or more of the preceding characters or expressions. For example, ba@c matches bc, bac, baac, baaac, and so on.
+	At least one or more of the preceding characters or expressions. For example, ba+c matches bac, baac, and baaac, but not bc.
[ ]	Any sequence of characters between the brackets. For example, [ju]+fruit finds jufruit, jujufruit, jujujufruit, and so on. Note that it will not find jfruit, ufruit, or ujfruit because the sequence ju is not in any of those strings.
[~]	Any character except those following the tilde character (~) in the brackets, or any of an ASCII range of characters separated by a hyphen (-). For example, x[~0-9] matches xa, xb, xc, and so on, but not x0, x1, x2, and so on.
[a-zA-Z0-9]	Any single alphanumeric character.
[\x09\]+	Any white-space character.

Regular expression	Description
[a-zA-Z]	Any single alphabetic character.
[0-9]	Any decimal digit.
[0-9a-fA-F]+	Any hexadecimal number.
{[0-9]+.[0-9]@} | {[0-9]@.[0-9]+} | {[0-9]+}	Any unsigned number. For example, {[0-9]+.[0-9]@} | {[0-9]@.[0-9]+} | {[0-9]+} should match 123, .45, and 123.45.
[0-9]+	Any unsigned decimal integer.
[a-zA-Z_$] [a-zA-Z0-9_$]@	C/C++ identifier.
[a-zA-Z]+	Any English word (that is, any string of alphabetic characters).
"[~"]@"	Any quoted string.
\	Removes the pattern match characteristic in the Find What text box from the special characters listed above. For example, 100$ matches 100 at the end of a line, but 100\$ matches the character string 100$ anywhere on a line.

Note   You can use regular expressions with the Find button on the toolbar if you have previously selected the Regular Expression check box in the Find dialog box or the Replace dialog box.

Using Regular Expressions with Epsilon Emulation

A regular expression is a search string that uses special characters to match a text pattern in a file. You can use regular expressions with both the Find and Replace commands.

▶ To use a regular expression

1 From the Edit menu, choose either Find or Replace.

2 In the Find What text box, type a regular expression.

3 In the Replace With text box, type a regular expression if required.

Tip   Select the menu button to the right of the combo box to display a list of regular search expressions. When you select an expression from this list, the expression is substituted as the search text in the Find What text box. You can also use the drop-down list to select from a list of up to 16 previous search strings. If you do use regular expressions, be sure the Regular Expression check box is selected.

The following table lists valid regular expressions for the Epsilon emulation.

Regular expression	Description
.	Any single character.
[ ]	Any one of the characters contained in the brackets or any of an ASCII range of characters separated by a hyphen (-). For example, b(aeiou)d matches bad, bed, bid, bod and bud, and r(eo)+d matches red, rod, reed and rood, but not reod or roed. x(0-9) matches x0, x1, x2, and so on.
	If the first character in the brackets is a caret (^), then the regular expression matches any characters except those in the brackets.
^	The beginning of a line.
$	The end of a line.
( )	Indicates a tagged expression to retain for replacement purposes. If the expression in the Find What text box is (lpsz)BigPointer, and the expression in the Replace With box is #1NewPointer, all selected occurrences of lpszBigPointer are replaced with lpszNewPointer.
	Each occurrence of a tagged expression is numbered according to its order in the Find What text box, and its replacement expression is #n, where 1 corresponds to the first tagged expression, 2 to the second, and so on. You can have up to nine tagged expressions.
~	Not the following character. For example, b~ad matches bbd, bcd, bdd, and so on, but not bad.
(c|c)	Any one of the characters separated by the alternation symbol (|). For example, (j|u)+fruit finds jfruit, jjfruit, ufruit, ujfruit, uufruit, and so on.
*	None or more of the preceding characters or expressions. For example, ba*c matches bc, bac, baac, baaac, and so on.
+	At least one or more of the preceding characters or expressions. For example, ba+c matches bac, baac, and baaac, but not bc.
[^]	Any character except those following the caret (^) in the brackets, or any of an ASCII range of characters separated by a hyphen (-). For example, x[^0-9] matches xa, xb, xc, and so on, but not x0, x1, x2, and so on.
[a-zA-Z0-9]	Any single alphanumeric character.
[<tab>]+	Any white-space character.
[a-zA-Z]	Any single alphabetic character.
{0-9]	Any decimal digit.
[0-9a-fA-F]+	Any hexadecimal number.
([0-9]+.[0-9]*| [0-9]*.[0-9]+| [0-9]+)	Any unsigned number. For example, ([0-9]+.[0-9]*|[0-9]*.[0-9]+|[0-9]+) should match 123, .45, and 123.45.

Regular expression	Description
`[0-9]+`	Any unsigned decimal integer.
`[a-zA-Z_$]` `[a-zA-Z0-9_$]*`	C/C++ identifier.
`[a-zA-Z]+`	Any English word (that is, any string of alphabetic characters).
`"[~"]*"`	Any quoted string.
`\`	Removes the pattern match characteristic in the Find What text box from the special characters listed above. For example, `100$` matches `100` at the end of a line, but `100\$` matches the character string `100$` anywhere on a line.

Note   You can use regular expressions with a search in a single source file with the Find button on the toolbar if you have previously selected Regular Expression in the Find or Replace dialog box.

Selecting Text

You can select lines, multiple lines, and column blocks of text to cut, copy, delete, indent, and unindent. Most of the selection commands have extensions (the word "Extend" is appended to the name of the command) that move the cursor and extend the selection. By default, these commands are bound to the same key combination as the primary selection command plus the SHIFT key (such as SHIFT+LEFT ARROW for CharLeftExtend).

▶ **To select a line of text**

- In the selection margin, point to the beginning of the text you want to select and click the left mouse button.

▶ **To select multiple lines of text**

1 In the selection margin, point to the beginning of the text you want to select.

2 Drag either up or down to select the lines of text.

▶ **To select a column block of text**

1 Point to the beginning of the text you want to select.

2 Hold down the ALT key and click the left mouse button.

3 Release the ALT key and point to the end of the text you want to select.

When you release the left mouse button, the block of text is selected, and the text is available for cut, copy, delete, and indent operations. To cancel column-select mode, click the left mouse button.

Note When you use proportional fonts in the editor window, the column positions you select in the first line may not correspond exactly to the subsequent lines you select. The text editor selects the character most directly in line with the start and end columns, ignoring the actual character count.

The text editor commands for selection are described in the following table.

Command	Description
CharLeftExtend	Extends the selection one character to the left.
CharRightExtend	Extends the selection one character to the right.
ConditionalDownExtend	Selects to the next matching preprocessor condition.
ConditionalUpExtend	Selects to the previous matching preprocessor condition.
DocumentEndExtend	Extends the selection to the end of the file.
DocumentStartExtend	Extends the selection to the beginning of the file.
HomeExtend	Extends the selection alternately between the start of the current line and the start of the text on that line.
LineDownExtend	Extends the selection one line downward.
LineEndExtend	Extends the selection to the end of the text on the current line.
LineUpExtend	Extends the selection one line upward.
PageDownExtend	Extends the selection one page downward.
PageUpExtend	Extends the selection one page upward.
SelectAll	Selects the entire document.
SelectChar	Starts the character-selection mode. While this mode is active, all other navigation commands will select the characters from the position where the command was executed to the current cursor location.
SelectLine	Starts the line-selection mode. While this mode is active, all other navigation commands will select lines from the position where the command was executed to the current cursor location.
SelectColumn	Starts the column-select mode. In column-select mode, the navigation keys act as if virtual space is enabled.
WordLeftExtend	Extends the selection backward one word.
WordRightExtend	Extends the selection forward one word.

See Also Viewing and Changing the Shortcut Keys

Editing with the Text Editor

With the text editor, you can cut, copy, and paste text using menu commands or drag-and-drop. You can also undo and redo selected editing actions.

The text editor provides the following editing commands:

- Cutting, copying, pasting, and deleting text
- Undoing and redoing editing actions
- Using drag-and-drop
- Specifying column blocks for editing

All editing commands require a selection in order to work. Some of the commands can make a selection based on the current cursor location. Command names that begin with an object (such as WordCapitalize) assume that object for a default selection; otherwise, the default selection will be the character adjacent to the cursor. For example, the Delete command removes the character to the right of the cursor if there is no selection.

Note   You can enable the copy command to work on the current line even if there is no selection. From the Tools menu, select Options. Select the Compatibility tab, and select the Enable Copy Without Selection option. This enables the copy command to work on the current line if there is no selection.

When you cut text from the file, the text is removed from your file and placed on the Clipboard. When you delete text from the file, the text is removed from your file, and the Clipboard is not used. All Windows applications share one single Clipboard. Commands that use the Clipboard will overwrite whatever was previously placed onto the Clipboard by other commands or other Windows applications. This single-Clipboard behavior is true even when Developer Studio is emulating an editor, such as Epsilon, that supports multiple Clipboards.

The text editor commands for editing are described in the following table.

Command	Description
CharTranspose	Swaps characters around the cursor.
Copy	Copies the selection to the Clipboard.
Cut	Removes the selection and copies it to the Clipboard.
Delete	Deletes the selection.

Command	Description
DeleteBack	Deletes the selection, or if there is no selection, deletes the character to the left of the cursor.
DeleteBlankLines	Deletes the blank lines adjacent to the cursor.
DeleteHorizontalSpace	Deletes the spaces and tabs around the cursor.
FormatSelection	Formats the selection using the smart indent settings.
IndentSelection	Indents the selected text right one tab stop.
IndentSelectionToPrev	Indents the selection to line up with the previous line's indention.
LevelCutToEnd	Cuts the text between the cursor and the end of the next bracketed level.
LevelCutToStart	Cuts the text between the cursor and the beginning of the previous bracketed level.
LineCut	Deletes the selected lines and places them on the Clipboard.
LineDelete	Deleted the selected line.
LineDeleteToEnd	Deletes to the end of the current line.
LineDeleteToStart	Deletes to the beginning of the current line.
LineOpenAbove	Opens a new line above the cursor.
LineOpenBelow	Opens a new line below the cursor.
LineTranspose	Swaps the current and previous lines.
LowerCaseSelection	Makes the selection all lowercase.
Paste	Inserts the Clipboard contents at the cursor.
SentenceCut	Deletes the remainder of the sentence.
TabifySelection	Replaces spaces with tabs in the selection.
UnindentSelection	Indents the selected text left one tab stop.
UntabifySelection	Replaces tabs with spaces in the selection.
UpperCaseSelection	Makes the selection all uppercase.
WordCapitalize	Makes the first character uppercase.
WordDeleteToEnd	Deletes a word to the right.
WordDeleteToStart	Deletes a word to the left.
WordLowerCase	Makes the current word lowercase.
WordTranspose	Swaps the current and previous words.
WordUpperCase	Makes the current word uppercase.

See Also   Viewing and Changing the Shortcut Keys

Cutting, Copying, Pasting, and Deleting Text

You can edit your text using the following actions.

Action	Description
Cut	Removes selected text from the active window.
Copy	Duplicates selected text in the active window.
Paste	Pastes cut or copied text into an active window.
Delete	Deletes text without copying it to the Clipboard.
Undo	Restores the text.
Redo	Re-applies the prior edit.

▶ To cut or copy and paste text

1 Select the text you want to cut or copy.

2 From the Edit menu, choose Cut or Copy.

   The cut or copied text is placed onto the Clipboard and is available for pasting.

3 Move the insertion point to any source window where you want to insert the text.

4 From the Edit menu, choose Paste.

▶ To delete text

1 Select the text you want to delete.

2 From the Edit menu, choose Delete.

   The deleted text is not placed onto the Clipboard, and cannot be pasted.

Undoing and Redoing Editing Actions

Use the Undo command to undo previous editing actions. Use the Redo command to reapply editing actions that have been undone. Redo is unavailable unless you have used the Undo command.

The number and scope of editing actions you can undo is determined by the size of the text editor's UndoRedoSize buffer in the registry. For information on how to modify the Registry, see Appendix B, Initializing and Configuring Microsoft Developer Studio.

Note You can also undo automated edits. For example, if you have used ClassWizard to add a command handler, you can undo the ClassWizard edits by choosing AutomatedEdit in the Undo drop-down list.

▶ **To undo an editing action**

• From the Edit menu, choose Undo.

▶ **To redo an undo action**

• From the Edit menu, choose Redo.

Using Drag-and-Drop

Drag-and-drop editing is the easiest way to move or copy a selection of text in a file or between files.

▶ **To move text using drag-and-drop editing**

1 Select the text you want to move.

2 Drag the selected text to the new location.

Note You can also use the right mouse button for drag-and-drop editing. Select the text you want, and then use the right mouse button to drag the text to a new location. A pop-up menu appears, asking if you want to move or copy the selected text.

 Tip At any time during a drag-and-drop, you can click the other mouse button to cancel the operation.

▶ **To copy text using drag-and-drop**

1 Select the text you want to copy.

2 While holding down the CTRL key, drag the selected text to the new location.

Recording and Playing Back Keystrokes

With the text editor, you can automate repetitive keyboard tasks by recording and playing back keystrokes. The playback feature is available until you record a new set of keystrokes or end the editing session.

You can play back recorded keystrokes only into a single editor view. If you activate a new editor view while recording keystrokes, the recorder will remain in record mode and continue recording keystrokes. However, when the recorded keystrokes are played back, they will be played back into the view they were recorded from. If a window is closed, the playback stops.

Note During recording, all mouse-driven selections in text windows are disabled.

▶ **To record keystrokes**

1 Move the mouse pointer to where you want to begin typing.

2 From the Tools menu, choose Record Keystrokes.

   The Record toolbar appears.

3 Record the keystrokes that you want.

During recording, all mouse-driven selections are disabled. Keystrokes are entered at the location you have selected.

4 From the Tools menu, choose Stop Recording when you have finished recording your keystrokes.

▶ **To play back keystrokes**

1 Move the mouse pointer to where you want to play back the recorded keystrokes.

2 From the Tools menu, choose Playback Recording.

The recorded keystrokes will be played back into the active editor window at the location you have selected.

Setting Text Editor Options

With Developer Studio, you can set the text editor's behavior to suit your preferences and work habits. You can customize the text editor by:

- Setting editor emulation.
- Setting file save preferences.
- Setting and using the selection margin.
- Setting tabs and indents.
- Setting the font style, size, and color.
- Setting syntax coloring.
- Setting syntax coloring for user-defined types.

The text editor commands for editor settings are described in the following table.

Command	Description
EditToggleCaseSensitivity	Toggles the search case sensitivity.
EditToggleFindMatchWord	Toggles match whole word.
EditToggleOvertype	Toggles between inserting and replacing typing.
EditToggleRE	Toggles the regular expression search.
EditToggleTabDisplay	Shows or hides the tab characters.

See Also   Viewing and Changing the Shortcut Keys, Using Virtual Space

Setting Editor Emulation

The Microsoft Developer Studio text editor can emulate two popular text editors: BRIEF and Epsilon. With the emulation feature, the text editor can emulate the key bindings, text selection, caret display, and window display, as well as most editing commands of the selected editor.

▶ **To set an editor emulation**

1 From the Tools menu, choose Options.

The Options dialog box appears.

2 Select the Compatibility tab.

3 In the Recommended Options For list box, select the editor that you want to emulate.

The default editor is Developer Studio.

The Options box displays the status of pre-defined editor options.

4 Choose the OK button.

See Also Setting Editor Behavior, Using Epsilon Emulation, Using BRIEF Emulation, Viewing and Changing the Shortcut Keys

Setting Save Preferences

You can set save preferences—such as whether to be prompted before saving a file— in the Options dialog box. As a default, the text editor saves all changed files prior to building an application. The following table lists the save preferences:

Save Option	Description
Save before running tools	Saves files before you build a project or run a build utility such as NMAKE.
Prompt before saving files	Confirms (with a dialog box prompt) that you want to save files.
Automatic reload of externally modified files	Automatically reloads externally modified files that have been loaded (but not yet changed) by the editor.

▶ **To change the save options**

1 From the Tools menu, choose Options.

The Options dialog box appears.

2 Select the Editor tab.

3 Select any of the Save Options.

4 Choose the OK button.

Setting and Using the Selection Margin

The selection margin is an area to the left of each line of text. You can use the mouse in this area to select text. The selection margin also displays information about source lines. Breakpoints, bookmarks, the extended instruction pointer (EIP), and the tag pointer are all indicated by icons in the selection margin.

▶ To set the selection margin

1 From the Tools menu, choose Options.

The Options dialog box appears.

2 Select the Editor tab.

3 Select the Selection Margin check box.

4 Choose the OK button.

▶ To use the selection margin

When the mouse pointer is moved into the selection margin, it changes to an up-and-right-pointing select arrow (a mirror image of the standard select arrow).

- Do any of the following:
  - Click in the margin to select the entire line to the right of the mouse pointer.
  - Click in the margin and move the mouse pointer to select multiple consecutive lines.
  - While holding down SHIFT, click in the margin and move the mouse pointer to extend a selection.
  - While holding down CTRL, click anywhere in the margin to select the entire file. (This is equivalent to choosing the Select All command from the Edit menu.)

Setting Tabs and Indents

You can indent text with tab characters several ways:

- Use the INDENT SELECTION key.
- Use Auto Indent (without Smart Indent)
- Use Auto Indent (with Smart Indent enabled)

When you press the TAB key, the insertion point moves to the next indent level. You can display (or hide) the tab symbols by pressing the EditToggleTabDisplay key combination.

Note You can display all of the current keyboard shortcuts. For more information, see "Displaying the Keyboard Shortcuts" in Chapter 22, "Customizing Microsoft Developer Studio."

You can also use Auto Indent (without Smart Indent) to automatically indent new lines to match the previous line.

▶ **To set Auto Indent**

1 From the Tools menu, choose Options.

  The Options dialog box appears.

2 Select the Tabs tab.

3 Under Auto Indent, select the appropriate setting. To use Smart Indent, select the Smart option. Select the Default option to set the tab and indent size to match that of the previous level.

4 Choose the OK button.

If you use Auto Indent (with Smart Indent enabled), the text editor automatically indents the text based on the context of the previous lines.

▶ **To set Smart Indent**

1 From the Tools menu, choose Options.

  The Options dialog box appears.

2 Select the Tabs tab.

3 Under Auto Indent, select the Smart option.

4 Under Smart Indent Options, select the language element and specify the number of previous lines to use for the context of smart indenting.

5 Choose the OK button.

Backspacing over a tab character deletes the tab character, regardless of the indent setting.

If you select the Insert Spaces option, a tab character is not inserted, and only spaces are inserted to reach the next indent level.

Note The File Type list box on the Tabs tab contains a list of file types. The initial tab settings for each file you load are assigned based on the file extension and the setting of this list box. You can use the Tab Size box and Indent Size box on the Tabs tab or on the Source Window property page to specify individual settings for these two fields on a per-file basis, as needed.

▶ **To change tab and indent settings**

1 From the Tools menu, choose Options.

  The Options dialog box appears.

2 Select the Tabs tab.

3 In the Tab Size box, type the number of spaces to use as a tab stop. The default is four spaces.

4 In the Indent Size box, type the number of spaces to use for indents. The default is four spaces.

5 Select the Keep Tabs option to treat each tab as a single tab character when the file is saved.

−or−

Select the Insert Spaces option to use spaces as specified in the Tab Size box.

6 Choose the OK button.

▶ **To change tab and insert settings using the Source Window property page**

1 Click the right mouse button with the mouse pointer in the source window,

2 From the pop-up menu, choose Properties.

The Source Window property page appears.

3 In the Tab Size box and Indent Size box, type the tab and indent setting.

▶ **To display or hide tab symbols**

• Press the EditToggleTabDisplay key combination to toggle the display of tab symbols. Tab symbols are displayed as >> whenever there is a tab in a source file.

You can press the TAB key to move the caret to the next indent level. You can also move a block of lines one tab to the right or left.

▶ **To indent a group of lines**

1 Select the group of lines.

2 Press the IndentSelection key combination.

▶ **To unindent a group of lines**

1 Select the group of lines.

2 Press the UnindentSelection key combination.

   Note   The UnindentSelection command only returns to previous tab stops.

See Also   Viewing and Changing the Shortcut Keys

Setting the Font Style, Size, and Color

You can change the font style, size, and color settings for any window within Developer Studio with the Format command. You may find different fonts in various windows give visual clues about the function of the windows—the default setting for source windows, a different font for the Watch window, and so on. You can use the text font and size to better manage your window display of information.

Note   In addition to setting font coloring, you must enable syntax coloring in order to view colored text elements.

▶ **To change a font style, size, or color**

1 From the Tools menu, choose Options.

The Options dialog box appears.

2 Select the Format tab.

3 In the Category box, select the category of information to be formatted.

The Category list box displays the windows that have formatting options.

4 In the font box, select the font to be used for the category you selected.

The Font drop-down list box displays the different fonts installed on your system. The text sample in the sample box changes to the font you select.

5 In the Size box, select the Size to be used for the font you selected.

The Size drop-down list displays the sizes available for the selected font. The text sample in the sample box changes to the size you select.

6 In the Colors list box, select the type of text you want to color.

7 In the Background list box, select a background color.

8 In the Foreground list box, select a foreground color.

Note The Background and Foreground lists display the 16 standard colors and the Automatic setting. The text sample displayed in the Sample box changes to the color you select.

The behavior of the Automatic color setting depends on the element selected. For colors that map to standard system elements (such as Foreground color, Background color, or Text Selection color), the Automatic setting sets the element to the appropriate system color. For syntax coloring elements and other non-system defined colors, the Automatic setting indicates that the foreground color or background color from the same category is to be used.

9 Choose the OK button.

Text within one category of window can be only one font and size. Multiple fonts cannot be displayed in the same category of source window.

The font and size settings apply to everything within the selected category, while the foreground and background color settings apply only to the selected element of that category.

 Tip You can reset the formatting options for a selected Category to the default settings by choosing Reset.

Setting Syntax Coloring

Using different colors for various elements of your display, such as functions or variables lines, gives you visual cues about the structure of your source code. These changes are global and affect all source files with extensions recognized by the installed language.

▶ **To set syntax coloring in an individual source file**

1 Click the source file window or use the Window menu to make the source window active.

If there are multiple windows open on the source file, select one. Syntax coloring changes will appear in all windows opened on the source file.

2 From the Edit menu, choose Properties.

The Source Window property page appears. The Language list box displays the current language setting for syntax coloring. The drop-down list contains the installed language choices.

3 In the Language list box, select C/C++ to set syntax coloring for that source file, or select None to turn syntax coloring off.

Note   Global syntax coloring for C++ is enabled by default.

Setting Syntax Coloring for User-Defined Types

The text editor can display custom coloring of user-defined data types as well as predefined language elements.

The process of setting colors for user-defined types has three stages:

- Create an ASCII text file containing a list of user-defined types.

- Enable syntax coloring.

- Select appropriate colors for the user-defined types.

▶ **To set syntax coloring for user-defined types**

1 In the same directory as MSDEV.EXE, create a text-only file named USERTYPE.DAT, containing a list of user-defined type names.

Note   You must save USERTYPE.DAT as a text-only file. You can use the text editor or the Windows Notepad to create this file. The file should contain a list (one per line) of the user-defined strings that should be colored.

2 Click the source file window or use the Window menu to make the source window active.

If there are multiple windows open on the source file, select one. Syntax coloring changes will appear in all windows opened on the source file.

3 From the Edit menu, choose Properties.

The Source Window Properties page appears. The Language list box displays the current language setting for syntax coloring. The drop-down list contains the installed language choices.

4 In the Language list box, select C/C++ to set syntax coloring for that source file, or select None to turn syntax coloring off.

Note Global syntax coloring for C++ is enabled by default.

5 From the Tools menu, choose Options.

The Options dialog box appears.

6 Select the Format tab.

7 In the Category box, select the category of information to be formatted.

The Category list box displays the windows that have formatting options.

8 In the Font box, select the font to be used for the category you selected.

The Font list box displays the different fonts installed on your system. The text sample in the sample box changes to the font you select.

9 In the Size box, select the Size to be used with the font you selected.

The Size list box displays the sizes available for the selected font. The text sample in the sample box changes to the size you select.

10 In the Colors list box, select the type of text you want to color.

11 In the Background list box, select a background color.

12 In the Foreground list box, select a foreground color.

Note The Background and Foreground lists display the 16 standard colors and the Automatic setting. The text sample displayed in the Sample box changes to the color you select.

The behavior of the Automatic color setting depends on the element selected. For colors that map to standard system elements (such as Foreground Color, Background Color, or Selected Text Color), the Automatic setting sets the element to the appropriate system color. For syntax coloring elements and other non-system defined colors, the Automatic setting indicates that the foreground color or background color from the same category is to be used.

13 Choose the OK button.

The USERTYPE.DAT file is read during initialization. It cannot be renamed, nor can it be reloaded during an editing session. The syntax coloring mechanism checks the USERTYPE.DAT file last. Thus, all previously defined color settings take precedence over the user-defined types.

 Tip   For any source file, you can use the Source Window property page to specify which language syntax coloring to apply (or turn off syntax coloring altogether). For more information, see "Setting the Font Style, Size, and Color" earlier in this chapter.

Managing Open Windows

The text editor features options that control the display of source windows. You can switch between windows, open new windows, split window views, and view a source file in full-screen mode.

▶ **To switch to a source window**

- Click anywhere in the window.

    −or−

- From the Window menu, choose the filename.

    −or−

1 From the Window menu, choose Windows.

   The Windows dialog box appears.

2 Select a window from the Select Window list.

3 Choose the Activate button, or double-click the selection.

▶ **To create a new window for an open source file**

1 Switch to the source window.

2 From the Window menu, choose the New Window command.

   A second copy of the source file is displayed with an :*n* suffix. As you open more windows on the source file, the value of *n* increases. You can scroll and split each window independently. You can make changes to the source file from any window.

   Note   When you first open a file, if you select the Read Only check box in the Open dialog box, the current window and any duplicates of the window remain read only.

▶ **To split a source window**

- Click the split bar at the top of the vertical scroll bar, and drag it down to the location you want.

  −or−

1 Switch to the source window.

  If there are multiple windows open on the source file, select one of them.

2 From the Window menu, choose Split.

  The split bar appears.

3 Drag the split bar to the location you want.

▶ **To view a source file in full-screen mode**

1 Switch to the source window.

2 From the View menu, select Full Screen.

  The source window is displayed in full-screen mode. A small button appears at the top that allows you to reset the screen to regular mode.

  Initially, the toolbars, status bar, and scroll bars are hidden. From the Tools menu (ALT+T), choose Options and then use the Editor tab to control window settings.

▶ **To end full screen mode**

- Press the ESC key.

  −or−

- Click the Full-Screen button.

All files are automatically closed when you quit Developer Studio (you will be prompted to save any changed files). You can also close any individual source file without quitting the application.

▶ **To close a source file**

1 From the Window menu, choose Windows.

  The Windows dialog box appears.

2 Select one or more files from the Select Window list box.

3 Choose the Close Window button.

−or−

4 Switch to the source window.

5 From the File menu, choose Close to close the active window and any additional views of the window.

−or−

If the window is not maximized, double-click the window's Control-menu box. When you double-click the Control-menu box, the window is closed, but additional views of the document remain open.

CHAPTER 4

Working with Source-Code Control

Source-code control systems enable you to track changes to source-code files during the course of software development. With source-code control systems, you can ensure that changes are not overwritten in projects with multiple authors, and that authors are working with the most up-to-date code. You can also return to earlier versions of code, if necessary.

Microsoft Developer Studio provides facilities for integrating a source-code control system into the development environment. If you install a source-code control system that conforms to the Microsoft Common Source Code Control Interface, you can directly access source-code control functionality from the Developer Studio menus.

Note Until you install a source-code control system that conforms to the Microsoft Common Source Code Control Interface, the menu commands for source-code control will not appear. In addition, either you or the installation program must make the correct entries in the Registry.

Setting Up Source-Code Control

To use the integrated source-code control capabilities in Microsoft Developer Studio, you must take the following steps:

- Install a source-code control system that conforms to the Microsoft Common Source Code Control Interface.

- Ensure that the installation program for the source-code control system writes the correct information to the Registry, and if it doesn't, make the correct entries.

- Complete all the administrative tasks required by your source-code control system. These tasks may include designating locations for master versions of files, creating network connections, setting permissions for drives and/or directories, or adding user information and permissions to the system.

Supported Source-Code Control Functionality

Microsoft Developer Studio provides commands for a number of common source-code control operations used in everyday work. It supports the following operations:

- Putting an entire project under source-code control.
- Putting individual files under source-code control.
- Getting current versions of files.
- Checking files out of the source-code control system.
- Checking files into the source-code control system and merging others' changes.
- Checking files into the source-code control system and ignoring changes.
- Removing files from the source-code control system.
- Viewing the history of changes made to a file.
- Viewing the differences between the local copy of a file and its master copy.

If your installed source-code control system supports other operations in addition to these basic ones, Microsoft Developer Studio provides access to them from the Advanced button on the relevant dialog box. These other operations could include such things as checking out files exclusively to prevent other users from working on them at the same time.

Unsupported Source-Control Functionality

Microsoft Developer Studio supports basic functionality in installed source-code control systems, as outlined in the section "Supported Source-Code Control Functionality" earlier in this chapter. This integrates common source-code control operations into your customary working environment.

These integrated operations do not encompass all possible capabilities of source-code control systems. For certain source-code control operations, you will have to use the programs or features of your installed source-code control system. These operations include adminstrative tasks, such as designating locations for master versions of files, creating network connections, setting permissions for drives and/or directories, or adding user information and permissions to the system.

In addition, if your source-code control system allows certain operations on files in the source-code control tree, such as getting specific versions of files, branching, or merging branches, you need to use the installed source-code control program for those operations.

Putting Files Under Source-Code Control

When you add a file to your source-code control system, the system manages access to the file and maintains a record of all changes made to the file. It also records when a file was changed and who changed the file. From Microsoft Developer Studio, you can put entire projects under source-code control, or you can put individual files under source-code control.

Displaying the Source-Code Control Toolbar

You can access the integrated source-code control commands from buttons on a standard toolbar.

▶ **To display the Source-Code Control toolbar**

1 From the View menu, choose Toolbars.

The Toolbars dialog box appears.

2 From the Toolbars list, select Source Control.

The Source-Code Control toolbar immediately appears.

3 Choose the Close button.

You can also remove buttons from the toolbar, add other buttons, or add source-code control buttons to other toolbars. For information on customizing toolbars, see the section "Working with Toolbars" in Chapter 22.

Adding a Project to Source-Code Control

You can add a project to your source-code control system any time after you have created it.

Note Before you can add any files to source-code control, you must complete any administrative tasks required by your source-code control system, using the administrative program supplied by your system. This may include adding users or creating a source-code control project database, for instance.

▶ **To add a project to source-code control**

1 Open an existing project or create a new project.

2 From the Tools menu, choose Source Control, and from the cascading menu, choose Add To Source Control.

The installed source-code control displays one or more dialog boxes, requesting source-code control project information.

3 Specify the information required by the installed source-code control system.

The Add To Source Control dialog box appears, with files in the project workspace selected.

4 If you want to add the files to source-code control, but immediately check them out, select the Keep Checked Out check box.

5 In the Comment text box, type a comment about the files, if you want.

Note If your source-code control system supports additional options, an Advanced button appears on the Add To Source Control dialog box, and you can select those options at this point.

6 Choose the OK button.

Adding Individual Files to Source-Code Control

You can set Developer Studio options to prompt you automatically each time you insert files into your project, or you can explicitly choose to put them under source-code control.

▶ **To prompt automatically for inclusion under source-code control**

1 From the Tools menu, choose Options.

The Options dialog box appears.

2 Select the Source Control tab.

3 Select the Prompt To Add Files When Inserted check box.

4 Choose the OK button.

Now, each time you insert files into the project, Developer Studio prompts you to add the inserted files to your source-code control system.

If some or all of the files currently included in your project are not under source-code control, you can add them individually to the source-code control system.

▶ **To add individual files to source-code control**

1 In the FileView pane of the Project Workspace window, select the files that you want to put under source-code control.

2 From the Tools menu, choose Source Control, and then choose Add To Source Control from the cascading menu.

The Add To Source Control dialog box appears, with checks in the Files list next to the files that you have selected. The list includes all files in the project directory that are not already under source-code control, and you may check or uncheck any files in the list.

3 In the Comment text box, type a comment about the files, if you want.

4 Choose the OK button.

The files are now under source-code control, and the file icons in the FileView pane are now grayed to indicate this.

Removing Files from Source-Code Control

When you remove files from your Microsoft Developer Studio project, you may first want to remove them from source-code control.

▶ **To remove a file from source-code control**

1 In the FileView pane of the Project Workspace window, select the files that you want to remove from source-code control.

2 From the Tools menu, choose Source Control, and from the cascading menu, choose Remove From Source Control.

The Remove From Source Control dialog box appears, with checks in the Files list next to the files that you have selected. You may check or uncheck any files in the list.

3 Choose OK.

Note Not all source-code control systems allow individual users to remove files from source-code control. Some systems require source-code control administrators to remove them, and the administrator may need to use the source-code control system's administrative program.

Determining the Status of Files

When you are using a source-code control system, it is important to be able to determine the status of files within the system. This can help prevent collisions in groups with multiple authors, ensure that you are working on current files, determine whether you have access to a file, and so on. You can also examine the historical status of files to determine when and what changes were made, and who made them.

You can determine some information from the FileView pane, other information from the property pages for a file, and other information from examining the file's history.

Reading the FileView Pane

The FileView pane of the Project Workspace window displays all the files that are currently in the project workspace. If a project is under source-code control, the file icons are grayed, and if a file is checked out, a check mark appears to the left of the file icon. Figure 4.1 shows a file under source-code control that has been checked out.

Figure 4.1   FileView Showing a Checked Out File

Examining File Status on Property Pages

Each file in a project has a property page associated with it. The property page includes information about the file, including its current status in the source-code control system if it is under source-code control.

Note If the file is not under source-code control, no status information appears on the property page.

▶ **To examine a property page from the FileView pane**

- Select the file in the FileView pane of the Project Workspace window, and press ALT+ENTER.

  –or–

- Select the file in the FileView pane of the Project Workspace window, click the right mouse button to display the pop-up menu, and choose Properties.

  –or–

- Select the file in the FileView pane of the Project Workspace window, and from the Edit menu, choose Properties.

▶ **To examine a property page from a source editor window**

- Press ALT+ENTER and select the General tab.

  –or–

- Click the right mouse button to display the pop-up menu, choose Properties, and then select the General tab.

  –or–

- From the Edit menu, choose Properties, and then select the General tab.

Examining File Histories

In some cases, you may want to know what changes were made to a file, either recently or throughout its existence. You can request the source-code control system to show a history for a file or files that you have added to source-code control. Some source-code control systems allow you to select only a single file. The type of detail shown in the file histories depends on the source-code control system.

▶ **To show file histories**

1 In the FileView pane of the Project Workspace window, select the file or files for which you want a history.

2 From the Tools menu, choose Source Control, and then choose Show History from the cascading menu.

  Your source-code control system displays the history for the selected file or files.

Getting Current Versions of Files

Updating your local copies of files to versions from the master source-code control files is called "getting" or "synchronizing" files. In any software project with multiple authors, you need to update your local copies frequently to ensure that you incorporate changes that other authors have made.

In a large project, changes can be made in files that you normally do not work in, but that do contain information that you use. For instance, project-wide header files may define manifest constants or macros that appear in your source files. When you get or synchronize your local files, the master versions of files are copied to your local project. The files are not checked out, and you cannot modify them and check in changes, but you can build with the most up-to-date versions.

If you have checked out files and made changes to your local copies, and other authors have made changes to those same files and checked them in, your source-code control system reports that you have changes to merge. You then need to follow the recommended procedures in your source-code control system to reconcile and verify those changes.

▶ **To get current files in your project**

1 In the FileView pane of the Project Workspace window, select the files that you want to get.

2 From the Tools menu, choose Source Control, and from the cascading menu, choose Get Latest Version.

   The Get Latest Version dialog box appears, with checks next to the files that you have selected. The list includes all files in the project directory that are under source-code control, and you may check or uncheck any files in the list.

   Tip You can quickly select all the items in the list by selecting the first item, pressing SHIFT+END to select all the items, and then pressing the SPACEBAR to change the check box state. If one or more files are checked, they now are unchecked. Pressing the SPACEBAR again checks them all.

3 Choose the OK button.

The source-code control system copies all the selected files with changes by other authors to your local directory.

You can also have Developer Studio automatically prompt you to get the current versions of files when you open a project workspace.

▶ **To get current versions of files when opening a project workspace**

1 From the Tools menu, choose Options.

   The Options dialog box appears.

2 Select the Source Control tab.

3 Select the Get Files When Opening The Workspace check box.

4 Choose the OK button.

Checking Files In and Out

When you begin work on your project, normally you open the project in the project workspace and get the current versions of the project files to make sure that you are looking at the most up-to-date sources. Before you begin to modify the source files, you check them out; after you have completed the modifications, you check the files in.

When you have a file checked in, your local copy of the file is read-only, and you cannot save any changes to it. When you check out a file, you can make changes to your local copy of the file, and save those changes to the file. When you check the file in, you copy those changes to the master copy of the file in the source-code control project. This makes those changes available to your coworkers. Depending on the characteristics of your source-code control system, only one author can check out a file, or more than one author can check out a file simultaneously.

In Microsoft Developer Studio, in addition to selecting files directly from the FileView pane, you can also check them in and out by selecting from the other panes. For instance, if you select a class to check out in the ClassView pane, Developer Studio prompts you to check out files associated with that class. In the ResourceView pane, if you select a bitmap resource to check out, Developer Studio prompts you to check out the resource file and the bitmap file.

Checking Files Out

When you check a file out, your installed source-code control system changes the status of the file from read-only to writeable, and records that you have the file checked out. You then have the necessary permissions to revise the file. Your source-code control system may include a mechanism for exclusive use. You can then specify that you have the file checked out, and that no one else may check out that file.

Some source-code control systems allow multiple authors to check out the same file. In this case, the source-code control system merges the changes from the authors when each checks in the file.

▶ **To check files out**

1 In the FileView pane of the Project Workspace window, select the files that you want to check out.

2 From the Tools menu, choose Source Control, and from the cascading menu, choose Check Out.

The Check Out File(s) dialog box appears, with checks next to the files that you have selected. The list includes all checked-in files in the project directory, and you may check or uncheck any files in the list.

3 Type a comment in the Comment text box, if you want.

Note Not all source-code control systems support comments when checking files out. If yours does not, this text box does not appear.

4 Choose the OK button.

You can also check out a file using the pop-up menu in the text editor windows. Press the right mouse button to display the menu. From the menu, choose Check Out.

You can have Developer Studio prompt you to check out a file if you start to edit it, but have not checked it out.

▶ **To prompt for check out from editor windows**

1 From the Tools menu, choose Options.

The Options dialog box appears.

2 Select the Source Control tab.

3 Select the Check Out Source File(s) When Edited check box.

4 Choose the OK button.

Checking Files In

When you check a file in, the source-code control system changes the status of the file from writeable to read-only, and records that you have checked in the file. It also records the differences between the contents of the file when you checked it out and when you checked it in.

You generally want to view the changes to the file before you check it in to confirm the changes that you made. In some cases, you may want to discard all changes to your file before checking it in. In other cases, you may need to merge changes that coworkers have made to the file after you checked it out. If you had the file checked out exclusively, after you check it in, others can check out the file.

Viewing Your Changes to a File

It is best to review the changes that you have made in a file before you check in the file. Your source-code control system displays the differences between your local version of the file and the master version in your source-code control project.

▶ **To view your changes**

1 Select the file with the changes that you want to view.

Note You can select only a single file, which must already be checked out. This method reports only the differences between this version and the master version. You cannot use this method to examine differences between two files in your project, for instance.

2 From the Tools menu, choose Source Control, and from the cascading menu, choose Show Differences.

Your source-code control system displays the differences, or reports that the files are identical.

Checking Files In and Removing Your Changes

In some cases, you may make changes to your local files, and then decide that you do not want to check the changes in to the source-code control system. You may, for instance, have viewed the local changes and discovered errors, you may have pursued some modifications that were not fruitful, or you may not have had time to completely implement some changes and do not care to check in incomplete code. In these cases, you can have the source-code control system check the files in, but ignore any changes you made.

Note If you want to save the changes before checking the files in without the changes, you can always copy the files to another location, or save them under another name using the Save As command.

▶ **To check files in but ignore changes**

1 In the FileView pane of the Project Workspace window, select the files that you want to check in without incorporating changes.

2 From the Tools menu, choose Source Control, and from the cascading menu, choose Undo Check Out.

The Undo Check Out dialog box appears, with checks next to the files that you have selected. The list includes all checked-out files in the project directory, and you may check or uncheck any files in the list.

3 Choose the OK button.

The source-code control system changes the status of the files to checked in, but does not copy any of your changes to the master files. It does not record any differences. It also restores your local copy of the file so that it matches the master file.

Checking Files In and Merging Others' Changes

If your source-code control system does not support exclusive use, while you have had the file checked out, another author may have also checked the file out, made changes, and then checked the file in. In this case, before you check your local copy of the file in, you need to find out if there were changes by other authors. If so, you need to merge those changes into your local copy. You can then verify that all the changes are compatible and that none cause problems when you use the file. After you have verified the changes, you can check in the file.

▶ **To check files in and merge others' changes**

1 In the FileView pane of the Project Workspace window, select the files that you want to check in.

2 From the Tools menu, choose Source Control, and from the cascading menu, choose Get Latest Version.

The Get Latest Version dialog box appears, with checks next to the files that you have selected. The list includes all files in the project directory under source-code control, and you may check or uncheck any files in the list.

3 Choose the OK button.

The source-code control system copies master files to your local copies. If there is a file with changes in both your local copy and the master copy, your source-code control system notifies you that you have changes to merge. You then need to follow the recommended procedures in your source-code control system to reconcile the changes and verify those changes.

4 Repeat steps 1 through 3.

Remember that while you are verifying the last set of changes, another set may have appeared.

5 When your source-code control system reports that there are no more files to merge, select the files that you want to check in.

6 From the Tools menu, choose Source Control and from the cascading menu, choose Check In.

The Check In File(s) dialog box appears, with checks next to the files that you have selected. The list includes all files in the project directory, and you may check or uncheck any files in the list.

7 Choose the OK button.

You can also check in a file using the pop-up menu in the text editor windows. Press the right mouse button to display the menu, and choose Check In.

Checking Files In When Closing the Workspace

You can choose to have Developer Studio prompt you to check in files when you close the current workspace.

▶ **To check in files when closing the workspace**

1 From the Tools menu, choose Options.

The Options dialog box appears.

2 Select the Source Control tab.

3 Select the Check In Files When Closing The Workspace check box.

4 Choose OK.

Maintaining Makefiles Under Source-Code Control

If you work in a group, you generally want to share the makefile for a project workspace with other members of your group. This ensures that everyone in the group can build the projects defined in the project workspace using the same files, settings, tools, and so on, as well as ensuring that everyone gets the changes to the makefile and builds with the most up-to-date settings.

Updating the makefile in a group setting requires some coordination among the members of the group in order for the process to work smoothly. In the optimal case, all members of the group get the makefile from source-code control when they open the project, but no one checks it out.

The following actions cause the makefile to change:

- Adding or deleting files.
- Adding or deleting projects, subprojects, or project configurations.
- Changing settings for any configuration.

If you want to take any of these actions, you need to take the following steps:

1. Plan the changes to make in your project workspace.
2. Check out the makefile.
3. Make the changes.
4. Save the changes to the makefile by choosing the Save All command from the File menu. (Closing the project workspace or closing Developer Studio also saves the changes to the makefile.)
5. Check in the makefile.
6. Notify the members of the group that the makefile has changed.

   At this point, the other members of the group need to close the project workspace, then reopen it and get the new version of the makefile. If they have set the option to prompt to get the latest versions of files, opening the project workspace reminds them to get the latest version.

If two or more members of the group simultaneously check out the makefile and revise it, checking the makefile in could require merging changes. Because Developer Studio may write multiple settings to a single line of the makefile, and changes to settings by different users may alter a single line in two (or more) different places, reconciling those changes manually could result in errors.

Note If your source-code control system supports exclusive check-outs, you should check the makefile out for exclusive use if you need to alter it.

Working with Resources

In Microsoft Developer Studio, a resource is an interface element that the user gains information from or manipulates to perform an action. Some basic resources are created for your project by AppWizard in Visual C++.

The following are common areas in the resources:

- The resource editing procedures common to all the editors
- Common operations for working with symbols (resource identifiers)
- Working with resource files

Using the Resource Editors

The Microsoft Developer Studio resource editors share techniques and interfaces to create and modify application resources quickly and easily. You can use the resource editors to create new resources, modify existing resources, copy existing resources, and delete old resources. The resource editors are functionally consistent for ease of use.

With Developer Studio you can edit all of the Microsoft Windows resources that your application uses:

- Accelerator tables (described in Chapter 8, "Using the Accelerator Editor")
- Binary data information (Chapter 12, "Using the Binary Data Editor")
- Bitmaps (Chapter 10, "Using the Graphic Editor")
- Cursors (Chapter 10, "Using the Graphic Editor")
- Dialog boxes (Chapter 6, "Using the Dialog Editor")
- Icons (Chapter 10, "Using the Graphic Editor")
- Menus (Chapter 7, "Using the Menu Editor")

- String tables (Chapter 9, "Using the String Editor")
- Toolbar resources (Chapter 11, "Using the Toolbar Editor")
- Version Information (Chapter 13, "Using the Version Information Editor")

When you create or open a resource, the appropriate editor opens automatically. For example, graphical resources like toolbar buttons, cursors, and icons are modifiable bitmaps. The accelerator tables, string tables, and version information consist of formatted text. Dialog boxes are a combination of graphical components and text strings. Menus consist of text strings that appear in the menu bar.

The resource editors have many commands and procedures in common. For example, once you learn how to create and open a dialog box, you know the steps for creating and opening any of the other resources. The most common resource editing activities are:

- Viewing resources
- Creating new resources
- Using resource templates
- Using language ID and conditionals
- Copying resources
- Editing resources
- Importing or exporting resources
- Using the property pages

Viewing Resources

You can access resources from the ResourceView pane of the project window. Select the resource tab if ResourceView is not the topmost pane.

▶ **To view the ResourceView pane**

- With the *PRJNAME*.MAK project window open, double-click the *PRJNAME*.RC item.

    ResourceView appears (Figure 5.1).

Figure 5.1 The ResourceView Pane

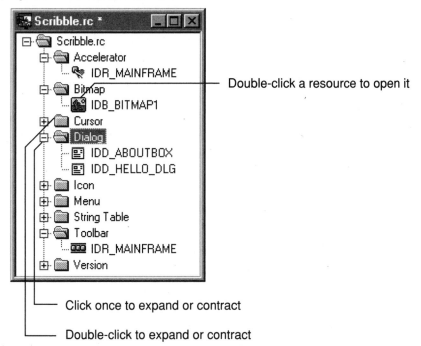

Double-click a resource to open it

Click once to expand or contract

Double-click to expand or contract

When the ResourceView pane is first displayed, each of the resource categories is condensed. You can expand any category by clicking its plus sign (+).

While viewing the ResourceView pane, standard Edit menu commands such as Undo, Cut, Copy, Paste, and Delete are available by using either the menu commands or the accelerator keys.

Creating a New Resource

You can create a resource as a new default resource, or as a resource patterned after a template. Creating a new default resource is as easy as clicking the appropriate button on the Resource toolbar (see Figure 5.2). For more information on creating a resource from a template file, see "Using Resource Templates" later in this chapter.

When you create a resource, Developer Studio assigns it a unique symbol name and value. If you need to change the symbol value, you can use the ID box on the resource's property page. For more information on the property page, use the Help button.

▶ **To create a new resource**

1 From the Insert menu, choose Resource.

The Insert Resource dialog box appears.

2 Select a resource from the Resource Type list box and choose the OK button.

−or−

• Click the corresponding toolbar button.

Figure 5.2 The Resource Toolbar

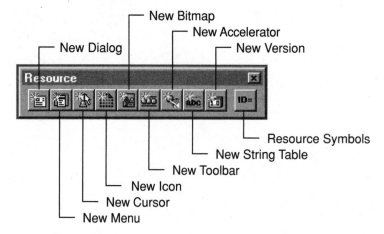

▸ **To display the Resource toolbar**

• For information on displaying toolbars and customizing your workspace, see "Showing and Hiding Toolbars" in Chapter 22, "Customizing Microsoft Developer Studio."

Using Resource Templates

A template file is a copy of an edited resource that you can use to create additional resources. Resource templates save time in developing additional resources or groups of resources that share a particular feature.

For instance, you might want to include a Help button and an icon of a company logo in several dialog boxes. Create a new template, and customize that template dialog box with the logo and Help button. Now, when you want to create a new dialog box, you can choose this template dialog box with the features already added.

▸ **To create templates for resources**

1 From the Insert menu, choose Resource.

The Insert Resource dialog box (Figure 5.3) appears.

2 Select a resource from the Resource Type list box, and choose the OK button.

−or−

Copy a resource from another resource file. Hold down CTRL and drag the new resource to the resource template directory.

Figure 5.3   The Insert Resource Dialog Box

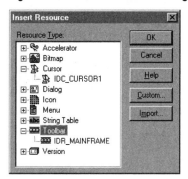

3 Modify the resource.

This resource, once saved as a template, can be copied numerous times to save effort on positioning controls, inserting text, and so on.

4 From the File menu, choose Save As.

5 In the Save File As Type drop-down list box, select Resource Template (*.rct).

6 Select the TEMPLATE subdirectory under your MSDEV installation.

7 Choose the OK button to save the template.

Repeat for any remaining templates.

▶ **To create new resources from the templates**

1 From the Insert menu, choose Resource.

The Insert Resource dialog box appears.

2 Select a resource type. Click the resource icon to create a default resource template object.

−or−

Click the plus sign (+) next to a resource to move down the hierarchy to the template files grouped under that resource. Then click the specific template file under that resource to create a resource template object.

3 Choose the OK button.

Copying Resources

You can duplicate resources exactly, change their language IDs or conditions, or duplicate them from a template (see "Using Resource Templates" earlier in this chapter).

When you create or copy a resource with a different language or condition, this is displayed after the symbol name in the project window. The language identifies the language used for text in the resource. The condition is a symbol that identifies a condition under which this copy of the resource is used.

▶ **To copy an existing resource exactly**

1 In ResourceView, select the resource you want to copy.

2 From the Edit menu, choose Copy and then Paste.

▶ **To copy an existing resource and change the language or condition**

1 In ResourceView, select the resource you want to copy.

2 From the Insert menu, choose Resource Copy.

The Insert Resource Copy dialog box appears.

3 In the Language list box, select the language.

−or−

In the Condition box, type the condition.

4 Choose the OK button.

▶ **To modify the language or property conditions of a resource**

1 In ResourceView, select the resource you want to edit.

2 From the Edit menu, choose Properties.

−or−

Click the right mouse button to display the pop-up menu, and choose Properties.

3 Edit the Language or Condition properties.

The easiest way to copy resources from either an existing resource or an executable file to your current resource file is to have both .RC files open in Developer Studio at the same time. Then use drag-and-drop to move items from one ResourceView pane to another (see Figure 5.4).

Figure 5.4 Using Drag-and-Drop to Copy Resources Between Files

Note Developer Studio includes sample resource files that you can use in your own application. For more information, see "COMMON.RES Sample Resources" in Part 2 of *Programming with MFC.*

▶ **To copy resources from one file to another**

1 Open both files. Make sure both resource files are visible at the same time.

2 In the ResourceView pane of the "from" file, select the resource you want to copy.

3 Hold down the CTRL key and drag the resource to the ResourceView pane of the "to" file.

Dragging the resource without holding down the CTRL key moves the resource rather than copying it.

Note To avoid conflicts with symbol names or values in the existing file, Developer Studio may change the transferred resource's symbol value, or symbol name and value, when you copy it to the new file.

Editing Resources

The editors for the different resources share many of the same procedures. For more detailed information on editing the individual resources, see the chapter for that resource.

▶ **To open an existing resource for editing**

• In ResourceView, select the resource you want to edit, and press ENTER.

–or–

Double-click the resource.

The resource editor window opens for editing.

▶ **To save an edited resource file**

• From the File menu, choose Save.

The resource is saved using its current name.

–or–

1 From the File menu, choose Save As.

2 In the Drives list box, select the target drive.

3 In the Directories list box, select the directory path.

4 In the File Name box, type the name for the file.

5 Choose the OK button.

The resource is saved using the Save As name.

▶ **To delete an existing resource**

1 In ResourceView, select the resource you want to delete.

2 From the Edit menu, choose Delete.

The resource is deleted.

Importing and Exporting Resources

▶ **To import a separate bitmap, icon, or cursor file into your current resource file**

1 From the right mouse pop-up menu, choose Import.

The Import Resource dialog box appears.

2 Select the name of the .EPS, .ICO, or .CUR file you want to import.

3 Choose the OK button to add the file to the current resource file.

 Tip You can also copy a bitmap, icon, or cursor into your current resource file by dragging it from File Manager and dropping it into the Developer Studio ResourceView pane.

▶ **To export a bitmap, icon, or cursor as a separate file**

1 Select the bitmap, icon, or cursor you want to export.

Developer Studio exports the graphic selected in the ResourceView pane or the graphic in the currently active image editor window.

2 From the right mouse pop-up menu, choose Export.

The Export Resource dialog box appears.

3 If you do not want to accept the current filename, type a new one.

4 Choose the OK button to save the graphics file on the disk.

Using Property Pages

Property pages control the appearance and the behavior of resources and differ according to their purpose. For example, a bitmap resource property page contains information on the ID, language, condition, and filename, as well as a preview of the resource. But a property page for a pushbutton control in a dialog box contains several tabs of information, General and Extended Styles, each with many style bits to modify the control's behavior.

OLE controls supplied from independent vendors may come equipped with their own property pages and characteristics. OLE controls always have General and All pages, plus whatever the vendor has attached to a particular control.

Accelerator keys have many legal entries in the key box on the property page. For more information, see "Setting Accelerator Properties" in Chapter 8.

Note Whenever you make a change on a property page, it is made immediately. You cannot cancel any changes made on a property page.

Manipulating a Property Page

You can use any of the editing keyboard shortcut keys to cut, copy, and paste text. In general these shortcut keys can be used in any edit control on the property page.

You can control the behavior of the Properties window to suit your working style or the nature of the resource editing task. Use the Pushpin button in the upper-left corner of the property page.

Button position	Result
	When the button is in the down position, the Properties window stays visible even when you are working in another window. This is convenient if, during an editing session, you want to move back and forth frequently between setting properties and editing objects. Pressing ENTER after you change a value in the Properties window returns you to the editing window but leaves the Properties window visible.
	When the button is in the up position, you can dismiss the active Properties window by pressing ENTER or ESC. This is useful if you want to concentrate on working in an editing window but need to bring up the Properties window briefly to change one or two values.

Working with Symbols

A symbol is a resource identifier that consists of a text string (name) mapped to an integer value. Symbols provide a descriptive way of referring to resources and user interface objects, both in your source code and while you're working with them in the resource editors.

When you create a new resource or resource object, Microsoft Developer Studio provides a default name for the resource (for example, IDC_RADIO1) and assigns a value to it. The name-plus-value definition is stored in the Developer Studio-generated file RESOURCE.H.

In working with symbols from within Developer Studio, you can:

- Change the symbol associated with a resource or object.

- Change a symbol's name or value in the Resource Symbols browser (if the symbol hasn't been used yet).

- Change a symbol's name in the Properties window (if the symbol is already in use by a single object).

- Manage symbols (add, delete, or change the symbols) in the Resource Symbols browser.

Note   When you are copying resources or resource objects from one .RC file to another, Developer Studio may change the transferred resource's symbol value, or symbol name and value, to avoid conflicts with symbol names or values in the existing file.

Changing a Symbol or Symbol Name

When you create a new resource or resource object, Developer Studio assigns it a default name—for example, `IDD_DIALOG1`. Use the resource's property page to change the default symbol name or to change the name of any symbol already associated with a resource.

▶ **To change a resource's symbol name**

1 In ResourceView, select the resource.

2 From the Edit menu, choose Properties to move directly to the resource's property page.

3 In the ID box, type a new symbol name or select from the list of existing symbols. If you type a new symbol name, Developer Studio assigns it a value automatically.

You can use the Resource Symbols browser to change the names of symbols not currently assigned to a resource. For more information, see "Changing Unassigned Symbols" later in this chapter.

Changing a Symbol's Numerical Value

Usually you can let Microsoft Developer Studio assign the numerical value associated with the symbol names you define. However, there may be times when you need to change the symbol value associated with a resource—for example, when you want a group of controls or a series of related strings in the string table to have sequential IDs.

For symbols already associated with a single resource, use the resource's property page to change the symbol value. For symbols associated with more than one resource or object, make the changes directly in RESOURCE.H using a text editor.

▶ **To change a symbol value assigned to a single resource or object**

1 Select the resource.

2 From the Edit menu, choose Properties.

3 In the property page ID box, type the symbol name followed by an equal sign and an integer. For example,

`IDC_EDITNAME=5100`

–or–

• From the View menu, choose Resource Symbols.

  The Resource Symbols browser appears.

• Select the symbol you want to change, and choose the Change button.

  The Change Symbol dialog box appears.

• Choose the View Use button.

  The resource and its property page are displayed.

- In the property page ID box, type the symbol name followed by an equal sign and an integer. For example,

```
IDC_EDITNAME=5100
```

The new value is stored in the symbol header file the next time you save the project. Only the symbol name remains visible in the ID box; the equal sign and value are not displayed after they are validated.

▶ To change the numeric value of a symbol assigned to more than one resource or object

1 End your editing session by closing the current resource file.

2 Open RESOURCE.H in a source window and make the necessary changes.

3 Save RESOURCE.H.

The next time you open the project's .RC file, Developer Studio uses the new symbol values.

Note While editing RESOURCE.H, take special care not to define duplicate symbols. Developer Studio can detect duplicates only of the symbols it creates.

You can use the Resource Symbols browser to change the value of symbols not currently assigned to a resource. For more information, see "Changing Unassigned Symbols" later in this chapter.

Managing Symbols with the Resource Symbols Browser

As your application grows in size and sophistication, so do the number of resources and symbols. Tracking large numbers of symbols scattered throughout several files can be difficult. The Resource Symbols browser (Figure 5.5) simplifies symbol management by offering a central tool through which you can:

- Quickly browse existing symbol definitions to see the value of each symbol, a list of symbols being used, and the resources assigned to each symbol.

- Create new symbols.

- Change the name and value of a symbol that is not in use.

- Delete a symbol if it is not being used.

- Move quickly to the appropriate Developer Studio resource editor where the symbol is being used.

Figure 5.5   The Resource Symbols Browser

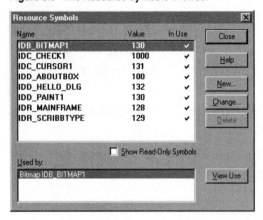

▶ **To open the Resource Symbols browser**

• From the View menu, choose Resource Symbols.

Creating New Symbols

When you are beginning a new project, you may find it convenient to map out the symbol names you need before creating the resources they will be assigned to.

▶ **To create a new symbol using the Resource Symbols browser**

1 In the Resource Symbols browser, choose the New button.

The New Symbol dialog box appears.

2 In the Name box, type a symbol name.

3 Accept the symbol value assigned by Developer Studio or, in the Value box, type a new value.

4 Choose the OK button to add the new symbol to the symbol list.

The symbols appear in alphabetic order.

If you type a symbol name that already exists, a message box appears stating that a symbol with that name is already defined. You cannot define two or more symbols with the same name, but you can define different symbols with the same numeric value. For more information, see "Symbol Name Restrictions" and "Symbol Value Restrictions" later in this chapter.

Changing Unassigned Symbols

While in the Resource Symbols browser, you can edit or delete existing symbols that are not already assigned to a resource or object. You can change existing symbols that are in use in only one place by using the Change command to move to the appropriate resource's property page or by moving to the property page directly. You cannot change read-only symbols.

A check mark in the In Use column of the Resource Symbols browser indicates that the symbol is being used. If Show Read-Only Symbols is selected, read-only symbols are also displayed. Editable symbols are displayed as bold text, and read-only symbols are displayed as normal text.

For more information on changing the name or value of a symbol already in use, see "Changing a Symbol or Symbol Name" earlier in this chapter.

▶ **To change an unassigned symbol using the Resource Symbols browser**

1 In the Name box, select the unassigned symbol you want, and choose the Change button.

The Change Symbol dialog box appears.

2 Edit the symbol's name or value in the boxes provided.

3 Choose the OK button.

▶ **To delete an unassigned symbol using the Resource Symbols browser**

• Select the unassigned symbol that you want to delete, and choose the Delete button.

Note Before deleting an unused symbol in a resource file, make sure it is not used elsewhere in the program or by resource files included at compile time.

Opening the Resource Editor for a Given Symbol

When you are browsing symbols in the Resource Symbols browser, you may want more information on how a particular symbol is used. The View Use command provides a quick way to get this information.

▶ **To move to the resource editor where a symbol is being used**

1 In the Name box of the Resource Symbols browser, select the symbol you want.

2 In the Used By box, select the resource type that interests you.

3 Choose the View Use button.

The resource appears in the appropriate editor window.

Symbol Name Restrictions

All symbol names must be unique within the scope of the application. This prevents conflicting symbol definitions in the header files. Legal characters for a symbol name include A-Z, a-z, 0-9, and the underscore (_). Symbol names cannot begin with a number and are limited to 247 characters. Symbol names are not case sensitive, but the case of the first symbol definition is preserved.

Symbol names can be used more than once in your application. For example, if you are writing a data-entry program with several dialog boxes containing a text box for a person's Social Security number, you may want to give all the related text boxes a symbol name of IDC_SSN. To do this, you can define a single symbol and use it as many times as needed.

While it is not required, symbol names are often given descriptive prefixes that indicate the kind of resource or object they represent. The Microsoft Foundation Class Library (MFC) uses the symbol naming conventions shown in the following table.

Category	Prefix	Use
Resources	IDR_	Accelerator or menu (and associated resources)
	IDD_	Dialog box
	IDC_	Cursor
	IDI_	Icon
	IDB_	Bitmap
Menu items	IDM_	Menu item
Commands	ID_	Command
Controls and child windows	IDC_	Control
Strings	IDS_	String in the string table
	IDP_	String-table string used for message boxes

For more information on framework naming conventions, see Technical Note 20 under MFC in Books Online.

Symbol Value Restrictions

In Developer Studio, a symbol value can be any integer expressed in the normal manner for **#define** preprocessor directives. Here are some examples of symbol values:

```
18
4001
0x0012
-3456
```

Note Symbol values for resources (accelerators, bitmaps, cursors, dialog boxes, icons, menus, string tables, and version information) must be decimal numbers in the range from 0 to 32,767 (but cannot be hexadecimal). Symbol values for parts of resources (such as dialog box controls or individual strings in the string table) can be from 0 to 65,534 or from -32,768 to 32,767.

Some number ranges are used by Developer Studio and MFC for special purposes. For more information, see Technical Note 20 under MFC in Books Online.

You cannot define a symbol value using other symbol strings. For example, the following symbol definition is not supported:

```
#define IDC_MYEDIT  IDC_OTHEREDIT  //not supported
```

You also cannot use preprocessor macros with arguments as value definitions. For example,

```
#define  IDD_ABOUT  ID(7) //not supported
```

is not a valid expression in Developer Studio regardless of what ID evaluates to at compile time.

Your application may have an existing file containing symbols defined with expressions. For more information on how to include the symbols as read-only symbols, see "Using Shared (Read Only) or Calculated Symbols" later in this chapter.

Working With Resource Files

You can work with resources that were not developed in the Microsoft Developer Studio environment or are not part of your current project. For example, you can:

- Work with nested and conditionally included resource files
- Update existing resources or convert them to Developer Studio format
- Import or export graphic resources to or from your current resource file.
- Include shared or read-only identifiers (symbols) that can't be modified by Developer Studio.
- Include resources in your executable (.EXE) file that don't require editing (or that you don't want to be edited) during your current project, such as resources that are shared between several projects.
- Include resource types not supported by Developer Studio

You can open the types of files shown in the following table and edit the resources they contain.

Filename	Description
.RC	16- and 32-bit resource script files.
.RES	16- and 32-bit resource files.
.EXE	16- and 32-bit executable files.
.DLL	16- and 32-bit dynamic-link library files.
.EPS, .DIB, .ICO, and .CUR	Bitmap, icon, and cursor files.

You can save your resources as shown in the following table.

Open file as	Save file as
.RC	.RC or 32-Bit .RES
16-Bit .RES	.RC or 16-Bit .RES
32-Bit .RES	.RC or 32-Bit .RES
16-Bit .EXE	16-Bit .EXE, .RC or 16-Bit .RES

Open file as	Save file as
32-Bit .EXE	32-Bit .EXE, .RC or 32-Bit .RES
16-Bit .DLL	16-Bit .DLL, .RC or 16-Bit .RES
32-Bit .DLL	32-Bit .DLL, .RC or 32-Bit .RES
.BMP or .DIB	.BMP or .DIB
.ICO	.ICO
.CUR	.CUR

Note Resource script files (.RC) are distinguished as being 16 or 32 bit by whether they contain 32-bit resource keywords (such as LANGUAGE, EXSTYLE, or DIALOGEX), not by some underlying file structure. You create a 32-bit .RC file only by adding 32-bit keywords to it.

Developer Studio also works with the files shown in the following table during your resource editing session.

Filename	Description
RESOURCE.H	Header file generated by Developer Studio; contains symbol definitions.
filename.APS	Binary version of the current resource script file; used by Developer Studio for quick loading.
projectname.CLW	File containing information about the current project; used by ClassWizard in Visual C++.
projectname.MAK	File containing project build instructions.
projectname.VCP	A project configuration file.

Importing Non-Microsoft Developer Studio Resource Script Files

▶ **To update an existing resource script file for use with Microsoft Developer Studio**

1 Make a backup copy of your existing resource script (.RC) file.

2 Add the .RC file to your project.

3 Open the .RC file in Developer Studio.

   Note Developer Studio uses the include path set using the Directories tab in the Options dialog box. In addition, relative include paths for a Developer Studio .RC file must be based on the directory where the .RC file is currently located.

4 Save the Developer Studio version of the .RC file.

Reading in and then saving .RC files not created by Developer Studio modifies the organization of your .RC files.

Features Supported Only in Microsoft Foundation Class Library Resource Files

Normally when you build an MFC application for Windows from scratch using AppWizard, you start by generating a basic set of files, including a resource script file (.RC), that contain the core features of the Microsoft Foundation classes. However, if you are editing an .RC file for an application for Windows that is not based on MFC, the following features specific to the framework are not available in Visual C++:

- ClassWizard
- Menu prompt strings
- List contents for combo-box controls

You can, however, add framework support to existing .RC files that do not have it.

▶ **To add framework support to .RC files that do not already have it**

1 Open the resource file.

2 In ResourceView, highlight the resource file.

3 From the Edit menu, choose Properties.

   The Resource File Properties page appears.

4 Select the Enable MFC Features check box.

5 Choose the OK button.

Using Advanced Resource File Techniques

You can use the Resource Includes command on the View menu to modify Microsoft Developer Studio's normal working arrangement of storing all resources in the project .RC file and all symbols in RESOURCE.H. For more information on symbols, see "Working with Symbols" earlier in this chapter.

In the Resource Includes dialog box, use the Symbol Header File box to change the name of the header file where Developer Studio stores the symbol definitions for your resource file.

Use the Read-Only Symbol Directives box to include header files that contain symbols that should not be modified during a Developer Studio editing session. For example, you can use the Read-Only Symbol Directives box to include a symbol file that has been created to be shared among several projects. You can also use this box to include MFC.H files.

Use the Compile-Time Directives box to include resource files that:

- Are created and edited separately from the resources in your main resource file.

- Contain compile-time directives, such as directives that conditionally include resources.

- Contain resources in a custom format.

The Compile-Time Directives box is also used to include standard MFC resource files.

Once you've made changes to your resource file using the Resource Includes dialog box, you need to close the file and then re-open it for the changes to take effect.

Changing the Name of the Symbol Header File

Normally Developer Studio saves all symbol definitions in RESOURCE.H. However, you may need to change this include filename so that you can, for example, work with more than one resource file in the same directory.

▶ **To change the name of the resource symbol header file**

1 From the View menu, choose Resource Includes.

The Resource Includes dialog box appears.

2 In the Symbol Header File box, type the new name for the include file.

3 Choose the OK button.

Using Shared (Read-Only) or Calculated Symbols

The first time Microsoft Developer Studio reads a non-Developer Studio resource file, it marks all included header files as read-only. Subsequently, you can use the Resource Includes command on the View menu to add additional read-only symbol header files.

One reason you may want to use read-only symbol definitions is for symbol files that you plan to share among several projects.

You would also use included symbol files when you have existing resources with symbol definitions that use expressions rather than simple integers to define the symbol value. For example,

```
#define   IDC_CONTROL1 2100
#define   IDC_CONTROL2 (IDC_CONTROL1+1)
```

Developer Studio will correctly interpret these calculated symbols as long as:

- The calculated symbols are placed in a read-only symbols file.

- Your resource file contains resources to which these calculated symbols are already assigned.

► **To include shared (read-only) symbols in your resource file**

1 From the View menu, choose Resource Includes.

The Resource Includes dialog box appears.

2 In the Read-Only Symbol Directives box, use the **#include** compiler directive to specify the file where you want the read-only symbols to be kept. (The file should not be called RESOURCE.H, since that is the filename normally used by Developer Studio's main symbol header file.)

Important   What you type in the Read-Only Symbol Directives box is included in the resource file exactly as you type it. Make sure what you type does not contain any spelling or syntax errors.

You should use the Read-Only Symbol Directives box to include files with symbol definitions only. Do not include resource definitions; otherwise, duplicate resource definitions will be created when it is saved.

3 Place the symbols in the file you specified.

The symbols in files included in this way are evaluated each time you open your resource file, but they are not replaced on the disk by Developer Studio when you save your file.

4 Choose the OK button.

Including Resources From Other Files

Normally it is easy and convenient to work with Developer Studio's default arrangement of all resources in one resource script (.RC) file. However, you can add resources in other files to your current project at compile time. Use the Resource Includes dialog box's Compile-Time Directives box.

There are several reasons to place resources in a file other than Developer Studio's main .RC file:

• To include resources that have already been developed and tested and need no further modification.

• To include resources that are being used by several different projects, or that are part of a source code version-control system, and thus must exist in a central location where modifications will affect all projects.

• To include resources (such as RCDATA resources) that are in a custom format.

• To include statements in your resource file that execute conditionally at compile time using compiler directives such as **#ifdef** and **#else**. For example, your project may have a group of resources that are bracketed by **#ifdef _DEBUG ... #endif** and are thus included only if the constant **_DEBUG** is defined at compile time.

• To include statements in your resource file that modify resource-file syntax by using **#define** to implement simple macros.

If you have sections in your existing .RC files that meet any of these conditions, you should place the sections in one or more separate .RC files and include them in your project using the Resource Includes dialog box. The *projectname*.RC2 file created by Developer Studio in the RES subdirectory of a new project is used for this purpose.

▶ **To include resource files that will be added to your project at compile time**

1 Place the resources in a resource script file with a unique filename. (Do not use *projectname*.RC, since this is the filename used for Developer Studio's main resource script file.)

2 From the View menu, choose Resource Includes.

The Resource Includes dialog box appears.

3 In the Compile-Time Directives box, use the **#include** compiler directive to include the new resource file in the main Developer Studio resource file.

The resources in files included in this way are made a part of your executable file at compile time. They are not directly available for editing or modification when you are working on your project's main .RC file. You need to open included .RC files separately.

4 Choose the OK button.

Using the Dialog Editor

The Mic   ft L   oper Studio dialog editor helps with the creation or editing of a
dialog b   or resource. You can place, arrange, or activate controls; add
OLE c   est the dialog box. Dialog boxes can be stored as templates. While
using   tial   itor, you can define message handlers and manage data collection
and v   h ClassWizard.

Wit   ...   ditor, you can:

•   , or edit controls.

•   ...   ab order or accelerator keys.

/   in the dialog layout.

•   Add and edit OLE controls.

•   Configure custom controls.

•   Create a form-view dialog box.

•   Import a Visual Basic form to a dialog resource.

•   Test a dialog box.

You can use resource templates to create dialog boxes to use later or copy dialog box
resources. For more information, see "Using Resource Templates" in Chapter 5,
"Working with Resources."

You can also use the dialog editor to create and edit templates used with form views
and dialog bars. A form view is a template for a program window whose client area
contains dialog box controls. For more information, see "Creating a Form View
Dialog Box" later in this chapter.

Figure 6.1 The Dialog Editor

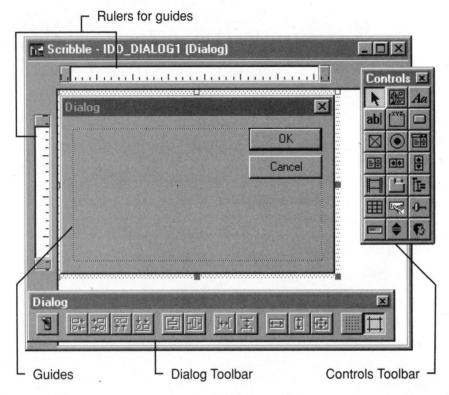

Rulers for guides

Guides   Dialog Toolbar   Controls Toolbar

 Tip   While using the dialog editor, in many instances you can click the right mouse button to display a pop-up menu of frequently used commands. The commands available depend on what the pointer is pointing to. For example, if you click while pointing to a dialog box, the pop-up menu shows the ClassWizard and Properties commands.

For information about common resource edit procedures such as creating new resources, opening existing resources, and deleting resources, see Chapter 5, "Working with Resources."

Adding and Editing Controls in a Dialog Box

One of the first steps to creating a new dialog box (or making a dialog box template) is to add controls to the dialog box. Controls can be edited to fit a certain size, shape, or alignment, or they can be moved around to work within the dialog box.

This section focuses on:

- Types of controls in dialog boxes
- Adding controls to dialog boxes
- Selecting specific controls or groups of controls
- Sizing individual controls

Types of Controls

With the dialog editor you can create dialog boxes that include the standard control types shown on the Controls toolbar in Figure 6.2.

Figure 6.2   The Controls Toolbar

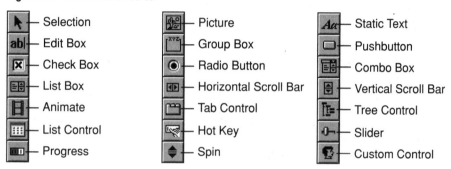

By default the Controls toolbar is displayed when the dialog editor is open, but you can modify this behavior.

▶ **To hide the Controls toolbar**

- Click the close box in the upper-left corner of the Controls toolbar.

▶ **To show the Controls toolbar**

1 From the View menu, choose Toolbars.

2 Select the Controls check box, and then choose Close.

Adding Controls

You add controls to a dialog box by using the Controls toolbar to choose the control you want and drag the control to the dialog box. When displayed, the toolbar stays positioned above other open windows in your workspace.

The fastest way to add controls to a dialog box, reposition existing controls, or move controls from one dialog box to another is to use the drag-and-drop method. (See Figure 6.3.) The control's position is outlined in a dotted line until it is dropped into the dialog box. When you add a control to a dialog box with drag-and-drop, the control is given a standard height appropriate to that type of control.

Figure 6.3 Dragging a Control from the Controls Toolbar

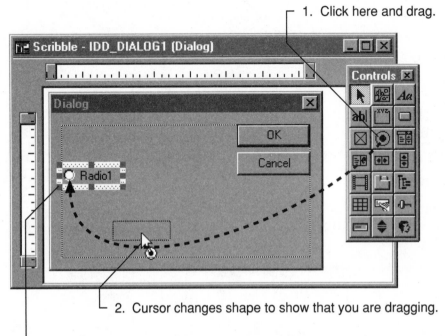

1. Click here and drag.

2. Cursor changes shape to show that you are dragging.

3. Release mouse button to place the control.

You can also add a new control by clicking the Controls toolbar button for the control you want and:

- "Drawing" the control in the dialog box. This is a good method when you want to specify the initial size of the object. Just place the pointer where you want the upper-left corner of the control to be. Drag the pointer to the right and downward to the appropriate size for that control.

- Clicking the dialog box at the location you want. This is an alternative method to dragging and dropping.

Holding down CTRL when selecting a control from the Controls toolbar places multiple controls using either method listed above. Pressing ESC stops placing controls.

When you add a control to a dialog box or reposition it, its final placement may be determined by guides or margins, or whether you have the Grid turned on. For more information about guides and margins, see "Using Guides and Margins" later in this chapter. For information about the Grid and other placement and alignment tools, see "Arranging Controls" later in this chapter.

When you have added a control to the dialog box, you can change its caption or any of its other properties in its property page.

Selecting Controls

To move, copy, delete, or align controls, you select them and then perform the operation you want. In most cases, you need to select more than one control to use the sizing and alignment tools on the Dialog toolbar.

When a control is selected, it has a shaded border around it with solid (active) or hollow (inactive) "sizing handles," small squares that appear in the selection border.

When you are sizing or aligning multiple controls, the dialog editor uses the "dominant control" to determine how the other controls are sized or aligned. When multiple controls are selected, the dominant control has solid sizing handles; all the other selected controls have hollow sizing handles.

▶ **To select multiple controls**

1 From the Controls toolbar, select the pointer tool.

2 Drag to draw a selection box around the controls you want to select (Figure 6.4). Controls partially outside the selection box are not selected.

When you release the mouse button, all controls inside the selection box are selected.

Figure 6.4 Selecting Multiple Controls

To select the controls you want, drag the mouse
pointer to draw a box around them...

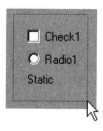
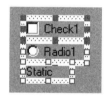

...then release the mouse button.

Once you have selected one or more controls, you can remove or add individual controls without disturbing the selection as a whole.

3 Hold down the SHIFT key and click the control you want to remove from or add to the existing selection.

▶ **To change the dominant control when more than one control is selected**

• Hold down the CTRL key and click the control you want to use to influence the size or location of the others.

The sizing handles change from hollow to solid. All further resizing or alignment is based on this control.

Sizing Individual Controls

Use the sizing handles to resize a control. When the pointer is positioned on a sizing handle, it changes shape to indicate the direction in which the control will be resized (see Figure 6.5). Active sizing handles are solid; if a sizing handle is hollow, the control cannot be resized along that axis.

Figure 6.5 Sizing a Control

You can also change the size of a control by snapping the control to guides or margins, or by moving a snapped control and guide away from another. For more information, see "Using Guides and Margins" later in this chapter. The final shape of the control may be affected by whether or not you have the Grid turned on. For more information, see "Using the Layout Grid" later in this chapter.

▸ **To size a control**

1 Click the control, or select it with the TAB key.

2 Drag the sizing handles to change the size of the control:

- Sizing handles at the top and sides change the horizontal or vertical size.
- Sizing handles at the corners change both horizontal and vertical size.

–or–

Hold down the SHIFT key and use the ARROW keys to resize the control one dialog unit (DLU) at a time.

As you type a caption to text within a control, the control will resize to fit the text caption. This function can be disabled by manually resizing the control with the sizing handles. To return to the automatic resizing of a control to fit the text within it, choose Size To Content from the Layout menu.

When you select a drop-down combo box or drop-down list box to size it, only the right and left sizing handles are active (Figure 6.6). Use these handles to set the width of the box as it is initially displayed.

You can also set the vertical size of the drop-down portion of the box.

Figure 6.6   Sizing the Drop-down Portion of a Combo Box

Click the button to change to drop-down view...

...then drag the sizing handle to change the size of the drop-down box.

▶ **To set the size of the combo box drop-down area**

1 Click the drop-down arrow at the right of the combo box (Figure 6.6).

The outline of the control changes to show the size of the combo box with the drop-down area extended.

2 Use the bottom sizing handle to change the initial size of the drop-down area.

3 Click the drop-down arrow again to close the drop-down portion of the combo box.

You can resize a group of controls based on the size of the dominant control. You can also resize a control based on the dimensions of its caption text.

▶ **To make controls the same width, height, or size**

1 Select the controls you want to resize.

2 Make sure the correct dominant control is selected.

The final size of the controls in the group depends on the size of the dominant control. For more information on selecting the dominant control, see "Selecting Controls" earlier in this chapter.

3 Choose one of the following tools on the Dialog toolbar:

- Make Same Width
- Make Same Height
- Make Same Size

Formatting the Layout of a Dialog Box

The dialog editor contains special tools for layout to help in arranging controls in the correct place and alignment. Some of these tools are contained on the Dialog toolbar, like guides and the Grid.

You can use the dialog editor in three different states for moving controls: with the guides and margins on (default setting), with Grid on, or plain, with no snapping or alignment features on at all.

You can:

- Arrange the controls using the Dialog toolbar.
- Align controls with each other or by spacing.
- Use guides and margins to align controls inside the dialog box.
- Use Grid to place controls inside the dialog box.

Arranging Controls

The dialog editor provides layout tools that align and size controls automatically. For most tasks, you can use the Dialog toolbar (Figure 6.7). All commands are also available on the Layout menu, and most have shortcut keys.

Figure 6.7 Dialog Toolbar

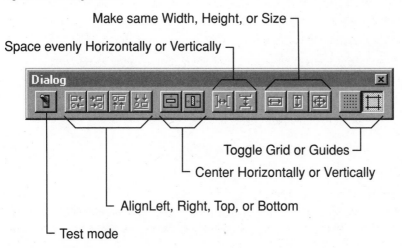

Many layout commands are available only when more than one control is selected. For information on selecting more than one control, see "Selecting Controls" earlier in this chapter.

The location, height, and width of the current control is displayed in the lower-right corner of the Developer Studio status bar (Figure 6.8). When more than one control is selected, the position indicators show the position of the dominant control (the control with solid sizing handles). When the dialog box is selected, the status bar displays the position of the dialog box and its height and width.

Figure 6.8   Dialog Editor Position Indicators

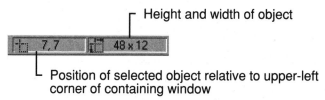

The location and size of a dialog box, as well as the location and size of controls within it, are measured in dialog units (DLUs). A DLU is based on the size of the dialog box font, normally 8-point MS Sans Serif. A horizontal DLU is the average width of the dialog box divided by four. A vertical DLU is the average height of the font divided by eight.

Aligning Controls

Once controls are in place, the dialog editor offers a variety of ways to refine their positions. You can:

- Align a group of controls along their left, right, top, or bottom edges.
- Align a group of controls on their center, either horizontally or vertically.
- Even the spacing between a group of three or more controls.
- Center one or more controls in the dialog box, vertically or horizontally.
- Automatically give pushbuttons a standard position along the bottom or on the right of the dialog box.

▶ **To align controls**

1 Select the controls you want to align.

2 Make sure the correct dominant control is selected.

The final position of the group of controls depends on the position of the dominant control. For more information on selecting the dominant control, see "Selecting . Controls" earlier in this chapter.

3 From the Layout menu, choose Align Controls, and then choose one of the following alignments:

- The Left command aligns the selected controls along their left side.
- The Right command aligns the selected controls along their right side.
- The Top command aligns the selected controls along their top edges.
- The Bottom command aligns the selected controls along their bottom edges.

▶ **To align controls on their center, vertically or horizontally**

1 Select the controls you want to center.

2 Make sure the correct dominant control is selected.

The final position of the group of controls depends on the position of the dominant control. For more information on selecting the dominant control, see "Selecting Controls" earlier in this chapter.

3 From the Layout menu, choose Align Controls, and then choose Vert. Center or Horiz. Center.

▶ **To even the spacing between controls**

1 Select the controls you want to rearrange.

2 From the Layout menu, choose Space Evenly, and then choose one of the following spacing alignments:

- Across: Controls are spaced evenly between the leftmost and the rightmost control selected.

- Down: Controls are spaced evenly between the topmost and the bottommost control selected.

▶ **To center controls in the dialog box**

1 Select the control or controls you want to rearrange.

2 From the Layout menu, choose Center In Dialog, and then choose one of the following arrangements:

- Vertical: Controls are centered vertically in the dialog box.

- Horizontal: Controls are centered horizontally in the dialog box.

▶ **To arrange pushbuttons along the right or bottom of the dialog box**

1 Select one or more pushbuttons.

2 From the Layout menu, choose Arrange Buttons, and then choose one of the following arrangements:

- Right

- Bottom

The selected buttons are positioned in a standard arrangement along the bottom or right side of the dialog box. If a control other than a pushbutton is selected, its position is not affected.

Using Guides and Margins

Whether you are moving controls, adding controls, or rearranging a current layout, guides can help you align controls accurately within a dialog box. Guides appear as blue dotted lines across the dialog box displayed in the editor and corresponding arrows in the rulers.

When you create a dialog box, four margins are provided. Margins are modified guides, appearing as blue dotted lines.

You can:

- Align controls on a guide or move controls with a guide.
- Disable the guides or move the guides without the controls.

Figure 6.9 shows the dialog editor with guides and margins.

Figure 6.9   Dialog Editor with Guides and Margins

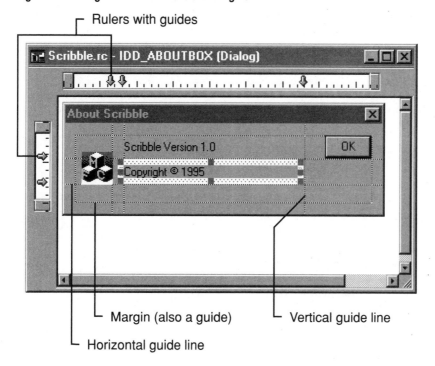

Rulers with guides

Margin (also a guide)   Vertical guide line

Horizontal guide line

▶ To create and set a guide

1 Click anywhere within the rulers to create a guide.

2 Drag the guide into position.

The number of DLUs is displayed in the ruler and below on the Developer Studio status bar. After the guide is dropped into position, hold the cursor over the guide's arrow in the ruler to see the exact position of the guide.

To delete a guide, drag the guide out of the dialog box that is being edited.

Aligning Controls on a Guide

The sizing handles of controls snap to guides when the controls are moved, and guides snap to controls (if there are no controls previously snapped to the guide). When a guide is moved, controls that are snapped to it move as well. Controls snapped to more than one guide are resized when one of the guides is moved.

The tick marks in the rulers that determine the spacing of guides and controls are determined by dialog units (DLUs). A DLU is based on the size of the dialog box font, normally 8-point MS Sans Serif. A horizontal DLU is the average width of the dialog box divided by four. A vertical DLU is the average height of the font divided by eight.

▶ To move guides

- Drag the guide to the new position.

  The coordinates of the guide are displayed in the status bar at the bottom of the Developer Studio window and in the ruler. Move the pointer over the arrow in the ruler to display the exact position of the guide.

▶ To move margins

- Drag the margin to the new position.

  −or−

  Move the gray spacing block in the ruler adjoining the margin.

  To make a margin disappear, move the margin to a zero position. To bring that margin back, place the pointer over the margin's zero position and move the margin into position.

▶ To size a group of controls with guides

1 Snap one side of the control (or controls) to a guide.

2 Drag a guide to the other side of the control (or controls).

  If necessary with multiple controls, size each to snap to the second guide.

3 Move either guide to size the control (or controls) on that side.

▶ **To change the intervals of the tick marks**

1 From the Layout menu, choose Guide Settings.

The Guide Settings dialog box appears.

2 In the Grid Spacing box, specify the new width and height in DLUs.

3 Choose the OK button.

Disabling the Guides

You can use special keys in conjunction with the mouse to disable the snapping effect of the guides. Using the ALT key disables the snapping effects of the guide selected. Moving a guide with the SHIFT key prevents snapped controls from moving with the guide.

▶ **To disable the snapping effect of the guides**

• Drag the control while holding down the ALT key.

▶ **To move guides without moving the snapped controls**

• Drag the guide while holding down the SHIFT key.

▶ **To clear all the guides**

1 Click the right mouse button in the ruler bar.

2 From the pop-up menu, choose Clear All.

▶ **To turn off the guides**

1 From the Layout menu, choose Guide Settings.

The Guide Settings dialog box appears.

2 Under Layout Guides, select None.

3 Choose the OK button.

Using the Layout Grid

When you are placing or arranging controls in a dialog box, you can use the layout grid for more precise positioning. When the grid is turned on, controls appear to "snap to" the dotted lines of the grid as if magnetized. You can turn this "snap to grid" feature on and off and change the size of the layout grid cells.

▶ **To turn the Grid on or off**

1 From the Layout menu, choose Guide Settings.

2 Select or clear the Grid radio button.

You can still control Grid in individual dialog editor windows using the Toggle Grid button on the Dialog toolbar.

▶ **To change the size of the layout grid**

1 From the Layout menu, choose Guide Settings.

2 Type the height and width in DLUs for the cells in the grid. The minimum height or width is 4 DLUs. For more information on DLUs, see "Arranging Controls" earlier in this chapter.

Editing the Dialog Box

Each dialog box has a property page, a tab order, and mnemonic keys. The tab order is the order that the focus moves from when using the TAB key. Alternatively, a keyboard user can press a mnemonic key to move the input focus from one control to another.

You can:

- Change the tab order for the input focus.
- Define the mnemonic keys for the input focus.

For more information on editing property pages, see "Using Property Pages" in Chapter 5, "Working with Resources."

Changing the Tab Order

The tab order is the order in which the TAB key moves the input focus from one control to the next within a dialog box. Usually the tab order proceeds from left to right in a dialog box, and from top to bottom. Each control has a property page with a Tabstop check box used to determine whether a control actually receives input focus or not.

Even controls that do not have the Tabstop property set need to be part of the tab order. This can be important, for example, when you define mnemonics for controls that do not have captions. Static text that contains a mnemonic for a related control must immediately precede the related control in the tab order.

Note If your dialog box contains overlapping controls, changing the tab order may change the way the controls are displayed. Controls that come first in the tab order are always displayed on top of any overlapping controls that follow them in the tab order.

▶ **To change the tab order for all controls in a dialog box**

1 From the Layout menu, choose Tab Order.

A number in the upper-left corner of each control shows its place in the current tab order.

2 Set the tab order by clicking each control in the order you want the TAB key to follow.

3 Press ENTER to exit Tab Order mode.

▶ **To change the existing tab order**

To change the existing tab order, specify the starting control; that is, select the control *prior to* the one where you want the changed order to begin. The selected control determines the number of the control you click next. For example, if you are in Tab Order mode, and control number 3 is selected, the next control you click is set to number 4.

1 From the Layout menu, choose Tab Order.

2 Specify where the change in order will begin. To do this, hold down the CTRL key and click the control *prior to* the one where you want the changed order to begin.

For example, if you want to change the order of controls 7 through 9, select control 6 first.

Note   To set a specific control to number 1 (first in the tab order), double-click the control.

3 Reset the tab order by clicking the controls in the order you want the TAB key to follow.

4 Press ENTER to exit Tab Order mode.

Defining Mnemonic Keys

Normally, keyboard users move the input focus from one control to another in a dialog box with the TAB and ARROW keys. However, you can define a mnemonic key that allows users to choose a control by pressing a single key.

Note   All the mnemonics within a dialog box should be unique.

▶ **To define a mnemonic key for a control with a visible caption (pushbuttons, check boxes, and radio buttons)**

1 Select the control.

2 From the Edit menu, choose Properties to open the control's property page.

3 In the Caption box, type an ampersand (&) in front of the letter you want as the mnemonic for that control.

An underline appears in the displayed caption to indicate the mnemonic key.

▶ **To define a mnemonic for a control without a visible caption**

1 Make a caption for the control by using a static text control. In the static text caption, type an ampersand (&) in front of the letter you want as the mnemonic.

2 Make sure the static text control immediately precedes the control it labels in the tab order.

Using OLE Controls in a Dialog Box

An OLE control is a custom control implemented as an object that fully supports OLE technology for its interface. Each OLE control has its own unique set of features. Some controls may not support all the features.

OLE controls can be imported to a project, installed on the toolbar and manipulated like other controls. You can:

- Add OLE controls to a dialog box.
- Edit the property pages associated with that control.

You can also edit the control's message map and data map with ClassWizard (for more information, see Chapter 14, "Working With Classes").

Adding OLE Controls

To place OLE controls on the dialog editor Controls toolbar, you must first add the OLE controls to your project in Component Gallery. Once inserted, the OLE controls appear on the dialog editor Controls toolbar and can be dragged to the dialog box that you are constructing. The controls that you apply are reloaded each time you start the project.

▶ **To add an OLE control to the project**

1 From the Insert menu, choose Component.

The Component Gallery dialog box appears.

2 Select the control you want by clicking the OLE control icon in the Component Gallery window.

3 Choose the Insert button.

An icon representing each control installed appears on the dialog editor Controls toolbar.

Note   You can also insert an OLE control using the right-mouse menu. This method inserts the control as a stand-alone control without the wrapper class.

Editing OLE Control Property Pages

Each of the OLE controls features a unique set of property pages that are appropriate to that control's purpose. These property pages enable you to customize the exact parameters of a control to certain specifications. The property pages for an OLE control usually contain General and All, and may have other property pages specific to that control.

For more information on property pages, see "Using Property Pages" in Chapter 5, "Working with Resources."

Using Custom Controls in a Dialog Box

A custom control is a special-format dynamic-link library (DLL) or object file used to add additional features and functionality to the user interface of the Windows NT operating system. A custom control can be a variation on an existing Windows dialog box control (for example, a text box suitable for use with Windows for Pen Computing) or a totally new category of control.

Working with User-Defined Controls

The dialog editor user-defined controls let you use existing custom controls regardless of their format.

With user-defined controls, you can:

- Set the location in the dialog box.
- Type a caption.
- Identify the name of the control's Windows class (your application code must register the control by this name).
- Type a 32-bit hexadecimal value that sets the control's style.

When you are designing a dialog box that contains custom controls, the custom control is displayed as a gray square. In test mode the custom control is also displayed as a gray square, and its run-time behavior is not simulated.

▶ **To edit user-defined control properties**

1 Select the control.

2 From the Edit menu, choose Properties.

3 Type or modify the information as appropriate.

Creating a Form View Dialog Box

You can use the dialog editor to create a template that is used as a "form view," a **CView**-compatible window that contains dialog box controls. An application that might need a form view is one in which the primary program function is data entry. In this case, the program's main view contains nothing but dialog box controls for entering data.

To construct a form view, you create a dialog box as you normally would but set several style properties differently. You then incorporate the form view into your program using the Microsoft Foundation Class Library **CFormView** class. You can use the same procedure to create a template for use with the **CDialogBar** class. For more information, see the *Class Library Reference*.

▶ **To create a dialog box template for use with the CFormView or CDialogBar class**

1 Use the dialog editor in the usual way to create a dialog box template with the controls arranged as you want them to appear in the form view.

2 From the Edit menu, choose Properties.

3 Select the Styles tab, and set the following properties:

- In the Style box, select Child.

- In the Border box, select None.

4 Select the More Styles tab, and clear the Visible check box.

5 Select the General tab, and clear the Caption box.

6 Incorporate the template into your program using the **CFormView** class.

Importing a Visual Basic Form

You can import a Visual Basic form into Visual C++ in the dialog editor. Some controls will also import with the form; OLE controls, if installed in the project, will import. Controls that are native to Visual Basic can be troublesome; nested controls also have limitations. Most of these limitations come from Visual Basic run-time differing from the Windows run-time and dialog behaviors.

▶ **To import a Visual Basic form**

1 From the Insert menu, choose Resource.

The Insert Resource dialog box appears.

2 Choose the Import button.

The Import Resource dialog box appears.

3 Type the name of the .FRM file.

4 Choose the Import button.

Warning Messages

When importing a Visual Basic form, several warning messages may appear, with information similar to this:

- The OLE control "FOOLIB.FOOCTRL" is not installed in the project.

    OLE controls have to be installed using the Component Gallery. (System registry alone will not work.)

- Syntax error in VB form description.

    The form is invalid because of customization. For example, editing or merging with a source-code file.

- The form's binary data file "FOO.FRX" can't be opened.

Limitations with Imported Visual Basic Controls

The following controls are implemented in a reduced-functionality way or ignored, due to differences between the Visual Basic run-time and the Windows dialog functionality:

- Drive and directory list boxes

  These are converted to a Windows list box, which can be filled.

- MDI forms

  Imported as a normal dialog box. Menus are ignored.

- Data controls

- Line and shape controls

- Horizontal and vertical scroll bars

- Timers

- Printers

- Screens

- Clipboards

- Queries

- Apps

Limitations with Visual Basic Properties and Nested Controls

Several properties of Visual Basic controls are implemented only by Visual Basic and have no equivalent in Windows dialog boxes and controls. Several examples include per/control font and per/control color.

Nested controls possible in Visual Basic do not translate into the Windows enviroment. In the Visual Basic environment, controls can be nested inside of each other, with the code turning one control of the many set to Visible. In the Visual C++ environment, the visibility of the controls is a run-time feature; in the editor you can see all the controls. One solution is to move the overlapping controls into separate dialog boxes. Then have the code create the dialog boxes as needed, with the main dialog box as a parent window.

Testing a Dialog Box

You can simulate the run-time behavior of a dialog box from within the dialog editor without compiling your program. This gives you immediate feedback on how the layout of controls appears and performs and thus speeds up the user-interface design process.

When you are in test mode, you can:

- Type text, select from combo-box lists, turn options on and off, and choose commands.

- Test the tab order.

- Test the grouping of controls, such as radio buttons or check boxes.

- Test the dialog box's keyboard shortcuts (for controls that have mnemonic keys defined for them).

Note Connections to dialog box code made using ClassWizard are not simulated during dialog box test mode.

When you test a dialog box, it is usually displayed at a location relative to the main Developer Studio program window. If the dialog box's Absolute Align property is selected, the dialog box is displayed at a position relative to the upper-left corner of the screen.

▶ To test a dialog box

1 From the Layout menu, choose Test.

2 To end the test session, do one of the following actions:

- Press ESC.

- Close the dialog box using its Control-menu box.

- Choose a pushbutton with a symbol name of IDOK or IDCANCEL.

CHAPTER 7

Using the Menu Editor

Menus allow you to arrange commands in a logical, easy-to-find fashion. With the Microsoft Developer Studio menu editor, you can create and edit menus by working directly with a menu bar that closely resembles the one in your finished application.

With the menu editor, you can:

- Create standard menus and commands.

- Create pop-up menus.

- Assign shortcut keys accelerator keys, and status bar prompts to menus and commands.

- Move menus or commands from one place to another.

In addition, you can use ClassWizard to hook menu items to code. For more information on connecting interface objects to message handling functions, see Chapter 14, "Working with Classes."

 Tip While using the menu editor, in many instances you can click the right mouse button to display a pop-up menu of frequently used commands. The commands available depend on what the pointer is pointing at. For example, if you click while pointing at a menu item, the pop-up menu shows Cut, Copy, Paste, and View As Popup commands, as well as commands to open ClassWizard and the properties page for the selected item.

For information about common resource edit procedures such as creating new resources, opening existing resources, and deleting resources, see Chapter 5, "Working with Resources."

Figure 7.1 Menu Terminology

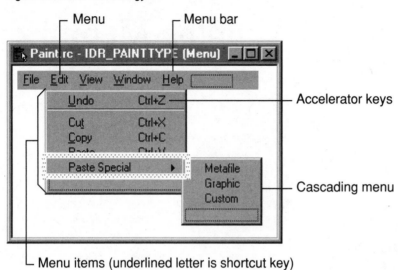

Creating Menus or Menu Items

You can create menus, cascading menus, and menu commands on the menu bar in the menu editor.

▸ **To create a menu on the menu bar**

1 Select the new-item box (an empty rectangle) on the menu bar (see Figure 7.2). Or move the new item box to a blank spot with the right and left arrow keys.

Figure 7.2 Menu Editor New-Item Boxes

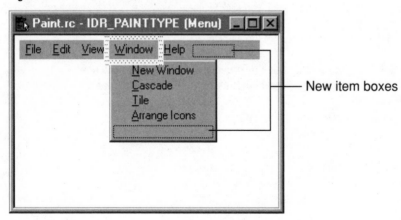

2 Type the name of the menu. When you start typing, focus automatically shifts to the Menu Item Properties page, and the text you type appears both in the Caption box and in the menu editor window.

You can define a mnemonic key that allows the user to select the menu with the keyboard. Type an ampersand (&) in front of a letter to specify it as the mnemonic. Make sure all the mnemonics on a menu bar are unique.

Once you have given the menu a name on the menu bar, the new-item box shifts to the right, and another new-item box opens below for adding menu items.

Note   To create a single-item menu on the menu bar, clear the Pop-up check box on the Menu Item Properties page.

▶ **To create a menu item**

1 First, create a menu according to the steps outlined in the previous procedure.

2 Select the menu's new-item box.

   –or–

Select an existing menu item and press INS. The new-item box is inserted before the selected item.

3 Type the name of the menu item. When you start typing, focus automatically shifts to the Menu Item Properties page, and the text you type appears in the Caption box.

You can define a mnemonic key that allows the user to select the menu command. Type an ampersand in front of a letter to specify it as the mnemonic. The mnemonic allows the user to select the menu command by typing that letter.

4 In the ID box, type the menu item ID, or select an existing command identifier. If you don't specify an ID, Visual C++ will generate an ID for you based on the command name.

5 On the properties page, select the menu item styles that apply.

6 In the Prompt box on the properties page, type the prompt string you want to appear in your application's status bar. This feature is only available with Microsoft Foundation Class Library resource script (.RC) files.

This creates an entry in the string table with the same resource identifier as the menu item you created.

7 Press ENTER to complete the menu item. The new-item box is selected so you can create additional menu items.

▶ **To create a cascading (hierarchical) menu**

1 Select the new-item box on the menu where you want the cascading menu to appear. Then type the name of the menu item that, when selected, will cause the cascading menu to appear.

When you start typing, focus automatically shifts to the Menu Item Properties page, and the text you type appears in the Caption box.

−or−

Select an existing menu item that you want to be the parent item of the cascading menu, and double-click.

2 On the properties page, select the Pop-up check box. This marks the menu item with the cascading menu symbol, and a new-item box appears to its right.

3 Add additional menu items to the cascading menu according to the instructions in the previous procedure.

Selecting Menus and Menu Items

▶ **To select a menu and display its menu items**

- Click the menu caption on the menu bar or the parent item of the cascading menu. Then click the menu item you want.

  −or−

  Move to the menu caption with the TAB (move right) and SHIFT+TAB (move left) keys or the right and left arrow keys.

▶ **To select one or more menu items**

1 Click the menu or cascading menu you want.

Its menu items are displayed.

2 Click to select a menu item, or press the SHIFT key while clicking to select multiple menu items. Hold down the SHIFT key and click an already-selected menu item to deselect it.

−or−

With the pointer outside the menu, drag to draw a selection box around the menu items you want to select.

Creating Pop-up Menus

Pop-up menus display frequently used commands with a right mouse click. They can be context sensitive to the location of the pointer. Using pop-up menus in your application requires building the menu itself and then connecting it to application code.

Once you have created the menu resource, your application code needs to load the menu resource and use the TrackPopupMenu command to cause the menu to appear. Once the user has dismissed it by clicking outside it, or has clicked on a command, that function will return. If the user chooses a command, that command message will be sent to the window whose handle was passed.

▶ **To create a pop-up menu**

1 Create a menu bar with an empty title. Type a temporary letter in the caption or choose an attribute to reverse later. This is to allow the menu to be created below.

2 Move to the next menu item below. Bring up the property page and type in the caption and any other information. Repeat this process for any other menu items in the pop-up menu.

3 Make the top menu bar empty again (if using a temporary letter in the caption) or reset the temporary attribute. The goal is to have a pop-up menu descending beneath a blank menu bar.

4 Save the menu resource.

▶ **To connect a pop-up menu to your application**

• Add the following code to your source file:

```
CMenu menu;
VERIFY(menu.LoadMenu(IDR_MENU1));
CMenu* pPopup = menu.GetSubMenu(0);
ASSERT(pPopup != NULL);

pPopup->TrackPopupMenu(TPM_LEFTALIGN | TPM_RIGHTBUTTON, x,
y, AfxGetMainWnd());
```

Moving and Copying Menus and Menu Items

▶ **To move or copy menus or menu items using drag-and-drop**

1 Drag or copy the item you want to move to:

• A new location on the current menu.

• A different menu. (You can navigate into other menus by dragging the mouse pointer over them.)

2 Drop the menu item when the insertion guide shows the position you want.

Figure 7.3   Moving a Menu to a Cascading Menu

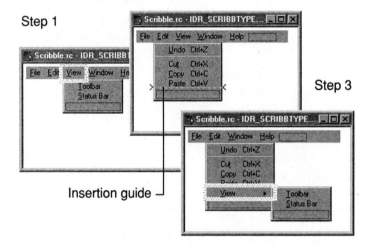

Step 1

Step 2

Step 3

Insertion guide

▶ **To move or copy menus or menu items using the menu commands**

1 Select one or more menus or menu items.

2 From the Edit menu, choose Cut (to move) or Copy.

3 If you are moving the items to another menu resource or resource script file, make that menu editor window active.

4 Select the position of the menu or menu item you want to move or copy to.

5 From the Edit menu, choose Paste. The moved or copied item is placed before the item you select.

Note   You can also drag, copy, and paste to other menus in other menu windows.

Viewing the Menu Resource as a Pop-up Menu

Normally, when you are working in the menu editor, a menu resource is displayed as a menu bar. However, you may have menu resources that are added to the application's menu bar while the program is running. To see what a menu resource looks like as a pop-up menu, use the menu editor's View As Popup command on the right mouse pop-up menu. To change back to the menu-bar view, choose View As Popup again.

Associating a Menu Item with an Accelerator Key

Many times you want a menu item and a keyboard combination to issue the same program command. You do this by assigning the same resource identifier to the menu item and to an entry in your application's accelerator table. You then edit the menu item's caption to show the name of the accelerator key.

▶ **To associate a menu item with an accelerator key**

1 In the menu editor, select the menu item you want. From the Edit menu, choose Properties or double-click the item.

2 In the Caption box, add the name of the accelerator key to the menu caption:

- Following the menu caption, type the escape sequence for a TAB (\t), so that all the menu's accelerator keys are left-aligned.

- Type the name of the modifier key (CTRL, ALT, or SHIFT) followed by a plus sign and the name, letter, or symbol of the additional key.

For example, to assign CTRL+O to the Open command on the File menu, you modify the menu item's caption so that it looks like this:

```
Open\tCtrl+O
```

The menu item in the menu editor is updated to reflect the new caption as you type it.

3 Create the accelerator-table entry in the accelerator editor and assign it the same identifier as the menu item. Use a key combination that you think will be easy to remember.

For more information on creating and naming accelerator resources, see Chapter 8, "Using the Accelerator Editor."

Associating a Menu Item with a Status Bar Prompt

Your application can display descriptive text for each of the menu items that may be selected. MFC can handle this for you if you have a string in the string table whose ID is the same as the command. You do this by assigning a text string to each menu item using the Menu Item Properties page.

▶ **To associate a menu item with a status bar text string**

1 Select the menu item.

2 In the Prompt box, type the associated status bar text.

CHAPTER 8

Using the Accelerator Editor

An accelerator table is a Windows resource that contains a list of accelerator keys (also known as shortcut keys) and the command identifiers that are associated with them. A program can have more than one accelerator table.

Normally, accelerators are used as keyboard shortcuts for program commands that are also available on a menu or toolbar. However, you can use the accelerator table to define key combinations for commands that don't have a user-interface object associated with them.

You can use ClassWizard to hook accelerator key commands to code. For more information on ClassWizard, see Chapter 14, "Working with Classes."

With the accelerator editor, you can:

- Add, delete, change, and browse the accelerator key assignments in your project.
- View and change the resource identifier associated with each entry in the accelerator table. The identifier is used to reference each accelerator table entry in program code.
- Associate an accelerator key with a menu item.

Figure 8.1 The Accelerator Editor

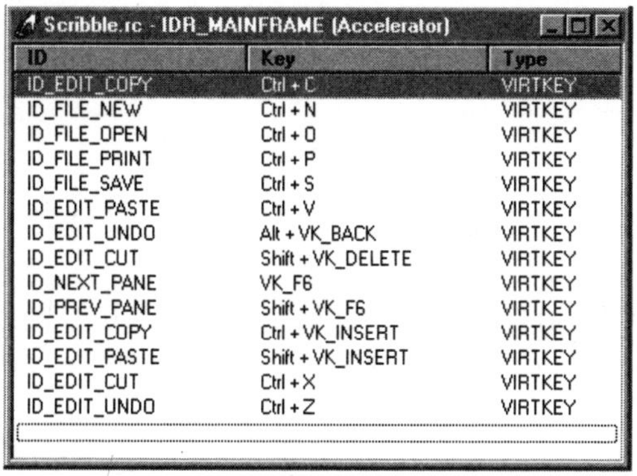

ID	Key	Type
ID_EDIT_COPY	Ctrl + C	VIRTKEY
ID_FILE_NEW	Ctrl + N	VIRTKEY
ID_FILE_OPEN	Ctrl + O	VIRTKEY
ID_FILE_PRINT	Ctrl + P	VIRTKEY
ID_FILE_SAVE	Ctrl + S	VIRTKEY
ID_EDIT_PASTE	Ctrl + V	VIRTKEY
ID_EDIT_UNDO	Alt + VK_BACK	VIRTKEY
ID_EDIT_CUT	Shift + VK_DELETE	VIRTKEY
ID_NEXT_PANE	VK_F6	VIRTKEY
ID_PREV_PANE	Shift + VK_F6	VIRTKEY
ID_EDIT_COPY	Ctrl + VK_INSERT	VIRTKEY
ID_EDIT_PASTE	Shift + VK_INSERT	VIRTKEY
ID_EDIT_CUT	Ctrl + X	VIRTKEY
ID_EDIT_UNDO	Ctrl + Z	VIRTKEY

Tip While using the accelerator editor, in many instances you can click the right mouse button to display a pop-up menu of frequently used commands. The commands available depend on what the pointer is pointing to. For example, if you click while pointing to an accelerator entry, the pop-up menu shows the Cut, Copy, New Accelerator, ClassWizard, and Properties commands.

Note Windows does not allow the creation of empty accelerator tables. If you create an accelerator table with no entries, it is deleted automatically when you exit Microsoft Developer Studio.

For information about common resource edit procedures such as creating new resources, opening existing resources, and deleting resources, see Chapter 5, "Working with Resources."

Editing an Accelerator Table

▶ **To add an entry to an accelerator table**

1 Select the new-item box at the end of the list, or press the INS key.

2 Type the accelerator key to define it.

The Accel Properties page appears, with the focus in the Key box.

Note Make sure all accelerators you define are unique. When duplicate accelerator keys are assigned, only the first one works correctly.

▶ **To delete an entry from an accelerator table**

1 Select the entry you want to delete. Hold down the CTRL or SHIFT key while clicking to select multiple entries.

2 From the Edit menu, choose Delete.

▶ **To move or copy an accelerator table entry from one resource script file to another**

1 Open the accelerator editor windows in both resource script files.

2 Select the entry you want to move.

3 Drag the entry to its new location.

-or-

Use the Copy (or Cut) and Paste commands on the Edit menu.

Note When you copy—rather than move—an entry, duplicate accelerator keys are created. Microsoft Developer Studio does not prompt you to resolve accelerator key conflicts.

Setting Accelerator Properties

The Accel Properties page allows you to control the features of each accelerator key. By default, the property page is dismissed when it does not have focus. If you want the property page to remain on the screen, even when it does not have focus, click the Pushpin button in the upper-left corner of the window.

The following are legal entries in the Key box of an accelerator property page:

- An integer between 0 and 255 in decimal, hexadecimal, or octal format. The setting of the Type property determines if the number is an ASCII or virtual key value.

  Single-digit numbers are always interpreted as the corresponding key, rather than as ASCII values. To enter an ASCII value from 0 to 9, precede it with two zeros (for example, 006).

- A single keyboard character. Uppercase A–Z or the numbers 0–9 can be either ASCII or virtual key values; any other character is ASCII only.

- A single keyboard character in the range A–Z (uppercase only), preceded by a caret (^) (for example, ^C). This enters the ASCII value of the key when it is pressed with the CTRL key held down.

  Note   When entering an ASCII value, the CTRL and SHIFT modifiers on the property page are not available. You cannot use a control-key combination entered with a caret to create a virtual accelerator key.

- Any valid virtual key identifier. The Key box on the property page contains a list of standard virtual key identifiers.

 Tip   Another way to define an accelerator key is to choose the Next Key Typed button in the property page and then press any of the keys on the keyboard.

Associating an Accelerator Key with a Menu Item

Many times you want a menu item and a keyboard combination to issue the same program command. You do this by assigning the same resource identifier to the menu item and to an entry in your application's accelerator table. You then edit the menu item's caption to show the name of the accelerator. For more information on menu items and accelerator keys, see "Associating a Menu Item with an Accelerator Key" in Chapter 7.

CHAPTER 9

Using the String Editor

A string table is a Windows resource that contains a list of IDs, values, and captions for all the strings of your application. For example, the status-bar prompts are located in the string table. An application can have only one string table.

With the string editor you can edit a program's string table resource. In a string table, strings are grouped into segments, or blocks, of 16 strings each. The segment a string belongs to is determined by the value of its identifier; for example, strings with identifiers of 0 to 15 are in one segment, strings with identifiers of 16 to 31 are in a second segment, and so on. Thus, to move a string from one segment to another you need to change its identifier.

Individual string segments are loaded on demand in order to conserve memory. For this reason, programmers usually try to group strings into logical groupings of 16 or less and then use each group or segment only when it is needed.

With the string editor (shown in Figure 9.1), you can:

- Find a string in the string table.
- Add a string table entry.
- Delete an individual string.
- Move a string from one segment to another.
- Move a string from one resource script (.RC) file to another.
- Change a string or its identifier.
- Add formatting or special characters to a string.

Figure 9.1 The String Editor

ID	Value	Caption
IDR_MAINFRAME	128	Paint
IDR_PAINTTYPE	129	\nPaint\nPaint\n\n\nPaint.Document\r
AFX_IDS_APP_TITLE	57344	Paint
AFX_IDS_IDLEMESSAGE	57345	Ready
ID_FILE_NEW	57600	Create a new document\nNew
ID_FILE_OPEN	57601	Open an existing document\nOpen
ID_FILE_CLOSE	57602	Close the active document\nClose
ID_FILE_SAVE	57603	Save the active document\nSave
ID_FILE_SAVE_AS	57604	Save the active document with a new r
ID_FILE_PAGE_SETUP	57605	Change the printing options\nPage Set
ID_FILE_PRINT_SETUP	57606	Change the printer and printing options\r

(Paint.rc - String Table (String Table))

Tip While using the string editor, in many instances you can click the right mouse button to display a pop-up menu of resource-specific commands. The commands available depend on what the pointer is pointing to. For example, if you click while pointing to a string table entry, the pop-up menu shows the Cut, Copy, New String, and Properties commands.

Note Windows does not allow the creation of empty string tables. If you create a string table with no entries, it is deleted automatically when you exit Microsoft Developer Studio.

For information about common resource edit procedures such as creating new resources, opening existing resources, and deleting resources, see Chapter 5, "Working with Resources."

Finding a String

With the string editor's Find command you can quickly locate a string in the string table by either the caption or resource identifier.

▶ **To find a string in the string table**

1 In ResourceView, open the string table by double-clicking its icon.

2 From the Edit menu, choose Find.

   The Find dialog box appears.

3 In the Find What box, type the caption text or resource identifier of the string you want to find. Select or clear the Match Case check box as appropriate.

4 Choose the Find Next button.

   If a string or its identifier in the string table matches what you typed, it is selected.

Adding or Deleting a String

When the string editor window is displayed, you can add or delete entries in the string table. String table segments are separated by horizontal lines in the string editor window.

▶ **To add a string table entry**

1 Select the new-item box (an empty rectangle) at the end of a string segment.

2 Type the new string.

Focus shifts to the String Properties page as you start typing. The text is entered in the Caption box, and the string is given the next identifier in sequence.

3 Press ENTER to place the new string in the string table.

New entries can also be inserted into the string table. Select an existing entry, and from the Insert menu, choose New String. The new string is placed after the currently selected string in the next available identifier.

Note   Null strings are not allowed in Windows string tables. If you create an entry in the string table that is a null string, the entry is deleted when you close the string editor.

▶ **To delete a string table entry**

1 Select the string you want to delete.

2 From the Edit menu, choose Delete.

Moving a String from One Segment to Another

▶ **To move a string from one segment to another**

1 Select the string you want to move.

2 From the Edit menu, choose Properties.

The String Properties page opens.

3 Change the string's value in the ID box so that it falls in the range you want.

For example, to move a string with a name of `IDS_MYSTRING` and a value of `100` to a segment in the `200` range, type the following in the ID box:

```
IDS_MYSTRING=201
```

4 Press ENTER to record the change.

Moving a String from One Resource Script File to Another

▶ **To move a string from one resource script file to another**

1 Open the string editor windows in both resource script files.

2 Select the string you want to move.

3 Drag the selected string from one string editor window and drop it in the target string editor window.

–or–

Use the Cut and Paste commands on the Edit menu.

Note If the symbol name or value of the moved string conflicts with an existing identifier in the destination file, the symbol name is changed (if a symbol with that name already exists) or the symbol value is changed (if a symbol with that value already exists).

Changing a String or Its Identifier

▶ **To change a string or its identifier**

1 Select the string you want to edit.

2 From the Edit menu, choose Properties, and modify the string in the Caption box.

3 In the ID box, modify the string's identifier:

- Type a new symbol name, or select one from the list.
- To change a string's value, type the symbol name followed by an equal sign and the new value; for example:

  ```
  IDS_ERROR_MSG=2350
  ```

For more information on editing symbols, see Chapter 16, "Browsing Through Symbols."

Adding Formatting or Special Characters to a String

▶ **To add formatting or special characters to a string**

- Use the standard escape sequences shown in Table 9.1.

Table 9.1 Formatting and Special Characters in Strings

To get this	Type this
New line	\n
Carriage return	\r
Tab	\t
Backslash (\)	\\
ASCII character	\ddd (octal notation)
Alert (bell)	\a

CHAPTER 10

Using the Graphic Editor

The Microsoft Developer Studio graphic editor has an extensive set of tools for drawing bitmaps, icons, and cursors, as well as features to support the creation of toolbar bitmaps and the management of icon and cursor images.

With the graphic editor, you can:

- Use the image editor window and docking toolbars.
- Customize and adjust the graphic editor workspace.
- Edit a graphic resource and draw new graphics.
- Customize colors, change palettes, and select colors.
- Edit icons and cursors, including 48 x 48 icons.

Most editing procedures are the same for bitmaps, icons, and cursors. This chapter first shows the procedures common to all graphical resources. Later sections detail procedures and graphic-editor capabilities specific to icons and cursors. For specific information on editing toolbar resources and converting bitmaps to toolbars, see Chapter 11, "Using the Toolbar Editor."

Note Many of the graphic editor's functions require a mouse or other pointing device. For keyboard shortcuts or accelerators, check the Help Keyboard Table in the Help menu. See Chapter 22, "Customizing the Microsoft Developer Studio Display."

 Tip While using the graphic editor, in many instances you can click the right mouse button to display a pop-up menu of frequently used commands. The commands available depend on what the pointer is pointing to. For example, if you click while pointing to a bitmap folder, the pop-up menu shows the New and New Bitmap commands.

For information about common resource edit procedures such as creating new resources, opening existing resources, and deleting resources, see Chapter 5, "Working with Resources."

Using the Image Editor Window and Tools

You edit bitmaps, icons, and cursors in the image editor window, using the tools on the Graphics toolbar (Figure 10.1).

Figure 10.1 Image Editor Window, Graphics Toolbar, and Colors Palette

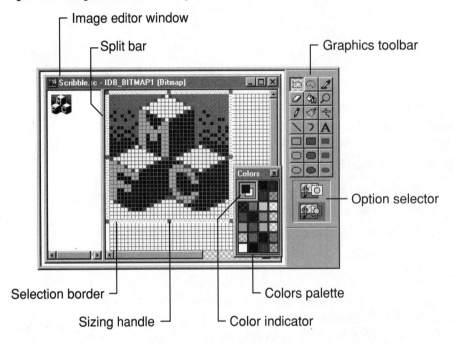

The figure shows three basic tools: the image editor window, the Graphics toolbar, and the Colors palette. Additionally, the Image menu provides useful commands, and the status bar shows helpful information.

The Image Editor Window

The image editor window shows two views of an image. A split bar separates the two panes. You can drag the split bar from side to side to change the relative sizes of the panes. The active pane displays a selection border, as shown in Figure 10.1.

The Graphics Toolbar

The Graphics toolbar has two parts, which are shown in Figure 10.1:

- The toolbar, which contains 21 tools for drawing, painting, entering text, erasing, and manipulating views.

- The option selector, which you click to select brush widths and other drawing options.

To use the Graphics toolbar, Colors palette, and option selector, click the tool, color, or option that you want.

The Colors Palette

The Colors palette has two parts, which are shown in Figure 10.1:

- The color indicator, which shows the foreground and background colors and (for icons and cursors) selectors for "screen" and "inverse" color.

- The Colors palette, which you click to select the foreground and background colors.

For large icons using the 256-color palette on the property page, see "Creating and Editing Icons and Cursors" later in this chapter.

The Status Bar

The status bar, at the bottom of the frame window, displays two panes when an image editor window is open. When the pointer is over an image, the left pane shows the cursor's current position, in pixels, relative to the upper-left corner of the image. During a dragging operation, such as selecting, moving, or drawing a rectangle, the right pane shows the size, in pixels, of the affected area.

The Image Menu

The Image menu, which appears only when the graphic editor is active, has commands for editing images, managing color palettes, and setting image editor window options.

Managing the Graphic Editor Workspace

By adjusting the graphic editor workspace to fit your needs and preferences, you can work more effectively and comfortably. This section describes procedures for:

- Selecting and sizing image-editor panes.

- Changing the magnification of image editor windows.

- Displaying and hiding pixel grids.

Using Image-Editor Panes

The image editor window typically displays a bitmap in two panes separated by a split bar. One view is actual size, and the other is enlarged (the default enlargement factor is 6). The views in these two panes are updated automatically: changes you make in one pane are immediately shown in the other. The two panes make it easy for you to work on an enlarged "picture" of your bitmap, in which you can distinguish individual pixels and, at the same time, observe the effect of your work on the actual-size view of the image.

If the bitmap is 200 x 200 pixels or larger, however, only one pane is displayed initially. Move the split bar to display both panes.

You can use the two panes in other ways. For example, you might enlarge the smaller pane and use the two panes to show different regions of a large bitmap. Click in the pane to select it.

You can change the relative sizes of the panes by positioning the pointer on the split bar and moving the split bar to the right or left. The split bar can move all the way to either side if you want to work on only one pane.

Changing the Magnification Factor

By default, the graphic editor displays the view in the left pane at actual size and the view in the right pane at 6 times actual size. The magnification factor is the ratio between the actual size of the bitmap and the displayed size. The default is 6, and the range is from 1 to 8.

▶ To change the magnification factor

1 Select the image-editor pane whose magnification factor you want to change.

2 On the toolbar, click the Magnify tool.

The pointer changes to the Magnify tool, and magnification-factor options appear in the option selector on the Graphics toolbar. If the current magnification factor matches an option, that option is highlighted.

3 Click the desired magnification factor.

–or–

Select the image-editor pane whose magnification factor you want to change.

Press SHIFT+RIGHT ANGLE BRACKET (>) to increase the magnification factor, or press SHIFT+LEFT ANGLE BRACKET (<) to decrease the magnification factor.

Displaying and Hiding the Pixel Grid

For all image-editor panes with a magnification factor of 4 or greater, you can display a grid that delimits the individual pixels in the image. For more information, see "Changing the Magnification Factor."

▶ To display or hide the pixel grid

1 From the Image menu, choose Grid Settings.

The Grid Settings dialog box appears.

2 Select the Pixel Grid check box to display the grid, or clear the box to hide the grid.

3 Choose the OK button.

–or–

- Press G to toggle the grid display.

Editing Graphical Resources

There are several editing operations involved in using the graphic editor. This section describes these graphics-editing tasks:

- Setting bitmap properties
- Showing and hiding the Graphics toolbar
- Drawing and erasing
- Drawing lines and closed figures
- Cutting, copying, clearing, and moving selected parts of a bitmap
- Creating a custom brush
- Flipping or resizing a bitmap

You can also import existing bitmaps, icons, and cursors and add them to your project, and you can open files that are not part of a project for stand-alone editing. For more information on importing resources, see "Using the Resource Editors" and "Working with Symbols," both in Chapter 5.

Note   Most graphic editor operations are the same for all kinds of graphical resources. Unless the text states otherwise, the procedures described in this section can be performed on bitmaps, cursors, or icons.

Setting Bitmap Properties

You use the Properties window to change most resource properties. Exceptions are new icons or cursors for additional target devices. For more information, see "Setting a Cursor's Hot Spot," later in this chapter, and Appendix B, "Initializing and Configuring Microsoft Developer Studio."

 Tip   By default the Properties window is hidden whenever it does not have focus. To keep the Properties window in view when it does not have focus, click the Pushpin command button in the upper-left corner of the Properties window.

▶ **To change a bitmap's properties**

1 Open the bitmap whose properties you want to change.

2 From the Edit menu, choose Properties to open its property page.

3 Change any or all of these properties on the General tab:

- In the ID box, modify the resource's identifier. For a bitmap, Microsoft Developer Studio by default assigns the next available identifier in a series: IDB_BITMAP1, IDB_BITMAP2, and so forth. Similar names are used for icons and cursors.

- In the Width and Height boxes, modify the bitmap's width and height (in pixels). The default value for each is 48.

  If you change the dimensions of a bitmap using the property page, the image is cropped or "blank" space is added to the right of or below the existing image.

- In the Colors list box, select Monochrome, 16, or 256. If you have already drawn the bitmap with a 16-color palette, selecting Monochrome causes substitutions of black and white for the colors in the bitmap. Contrast is not always maintained: for example, adjacent areas of red and green are both converted to black.

- In the File Name box, modify the name of the file in which the bitmap is to be stored. By default, Developer Studio assigns a base filename created by removing the first four characters ("IDB_") from the default identifier and adding the extension .EPS.

- Select the Save Compressed check box to save the bitmap in a compressed format.

4 Change any or all of the color properties on the Palette tab:

- Double-click to select a color and display the Custom Color Selector dialog box.

- Define the color by typing RGB or HSL values in the appropriate text boxes, or by moving the cross hairs on the color box.

- For more information, see "Changing Colors" later in this chapter.

Showing and Hiding the Graphics Toolbar

Since many of the drawing tools are available from the keyboard, sometimes it is useful to hide the Graphics toolbar.

▶ **To show or hide the Graphics toolbar**

1 Place the mouse pointer over the toolbar area and click the right mouse button.

A pop-up menu appears.

2 From the pop-up menu, choose Graphics.

Freehand Drawing and Erasing

The graphic editor's freehand drawing and erasing tools all work in the same way: you select the tool and, if necessary, select foreground and background colors and size and shape options. You then move the pointer to the bitmap and click or drag to draw and erase.

When you have selected the eraser tool, brush tool, or airbrush tool, the option selector displays that tool's options.

 Tip   Instead of using the eraser tool, you may find it more convenient to draw in the background color with one of the drawing tools.

Selecting and Using a Drawing Tool

The various drawing tools are easily selected using the Graphics toolbar. Figure 10.2 shows each toolbar button and its related drawing tool.

Figure 10.2   Drawing Tools in the Graphics Toolbar

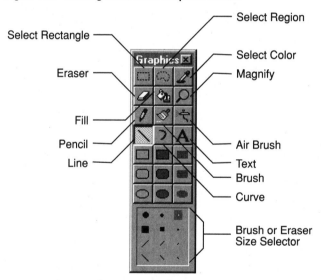

▶ **To select and use a drawing tool**

1 Click a button on the Graphics toolbar:

- The eraser tool "paints over" the image with the current background color when you press the left mouse button. When you press the right mouse button, it replaces the current foreground color with the current background color.

- The pencil tool draws freehand in a constant width of one pixel.

- The brush tool's shape and size are determined by the option selector.
- The airbrush tool randomly distributes color pixels around the center of the brush.

2 If necessary, select colors and a brush:

- In the Colors palette, click the left button to select a foreground color or the right button to select a background color.
- On the options selector of the Graphics toolbar, click a shape representing the brush you want to use. Your selection is highlighted.

3 Point to the place on the bitmap where you want to start drawing or painting. The brush or pointer appears on the bitmap.

4 Press the left mouse button (for the foreground color) or the right mouse button (for the background color), and hold it down as you draw.

5 Release the mouse button.

▶ **To change the size of the brush, airbrush, or eraser**

- Press the PLUS SIGN (+) key to increase the size or the MINUS SIGN (−) key to decrease it.

−or−

Press the PERIOD (.) to choose the smallest size.

−or−

Choose a brush in the option selector.

Drawing Lines and Closed Figures

The graphic editor tools for drawing lines and closed figures all work in the same way: you place the insertion point at one point and drag to another. For lines, these points are the endpoints. For closed figures, these points are opposite corners of a rectangle bounding the figure.

Lines are drawn in a width determined by the current brush selection, and framed figures are drawn in a width determined by the current width selection. Lines and all figures, both framed and filled, are drawn in the current foreground color if you press the left mouse button, or in the current background color if you press the right mouse button.

Drawing a Line

▶ **To draw a line**

1 From the toolbar, select the line tool.

2 If necessary, select colors: in the Colors palette, click the left button to select a foreground color or the right button to select a background color.

3 If necessary, select a brush: in the option selector, click a shape representing the brush you want to use. Your selection is highlighted.

4 Place the pointer at the line's starting point.

5 Drag to the line's endpoint.

Drawing a Closed Figure

The various closed-figure drawing tools are easily selected using the Graphics toolbar. Figure 10.3 shows the toolbar buttons for closed-figure drawing.

Figure 10.3   Closed-Figure Tools on the Graphics Toolbar

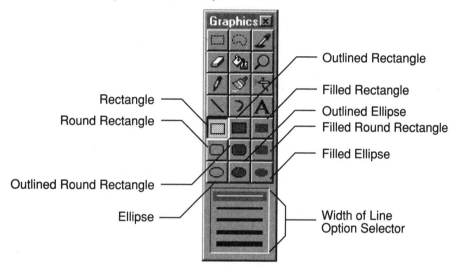

▶ **To draw a closed figure**

1 From the Graphics toolbar, select a closed-figure drawing tool:

- The outlined-rectangle tool draws a rectangle framed with the foreground or background color.

- The filled rectangle tool draws a rectangle filled with the foreground or background color.

- The outlined round rectangle tool draws a rectangle with rounded corners framed with the foreground or background color.

- The filled round rectangle tool draws a rectangle with rounded corners filled with the foreground or background color.

- The outlined ellipse tool draws an ellipse framed with the foreground or background color.

- The filled ellipse tool draws an ellipse filled with the foreground or background color.

2 If necessary, select colors: on the Colors palette, click the left button to select a foreground color or the right button to select a background color.

3 If necessary, select a line width: on the option selector, click a shape representing the brush you want to use. Your selection is highlighted.

4 Move the pointer to one corner of the rectangular area in which you want to draw the figure.

5 Drag it to the diagonally opposite corner.

Selecting an Area of the Bitmap

The selection tool defines an area of the bitmap that you can cut, copy, clear, resize, invert, or move. You can also create a custom brush from the selection. For more information on creating a custom brush, see "Creating a Custom Brush" later in this chapter.

▶ **To select an area of the bitmap**

1 In the Graphics toolbar, click the selection tool.

2 Move the insertion point to one corner of the bitmap area that you want to select.

Cross hairs appear when the insertion point is over the bitmap.

3 Drag the insertion point to the opposite corner of the area you want to select.

A rectangle shows which pixels will be selected. All pixels within the rectangle, including those "under" the rectangle, are included in the selection.

4 Release the mouse button.

The "selection border"—a rectangular frame—encloses the selected area. Now any operation you perform will affect only the pixels within the rectangle.

▶ **To select the entire bitmap**

- Click the bitmap outside of the current selection.

  −or−

- Press the ESC key.

  −or−

- Choose another tool on the toolbar.

Cutting, Copying, Clearing, and Moving

You can perform standard editing operations—cutting, copying, clearing, and moving—with the selection, whether the selection is the entire bitmap or just a part of it. Because the graphic editor uses the Windows Clipboard, you can transfer images between Developer Studio and other applications for Windows, such as Microsoft Paintbrush™ and Microsoft Word for Windows.

In addition, you can resize the selection, whether it includes the entire bitmap or just a part. For more information on resizing, see "Resizing a Bitmap" later in this chapter.

▶ To cut the current selection and move it to the Clipboard

- From the Edit menu, choose Cut.

  The original area of the selection is filled with the current background color, and the selection is now in the Clipboard.

▶ To clear the current selection without moving it to the Clipboard

- From the Edit menu, choose Clear.

  The original area of the selection is filled with the current background color.

▶ To paste the Clipboard contents into the bitmap

1 From the Edit menu, choose Paste.

  The Clipboard contents, surrounded by the selection border, appear in the upper-left corner of the pane.

2 Position the pointer within the selection border and drag the image to the desired location on the bitmap.

3 To anchor the image at its new location, click outside of the selection border or choose a new tool.

▶ To move the selection

1 Position the pointer inside the selection border or anywhere on it except the sizing handles.

2 Drag the selection to its new location.

  The original area of the selection is filled with the current background color.

3 To anchor the selection in the bitmap at its new location, click outside the selection border or choose a new tool.

▶ To copy the selection

1 Position the pointer inside the selection border or anywhere on it except the sizing handles.

2 Hold down the CTRL key as you drag the selection to a new location.

  The area of the original selection is unchanged.

3 To copy the selection into the bitmap at its current location, click outside the selection cursor or choose a new tool.

▶ **To draw with the selection**

1 Position the pointer inside the selection border or anywhere on it except the sizing handles.

2 Hold down the SHIFT key as you drag the selection.

Copies of the selection are left along the dragging path. The more slowly you drag, the more copies are made.

Flipping the Selection

▶ **To flip the selection along the horizontal axis**

• From the Image menu, choose Flip Horizontal.

▶ **To flip the selection along the vertical axis**

• From the Image menu, choose Flip Vertical.

▶ **To rotate the selection 90°**

• From the Image menu, choose Rotate 90°.

Creating a Custom Brush

A custom brush is a rectangular portion of a bitmap that you "pick up" and use like one of the graphic editor's ready-made brushes. All operations you can perform on a selection, you can perform on a custom brush as well.

▶ **To create a custom brush**

1 Select the part of the bitmap that you want to use for a brush. For more information, see "Selecting and Using a Drawing Tool" earlier in this chapter.

2 Press CTRL+B.

Pixels in a custom brush that match the current background color are normally "transparent," they do not paint over the existing image. You can change this behavior so that background-color pixels paint over the existing image.

You can use the custom brush like a "stamp" or a "stencil" to create a variety of special effects.

Using a Custom Brush

▶ **To draw custom brush shapes in the background color**

1 Select an opaque or transparent background. For more information, see "Choosing Opaque and Transparent Backgrounds" later in this chapter.

2 Set the background color to the color in which you want to draw.

3 Position the custom brush where you want to draw.

4 Press the right mouse button.

Any opaque regions of the custom brush are drawn in the background color.

▶ To double or halve the custom brush size

- Press the PLUS SIGN (+) key to double the brush size, or the MINUS SIGN (–) key to halve it.

▶ To cancel the custom brush

- Press ESC or choose another drawing tool.

Resizing a Bitmap

The behavior of the graphic editor while resizing a bitmap depends on whether the selection includes the entire bitmap or just part of it:

- When the selection includes only part of the bitmap, Microsoft Developer Studio shrinks the selection by deleting rows or columns of pixels and filling the vacated regions with the current background color, or it stretches the selection by duplicating rows or columns of pixels.

- When the selection includes the entire bitmap, Developer Studio either shrinks and stretches the bitmap, or crops and extends it.

There are two mechanisms for resizing a bitmap: the resizing handles and the property page. You can drag the sizing handles to change the size of all or part of a bitmap. Sizing handles that you can drag are solid, like those on the lower-right corner and the midpoints of the right and bottom sides of the bitmaps. You cannot drag handles that are hollow. You can use the property page to resize only the entire bitmap, not a selected part.

Note If you have the Tile Grid option selected (see Grid Settings command on the Image menu), then resizing snaps to the next tile grid line. If only the Pixel Grid option is selected, resizing snaps to the next available pixel. Usually, only the Pixel Grid option is selected.

Resizing an Entire Bitmap

▶ To resize an entire bitmap using the property page

1 From the Edit menu, choose Properties to open the property page.

2 In the Width and Height boxes, type the dimensions that you want.

If you are increasing the size of the bitmap, the graphic editor extends the bitmap to the right downward, or both, and fills the new region with the current background color. The image is not stretched.

If you are decreasing the size of the bitmap, the graphic editor crops the bitmap on the right or bottom edge, or both.

You can use the Width and Height properties to resize only the entire bitmap, not to resize a partial selection.

▶ **To crop or extend an entire bitmap**

1 Select the entire bitmap.

If part of the bitmap is currently selected, and you want to select the entire bitmap, click anywhere on the bitmap outside the current selection border, press ESC, or choose another drawing tool.

2 Drag a sizing handle until the bitmap is the desired size.

Normally, the graphic editor crops or enlarges a bitmap when you resize it by moving a sizing handle. If you hold down the SHIFT key as you move a sizing handle, the graphic editor shrinks or stretches the bitmap.

▶ **To shrink or stretch an entire bitmap**

1 Select the entire bitmap.

If a part of the bitmap is currently selected and you want to select the entire bitmap, click anywhere on the bitmap outside the current selection border, press ESC, or choose another drawing tool.

2 Hold down the SHIFT key and drag a sizing handle until the bitmap is the desired size.

▶ **To shrink or stretch part of a bitmap**

1 Select the part of the bitmap you want to resize. For more information, see "Selecting an Area of the Bitmap" earlier in this chapter.

2 Drag one of the sizing handles until the selection is the desired size.

Working With Colors in the Graphic Editor

The graphic editor comes equipped with many features specifically to help with the handling and customizing of colors. You can:

- Set foreground and background colors, and choose opaque and transparent backgrounds.
- Fill an area of a bitmap with a color or quickly "pick up" a color from the bitmap to use it elsewhere.
- Invert the colors in a selection.
- Customize or change the colors.
- Save and load different color palettes.

Selecting Foreground and Background Colors

Except for the eraser, these tools on the Graphics toolbar draw with the current foreground or background color when you press the left or right mouse button, respectively.

▶ **To select a foreground color**

- With the left mouse button, click the color you want on the Colors palette.

▶ **To select a background color**

- With the right mouse button, click the color you want on the Colors palette.

Filling Bounded Areas

The graphic editor provides the fill (or "paint-bucket") tool for filling any enclosed bitmap area with the current drawing color or the current background color.

▶ **To use the fill tool**

1 From the Graphics toolbar, choose the fill tool.

2 If necessary, choose drawing colors: in the Colors palette, click the left button to select a foreground color or the right button to select a background color.

3 Move the fill tool to the area you want to fill.

4 Click the left or right mouse button to fill with the foreground color or the background color, respectively.

Picking Up Colors

The color-pickup tool makes any color on the bitmap the current foreground color or background color, depending on whether you press the left or the right mouse button. To cancel the color pickup tool, choose another tool or press ESC.

▶ **To pick up a color**

1 From the Graphics toolbar, select the color-pickup tool.

The pointer changes to the "eyedropper."

2 Select the color you want to pick up from the Colors palette or from the Palette tab of the property page.

After you pick up a color, the graphic editor reactivates the most recently used tool.

3 Draw using the left mouse button for the foreground color, or the right mouse button for the background color.

Choosing Opaque and Transparent Backgrounds

When you move or copy a selection from a cursor or icon, any pixels in the selection that match the current background color are by default "transparent," they do not obscure pixels in the target location. A custom brush behaves in the same way. For more information on custom brushes, see "Creating a Custom Brush" earlier in this chapter.

▶ **To toggle the background-color transparency**

- In the Graphics toolbar option selector, click the appropriate button:
  - Opaque background: existing image is obscured by all parts of the selection.
  - Transparent background: existing image shows through parts of the selection that match the current background color.

You can change the background color while a selection is already in effect to change which parts of the image are transparent.

Inverting Colors in the Current Selection

So that you can tell how a bitmap would appear with inverted colors, the graphic editor provides a convenient way to invert colors in the selected part of the bitmap.

▶ **To invert colors in the current selection**

- From the Image menu, choose Invert Colors.

Changing Colors

The graphic editor's Colors palette initially displays 24 "ready-made" colors: 16 standard colors and 8 dithered colors. In addition to the ready-made colors, you can create your own custom colors. Colors palette selections can be saved on disk and individually reloaded as needed. The "most recently used" Colors palette definition is saved in the Registry and automatically loaded the next time you start Developer Studio.

The Palette tab in the Properties window displays up to 256 colors. Changing any of the colors on the Palette tab will immediately change the corresponding color in the bitmap. The colors on the Palette tab are always solid colors and can indicate any color your video card is capable of displaying.

Note The Palette tab in the Properties window displays for bitmaps only.

▶ To change colors on the Colors palette or Palette tab

1 From the Image menu, choose Adjust Colors.

−or−

Double-click one of the colors on the Colors palette.

−or−

Double-click one of the colors on the Palette tab of the Bitmap Properties page.

The Custom Color Selector dialog box (Figure 10.4) appears.

Figure 10.4 Custom Color Selector Dialog Box

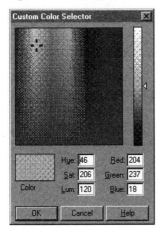

2 Define the color by typing RGB or HSL values in the appropriate text boxes, or by moving the cross hairs on the color box.

3 Set the luminance by moving the slider on the luminance bar.

4 Many custom colors are dithered. If you want the solid color closest to the dithered color, double-click the Color preview window. (If you later decide you want the dithered color, move the slider or the cross hairs again to restore the dithering.)

5 Choose OK to add the new color.

Saving and Loading Colors Palettes

You use commands on the Image menu save or load a palette.

▶ To save a custom Colors palette

1 From the Image menu, choose Save Palette.

2 Use the Save Palette Colors dialog box to navigate directories, and type a filename.

▶ **To load a custom Colors palette**

1 From the Image menu, choose Load Palette.

2 Use the Load Palette Colors dialog box to navigate directories and choose a filename.

 Tip Since the graphic editor has no means to restore the default Colors palette, save the default Colors palette under a name such as STANDARD.PAL or DEFAULT.PAL so that you can easily restore the default settings.

Creating and Editing Icons and Cursors

Icons and cursors are like bitmaps, and you edit them in the same ways. However, icons and cursors have attributes that distinguish them from bitmaps. For example, each icon or cursor resource can contain multiple images for different display devices. In addition, a cursor has a "hot spot"—the location Windows NT uses to track its position.

With the graphic editor, you can:

- Create a new image for icons and cursors.
- Select a display device or customize a display device.
- Draw with screen and inverse colors.
- Set a cursor's hot spot.
- Use 256 colors from the property page for large icons and cursors.

Creating a New Icon or Cursor Image

When you create a new icon or cursor, the graphic editor first creates an image for the VGA. The image is initially filled with the "screen" (transparent) color. If the image is a cursor, the hot spot is initially the upper-left corner (coordinates 0,0).

By default, the graphic editor supports the creation of images for the devices shown in Table 10.1.

Table 10.1 Devices for Icon or Cursor Images

Devices	Colors	Width	Height
Monochrome	2	32	32
Small	16	16	16
Normal	16	32	32
Large	256	64	64

You can create images for other devices by typing width, height, and color-count parameters into the custom device dialog box. See "Selecting a Display Device" later in this chapter for more information.

Selecting a Display Device

When you create a new icon or cursor image, you need to designate the target display device. When the icon or cursor resource is opened, the image most closely matching the current display device is opened by default (see Figure 10.5).

Figure 10.5   New Icon Image Dialog Box

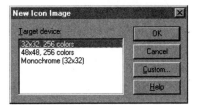

In addition to the standard types of devices listed, you can add a custom device for your icon or cursor image. You can enter width, height and color-count parameters in the Custom Image dialog box (Figure 10.6).

Figure 10.6   Custom Image Dialog Box

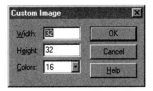

▶ **To select a target device image**

1 On the control bar of the image editor window, click the New Device Image button.

2 Select a target device image from the list box.

−or−

Choose the Custom button to define the width, height, and colors of a custom image.

3 Choose OK to select the new parameters.

Drawing with Screen and Inverse Colors

The initial icon or cursor image has a transparent attribute. Although icon and cursor images are rectangular, many do not appear so because parts of the image are "transparent," the underlying image on the screen shows through the icon or cursor. When you drag an icon, parts of the image may appear in an inverted color. You create this effect by choosing screen-color and inverse-color options from the color indicator on the Colors palette (see Figure 10.7).

The screen and inverse "colors" you apply to icons and cursors either shape and color the derived image or designate inverse regions. The colors indicate parts of the image possessing those attributes. You can change the colors that represent the screen-color and inverse-color attributes for your convenience in editing. These changes do not affect the appearance of the icon or cursor in your application.

Figure 10.7 Selectors for Screen Color and Inverse Color

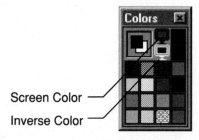

Screen Color
Inverse Color

▶ **To create transparent or inverse regions in an icon or cursor**

1 On the Colors palette, click a selector for screen or inverse color.

2 Apply the screen or inverse color.

▶ **To change the colors representing screen color and inverse color**

1 Select either the screen-color selector or the inverse-color selector.

2 Choose a color from the Colors palette.

  The complementary color is automatically designated for the other selector.

 Tip If you double-click the screen color or inverse-color indicator, the Custom Color Selector dialog box appears.

Creating 256 Color Icons and Cursors

Icons can be sized large (64 x 64) with a 256-color palette to choose from. For more information on large icons, see "Selecting a Display Device" earlier in this chapter. For more information on creating icons or cursors in general, see "Creating and Editing Icons and Cursors" earlier in this chapter.

To draw with a selection from the 256-color palette, you need to display the palette in the property page for the icon or cursor and select the colors from the property page.

Figure 10.8 Property Page with Palette for 256 Colors

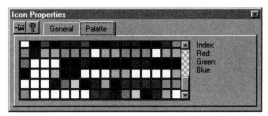

▶ **To choose a color from the 256-color palette for large icons:**

1 Select the large icon or cursor, or create a new large icon or cursor.

2 From the Edit menu, choose Properties. Select the Palette tab.

3 Choose the color from the 256 colors displayed in the palette.

–or–

Double-click a color to customize the color on the palette.

The initial palette used for 256-color images matches the palette returned by **CreateHalftonePalette**() Windows API. All icons intended for the Windows shell should use this palette to prevent flicker during palette realization.

Custom colors can be added by double clicking a color in the Palette property page.

Setting a Cursor's Hot Spot

The hot spot is the point to which Windows refers in tracking the cursor's position. By default, the hot spot is set to the upper-left corner (coordinates 0,0). The Cursor Properties page and the image editor control bar show the hot spot coordinates.

▶ **To set a cursor's hot spot**

1 On the control bar of the image editor window, choose the Hot Spot button.

2 Click the pixel you want to designate as the cursor's hot spot.

CHAPTER 11

Using the Toolbar Editor

The Visual C++ toolbar editor is a graphic tool to support the creation of toolbar resources and the conversion of bitmaps into toolbar resources. The toolbar editor uses a graphic display to show a subject toolbar and selected button that closely resembles the toolbar and buttons in a finished application. Toolbar buttons can be linked to code using ClassWizard.

With the toolbar editor, you can:

- Create new toolbars and buttons.
- Convert bitmaps to toolbar resources.
- Create, move, and edit toolbar buttons.

Figure 11.1 The Toolbar Editor

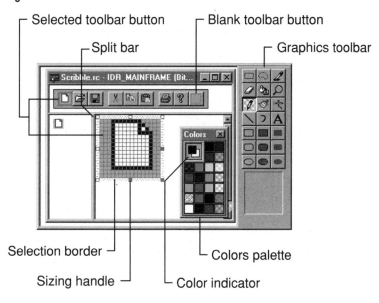

The toolbar editor window shows two views of a button image, the same as the graphic editor window. A split bar separates the two panes. You can drag the split bar from side to side to change the relative sizes of the panes. The active pane displays a selection border.

Above the two views of the image is the display of the subject toolbar, indicated by white space surrounding the subject toolbar, as shown in Figure 11.1. The selected button in this toolbar shows a fuzzy border.

The toolbar editor is similar to the graphic editor in functionality. The menu items, graphic tools, and bitmap grid are the same as those in the graphic editor. For more information on using the Graphics toolbar, Colors palette, or Image menu, see "Using the Image Editor Window and Tools" in Chapter 10, "Using the Graphic Editor."

Creating New Toolbar Resources

There are two methods for creating a new toolbar. One method is to select a new toolbar resource from the Insert Resource menu. The other method is to convert an existing bitmap to a toolbar. For more information on converting bitmaps, see "Converting Bitmaps to Toolbars" later in this chapter. For further editing of the new toolbar resource, see "Creating, Moving and Editing Toolbar Buttons" later in this chapter.

▶ **To create a new toolbar resource**

1 From the Insert menu, choose Resource.

   The Insert Resource dialog box appears.

2 In the Resource Type list, select Toolbar, and choose the OK button.

   −or−

   Click the plus sign (+) for the toolbar resource. Any toolbar resources listed are templates. Select a template to use, and choose the OK button.

Converting Bitmaps to Toolbars

You can create a new toolbar resource by converting a bitmap to a toolbar resource. You can also create a new toolbar from the Resource menu (see "Creating New Toolbar Resources" earlier in this chapter).

The graphic from the bitmap converts to the button images for a toolbar resource. Usually the bitmap contains several button images on a single bitmap, usually with one image for each button. Images can be any size; the default is 16 x 15 pixels. You can specify the size of the button images in the New Toolbar dialog box when you choose Toolbar Editor from the Image menu.

You can change the ID of the buttons of the new toolbar resource, using the property pages for the buttons. For information on editing the new toolbar, see "Creating, Moving and Editing Toolbar Buttons" later in this chapter.

▶ **To convert bitmaps to a toolbar resource**

1 Open an existing bitmap resource in the graphic editor.

2 From the Image menu, choose Toolbar Editor.

The New Toolbar Resource dialog box appears. You can change the width and height of the icon images to match the bitmap. The toolbar image is then displayed in the toolbar editor.

3 To finish the conversion, change the command IDs on the buttons in the toolbar.

- Open the property page on the toolbar button. (From the Edit menu, choose Properties.)

- Type in the new ID, or select an ID from the drop-down list.

 Tip   Click the Pushpin button on the property page to cycle through all the toolbar buttons without having to re-open the individual property pages.

Creating, Moving and Editing Toolbar Buttons

Toolbar buttons can be easily created, moved, copied, and edited. There are property pages for the buttons as well as the toolbar resource. Toolbar buttons can be connected to code by using ClassWizard while the toolbar editor is active.

A new or "blank" button is displayed, by default, at the right end of the toolbar. This button can be moved before it is edited. When a new button is created, another blank button appears to the right of that edited button. When a toolbar resource is saved, the blank button is not saved with the resource.

▶ **To create a new toolbar button**

- Assign an ID to the blank button at the right end of the toolbar. Open the property page on that toolbar button to edit the ID box.

  −or−

- Select the blank button at the right end of the toolbar, and begin drawing. A default button command ID is assigned (ID_BUTTON<n>).

▶ **To move a toolbar button**

- Drag the button that you want to move to its new location on the toolbar.

▶ **To copy buttons from a toolbar resource**

1 Hold down the CTRL key.

2 Drag the button from the originating toolbar to its new location on the same toolbar or to a location on another displayed toolbar.

► **To delete a toolbar button**

- Select the toolbar button on the subject toolbar, and drag the button off the toolbar.

► **To insert a space between buttons on a toolbar resource**

1 To insert a space before a button that is not followed by a space, drag the button to the right or down until it overlaps the next button about halfway.

2 To insert a space before a button that is followed by a space and retain the space following the button, drag the button until the right or bottom edge is just touching the next button or just overlaps it.

3 To insert a space before a button that is followed by a space and close up the following space, drag the button to the right or down until it overlaps the next button about halfway.

► **To close up a space between buttons on a toolbar**

- Drag the button on one side of the space toward the button on the other side of the space until it overlaps the next button about halfway.

  If there is no space on the side of the button that you are dragging away from, and you drag the button more than halfway past the adjacent button, Visual C++ also inserts a space on the opposite side of the button that you are dragging.

Editing the Property Page of a Toolbar Button

The property page of a toolbar button (see Figure 11.2) contains the ID box, the Width and Height boxes, and the Prompt box. The ID box has a drop-down list containing common ID names. The Prompt box is for the message displayed in the status bar. Adding \n and a name adds a tooltip to that toolbar button.

Figure 11.2 The Toolbar Button Property Page

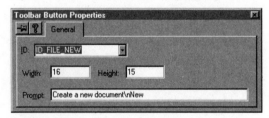

► **To change the ID of a toolbar button**

1 Select the toolbar button.

2 From the Edit menu, choose Properties to bring up the property page for that toolbar button.

3 Type the new ID in the ID box, or use the drop-down list to select a new ID.

▶ **To add a tooltip to a toolbar button**

1 Select the toolbar button.

2 From the Edit menu, choose Properties to bring up the property page for that toolbar button.

3 In the Prompt box, add a description of the button for the status bar; after the message, add \n and the tooltip name.

CHAPTER 12

Using the Binary Data Editor

The binary data editor allows you to edit a resource at the binary level in either hexadecimal or ASCII format. You should use the binary data editor only when you need to view or make minor changes to custom resources or resource types not supported by Microsoft Developer Studio.

Caution Editing nondata resources in the binary data editor can corrupt the resource. A corrupted resource can cause Microsoft Developer Studio and Windows NT to behave in unexpected ways.

 Tip While using the binary data editor, in many instances you can click the right mouse button to display a pop-up menu of resource-specific commands. The commands available depend on what the pointer is pointing to. For example, if you click while pointing to the binary data editor with selected hexadecimal values, the pop-up menu shows the Cut, Copy, and Paste commands.

Creating a New Data Resource or Custom Resource

You can create a new custom or data resource by placing the resource in a separate file using normal resource script (.RC) file syntax, and then including the file with the Resource Includes command on the View menu.

▶ **To create a new custom or data resource**

1 Create an .RC file that contains the custom or data resource.

Custom data can be typed in an .RC file as null-terminated quoted strings, or as integers in decimal, hexadecimal, or octal format. For more information, see the Win32 Software Development Kit documentation.

2 From the View menu, choose Resource Includes.

The Resource Includes dialog box appears.

3 In the Compile-Time Directives box, type an include statement that gives the name of the file containing your custom resource. For example:

```
#include mydata.rc
```

Make sure the syntax and spelling of what you type are correct. The contents of the Compile-Time Directives box are inserted into the resource script file exactly as you typed them.

4 Choose the OK button to record your changes.

The custom or data resource is included in your application at compile time.

Opening a Resource for Binary Editing

▶ **To open a resource for binary editing**

1 Open the project or resource script containing the resource to be edited.

2 Select the specific resource file you want to edit. Just highlight the resource.

3 Click the right mouse button and choose Open Binary Data.

The binary data editor appears (Figure 12.1).

If you want to use the binary data editor on a resource already being edited in another editor window, close the other editor window first.

Note If you use the ResourceView window to open a resource with a format that Microsoft Developer Studio does not recognize (such as a VERSION, RCDATA, or custom resource), the resource is automatically opened in the binary data editor.

Figure 12.1 Binary Data Editor

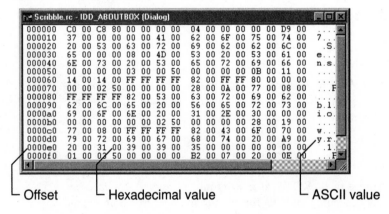

Editing Binary Data

▶ **To edit a resource in the binary data editor**

1 Select the byte you want to edit.

The TAB key moves the focus between the hexadecimal and ASCII sections of the binary data editor. You can use the PAGE UP and PAGE DOWN keys to move through the resource one screen at a time.

2 Type the new value, or paste a value you have copied.

CHAPTER 13

Using the Version Information Editor

Version information consists of company and product identification, a product release number, and copyright and trademark notification. The version information editor is a tool for creating and maintaining this data. Although the version information resource is not required by an application, it is a useful place to collect this information that identifies the application.

A single version information resource can contain multiple string blocks, each representing a different language or character set. All you need to do is define the character sets and languages that are specific to your product.

With the version information editor, you can add or delete string blocks, and you can modify individual string values.

Note The Windows standard is to have only one version resource, named VS_VERSION_INFO.

If you wish to access the version information from within your program, your application can make use of the **GetFileVersionInfo** function and the **VerQueryValue** function. For additional information on how to access version information, see the online *Microsoft Win32 Programmer's Reference, Volume 2*.

 Tip While using the version information editor, in many instances you can click the right mouse button to display a pop-up menu of resource-specific commands. For example, if you click while pointing to a block header entry, the pop-up menu shows the New String Block and Delete String Block commands.

For information about common resource edit procedures such as creating new resources, opening existing resources, and deleting resources, see Chapter 5, "Working with Resources."

Editing the Version Information

The version information resource (shown in Figure 13.1) has a single fixed information block (at the top of the resource) and one or more string information blocks (at the bottom of the resource). The top block has both editable numeric boxes and selectable drop-down lists. The bottom string block has editable text boxes.

Figure 13.1 Version Information Resource

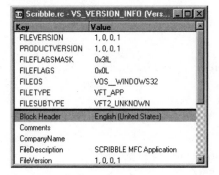

You can sort the information sequence of the string block by choosing either the Key button or the Value button. This choice automatically rearranges the information into the selected sequence.

▶ **To edit a version information resource**

• Click the item you want to edit.

 The selected text box or drop-down list appears for modification.

 Note When editing the FILEFLAGS property page, the DEBUG flag cannot be set for .RC files because Microsoft Developer Studio sets that flag with an **#ifdef** in the resource script, based on the **_DEBUG** build flag.

▶ **To add a new string block**

1 Open a version information resource.

2 From the Insert menu, choose New String Block.

 This command appends an additional string information block into the current version information resource and opens the Block Header property page.

3 On the Block Header property page, choose the appropriate language and character set for the new block.

▶ **To delete a string block**

1 With a version information resource open, select one of the block headers.

2 From the Insert menu, choose Delete String Block.

This command deletes the selected header and leaves the remaining version information intact.

CHAPTER 14

Working With Classes

ClassWizard and WizardBar simplify your use of the classes found in the Microsoft Foundation Class Library (MFC). ClassWizard assists you in creating classes, member variables, and message-handling functions. It also simplifies working with OLE and database classes. WizardBar is a shortcut from your implementation (.CPP) files into ClassWizard that further simplifies creating, modifying, or locating message-handling functions. For more information on these tools, see "Using ClassWizard" below, and "Using WizardBar" on page 222.

You can only use ClassWizard and WizardBar with applications that use MFC. Both work with MFC message-maps, OLE automation dispatch maps, and the **DoDataExchange** member function of your application's view class. For more information on the classes that ClassWizard and WizardBar handle, see "Classes Offered by ClassWizard" on page 224.

ClassWizard and WizardBar are used with Microsoft Foundation Class Library version 4.0 projects. For information on how to convert other projects (including Microsoft Foundation Class Library version 1 projects) for use with ClassWizard, see Technical Note 19 available under MFC in Books Online.

See Also   ClassWizard, WizardBar, Classes Offered by ClassWizard

Using ClassWizard

ClassWizard is like a programmer's assistant: it makes it easier for you to do certain routine tasks such as creating new classes, defining message handlers, overriding MFC virtual functions, and gathering data from controls in a dialog box, form view, or record view. ClassWizard works only with applications that use MFC.

With ClassWizard, you can:

- Create new classes derived from many of the main framework base classes that handle Windows messages and recordsets.

- Map messages to functions associated with windows, dialog boxes, controls, menu items, and accelerators.

- Create new message-handling member functions.

- Delete message-handling member functions.

- See which messages have message handlers already defined and jump to the handler program code.

- Define member variables that automatically initialize, gather, and validate data entered into dialog boxes or form views.

- Add OLE Automation methods and properties when creating a new class.

See Also   Adding a Class, Mapping Messages to Functions, Adding a Message Handler, Deleting a Message Hander, Editing a Message Handler, Working With Dialog Box Data

Using WizardBar

WizardBar is a shortcut into ClassWizard that simplifies routine tasks such as defining message handlers, overriding MFC virtual functions, and navigating in an implementation (.CPP) file. Like ClassWizard, WizardBar works only with applications that use MFC.

With WizardBar, you can:

- Browse the Windows messages associated with windows, dialog boxes, controls, menu items, and accelerators.

- Create new message-handling member functions.

- Delete message-handling member functions.

- See which messages have message handlers already defined and jump to the handler program code.

WizardBar Features

WizardBar resides at the top of any text-editing window that displays a .CPP file of a class that is in the ClassWizard database. You control whether WizardBar is displayed with the Toolbar command in the edit window's pop-up menu. The pop-up menu is activated with the right mouse button.

You can use WizardBar, shown in Figure 14.1, to select a class component quickly and modify the associated virtual functions, Windows messages, or **CCmdTarget** procedures. WizardBar has four parts that will be described in the following sections.

Figure 14.1 WizardBar

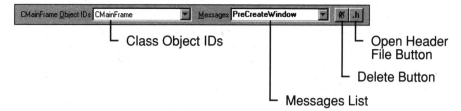

Class Object IDs

The Object IDs list, on the left side of WizardBar, displays the class name and ID names of a class that is in the currently opened implementation file. The first item in the list is always the class itself, which allows you to override virtual functions and Windows messages.

Messages List

The Messages drop-down list contains virtual functions, Windows messages, and **CCmdTarget** procedures associated with the class component currently selected in the Class Object IDs list. Messages in bold have already been mapped or overridden in the class. For more information, see "Overriding a Virtual Function" on page 240 and "Adding a Message Handler" on page 234.

Delete Function Button

If you've selected an overridden virtual function in the Messages box, the Delete Function button becomes active and will delete the associated function prototype in the class definition. If you've selected a command with a message handler in the Messages box, the Delete button will delete the message-map and declaration code.

After either use of the Delete button, the insertion point moves to the function definition, allowing you to check whether you want to delete the code in the function body. You must delete it yourself. For more information, see "Deleting a Message Handler" on page 238.

Open Header File Button

This button opens the current .CPP file's header (.H) file in a new window.

See Also Adding a Message Handler, Deleting a Message Handler, Overriding a Virtual Function, Mapping Messages to Functions, Editing a Message Handler, Using ClassWizard

Classes Offered by ClassWizard

Use ClassWizard to add error-free class declarations to your project for classes that contain message-handling functions.

Note ClassWizard is only for use with user-interface classes derived from **CCmdTarget** that handle messages or manage dialog box controls. To add a new class that does not handle messages, create the class directly in the text editor. (The exception to this rule is class **CRecordset**, for database support, which can be created with ClassWizard.)

ClassWizard enables you to create classes derived from the Microsoft Foundation Classes shown in Table 14.1.

Table 14.1   Types of MFC Classes Available from ClassWizard

Class	Description
CAnimateCtrl	Provides the functionality of the Windows common animation control.
CButton	Button control.
CCmdTarget	Base class for objects that can receive and respond to messages. It is the result of a selection based on a table query.
CColorDialog	Color-selection dialog box with a list of colors that are defined for the display system.
CComboBox	List box with static or edit control.
CDaoRecordSet	Represents a set of records selected from a data source. **CDaoRecordset** objects are available in three forms: table-type recordsets, dynaset-type recordsets, and snapshot-type recordsets.
CDaoRecordView	Displays database records in controls. This form view is directly connected to a **CDaoRecordset** object.
CDialog	Dialog box.
CDocument	Class for managing program data.
CDragListBox	Windows list box that allows the user to move list box items within the list box.
CEdit	Rectangular child window for text entry.
CEditView	Provides the functionality of a Windows edit control and can be used to implement simple text-editor functionality.
CFileDialog	Windows common file dialog box provides an easy way to implement File Open and File Save As dialog boxes.
CFontDialog	Font-selection dialog box that displays a list of fonts that are currently installed in the system.
CFormView	Window that can contain dialog box controls.
CFrameWnd	Single document interface (SDI) frame window.

Table 14.1   Types of MFC Classes Available from ClassWizard (Continued)

Class	Description
CHeaderCtrl	Provides the functionality of the Windows common header control.
CHotKeyCtrl	Provides the functionality of the Windows common hot key control.
CListBox	List box.
CListCtrl	Provides the functionality of the Windows common list view control.
CListView	List control that simplifies use of **CListCtrl**, the class that encapsulates list-control functionality.
CMDIChildWnd	Multiple document interface (MDI) child frame window.
COleDocument	Treats a document as a collection of **CDocItem** objects to handle OLE items. Both container and server applications require this architecture because their documents must be able to contain OLE items.
COleLinkingDoc	Base class for OLE container documents that support linking to the embedded items they contain.
COleServerDoc	Base class for OLE server documents.
CPrintDialog	Windows common dialog box for printing that provides an easy way to implement Print and Print Setup dialog boxes.
CProgressCtrl	Provides the functionality of the Windows common progress bar control.
CPropertyPage	Represents an individual page of a property sheet, otherwise known as a tab dialog box.
CPropertySheet	Represents property sheets, otherwise known as tab dialog boxes. A property sheet consists of a **CPropertySheet** object and one or more **CPropertyPage** objects.
CRecordset	Class for accessing a database table or query.
CRecordView	Window containing dialog box controls mapped to recordset fields.
CRichEditCtrl	Window in which the user can enter and edit text. The text can be assigned character and paragraph formatting, and can include embedded OLE objects.
CRichEditDoc	Maintains the list of OLE client items which are in the view.
CRichEditView	Maintains the text and formatting characteristics of text.
CScrollBar	Scroll bar.
CScrollView	Scrolling window, derived from **CView**.
CSliderCtrl	Provides a window containing a slider and optional tick marks.
CSpinButtonCtrl	Provides a pair of arrow buttons that the user can click to increment or decrement a value.

Table 14.1   Types of MFC Classes Available from ClassWizard *(Continued)*

Class	Description
CStatic	A simple text field, box, or rectangle used to label, box, or separate other controls.
CStatusBarCtrl	Provides a horizontal window, usually displayed at the bottom of a parent window, in which an application can display status information.
CTabCtrl	Allows an application to display multiple pages in the same area of a window or dialog box.
CToolBarCtrl	Provides the functionality of the Windows toolbar common control.
CToolTipCtrl	Provides the functionality of a "tooltip control," a small pop-up window that displays a single line of text describing the purpose of a tool in an application.
CTreeCtrl	Displays a hierarchical list of items.
CTreeView	Tree control that simplifies use of **CTreeCtrl**, the class that encapsulates tree-control functionality
CView	Class for displaying program data.
CWinThread	Represents a thread of execution within an application.
generic CWnd	Custom window.
splitter	An MDI child window that contains a **CSplitterWnd** class. The user can split the resulting window into multiple panes.

For more information on these classes, see the *Class Library Reference*.

When you use ClassWizard to create a new class derived from one of the framework classes listed in Table 14.1, it automatically places a complete and functional class in the header (.H) and implementation (.CPP) files you specify. ClassWizard keeps track of the class's message-handling and data-exchange members, so that you can update the class at a later time.

See Also   Adding a Class, Creating a Class That Does Not Require a Resource ID, Creating a Class That Requires a Resource ID, Using Component Gallery, MFC Message Maps, Importing a Class, Importing the Elements of an OLE Type Library, Selecting an Existing Class, Creating a Reusable Control Class

Adding a Class

ClassWizard enables you to easily bind user-interface classes that are derived from the MFC library to the messages generated by the resources of your application. It uses MFC message maps to create the binding. You can use one of the following three ways to add MFC classes to a project:

- Click ClassWizard's Add Class menu button and choose the New command to create an entirely new class and add it to the ClassWizard database.

With ClassWizard you can create two kinds of classes:

- Those, such as **CButton**, that do not require a resource ID. For more information, see "Creating a Class That Does Not Require a Resource ID" below.

  - Those, such as **CDialog**, that require a resource ID. For more information, see "Creating a Class That Requires a Resource ID" on page 229.

- Click ClassWizard's Add Class menu button and choose the From A File command to import an existing class from another project into the ClassWizard database. For more information on importing a class, see "Importing a Class" on page 231.

- Click ClassWizard's Add Class menu button and choose the From An OLE TypeLib command to select elements from an OLE Type library, wrap them in an MFC C++ class, import the resulting class into a project, and add the class to the ClassWizard database. For more information on this command, see "Importing the Elements of an OLE Type Library" on page 233.

See Also   Classes Offered by ClassWizard, Creating a Class That Does Not Require a Resource ID, Creating a Class That Requires a Resource ID, Using Component Gallery, MFC Message Maps, Importing a Class, Importing the Elements of an OLE Type Library, Selecting an Existing Class, Creating a Reusable Control Class

Creating a Class That Does Not Require a Resource ID

The following procedure describes how to create classes that do not require a resource ID—classes, such as **CButton** or **CEdit**, that are derived from base classes other than **CDaoRecordView**, **CDialog**, **CFormView**, **CPropertyPage**, or **CRecordView**.

▶ **To add a class to a project**

1 From the View menu, choose ClassWizard.

ClassWizard appears.

2 Choose the Add Class button.

3 Choose the New command to create an entirely new class and add it to the ClassWizard database as described in the following procedure.

–or–

Choose the From A File command to import an existing class from another project into the ClassWizard database. For more information on importing a class, see "Importing a Class" on page 231.

–or–

Choose the From An OLE TypeLib command to select elements from an OLE Type library, wrap them in an MFC C++ class, import the resulting class into a project, and add the class ClassWizard database. For more information on this command, see "Importing the Elements of an OLE Type Library" on page 233.

▶ **To create a new class that does not require a resource ID**

1 From ClassWizard, choose the Add Class menu button.

2 Choose the New command.

The Create New Class dialog box appears.

3 Type the name of your new class in the Name text box.

4 From the Base Class combo box, select a base class from which to derive your current class (see Table 14.1, "Types of MFC Classes Available From ClassWizard" on page 224).

5 Choose the Change button if you want to see and/or change the default names of the header (.H) and implementation (.CPP) files where the class is to be defined.

The Change Files dialog box appears.

6 Accept the default file names by choosing the OK button or use the Header File and Implementation File text boxes to change them. By default, ClassWizard assigns the same name to .H and .CPP files.

As this class does not require a resource ID, the Dialog ID drop-down list is not active.

7 From the OLE Automation group box, select one of the following options:

- Select None for no OLE Automation.

- Select Automation if you want to expose the capabilities of this class through OLE Automation.

  If you select this option, the newly created class will be available as a programmable object by automation client applications, such as Microsoft Visual Basic™ or Microsoft Excel. This option is available only for some classes.

- Select Createable By Type ID if you want to allow other applications to create objects of this class by using OLE Automation.

  With this option, automation clients can directly create an OLE Automation object. The type ID in the text box is used by the client application to specify the object to be created; it is systemwide and must be unique. This option is available only for some classes.

Note Use ClassWizard's OLE Automation tab to add OLE Automation methods and properties to an existing class. These methods and properties define a dispatch interface that OLE Automation clients can use.

8 Select the Add To Component Gallery option to add this class to the Component Gallery. For more information on the Component Gallery, see Chapter 15, "Using Component Gallery."

9 Choose the Create button to create the class in the files you spec

The name of your new class is displayed in the Class Name drop-α,   ˙he
ClassWizard dialog box.

If you specify filenames that don't yet exist, ClassWizard creates the new
adds them to your project. It adds skeletal information on the new class to ι   .ᵕ
header and implementation files.

10 Choose OK.

For information about creating database classes (**CRecordView**, **CRecordset**) and
OLE classes, see the article "ClassWizard" in *Programming with MFC*.

See Also Classes Offered by ClassWizard, Adding a Class, Creating a Class That
Requires a Resource ID, Importing a Class, Importing the Elements of an OLE Type
Library, Selecting an Existing Class, Creating a Reusable Control Class

Creating a Class That Requires a Resource ID

For classes that require a resource ID (classes derived from **CDaoRecordView**,
CDialog, **CFormView**, **CPropertyPage**, or **CRecordView**), you should first use the
dialog editor to create the resource and its ID and then use ClassWizard to create the
associated class. This is true for for the following reasons:

- Most importantly, if you plan to add your new resource class to Component
  Gallery, you must do so from the Create New Class dialog box at the time the class
  is created. The resource must already exist or it will not be added into Component
  Gallery along with the new class. You cannot retroactively add the resource into
  Component Gallery. For more information on Component Gallery, see Chapter 15,
  "Using Component Gallery."

- If you first create the class and then the resource, you must perform more steps
  and your work flow will be less efficient.

The following procedure describes how to create classes that require a resource ID.

▶ **To create a new class and bind it to an existing resource**

1 Use the dialog, menu, toolbar, or accelerator editor to create a resource. For
information on using these editors, see Using the Resource Editors.

2 Save the resource and ensure that the editor has the focus.

3 From the View menu, choose ClassWizard.

ClassWizard appears with the Adding A Class dialog box in front of it.

4 Choose Create A New Class to create an entirely new class and add it to the
ClassWizard database.

For information on importing a class, see"Importing a Class" on page 231. For
information on selecting an existing class, see "Selecting an Existing Class" on
page 232.

5 Choose OK.

The Create New Class dialog box appears.

6 In the Name text box, type the name of your new class.

7 From the Base Class combo box, select a base class from which to derive your current class (see Table 14.1, "Types of MFC Classes Available From ClassWizard," on page 224).

8 Choose the Change button if you want to see and/or change the default names of the header (.H) and implementation (.CPP) files where the class is to be defined.

The Change Files dialog box appears.

9 Accept the default file names by choosing the OK button or use the Header File text box and Implementation File text box to change them. By default, ClassWizard assigns the same name to .H and .CPP files.

10 If the resource for which you are creating a class is a dialog box, choose the new resource's ID from the Dialog ID combo box. It may already be selected.

11 From the OLE Automation group box, select one of the following options:

- Select None for no OLE Automation.

- Select Automation if you want to expose the capabilities of this class through OLE Automation.

  If you select this option, the newly created class will be available as a programmable object by automation client applications, such as Microsoft Visual Basic™ or Microsoft Excel. This option is available only for some classes.

- Select Createable By Type ID if you want to allow other applications to create objects of this class by using OLE Automation.

  With this option, automation clients can directly create an OLE Automation object. The type ID in the text box is used by the client application to specify the object to be created; it is systemwide and must be unique. This option is available only for some classes.

Note Use ClassWizard's OLE Automation tab to add OLE Automation methods and properties to an existing class. These methods and properties define a dispatch interface that OLE Automation clients can use.

12 Select the Add To Component Gallery check box to add this class to the Component Gallery. For more information on the Component Gallery, see Chapter 15, "Using Component Gallery."

13 Choose the Create button to create the class in the files you specified.

The name of your new class is displayed in the Class Name drop-down list of the ClassWizard dialog box.

If you specify filenames that don't yet exist, ClassWizard creates the new files and adds them to your project. It adds skeletal information on the new class to both the header and implementation files.

14 Choose OK.

For information about creating database classes (**CRecordView**, **CRecordset**) and OLE classes, see the article "ClassWizard" in *Programming with MFC*.

See Also Classes Offered by ClassWizard, Adding a Class, Creating a Class That Does Not Require a Resource ID, Using Component Gallery, Using the Resource Editors, Importing a Class, Importing the Elements of an OLE Type Library, Selecting an Existing Class, Creating a Reusable Control Class

Importing a Class

If you add a message-handling class to your current project by copying code from another project, you can update ClassWizard so that it recognizes the new class.

Note If the new code you copy contains more than two or three new message-handling classes, you can save time by completely rebuilding the ClassWizard file rather than importing each new class individually. For more information, see "Rebuilding the ClassWizard (.CLW) File" on page 252.

If the code you are importing does not already have ClassWizard comments in it, manually add the special-format comments ClassWizard uses to locate message-map entries. For information on the ClassWizard special-format comments, see Technical Note 6, available under MFC in Books Online.

▶ **To import a class from another project**

1 From the View menu, choose ClassWizard.

ClassWizard appears.

2 From any of ClassWizard's tabs, choose the Add Class button and select the From A File command.

The Import Class Information dialog box appears.

3 Type the name of the class to import and the name of the header and implementation files where the class source code can be found. You can also use the Browse buttons to locate the files.

By default, the header file and the implementation file have the same name as the class file.

4 Choose OK to add the new class to the ClassWizard file.

See Also Classes Offered by ClassWizard, Adding a Class, Creating a Class That Does Not Require a Resource ID, Creating a Class That Requires a Resource ID, Rebuilding the ClassWizard (.CLW) File, Importing the Elements of an OLE Type Library, Selecting an Existing Class, Creating a Reusable Control Class

Selecting an Existing Class

Use the Select Class dialog box to associate a new dialog box, menu, toolbar, or accelerator resource with an existing class. You will use this dialog box if you created a class before you created the resource that the class should be associated with. The association will cause ClassWizard to make the resource command IDs available for mapping when the class is selected in the ClassWizard Message Maps tab or in WizardBar.

Note Your can work more efficiently if you first create a resource and then use ClassWizard to associate a class with the resource.

▸ **To select an existing class from the project**

1 Use the dialog, menu, toolbar, or accelerator editor to create a resource. For information on using these editors, see Using the Resource Editors in Chapter 5, "Working with Resources."

2 Save the resource and ensure that the editor has the focus.

3 From the View menu, choose ClassWizard.

The Adding A Class dialog box appears.

4 Select the Select An Existing Class option.

5 Choose OK.

The Select Class dialog box appears.

6 From the Class Name list, select an existing class.

7 Choose Select.

A message box asks if you want to subsitute your dialog box's resource ID for the class's current resource ID.

8 Choose Yes.

ClassWizard reappears.

9 Choose OK.

ClassWizard associates the user-interface component with the specified class.

See Also Classes Offered by ClassWizard, Using the Resource Editors, Adding a Class, Creating a Class That Does Not Require a Resource ID, Creating a Class That Requires a Resource ID, Importing a Class, Importing the Elements of an OLE Type Library, Creating a Reusable Control Class

Importing the Elements of an OLE Type Library

You can use ClassWizard to wrap the elements of an OLE type library in an MFC C++ class and add the new class to a project.

▶ **To import the elements of an OLE type library**

1 From the View menu, choose ClassWizard.

ClassWizard appears.

2 From any of ClassWizard's tabs, choose the Add Class button, and select the From An OLE TypeLib command.

The Import From OLE TypeLib dialog box appears.

3 Use the File Name, Drives, and Directories controls to select an OLE type library.

4 Choose OK.

The Confirm Classes dialog box appears. This dialog box contains a list of classes that ClassWizard can create from information in the type library. The class names are generated by ClassWizard.

5 Use the Name text box to rename the class that is currently selected from the list.

6 Use the Header File and Implementation File text boxes to rename the .H and .CPP files, if you choose to. Also, you can use the Browse buttons to rename the files or cause the files to be generated in a different directory.

All classes selected from the class list are added to these two files.

7 Choose OK.

ClassWizard generates the specified class.

See Also Classes Offered by ClassWizard, Adding a Class, Creating a Class That Does Not Require a Resource ID, Creating a Class That Requires a Resource ID, Importing a Class, Selecting an Existing Class, Creating a Reusable Control Class

Mapping Messages to Functions

Both ClassWizard and WizardBar let you browse the messages associated with a user-interface object in your application and quickly define message-handling functions for them. Both tools automatically update the message-dispatch table, or message map, and your class header file when you use them to define message-handling functions.

Table 14.2 shows the types of objects you work with in ClassWizard and the types of messages associated with them.

Table 14.2 User-Interface Objects and Associated Messages

Object ID	Messages
Class name, representing the containing window (see Table 14.1)	Windows messages appropriate to a **CWnd**-derived class: a dialog box, window, child window, MDI child window, or topmost frame window
Menu or accelerator identifier	**COMMAND** message (executes the program function)
	UPDATE_COMMAND_UI message (dynamically updates the menu item)
Control identifier	Control notification messages for the selected control type

See Also   Classes Offered by ClassWizard, Creating a Reusable Control Class, Adding a Message Handler, Shortcut for Defining Message Handlers for Dialog Buttons, Shortcut for Defining Member Variables for Dialog Controls, Deleting a Message Handler, Editing a Message Handler, Overriding a Virtual Function

Adding a Message Handler

After creating a class with ClassWizard, or importing an existing class, you can use either ClassWizard or WizardBar to browse the messages or control notifications associated with each object and to create handler routines (member functions) as appropriate.

▶ **To define a message handler with ClassWizard**

1 From the View menu, choose ClassWizard.

ClassWizard appears and displays information about the currently selected class or the class you last edited with ClassWizard.

2 Select the Message Maps tab.

3 From the Class Name drop-down list box, select the class name of the user-interface component (such as a menu, accelerator, or dialog resource) you want to work with.

ClassWizard displays information about the user-interface object that is currently selected.

4 In the Object IDs box, select the name of the user-interface object for which you want to define a message handler.

5 In the Messages box, select the message for which you want to define a handler. Choose Add Function (or double-click the message name).

A message with a handler already defined is displayed in bold.

Note The messages you see in the Messages box are those most appropriate to your class. If your class is not associated with the menu resource that contains the command that you want to handle, set the focus on the menu or accelerator resource, open ClassWizard, and then use the Class Name drop-down list to switch to the class from which you want the message handled.

In addition, you can change the set of messages you handle by selecting the Class Info tab and selecting a new set of messages in the Message Filter box. For information on handling custom messages, see Technical Note 6, available under MFC in Books Online.

Tip Selecting a message displays a brief description of it at the bottom of the MFC ClassWizard dialog box. You can get a more complete description of the message by pressing the F1 KEY.

For messages that do not already have a predefined name for the handler function, the Add Member Function dialog box appears.

6 If the Add Member Function dialog box appears, type a name for the member function and press ENTER.

–or–

From the Add Member Function dialog box, press ENTER to accept the proposed name.

Either action returns you to the ClassWizard Message Maps tab.

The message name is displayed in bold to show that a message handler is defined. The name of the new message hander appears in the Member Functions box.

7 At this point you have several options. You can:

- Choose Cancel to avoid updating your source code with the selected member functions. Note that ClassWizard does not remove any functions or code that it has already added.

- Add more message handlers.

- Choose OK to automatically update your source code with selected member functions and close ClassWizard. You can return to ClassWizard any time during the development process.

- Choose Edit Code to jump to the empty function body just created by ClassWizard and begin defining the function's behavior.

When you choose OK or Edit Code, ClassWizard updates your source code as follows:

- A function declaration is inserted into the header file.

- A complete, correct function definition with a skeletal implementation is inserted into the implementation file.

- The class's message map is updated to include the new message-handling function.

▶ **To define a message handler with WizardBar**

1 Use ClassView to navigate to the implementation (.CPP) file in which you want the new message handler placed. For information on using ClassView, see "Using ClassView" in Chapter 2, "Working with Projects."

2 In the WizardBar Object List, select the name of the user-interface object for which you want to define a message handler. Table 14.3, "User-Interface Objects and Associated Messages" shows the types of classes that will appear in the Object List and the messages appropriate to each type.

The WizardBar Messages List contains the messages associated with the selected user-interface object. Messages that are bold already have handlers.

3 In the Messages List, click the message for which you want to define a handler.

4 If the user-interface object you selected in step 1 was a virtual member function, a message box informs you that the message is not handled and asks if you want to add a handler. Choose Yes.

–or–

If the user-interface object that you selected in step 1 was a message, such as COMMAND or UPDATE_COMMAND, the Add Member Function dialog box appears.Type a name for the member function and press ENTER.

–or–

Press ENTER to accept the default name.

In all of these three cases,WizardBar updates your source code as follows:

- A function declaration is inserted into the header file.

- A complete, correct function definition with a skeletal implementation is inserted into the implementation file.

- The class's message map is updated to include the new message-handling function.

WizardBar then moves the text-editor's insertion point to the body of the function.

Note The messages you see in the Members list are those most appropriate to your class. If your class is a dialog class, form view, or record view, then the messages will normally include window messages but not menu commands. To list menu commands as well as window messages, set the focus on a menu or accelerator resource, open ClassWizard, and then use the Class Name drop-down list to switch to the class you want to use.

In addition, you can change the set of messages you handle by selecting ClassWizard's Class Info tab and selecting a new set of messages in the Message Filter box. For information on handling custom messages, see Technical Note 6, available under MFC in Books Online.

See Also Mapping Messages to Functions, Creating a Reusable Control Class, Shortcut for Defining Message Handlers for Dialog Buttons, Shortcut for Defining Member Variables for Dialog Controls, Deleting a Message Handler, Editing a Message Handler, Overriding a Virtual Function

Shortcut for Defining Message Handlers for Dialog Buttons

To define a message handler for a dialog box button, you can use the following convenient shortcut to bypass some intermediate steps.

▶ **To define a message handler for a dialog box button**

1 In the dialog editor, select a button.

2 While holding down the CTRL key, double-click the button.

ClassWizard automatically creates a message handler in the class associated with the dialog box. The message handler is named according to the control ID of the dialog box button. Finally, the insertion point moves to the newly created function in your source code.

See Also Mapping Messages to Functions, Creating a Reusable Control Class, Adding a Message Handler, Shortcut for Defining Member Variables for Dialog Controls, Deleting a Message Handler, Editing a Message Handler, Overriding a Virtual Function

Shortcut for Defining Member Variables for Dialog Controls

To define a member variable for a dialog box control, you can use the following shortcut to bypass explicitly invoking ClassWizard from the dialog editor.

▶ **To define a member variable for a dialog box control**

1 In the dialog editor, select a control.

2 While holding down the CTRL key, double-click the dialog box control.

The Add Member Variable dialog box appears.

3 Type the appropriate information in the Add Member Variable dialog box. For more information, see "Defining Member Variables" on page 246.

4 Choose OK.

ClassWizard returns you to the dialog editor.

 Tip To jump from a dialog box button to its existing handler, hold down the CTRL key while double-clicking the button.

See Also Mapping Messages to Functions, Creating a Reusable Control Class, Adding a Message Handler, Shortcut for Defining Message Handlers for Dialog Buttons, Deleting a Message Handler, Editing a Message Handler, Overriding a Virtual Function

Deleting a Message Handler

Once you have defined a message handler with ClassWizard or WizardBar, you can use either tool to delete it. However, you must remove the function definition, as well as any references to the function, from the implementation file. Neither ClassWizard nor WizardBar make changes to your implementation code—only to the message and data maps.

▶ **To delete a message-handling function with ClassWizard**

1 In the ClassWizard dialog box, select the Message Maps tab.

2 In the Class Name box, select the class containing the message-handling function you want to delete.

3 In the Member Functions box, select the name of the member function to delete.

4 Choose Edit Code to open the implementation file containing the member function.

5 Comment out or delete the function header and function body.

6 Return to ClassWizard and choose Delete Function. This deletes the member function entries from the message map for that class in both the header and implementation files.

▶ **To delete a message-handling function with WizardBar**

1 Use ClassView to navigate to the implementation (.CPP) file that contains the message-handling function. For information on using ClassView, see "Using ClassView" in Chapter 2, "Working with Projects."

2 From the Object IDs list, select the name of the user-interface object for which you want to delete the associated message-handling function.

3 From the Messages List, select the name of the message that has the handler you want to delete. Messages with handlers are bold.

WizardBar moves the insertion point to the member function.

4 Choose the Delete button, to the right of the Members list.

WizardBar displays a message box informing you that deleting the handler will require manually removing the implementation code. If you choose Yes, WizardBar deletes the member function entries from the message map for that class in both the header and implementation files. You must remove the handler's function body.

See Also   Mapping Messages to Functions, Creating a Reusable Control Class, Adding a Message Handler, Shortcut for Defining Message Handlers for Dialog Buttons, Shortcut for Defining Member Variables for Dialog Controls, Editing a Message Handler, Overriding a Virtual Function

Editing a Message Handler

Once you have defined a procedure with ClassWizard or WizardBar, you can use either tool to jump to the member function's definition and begin to add or modify code.

▶ To jump to a member function definition with ClassWizard

1 In the ClassWizard dialog box, select the Message Maps tab.

2 In the Class Name box, select the class containing the message-handling function you want to edit.

3 In the Member Functions box, select the function you want to edit.

4 Choose Edit Code.

–or–

Double-click the function name.

The insertion point moves to the function.

▶ To jump to a member function definition with WizardBar

1 In the Object IDs list, select the class name or the user-interface ID for which you want to edit an associated function.

2 In the Messages list, select the virtual function you want to edit or the message that has a handler you want to edit. Virtual functions and messages with handlers are bold.

The insertion point moves to the function.

See Also Mapping Messages to Functions, Creating a Reusable Control Class, Adding a Message Handler, Shortcut for Defining Message Handlers for Dialog Buttons, Shortcut for Defining Member Variables for Dialog Controls, Deleting a Message Handler, Overriding a Virtual Function

Overriding a Virtual Function

Both ClassWizard and WizardBar can override virtual functions defined in a base class. The mechanism is similar to creating message handlers for Windows messages.

▶ **To override a virtual function with ClassWizard**

1 From the View menu, choose ClassWizard.

ClassWizard appears.

2 On the Message Maps tab, select the name of the class in which you want to override a virtual function.

3 In the Object IDs box, select the class name again.

The Object IDs box displays a list of virtual functions you can override and a list of Windows messages. The virtuals come before the messages and appear in mixed case.

4 In the Messages box, select the name of the virtual function you want to override.

5 Choose Add Function.

The function is created and its name displayed in the Member Functions box. The names of virtual overrides are preceded by a gray glyph containing the letter "V" (handlers have a "W").

6 Choose Edit Code to jump to the Windows message code.

▶ **To override a virtual function with WizardBar**

1 In the Object IDs list, select the name of the class containing the virtual function you want to override.

The Messages list contains the virtual functions and the messages associated with the class that you've selected. The virtuals come before the messages and appear in mixed case. Virtual function names that are bold are already overridden.

2 In the Messages list, click the virtual function you want to override.

A message box appears to inform you that the virtual function is not handled and asks if you want to add a handler.

3 Choose the Yes button.

WizardBar updates your source code as follows:

- A member function declaration is inserted into the class's header file.

- A complete, correct function definition with a skeletal implementation is inserted into the class's implementation file.

WizardBar then moves the text-editor's insertion point to the body of the function.

See Also Mapping Messages to Functions, Creating a Reusable Control Class, Adding a Message Handler, Shortcut for Defining Message Handlers for Dialog Buttons, Shortcut for Defining Member Variables for Dialog Controls, Deleting a Message Handler, Editing a Message Handler

Creating a Reusable Control Class

With ClassWizard you can build reusable control classes that are derived from any of the following MFC control classes:

CAnimateCtrl	**CListBox**	**CStatic**
CButton	**CListCtrl**	**CTabCtrl**
CComboBox	**CProgressCtrl**	**CTreeCtrl**
CEdit	**CSliderCtrl**	
CHotKeyCtrl	**CSpinButtonCtrl**	

You can define handlers for the messages received by these controls in the same way that you would for any other type of window. You can also define reflected message handlers that allow your class to handle its own messages before the message is received by the parent.

With this functionality you could, for example, create a list box that will redraw itself rather than relying on the parent window to do so (owner drawn). For more information on reflected messages, seeMFC: OLE and Other Enhancements in MFC Version 4.0 in *Programming with MFC*.

You can develop a reusable class in your current project. To create an OLE control with the same functionality, you would have to create a project for the OLE control. The following procedure describes how to create a new MFC control class.

▶ **To create a new MFC control class**

1 From the View menu, choose ClassWizard.

ClassWizard appears.

When you finish your new class, it will be added to the project selected in the Project drop-down list box.

2 Choose the Add Class button.

3 Choose the New command.

The Create New Class dialog box appears.

4 In the Name text box, type the name of your new class.

5 From the Base Class combo box, select one of the MFC control classes as a base class from which to derive your class. An MFC control is one that you can add to a dialog box.

6 Select the Add To Component Gallery option to add this class to the Component Gallery. For more information on Component Gallery, see Chapter 15, "Using Component Gallery."

7 Choose the Create button to create the class in the files specified in the File control group.

ClassWizard reappears. The name of your new class is displayed in the Class Name drop-down list.

8 Choose OK.

If you chose to add your new class to Component Gallery, you can now add it to other projects. You can also use ClassWizard to create variables that are based on your new class. Before doing either, you will probably want to add some message handlers to your new class. The following procedure explains how.

For more information on adding a new class, see "Adding a Class" on page 226.

See Also   Defining a Message Handler for a Reflected Message, Declaring a Variable Based on Your New Reusable Class, Mapping Messages to Functions, Adding a Message Handler, Shortcut for Defining Message Handlers for Dialog Buttons, Shortcut for Defining Member Variables for Dialog Controls, Deleting a Message Handler, Editing a Message Handler, Overriding a Virtual Function

Defining a Message Handler for a Reflected Message

Once you have created your new class derived from an MFC control class, you can use either ClassWizard or WizardBar to define message handlers for it. Thus, your control can handle its own messages. You can use the MFC **CWnd::SendMessage** function to send messages from your control to a parent window.

▶ **To define a message handler for a reflected message with ClassWizard**

1 From ClassWizard, select the Message Maps tab.

2 From the Class Name drop-down list box, select the name of your reusable class.

3 In the Object IDs box, select the name of your reusable class.

4 In the Messages box, select the message for which you want to define a handler. Your class's reflected messages are marked with an equal sign (=).

A message with a handler already defined is displayed in bold.

Tip Selecting a message displays a brief description of it at the bottom of the MFC ClassWizard dialog box. You can get a more complete description of the message by pressing the F1 KEY.

5 Choose Add Function (or double-click the message name).

For messages that do not already have a predefined name for the handler function, the Add Member Function dialog box appears.

6 Choose OK to accept the proposed name.

ClassWizard reappears. The message name is displayed in bold to show that a message handler is defined. The name of the new message hander appears in the Member Functions box.

7 At this point you have several options. You can:

- Choose Cancel to avoid updating your source code with the selected member functions. Note that ClassWizard does not remove any functions or code that it has already added.

- Add more message handlers.

- Choose OK to automatically update your source code with selected member functions and close ClassWizard. You can return to ClassWizard any time during the development process.

- Choose Edit Code to jump to the empty function body just created by ClassWizard and begin defining the function's behavior.

When you choose OK or Edit Code, ClassWizard updates your source code as follows:

- A function declaration is inserted into the header file.

- A complete, correct function definition with a skeletal implementation is inserted into the implementation file.

- The class's message map is updated to include the new message-handling function.

▶ **To define a message handler for a reflected message with WizardBar**

1 Use ClassView to navigate to your reusable class's implementation (.CPP) file. For information on using ClassView, see "Using ClassView" in Chapter 2, "Working with Projects."

2 In the WizardBar Object List, select the name of your reusable class.

The WizardBar Messages List contains the messages associated with the selected user-interface object. Messages that are bold already have handlers.

3 In the Messages List, click the message for which you want to define a handler. Your class's reflected messages are marked with an equal sign (=).

For messages that do not already have a predefined name for the handler function, the Add Member Function dialog box appears.

4 Choose OK to accept the proposed name.

WizardBar updates your source code as follows:

- A function declaration is inserted into the header file.

- A complete, correct function definition with a skeletal implementation is inserted into the implementation file.

- The class's message map is updated to include the new message-handling function.

WizardBar then moves the text-editor's insertion point to the body of the function.

See Also   Creating a Reusable Control Class, Declaring a Variable Based on Your New Reusable Class, Mapping Messages to Functions, Adding a Message Handler, Shortcut for Defining Message Handlers for Dialog Buttons, Shortcut for Defining Member Variables for Dialog Controls, Deleting a Message Handler, Editing a Message Handler, Overriding a Virtual Function

Declaring a Variable Based on Your New Reusable Class

Once you have created a reusable control, you can use ClassWizard to declare a variable based on it. To provide a context that ClassWizard can use to place the new variable, you must open the dialog editor and edit the dialog box in which you want to use your reusable control. Moreover, the dialog box must already have a class associated with it. For information on using the dialog editor, see Chapter 6, "Using the Dialog Editor." For information on using ClassWizard to add a class, see "Adding a Class" on page 226.

▶ **To declare a variable based on your reusable class**

1 While editing the dialog box, drag a control of the same type as your new control from the Controls toolbar onto the dialog box.

2 Place the mouse cursor over the dropped control.

3 While holding down the CTRL key, double-click the control.

The Add Member Variable dialog box appears.

4 In the Member Variables Name text box, type a name.

5 From the Category drop-down list, select Control.

6 From the Variable Type drop-down list, select the name of your reusable control.

7 Choose OK.

A message box reminds you to include (**#include**) your reusable control's header (.H) file into the project so that the compiler has access to its symbols. ClassWizard has no safe way of guaranteeing that your control class is in the scope of the dialog class.

8 Choose OK, and remember to include your control's .H file.

ClassWizard generates dialog data exchange (DDX) code to attach your control class to the dialog box.

See Also Creating a Reusable Control Class, Defining a Message Handler for a Reflected Message, Mapping Messages to Functions, Adding a Message Handler, Shortcut for Defining Message Handlers for Dialog Buttons, Shortcut for Defining Member Variables for Dialog Controls, Deleting a Message Handler, Editing a Message Handler, Overriding a Virtual Function

Working with Dialog Box Data

ClassWizard offers an easy way to take advantage of the dialog data exchange (DDX) and dialog data validation (DDV) capabilities of MFC.

To use DDX, you define member variables in the dialog box, form view, or record view class, and associate each of them with a dialog box control. The framework transfers any initial values to the controls when the dialog box is displayed. When you choose OK, it updates the variables with the data that you entered.

With DDV, dialog box information entered by the user is validated automatically. You can set the validation boundaries: the maximum length for string values in an edit-box control or the minimum or maximum numeric values when you expect a number to be entered. You can also use ClassWizard to connect dialog box controls to your own custom data-validation routines.

See Also Dialog Data Exchange, Defining Member Variables, Table 14.4 DDX Variable Types Defined with the Control Property, Table 14.3 DDX Variable Types for the Value Property, Setting Initial Values for Member Variables, Dialog Data Validation

Dialog Data Exchange

ClassWizard lets you create variables that use the framework's automatic dialog data exchange capabilities. When you want to set an initial value for or gather data from a dialog box control, use ClassWizard to define a data member in the dialog box class. The framework then transfers the initial value of the variable to the dialog box when it is created and updates the associated member variable when the dialog box is dismissed.

Note You can also use **CWnd::UpdateData** to transfer data back and forth between controls and member variables while a dialog box is open.

See Also Working with Dialog Box Data, Defining Member Variables, Table 14.4 DDX Variable Types Defined with the Control Property, Table 14.3 DDX Variable Types for the Value Property, Setting Initial Values for Member Variables, Dialog Data Validation

Defining Member Variables

You can use ClassWizard to define member variables for dialog box controls.

▶ **To define data members for dialog data exchange**

1 Create your dialog box, place in it the controls you want, and set the appropriate control styles in the Properties window. Then use ClassWizard to define a new dialog box class. For more information on adding a class, see "Adding a Class" on page 226.

2 In the MFC ClassWizard dialog box, select the Member Variables tab.

Note For a recordset class, the Update Columns button updates the current static list with the current database list. Members assigned to a deleted column may be deleted.

The Bind All button creates an initial recordset with a default member name for every column in the table.

3 In the Control IDs box, select the control for which you want to set up dialog data exchange (DDX), and choose Add Variable.

The Add Member Variable dialog box appears.

4 In the Member Variable Name box, type the name of the new variable. ClassWizard provides the m_ prefix to identify it as a member variable.

5 In the Category box, select whether this variable is a Value variable or a Control variable.

For standard Windows controls, choose Value to create a variable that contains the control's text or status as typed by the user. The framework automatically converts the control's data to the data type selected in the Variable Type box (see Table 14.4, "DDX Variable Types Defined with the Control Property").

You can also choose Control in the Category drop-down list to create a Control variable that gives you access to the control itself (see Table 14.4, "DDX Variable Types Defined with the Control Property").

6 In the Variable Type box, choose from a list of variable types appropriate to the control (see Table 14.3, "DDX Variable Types for the Value Property" and Table 14.4, "DDX Variable Types Defined with the Control Property").

7 Choose OK.

The new member variable is added to the Control IDs list.

Once you've defined a DDX Value variable for a standard Windows control, the framework automatically initializes and updates the variable for you.

Table 14.4 shows the type of DDX Value variables ClassWizard initially provides. T create additional variable types, see Technical Note 26, available under MFC in Books Online.

Table 14.3 DDX Variable Types for the Value Property

Control	Variable type
Edit box	**CString, int, UINT, long, DWORD, float, double, short, BOOL, COleDateTime, COleCurrency**
Normal check box	**BOOL**
Three-state check box	**int**
Radio button (first in group)	**int**
Nonsorted list box	**CString, int**
Drop-down combo box	**CString, int**
All other list box and combo box types	**CString**

The following additional notes apply to using DDX Value variables:

- Possible values for three-state check boxes are 0 (off), 1 (on), and 2 (indeterminate).

- Values for a group of radio buttons range from 0 for the first button in the group to $n-1$ for a group with n buttons. A value of -1 indicates that no buttons are selected.

- When you are using a group of check boxes or radio buttons with a DDX variable, set the Auto property from each control's Property window.

- Set the Group property for the first radio button in a group, and make sure all the other radio buttons immediately follow the first button in the tab order.

- To use an integer value with a combo box or list box, turn off the Sort property found on each control's Property window Styles tab.

You can now use ClassWizard to bind a member variable to the value of a scroll-bar control, using the Value property and the **int** data type, as well as to a **CScrollBar** object, using the Control property. The Value property binds the value of a scroll-bar control (the position of the scroll box, or "thumb"). ClassWizard enables DDX for a scroll bar by calling **DDX_Scroll** in your `DoDataExchange` override.

If your `DoDataExchange` function contains a call to **DDX_Scroll**, you must additionally set the scroll-bar range before that call, as shown in the following code:

```
void CMyDlg::DoDataExchange( CDataExchange* pDX )
{
    CScrollBar* pScrollBar = (CScrollBar*)GetDlgItem( IDC_SCROLLBAR1 );
    pScrollBar->SetScrollRange( 0, 100 );
    CDialog::DoDataExchange( pDX );
    //{{AFX_DATA_MAP(CMyDlg)
    DDX_Scroll(pDX, IDC_SCROLLBAR1, m_nScroll );
    //}}AFX_DATA_MAP
}
```

Table 14.4 shows the type of DDX Control variables you can define with ClassWizard.

Table 14.4   DDX Variable Types Defined with the Control Property

Control	Variable type
Edit box	**CEdit**
Check box	**CButton**
Radio button	**CButton**
Pushbutton	**CButton**
List box	**CListBox**
Combo box or drop-down combo box	**CComboBox**
Static text	**CStatic**
Scroll bar	**CScrollBar**

See Also   Working with Dialog Box Data, Dialog Data Exchange, Setting Initial Values for Member Variables, Dialog Data Validation

Setting Initial Values for Member Variables

You can set the initial value of dialog data exchange (DDX) variables by editing the initialization code that ClassWizard places in the constructor for the dialog box class. (ClassWizard does not disturb these initialization statements once they are put in place.) The framework transfers the values to the dialog box when it is created.

To see what the user typed once the dialog box is dismissed, access the values of the DDX variables just as you would any other C++ member variable.

See Also Working with Dialog Box Data, Dialog Data Exchange, Defining Member Variables, Table 14.4, DDX Variable Types Defined with the Control Property, Table 14.3, DDX Variable Types for the Value Property, Dialog Data Validation

Dialog Data Validation

By default, ClassWizard supports the types of dialog data validation (DDV) shown in Table 14.5, but you can add additional types (see Technical Note 26, available under MFC in Books Online).

Table 14.5 DDV Variable Types

Variable type	Data validation
CString	Maximum length
Numeric (**int**, **UINT**, **long**, **DWORD**, **float**, **double**)	Minimum value, maximum value

You can define the maximum length for a **CString** DDX variable or the minimum or maximum values for a numeric DDX variable at the time you create it.

At run time, if the value entered by the user exceeds the range you specify, the framework automatically displays a message box asking the user to reenter the value. The validation of DDX variables takes place all at once when the user chooses OK to accept the entries in the dialog box.

See Also Working with Dialog Box Data, Dialog Data Exchange, Defining Member Variables, Table 14.4, DDX Variable Types Defined with the Control Property, Table 14.3, DDX Variable Types for the Value Property

Custom Data Exchange and Validation

Although you can write a dialog box class that gathers and validates its own dialog box data using custom message handlers, you may find that you have routines for data exchange and validation (containing your own variable types and data formats) that you want to use repeatedly. You can extend the ClassWizard user interface to reuse your own DDX and DDV routines. For more information on this subject, see Technical Note 26, available under MFC in Books Online.

See Also Working with Dialog Box Data, Dialog Data Exchange, Defining Member Variables, Table 14.4, DDX Variable Types Defined with the Control Property, Table 14.3, DDX Variable Types for the Value Property, Setting Initial Values for Member Variables

Keeping ClassWizard Updated When Code Changes

As your program develops, it's very likely that you'll need to delete or modify classes, delete or add resources, or move a class from one source file to another. ClassWizard will track your code as you make these changes: it asks you for the updated information when you next edit the affected class.

ClassWizard stores the information about your project's classes in a file with the file extension .CLW. To accommodate source files that have changed, ClassWizard displays the Repair Class Information dialog box whenever it finds that the information in the .CLW file is out of date.

The Repair Class Information dialog box has two main functions:

- Deleting obsolete classes from the ClassWizard file
- Updating the ClassWizard file with the new name or location of classes that you have changed or moved

See Also   Deleting Classes, Renaming or Moving Classes, Rebuilding the ClassWizard (.CLW) File

Deleting Classes

To delete a ClassWizard-created class from your project, you can either delete it from the header (.H) and implementation (.CPP) files in which it coexists with other classes or delete the .H and .CPP files altogether. In either case, you must update the information in the ClassWizard (.CLW) file.

▶ **To delete a class**

1 Delete all references to the class from its .H and .CPP files or delete the files from the disk.

2 From the View menu, choose ClassWizard.

   If ClassWizard appears, the active project does not contain the deleted class.

3 From ClassWizard's Project drop-down list, select the project that contains the deleted class.

4 If ClassWizard asks you to close any files, close ClassWizard, close the files, and then restart ClassWizard.

   A message box informs you that ClassWizard cannot find the deleted class.

5 Choose OK.

   ClassWizard displays the Repair Class Information dialog box.

6 Choose Remove.

The class is deleted from the .CLW file.

ClassWizard appears.

7 Choose OK.

See Also Keeping ClassWizard Updated When Code Changes, Renaming or Moving Classes, Rebuilding the ClassWizard (.CLW) File

Renaming or Moving Classes

When you change the name of a class or move it from one implementation file to another, you're prompted to update the information in the ClassWizard (.CLW) file the next time you start ClassWizard.

▶ **To change the name of a class or move it from one file to another**

1 Make the desired changes to your source files.

Note When you change the name of a class, remember to change it everywhere, including in the special-format comments ClassWizard uses. For example,

`//{{AFX_MSG_MAP(OldClass)` becomes `//{{AFX_MSG_MAP(NewClass)`

2 From the View menu, choose ClassWizard.

If ClassWizard appears, the active project does not contain the renamed or moved class.

3 From ClassWizard's Project drop-down list, select the project that contains the renamed or moved class.

4 If ClassWizard asks you to close any files, close ClassWizard, close the files, and then restart ClassWizard.

ClassWizard displays a message box warning you that the old class could not be found.

5 Choose OK.

The Repair Class Information dialog box appears.

Supply the new information about the class in the Class Name, Header File, and Implementation File text boxes. If necessary, use the Browse button to supply the correct name of the header file or the implementation file.

6 Choose OK to update the .CLW file.

See Also Keeping ClassWizard Updated When Code Changes, Deleting Classes, Rebuilding the ClassWizard (.CLW) File

Rebuilding the ClassWizard (.CLW) File

If you have made numerous changes to your code or have added a large number of existing user-interface classes to your current project, you may find it convenient to rebuild the associated ClassWizard (.CLW) file from scratch rather than update it one class at a time. To do this, delete your project's .CLW file and use ClassWizard to generate a new one. The newly-generated .CLW file contains information about all the classes that have the special-format ClassWizard comments. For information on the ClassWizard special-format comments, see Technical Note 6, available under MFC in Books Online.

▶ **To rebuild the ClassWizard file**

1 Delete your project's .CLW file.

2 From the View menu, choose ClassWizard.

If ClassWizard appears, the project for which you deleted the .CLW file is not the active project. From ClassWizard's Project drop-down list, select the project for which you want to rebuild the .CLW file.

3 If ClassWizard asks you to close any files, close ClassWizard, close the files, and then restart ClassWizard.

A message box asks if you want to rebuild the ClassWizard file from your source files.

4 Choose Yes.

The Select Source Files dialog box appears.

5 Use the Add and Add All buttons to transfer all of the project's .H and .CPP files, and the .RC file from the File Name list to the Files In Project box. Use the Remove button to remove any files other than .H, .CPP, or .RC from the Files In Project box.

6 Choose OK.

ClassWizard appears and generates a new .CLW file.

7 Choose OK to close ClassWizard.

See Also   Keeping ClassWizard Updated When Code Changes, Deleting Classes, Renaming or Moving Classes

CHAPTER 15

Using Component Gallery

Have you ever wanted an easy way to reuse a new dialog box or dialog box control you have just created? A way that doesn't require that you cut and paste across multiple files or require hit-or-miss checking for name collisions? With Component Gallery, you can do just that. Component Gallery contains reusable code such as OLE controls, your own reusable C++ classes with any associated resources, or components created by a third-party vendor. Third-party-created components can range from reusable code to useful tools, such as a code analysis tool.

Figure 15.1 Component Gallery

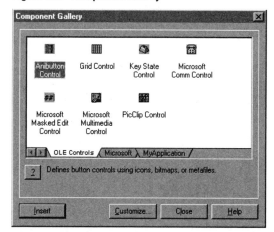

As you can see in Figure 15.1, Component Gallery uses tabbed panes to organize components. Each tab is labeled with a category name. You can easily create and/or add components to Component Gallery. You can also create and name your own categories and move components from one category to another.

See Also Inserting Components into a Project, Creating Your Own Components, Sharing Components with Others, Managing Components, Managing Categories

Inserting Components into a Project

One of the most important uses of Component Gallery is inserting components, such as OLE controls, into your project. To do this, use the Insert button, found in the Component Gallery's main dialog box. Usually, inserting a component adds the associated header (.H) and implementation (.CPP) files to the currently selected default project and updates the information in the Project Workspace window. However, the result of inserting a component depends on the component. Refer to each component's documentation to determine its functionality. Each component shipped with Visual C++ has a help system that you can view by selecting the component from the main Component Gallery dialog box and pressing the question-mark button found in the Component Gallery dialog box. In addition, each component you buy from a third-party vendor will have its own documentation.

▶ **To insert components into your project**

1 Open the project workspace to which you want to add a component.

2 From the Build menu, choose Set Default Project, and select a project and one of its configuration in the Default Project Configuration dialog box.

3 From the Insert menu, choose Component.

Component Gallery appears.

4 If there is more than one tabbed pane, use the mouse and the CTRL+PAGE UP and CTRL+PAGE DOWN keys to tabbed select the pane containing the component to apply.

5 Use the mouse or the UP, DOWN, LEFT OR RIGHT ARROW keys to move to the component that you want to apply.

6 Choose the Insert button.

The component makes changes to your project, prompting you for any information it needs.

For example, if you insert an OLE control into your project, Component Gallery will:

- Register, if not already registered, the OLE control with the Windows OLE registration database.

- Add the OLE control to the dialog editor's toolbar of controls.

- Generate a programmatic interface, called an OLE wrapper, which allows the OLE control to communicate with your program. If, for example, you added an OLE control that looks like a measuring gauge to a dialog box, the associated wrapper (a header file and an implementation file) would allow you to write code allowing the gauge to visually represent some program action.

Note OLE controls are per-project components. You must insert an OLE control into each project in which you want to use it.

See Also Creating Your Own Components, Adding Components to Component Gallery, Sharing Components with Others, Managing Components, Managing Categories

Sharing Components with Others

Through Component Gallery, you can share the components that you have created using the Create New Class dialog box with others. However, the component must be exported to a file before it can be shared. The resulting file contains a component's classes and resources. The file extension is, by convention, .OGX. Use the Export Component dialog box, accessed from the Custom tab of the Properties dialog box, to export a component to a file.

▶ **To export a component**

1 From the Insert menu, choose Component.

  Component Gallery appears.

2 From the tabbed panes, choose the component that you want to distribute.

  You can only export components that you have created using the Create New Class dialog box.

3 Choose the Customize button.

  The Customize Component Gallery dialog box appears.

4 Choose the Properties button.

  The Properties dialog box appears.

5 Using the mouse or the LEFT ARROW or RIGHT ARROW keys, select the Custom tab.

  If the Export button is grayed out, an export file already exists for the component and you need not finish the following steps.

6 Choose the Export button.

  The Export Component dialog box appears.

7 Select the drive and directory on which to store the exported file.

8 Set the exported component's file extension, displayed in the File Name box, using the Save Files As Type list. The recommended file extension is .OGX.

  Alternatively, you can specify the file extension directly in the File Name box.

9 In the File Name box, type a filename.

10 Choose OK.

The exported component can be shared with others. They need only import it into their own Component Gallery.

See Also   Inserting Components into a Project, Importing Components, Creating Your Own Components, Renaming a Component, Moving Components Between Categories, Deleting a Component from a Category, Changing a Component's Icon, Providing a Description of a Component to Users

Adding Components to Component Gallery

You can build your own gallery of components from components you have created, components others have shared with you, and/or components you have purchased from third-party vendors. There are four ways to add components to Component Gallery:

- Use the Import dialog box, accessible from the Customize Component Gallery dialog box. For more information on this technique, see Importing Components.

- Use the Create New Class dialog box to create a new component. For more information on this technique, see Creating Your Own Components.

- Run the setup program supplied with the component. Not all components provide setup programs.

- Register an OLE control with the Windows OLE registration database. Any registered OLE control is automatically added to Component Gallery.

You need not have a project open to add these to Component Gallery.

See Also   Importing Components, Creating Your Own Components, Sharing Components with Others, Renaming a Component, Moving Components Between Categories, Deleting a Component from a Category, Changing a Component's Icon, Providing a Description of a Component to Users

Importing Components

You can use the Import button in the Customize Component Gallery dialog box to add components to Component Gallery. The Customize Component Gallery dialog box is accessed from the Component Gallery's main dialog box, as described below.

▶ **To import components into Component Gallery**

1 From the Insert menu, choose Component.

Component Gallery appears.

2 Select the pane to which you want to add the component.

3 Choose the Customize button.

The Customize Component Gallery dialog box appears.

4 Choose the Import button.

The Import Component dialog box appears.

5 Select the drive and directory where the component that you want to import is stored.

6 Set the types of files to display in the List Files Of Type box.

Files with the chosen extension are displayed in the File Name box. This box serves as a filter to display all files with a given extension. For example, selecting the OLE Control Files (.ocx) list item displays all files with the .OCX extension.

Alternatively, you can specify wildcard patterns in the File Name box to display file types. The new wildcard pattern is retained until the dialog box is closed. You can also use any combination of wildcard patterns, delimited by semicolons.

7 Select the Copy To Gallery directory option in order to physically copy a component to the Component Gallery's directory —\MSDEV\TEMPLATE.

If you do not select the Copy To Gallery directory box, no physical copy is made of the component. Instead, Component Gallery stores information about the location of the component in its database. As long as the location information in the database is valid, these "reference components" can be applied to a project. You cannot, however, export them. You can only export components created from the Create New Class dialog box. For more information on exporting see, Sharing Components with Others.

In the File Name box, enter a filename, and then choose the Import button.

– or–

Double-click the filename.

See Also   Inserting Components into a Project, Creating Your Own Components, Sharing Components with Others, Renaming a Component, Moving Components Between Categories, Deleting a Component from a Category, Changing a Component's Icon, Providing a Description of a Component to Users

Creating Your Own Components

You can use the Add To Component Gallery option in the Create New Class dialog box to leverage your code into a component that you can use over and over again. The Create New Class dialog box is accessed from ClassWizard. You can create a component that includes a new class and any associated resource.

▶ **To create a new component**

1 From the View menu, choose ClassWizard.

Note If your new component uses a class associated with a dialog box resource—classes derived from **CDialog**, **CFormView**, **CPropertyPage**, or **CRecordView**—create the resource in the dialog editor before you use ClassWizard to create the class. This gives ClassWizard access to the resource ID. If ClassWizard has access to the resource ID, the Adding A Class dialog box appears. This dialog box enables you to add a class, import a class into the ClassWizard database, or select a class from the ClassWizard database.

2 If the Create New Class dialog box does not appear, choose the Add Class menu button, and then choose the New command.

The Create New Class dialog box appears.

3 In the Name text box, type the name of your new class.

4 In the Base Class drop-down list, select a base class to derive your current class from (see Table 14.1, Types of MFC Classes Created in ClassWizard, on page 224).

5 Choose the Change button only if you want to see and/or change the default names of the header (.H) and implementation (.CPP) files where the class is to be defined.

The Change Files dialog box appears.

6 In the Change Files dialog box, accept the default filenames by choosing the OK button, or use the Header File box and Implementation File box to change them.

By default, ClassWizard assigns the same name to .H and .CPP files.

7 If you're adding a class to describe a user-interface component that contains controls and acts like a dialog box (**CDialog**, **CFormView**, **CPropertyPage**, or **CRecordView**), use the Dialog ID combo box to select and associate the class you are adding with an existing resource ID.

8 Select Automation if you want to expose the capabilities of this class through OLE Automation.

If you select this option, the newly created class will be available as a programmable object by automation client applications, such as Microsoft Visual Basic™ or Microsoft Excel.

9 Choose Createable By Type ID if you want to allow other applications to create objects of this class by using OLE Automation.

With this option selected, an OLE client application can create one of these objects at any time. The type ID in the box is used by the client application to specify the object to be created. The type ID is system-wide and must be unique. This option is enabled only if you select OLE Automation.

10 Select the Add To Component Gallery option.

This option places a path to the associated header, implementation, and resource files into the Component Gallery database and adds the component to Component Gallery.

11 Choose the Create button to create the class in the files you specified in steps 5 and 6.

When you use ClassWizard to create a new class, it adds skeletal information on the new class to both the header and implementation files. If you specify filenames that don't yet exist, ClassWizard creates the new files and adds them to your project.

12 Choose OK to close ClassWizard.

Once you have used the Create New Class dialog box to create a component, be sure to provide a description of the component for display in Component Gallery's main dialog box. For more information on adding a description, see "Providing a Description of a Component to Users," on page 263.

See Also   Inserting Components into a Project, Importing Components, Sharing Components with Others, Renaming a Component, Moving Components Between Categories, Deleting a Component from a Category, Changing a Component's Icon, Providing a Description of a Component to Users

Managing Components

You can create components, add components to Component Gallery, distribute them to others, rename components, move components between categories, and delete components. You can also change a component's icon and the description it displays in the Component Gallery's main dialog box. The following topics describe how to do all of these procedures.

See Also   Inserting Components into a Project, Importing Components, Creating Your Own Components, Sharing Components with Others, Renaming a Component, Moving Components Between Categories, Deleting a Component from a Category, Changing a Component's Icon, Providing a Description of a Component to Users

Renaming a Component

To rename a component, overwrite the existing name in the Components pane of the Customize Component Gallery dialog box.

▶ **To rename a component**

1 From the Insert menu, choose Component.

Component Gallery appears.

2 Choose the Customize button.

The Customize Component Gallery dialog box appears.

3 In the Categories pane, select the category containing the component to rename.

You can use the mouse or the CTRL+TAB (move right) and the SHIFT+CTRL+TAB (move left) keys to move the focus to and from the Categories pane. With the focus on the Categories pane, you can move to a category using the mouse or the UP and DOWN ARROW keys.

The components contained in the selected category are displayed in the component pane.

4 In the Components pane, select the component to rename.

5 Type a new name for the component.

6 Choose the OK button to accept the new name.

The main Component Gallery dialog box appears, and the component has a new name.

Because components are sorted by name within a category, the renamed component will most likely be relocated.

See Also   Inserting Components into a Project, Importing Components, Creating Your Own Components, Sharing Components with Others, Moving Components Between Categories, Deleting a Component from a Category, Changing a Component's Icon, Providing a Description of a Component to Users

Moving Components Between Categories

To move components between categories, use the Move dialog box, accessed from the Customize Component Gallery dialog box.

▶ **To move components between categories**

1 From the Insert menu, choose Component.

Component Gallery appears.

2 Choose the Customize button.

The Customize Component Gallery dialog box appears.

3 In the Categories pane, select the category containing the component to move.

You can use the mouse or the CTRL+TAB (move right) and the SHIFT+CTRL+TAB (move left) keys to move the focus to and from the Categories pane. With the focus on the Categories pane, you can move to a category using the mouse or the UP and DOWN ARROW keys.

The components contained in the selected category are displayed in the Component pane.

4 In the Components pane, select the component to move.

5 Choose the Move button.

The Move dialog box appears.

6 In the Move To pane, select the category to which you want to move the selected component.

7 Choose the OK button from the Move dialog box and then the Customize Component Gallery dialog box.

The main Component Gallery dialog box appears.

8 Select the tabbed pane into which you have moved the component and note that the component has moved.

Note You can select multiple components to move several at once.

See Also Inserting Components into a Project, Importing Components, Creating Your Own Components, Sharing Components with Others, Renaming a Component, Deleting a Component from a Category, Changing a Component's Icon, Providing a Description of a Component to Users

Deleting a Component from a Category

To delete a component from a category, select the component from the Components pane of the Customize Component Gallery dialog box and press the DEL key.

▶ **To delete a component from a category**

1 From the Insert menu, choose Component.

Component Gallery appears.

2 Choose the Customize button.

The Customize Component Gallery dialog box appears.

3 In the Categories pane, select the category containing the component to delete.

You can use the mouse or the CTRL+TAB (move right) and the SHIFT+CTRL+TAB (move left) keys to move the focus to and from the Categories pane. With the focus on the Categories pane, you can move to a category using the mouse or the UP and DOWN ARROW keys.

The components contained in the selected category are displayed in the Components pane.

4 In the Components pane, select the component to delete.

5 Press the DEL key.

The selected component disappears from the Components pane. Deleted components are removed from Component Gallery only. The associated files are not deleted. Deleting the files is left to your discretion.

6 Choose OK.

The main Component Gallery dialog box appears. Note that the component has been removed from its pane.

See Also Inserting Components into a Project, Importing Components, Creating Your Own Components, Sharing Components with Others, Renaming a Component, Moving Components Between Categories, Changing a Component's Icon, Providing a Description of a Component to Users

Changing a Component's Icon

To change a component's icon, use the Change Icon dialog box, accessed from the General tab of the Properties dialog box. You can use any standard 32 x 32 icon created by the graphic editor. For information on creating icons, see Chapter 10, "Using the Graphic Editor."

▶ **To change a component's icon**

1 From the Insert menu, choose Component.

Component Gallery appears.

2 From the tabbed panes, choose the component for which you want to change the icon.

3 Choose the Customize button.

The Customize Component Gallery dialog box appears.

4 Choose the Properties button.

The Properties dialog box appears.

5 Select the General tab.

6 Choose the Change Icon button.

The Change Icon dialog box appears.

7 Select the drive and directory where the desired icon file resides.

The default is the current drive and directory.

8 Set the icon's file extension, displayed in the File Name box, using the List Files Of Type box.

The default file extension is .ICO.

Alternatively, you can type the file extension directly in the File Name box.

9 In the File Name box, type a filename, and then choose the OK button.

10 Choose OK for the General tab and then for the Customize Component Gallery dialog box.

The component's new icon appears in its tabbed pane.

See Also Inserting Components into a Project, Importing Components, Creating Your Own Components, Sharing Components with Others, Renaming a Component, Moving Components Between Categories, Deleting a Component from a Category, Providing a Description of a Component to Users

Providing a Description of a Component to Users

When you have selected a component in Component Gallery, it should display a simple description just under the tabbed panes in Component Gallery's main dialog box. If it does not, you can write a description for it in the Description box that is located on the General tab of Component Gallery's Properties dialog box.

▶ **To write a simple description of a component**

1 From the Insert menu, choose Component.

Component Gallery appears.

2 From the tabbed panes, select the component for which you want to write a description.

3 Choose the Customize button.

The Customize Component Gallery dialog box appears.

4 Choose the Properties button.

The Properties dialog box appears.

5 Select the General tab.

6 In the Description box, type a description of the selected component.

7 Choose the OK button for the Properties dialog box and then for the Customize Component Gallery dialog box.

The main Component Gallery dialog box appears.

The component's description is displayed just under Component Gallery's tabbed panes.

See Also Inserting Components into a Project, Importing Components, Creating Your Own Components, Sharing Components with Others, Renaming a Component, Moving Components Between Categories, Deleting a Component from a Category, Changing a Component's Icon

Managing Categories

Component Gallery organizes components by the tabbed panes that you see in its main dialog box. You can create new categories and delete, rename, and rearrange existing categories. The following topics describe how to do all of these procedures.

See Also   Creating a Category in Which to Store Components, Deleting a Category of Components, Renaming a Category of Components, Rearranging the Order of Existing Categories

Creating a Category in Which to Store Components

To create a new category in Component Gallery, type the name for the new category in the Categories pane of the Customize Component Gallery dialog box.

▶ **To create a category**

1 From the Insert menu, choose Component.

Component Gallery appears.

2 Choose the Customize button.

The Customize Component Gallery dialog box appears.

3 In the Categories pane, select the new-category box (an empty rectangle).

You can use the mouse or the CTRL+TAB (move right) and the SHIFT+CTRL+TAB (move left) keys to move the focus to and from the Categories pane. With the focus on the Categories pane, you can move to the new-category box using the mouse, UP and DOWN ARROW keys, or the END key.

4 Type the name of the new category.

5 Choose the OK button to accept the new category.

The main Component Gallery dialog box appears. Note the existence of your newly-named tabbed pane.

See Also   Deleting a Category of Components, Renaming a Category of Components, Rearranging the Order of Existing Categories

Deleting a Category of Components

To delete a category from Component Gallery, select the name of the category in the Categories pane of the Customize Component Gallery dialog box and press the DEL key. The category must first be empty of components. For information on deleting components, see "Deleting a Component from a Category" on page 261. For information on moving components between categories, see "Moving Components Between Categories" on page 260.

▶ **To delete a category**

1 From the Insert menu, choose Component.

Component Gallery appears.

2 Choose the Customize button.

The Customize Component Gallery dialog box appears.

3 In the Categories pane, select the category to delete.

You can use the mouse or the CTRL+TAB (move right) and the SHIFT+CTRL+TAB (move left) keys to move the focus to and from the Categories pane. With the focus on the Categories pane, you can move to a category using the mouse or the UP and DOWN ARROW keys.

4 Press the DEL key.

The selected category disappears from the Categories pane. You cannot delete a category that contains components without first moving or deleting the components it contains. Deleted components are removed from Component Gallery only. The associated files are not deleted. Deleting the files is left to your discretion.

5 Choose OK.

The main Component Gallery dialog box appears. Note that the tabbed pane associated with the deleted category is gone.

See Also   Deleting a Component from a Category, Moving Components Between Categories, Creating a Category in Which to Store Components, Renaming a Category of Components, Rearranging the Order of Existing Categories

Renaming a Category of Components

To rename a category of components, overwrite the existing name in the Categories pane of the Customize Component Gallery dialog box.

▶ **To rename a category**

1 From the Insert menu, choose Component.

Component Gallery appears.

2 Choose the Customize button.

The Customize Component Gallery dialog box appears.

3 In the Categories pane, select the category to rename.

You can use the MOUSE OR THE CTRL+TAB (move right) and the SHIFT+CTRL+TAB (move left) keys to move the focus to and from the Categories pane. With the focus on the Categories pane, you can move to a category using the mouse or the UP and DOWN ARROW keys.

4 Type a new name for the category.

5 Choose the OK to button to accept the new name.

The main Component Gallery dialog box appears, and the pane associated with the renamed category has a new name.

See Also Creating a Category in Which to Store Components, Deleting a Category of Components, Rearranging the Order of Existing Categories

Rearranging the Order of Existing Categories

To rearrange the order of existing categories in Component Gallery, use the Categories pane of the Customize Component Gallery dialog box.

▶ **To rearrange the order of existing categories**

1 From the Insert menu, choose Component.

Component Gallery appears.

2 Choose the Customize button.

The Customize Component Gallery dialog box appears.

3 In the Categories pane, select the category to move. Select the name, not the file-folder icon.

To move the category with the mouse, drag it to a new location. A gray, horizontal bar indicates the insertion point. To move the category with the keyboard, hold down the ALT key and press the UP or DOWN ARROW keys to reposition the category.

The category is moved to the insertion point.

4 Choose OK.

The main Component Gallery dialog box appears, and the pane associated with the rearranged category has moved.

Note Components are sorted by name within a category and so cannot be reordered.

See Also Creating a Category in Which to Store Components, Deleting a Category of Components, Renaming a Category of Components

CHAPTER 16

Browsing Through Symbols

Browse windows display information about the symbols (classes, functions, data, macros, and types) in your program. If you have browse information turned on when you build a project, the compiler creates .SBR files with information about each program file in your project. The BSCMAKE utility (BSCMAKE.EXE) assembles these .SBR files into a single browse file. This browse file has the project's base name and the extension .BSC.

Note For information on how to modify your project settings so that a browse file is always generated, see "Disabling and Enabling BSCMAKE" on page 271.

You view browse information in browse windows, which have different appearances and different controls depending on the type of information displayed.

Using browse commands, you can examine:

- Information about all the symbols in any source file.
- The source code line in which a symbol is defined.
- Each source code line where there is a reference to a symbol.
- The relationships between base classes and derived classes.
- The relationships between calling functions and called functions.

 Tip If you do not require browse information, you can speed up the build process by turning browse information off. When the browse option is off, .SBR files are not generated, and the .BSC file is not updated.

Opening and Closing Browse Files

When you open a project workspace, Microsoft Developer Studio opens the project browse file automatically.

If you want to browse information on a symbol in another project, you must open the browse file for that project.

▶ **To open a browse file for another project**

1 From the File menu, choose Open.

2 In the List Files of Type list box, select Browse Info Files (*.BSC).

3 Select the drive, directory, and browse file that you want.

4 Choose the Open button.

Note Some browser queries may open source files. The current browse file determines which project the browser can open source files from.

▶ **To close a browse file**

• From the Tools menu, choose Close Browse Info File.

 Tip When you use a browse information file, the .BSC file stays open for the duration of the session unless you close it. If you run NMAKE outside of Developer Studio, you should close the .BSC file to allow updating. If the .BSC file remains open, it cannot be updated.

Modifying the Browse Window Display

A browse window appears in response to queries. For example, if you query on name **CWinApp** and select Definitions and References, a browse window for the **CWinApp** class, with all of its definitions and references, is displayed.

By default, a browse window disappears when you move the focus away from the window. You can keep the browse window in view with the pushpin button at the top of the window as shown in Figure 16.1.

Figure 16.1 Browse Window with Active Pushpin

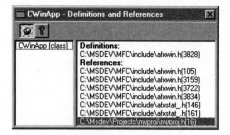

Fixing a browse window on your screen with the pushpin has these two effects:

• The browse window remains visible even if you move the focus to another window, for instance, to edit a source file.

• The browse window remains on top of all other Developer Studio windows.

▶ **To keep a browse window visible**

• Click the pushpin button at the top of the window.

▶ **To change the size of a pane in a browse window**

• With the mouse pointer, point to the split bar between panes, and drag the split bar to its new location.

▶ **To move the focus from pane to pane in a browse window**

• Press TAB to move to the next pane.

• Press SHIFT+TAB to move to the previous pane.

Nodes in a graph display a plus sign or a minus sign in the left margin of the graph. If a node has a plus sign, you can expand that node. If a node has a minus sign, you can contract that node.

▶ **To expand or contract a node in a graph**

• Click the plus sign or minus sign.

  –or–

  Select the node with the arrow keys, and then press ENTER.

Using Browse Files

Whenever you open a project, Developer Studio opens the browse file for the project if it exists. If you close the browse file, Developer Studio reopens the file when you do a query.

▶ **To query the current information file about a symbol**

1 From the Tools menu, choose Browse.

  The Browse dialog box appears.

2 In the Query On Name text box, type the name of the symbol you want to query for.

  You can use the asterisk as a wildcard to match any string.

3 In the Select Query list box, select the type of query you want.

4 If necessary, select the Case Sensitive Queries option.

5 Choose the OK button.

  A browse window specific to the query type appears. The query results for the symbol you selected are displayed.

Tip If you select a symbol in a source file, the symbol appears in the Query On Name box when you open the Browse dialog box. This eliminates step 2 in the procedure above.

When the browse information file is open, you can use it to find where a symbol used in a source file is defined or first referenced.

▶ **To find the definition of a symbol**

1 Select the symbol in a source file or the standard toolbar Find box.

2 From the Edit menu, choose Go To.

   The Go To dialog box appears.

3 In the Go To What list, select Definition.

4 Choose the Go To button.

▶ **To find the first reference to a symbol**

1 Select the symbol in a source file or the standard toolbar Find box.

2 From the Edit menu, choose Go To.

   The Go To dialog box appears.

3 In the Go To What list, select Reference.

4 Choose the Go To button.

Note The browse file is based on the state of the source files at the time of the last build. If you edit source files and then go to a definition or a reference, the location in the browse file may no longer be accurate. If the browse file has not been built, a dialog box provides the option of building the browse file.

 Tip You can jump to the previous or next definition or reference by choosing one of the navigation buttons on the Go To dialog box: Previous or Next.

Symbol Codes in the Browse Window

A browse window uses symbol codes to describe the displayed query types. For example, f V CAboutDlg::GetMessageMap(void) indicates a virtual (V) function (f).

The following table shows the codes and their meanings.

Table 16.1 Browse Window Symbol Codes

Code	Meaning
c	Class
f	Function
d	Data
m	Macro

Table 16.1   Browse Window Symbol Codes *(continued)*

Code	Meaning
t	Type (other than class)
V	Virtual function
S	Static function or data member

Disabling and Enabling BSCMAKE

In a large project, creating the browse information file (.BSC file) can take a significant amount of time. To create browse information, a separate .SBR file is generated for each program file, and then these files are assembled into a single browse file (.BSC file).

You can build your project more quickly if you turn off creation of both the .SBR files and .BSC file. As a default, browse information is turned off. You will not be able to browse current information until you turn the browse options on and build your project again.

▶ **To turn on creation of the .SBR files at compile time**

1 Open the project if it is not currently open.

2 From the Build menu, choose Settings.

   The Project Settings dialog box appears.

3 Select the C/C++ tab.

4 Select the Generate Browse Info check box.

5 Choose the OK button.

▶ **To turn on updating of the .BSC file at compile time**

1 Open the project if it is not currently open.

2 From the Build menu, choose Settings.

   The Project Settings dialog box appears.

3 Select the Browse Info tab.

4 Select the Build Browse Info File check box.

5 Choose the OK button.

Note   You must turn on creation of the .SBR files at compile time for this option to work; otherwise, the browse file will be updated using old .SBR information.

Tip   If you want to speed up your builds and also want to update your browse information file quickly, turn on creation of .SBR files and turn off updating of the .BSC file. When you want to update your browse information file, turn on updating of the .BSC file and build your project.

▶ **To turn off creation of the .SBR files at compile time**

1 Open the project if it is not currently open.

2 From the Build menu, choose Settings.

   The Project Settings dialog box appears.

3 Select the C/C++ tab.

4 Clear the Generate Browse Info check box.

5 Choose the OK button.

▶ **To turn off updating of the .BSC file at compile time**

1 Open the project if it is not currently open.

2 From the Build menu, choose Settings.

   The Project Settings dialog box appears.

3 Select the Browse Info tab.

4 Clear the Build Browse Info File check box.

5 Choose the OK button.

Note Turning this option off prevents BSCMAKE from updating the .BSC file, but does not prevent the compiler from creating .SBR files. To bring the browse file up to date, you must turn this update option back on.

Displaying the Symbols in a File

You can display an outline of all the symbols in a specific source file and filter the information that is displayed.

▶ **To display the symbols in a file**

1 Open the source file that you want to examine. If it is already open, click that window to move the focus there.

   –or–

   Select the file in the Project Workspace window.

2 From the Tools menu, choose Browse.

   The Browse dialog box appears.

3 From the Select Query list box, select File Outline.

4 Choose the OK button.

   The File Outline browse window appears, with classes and functions displayed at the top of the left pane, as shown in Figure 16.2.

Figure 16.2   Browse Window with File Outline

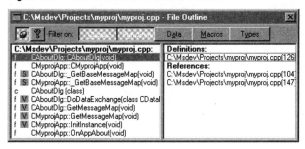

The following table describes the window elements, the function of each element, and the user's actions.

Table 16.2   File Outline Window

Window Element	Function	Action
Left pane	Lists the symbols (classes, functions, data, macros, and types) for the selected file. One or more codes identify each symbol.	Select a symbol.
Right pane	Lists the available definitions and references for the symbol selected in the left pane.	Double-click the definition or reference you want to see.
Pushpin	Determines whether or not the window is held open or allowed to close. The window remains open when the pin is pushed in.	Select to push or pull the pin.
Filter buttons	Filter the symbols shown in the current display. For more information, see Filtering Browse Information for Files.	Select to toggle filter.

Tip   You can display symbols in multiple files by using the asterisk as a wildcard character in the filename. If you type a filename specification followed by the asterisk wildcard but no extension (oc*, for example), the search finds files without extensions, such as "oc1," but not files with extensions, such as "oc1.cpp".

Filtering Browse Information for Files

When you do a file outline query, five buttons appear at the top of the browse window. These buttons are filter buttons. Their settings determine which symbols are displayed in the left pane of the browse window. When a button is selected (pushed in), the corresponding symbols are displayed.

▶ **To filter the symbol display**

• Select the buttons corresponding to the symbols you want to see, as shown in the
  following table.

Button	Keyboard	Displays
Classes	ALT+C	Classes
Functions	ALT+U	Functions
Data	ALT+A	Data symbols
Macros	ALT+M	Macros
Types	ALT+Y	Types (other than classes)

Displaying Class Information

You can view C++ class hierarchies as graphs. You can select a class and display
either of the following two types of graphs for class hierarchies.

Derived Class Graph: All the classes that inherit attributes from the selected class.

Base Class Graph: All the classes from which the selected class inherits attributes, up
to its ultimate base class, or base classes if it has multiple inheritance.

In each graph, a node represents a class.

Displaying the Graph of Classes Derived from a Class

▶ **To display a derived class graph**

1 Select the class name in a source file or the standard toolbar Find box.

2 From the Tools menu, choose Browse.

3 In the Select Query list box, select Derived Classes And Members.

4 Choose the OK button.

The Derived Classes And Members window appears, with the selected class name
displayed at the top of the left pane. Figure 16.3 shows an example of this window.

Figure 16.3   Derived Classes and Members Window

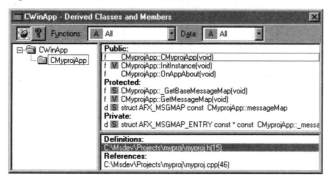

The following table describes the window elements, the function of each element, and the user's actions.

Table 16.3   Derived Classes and Members Window

Window Element	Function	Action
Left pane	Displays the derived class graph.	Click the plus sign or minus sign to expand or contract the graph. To display information for a class, click the class name or folder icon. To open the source file for a class, double-click the class name or folder icon.
Top right pane	Displays member functions and member variables of the class selected in the left pane.	Double-click the member whose definition you want to see.
Bottom right pane	Displays available definitions and references for the symbol selected in the left pane or top right pane.	Double-click the definition or reference you want to see.
Pushpin	Determines whether or not the window disappears after it loses focus.	Select to push or pull the pin.
Help button	Displays help for the window.	Select for help.
Filter buttons	Filter the browse query to display selected types of information. For more information on filters, see Filtering Browse Information for Classes.	Select filter types from the lists.

Displaying the Base Class Graph for a Class

▶ **To display a base class graph**

1 Select the class name in a source file or the standard toolbar Find box.

2 From the Tools menu, choose Browse

3 In the Select Query list box, select Base Classes And Members.

4 Choose the OK button.

The Base Classes And Members window appears, with the selected class name displayed at the top of the left pane. Figure 16.4 shows an example of this window.

Figure 16.4 Base Classes and Members Window

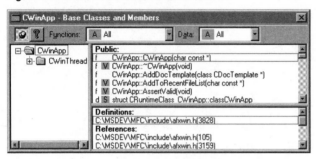

The following table describes the window elements, the function of each element, and the user's actions.

Table 16.4 Base Classes and Members Window

Window Element	Function	Action
Left pane	Displays the base class graph.	Click the plus sign or minus sign to expand or contract the graph. To display information for a class, click the class name or folder icon. To open the source file for a class, double-click the class name or folder icon.
Top right pane	Displays member functions and member variables of the class selected in the left pane. One or more codes identify each symbol.	Double-click the member whose definition you want to see.
Bottom right pane	Displays available definitions and references for the symbol selected in the left pane or top right pane.	Double-click the definition or reference you want to see.
Pushpin	Determines whether or not the window disappears after it loses focus.	Select to push or pull the pin.

Table 16.4   Base Classes and Members Window *(continued)*

Window Element	Function	Action
Help button	Displays help for the window.	Select for help.
Filter buttons	Filter the browse query to display selected types of information. For more information on filters, see Filtering Browse Information for Classes.	Select filter type from the lists.

If the class has multiple inheritance, and one base class appears in more than one inheritance path, the second and subsequent instances of the class name have an ellipsis (...) after them. You cannot expand nodes that have ellipses.

Filtering Browse Information for Classes

When you open the Derived Classes And Members window, two drop-down list boxes appear at the top. You can use these lists to filter the display of information about member functions and data members.

▶ To filter information on member functions

- From the Functions drop-down list box, select the desired filter.

Filter	Displays
All	All member functions
Virtual	Virtual member functions only
Static	Static member functions only
Non-Virtual	Non-virtual member functions only
Non-Static	Non-static member functions only
Non-Virtual Non-Static	Non-virtual, non-static member functions only
None	No member functions

▶ To filter information on data members

- From the Data drop-down list box, select the desired filter.

Filter	Displays
All	All member data
Static	Static member data only
Non-Static	Non-static member data only
None	No member data

The graphic symbols displayed in the drop-down list boxes for the function and data filters identify corresponding entries in the top right pane of the browse window.

Displaying Function Information

You can display the relationships among functions in your program as a graph. You can select a function and display either of the following two types of graphs for function relationships:

- Call Graph: All the functions that the selected function calls.
- Callers Graph: All the functions that call the selected function.

In each graph, a node represents a function.

Displaying a Call Graph

The call graph displays all the functions called by a selected function.

▶ **To display the graph of all functions that a selected function calls**

1 Select the function name in a source file or the standard toolbar Find box.

2 From the Tools menu, choose Browse.

3 In the Select Query list box, select Call Graph.

4 Choose the OK button.

5 If the function is an overloaded function or a member function of more than one class, the Resolve Ambiguity dialog box appears. Select the function that you want from the list.

The Call Graph window appears, with the selected function displayed at the top of the left pane. Figure 16.5 shows the Call Graph window for a sample function.

Figure 16.5   Call Graph Window

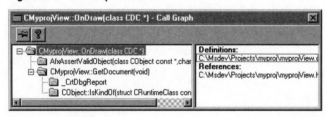

The following table describes the window elements, the function of each element, and. the user's actions.

Table 16.5   Call Graph Window

Window Element	Function	Action
Left pane	Displays the call graph for the selected function.	Click the plus sign or minus sign to expand or contract the graph. To display information for a function, click the class name or folder icon. To open the source file for a function, double-click the class name or folder icon.
Right pane	Displays a list of available definitions and references for the function selected in the left pane.	Double-click the definition or reference you want to see.
Pushpin	Determines whether or not the window disappears after it loses focus.	Select to push or pull the pin.
Help button	Displays help for the window.	Select for help.

Displaying a Graph of Calling Functions

A callers graph displays all the functions that call a selected function.

▶ **To display the graph of all functions that call a selected function**

1 Select the function name in a source file or the standard toolbar Find box.

2 From the Tools menu, choose Browse.

3 In the Select Query list box, select Callers Graph.

4 Choose the OK button.

5 If the function is an overloaded function or a member function of more than one class, the Resolve Ambiguity dialog box appears. Select the function that you want from the list.

The Callers Graph window appears, with the selected function displayed at the top of the left pane. Figure 16.6 shows the Callers Graph window for a sample function.

Figure 16.6   Callers Graph Window

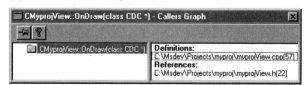

The following table describes the window elements, the function of each element, and the user's actions.

Table 16.6   Callers Graph Window

Window Element	Function	Action
Left pane	Displays the callers graph for the selected function.	Click the plus sign or minus sign to expand or contract the graph. To display information for a function, click the class name or folder icon. To open the source file for a function, double-click the class name or folder icon.
Right pane	Displays a list of available definitions and references for the function selected in the left pane.	Double-click the definition or reference you want to see.
Pushpin	Determines whether or not the window disappears after it loses focus.	Select to push or pull the pin.
Help button	Displays help for the window.	Select for help.

Finding Definitions and References

Browse windows make it easy to move from one location of a symbol in a file to another location in another file. For instance, if you are in a source file examining the use of a symbol, you can immediately jump to the definition of that symbol. Or if you have changed the definition of a symbol, you can jump to every place in every file where the symbol is used.

Note   The browse file is based on the state of the source files at the time of the last build. If you edit source files and then go to a definition or a reference, the location in the browse file may no longer be accurate. When you issue a query, if the browse file has not been built (or is not current), a dialog box is displayed with the option of building the browse file.

Displaying a Symbol Definition or Reference

You can quickly display the definition or reference of a symbol using the Browse toolbar. Developer Studio opens the source file containing the first definition or reference and highlights the symbol. To see the next definition or reference, choose the Next Ref./Def. button on the toolbar.

▶ **To display the definition or reference of a symbol using the Browse toolbar**

1 Select the symbol in a source file or the standard toolbar Find box.

   You can use the asterisk as a wildcard to match any string.

2 From the Browse toolbar, choose either the Go To Definition or Go To Reference button.

3 If the symbol is a member of more than one class, the Resolve Ambiguity dialog box appears. Select the symbol that you want from the list.

▶ To display the definition or reference of a symbol using the right mouse button

1 Point to the symbol in a source file (either a text editor window or the pane containing ClassView), and click the right mouse button.

2 From the pop-up menu, choose either Go To Definition or Go To Reference.

▶ To display the definition or reference of a symbol using the Go To dialog box

1 From the Edit menu, choose Go To.

2 In the Go To What list box, select either Definition or Reference.

3 Enter the additional selection criteria.

4 Choose one of the navigation buttons: Go To, Previous, or Next.

▶ To display the definition or reference of a symbol using the Definitions And References window

1 Select the symbol in a source file or the standard toolbar Find box.

You can use the asterisk as a wildcard to match any string.

2 From the Tools menu, choose Browse.

3 In the Select Query list box, select Definitions And References.

4 Choose the OK button.

5 If the symbol is a member of more than one class, the Resolve Ambiguity dialog box appears. Select the symbol that you want from the list.

6 In the Definitions And References window, double-click the definition or reference you want to see.

The Definitions And References window appears, with the selected symbol displayed at the top of the left pane. Figure 16.7 shows an example.

Figure 16.7   Definitions and References Window

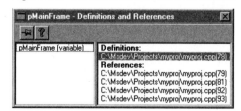

The following table describes the Definitions And References window elements, the function of each element, and the user's actions.

Table 16.7   Definitions and References Window

Window Element	Function	Action
Left pane	Displays the selected symbol, or a list of the matching symbols if you used a wildcard. If the symbol is not fully qualified, it is followed by the symbol's type.	To display information for a symbol, click the symbol name. To open the source file for a symbol, double-click the class name or folder icon.
Right pane	Displays definitions and references for the symbol currently selected in the left pane.	Double-click the definition or reference you want to see.
Pushpin	Determines whether or not the window disappears after it loses focus.	Select to push or pull the pin.
Help button	Displays help for the window.	Select for help.

Note   The browse file is based on the state of the source files at the time of the last build. If you edit source files and then go to a definition or a reference, the location in the browse file may no longer be accurate. When you issue a query, if the browse file has not been built (or is not current), a dialog box is displayed with the option of building the browse file.

Using the Debugger

Microsoft Developer Studio provides an integrated debugger to help locate bugs in an executable program, dynamic-link library (DLL), thread, or OLE client or server. Using the debugger, you can:

- Use multiple debug windows displaying the call stack, variables, memory contents, register contents, and assembly language code.

- Use Just-in-Time debugging to catch faults that occur while the program is running outside the development environment.

- Control and manage breakpoints.

- Control threads in multithreaded environments.

- Debug DLLs and OLE applications.

- Remotely debug programs operating on other operating systems.

Using the debugger, you can control the execution of your program and examine the program state at selected points through multiple windows and dialog boxes. You can set breakpoints to halt execution at critical locations or when a specified condition occurs.

When running a program with the debugger, you can single-step to observe the effects of your code. You can choose to enter a function call, using the Step Into command, or step past a function call, using the Step Over command. You can exit a called function and return to the calling statement using the Step Out command.

When you end a debugging session, the project retains any breakpoints you have set. When you reopen the project, the debugger restores the breakpoints in the proper locations. When the program is halted at a breakpoint, you can use the debug windows and dialog boxes to examine the state of your program.

Using the Debugger Interface Components

To use the debugger, you use interface components including menus, windows, dialog boxes, and spreadsheet fields. Drag-and-drop functionality is available for moving debug information between components. This chapter provides basic information to help you locate and operate these components.

Debugger Menu Items

Commands for debugging can be found on the Debug menu, the Build menu, the View menu, and the Edit menu.

The Debug menu appears in the menu bar while the debugger is running (even if it is stopped at a breakpoint). From the Debug menu, you can control program execution and access the QuickWatch window. When the debugger is not running, the Debug menu is replaced by the Build menu. The Build menu contains a command called Debug, which contains a subset of the commands on the full Debug menu. These commands start debugging (Go, Step Into, and Run To Cursor). For a description of the Debug menu commands and the Debug commands on the Build menu, see "Controlling Program Execution" on page 287 in this chapter.

The View menu contains commands that display the various debugger windows, such as the Variables window and the Memory window. For more information about the debugger windows, see "Viewing and Modifying Variables and Expressions" on page 307 in this chapter. From the Edit menu, you can access the Breakpoints dialog box, from which you can insert, remove, enable, or disable different types of breakpoints. For details, see "Using Breakpoints" on page 293 in this chapter.

The Edit menu contains a command to open the Breakpoint dialog to insert or edit a breakpoint.

A pop-up menu appears whenever you click the right mouse button in a debugger window. This menu provides commonly used commands applicable to that window.

Debugger Windows

Several specialized windows display debugging information for your program. When you are debugging, you can access these windows using the View menu.

Table 17.1 lists the debugger windows and describes the information they display.

Table 17.1   Debugger Windows

Window	Displays
Output	Information about the build process, including any compiler, linker, or build-tool errors, as well as output from the **OutputDebugString** function or the **afxDump** class library, thread termination codes, and first-chance exception notifications.
Watch	Names and values of variables and expressions.
Variables	Information about variables used in the current and previous statements and function return values (in the Auto tab), variables local to the current function (in the Locals tab), and the object pointed to by **this** (in the This tab).
Registers	Contents of the general purpose and CPU status registers.
Memory	Current memory contents.
Call Stack	Stack of all function calls that have not returned.
Disassembly	Assembly-language code derived from disassembly of the compiled program.

Debugger windows can be docked or floating. For information on docked and floating windows, see "Working with Docking Tool Windows," in Chapter 22, on page 433.

When a window is in floating mode, you can resize or minimize it to increase the visibility of other windows. You can copy information from any debugger window. You can print information only from the Output window.

 Tip   To set formatting and other options for these windows, use the Debug tab in the Options dialog box (accessed from the Tools menu).

Pop-up Menus

Each debugger window has a pop-up menu, which contains frequently used commands for that window.

▶ To display the pop-up menu for a window

- Click the right mouse button inside the window.

For example, if you click the right mouse button in the Variables window, you see a pop-up menu with several formatting options. If you click the right mouse button in a source/text window, you see a pop-up menu with several commands, including Insert/Remove Breakpoint. If you click a variable *Var* within a source window while you are debugging, the pop-up menu includes the command QuickWatch *Var*, which displays the variable *Var* in the QuickWatch dialog box.

Debugger Dialog Boxes

In addition to windows, the debugger uses a number of dialog boxes to manipulate breakpoints, variables, threads, and exceptions. You can access the Breakpoints dialog box using the Breakpoints command on the Edit menu. You can access the other dialog boxes using commands from the Debug menu.

Table 17.2 lists the debugger dialog boxes and describes the information they display.

Table 17.2 Debugger Dialog Boxes

Dialog Box	Displays
Breakpoints	List of all breakpoints assigned to your project. Use the tabs in the Breakpoints dialog box to create new breakpoints of various types.
Exceptions	System and user-defined exceptions for your project. Use the Exceptions dialog box to control how the debugger handles exceptions.
QuickWatch	A variable or expression. Use QuickWatch to quickly view or modify a variable or expression or to add it to the Watch window.
Threads	Application threads available for debugging. Use the Threads dialog box to suspend and resume threads and to set focus.

Spreadsheet Fields

The debugger interface uses spreadsheet fields, with an interface similar to that of Microsoft Excel. These spreadsheet fields appear in the Watch window, the Variables window, and the QuickWatch dialog box.

When working with these fields, you can autosize a column to fit its contents by double-clicking the divider. You can size a column manually by dragging the divider at the right edge of the column.

Note Rows fit the current font and cannot be resized. To change the font size, use the Format tab of the Options dialog box, accessed from the Tools menu.

Spreadsheet fields contain controls for easy viewing of array, object, structure, and pointer variables. These variables are marked with a box containing a plus sign (+) in the Name column. You can expand the variable by clicking the + box, which opens into a tree that may contain additional boxes.

If the variable is a pointer, the branch immediately below the pointer contains the value pointed to. If the variable is an array, object, or structure, the branch below the variable contains the component elements or members. When a variable is expanded, the box in the Name column contains a minus sign (−). You can collapse an expanded variable by clicking the − box. As an alternative, you can expand a variable by selecting it and pressing the PLUS SIGN or RIGHT ARROW key. You can collapse a variable by selecting it and pressing the MINUS SIGN or LEFT ARROW key.

Scalar variables, which have no components to expand, do not have boxes in the Name column.

▶ **To select a spreadsheet cell for editing**

1 Select the spreadsheet.

2 Use the UP ARROW and DOWN ARROW keys to move to the correct line.

3 To select the cell, press TAB to advance the selection to the next editable cell, or press SHIFT+TAB to move the selection back to the previous editable cell.

The window where the spreadsheet field is located determines which cells are editable. In the Variables window, you can edit the cells in the Value column. In the Watch window, you can edit the cells in the Name and Value columns.

Dragging and Dropping Debugger Information

You can move information between debugger windows using drag-and-drop or cut-and-paste features. When you select information and drag it with the mouse, the mouse pointer changes. A small gray rectangle appears at the base of the arrow to indicate that the information can be dropped. If you move the mouse pointer across a window or area that cannot accept a drop, the mouse pointer temporarily changes into the "No" symbol — a circle with a slash through it.

The debugger interface supports intelligent drag-and-drop. The result of a drag-and-drop operation depends, in part, on the location where the drop takes place.

For example, you can drag a variable from the Variables window to the Watch window. This action puts the variable information into the Watch window, where it is updated each time the Watch window is updated. If you drag the variable to a text window, instead, the variable information is converted into text. But if you drag the variable to the Memory window or the Disassembly window, the variable is used as a pointer, and the window scrolls to display the memory contents or instructions at the indicated address.

If you expand an object (Obj, for example) in the Variables window, you can drag a member of that object (such as Obj.child) to the Watch window.

Controlling Program Execution

To start debugging, choose the Go, Step Into, or Run To Cursor command under Debug on the Build menu. Table 17.3 lists the Build Debug menu commands and their actions.

Table 17.3 Build Menu Debug Commands

Build Menu Command	Action
Go	Executes code from the current statement until a breakpoint is reached or the end of the program is reached. (Equivalent to the Go button on the toolbar.)
Step Into	Single-steps through instructions in the program, and enters each function call that is encountered.
Run to Cursor	Executes the program as far as the line that contains the insertion point. This is equivalent to setting a temporary breakpoint at the insertion point location.

When you begin debugging, the Debug menu appears, replacing the Build menu on the menu bar. You can then control program execution using the commands listed in Table 17.4.

Table 17.4 Debug Menu Commands that Control Program Execution

Debug Menu Command	Action
Go	Executes code from the current statement until a breakpoint is reached or the end of the program is reached. (Equivalent to the Go button on the Standard toolbar.) When the Debug menu is not available, you can choose from Go from the Debug submenu of the Build menu.
Restart	Resets execution to the first line of the program. This command reloads the program into memory, and discards the current values of all variables (breakpoints and watch expressions still apply). It automatically halts at the **main()** or **WinMain()** function.
Stop Debugging	Terminates the debugging session, and returns to a normal editing session.
Break	Halts the program at its current location.
Step Into	Single-steps through instructions in the program, and enters each function call that is encountered. When the Debug menu is not available, you can choose Step Into from the Debug submenu of the Build menu.
Step Over	Single-steps through instructions in the program. If this command is used when you reach a function call, the function is executed without stepping through the function instructions.

Table 17.4   Debug Menu Commands that Control Program Execution *(continued)*

Debug Menu Command	Action
Step Out	Executes the program out of a function call, and stops on the instruction immediately following the call to the function. Using this command, you can quickly finish executing the current function after determining that a bug is not present in the function.
Run to Cursor	Executes the program as far as the line that contains the insertion point. This command is equivalent to setting a temporary breakpoint at the insertion point location. When the Debug menu is not available, you can choose Run To Cursor from the Debug submenu of the Build menu.

Running to a Location

▶ **To run until a breakpoint is reached**

• From the Debug menu, choose Go.

▶ **To run to the cursor**

1 Open a source file, and move the insertion point to the location where you want the debugger to break.

2 From the Debug menu, choose Run To Cursor.

The Run To Cursor command also works in the Call Stack window, the Disassembly window, and the Find box on the standard toolbar.

▶ **To run to the cursor location in object code**

1 In the Disassembly window, move the insertion point to the location where you want the debugger to break.

2 From the Debug menu, choose Run To Cursor.

▶ **To run to the cursor location in the call stack**

1 In the Call Stack window, select the function name.

2 From the Debug menu, choose Run To Cursor.

▶ **To run to a specified function**

1 In the Find box on the standard toolbar, type the function name.

2 From the Debug menu, choose Run To Cursor.

 Tip   You can use the Run To Cursor command to return to an earlier statement to retest your application, using different values for variables.

You can use the Set Next Statement command to set the next statement or assembly instruction to execute.

▶ **To set the next statement to execute**

1 In a source window, move the insertion point to the statement or instruction that you want to execute next.

2 Click the right mouse button.

3 From the pop-up menu, choose Set Next Statement.

▶ **To set the next assembly instruction to execute**

1 In the Disassembly window, move the insertion point to the assembly instruction you want to execute next.

2 Click the right mouse button.

3 From the pop-up menu, choose Set Next Statement.

 Tip You can use the Set Next Statement command to skip a section of code—for instance, a section that contains a known bug—and continue debugging other sections.

Caution The Set Next Statement command causes the CPU program counter to jump to the new location. The intervening code is not executed. Use this command with caution.

Stepping Into Functions

Once your program has stopped at a breakpoint, you can step through the code one statement at a time using the Step Into command from the Debug menu or the Step Into button on the Debug toolbar.

▶ **To run the program and execute the next statement (Step Into)**

1 While the program is paused at a breakpoint, choose Step Into from the Debug menu.

The debugger executes the next statement, then pauses execution. If the next statement is a function call, the debugger steps into that function, then pauses execution at the beginning of the function.

2 Repeat step 1 to continue executing the program one statement at a time.

If you use this technique to step into a nested function call, the debugger steps into the most deeply nested function. Consider, for example, the following line of code:

```
Fun(Fun2);
```

If you use the Step Into command, the debugger steps into the function Fun2, then pauses. If you use the Step Into Specific Function command instead, you can control which function the debugger steps into. In the following example, you can use the Step Into Specific Function command to step into Fun without first stepping through Fun2.

▶ **To step into a specific function**

1 Set a breakpoint just before the nested function call

–or–

Use the Step Into, Step Over, or Run To Cursor command to advance the program execution to that point.

2 In a source window, select the function that you want to step into.

3 From the Debug menu, or from the source window pop-up menu, choose Step Into *Name*, where *Name* is the name of the selected function.

The debugger executes the function call and pauses execution at the beginning of the selected function.

For example, if you want to step into the function Fun in this nested function call:

```
Fun(Fun2);
```

select the function name Fun and choose Step Into Fun from the Debug menu.

The Step Into Specific Function command works for any number of nesting levels. In the following statement, for example, you can select Fun, Fun2, or Fun3, and step into the selected function:

```
Fun(Fun2(Fun3));
```

In some cases, you can use the Step Into Specific Function command to step into a function pointer or a member function. In the following call, for example, you might use it to step into MemberFn:

```
CMyClass::MemberFn();
```

Note   Because function pointers and member functions are bound at run time, the binding can change before a function call occurs. As a result, it is not always possible to step into a function pointer or member function.

Using Step Into with SendMessage and DispatchMessage

When the debugger is stopped on a line of source code with a call to the **SendMessage** or **DispatchMessage** function, you can use the Step Into command to step into the WndProc called by the function. To avoid stepping into the WndProc, use the Step Over command instead.

Although **SendMessage** and **DispatchMessage** are the most common applications of this feature, you can also step into the following WndProc functions:

- **SendMessageTimeout**
- **SendMessageCallback**
- **SendNotifyMessage**

- **SendDlgItemMessage**
- **CallWindowProc**

Note If the source for the target WndProc is not available, the debugger cannot step into the WndProc.

Stepping Over or Out of Routines

You can step through your program one statement at a time in a chosen function, starting from a breakpoint, without entering any other functions, by using the Step Over command. You can also exit from a function immediately and return to the line where the function was called by using the Step Out command.

Caution In general, to avoid very slow execution, you should not step out of a function containing a loop. Instead, you should set a breakpoint at the end of the function, and then choose Go from the Debug menu to execute to the end of the function.

▶ **To run the next statement in the current function**

1 Open a source file, and set a breakpoint in the function.

2 From the Debug menu, choose Go.

When the program comes to the breakpoint, the debugger pauses.

3 From the Debug menu, choose Step Over.

The debugger executes the next function, but pauses after the function returns.

4 Repeat step 3 to continue executing the program, one statement at a time.

You can stop the debugger after it has executed the return statement in a function. It stops on the line following the function call.

▶ **To run the program and stop execution after the current function returns to the calling function**

1 Open a source file, and set a breakpoint in the function.

2 From the Debug menu, choose Go.

When the program comes to the breakpoint, the debugger pauses.

3 From the Debug menu, choose Step Out.

The debugger continues until it has completed execution of the return from the current function, then pauses.

Interrupting Your Program

There may be times when you cannot set a breakpoint to halt the program, such as when your program encounters an infinite loop. In such cases, you can interrupt your program by choosing Break on the Debug menu. This action returns control to

Microsoft Developer Studio and opens the Disassembly window. You can then use the Go, Step Into, or Step Over commands to regain control of your program.

With Win32s, you must press the CTRL+SHIFT+F11 key combination on the remote computer to return control to Developer Studio.

Note   If you interrupt execution while Windows or other system code is running, the results can be unpredictable.

Just-in-Time Debugging

Using Microsoft Developer Studio, you can edit, compile, link, debug, and test a program within a single integrated environment. Sometimes, however, you may want to test a program outside of Developer Studio. With Just-in-Time debugging, you can run a program outside Developer Studio. When an application error occurs, it calls the Developer Studio debugger.

To use Just-in-Time debugging, you must set the Just-in-Time debugging option before you execute your program. If you do not set this option, the debugger cannot respond to an application error that occurs in your program.

▶ **To enable Just-in-Time debugging**

1 From the Tools menu, choose Options.

2 Select the Debug tab.

3 Select the Just-in-Time Debugging check box.

4 Choose OK.

5 From the Build menu, choose Build *Project*.exe.

Note   If you are running Windows NT, you must have administrator privileges to set the Just-in-Time option.

Using Breakpoints

Breakpoints tell the debugger where or when to break execution of a program. When the program is halted at a breakpoint, you can examine the state of your program, step through your code, and evaluate expressions using the debugger windows.

The debugger supports the following types of breakpoints:

- Location breakpoints that halt the debugger at a specified location
- Data breakpoints that halt the debugger when an expression becomes true or changes value
- Message breakpoints that halt the debugger at a WndProc function when a message is received

- Conditional breakpoints that halt the debugger at a specified location when an expression is true or changes value

The Breakpoints dialog box displays a list of all breakpoints set in the project. You can use this dialog box to set, remove, disable, and enable breakpoints. When you close a project, the debugger saves all breakpoints you have set as part of the project information. The next time you open the project, the breakpoints remain as you left them.

The debugger also provides quick methods for setting location breakpoints and data breakpoints without using the Breakpoints dialog box.

Quick Methods for Location Breakpoints

The most common type of breakpoint is a location breakpoint. With the debugger, you can set location breakpoints:

- On a specific line of source code.
- At the beginning or the return point of a function.
- At a label.
- At a specified memory address.

You can set or remove any of these location breakpoints without using the Breakpoints dialog box. You can disable and enable breakpoints on a source-code line or in the Disassembly or Call Stack window.

▸ **To set a breakpoint at a source-code line**

1 In a source window, move the insertion point to the line where you want the program to break.

2 Choose the Insert/Remove Breakpoint toolbar button.

A red dot appears in the left margin, indicating that the breakpoint is set.

Note If you want to set a breakpoint on a source statement extending across three or more lines, you must set the breakpoint on the first or last line of the statement.

▸ **To set a breakpoint at the beginning of a function**

1 In the Find box on the Standard toolbar, type the function name, and press ENTER.

2 Choose the Insert/Remove Breakpoint toolbar button.

–or–

Click the right mouse button, and choose Insert/Remove Breakpoint from the pop-up menu.

In the source code, a red dot appears in the left margin at the beginning of the function, indicating that the breakpoint is set.

▶ **To set a breakpoint at the return point of a function**

1 In the Call Stack window, move the insertion point to the function where you want the program to break.

−or−

Click the right mouse button, and choose Insert/Remove Breakpoint from the pop-up menu.

2 Choose the Insert/Remove Breakpoint toolbar button.

A red dot appears in the left margin, indicating that the breakpoint is set.

▶ **To set a breakpoint at a label**

1 In the Find box on the Standard toolbar, type the name of the label, and press ENTER.

−or−

Click the right mouse button, and choose Insert/Remove Breakpoint from the pop-up menu.

2 Choose the Insert/Remove Breakpoint toolbar button.

A red dot appears in the left margin at the line containing the label, indicating that the breakpoint is set.

▶ **To set a breakpoint at a memory address**

1 In the Disassembly window, move the insertion point to the line where you want the program to break.

2 Choose the Insert/Remove Breakpoint toolbar button.

−or−

Click the right mouse button, and choose Insert/Remove Breakpoint from the pop-up menu.

A red dot appears in the left margin, indicating that the breakpoint is set.

▶ **To disable a breakpoint**

1 In a source window, or in the Call Stack or Disassembly window, move the insertion point to the line containing the breakpoint you want to disable.

2 Choose the Enable/Disable Breakpoint toolbar button.

−or−

Click the right mouse button, and choose Disable Breakpoint from the pop-up menu.

The red dot in the left margin changes to a hollow circle.

▶ **To disable all breakpoints**

• Choose the Disable All Breakpoints toolbar button.

  The red dots in the left margin change to hollow circles.

▶ **To enable a breakpoint**

1 In a source window, or in the Call Stack or Disassembly window, move the insertion point to the line containing the breakpoint you want to enable.

2 Choose the Enable/Disable Breakpoint toolbar button.

  −or−

  Click the right mouse button, and choose Enable Breakpoint from the pop-up menu.

  The hollow circle in the left margin changes to a red dot.

Note If you set more than one breakpoint on a line, and some breakpoints are disabled while others are enabled, a gray dot appears in the left margin. The first time you choose the Enable/Disable Breakpoint toolbar button, all breakpoints on the line become disabled, and the gray dot changes to a hollow circle. If you choose the Enable/Disable Breakpoint button again, all breakpoints on the line become enabled, and the hollow circle changes to a red dot.

▶ **To remove a breakpoint**

1 In a source window, or in the Call Stack or Disassembly window, move the insertion point to the line containing the breakpoint you want to remove.

2 Choose the Insert/Remove Breakpoint toolbar button.

  −or−

  Click the right mouse button, and choose Remove Breakpoint from the pop-up menu.

  The red dot in the left margin disappears.

Note If a line contains enabled and disabled breakpoints, the Insert/Remove Breakpoint button removes all enabled breakpoints. Disabled breakpoints are not affected

Quick Methods for Data Breakpoints

Without using the Breakpoints dialog box, you can set two types of data breakpoints: breakpoints that halt execution when a variable changes value, and breakpoints that halt execution when an expression evaluates to true.

▶ **To set a breakpoint when a variable changes value**

1 In the Find box on the Standard toolbar, type the name of the variable.

2 Choose the Insert/Remove Breakpoint toolbar button.

  A red dot appears in the margin, indicating that the breakpoint is set.

▶ **To set a breakpoint when an expression is true**

1 In the Find box on the Standard toolbar, type an expression, such as Fun==3, that evaluates to true or false.

2 Choose the Insert/Remove Breakpoint toolbar button.

   A red dot appears in the margin, indicating that the breakpoint is set.

To set other types of data breakpoints, or to remove a data breakpoint, use the Breakpoints dialog box.

Using the Breakpoints Dialog Box

Using the Breakpoints dialog box, accessed by the Breakpoints command on the Edit menu, you can set, remove, disable, enable, or view:

- Location breakpoints
- Data breakpoints
- Message breakpoints
- Conditional breakpoints

The Breakpoints dialog box contains three tabs that correspond to the first three types of breakpoints listed above. The Location tab is also used, together with the Breakpoint Condition dialog box, to set conditional breakpoints.

Location breakpoints are set at a specific line of source code, the start of a function, or a specified memory address. They break execution of the program when the location counter reaches that point in the program.

Data breakpoints are set on a variable or expression. They break execution when the value of the variable or expression changes, or (for a boolean expression) when the value becomes true.

Message breakpoints are set on a WndProc. They break execution when a specified message is received.

Conditional breakpoints are location breakpoints that break execution only if a specified condition is true. (Data breakpoints can also have a length condition attached to them, but this is not set in the Breakpoint Condition dialog box. Thus, they are not considered conditional breakpoints for the purposes of this discussion.)

All four types of breakpoints appear in the Breakpoints list at the bottom of the Breakpoints dialog box.

The Breakpoints List

The Breakpoints dialog box contains a list of all breakpoints currently set in your program. You can use this list to examine all breakpoints in your program, to disable breakpoints, or to enable breakpoints that you previously disabled. You can also use the list to remove (delete) a breakpoint.

▶ **To view the list of current breakpoints**

1 From the Edit menu, choose Breakpoints.

The Breakpoints dialog box appears.

2 Use the scroll bars to move up or down the Breakpoints list.

▶ **To disable a breakpoint**

1 In the Breakpoints dialog box, find the breakpoint in the Breakpoints list.

2 Clear the check box corresponding to the breakpoint that you want to disable.

3 Choose OK.

For a location breakpoint, the red dot in the left margin changes to a hollow circle.

▶ **To enable a breakpoint**

1 In the Breakpoints dialog box, find the breakpoint in the Breakpoints list.

2 Select the empty check box corresponding to the breakpoint that you want to enable.

3 Choose OK.

For a location breakpoint, the red dot in the left margin changes to a hollow circle.

 Tip You can also use the SPACEBAR to toggle the state of a breakpoint in the Breakpoints list.

Note An asterisk (*) in the breakpoint check box indicates that the breakpoint is not supported on the current platform.

▶ **To remove a breakpoint**

1 In the Breakpoints dialog box, select one or more breakpoints in the Breakpoints list.

2 Choose the Remove button.

–or–

Press the DELETE key.

3 Choose OK.

When you select a breakpoint in the Breakpoints list, the breakpoint information automatically appears in the text box of the Location, Data, or Messages tab (depending on the breakpoint type). You can edit the breakpoint using the procedures described in the section for that tab.

Note For a location breakpoint, you can use the Edit Code button to navigate to the source or object code where the breakpoint is set.

▶ **To view the source code or disassembled object code where a breakpoint is set**

1 In the Breakpoints list, select a line-number or memory-address breakpoint.

2 Choose the Edit Code button.

This action takes you to the source code for a breakpoint set at a line number, or to the disassembled object code for a breakpoint set at a memory address.

The Location Breakpoints Tab

You can use the Location tab in the Breakpoints dialog box to set a location breakpoint:

• On a specific line of source code.

• At a label.

• At the start of a function.

• At a specified memory address.

Note Except where noted, the following procedures work only within the current context (function, source file, or executable). To set a breakpoint outside the current context, you must specify the context using the Advanced Breakpoint dialog box.

▶ **To set a breakpoint at the current location**

1 From the Edit menu, choose Breakpoints.

The Breakpoints dialog box appears.

2 Select the Location tab.

3 Select the drop-down arrow next to the Break At text box.

4 From the menu that appears, choose the current line number or memory location.

5 Choose OK to set the breakpoint.

Note If you want to set a breakpoint on a source statement extending across three or more lines, you must set the breakpoint on the first or last line of the statement.

▶ **To set a breakpoint at another location**

1 On the Location tab, type a source-code line number (if the current location is in a source file) or memory address directly into the Break At text box. For source locations, type a period immediately before the line number.

2 Choose OK to set the breakpoint.

Note If you want to set a breakpoint on a source statement extending across three or more lines, you must set the breakpoint on the first or last line of the statement.

▶ **To set a breakpoint at a label**

1 In the Location tab, type the name of the label in the Break At text box.

2 Choose OK to set the breakpoint.

▶ **To set a breakpoint at the beginning of the current function**

1 In the Location tab, click on the drop-down menu next to the Break At box.

2 From the menu choose the current function name that appears.

3 Choose OK to set the breakpoint.

> **Note** If the debugger is halted in disassembled object code, rather than source code, this option is not available.

▶ **To set a breakpoint at the beginning of another function**

1 In the Location tab, type the function name directly into the Break At text box.

2 Choose OK to set the breakpoint.

▶ **To set a breakpoint outside the current context**

1 In the Breakpoints dialog box, select the Location tab.

2 Select the drop-down arrow next to the Break At text box.

3 From the menu that appears, choose Advanced. The Advanced Breakpoint dialog box appears.

4 In the Location text box, type the location (source line number, memory address, or function name) where you want to set the breakpoint.

5 Under Context, type any necessary information in the Function, Source File, and Executable File text boxes. (It is not necessary to fill in all fields —only the ones you need to qualify the context.

For example, to set a breakpoint at a line number in another source file, specify only the source file. To set a breakpoint in a dynamic-link library (DLL), you must specify the function, source file, and DLL. The DLL filename goes in the Executable File text box.)

6 Choose OK to close the Advanced Breakpoint dialog box.

The information that you specified appears in the Break At text box in the Breakpoints dialog box.

7 Choose OK to set the breakpoint.

> **Note** You can enter context information directly into the Break At text box, using the advanced breakpoints syntax. For details, see "Advanced Breakpoint Syntax" on page 306 in this chapter.

▶ **To edit a location breakpoint**

1 In the Location tab, select the location breakpoint in the breakpoints list.

2 Edit the location that appears in the Break At text box.

3 Choose OK to set the breakpoint.

The Data Breakpoints Tab

You can use the Data tab in the Breakpoints dialog box to set a breakpoint on a variable or expression. A data breakpoint breaks execution of the program when the value of the variable or expression changes or (for a boolean expression) when the value becomes true. The debugger automatically knows which option ("changes" or "becomes true") makes sense for the variable or expression you have entered — you don't need to set this yourself.

You can set a breakpoint on any valid C or C++ expression. Breakpoint expressions can also use memory addresses and register mnemonics. The debugger interprets all constants as decimal numbers unless they begin with '0' (octal) or '0x' (hexadecimal).

Note   Except where noted, the following procedures work only for variables within the current scope. To set a breakpoint using a variable outside the current scope, you must specify the context using the Advanced Breakpoint dialog box.

▶ **To break when a variable changes value**

1 From the Edit menu, choose Breakpoints.

The Breakpoints dialog box appears.

2 Select the Data tab.

3 In the Enter The Expression To Be Evaluated text box, type the variable name, such as Var2 or obj.mem.

4 Choose OK to set the breakpoint.

▶ **To break when an expression is true**

1 In the Expression text box, type an expression that contains a boolean comparison operator, such as x==1 or y<7.

2 Choose OK to set the breakpoint.

▶ **To break when an expression changes value**

1 In the Expression text box, type an expression such as x+y.

2 Choose OK to set the breakpoint.

▶ **To break on a variable outside the current scope**

1 In the Expression text box, type the variable name.

2 Select the drop-down arrow to the right of the text box.

3 From the menu that appears, choose Advanced.

The Advanced Breakpoint dialog box appears.

4 In the Expression text box, type the function name and (if necessary) the filename of the variable.

5 Choose OK to close the Advanced Breakpoint dialog box.

The information that you specified appears in the Expression text box in the Breakpoints dialog box.

6 In the Breakpoints dialog box, choose OK to set the breakpoint.

Note You can enter context information directly into the Expression field, using the advanced breakpoints syntax. For details, see "Advanced Breakpoint Syntax" on page 306.

To set a breakpoint on an array, use the Number Of Elements text box on the Data tab. The number you enter in this field determines how many elements of the array the debugger will monitor. Here are some examples of how to use this field:

▶ **To break when the initial element of an array changes value**

1 In the Expression text box, type the first element of the array (myArray[0], for example).

2 In the Number Of Elements text box, type 1.

3 Choose OK to set the breakpoint on myArray [0].

▶ **To break when the initial element of an array has a specific value**

1 In the Expression text box, type an expression containing the initial element of the array (myArray[0]==1, for example).

2 In the Number Of Elements text box, type 1.

3 Choose OK to set the breakpoint on myArray [0].

▶ **To break when the twelfth element of an array changes value**

1 In the Expression text box, type the twelfth element of the array (myArray[12], for example).

2 In the Number Of Elements text box, type 1.

3 Choose OK to set the breakpoint on myArray [12].

▶ **To break when any element of an array changes value**

1 In the Expression text box, type the first element of the array (myArray[0]).

2 In the Number Of Elements text box, type 1.

3 Choose OK to set the breakpoint on myArray.

▶ **To break when any of the first 10 elements of an array change value**

1 In the Expression text box, type the first element of the array (myArray[0], for example).

2 In the Number Of Elements text box, type 10.

3 Choose OK to set the breakpoint on `myArray[0]` through `myArray[10]`.

If you set a breakpoint on a pointer variable, the debugger does not automatically dereference the pointer. If you want to set a breakpoint on the value pointed to, instead of the location pointed to, you must explicitly dereference the pointer, as described in the following procedures. (These procedures also apply to structure pointers.)

▶ **To break when the location value of a pointer changes**

1 In the Expression text box, type the pointer variable name (p, for example).

2 Choose OK to set the breakpoint.

▶ **To break when the value at a location pointed to changes**

1 In the Expression text box, type the dereferenced pointer variable name (`*p` or `p->next`, for example).

2 Choose OK to set the breakpoint.

▶ **To break when an array pointed to by a pointer changes**

1 In the Expression text box, type the dereferenced pointer variable name (`*p`, for example).

2 In the Number Of Elements text box, type the length of the array in elements. For example, if the pointer is a pointer to **double**, and the array pointed to contains 100 values of type **double**, type `100`.

3 Choose OK to set the breakpoint.

In addition to C/C++ variable names, you can use memory addresses and registers in your breakpoint expressions. The following examples show how to use memory addresses and registers.

▶ **To break when the value at a specified memory address changes**

1 In the Expression text box, type the memory address for the byte.

For a word or doubleword memory address, enclose the address in parentheses, and precede it with a cast operator. For example, `WO(00406036)` for the word at memory location 00406036. Use the cast operator `BY` for a byte (optional), `WO` for a word, or `DW` for a doubleword.

2 In the Number Of Elements text box, type the number of bytes, words, or doublewords to monitor. If you used the `BY` operator in the Expression field, specify the number of bytes. If you used `WO`, specify the number of words. If you used `DW`, specify the number of doublewords.

3 Choose OK to set the breakpoint.

▶ **To break when a register changes**

1 In the Expression text box, type a register mnemonic, such as `CS`.

2 In the Number Of Elements text box, type the number of bytes to monitor.

3 Choose OK to set the breakpoint.

▶ **To break when a register expression is true**

1 In the Expression text box, type an expression that contains a boolean comparison operator, such as `CS==0`.

2 In the Number Of Elements text box, type the number of bytes to monitor.

3 Choose OK to set the breakpoint.

Note When you set a data breakpoint, the debugger places the variable or variables used into a special debug register, if possible. The number of debug registers is limited. (Intel 80386 and later CPUs provide four debug registers. Motorola 680X0 and PowerPC chips have no debug registers.) Furthermore, stacked-based variables (parameters) cannot be placed into debug registers. If a breakpoint variable cannot be placed into a debug register, the debugger must examine the variable's memory location after every instruction to determine whether the contents have changed. These extra memory accesses reduce execution speed of the program with the debugger. In some cases, the program may appear to hang. Performance may be especially slow if you are debugging a remote application.

The Messages Breakpoints Tab

You can use the Messages tab in the Breakpoints dialog box to set a breakpoint on a message received by an exported Windows function. You can select whether to break on a specific message or on any message from a class of messages.

Note Message breakpoints work only on x86- or Pentium-based systems.

▶ **To set a breakpoint on a message**

1 From the Edit menu, choose Breakpoints.

The Breakpoints dialog box appears.

2 Select the Messages tab.

3 In the Break At WndProc text box, type the name of the Windows function.

If you are setting a breakpoint during a debug session, the list contains the exported functions in your project.

4 In the Set One Breakpoint For Each Message To Watch drop-down list box, select the message.

5 To set another breakpoint, press ENTER, and then repeat steps 3 and 4.

The Breakpoints list displays the currently active breakpoints.

6 Choose OK to set the breakpoints.

Conditional Breakpoints

Conditional breakpoints are location breakpoints that break execution only if a specified condition is met. This condition can be:

- When the value of the variable or expression changes, or
- When the value of a boolean expression is true.

To set conditional breakpoints, use the Breakpoint Condition dialog box. This dialog box appears when you choose the Condition button on the Location tab.

The Breakpoint Condition dialog box looks and operates much like the Data tab, with one additional field. The Enter The Number Of Times To Skip Before Stopping text box allows the debugger to skip the breakpoint a specified number of times. If you type 4 in this text box, for example, the debugger stops the fifth time your program reaches that location and the condition is met. If you set this field to 9, the debugger stops the tenth time your program reaches that location and the condition is met.

▶ To set a conditional breakpoint

1 From the Edit menu, choose Breakpoints.

The Breakpoints dialog box appears.

2 Select the Location tab.

3 In the Break At text box, type a location as described in "Location Breakpoints Tab" on page 299.

4 Choose the Condition button.

The Breakpoint Condition dialog box appears.

5 Fill in the Expression and Number Of Elements text boxes as you would for a data breakpoint. (See "Data Breakpoints Tab" on page 301 of this chapter for detailed information.)

6 In the Breakpoint Condition dialog box, choose OK to set the condition.

7 In the Breakpoints dialog box, choose OK to set the breakpoint.

▶ To set a conditional breakpoint with a skip count

1 In the Breakpoints dialog box, select the Location tab.

2 In the Break At text box, type a location as described in "Location Breakpoints Tab" on page 299.

3 Choose the Condition button.

The Breakpoint Condition dialog box appears.

4 Fill in the Expression and Number Of Elements text boxes, as you would for a data breakpoint. (See "Data Breakpoints Tab" on page 301 of this chapter for detailed information.)

5 Fill in the Enter The Numbers Of Times To Skip Before Stopping text box. If you want your program to break every Nth time the condition is met at the specified location, set the Enter The Numbers Of Times To Skip Before Stopping to N - 1. (The debugger skips the breakpoint the first N times.)

6 In the Breakpoint Condition dialog box, choose OK to set the condition.

7 In the Breakpoints dialog box, choose OK to set the breakpoint.

You cannot set both Enter The Numbers Of Times To Skip Before Stopping and Number Of Elements for the same breakpoint.

Advanced Breakpoint Syntax

If you want to set a breakpoint on a location or variable that is not within the current scope, there are two ways to do it:

- Use the Advanced Breakpoint dialog box.

- Specify the breakpoint directly on the Location or Data tab of the Breakpoints dialog box, using advanced breakpoint syntax.

Both methods achieve the same result, but the Advanced Breakpoint dialog box handles many details for you and does not require you to learn any special syntax.

To use advanced breakpoints syntax, you must qualify a breakpoint location or variable with a special context operator, as follows:

- {[*function*],[*source*],[*exe*]}*location*

- {[*function*],[*source*],[*exe*]}*variable_name*

- {[*function*],[*source*],[*exe*]}*expression*

The context operator is a pair of braces ({ }) containing two commas, and some combination of function name, source filename, and executable filename. If you omit either *function* or *exe*, the two commas cannot be omitted. The following syntax, for example, is illegal:

```
{File.c, File.exe}.143 —Bad
```

If you omit both *source* and *exe*, however, you can omit the commas. The following syntax is legal:

```
{Fun}.143
```

The *location* can be any line number, function, or memory address at which you can set a breakpoint. For example,

- {[*function*],[*source*],[*exe*]}.100 —A line number

- {[*function*],[*source*],[*exe*]} Traverse —A function name
- {[*function*],[*source*],[*exe*]} CMyWindow::OnCall —A function name
- {[*function*],[*source*],[*exe*]} 00406030 —A memory address (decimal)
- {[*function*],[*source*],[*exe*]} 0x1002A —A memory address (hexadecimal)

If the *source* or *exe* filename includes a comma, an embedded space, or a brace, you must use quotation marks around the filename so that the context parser can properly recognize the string. Single quotation marks are considered to be part of a Windows NT/Windows 95 filename, so you must use double quotation marks. For example,

{,"a long, long, name.c", }.143

Another form of advanced breakpoints syntax uses the exclamation point instead of the context operator:

source!.location

This form of advanced breakpoint syntax does not include a function name or .EXE specifier. If you use this syntax to specify a filename that contains an exclamation point, you must surround the filename with double quotes:

"File.!c"!.115

Viewing and Modifying Variables and Expressions

The debugger provides several ways to view the value of a variable or expression:

- DataTips Pop-up Information™
- QuickWatch
- The Watch window
- The Variables window

It also provides several ways to modify the value of a variable:

- QuickWatch
- The Watch window
- The Variables window

Using DataTips Pop-up Information

The easiest way to see the value of a variable or expression when the debugger is stopped at a breakpoint is to use DataTips pop-up information.

You can view a DataTips pop-up information box for any variable or expression that appears in a source window and is within the current scope. To see a pop-up box for a variable, place the mouse pointer over the variable. To see a pop-up box for an expression, select the expression.

DataTips pop-up information is not available for invalid expressions, such as a division by zero. If you select an expression such as 1/0, no pop-up information box appears.

Using QuickWatch

You can use QuickWatch to quickly examine the value of a variable or expression. You can also use QuickWatch to modify the value of a variable or to add a variable or expression to the Watch window.

The QuickWatch dialog box contains a text box, where you can type an expression or variable name, and a spreadsheet field that displays the current value of the variable or expression that you specified.

The Current Value spreadsheet field displays only one variable or expression at a time. If you type a new variable or expression in the text box and press ENTER, the previous variable or expression in the Current Value field is replaced.

If you type a scalar variable or expression in the text box, QuickWatch displays the result on the first line of the spreadsheet. If you type an array, object, or structure variable, however, QuickWatch uses the spreadsheet to show additional detail. Plus sign (+) and minus sign (-) boxes appear. Click these boxes to expand or collapse your view of the variable.

If the variable is an object or a pointer to an object, QuickWatch automatically expands the variable to show the most important data at the top level. For example, suppose you had the following object:

```
CString String  =   {...}
char *   m_pchData =0x7ffdf000 "abc"
    int          m_nDataLength=4
    int          m_nAllocLength=1244628
```

QuickWatch would display the following:

```
CString String  =   {"abc"}
```

If the variable is a pointer to a C++ object, QuickWatch automatically downcasts the pointer. QuickWatch adds an extra member to the expanded object. This extra member, which looks like another base class, indicates the derived subclass. For example, if a variable declared as a pointer to **CObject** really points to **CComboBox**, QuickWatch recognizes this fact and adds an extra member so that you can access the **CComboBox** members.

QuickWatch displays values in their default format. You can change the display format (to display Unicode characters, for example) using formatting symbols. For details, see "Formatting Watch Variables" on page 312.

▶ **To view the value of a variable or expression using QuickWatch**

1 Wait for the debugger to stop at a breakpoint.

–or–

On an x86- or Pentium-based computer, choose Break from the Debug menu to halt the debugger.

2 From the Debug menu, choose QuickWatch.

The QuickWatch dialog box appears.

3 Type or paste the variable name or expression into the Expression text box.

4 Choose the Recalculate button.

5 Choose the Close button.

 Tip   The Expression drop-down list box contains the most recently used QuickWatch expressions.

▶ **To quickly view the value of a variable using QuickWatch**

1 When the debugger is stopped at a breakpoint, switch to a source window, and click the right mouse button on a variable (*Var*, for example).

2 From the pop-up menu, choose QuickWatch *Var*.

3 Choose the Recalculate button.

4 Choose the Close button.

When the program is paused at a breakpoint or between steps, you can change the value of any non-**const** variable in your program. This gives you the flexibility to try out changes and see their results in real time or to recover from certain logic errors.

▶ **To modify the value of a variable using QuickWatch**

1 From the Debug menu, choose QuickWatch.

2 In the Expression text box, type the variable name.

3 Choose the Recalculate button.

4 If the variable is an array, object, or structure, use the + box to expand the view until you see the value you want to modify.

5 Use the TAB key to move to the value you want to modify.

6 Type the new value, and then press ENTER.

7 Choose the Close button.

 Tip   To change the value of a structure or array (including strings), modify the individual fields or elements. You cannot edit an entire array or structure at once.

▶ **To add a QuickWatch variable or expression to the Watch window**

1 Use any of the procedures described previously to view the variable or expression in QuickWatch.

2 Choose the Add Watch button.

Using the Watch Window

Use the Watch window to specify variables and expressions that you want to watch while debugging your program. You can also modify the value of a variable using the Watch window.

The Watch window contains four tabs: Watch1, Watch2, Watch3, and Watch4. Each tab displays a user-specified list of variables and expressions in a spreadsheet field. You can group variables that you want to watch together onto the same tab. For example, you could put variables related to a specific window on one tab and variables related to a dialog box on another tab. You could watch the first tab when debugging the window and the second tab when debugging the dialog box.

▶ **To add a variable or expression to the Watch window**

1 From the View menu, choose Watch.

The Watch window appears.

2 Select a tab for the variable or expression.

3 Type, paste, or drag the variable name or expression into the Name column on the tab.

4 Press ENTER.

The Watch window evaluates the variable or expression immediately and displays the value or an error message.

If you add an array, object, or structure variable to the Watch window, plus sign (+) or minus sign (–) boxes appear in the Name column. You can use these boxes to expand or collapse your view of the variable, as described in "Spreadsheet Fields" on page 286.

If the variable is an object or a pointer to an object, the Watch window automatically expands the variable to show the most important data at the top level. For example, suppose you had the following object:

```
CString String  =   {...}
char *   m_pchData =0x7ffdf000 "abc"
    int          m_nDataLength=4
    int          m_nAllocLength=1244628
```

The Watch window displays the following:

```
String  =   {"abc"}
```

If the variable is a pointer to a C++ object, the Watch window automatically downcasts the pointer. The Watch window adds an extra member to the expanded object. This extra member, which looks like another base class, indicates the derived subclass. For example, if a variable declared as a pointer to **CObject** really points to a **CComboBox**, the Watch window recognizes this fact and adds an extra member so that you can access the **CComboBox** members.

The Watch window displays values in their default format. You can change the display format (to display Unicode characters, for example) using formatting symbols. For details, see "Formatting Watch Variables" on page 312.

 Tip The Watch window does not display variable type information. You can view information for a variable type by using the window's property page.

▶ **To view type information for a variable**

1 In the Watch window, select the line containing the variable whose type you want to see.

2 Click the right mouse button in the Watch window and choose Properties from the pop-up menu.

   −or−

   From the Edit menu, choose Properties.

▶ **To remove a variable or expression from the Watch window**

1 In the Watch window, select the line containing the variable or expression you want to remove.

2 Press the DEL key.

When the program is paused at a breakpoint or between steps, you can change the value of any non-**const** variable in your program. This gives you the flexibility to try out changes and see their results in real time, or to recover from certain logic errors.

▶ **To modify the value of a variable using the Watch window**

1 In the Watch window, double-click the value.

   −or−

   Use the TAB key to move the insertion point to the value you want to modify.

2 If the variable is an array, object, or structure, use the + box to expand the view until you see the value you want to modify.

3 Type the new value, and press ENTER.

 Tip To change the value of a structure or array (including strings), modify the individual fields or elements. You cannot edit an entire array or structure at once.

Formatting Watch Variables

You can change the display format of variables in the QuickWatch dialog box or in the Watch window using the formatting symbols in the following table.

Symbol	Format	Value	Displays
d,i	**signed** decimal integer	0xF000F065	-268373915
u	**unsigned** decimal integer	0x0065	101
o	**unsigned** octal integer	0xF065	0170145
x,X	Hexadecimal integer	61541 (decimal)	0x0000F065
l,h	**long** or **short** prefix for: d, i, u, o, x, X	00406042,hx	0x0c22
f	**signed** floating-point	3./2.	1.500000
e	**signed** scientific notation	3./2.	1.500000e+000
g	**signed** floating-point or **signed** scientific notation, whichever is shorter	3./2.	1.5
c	Single character	0x0065	'e'
s	String	0x0012fde8	"Hello world"
su	Unicode string		"Hello world"

To use a formatting symbol, type the variable name, followed by a comma and the appropriate symbol. For example, if var has a value of 0x0065, and you want to see the value in character form, type var,c in the Name column on the tab of the Watch window. When you press ENTER, the character-format value appears:

```
var,c = 'e'
```

You can use the formatting symbols shown in the following table to format the contents of memory locations.

Symbol	Format	Displays
ma	64 ASCII characters	0x0012ffac .4...0...".0W&.......1W&.0.:W..1...."..1.JO &.1.2.."..1...0y....1
m	16 bytes in hexadecimal, followed by 16 ASCII characters	0x0012ffac B3 34 CB 00 84 30 94 80 FF 22 8A 30 57 26 00 00 .4...0...".0W&..
mb	16 bytes in hexadecimal, followed by 16 ASCII characters	0x0012ffac B3 34 CB 00 84 30 94 80 FF 22 8A 30 57 26 00 00 .4...0...".0W&..
mw	8 words	0x0012ffac 34B3 00CB 3084 8094 22FF 308A 2657 0000

Symbol	Format	Displays
md	4 doublewords	0x0012ffac 00CB34B3 80943084 308A22FF 00002657
mu	2-byte characters (Unicode)	0x0012fc60 8478 77f4 ffff ffff 0000 0000 0000 0000

With the memory location formatting symbols, you can type any value or expression that evaluates to a location.

To display the value of a character array as a string, precede the array name with an ampersand (&):

```
&yourname
```

A formatting character can follow an expression also:

```
rep+1,x
alps[0],mb
xloc,g
count,d
```

To watch the value at an address or the value pointed to by a register, use the **BY**, **WO**, or **DW** operator.

- **BY** returns the contents of the byte pointed to.
- **WO** returns the contents of the word pointed to.
- **DW** returns the contents of the doubleword pointed to.

Follow the operator with a variable, register, or constant. If the **BY**, **WO**, or **DW** operator is followed by a variable, then the environment watches the byte, word, or doubleword at the address contained in the variable.

You can also use the context operator { } to display the contents of any location.

To display a Unicode string in the Watch window or the QuickWatch dialog box, use the **su** format specifier. To display data bytes with Unicode characters in the Watch window or the QuickWatch dialog box, use the **mu** format specifier.

Note   You can apply formatting symbols to structures, arrays, pointers, and objects as unexpanded variables only. If you expand the variable, the specified formatting affects all members. You cannot apply formatting symbols to individual members.

Microsoft Developer Studio has autoexpand capability for Microsoft Foundation Class library classes. The string (or other information) between the braces ({ }) is automatically expanded.

Using the Variables Window

The Variables window provides quick access to variables that are important in the program's current context. The window includes three tabs:

- The Auto tab displays variables used in the current statement and the the previous statement. It also displays return values when you step over or out of a function.

- The Locals tab displays the variables that are local to the current function.

- The This tab displays the object pointed to by **this**.

Each tab contains a spreadsheet with fields for the variable name and value. The debugger automatically fills in these fields.

You cannot add variables or expressions to the Variables window (use the Watch window for that), but you can expand or collapse the variables shown using the tree controls. You can expand an array, object, or structure variable in the Variables window if it has a plus sign (+) box in the Name field. If an array, object, or structure variable has a minus sign (–) box in the Name field, the variable is already fully expanded. To expand or collapse the variable, click the + or – box, as described in "Spreadsheet Fields" on page 286.

If the variable is an object or a pointer to an object, the Variables window automatically expands the variable to show the most important data at the top level. For example, suppose you had the following object:

```
CString String  =   {...}
char *    m_pchData =0x7ffdf000 "abc"
    int          m_nDataLength=4
    int          m_nAllocLength=1244628
```

The Variables window would display the following:

```
String  =   {"abc"}
```

If the variable is a pointer to a C++ object, the Variables window automatically downcasts the pointer. The Variables window adds an extra member to the expanded object. This extra member, which looks like another base class, indicates the derived subclass. For example, if a variable declared as a pointer to **CObject** really points to a **CComboBox**, the Variables window recognizes this fact and adds an extra member so that you can access the **CComboBox** members.

In addition to the tabs, the Variables window has a Context box on the toolbar that contains a copy of the current call stack in a drop-down list box. Use this list to specify the current scope of the variables displayed. The Content box is part of a toolbar, which you can hide using the right mouse button.

▶ **To display the Variables window**

1 From the View menu, choose Variables.

The Variables window appears.

2 Select the Auto tab, Locals tab, or This tab, according to the type of variables you want to see.

When the program is paused at a breakpoint or between steps, you can change the value of any non-**const** variable in your program. This gives you the flexibility to try out changes and see their results in real time or to recover from some logic error and continue.

The Variables window does not display variable type information. You can view type information for a variable by using the window's property page.

▶ **To view type information for a variable**

1 In the Variables window, select the Auto tab, the Locals tab, or the This tab.

2 Select the line containing the variable whose type you want to see.

3 Click the right mouse button in the Variables window, and choose Properties from the pop-up menu.

–or–

From the Edit menu, choose Properties.

Although you cannot delete variables from the Variables window, you can edit their values.

▶ **To modify the value of a variable**

1 In the Variables window, select the Auto tab, Locals tab, or This tab.

2 Select the line containing the variable whose type you want to modify.

3 If the variable is an array, object, or structure, use the + box to expand the view until you see the value you want to modify.

4 Double-click the value, or use the TAB key to move the insertion point to the value you want to modify.

5 Type the new value, and press ENTER.

 Tip   To change the value of a structure or an array (including strings), modify the individual fields or elements. You cannot edit an entire array or structure at once.

You can use the Variables window to examine function return values as well as variables.

▶ **To view the return value of a function**

1 Step over or out of the function.

2 In the Variables window, select the Auto tab.

3 Click the Return Value icon, which appears in the Name column, as shown in Figure 17.1 .

The function return value appears in the Auto tab. The Name column displays the return value as *Name* Returned, where *Name* is the name of the function.

Figure 17.1   Return Value Icon in Name Column

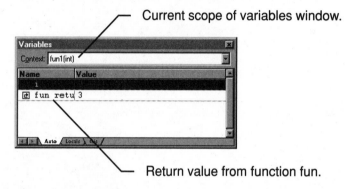

Current scope of variables window.

Return value from function fun.

You can turn off the display of return values.

▶ **To turn off the display of return values**

1 From the Tools menu, select Options.

2 In the Options dialog box, select the Debug tab.

3 Under Variables Window, clear the Return Value check box.

4 Choose OK.

Limitations on the Variables Window

Some project settings and programming practices limit the ability of the Variables window to display variables:

- The Auto tab uses syntax coloring to determine which variables to display. If you turn off syntax coloring for a file, the Auto tab cannot display any variables for that file. To turn syntax coloring back on, select a source window, choose Properties from the Edit menu, and set Language to C/C++ in the Source Windows property page.

- All three tabs use debugging information. If you build a section of code without debugging information, the tabs cannot display variables for that code.

- The Variables window does not expand macros and cannot display information on variables used within macros.

Navigating From the Variables Window

You can navigate to a function's source code or disassembled object code from the Context box in the Variables window. This procedure displays the function's source code, if it is available, in a source window. If source code for the selected function is not available, it displays the function's object code in the Disassembly window.

▶ **To navigate from the Variables window to a function's source or object code**

- Select the function name from the Context drop-down list box in the Variables window toolbar.

This procedure changes the view of the program displayed in the Variables window and other debugger windows, but does not change the next line of execution or the value stored in the program counter.

Using the Call Stack Window

During a debug session, the Call Stack window displays the stack of currently active function calls. When a function is called, it is pushed onto the stack. When the function returns, it is popped off the stack.

The Call Stack window displays the currently executing function at the top of the stack and older function calls below that. By default, the window also displays parameter types and values for each function call. You can display or hide parameter types and values using the Debug tab of the Options dialog box or the right mouse button pop-up menu.

▶ **To display the Call Stack window**

- From the View menu, choose Call Stack.

▶ **To view the call stack for a function**

1 Place the insertion point in the function.

2 From the Debug menu, choose Run To Cursor to execute your program to the location of the insertion point.

The Locals tab of the Variables window is updated automatically to display the local variables for the function or procedure.

3 From the View menu, choose Call Stack.

The calls are listed in the calling order, with the current function (the most deeply nested) at the top.

 Tip   To run the program to the return address, select the function in the Call Stack window, and choose Run To Cursor from the Debug menu.

Tip To set or remove a breakpoint at a function return address, select the function in the Call Stack window, and choose the Insert/Remove Breakpoint toolbar button.

You can navigate to a function's source code or disassembled object code from the Call Stack window. This procedure displays the function's source code, if it is available, in a source window. If source code for the selected function is not availabile, it displays the function's object code in the Disassembly window.

▶ **To navigate from the Call Stack window to a function's source or object code**

- Double-click the function name in the Call Stack window.

  −or−

  Select the function name, and press ENTER.

This procedure changes the view of the program shown in the Variables window and other debugger windows, but does not change the next line of execution or the value stored in the program counter.

Controlling Call Stack Display

By default, the Call Stack window displays parameter values and types for each function. You can turn off the display of parameter values, types, or both using the Debug tab in the Options dialog box or by using the right mouse button pop-up menu. You cannot turn off the display of function names.

▶ **To change the call stack display**

1 From the Tools menu, choose Options.

2 Select the Debug tab.

3 Under Call stack window, select the check boxes for Parameter Values or Parameter Types, according to the information you want to display.

  −or−

- In the Call Stack window, click the right mouse button, and from the pop-up menu, choose Parameter Values or Parameter Types to toggle the display of that information.

 Tip The Context box at the top of the Variables window contains a drop-down list of call stack functions. If you select one of these functions, the debugger window views change accordingly.

Using the Registers Window

The Registers window displays the contents of the CPU registers, flags, and floating-point stack. Using the Registers window, you can change the value of any register or flag while the program is being debugged.

▶ **To display the Registers window**

• From the View menu, choose Registers.

▶ **To change the value of a register**

1 In the Registers window, use the TAB key or the mouse to move the insertion point to the register value you want to change.

2 Type the new value.

3 Press ENTER.

Caution   Changing register values (especially in the EIP and EBP registers) can affect program execution.

Table 17.5 lists the flags displayed in the Registers window and their set values for Intel x86 processors.

Table 17.5   Register Window Flags

Flag	Set
Overflow	O=1
Direction	D=1
Interrupt	I=1
Sign	S=1
Zero	Z=1
Auxiliary carry	A=1
Parity	P=1
Carry	C=1

▶ **To set or clear a flag**

1 In the Registers window, use the TAB key or the mouse to move the insertion point to the left of the value you want to change.

2 Type the new value.

3 Press ENTER.

Using the Memory Window

Using the Memory window, you can view memory contents starting at any specified address.

▶ **To display the Memory window**

• From the View menu, choose Memory.

Using the scroll bars in the Memory window, you can view any memory location in the program's available address space. Using options on the Debug tab in the Options dialog box, you can control the starting address, numeric display format, and number of values displayed on each line.

By default, the Memory window displays numbers in decimal (base 10) format. If you prefer, you can change the display to hexadecimal (base 16) format.

▶ **To change the Memory window display format**

1 From the Tools menu, choose Options.

The Options dialog box appears.

2 Select the Debug tab.

3 In the Format drop-down list box, select the format.

4 Choose OK.

Note To view Unicode in the Memory window, set the Format option to Wide Char. To display data bytes with Unicode characters, select the Show Data Bytes check box also.

You can set the address for the Memory window display by using drag-and-drop, by directly editing the memory address, or by choosing Go To from the Edit menu.

▶ **To view memory contents at a specified location using drag-and-drop**

1 In any window, select a memory address or pointer variable containing a memory address.

2 Drag the address or pointer to the Memory window, and drop it.

▶ **To view memory contents at a specified location by editing**

1 Select the Memory window.

2 In the Address box, select the memory address.

3 Type the new memory address and press ENTER.

The Memory window displays the contents of memory locations beginning at the address specified in the Address box.

▶ **To view memory contents at a specified location using Go To**

1 Select the Memory window.

2 From the Edit menu, choose Go To.

The Go To dialog box appears.

3 In the Go To What box, select Address.

4 In the Enter Address/Expression box, type or paste an address.

5 Choose the Go To button.

You can also specify a memory address for the Memory window in the Options dialog box. You can type an expression for the memory location that changes dynamically as the program runs (a "live expression").

▶ **To specify a live expression for the memory location**

1 From the Tools menu, choose Options.

The Options dialog box appears.

2 Select the Debug tab.

3 In the Address box, type an address expression.

You can type `*pPtr`, for example, to display memory contents starting at the address pointed to by `pPtr`.

4 Select the Re-evaluate Expression check box.

5 Choose OK.

You can view some items more easily using live expressions. On an Intel-compatible system, for example, you can examine the top of the stack by typing `ESP` as a live expression. By specifying a pointer variable, you can use the Memory window to follow the pointer as it increments through an array.

Using the Disassembly Window

By default, the Disassembly window displays disassembled code with source-code annotations and symbols. You can change these display options using the Options dialog box.

▶ **To change the Disassembly window display options**

1 From the Tools menu, choose Options.

The Options dialog box appears.

2 Select the Debug tab.

3 Under Disassembly Window, select the appropriate check box for the display you want.

4 Choose OK.

The Disassembly window can be especially useful for debugging optimized code, as well as source-code lines that contain multiple statements. Consider, for example, the following line of code:

```
x=1; y=7; Z=3;
```

The source window treats each line of code as a unit. Using the source window, you cannot step from one statement on a source-code line to the next, or set a breakpoint on any statement other than the first.

The Disassembly window operates on assembly-language instructions instead of source-code statements or lines. Using the Disassembly window, you can set a breakpoint on any instruction. If you use the Step Into or Step Over command while the Disassembly window has focus, the debugger steps through your program instruction-by-instruction instead of line-by-line. Viewing and stepping through your code by assembly-language instructions can be especially useful when you are debugging optimized code.

Using the Disassembly window, you can display the assembly code created for the source code being debugged.

▶ **To display the Disassembly window**

- From the View menu, choose Disassembly.

▶ **To switch between corresponding locations in the source and Disassembly windows**

- In the source window, click the right mouse button, and choose Go To Disassembly from the pop-up menu.

  −or−

  In the Disassembly window, click the right mouse button, and choose Go To Source from the pop-up menu.

You can set the address at which the Disassembly window begins displaying code using drag-and-drop or by choosing Go To from the Edit menu or the right mouse button pop-up menu.

▶ **To view disassembly code at a specified location using drag-and-drop**

1 In any window, select a memory address or pointer variable containing a memory address.

2 Drag the address or pointer to the Disassembly window, and drop it.

▶ **To view disassembly code at a specified location using the Go To command**

1 Select the Disassembly window.

2 From the Edit menu, choose Go To.

  The Go To dialog box appears.

3 In the Go To What box, select Address.

4 In the Enter Address Expression box, type or paste an address.

5 Choose the Go To button.

Debugging Methods and Strategies

Debugging Compiler and Linker Errors offers some suggestions for debugging problems that stop you from building.

How Can I...?, offers some suggestions for assorted situations you may encounter while debugging.

Suggestions for debugging specific types of code are found in:

- Debugging Assertions
- Debugging Exceptions
- Debugging Threads
- Debugging DLLs
- Debugging Optimized Code
- Debugging OLE Applications

Some advanced debugging methods are found in:

- Debugging Remote Applications
- Using I/O Redirection

Debugging Compiler and Linker Errors

The first step in debugging is to fix language syntax errors. The Output window displays errors that prevent a program from being built and provides the filename, line number, and error number. The Output window behaves like a source window; you can copy and print information from the window. If the status bar is displayed, it gives a summary of the current error.

If you don't understand an error message, move the insertion point to the error number, and press the F1 KEY (IN THE DEFAULT KEYBOARD MAPPING) to display online information about it.

▶ **To move through the list of errors**

- In the Output window, double-click the error, or select the error and press ENTER.

  –or–

- Click the right mouse button in the Output window, and choose Go To Error/Tag from the pop-up menu.

  –or–

- Press F4 (in the default keyboard mapping) to select the next error.

  –or–

- Press SHIFT+F4 (in the default keyboard mapping) to select the preceding error.

As each error is selected in the Output window, the corresponding line containing the error is selected in the source window.

You can move to any line number in a source file.

▶ **To move to a specific line**

1 From the Edit menu, choose Go To.

The Go To dialog box appears.

2 In the Line Number box, type a line number.

3 Choose the Go To button.

If you type a line number greater than the last line in your source file, the editor moves to the end of the file.

How Can I...?

This section provides suggestions on how to handle some common, and some not-so-common, debugging situations.

▶ **My program runs fine in the Visual C++ environment, but when I run it standalone with Windows, it produces an access violation. How can I debug this problem?**

- Use Just-in-Time debugging. If you set the Just-in-Time debugging option before you compile, you can run your program standalone until the access violation occurs. Then, in the Access Violation dialog box, you can choose the Cancel button to launch the debugger. For more information, see "Just-in-Time Debugging" on page 293.

▶ **I'm using the Registers window to view a function's return value, but the register contents are hard to read. How can I format the register contents?**

- Use the Variables window, instead of the Registers window, to view return values. The Auto tab on the Variables window formats and displays the function return value for you. For more information, see "Using the Variables Window" on page 314.

▶ **My program has a window-activation problem. Stepping through the program with the debugger interferes with my ability to reproduce the problem, because my program keeps losing focus. Is there any way to avoid this?**

- If you have a second computer, use remote debugging. You can operate your program on the remote computer while you run the debugger on the host. For more information, see "Remote Debugging" on page 340.

▶ **I'm trying to debug a screen painting problem. To observe this problem, I have to keep my program in the foreground, which means I don't have access to the debugger windows. What can I do?**

- Again, if you have a second computer, you can use remote debugging. With a two-computer setup, you can watch the screen painting on the remote computer while you operate the debugger on the host.

▶ **I'm using remote debugging, but performance seems to be slow. What can I do to improve this?**

- Don't open all the debugger windows. Updating all the windows slows remote debugging down, so open only those that you need.

- If you're remote debugging on a Macintosh® or Power Macintosh®, avoid using data breakpoints unless you really need them. These computers do not have breakpoint registers, so data breakpoints must be implemented in software, which reduces performance.

▶ **I want to look at a large byte buffer, but the Watch window is too cramped to view all of it. What can I do?**

- Use the Memory window to view large buffers, strings, and other data that do not display well in the Watch or Variables window. For more information, see "Using the Memory Window" on page 319.

▶ **I think that one of my pointers may be corrupting memory at address 0x00408000. How can I find out what is happening there?**

- Use the Memory window to view memory contents starting at that address. Set a breakpoint on that memory address. For more information, see "Using the Memory Window" on page 319 and "Quick Methods for Location Breakpoints" on page 294.

▶ **My pointer, `ptr`, should be pointing to a specific memory block, but it's pointing somewhere else. How can I find out where it's getting changed?**

- Set a data breakpoint on `ptr`. This breakpoint causes the program to halt when the address pointed to by `ptr` changes. If you set the breakpoint on `*ptr` instead, the breakpoint halts the program when data at the location pointed to by `ptr` changes. For more information, see "Quick Methods for Data Breakpoints" on page 296.

▶ **I'm trying to debug some library object code in the Disassembly window, and I want to see the contents of certain registers. How can I do this?**

- Use the Registers window to view the contents of registers and flags or to add registers (such as `@EAX`) to the Watch window. For more information, see "Using the Register Window" on page 318.

▶ **When my program began drawing erratically, I used the Break command in the Debug menu to halt the program. Unfortunately, I ended up in MFC. I'm pretty sure the problem is in my code, not MFC. How can I get back to it?**

- Use the Call Stack window to navigate to the function from which MFC was called. For more information, see "Using the Call Stack Window" on page 317.

▶ **I've discovered that the wrong parameter value is being passed to one of my functions. This function is called from all over the place. How can I find out who's passing it the wrong value?**

- Using the Breakpoints dialog box, set a location breakpoint at the beginning of the function. Then choose the Condition button, and use the Breakpoints Condition dialog box to enter an expression, such as Var==3, where Var is the name of the function being passed the bad value, and 3 is the bad value passed to it.

  Now, run the program again. The breakpoint causes the program to halt at the beginning of the function when Var has the value 3. You can then use the Call Stack window to find the calling function and navigate to its source code. For more information, see "Quick Methods for Location Breakpoints" on page 294 and "Using the Call Stack Window" on page 317 of this chapter.

▶ **My program produces an access violation. How can I debug this?**

- Use the Call Stack window to work your way back up the call stack, looking for corrupted data being passed as a parameter to a function. If that fails, try setting a breakpoint at a point before the location where the access violation occurs. Check to see if data is good at that point. If so, try stepping your way toward the location where the access violation occured. If you can identify a single action, such as a menu command, that led to the access violation, you can try another technique: setting a breakpoint between the action (in this example, the menu command) and the access violation. You can then look at the state of your program during the moments leading up to the access violation. You can use a combination of these techniques to work forward and backward until you have isolated the location where the access violation occurred. For more information, see "Using the Call Stack Window" on page 317 of this chapter.

▶ **How can I debug inline assembly code?**

- Use the Disassembly window to view the assembly instructions. Use the Registers window to view register contents. For more information, see "Using the Disassembly Window" on page 321 and "Using the Register Window" on page 318 of this chapter.

▶ **I set a breakpoint at a line in my source code, but I'm actively editing the code as I debug. When I rebuild the project, I get an error message telling me that the breakpoint has moved. How can I stop this from happening?**

- If possible, set the breakpoint at the beginning of the function, by specifying the function name, instead of setting the breakpoint on a line number. Breakpoints on source-code lines stay on the same line number. If you edit the code, changing the number of lines, the breakpoint may no longer be on a line with a valid statement. Breakpoints set at the beginning of the function remain with the function, regardless of what source-code line the function begins on. For more information, see "Quick Methods for Location Breakpoints" on page 294.

▶ **My program fails on a call to a certain function, CnvtV. The program probably calls that function a couple hundred times before it fails. If I set a location breakpoint on CnvtV, the program stops on every call to that function, and I don't want that. I don't know what conditions cause the call to fail, so I can't set a conditional breakpoint. What can I do?**

- You can set a conditional breakpoint without specifying a condition. Set the Skip Count field to a value so high that it will never be reached. In this case, since you believe the function CnvtV is called a couple hundred times, set Skip Count to 1000 or more. Then, run the program and wait for it to fail. When it does, open the Breakpoints dialog box and look at the list of breakpoints. The breakpoint you set on CnvtV appears, followed by the skip count and number of iterations remaining:

```
at "CnvtV(ParamList)" skip 1000 times (750 remaining)
```

You now know that the breakpoint was skipped 250 times before the function failed. If you reset the breakpoint with a skip count of 250 and run the program again, the program stops at the call to CnvtV that caused it to fail last time. For more information, see "Quick Methods for Location Breakpoints" on page 294 of this chapter.

Debugging Assertions

An assertion statement specifies a condition at some particular point in your program. Visual C++ supports assertion statements based on the following constructs:

- The ANSI C/C++ **assert** function
- The C runtime library **_ASSERT** macro
- The Microsoft Foundation Class (MFC) **ASSERT** macro

Programs that use the MFC library should use the MFC **ASSERT** macro. Programs that use the runtime library should use the runtime **_ASSERT** macro. Other programs should use the ANSI assert function.

Assertion statements compile only when **_DEBUG** is defined. When **_DEBUG** is not defined, the compiler treats assertions as null statements. Therefore, assertion statements have zero overhead in your final release program; you can use them liberally in your code without affecting the performance of your release version.

Assertion statements are useful for catching logic errors. If you set an assertion on a condition that must be true according to the logic of your program, the assertion has no effect unless a logic error occurs. For example, suppose you are writing a simulation of gas molecules in a container, and the variable numMols represents the total number of molecules. Obviously, this number cannot be less than zero, so you might include an MFC assertion statement like this:

```
ASSERT(numMols >= 0);
```

This statement does nothing if your program is operating correctly. If a logic error has caused numMols to be less than zero, however, the statement halts the execution of your program and displays an MFC dialog box called Assertion Failed. This dialog box has three buttons, with the functions described in the following table.

Choose this button	To do this
Retry	Debug the assertion or get help on asserts.
Ignore	Ignore the assertion and continue running the program.
Abort	Halt execution of the program and end the debugging session.

When the debugger halts due to an MFC or C runtime library assertion, it navigates to the point in the source file where the assertion occured, if the source is available. The Debug tab of the Output window displays the assertion message that appeared in the Assertion dialog box. If you want to keep a copy of the message for future reference, you can copy it from the Output window to a text window using copy and paste or drag-and-drop. The Output window may contain other error messages as well. Examine these carefully; some may provide clues to the cause of the assertion failure.

When you add assertions to your code, avoid writing assertions that have side effects. For example:

```
ASSERT(numMols++ > 0); -- Don't do this!
```

This assertion statement changes the value of numMols. If you write assertion statements that have side effects like this, the debug and release versions of your code will produce different results, because the side effects occur only when **_DEBUG** is defined. Be careful using assertion statements on library or system calls, which may have side effects.

Use assertion statements when you need to check the result of an operation. Assertions are most valuable for testing operations whose results are not obvious from quick visual inspection. Consider, for example, the following code, which updates the variable iMols based on the contents of the linked list pointed to by mols:

```
while (mols->type <> "H2O")
{
 iMols += mols->num;
 mols = mols->next;
}
ASSERT(iMols<=numMols);
```

The number of molecules counted by iMols must always be less than or equal to the total number of molecules, numMols. A visual inspection of this loop does not guarantee that this must be the case, so an assertion statement is used after the loop to test for that condition.

Another use of assertion statements is to test for error conditions. Assertion statements are not a subsitute for error-handling code, however. The following example shows an assertion statement that can lead to problems in the final release code:

```
myErr = myGraphRoutine(a, b);
ASSERT(!myErr); -- Don't do this!
```

This code relies on the assertion statement to handle the error condition. As a result, any error code returned by myGraphRoutine will be unhandled in the final release code.

You can, however, use assertion statements to check for error conditions at a point in your code where any errors should have been handled by preceding code. In the following example, a graphic routine returns zero if it succeeds and an error code if an error (such as running out of memory) occurs. You can use an MFC assertion statement as follows:

```
myErr = myGraphRoutine(a, b);
...
/* Code to handle errors and
   reset myErr if successful */
...
ASSERT(!myErr);
```

If the error-handling code works properly, any error that occurs is handled, and myErr is restored to a value of zero, indicating no error, before the assertion statement is reached. The assertion succeeds, and control passes to the next statement. However, if myErr has another value, the assertion fails, the program halts, and the MFC Assertion Failed dialog box appears.

When an assertion fails, you must examine your program to determine the cause of the failure. If the assertion statement and the cause of the failure occur close to one another, debugging can be relatively straightforward. Sometimes, however, an assertion failure may provide little or no clue as to where the cause is located. For example, suppose your code contained the following assertion statement:

```
ASSERT(ialloc %50 == 0);
```

The program in this example allocates memory in blocks of 50 bytes. This assertion tests to see that memory is allocated in multiples of the proper size. If the assertion fails, you know that a memory leak exists in your program. Your next task, of course, is to find out where.

To isolate the location where the memory leak occurs, you might add copies of this assertion statement to other parts of your program where memory is allocated. Another alternative is to set a data breakpoint.

▶ **To find the locations where a condition fails**

1 From the Edit menu, choose Breakpoints.

The Breakpoints dialog box appears.

2 Select the Data tab.

3 In the Enter The Expression To Be Evaluated text box, type the negation of the expression that caused the asertion failure.

In general, for ASSERT (*anyExpression*), you can specify a data breakpoint as ! (*anyExpression*).

For example, if your program failed on the assertion:

```
ASSERT(ialloc %50 == 0);
```

In the Breakpoints dialog box, you would type:

```
!(ialloc %50 == 0)
```

4 Run your program again.

Execution halts when the condition specified in the data breakpoint becomes true. This is the point where the condition in the assertion statement becomes false.

If you choose to use a data breakpoint instead of additional assertion statements, remember that data breakpoints significantly slow program execution on Macintosh and Power Macintosh platforms, which do not have breakpoint registers. Assertion statements have minimal overhead on all platforms.

Another tool that is often useful for finding the cause of an assertion failure is the Call Stack window. Using the Call Stack window, you can examine previous functions and look for problems that may have caused the failure.

▶ **To navigate from the Call Stack window to a function's source or object code**

- In the Call Stack window, double-click the function name.

  –or–

  Select the function name, and press ENTER.

On rare occasions, you might want to look at the assertion-handling code rather than the code that caused the assertion to fail. You can use the Call Stack window for that purpose as well.

Debugging Exceptions

The exception-handling facility in C++ allows programs to handle abnormal and unexpected situations in an orderly, structured manner. When a function detects an exception that must be handled, it notifies the handler using **throw**. The exception handler receives the notification using **catch**. If no catch handler exists for an exception, the program typically calls **terminate**(). If you are debugging a program in Visual C++, however, the debugger notifies you that the exception was not caught.

C programs can use structured exception handling, a mechanism based on the Win32-specific **__try** and **__except** macros rather **throw** and **catch**. For information on writing code that uses exception handling or structured exception handling, see "C++ Exception Handling and Structured Exception Handling" in *Programming Techniques*.

When you are debugging in Visual C++, you can use the Exceptions dialog box to specify how the debugger is to handle each specific type of exception. In this dialog box, you can set one of two options —Stop Always or Stop If Not Handled —for each exception type that can occur in your program.

If you select Stop If Not Handled for an exception, the debugger writes a message to the Output window when an exception occurs, but does not halt the program and notify you with a dialog box unless the exception handler fails to handle the exception. At that point, it is too late to fix the problem or examine the source code to see where the exception occured. (The program is already past the point where the exception occurred and is executing in the exception handler.)

If you select Stop Always for an exception, the debugger stops the program and notifies you immediately when an exception occurs, before any handler code is invoked. When this happens, you can look at the source window to see where the exception occured. You can use the Watch and Variables windows and QuickWatch to see current variable contents. In some cases, you can fix the exception yourself by modifying the variable contents. When you continue the program after the exception, a dialog box appears asking if you want to pass the exception back to the program's exception handlers. If you fixed the problem, choose the No button. Otherwise, choose the Yes button, and the exception handler is invoked. If the exception handler cannot fix the problem, the debugger halts the program and notifies you again, just as if you had selected Stop If Not Handled.

Note The Stop Always option depends on the debug registers in Intel and Intel-compatible processors. As a result, this option is not available when you are debugging a program on Macintosh (including Power Macintosh) hardware.

The Exceptions list box in the Exceptions dialog box contains a default list of system exceptions. You can remove system exceptions or add exceptions of your own. This information is saved in the *project*.MDP file, which persists with the project. If an exception is not included in this list, the debugger treats it as a Stop If Not Handled exception.

Each exception has a unique number. System exceptions are defined in WINBASE.H with the prefix EXCEPTION (for example, EXCEPTION_ACCESS_VIOLATION).

▶ **To add a new exception to the Exceptions list box**

1 From the Debug menu, choose Exceptions.

The Exceptions dialog box appears.

2 In the Number box, type the exception number for the user-defined exception.

3 Optionally, type the name of the exception in the Name box.

4 Optionally, under Action, select the Stop Always or Stop If Not Handled option button.

5 Choose the Add button.

6 Choose OK.

You can change any parameter associated with an exception.

▶ **To change an exception parameter**

1 From the Debug menu, choose Exceptions.

The Exceptions dialog box appears.

2 In the Exceptions list box, select the exception.

3 Change any parameter, such as the name or the action.

4 Choose the Change button.

5 Choose OK.

You can remove any exception from the Exceptions list box.

▶ **To remove an exception from the Exceptions list box**

1 From the Debug menu, choose Exceptions.

The Exceptions dialog box appears.

2 In the Exceptions list box, select the exception.

3 Choose the Remove button.

When you delete an exception from the Exceptions list box, its action reverts to Stop If Not Handled.

4 Choose OK.

If you wish to restore system exceptions to the list, choose the Reset button.

▶ **To restore all default system exceptions to the Exceptions list**

1 From the Debug menu, choose Exceptions.

The Exceptions dialog box appears.

2 Choose the Reset button.

All default system exceptions are restored to the Exceptions list box without disturbing any of the user-defined exceptions that have been added.

3 Choose OK.

Debugging Threads

You can use the Microsoft Developer Studio debugger to debug multithreaded applications.

A thread is a path of execution within a process. A process is an executing instance of an application. Launching Notepad, for example, starts a process that has a single thread. The startup code passes this primary thread to the operating system in the form of a function address (usually the address of **main** or **WinMain**). When the primary thread terminates, so does the process.

You can create additional threads in your application code. These threads can handle background or maintenance tasks that proceed without the user's attention.

When debugging a multithreaded program, you can select a single thread using the Threads dialog box.

▶ **To display the Threads dialog box**

• From the Debug menu, choose Threads.

The Threads dialog box displays a list of all threads that exist in the application. Using this list, you can set focus on, suspend, or resume a thread.

▶ **To set focus on a thread**

1 In the Threads dialog box, select a thread from the Thread list.

2 Choose the Set Focus button.

▶ **To suspend a thread**

1 In the Threads dialog box, select a thread from the Thread list.

2 Choose the Suspend button.

▶ **To resume execution of a thread**

1 In the Threads dialog box, select a thread from the Thread list.

2 Choose the Resume button.

The Thread list in the Threads dialog box displays status information on each thread as follows:

The Thread ID column contains the DWORD that uniquely identifies each thread. When you set focus on a thread, an asterisk (*) appears next to its thread ID.

The Suspend column contains the suspension number of each thread. This number, which can vary from 0 through 127, is incremented each time you suspend the thread and decremented each time you resume the thread.

The Priority column contains the thread priority. A thread priority can be any of the following: Idle, Lowest, Below Normal, Normal, Above Normal, Highest, or Time Critical.

The Location column contains the function name or address associated with the thread. You can choose to see either the function name or address.

▶ **To view the function name associated with each thread**

• In the Threads dialog box, select Name.

▶ **To view the address associated with each thread**

• In the Threads dialog box, select Address.

If Name is selected, the current function name is displayed if it is known by the debugger. If no function is known, the address is displayed. If Address is selected, the current address is displayed.

Note If you are displaying thread locations by Name instead of by Address, each thread is typically shown with the function name in which its EIP currently resides. However, if the EIP is in a location where Developer Studio has no symbols (for example, in the NT kernel), then Visual C++ displays, in brackets, the name of the topmost function on the stack for which Developer Studio has symbols.

Debugging DLLs

You can debug a dynamic-link library (DLL) in one of two ways.

If you have the source for both the DLL and the calling program, you can open the project for the calling executable and debug the DLL from there. If you load a DLL dynamically, you must specify it in the Additional DLLs category of the Debug tab in the Project Settings dialog box.

If you have the source for the DLL only, you can open the project that builds the DLL. Use the Debug tab in the Project Settings dialog box to specify the executable that calls the DLL.

▶ **To debug a DLL using the project for the executable**

1 From the Build menu, choose Settings.

The Project Settings dialog box appears.

2 Select the Debug tab.

3 In the Category drop-down list box, select General.

4 In the Program Arguments text box, type any command-line arguments required by the executable.

5 In the Category drop-down list box, select Additional DLLs.

6 In the Local Name column, type the names of DLLs to debug.

If you are debugging remotely, the Remote Name column appears. In this column, type the complete path for the remote module to map to the local module name.

7 In the Preload column, select the check box if you want to load the module before debugging begins.

8 Choose OK to store the information in your project.

9 From the Build menu, choose Go to start the debugger.

You can set breakpoints in the DLL or the calling program. You can open a source file for the DLL and set breakpoints in that file, even though it is not a part of the executable's project.

▶ **To debug a DLL using the project for the DLL**

1 From the Build menu, choose Settings.

The Project Settings dialog box appears.

2 Select the Debug tab.

3 In the Category drop-down list box, select General.

4 In the Executable For Debug Session text box, type the name of the executable that calls the DLL.

5 In the Category list box, select Additional DLLs.

6 In the Local Module Name column, type the name of the DLLs you want to debug.

7 Choose OK to store the information in your project.

8 Set breakpoints as required in your DLL source files or on function symbols in the DLL.

9 From the Build menu, choose Go to start the debugger.

▶ **To debug a DLL created with an external project**

1 From the Build menu, choose Settings.

The Project Settings dialog box appears.

2 Select the Debug tab.

3 In the Category drop-down list box, select General.

4 In the Executable For Debug Session text box, type the name of the DLL that your external makefile builds.

5 Choose OK to store the information in your project.

6 Build a debug version of the DLL with symbolic debugging information, if you don't already have one.

7 Follow one of the two procedures immediately preceding this one to debug the DLL.

Debugging Optimized Code

To create more efficient code, the compiler can optimize, or reposition and reorganize, instructions derived from your source code. Because of optimization, the debugger cannot always identify the source code corresponding to a set of instructions. This makes it more difficult to debug optimized code. This section describes techniques for debugging optimized code.

If possible, try to debug your code without optimization.

▶ **To prevent the compiler from optimizing code**

- When you create a new project, select the Win32 Debug target. Build and debug the Debug target until you are ready to build a Win32 Release target. The compiler does not optimize the Debug target.

    −or−

- Use the /Od compiler option on the command line.

    −or−

1 From the Build menu, choose Settings.

The Project Settings dialog box appears.

2 Select the C/C++ tab.

3 In the Optimizations drop-down list box, select Disable (Debug).

You can enable optimizations after you finish debugging.

Some bugs affect optimized code but do not affect unoptimized code. If you must debug optimized code, use the following techniques:

- Use the /Zi compiler option to get maximum symbolic information for your program.

- Use the Disassembly and Registers windows. Set breakpoints at the appropriate locations using the Disassembly window.

To see why the Disassembly window is useful, consider the following example:

```
for (x=0; x<10; x++)
```

Suppose you set a breakpoint at this line. You might expect the breakpoint to be hit 10 times. But if this code is optimized, the breakpoint is only hit once, because the compiler recognizes that the first instruction associated with this line, which assigns the value of 0 to x, only needs to execute once. The compiler moves this instruction out of the loop. If you set a breakpoint on this source-code line, the debugger sets the breakpoint on the first instruction, which only executes once.

The instructions that compare and increment x remain inside the loop. To set a breakpoint on these instructions, use the Disassembly window. By viewing the object code the source-code line creates, you can set a breakpoint at the approriate instruction. You can set a breakpoint at the location where the condition is checked or the variable is incremented. You can use the Step Into or Step Over commands in the Disassembly window to step by assembly instruction, which allows greater control than stepping by source-code line.

Debugging an OLE Application

The Microsoft Developer Studio debugger supports debugging OLE client and server applications. When you are debugging an application that steps into an OLE remote procedure call (RPC), a second instance of the debugger appears. The second instance of the debugger handles the OLE server that you are stepping into through the RPC. It opens the source for the server code you have stepped into, if it is available. If the source for the server code is not available, the disassembled object code appears in the Disassembly window. You can use all Developer Studio debugging facilities to debug your OLE application.

▶ **To debug an OLE client or server application**

1 Open the project for the OLE application, and build a version of the OLE application with symbolic debugging information.

2 From the Tools menu, choose Options.

The Options dialog box appears.

3 Select the Debug tab.

4 Select the OLE RPC Debugging check box.

Note With Windows NT, you must have administrator privileges to select the OLE RPC Debugging check box.

5 Choose OK.

6 Set breakpoints at the points in the source files for your OLE application where you want to determine the state of the application.

7 From the Debug menu, choose Go to start the debugger.

Debugging Remote Applications

You can use Microsoft Developer Studio to debug programs running remotely on Intel, Macintosh, and Power Macintosh platforms. During remote debugging, the host computer controls debugging from a small remote monitor program on the remote (target) computer. The host computer communicates with the remote computer and sends debug commands through a serial or network connection.

There are three stages to remote debugging:

- Setting up the remote monitor
- Connecting the host and target computers
- Debugging the program

 Tip To improve the speed of remote debugging, close any unneeded debugger windows to minimize the amount of information that must be sent across the connection and minimize the use of data breakpoints.

Setting up the Remote Debug Monitor

The remote debug monitor is a small program on the target computer that communicates with the debugger and controls the execution of the program you are debugging.

▶ **To install the remote debug monitor**

- On a Windows 95 or NT computer, the remote debug monitor consists of the following files: MSVCMON.EXE, MSVCRT40.DLL, TLN0COM.DLL, TLN0T.DLL, and DMN0.DLL. Copy these files to the remote computer.

- On a Win32s computer, the remote debug monitor consists of MSVCMON.EXE, TLW3COM.DLL, and DMW3.DLL. These files are installed automatically during setup.

- On a Macintosh, the remote monitor is a control panel, called VC++ Debug Monitor, installed automatically by the Visual C++ for Macintosh Setup program.

- On a Power Macintosh, the remote debugger is an application, called VC++ PowerMac Remote Monitor, installed automatically by the Visual C++ for Macintosh Setup program. Setup also installs the following files: VC++ Power Macintosh File Utility, VC++ Power Macintosh ADSP Transport, VC++ Power Macintosh TCP/IP Transport, and VC++ Power Macintosh Serial Transport.

Connecting the Host and Target Machines

Once remote debugging is enabled, you must specify the type of connection between the host and target computers. The remote platform type determines the connections available. For Intel platforms, serial and TCP/IP connections are available. For Macintosh and Power Macintosh platforms, serial, TCP/IP, and AppleTalk connections are available. The AppleTalk connection is available only if the host is running Windows NT.

▶ **To configure a remote connection on the host computer**

1 From the Tools menu, choose Remote Connection.

The Remote Connection dialog box appears.

2 In the Platform drop-down list box, select the appropriate platform.

3 In the Connection drop-down list box, select the appropriate connection type.

4 Choose the Settings button.

The appropriate settings dialog box appears —the Serial Communication Settings dialog box for a serial connection, the Network (TCP/IP) Settings dialog box for a TCP/IP network connection, or the Network (AppleTalk) Settings dialog box for an AppleTalk network connection.

5 Specify the appropriate communication settings.

For remote debugging via an AppleTalk or TCP/IP network, the settings you must specify include a password, which must match the password set on the target computer. For TCP/IP debugging when the remote computer is a Macintosh or Power Macintosh, be sure to specify the TCP/IP address instead of the computer name.

6 Choose OK.

You must also configure the remote computer at this time, if you haven't done so previously.

▶ **To configure a remote connection on the remote computer (Macintosh)**

1 From the Apple menu, choose the Control Panels folder.

2 In the Control Panels folder, double-click to launch the VC++ Debug Monitor control panel.

3 In the Connection list box, select Serial, Network (AppleTalk), or Network TCP/IP.

4 Choose the Settings button.

The appropriate settings dialog box appears. For network debugging, this is where you set the password.

5 Specify the appropriate communication settings.

6 Choose OK.

▶ **To configure a remote connection on the remote computer (Power Macintosh)**

1 Double-click the VC++ PowerMac Remote Monitor application icon.

2 In the Connection list box, select Serial, Network (AppleTalk), or Network TCP/IP.

3 Choose the Settings button.

The appropriate settings dialog box appears. For network debugging, this is where you set the password.

4 Specify the appropriate communication settings.

5 Choose OK.

Note If the Macintosh or Power Macintosh fails when you try to change a setting in the debug monitor, the preferences file (VC++ Debug Preferences) may have become corrupted. Delete VC++ Debug Preferences (under Preferences in the System Folder), and restart the computer.

▶ **To configure a remote connection on the remote computer (Windows 95 or Windows NT)**

1 Launch MSVCMON.EXE.

2 In the Connection list box, select Serial or Network TCP/IP.

The appropriate settings dialog box appears.

3 Specify the appropriate communication settings.

4 Choose OK.

Remote Debugging

After you have configured the connection on both ends, you can begin remote debugging.

▶ **To begin remote debugging**

1 From the Build menu, choose Settings.

The Project Settings dialog box appears.

2 Select the Debug tab.

3 Verify that the Remote Executable Path And File Name text box contains the correct full-path entry.

4 Choose OK.

5 Start the remote debug monitor on the remote computer, if it is not already started.

6 From the Build menu, choose Go, Step Into, or Run To Cursor to start the debugger.

Note   The remote computer must remain operational while debugging. If you are using a Macintosh Powerbook, do not choose the Sleep button, choose the Sleep menu command, or close the Powerbook lid while debugging.

Using I/O Redirection

You can use input/output (I/O) redirection while debugging in Visual C++. The debugger supports I/O redirection in the same manner as Windows NT and Windows 95.

▸ **To set input/output redirection**

1 From the Build menu, choose Settings.

The Project Settings dialog box appears.

2 Select the Debug tab.

3 In the Program Arguments text box, specify one or more I/O redirection commands from the following table.

4 Set any other debug options that you want.

The table below lists the format and meaning of the available I/O redirection commands. You can combine I/O redirection commands in any order.

Command	Action
<file	Reads stdin from file
>file	Sends stdout to file
>>file	Appends stdout to file
2>file	Sends stderr to file
2>>file	Appends stderr to file
2>&1	Sends stderr (2) output to same location as stdout (1)
1>&2	Sends stdout (1) output to same location as stderr (2)

Note   You cannot set redirection commands from the command line of Microsoft Developer Studio.

Profiling Code

The profiler is a powerful analysis tool that you can use to examine the run-time behavior of your programs. By using the information given by the profiler, you can find out which sections of your code are working efficiently and which need to be examined more carefully. The profiler can also give you diagnostic information that shows areas of code that are not being executed.

Because profiling is a tuning process, you should use the profiler to make your programs run better, not to find bugs. Once your program is fairly stable, you should start profiling to find out where to devote your attention to optimize your code. Use the profiler to determine whether an algorithm is effective, a function is being called frequently (if at all), or a piece of code is being covered by software testing procedures.

The profiler is run from within Developer Studio, but can also be run from the command line. For information on using the profiler from the command line, see Chapter 27, "Profiler Reference." Chapter 27 includes descriptions of the PREP, PROFILE, and PLIST command-line tools and the profiler batch files. To learn more about profiling, see Chapter 12, "Advanced Profiling," in *Programming Techniques*. For information on profiling your applications on Win32s, see "Profiling Under Win32s," later in this chapter.

The following topics are covered:

- Setting up the profiler
- Building code for profiling
- Running the profiler
- Types of profiling
- Selective profiling
- Other profiler features
- Profiling under Win32s®

Setting Up the Profiler

The profiler uses the INIT environment variable to find TOOLS.INI, which contains information used by the profiler. Typically, the Setup program creates TOOLS.INI and sets INIT for you. If not, use the System icon in the Control Panel to set this variable.

For information on using TOOLS.INI to narrow profiling regions, see "Modifying TOOLS.INI" on page 350.

Building Code for Profiling

Before using the profiler, you must build the current project with profiling enabled (equivalent to LINK /PROFILE). If you want to do line profiling, you also need to include debugging information.

Note Selecting the Enable Profiling option turns off incremental linking. To re-enable incremental linking, clear the Enable Profiling option described below.

▶ **To build your project for profiling**

1 From the Build menu, choose Settings.

   The Project Settings dialog box appears.

2 Select the Link tab.

3 In the Category drop-down list box, select General.

4 Select the Enable Profiling check box. This setting also enables map (.MAP) file generation.

5 Select the Generate Debug Info check box.

6 Select the C/C++ tab.

7 In the Category drop-down list box, select General.

8 In the Debug Info drop-down list box, select Program Database or Line Numbers Only.

9 Choose the OK button.

10 From the Build menu, choose Build *projectname*.exe.

When the build is complete, the project is ready to be profiled.

Note If you are function profiling, the profiler ignores debug information, so you can skip steps 5 through 8.

Running the Profiler

▶ **To run the profiler**

1 From the Tools menu, choose Profile.

The Profile dialog box appears, as shown in Figure 18.1.

2 In the Profile Type box, select one of the following radio buttons:

- Function Timing
- Function Coverage
- Line Coverage

3 Choose the OK button.

Figure 18.1   Profile Dialog Box

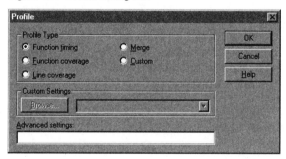

Note   If you haven't built your current project with profiling enabled, an error message lets you know that you need to rebuild your project. See "Building Code for Profiling" for more information.

From the Profile dialog box, you can also:

- Merge multiple profiling sessions
- Use Custom Settings to run a profiler batch file and perform other functions, including:
  - Function Counting
  - Line Counting
- Specify additional profiler options through Advanced Settings

Types of Profiling

The profiler can analyze the execution of your code with two levels of detail: function or line. Function profiling is good for detecting inefficient code and is faster than line profiling, because there is less information to collect. Line profiling can be useful for checking the validity of an algorithm, because it shows how many times each line is executed in response to certain input data, and you can see which lines aren't executed at all.

In many cases, you will want to profile only part of your project, such as a single function or library. To learn how to specify when to start and stop profiling certain areas, see "Selective Profiling," later in this chapter.

Function Profiling

The profiler provides three ways to profile by function:

- Function timing lists time spent in functions together with "hit count"—the number of times the function was called.
- Function counting lists only hit counts, but it is faster than function timing.
- Function coverage lists functions that are or are not executed.

Debugging information is not required for function timing, function counting, or function coverage. The profiler reads the project's .MAP file to match addresses with function names. It also creates a modified executable module and saves it in a temporary file with an ._XE or ._LL extension. This modified file contains thunks (substitutions for function calls), enabling the profiler to count and time the functions.

Caution With function timing, function counting, or function coverage, the function calls go through thunks for the profiler to record all the relevant information, which requires modification of the stack of the original executable (.EXE) file. As a result, it is not possible to profile functions that modify the stack themselves.

For example, the function **AfxDispatchCall** in the Microsoft Foundation Class dynamic-link library (.DLL) cannot be profiled, because it modifies the stack. However, the rest of the application or the .DLL can be profiled by excluding the object module that contains this offending function. (PREP automatically excludes the object module that defines **AfxDispatchCall**, olecall.obj.) The module that contains the offending function can be identified using the .MAP file (see "Generate Mapfile" on page 419 of Chapter 21, "Setting Linker Options"). For more information on how to exclude modules, see the /EXC option of PREP on page 594 of Chapter 27, "Profiler Reference."

Function Timing

The Function Timing option in the Profile dialog box profiles the current project, recording how many times each function was called (hit count) as well as how much time was spent in each function and called functions.

Here is a sample of the data provided by function timing.

```
Func              Func+Child
Time      %       Time        %        Hit Count     Function
------------------------------------------------------------------------
---------
2.606    48.1    2.606       48.1     2              _SetCursor@4
                                                     user32.def)
```

Function Counting

The Function Counting option in the Profile dialog box records how many times each function was called (hit count). To start a function counting profile run, use a custom batch file that specifies the source module and lines to profile.

1 From the Tools menu, choose Profile. The Profile dialog box appears.

2 In the Profile Type box, select the Custom radio button.

3 In the Custom Settings box, select the FCOUNT.BAT batch file (usually found in \MSDEV\BIN).

Function counting is similar to function timing, but only hit counts (greater than zero) are recorded, so profiled program execution is slightly faster. Here is a sample output line with column headings:

```
Hit Count         %               Function
-----------------------------------------------------------------
1                25.0            LoadCursorA@8(user32.def)
```

Function Coverage

The Function Coverage option in the Profile dialog box profiles the current project, recording whether a function was called.

Function coverage profiling is useful for determining which sections of your code are not being executed. The profiler lists all profiled functions, with an asterisk (*) marking those that were executed. The profiling overhead for function coverage matches the overhead for function counting. Here is a sample function coverage report:

```
Covered Function
-------------------------------------------
     .      _InitInstance (generic.obj)
     .      _LoadAcceleratorsA@8 (user32.def)
     *      _LoadCursorA@8 (user32.def)
     .      _LoadIconA@8 (user32.def)
     .      _SendMessageA@16 (user32.def)
     *      _SetCursor@4 (user32.def)
     .      _SetDlgItemTextA@12 (user32.def)
```

Line Profiling

With the profiler's two line profiling options, you can see which source lines are being executed.

- Line counting shows you how many times each line was executed.
- Line coverage shows you which lines were executed at least once.

Line profiling uses debugging information in your .EXE file to trigger the profiler, so it does not need a .MAP file.

Line Counting

The Line Counting option in the Profile dialog box records how many times each line was called (hit count). To start a line count profile, use a custom batch file that specifies the source module and the lines to profile.

▶ **To profile by line counting**

1 From the Tools menu, choose Profile. The Profile dialog box appears.

2 In the Profile Type box, select the Custom radio button.

3 In the Custom Settings box, type in the LCOUNT.BAT batch file (usually found in \MSDEV\BIN).

4 Choose the OK button.

Here is a sample of the output of a line counting profile run:

```
          Hit
Line count    %   Source
---------------------------------------------------------------
   1:                    // test.c
   2:
   3:                    #include <windows.h>
   4:
   5:                    void WasteTime(HANDLE hInstance, HWND hWnd)
   6:     1     0.0      {
   7:                        LONG lCount, lX;
   8:                        HCURSOR hOldCursor;
   9:     1     0.0         hOldCursor = SetCursor(LoadCursor(NULL,
                                IDC_WAIT));
  10:     1     0.0         for(lCount = 0; lCount < 1000L; lCount++)  {
  11:  1000    49.9            lX = 57L;
  12:  1000    49.9         }
  13:     1     0.0         SetCursor(hOldCursor);
  14:     1     0.0      }
```

Note that all included source lines are printed, even if they are not executed.

Line counting profiling is very slow because the profiler inserts a debugging breakpoint for every source code line, and these breakpoints remain for the duration of the profile session. To speed up profiling, reduce the number of lines selected for profiling. For more information, see "Selective Profiling," later in this chapter.

Line Coverage

The Line Coverage option in the Profile dialog box profiles the current project, recording whether a line was executed.

Line coverage profiling is useful for determining which sections of your code are not being executed. The profiler lists all profiled lines, with an asterisk (*) marking those that were executed. The profiling overhead for line coverage is lower than for line counting, because the profiler only needs to stop at a line once. Here is a sample line coverage report:

```
Line Covered  Source
-----------------------------------------------------------
   1:              // waste.c
   2:
   3:              #include <windows.h>
   4:
   5:              void WasteTime(HANDLE hInstance, HWND hWnd)
   6:      *       {
   7:                  LONG lCount, lX;
   8:                  HCURSOR hOldCursor;
   9:      *           hOldCursor = SetCursor(LoadCursor(NULL, IDC_WAIT));
  10:      *           for(lCount = 0; lCount < 1000L; lCount++) {
  11:      *               lX = 57L;
  12:      *           }
  13:      *           if(lCount == 0) {
  14:      .               lCount = 1; // should never execute
  15:                  }
  16:      *           SetCursor(hOldCursor);
  17:      *       }
```

Note that all included source lines are printed, even if they are not executed.

Line coverage profiling is much faster than line counting profiling, because the profiler can remove the inserted breakpoints when those lines are first executed.

Selective Profiling

It usually doesn't make much sense to profile an entire program because in most applications for Windows, the majority of the application's time is spent waiting for messages. Often, only one section of a program, such as repagination, might be performing poorly. Narrowing the region of code being profiled can speed up the execution of profiler sessions.

To narrow the area being profiled, see the following sections:

- Modifying TOOLS.INI
- Specifying Functions to Profile
- Specifying Lines to Profile
- Choosing Starting Functions for Profiling

Modifying TOOLS.INI

When setting up the profiler, the Setup program creates a TOOLS.INI file in the install directory (\MSDEV by default). The INIT environment variable should point to the directory containing TOOLS.INI.

The [profiler] section of TOOLS.INI specifies libraries and object (.OBJ) files for the profiler to ignore. By default, TOOLS.INI excludes the Win32 libraries, Microsoft Foundation Class (MFC) libraries, and C run-time libraries.

The following lines (taken from the default TOOLS.INI) exclude the common dialog and graphics device interface (GDI) libraries from profiling:

```
[profiler]
exclude:comdlg32.lib
exclude:gdi32.lib
```

Specifying Functions to Profile

By default, all functions in all modules are profiled, except those listed in the [profiler] section of TOOLS.INI. You can exclude and include functions from profiling by specifying options in the Advanced Settings text box of the Profile dialog box. For example, to exclude all functions in MYOBJ.OBJ except the MyFunc function, use these options:

```
/EXC MYOBJ.OBJ /INC MyFunc
```

Note Do not insert spaces in the text following /INC.

For more information on excluding and including functions, see the list of options for PREP in Chapter 27, "Profiler Reference," on page 594.

Specifying Lines to Profile

By default, all lines in all modules are profiled, except those listed in the [profiler] section of TOOLS.INI. You can exclude and include areas of code from profiling by specifying options in the Advanced Settings text box of the Profile dialog box. For example, to include all lines in the TEST module, specify the .OBJ filename with these options:

```
/EXCALL /INC test.obj
```

If you need specific lines, specify the source module with line numbers, as shown below:

```
/EXCALL /INC test.c(5-14)
```

Note Do not insert spaces in the text following /INC.

For more information on excluding and including lines, see the list of options for PREP in Chapter 27, "Profiler Reference," on page 594.

Choosing Starting Functions for Profiling

With the /SF option you can profile only a selected function and the functions it calls, so you can easily isolate a routine and its children for analysis.

To profile only MyFunc and the functions it calls, type the following in the Advanced Settings text box of the Profile dialog box:

```
/SF MyFunc
```

Using function selection can give you more useful results than function exclusion/inclusion, but function selection can be slower.

Note When you specify a C++ function name to the profiler, you must provide its decorated name. The easiest way to get the decorated name is to look it up in the project's .MAP file. For more information on C++ decorated names, see Appendix A, Decorated Names.

Other Profiler Features

Several other profiler features can be accessed from the Profile dialog box. With these features, you can perform advanced operations such as:

- Merging profiler output
- Running a custom batch file
- Advanced profiler settings

Merging Profiler Output

The Merge option in the Profile dialog box starts another profiler run of the same type as the most recent profiler run. The results of the current profile session are merged with those of the previous session, and the Profile tab of the Output window shows the results of the merge.

With this option, you can obtain more accurate results by combining profiling information from several sessions into a composite report.

For more information on merging profiler output, see "Combining Profile Sessions" in Chapter 12 of *Programming Techniques*.

Running a Custom Batch File

When a batch file is executed using the Custom option in the Profile dialog box, Developer Studio substitutes the project's program name for the %1 parameter.

▶ **To specify your program's command-line arguments**

1 From the Build menu choose Settings.

The Project Settings dialog box appears.

2 Select the Debug tab and type the arguments in the Program Arguments text box.

For more information on creating and running profiler batch files, see "Profiler Batch Processing" in Chapter 27, "Profiler Reference," on page 591.

Advanced Profiler Settings

With the Advanced Settings text box in the Profile dialog box, you can specify additional command-line options for PREP Phase I.

For more information, see PREP in Chapter 27, "Profiler Reference," on page 594.

Profiling Under Win32s

When developing an application for Win32s®, you may find that your code performs differently than under Windows NT. To help optimize your code for Win32s, profile it using PROFW32S, a special version of the profiler that runs under Win32s.

Installing the Win32s Profiler

The Win32s Setup program (SETUP.EXE) installs all the necessary profiler files for Win32s and correctly configures the profiler for your selected environment.

If you have already installed Win32s but did not choose to install the profiler at that time, you can run the Setup program again and install just the profiler components.

Win32s Profiling Procedure

The Developer Studio Profile dialog box is not supported under Win32s. Instead, run PREP and PLIST directly from the command line on the host (Windows NT) system, then run the Win32s profiler, PROFW32S, from the Program Manager or File Manager on the Win32s target system.

For more information on profiling from the command line, see Chapter 27, "Profiler Reference."

CHAPTER 19

Using Spy++

Spy++ (SPYXX.EXE) is a Win32-based utility that gives you a graphical view of the system's processes, threads, windows, and window messages. With Spy++, you can:

- Display a graphical tree of relationships among system objects, including processes, threads, and windows.
- Search for specified windows, threads, processes, or messages.
- View the properties of selected windows, threads, processes, or messages.
- Select a window, thread, process, or message directly from the view.
- Use the Finder Tool to select a window by mouse positioning.
- Set complex message log selection parameters.

 Tip While using Spy++, in many instances you can click the right mouse button to display a pop-up menu of frequently used commands. The commands available depend on where the pointer is. For example, if you click while pointing at a window, and the selected window is visible, the pop-up Highlight menu item will cause the border of the selected window to flash so that the window can be easily located on the screen.

Working In Spy++

Spy++ has a toolbar and hyperlinks to help you work faster. It also provides a Refresh command to update the active view, a Window Finder Tool to make spying easier, and a Font dialog box to customize view windows. Additionally, Spy++ saves and restores user preferences.

There are two utilities similar to Spy++: PVIEW.EXE, which shows details on processes and threads, and DDESPY.EXE, a monitoring program for Dynamic Data Exchange (DDE) messages. Books Online documents each utility.

Starting Spy++

▶ **To start Spy++**

• From the Tools menu, choose Spy++.

  −or−

  Click the Spy++ icon in the Visual C++ program group.

  Note   You can run only one copy of Spy++. Attempting to run additional copies of Spy++ will bring the currently running Spy++ to the front.

  Spy++ is a read-only program. Using Spy++ does not change program operation, but can slow program execution.

Viewing with Spy++

When Spy++ starts, it opens a window titled "Windows 1," which shows a tree view of all windows and controls in the system. There are also three other "views" available in Spy++: messages, processes, and threads.

The Spy++ Toolbar

The Spy++ toolbar appears beneath the menu bar. It provides shortcut commands for opening new views, starting or stopping the message stream display, changing message stream options, clearing message stream windows, and finding windows. You can display or hide the toolbar with the Toolbar command on the View menu.

Button	Effect
	Creates a window to display a tree view of all windows and controls in the system. See "The Windows View."
	Creates a window to display a tree view of all processes in the system. See "The Processes View."
	Creates a window to display a tree view of all threads in the system. See "The Threads View."
	Creates a window to display window messages. This button calls up the Message Options dialog box to let you select the window whose messages will be displayed, in addition to other options. See "The Messages View."
	Starts the message logging and displays the message stream. This button is available only when a Messages window is active (has the focus). See "Starting and Stopping the Message Log Display."
	Stops the message logging and display of the message stream. This button is available only when a Messages window is active (has the focus). See "Starting and Stopping the Message Log Display."

Button	Effect
	Displays the Message Options dialog box. Use this dialog box to select windows and message types for viewing. This button is available only when a Messages window is active (has the focus). See "Choosing Message Options."
	Clears the contents of the active Messages window. This button is available only when a Messages window is active (has the focus).
	Opens the Find Window dialog box, which lets you select a window to view messages or find properties. See "The Window Finder Tool."
	Expands one level of the selected tree. See "Expanding and Collapsing Spy++ Trees."
	Fully expands the selected branch of the tree.
	Fully expands every branch of the entire tree.
	Collapses the selected branch of the tree.
	Searches the current view for a matching window, process, thread, or message.
	Searches the current view for the next matching window, process, thread, or message. This button (and the related menu item) is available only when there is a valid search result that is not unique. For example, when you use a window handle as the search criteria in the window tree, it will produce unique results, since there is only one window with that handle in the window tree. In this instance, Find Next is not available.
	Searches the current view for the previous matching window, process, thread, or message. This button (and the related menu item) is available only when there is a valid search result that is not unique. For example, when you use a window handle as the search criteria in the window tree, it will produce unique results, since there is only one window with that handle in the window tree. In this instance, Find Previous is not available.
	Cascades the windows.
	Tiles the view windows horizontally.
	Tiles the view windows vertically.

Refreshing the View

Spy++ takes a "snapshot" of the system tables and refreshes a view based on this information. It is important that you periodically refresh your system views. If you have a Spy++ view open and have not refreshed the view, you will not see those processes, threads, and windows that are subsequently created. Also, you may see items that no longer exist. The Refresh command is available for all views except the Messages view.

▶ **To refresh the currently active view**

• From the Window menu, choose Refresh.

Changing Fonts

You can change the font, font style, and font size for Spy++ windows.

▶ **To change font options**

1 From the View menu, choose Font.

   The Font dialog box appears.

2 Choose a font, font style, and font size.

3 Choose the OK button.

Selecting Save Font As Default will cause all future Spy++ windows to use this font.

Expanding and Collapsing Spy++ Trees

You can expand and collapse the Windows, Processes, and Threads views using several methods: by clicking the icons in the window, by using the Tree menu, and by clicking the expansion toolbar buttons. The + and – icons in the tree act as they do in the Developer Studio Project Workspace window.

The Tree menu contains four commands.

Menu command	Description
Expand One Level	Expands the currently selected item to the next level.
Expand Branch	Fully expands the currently selected item.
Expand All	Fully expands all items in the window.
Collapse	Fully collapses the currently selected item.

 Tip If you expand a process, you see all the threads the process owns. If you expand a thread, you see a list of all the windows it owns.

▶ **To expand or collapse Spy++ trees**

1 Select one of the items in a Windows, Processes, or Threads view.

2 From the Tree menu, choose one of the expand or collapse commands.

   –or–

   Click the + and – icons in the tree.

The Windows View

The Windows view displays a tree of all windows and controls in the system. The Windows view shows only windows.

▶ To open the Windows view

- From the Spy menu, choose Windows.

Figure 19.1   shows the Spy++ representation of the Windows view with the first level expanded.

Figure 19.1   The Spy++ Windows View

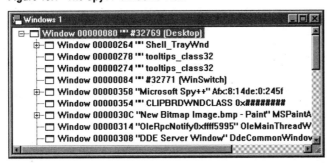

The current desktop window is at the top of the tree. All other windows are children of the desktop, and are listed according to the standard window hierarchy, with sibling windows ordered by Z-order. You can collapse or expand the whole tree by clicking the + or – symbol for the top-level window.

The Windows view is most useful if you need to find a particular window. If you start with a tree expanded at the second level (all windows that are children of the desktop), then you can identify the desktop-level window that you want by its class name and title. Once you have found the desktop-level window, you can expand the level to find a specific child window.

See Also   The Processes View, The Threads View, The Messages View

The Window Finder Tool

With the Window Finder Tool you can find the properties of a selected window. The Finder Tool can find disabled child windows and discern which window to highlight if disabled child windows overlap.

▶ To find a window to spy on

1 Arrange your windows so that Spy++ and the subject window are visible.

2 From the Spy menu, choose Find Window to open the Find Window dialog box.

3 Drag the Finder Tool to the window that you want.

As you drag the tool, window details appear in the dialog box.

−or−

If you know the handle of the window you want (for example, from the debugger), type it in the Handle box.

4 Under Show, choose Properties or Messages to select what kind of information to display.

5 Choose the OK button.

 Tip To reduce screen clutter, select the Hide Spy option in the Find Window dialog box. This removes the main Spy++ window and leaves the Find Window dialog box visible on top of your other applications. The Spy++ main window will be restored when you choose the OK or Cancel button, or by clearing the Hide Spy option.

In Figure 19.2, the Finder Tool was dragged over the "Exploring" window.

Figure 19.2 Showing Properties with the Find Window

Searching for a Window

You can search for a specific window by using its handle, caption, class, or a combination of its caption and class as search criteria. You can also specify the initial direction of the search.

▶ **To search for a window**

1 Arrange your windows so that Spy++, an active Windows view, and the subject window are visible.

2 From the Search menu, choose Find Window.

The Window Search dialog box appears.

3 Drag the Finder Tool to the subject window that you want.

As you drag the tool, window details appear in the dialog box.

−or−

If you know the handle of the window you want (for example, from the debugger), type it in the Handle box.

−or−

If you know the caption and/or class of the window you want, type them in the Caption and Class box and delete the Handle box.

4 Choose Up or Down for the initial direction of the search.

5 Choose the OK button.

If a matching window is found, it is highlighted in the Windows view.

 Tip   To reduce screen clutter, select the Hide Spy option in the Find Window dialog box. This removes the main Spy++ window and leaves the Find Window dialog box visible on top of your other applications. The Spy++ main window will be restored when you choose the OK or Cancel button, or by clearing the Hide Spy option.

Opening Window Properties

You can find out more about entries in the Windows view with the Window Properties dialog box.

▶ **To open the Window Properties dialog box, do one of the following**

- Double-click an item in one of the Windows views.

- Click the item, then choose Properties from the View menu.

- Point to the item and click the right mouse button, and then choose Properties from the pop-up menu.

Properties dialog boxes are not modal, so you can click another item in a view window and the dialog box will show information on the selected item.

See Also   Window Properties for Windows

Window Properties

The Window Properties dialog box contains five tabs, as shown in Figure 19.3: General, Styles, Windows, Class, and Process. Click the title of the tab to display that tab's options.

Figure 19.3 The Window Properties Dialog Box

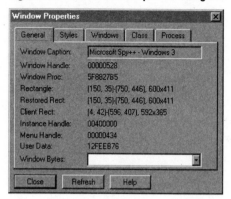

The options on the Window Properties General tab are:

Entry	Description
Window Caption	The text in the window caption.
Window Handle	The unique ID of this window. Window handle numbers are reused; they identify a window only for the lifetime of that window.
Window Proc	The virtual address of the window procedure function for this window. This field also indicates whether this window is a Unicode window, and whether it is subclassed.
Rectangle	The bounding rectangle for the window. The size of the rectangle is also displayed. Units are pixels in screen coordinates.
Restored Rect	The bounding rectangle for the restored window. The size of the rectangle is also displayed. Restored Rect will differ from Rectangle only when the window is maximized or minimized. Units are pixels in screen coordinates.
Client Rect	The bounding rectangle for the window client area. The size of the rectangle is also displayed. Units are pixels relative to the top left of the window client area.
Instance Handle	The instance handle of the application. Instance handles are not unique.
Control ID or Menu Handle	If the window being displayed is a child window, the Control ID label is displayed. Control ID is an integer that identifies this child window's control ID. If the window being displayed is not a child window, the Menu Handle label is displayed. Menu Handle is an integer that identifies the handle of the menu associated with this window.
User Data	Application-specific data that is attached to this window structure.
Window Bytes	The number of extra bytes associated with this window. The meaning of these bytes is determined by the application. Expand the list box to see the byte values in DWORD format.

The options on the Window Properties Styles tab are:

Entry	Description
Window Styles	A combination of window style codes.
Extended Styles	A combination of extended window style codes.

The options on the Window Properties Windows tab are:

Entry	Description
Next Window	The handle of the next sibling window in the same sequence (Z-order) shown in the window tree view ("none" if there is no next window). Click this entry to view the properties of the next window.
Previous Window	The handle of the previous sibling window in the same sequence (Z-order) shown in the window tree view ("none" if there is no previous window). Click this entry to view the properties of the previous window.
Parent Window	The handle of this window's parent window ("none" if there is no parent). Click this entry to view the properties of the parent window.
First Child	The handle of this window's first child window, in the sequence (Z-order) shown in the window tree view ("none" if there are no child windows). Click this value to view the properties of the first child window.
Owner Window	The handle of this window's owner window. An application's main window typically owns system-modal dialog windows, for example ("none" if there is no owner). Click this entry to view the properties of the owner window.

The options on the Window Properties Class tab are:

Entry	Description
Class Name	The name (or ordinal number) of this window class.
Class Styles	A combination of class style codes.
Class Bytes	Application-specific data associated with this window class.
Class Atom	The atom for the class returned by the RegisterClass call.
Instance Handle	The instance handle of the module that registered the class. Instance handles are not unique.
Window Bytes	The number of extra bytes associated with each window of this class. The meaning of these bytes is determined by the application. Expand the list box to see the byte values in DWORD format.
Window Proc	The current address of the WndProc function for windows of this class. This differs from Window Proc on the General tab if the window is subclassed.

Entry	Description
Menu Name	The name of the main menu that is associated with windows of this class ("none" if there is no menu).
Icon Handle	The handle for the icon that is associated with windows of this class ("none" if there is no icon).
Cursor Handle	The handle for the cursor that is associated with windows of this class ("none" if there is no cursor).
Bkgnd Brush	The handle for the background brush that is associated with windows of this class, or one of the predefined COLOR_* colors for painting the window background ("none" if there is no brush).

The options on the Window Properties Process tab are:

Entry	Description
Process ID	The ID of the process that owns the thread that created this window. Click this value to view the properties of this process.
Thread ID	The ID of the thread that created this window. Click this value to view the properties of this thread.

See Also   Opening Window Properties

The Processes View

Microsoft Windows® supports multiple processes. Each process can have one or more threads, and each thread can have one or more associated top-level windows. Each top-level window can own a series of windows. A + symbol indicates that a level is already collapsed. Click the + symbol to expand the level. The collapsed view consists of one line per process.

Use the Processes view if you want to examine a particular system process, which usually corresponds to an executing program. Processes are identified by module names, or they are designated "system processes." To find a process, collapse the tree and search the list.

▶ **To open the Processes view**

• From the Spy menu, choose Processes.

The Processes view window appears, as shown in Figure 19.4.

Figure 19.4   The Processes View Window

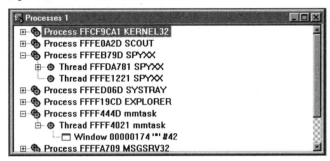

See Also   The Windows View, The Threads View, The Messages View

Searching for a Process

You can search for a specific process by using its process ID or module string as search criteria. You can also specify the initial direction of the search. The fields in the dialog box will show the attributes of the selected process in the process tree.

▶ **To search for a process**

1 Arrange your windows so that Spy++ and an active Processes view are visible.

2 From the Search menu, choose Find Process to open the Process Search dialog box (shown in Figure 19.5).

Figure 19.5   Process Search Dialog Box

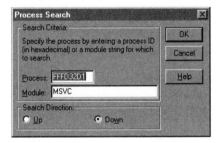

3 Type the process ID or a module string as search criteria.

4 Choose Up or Down for the initial direction of the search.

5 Choose the OK button.

If a matching process is found, it is highlighted in the Processes view.

 Tip   To find all the processes owned by a module, clear the Process box and type the module name in the Module box. Then use Find Next to continue searching for processes.

Opening Process Properties

You can find out more about entries in the Processes view with the Process Properties dialog box.

▶ **To open the Process Properties dialog box, do one of the following**

- Double-click an item in one of the Processes views.

- Click the item, then choose Properties from the View menu.

- Point to the item and click the right mouse button, and then choose Properties from the pop-up menu.

Properties dialog boxes are not modal, so you can click another item in a view window and the dialog box will show information on the selected item.

See Also   Process Properties for Windows 95, Process Properties for Windows NT

Process Properties for Windows 95

For Windows 95™, the Process Properties dialog box contains one tab as shown in Figure 19.6: General.

Figure 19.6   Process Properties Dialog Box for Windows 95

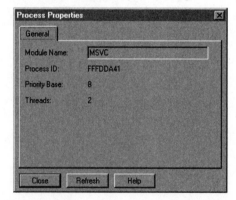

The options on the Process Properties General tab for Windows 95 are:

Entry	Description
Module Name	The name of the module.
Process ID	The unique ID of this process. Process ID numbers are reused, so they identify a process only for the lifetime of that process. The Process object type is created when a program is run. All the threads in a process share the same address space and have access to the same data.

Entry	Description
Priority Base	The current base priority of this process. Threads within a process can raise and lower their own base priority relative to the process's base priority.
Threads	The number of threads currently active in this process.

See Also   Opening Process Properties

Process Properties for Windows NT

For Windows NT, the Process Properties dialog box contains four tabs as shown in Figure 19.7: General, Memory, Page File, and Space. Click the title of a tab to display that tab's options.

Figure 19.7   Process Properties Dialog Box for Windows NT

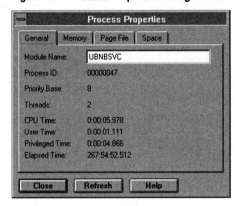

The options on the Process Properties General tab for Windows NT are:

Entry	Description
Module Name	The name of the module.
Process ID	The unique ID of this process. Process ID numbers are reused, so they identify a process only for the lifetime of that process. The Process object type is created when a program is run. All the threads in a process share the same address space and have access to the same data.
Priority Base	The current base priority of this process. Threads within a process can raise and lower their own base priority relative to the process's base priority.
Threads	The number of threads currently active in this process.
CPU Time	Total CPU time spent on this process and its threads. Equal to User Time plus Privileged Time.

Entry	Description
User Time	The cumulative elapsed time that this process's threads have spent executing code in User Mode in non-idle threads. Applications execute in User Mode, as do subsystems such as the window manager and the graphics engine.
Privileged Time	The total elapsed time this process has been running in Privileged Mode in non-idle threads. The service layer, the Executive routines, and the Kernel execute in Privileged Mode. Device drivers for most devices other than graphics adapters and printers also execute in Privileged Mode. Some work that Windows does for your application may appear in other subsystem processes in addition to Privileged Time.
Elapsed Time	The total elapsed time this process has been running.

The options on the Process Properties Memory tab for Windows NT are:

Entry	Description
Virtual Bytes	The current size (in bytes) of the virtual address space the process is using. The use of virtual address space does not necessarily imply corresponding use of either disk or main memory pages. However, virtual space is finite, and using too much may limit the ability of the process to load libraries.
Peak Virtual Bytes	The maximum number of bytes of virtual address space the process has used at any one time.
Working Set	The set of memory pages touched recently by the threads in the process. If free memory in the computer is above a threshold, pages are left in the Working Set of a process even if they are not in use. When free memory falls below a threshold, pages are trimmed from the Working Set. If they are needed, they will be soft-faulted back into the Working Set before they leave main memory.
Peak Working Set	The maximum number of pages in the working set of this process at any point in time.
Paged Pool Bytes	The current amount of paged pool the process has allocated. Paged pool is a system memory area where operating system components acquire space as they accomplish their appointed tasks. Paged pool pages can be paged out to the paging file when not accessed by the system for sustained periods of time.
Nonpaged Pool Bytes	The current number of bytes in the nonpaged pool allocated by the process. The nonpaged pool is a system memory area where space is acquired by operating system components as they accomplish their appointed tasks. Nonpaged pool pages cannot be paged out to the paging file; they remain in main memory as long as they are allocated.
Private Bytes	The current number of bytes this process has allocated that cannot be shared with other processes.

Entry	Description
Free Bytes	The total unused virtual address space of this process.
Reserved Bytes	The total amount of virtual memory reserved for future use by this process.
Free Image Bytes	The amount of virtual address space that is not in use or reserved by images within this process.
Reserved Image Bytes	The sum of all virtual memory reserved by images run within this process.

The options on the Process Properties Page File tab for Windows NT are:

Entry	Description
Page File Bytes	The current number of pages that this process is using in the paging file. The paging file stores pages of data used by the process but not contained in other files. The paging file is used by all processes, and lack of space in the paging file can cause errors while other processes are running.
Peak Page File Bytes	The maximum number of pages that this process has used in the paging file.
Page Faults	The number of Page Faults by the threads executing in this process. A page fault occurs when a thread refers to a virtual memory page that is not in its working set in main memory. Thus, the page will not be retrieved from disk if it is on the standby list and hence already in main memory, or if it is being used by another process with which the page is shared.

The options on the Process Properties Space tab for Windows NT are:

Entry	Description
Show For Space Marked As	Use this list box to select the category of space (image, mapped, reserved, or unassigned).
Executable Bytes	For the selected category, the sum of all the address space that this process is using. Executable memory is memory that can be executed by programs, but may not be read or written.
Exec-Read-Only Bytes	For the selected category, the sum of all the address space in use with read-only properties that this process is using. Exec-read-only memory is memory that can be executed as well as read.
Exec-Read-Write Bytes	For the selected category, the sum of all the address space in use with read-write properties that this process is using. Exec-read-write memory is memory that can be executed by programs as well as read and modified.

Entry	Description
Exec-Write-Copy Bytes	For the selected category, the sum of all the address space that can be executed by programs as well as read and written. This type of protection is used when memory needs to be shared between processes. If the sharing processes only read the memory, then they will all use the same memory. If a sharing process desires write access, then a copy of this memory will be made for the process.
No-Access Bytes	For the selected category, the sum of all the address space that prevents a process from using it. An access violation is generated if writing or reading is attempted.
Read-Only Bytes	For the selected category, the sum of all the address space that can be executed as well as read.
Read-Write Bytes	For the selected category, the sum of all the address space that allows reading and writing.
Write-Copy Bytes	For the selected category, the sum of all the address space that allows memory sharing for reading but not for writing. When processes are reading this memory, they can share the same memory. However, when a sharing process wants to have read/write access to this shared memory, a copy of that memory is made for writing.

See Also Opening Process Properties

The Threads View

The Threads view is a flat listing of all threads with associated windows. Processes are not included. You can easily find the process that owns a selected thread. Use the Threads view to search for a particular thread.

▶ **To open the Threads view**

• From the Spy menu, choose Threads.

The Threads view window appears as shown in Figure 19.8.

Figure 19.8 The Threads View Window

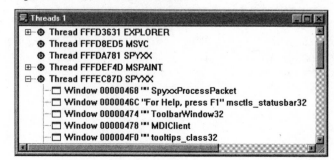

See Also   The Windows View, The Processes View, The Messages View

Searching for a Thread

You can search for a specific thread by using its thread ID or module string as search criteria. You can also specify the initial direction of the search. The fields in the dialog box will show the attributes of the selected thread in the thread tree.

▶ **To search for a thread**

1 Arrange your windows so that Spy++ and an active Threads view are visible.

2 From the Search menu, choose Find Thread.

   The Thread Search dialog box appears (shown in Figure 19.9).

3 Type the thread ID or a module string as search criteria.

4 Choose Up or Down for the initial direction of the search.

5 Choose the OK button.

If a matching thread is found, it is highlighted in the Threads view.

Figure 19.9   Thread Search Dialog Box

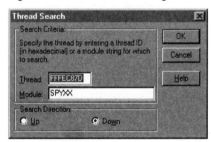

 Tip   To find all the threads owned by a module, clear the Thread box and type the module name in the Module box. Then use Find Next to continue searching for processes.

Opening Thread Properties

You can find out more about entries in the Threads view with the Thread Properties dialog box.

▶ **To open the Thread Properties dialog box, do one of the following**

• Double-click an item in one of the Threads views.

• Click the item, then choose Properties from the View menu.

• Point to the item and click the right mouse button, and then choose Properties from the pop-up menu.

Properties dialog boxes are not modal, so you can click another item in a view window and the dialog box will show information on the selected item.

See Also   Thread Properties for Windows 95, Thread Properties for Windows NT

Thread Properties for Windows 95

For Windows 95, the Thread Properties dialog box contains one tab as shown in Figure 19.10: General.

Figure 19.10   Thread Properties Dialog Box for Windows 95

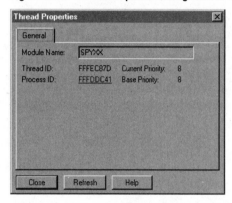

The options on the Thread Properties General tab for Windows 95 are:

Entry	Description
Module Name	The name of the module.
Thread ID	The unique ID of this thread. Note that Thread ID numbers are reused; they identify a thread only for the lifetime of that thread.
Process ID	The unique ID of this process. Process ID numbers are reused, so they identify a process only for the lifetime of that process. The Process object type is created when a program is run. All the threads in a process share the same address space and have access to the same data. Click this value to view the properties of the process ID.
Current Priority	The current dynamic priority of this thread. Threads within a process can raise and lower their own base priority relative to the base priority of the process.
Base Priority	The current base priority of this thread.

See Also   Opening Thread Properties

Thread Properties for Windows NT

For Windows NT, the Thread Properties dialog box contains one tab as shown in Figure 19.11: General.

Figure 19.11   Thread Properties Dialog Box for Windows NT

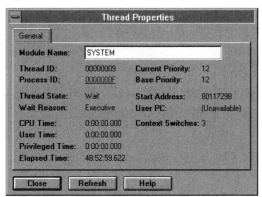

The options on the Thread Properties General tab for Windows NT are:

Entry	Description
Module Name	The name of the module.
Thread ID	The unique ID of this thread. Note that thread ID numbers are reused; they identify a thread only for the lifetime of that thread.
Process ID	The unique ID of this process. Process ID numbers are reused, so they identify a process only for the lifetime of that process. The Process object type is created when a program is run. All the threads in a process share the same address space and have access to the same data. Click this value to view the properties of the process ID.
Thread State	The current state of the thread. A Running thread is using a processor; a Standby thread is about to use one. A Ready thread is waiting to use a processor because one is not free. A thread in Transition is waiting for a resource to execute, such as waiting for its execution stack to be paged in from disk. A Waiting thread does not need the processor because it is waiting for a peripheral operation to complete or a resource to become free.
Wait Reason	This is applicable only when the thread is in the Wait state. Event Pairs are used to communicate with protected subsystems.
CPU Time	Total CPU time spent on this process and its threads. Equal to User Time plus Privileged Time.
User Time	The total elapsed time that this thread has spent executing code in User Mode. Applications execute in User Mode, as do subsystems such as the window manager and the graphics engine.

Entry	Description
Privileged Time	The total elapsed time that this thread has spent executing code in Privileged Mode. When a Windows system service is called, the service will often run in Privileged Mode to gain access to system-private data. Such data is protected from access by threads executing in User Mode. Calls to the system may be explicit, or they may be implicit, such as when a page fault or an interrupt occurs.
Elapsed Time	The total elapsed time (in seconds) this thread has been running.
Current Priority	The current dynamic priority of this thread. Threads within a process can raise and lower their own base priority relative to the base priority of the process.
Base Priority	The current base priority of this thread.
Start Address	Starting virtual address for this thread.
User PC	The user program counter for the thread.
Context Switches	The number of switches from one thread to another. Thread switches can occur either inside a single process or across processes. A thread switch may be caused by one thread asking another for information, or by a thread being preempted when a higher priority thread becomes ready to run.

See Also   Opening Thread Properties

The Messages View

Each window has an associated message stream. You can view this message stream in the Messages view. You can create a Messages view for a thread or process as well. This allows you to view messages sent to all windows owned by a specific process or thread, which is particularly useful for capturing window initialization messages.

▶ **To quickly open the Messages view for a window, process, or thread**

1 Move the focus to either a Windows, Processes, or Threads view window.

2 Click the right mouse button to display the pop-up menu.

   Note   There are some windows that can't be spied on. The pop-up menu will indicate the available selections.

3 Choose Messages.

   Spy++ begins logging messages.

   Note   The messages that appear depend on the current message options.

4 From the Messages menu, choose Stop Logging.

   Spy++ stops logging messages.

The Messages view appears as shown in Figure 19.12. Note that the first column contains the window handle, and the second column contains a message code (explained in Message Codes). Decoded message parameters and return values are on the right.

Figure 19.12 The Messages View Window

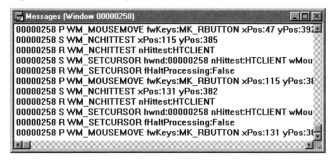

▶ **To open the Messages view for a window, process, or thread**

1 Move the focus to either a Windows, Processes, or Threads view window.

2 Find the name of the window, process, or thread that you want to examine, and select it.

3 From the Spy menu, choose Messages.

The Message Options dialog box appears.

4 Select the message options you want.

5 Choose the OK button.

Spy++ begins logging messages.

6 From the Messages menu, choose Stop Logging.

Spy++ stops logging messages.

For a more direct way to select a window for message stream viewing, use the following procedure.

▶ **To open the Messages view for a visible window using the Message Options dialog box**

1 Arrange your windows so that both Spy++ and the subject window are visible.

2 From the Spy menu, choose Messages.

The Message Options dialog box appears.

3 From the Windows tab, drag the Finder Tool to the window you want.

As you drag the tool, Window details appear in the dialog box.

4 Choose the OK button.

Spy++ begins logging messages.

5 From the Messages menu, choose Stop Logging.

Spy++ stops logging messages.

 Tip To reduce screen clutter, select the Hide Spy option in the Find Window dialog box. This removes the main Spy++ window and leaves the Find Window dialog box visible on top of your other applications. The Spy++ main window will be restored when you choose the OK or Cancel button, or by clearing the Hide Spy option.

See Also The Windows View, The Processes View, The Threads View

Message Codes

Each message line in the Messages view contains a 'P,' 'S,' 's,' or 'R' code. These codes have the following meanings:

Code	Meaning
P	The message was posted to the queue with the **PostMessage** function. No information is available concerning the ultimate disposition of the message.
S	The message was sent with the **SendMessage** function. This means that the sender doesn't regain control until the receiver processes and returns the message. The receiver can, therefore, pass a return value back to the sender.
s	The message was sent, but security prevents access to the return value.
R	Each 'S' line has a corresponding 'R' (return) line that lists the message return value. Sometimes message calls are nested, which means that one message handler sends another message.

Controlling the Messages View

With Spy++, you have considerable control over the content of the Messages view. You can start and stop displaying the messages at any time, and you can specify:

- Which message types you want to see.
- Which windows you want to monitor.
- The display format for message lines.

These settings are available from the Message Options dialog box and apply only to the selected Messages view.

Starting and Stopping the Message Log Display

When a Messages view window is active, a Start or Stop Logging choice appears on the Spy++ Messages menu, and the Start or Stop Logging toolbar button becomes active.

▶ **To stop the message log display**

- From the Messages menu, choose Stop Logging.

▸ **To start the message log display**

• From the Messages menu, choose Start Logging.

See Also   The Messages View

Choosing Message Options

The Options command on the Messages menu opens the Message Options dialog box (shown in Figure 19.13) with three tabs: Windows, Messages, and Output. Click the title of a tab to display that tab's options.

Figure 19.13   Message Options Dialog Box

The Windows Tab

The Windows tab on the Message Options dialog box contains the Window Finder Tool. Other options on the Windows tab include:

Option	Description
Parent	Display messages for the selected window and its immediate parent window.
Children	Display messages for the selected window and all its child windows, including nested child windows.
Windows Of Same Thread	Display messages for the selected window and all other windows owned by the same thread.
Windows Of Same Process	Display messages for the selected window and all other windows owned by the same process.
All Windows In System	Display messages for all windows.
Save Settings As Default	Save the preceding settings for new message stream windows. These settings are saved when Spy++ quits.

The Messages Tab

You can use the Messages tab in the Message Options dialog box to select message types for viewing. Typically, you first select message groups, and then fine-tune the selection by selecting individual messages. The All button selects all message types, and the None button clears all types.

Note that three entries under Message Groups do not map to specific entries under Messages To View. These include:

- WM_USER: with a code greater than WM_USER
- Registered: registered with the **RegisterWindowMessage** call
- Unknown: unknown messages in the range 0 to (WM_USER − 1)

If you select these "groups," the selection is applied directly to the message stream.

When you create a new Messages window, it can display all messages. When you filter messages from the Messages tab, that filter only applies to new messages, not messages that have already been displayed in the Windows view.

A grayed check box within Message Groups indicates that the Messages To View list box has been modified for messages in that group; not all of the message types in that group are selected.

If you select Save Settings As Default, the current settings are saved for later use as message search options. These settings are also saved when exiting Spy++.

The Output Tab

You can use the Output tab in the Message Options dialog box to select the following options:

Option	Description
Message Nesting Level	Prefix nested messages with one period per level.
Raw Message Parameters	Display the hexadecimal **wParam** and **lParam** values.
Decoded Message Parameters	Display the results of message-specific decoding of the **wParam** and **lParam** values.
Raw Return Values	Display the hexadecimal **lResult** return value.
Decoded Return Values	Display the results of message-specific decoding of the **lResult** return value.
Message Origin Time	The elapsed time since the Windows system was started (for posted messages only).
Message Mouse Position	The screen coordinates of the mouse when the message was posted (for posted messages only).

Option	Description
Lines Maximum	Limit the number of lines that are retained in the currently selected Messages view.
Also Log To File	Specify an output file for the message log. This output file is written simultaneously with the message log window.
Save Settings As Default	Save the preceding settings for new message stream windows. These settings are saved when you quit Spy++.

Searching for a Message

You can search for a specific message by using its handle, type, or message ID as search criteria. Any one of these criteria—or a combination—is valid search criteria. The initial direction of the search can also be specified. The fields in the Message Search dialog box (shown in Figure 19.14) will be preloaded with the attributes of the selected message in the message log.

Figure 19.14 Message Search Dialog Box

▶ **To search for a message**

1 Arrange your windows so that Spy++ and an active Messages view are visible.

2 From the Search menu, choose Find Message to open the Message Search dialog box.

3 Drag the Finder Tool to the window that you want.

As you drag the tool, window details appear in the dialog box.

−or−

If you know the window handle of the message you want, type it in the Handle box.

−or−

If you know the message type and/or message ID you want, make a selection using the Type and Message boxes and delete the Handle box.

You can clear any fields for which you do not want to specify values.

4 Type the message type, or message ID to search for.

5 Choose Up or Down for the initial direction of the search.

6 Choose the OK button.

If a matching message is found, it is highlighted in the Messages view window.

 Tip   To reduce screen clutter, select the Hide Spy option in the Find Window dialog box. This removes the main Spy++ window and leaves the Find Window dialog box visible on top of your other applications. The Spy++ main window will be restored when you choose the OK or Cancel button, or by clearing the Hide Spy option.

Opening Message Properties

You can find out more about entries in the Messages view with the Message Properties dialog box.

▶ **To open the Message Properties dialog box, do one of the following**

- Double-click an item in one of the Messages views.

- Click the item, then choose Properties from the View menu.

- Point to the item and click the right mouse button, and then choose Properties from the pop-up menu.

See Also   Message Properties

Message Properties

The Message Properties dialog box contains one tab as shown in Figure 19.15: General.

Figure 19.15   Message Properties Dialog Box

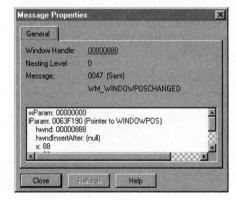

The options on the Message Properties General tab are:

Entry	Description
Window Handle	The unique ID of this window. Window handle numbers are reused; they identify a window only for the lifetime of that window. Click this value to view the properties of this window.
Nesting Level	Depth of nesting of this message, where 0 is no nesting.
Message	Number, status, and name of the selected windows message.
lResult	The value of the **lResult** parameter, if any.
wParam	The value of the **wParam** parameter, if any.
lParam	The value of the **lParam** parameter, if any. This value is decoded if it is a pointer to a string or structure.

See Also   Opening Message Properties

Setting Compiler Options

This chapter describes the compiler option categories that are available from the Category list box on the C/C++ tab of the Project Settings dialog box.

▶ **To view the Project Settings dialog box**

- From the Build menu, choose Settings.

The compiler option categories are described in the following sections:

- General
- C++ Language
- Code Generation
- Customize
- Listing Files
- Optimizations
- Precompiled Headers
- Preprocessor

Note The compiler options that are not available as controls within option categories on the C/C++ tab of the Project Settings dialog box are described in Chapter 25, "CL Reference."

General

General category options are the most commonly used options. All General category options, with the exception of the Debug Info option, are also available as settings in other option categories. Warning Level, Warnings as Errors, Debug Info, Common/Project/Source File Options, and Reset are described in this section.

The General category on the C/C++ tab is shown in Figure 20.1.

Figure 20.1 General Category on the C/C++ Tab

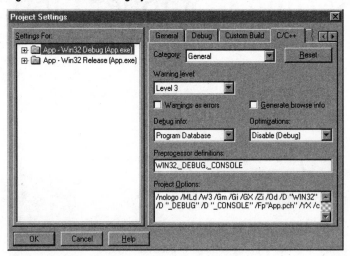

Warning Level

These options control the number of warning messages produced by the compiler. They affect only source files, not object (.OBJ) files.

None   Turns off all warning messages. Command-line equivalent: /W0 or /w

Level 1   Displays only severe warnings. Command-line equivalent: /W1

Level 2   Displays less severe warnings, such as the use of functions with no declared return type, failure to put return statements in functions that aren't void, and data conversions that would cause loss of data or precision. Command-line equivalent: /W2

Level 3   Displays less severe warnings, such as warnings about function calls that precede their function prototypes. Command-line equivalent: /W3

Level 4   Displays least severe warnings, such as non-ANSI features and extended keywords. Command-line equivalent: /W4

Compiler warning messages begin with C4. Books Online describes the warnings, indicates each warning's level, and indicates potential problems (rather than actual coding errors) with statements that may not compile as you intend.

You can also use the **warning** pragma to control the level of warning reported at compile time. For more information on the **warning** pragma, see "warning" in Chapter 2 of the *Preprocessor Reference*.

Warnings as Errors

This option instructs the compiler to issue an error message (and stop compilation) rather than a warning. Command-line equivalent: /WX

Debug Info

The Debug Info options select the type of debugging information created for your program and whether the debugging information is kept in .OBJ files or in a program database (PDB).

None   Produces no debugging information, so compilation is faster. No command-line equivalent.

Line Numbers Only   Produces an .OBJ file or executable (.EXE) file containing only global and external symbol and line-number information (no symbolic debugging information). Use this option if you want to reduce the size of the .EXE file, or if you don't want to use the debugger's expression evaluator (requires symbolic information). Command-line equivalent: /Zd

C7 Compatible   Produces an .OBJ file and an .EXE file containing line numbers and full symbolic debugging information for use with the debugger. The symbolic information includes the names and types of variables, as well as functions and line numbers. Command-line equivalent: /Z7

> **Note**   This option has the same effect as /Zi in Microsoft C/C++ version 7.

Program Database   Produces a program database (PDB) that contains type information and symbolic debugging information for use with the debugger. The symbolic debugging information includes the names and types of variables, as well as functions and line numbers. Command-line equivalent: /Zi

The compiler names the program database *project*.PDB. If you compile a file without a project, the compiler creates a database named VC40.PDB. The compiler embeds the name of the PDB in each .OBJ file created using this option, pointing the debugger to the location of symbolic and line-number information. When you use this option, your .OBJ files will be smaller, because debugging information is stored in the .PDB file rather than in .OBJ files.

If you create a library from objects that were compiled using this option, the associated .PDB file must be available when the library is linked to a program. Thus, if you distribute the library, you must distribute the PDB.

> **Note**   To create a library that contains debugging information without using .PDB files, you must select the compiler's C7 Compatible (/Z7) option and clear the linker's Use Program Database (/PDB:NONE) option. If you use the precompiled headers options, debugging information for both the precompiled header and the rest of the source code is placed in the PDB. The /Yd option is ignored when the Program Database option is specified.

Common/Project/Source File Options

The Common/Project/Source File Options text box displays the compiler options that are currently selected. The options are displayed using their command-line equivalents.

The name of the text box changes depending on the object selected in the Settings For pane. When a project is selected, the text box is named Project Options. When a source file is selected, the text box is named Source File Options. When multiple projects or files are selected, the text box is named Common Options, and it displays the options that are common to the selections.

You cannot type in the text box when it is named Common Options. However, when it is named Project Options or Source File Options, the text box accepts any option that is available from the C/C++ tab. It also accepts those compiler options that are otherwise available only from the command line.

You are responsible for the accuracy of any option you type in the text box. If an option is recognized as one that can be set using a dialog box control, the dialog box control is changed to reflect the option. However, if the option is not recognized, it is left in the options string and passed to the compiler as is.

Reset

The Reset button resets the project settings of a project or a file to the settings that existed when the project or file was created. This button is available if both of the following conditions are met:

- A single project or a single file is selected in the Settings For pane of the Project Settings dialog box.

- The settings of the selection have changed.

The Reset button is not available when multiple projects or files (including groups) are selected.

C++ Language

The C++ Language category options (see Figure 20.2) specify an inheritance representation for the C++ pointers to class members in your application, control exception handling, and control the creation of hidden virtual constructor/destructor displacement fields in classes with virtual bases.

Figure 20.2   C++ Language Category on the C/C++ Tab

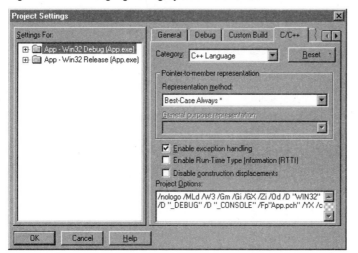

Pointer-to-Member Representation

Visual C++ supports pointers to members of any class. The number of bytes required to represent such a pointer and the code required to interpret the representation vary considerably, depending upon whether the class is defined with no, single, multiple, or virtual inheritance (no inheritance being smallest and virtual inheritance largest).

Representation Method

These options select the method that the compiler uses to represent pointers to class members. You can also use the **pointers_to_members** pragma in your code to specify a pointer representation. For more information on the **pointers_to_members** pragma, see "pointers_to_members" in Chapter 2 of the *Preprocessor Reference*.

Best-Case Always   Use this option if you always define a class before you declare a pointer to a member of the class. Command-line equivalent: /vmb

> If you define a class before declaring a pointer to a member of the class using the Best-Case Always option, the compiler knows the kind of inheritance used by the class when it encounters the declaration of the pointer. Thus, it can use the smallest possible representation of a pointer and create the smallest amount of code required to operate on the pointer for each kind of inheritance.

> With the Best-Case Always option, the compiler issues an error if it encounters the pointer declaration before the class definition. In this case, you must either reorganize your code or use the General-Purpose Always (/vmg) option. You can also use the **pointers_to_members** pragma or define the class using the **__single_inheritance**, **__multiple_inheritance**, or **__virtual_inheritance** keyword. These keywords allow control of the code created on a per-class basis.

For information on the use of the __single_inheritance, __multiple_inheritance, and __virtual_inheritance keywords, see "Representing Pointers to Members of Classes Using Inheritance" in Chapter 7 of the *C++ Language Reference*.

For the Best-Case Always options, the corresponding argument to the **pointers_to_members** pragma is **best_case**.

General-Purpose Always Use this option if you need to declare a pointer to a member of a class before defining the class. This need can arise if you define members in two different classes that reference each other. For such mutually referencing classes, one class must be referenced before it is defined. You must then choose an inheritance model from the General Purpose Representation drop-down list box. Command-line equivalent: /vmg

For General-Purpose Always, the corresponding argument to the **pointers_to_members** pragma is **full_generality**.

General Purpose Representation

If you select General-Purpose Always as the representation method, you must also specify an option to indicate the inheritance model of the not-yet-encountered class definition. You can select one of the following three options.

List entry	Command-line equivalent
Point to Any Class	/vmv
Point to Single- and Multiple-Inheritance Classes	/vmm
Point to Single-Inheritance Classes	/vms

When you specify one of these inheritance-model options, that model is used for all pointers to member classes, regardless of their inheritance type or whether the pointer is declared before or after the class.

Therefore, if you always use single-inheritance classes, you can reduce code size by selecting Point To Single-Inheritance Classes from the General Purpose Representation drop-down list box; however, if you want to compile using the most general case (at the expense of the largest data representation), you can select Point To Any Class, which allows pointers to classes of all inheritance types. Point To Any Class is the default.

Enable Exception Handling

This option controls whether destructors are called for automatic objects during a stack unwind that is caused by either a Windows NT-based structured exception or a C++ exception.

Select the Enable Exception Handling check box if you want the destructors of automatic objects to be called as the stack unwinds through the exception stack frames. Selecting this option produces code that is slightly larger than code created without this option. Code compiled using the /GX option can rely on the **_CPPUNWIND** predefined macro being defined. Command-line equivalent: /GX

Clear the Enable Exception Handling check box if you do not want destructors to be called as the stack unwinds. Command-line equivalent: /GX–

For more information on C++ exception handling, see Chapter 7, "C++ Exception Handling," in *Programming Techniques*.

Enable Run-Time Type Information (RTTI)

The Enable Run-Time Type Information (RTTI) option causes the compiler to add code to check object types at run time. When the Enable Run-Time Type Information (RTTI) check box is selected, the compiler defines the **_CPPRTTI** preprocessor macro. The option is cleared by default. Command-line equivalent: /GR

For more information on run-time type checking, see Run-Time Type Information (RTTI) in the *C++ Language Reference*.

Disable Construction Displacements

Select the Disable Construction Displacements check box to suppress the vtordisp constructor/destructor displacement member, but only if you are certain that all class constructors and destructors call virtual functions virtually. Command-line equivalent: /vd0

Clear the Disable Construction Displacements check box to enable the creation of hidden vtordisp constructor/destructor displacement members. Command-line equivalent: /vd1

Visual C++ implements C++ construction displacement support in situations where virtual inheritance is used. Construction displacements solve the problem created when a virtual function, declared in a virtual base and overridden in a derived class, is called from a constructor during construction of a further derived class.

The problem is that the virtual function may be passed an incorrect **this** pointer as a result of discrepancies between the displacements to the virtual bases of a class and the displacements to its derived classes. The solution provides a single construction displacement adjustment, called a vtordisp field, for each virtual base of a class.

By default, vtordisp fields are introduced whenever the code both defines user-defined constructors and destructors and also overrides virtual functions of virtual bases.

These options affect entire source files. You can use the **vtordisp** pragma to suppress and then re-enable vtordisp fields on a class-by-class basis. For more information on the **vtordisp** pragma, see "vtordisp" in Chapter 2 of the *Preprocessor Reference*.

Code Generation

- The Code Generation category options (see Figure 20.3) specify the CPU, run-time library, calling convention, and structure alignment.

Figure 20.3 Code Generation Category on the C/C++ Tab

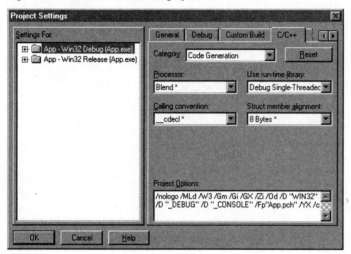

x86 Specific →

Processor

The Processor option directs the compiler to optimize code generation for the 80386, 80486, or Pentium® processors.

80386 Optimizes the code created in the same way as the Blend option. The 80386 option is retained for compatibility with previous versions of Visual C++ and to force a value of 300 for the **_M_IX86** preprocessor macro. Command-line equivalent: /GB or /G3

80486 Optimizes the code created in the same way as the Blend option. The 80486 option is retained for compatibility with previous versions of Visual C++. Command-line equivalent: /GB or /G4

Pentium Optimizes the code created to favor the Pentium. Use this option for programs meant only for the Pentium. Code created using the Pentium option does not perform as well on 80386- and 80486-based computers as code created using the Blend option. Command-line equivalent: /G5

Blend Optimizes the code created to favor the 80486, but includes many Pentium optimizations that do not seriously impact performance on the 80386 or 80486. Both the 80386 and the 80486 options now map to the Blend option. Command-line equivalent: /GB

The compiler creates a value for the **_M_IX86** preprocessor identifier that reflects the processor option, as shown in the following table.

Option	Value
Blend	**_M_IX86 = 400** (Default. Future compilers will issue a different value to reflect the dominant processor.)
80386	**_M_IX86 = 300**
80486	**_M_IX86 = 400**
Pentium	**_M_IX86 = 500**

END x86 Specific

Use Run-Time Library

With the Use Run-Time Library options, you can select either single-threaded or multithreaded run-time routines, indicate that a multithreaded module is a dynamic-link library (DLL), and select the retail or debug version of the library.

Note Having more than one copy of the run-time libraries in a process can cause problems, because static data in one copy is not shared with the other copy. To ensure that your process contains only one copy, avoid mixing static and dynamic versions of the run-time libraries. The linker will prevent you from linking with both static and dynamic versions within one .EXE file, but you can still end up with two (or more) copies of the run-time libraries. For example, a dynamic-link library linked with the static (non-DLL) versions of the run-time libraries can cause problems when used with an .EXE file that was linked with the dynamic (DLL) version of the run-time libraries. (You should also avoid mixing the debug and non-debug versions of the libraries in one process.)

Single-Threaded (LIBC.LIB)   Causes the compiler to place the library name LIBC.LIB into the .OBJ file so that the linker will use LIBC.LIB to resolve external symbols. This is the compiler's default action. LIBC.LIB does not provide multithread support. Command-line equivalent: /ML

Multithreaded (LIBCMT.LIB)   Defines **_MT** so that multithread-specific versions of the run-time routines are selected from the standard header (.H) files. This option also causes the compiler to place the library name LIBCMT.LIB into the .OBJ file so that the linker will use LIBCMT.LIB to resolve external symbols. Either /MT or /MD (or their debug equivalents /MTd or /MDd) is required to create multithreaded programs. Command-line equivalent: /MT

Multithreaded DLL (MSVCRT.LIB)   Defines **_MT** and **_DLL** so that both multithread- and DLL-specific versions of the run-time routines are selected from the standard .H files. This option also causes the compiler to place the library name MSVCRT.LIB into the .OBJ file. Command-line equivalent: /MD

Applications compiled with this option are statically linked to MSVCRT.LIB. This library provides a layer of code that allows the linker to resolve external references. The actual working code is contained in MSVCRT40.DLL, which must be available at run time to applications linked with MSVCRT.LIB.

The last three options select the debug versions of the library or DLL and define **_DEBUG**. For more information on using the debug versions, see "Debug Version of the C Run-Time Library" in Chapter 4 of the *C Run-Time Library Reference*.

Debug Single-Threaded (LIBCD.LIB)   Defines **_DEBUG** and causes the compiler to place the library name LIBCD.LIB into the .OBJ file so that the linker will use LIBCD.LIB to resolve external symbols. LIBCD.LIB does not provide multithread support. Command-line equivalent: /MLd

Debug Multithreaded (LIBCMTD.LIB)   Defines **_DEBUG** and **_MT**. Defining **_MT** causes multithread-specific versions of the run-time routines to be selected from the standard .H files. This option also causes the compiler to place the library name LIBCMTD.LIB into the .OBJ file so that the linker will use LIBCMTD.LIB to resolve external symbols. Either /MTd or /MDd (or their non-debug equivalents /MT or MD) is required to create multithreaded programs. Command-line equivalent: /MTd

Debug Multithreaded DLL (MSVCRTD.LIB)   Defines **_DEBUG**, **_MT**, and **_DLL** so that debug multithread- and DLL-specific versions of the run-time routines are selected from the standard .H files. It also causes the compiler to place the library name MSVCRTD.LIB into the .OBJ file. Command-line equivalent: /MDd

Applications compiled with this option are statically linked to MSVCRTD.LIB. This library provides a layer of code that allows the linker to resolve external references. The actual working code is contained in MSVCR40D.DLL, which must be available at run time to applications linked with MSVCRTD.LIB.

Calling Convention

The calling convention option determines the order in which arguments passed to functions are pushed onto the stack; which function, calling or called, removes the arguments from the stack; and the name-decorating convention that the compiler uses to identify individual functions.

__cdecl   Specifies the C calling convention for all functions that are not C++ member functions or are not marked as **__stdcall** or **__fastcall**. The called function's arguments are pushed onto the stack from right to left, and the calling function pops these arguments from the stack when control returns to the calling function. This is the default setting. Command-line equivalent: /Gd

For C, the **__cdecl** naming convention uses the function name preceded by an underscore (_); no case translation is performed. Unless declared as **extern "C"**, C++ methods use a different name-decorating scheme. For more information on decorated names, see Appendix A, "Decorated Names."

__*fastcall*__   Specifies the __fastcall__ calling convention for all functions that are not
C++ member functions or are not marked as __cdecl__ or __stdcall__. All __fastcall__
functions must have prototypes. Command-line equivalent: /Gr

Some of a __fastcall__ function's arguments are passed in registers **x86 Specific** →
ECX and EDX **END x86 Specific**, and the rest are pushed onto the stack from right
to left. The called routine pops these arguments from the stack before it returns.
Typically, /Gr decreases execution time.

Important   Be careful when using the __fastcall__ calling convention for any function written
in inline assembly language. Your use of registers could conflict with the compiler's use.

For C, the __fastcall__ naming convention uses the function name preceded and
followed by an at sign (@). The second is followed by the size of the function's
arguments in bytes. No case translation is performed. The compiler uses the
following template for the naming convention:

```
@function_name@number
```

Note   Microsoft does not guarantee the same implementation of the __fastcall__ calling
convention between compiler releases.

When using the __fastcall__ naming convention, use the standard include files.
Otherwise, you will get unresolved external references.

__*stdcall*__   Specifies the __stdcall__ calling convention for all prototyped C functions
that do not take a variable number of arguments and are not marked as __cdecl__ or
__fastcall__. All __stdcall__ functions must have prototypes. Command-line
equivalent: /Gz

A __stdcall__ function's arguments are pushed onto the stack from right to left, and
the called function pops these arguments from the stack before it returns.

For C, the __stdcall__ naming convention uses the function name preceded by an
underscore (_) and followed by an at sign (@) and the size of the function's
arguments in bytes. No case translation is performed. The compiler uses the
following template for the naming convention:

```
_functionname@number
```

x86 Specific →This option has no effect on the name decoration of C++ methods
and functions. Unless declared as **extern** "C", C++ methods and functions use a
different name-decorating scheme. For more information on decorated names, see
Appendix A, "Decorated Names." **END x86 Specific**

Note   x86 Specific →By default, C++ member functions use a calling convention in cases
where the member function's **this** pointer is passed in the ECX register. All other arguments
are pushed onto the stack from right to left, and the called routine pops the member function's
arguments from the stack. **END x86 Specific** A member function that is explicitly marked as
__cdecl__, __fastcall__, or __stdcall__ uses the specified calling convention. A member function
that takes a variable number of arguments always uses the __cdecl__ calling convention.

Struct Member Alignment

This option controls how the members of a structure are packed into memory and specifies the same packing for all structures in a module. When you specify this option, each structure member after the first is stored on either the size of the member type or n-byte boundaries (where n is 1, 2, 4, 8, or 16), whichever is smaller.

You should not use this option unless you have specific alignment requirements.

List entry	Command-line equivalent	Result
1 Byte	/Zp1	Packs structures on 1-byte boundaries
2 Bytes	/Zp2	Packs structures on 2-byte boundaries
4 Bytes	/Zp4	Packs structures on 4-byte boundaries
8 Bytes	/Zp8	Packs structures on 8-byte boundaries
16 Bytes	/Zp16	Packs structures on 16-byte boundaries

You can also use the **pack** pragma to control structure packing. For information on the **pack** pragma, see "pack" in Chapter 2 of the *Preprocessor Reference*.

Customize

The Customize category options (see Figure 20.4) disable Microsoft language extensions, enable function-level linking, eliminate duplicate strings, enable minimal rebuild, enable incremental compilation, and suppress the startup banner and informational messages.

Figure 20.4 Customize Category on the C/C++ Tab

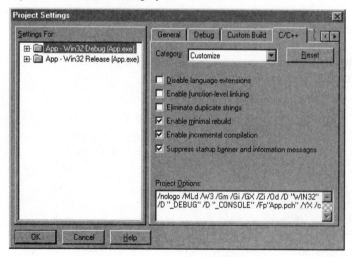

Disable Language Extensions

With the Disable Language Extensions option, you can ensure that a C program uses ANSI C only.

Check box	Command-line equivalent	Result
Selected	/Za	ANSI C compatibility. Language constructs not compatible with ANSI C are flagged as errors.
Cleared	/Ze	Enables Microsoft extensions.

Note If you use the Disable Language Extensions (/Za) option, the Improve Float Consistency (/Op) option is used to improve the consistency of floating-point tests for equality and inequality. This use of /Op with /Za is for strict ANSI conformance and is the only situation under which /Op is selected by default. The /Op– option is provided to override the default selection of /Op with /Za. Specify /Op– in the Common/Project/Source File Options text box (or on the command line), after /Za, to disable /Op. For more information, see "Generate Intrinsic Functions" on page 403 in this chapter and "Improve Float Consistency" on page 404 in this chapter.

Disable language extensions if you plan to port your program to other environments. The compiler treats extended keywords as simple identifiers, disables the other Microsoft extensions, and automatically defines the __STDC__ predefined macro for C programs. The following are Microsoft extensions:

Keywords The keywords __based, __cdecl, __except, __fastcall, __finally, __leave, __stdcall, __try, and __declspec are Microsoft specific.

Casts The Microsoft compiler supports the following two non-ANSI casts.

- Use of non-ANSI casts to produce l-values:

```
char *p;
(( int * ) p )++;
```

The preceding example could be rewritten to conform with the ANSI C standard as follows:

```
p = ( char * )(( int * )p + 1 );
```

- Non-ANSI casting of a function pointer to a data pointer:

```
int ( * pfunc ) ();
int *pdata;
pdata = ( int * ) pfunc;
```

To perform the same cast while maintaining ANSI compatibility, you must cast the function pointer to an int before casting it to a data pointer:

```
pdata = ( int * ) (int) pfunc;
```

Variable-Length Argument Lists   The Microsoft compiler supports use of a function declarator that specifies a variable number of arguments, followed by a function definition that provides a type instead:

```
void myfunc( int x, ... );

void myfunc( int x, char * c )
{ }
```

Single-Line Comments   The Microsoft C compiler supports single-line comments, which are introduced with two forward slash (//) characters:

```
// This is a single-line comment.
```

Scope   The Microsoft C compiler supports the following scope-related features:

- Redefinitions of **extern** items as **static**:

```
extern int clip();
static int clip()
{}
```

- Use of benign **typedef** redefinitions within the same scope:

```
typedef int INT;
typedef int INT;
```

- Scope of function declarators is file scope:

```
void func1()
{
    extern int func2( double );
}

void main( void )
{
    func2( 4 );    //  /Ze passes 4 as type double
}              //  /Za passes 4 as type int
```

- Use of block-scope variables initialized with nonconstant expressions:

```
int clip( int );
int bar( int );

void main( void )
{
    int array[2] = { clip( 2 ), bar( 4 ) };
}

int clip( int x )
{
    return x;
}

int bar( int x )
```

```
{
    return x;
}
```

Data Declarations and Definitions   The Microsoft C compiler supports the
following data declaration and definition features:

- Mixed character and string constants in an initializer:

```
char arr[5] = {'a', 'b', "cde"};
```

- Bit fields with base types other than **unsigned int** or **signed int**.

- Declarators without either a storage class or a type:

```
x;

void main( void )
{
    x = 1;
}
```

- Unsized arrays as the last field in structures and unions:

```
struct zero
{
    char *c;
    int zarray[];
};
```

- Unnamed (anonymous) structures:

```
struct
{
    int i;
    char *s;
};
```

- Unnamed (anonymous) unions:

```
union
{
    int i;
    float fl;
};
```

- Unnamed members:

```
struct s
{
    unsigned int flag : 1;
    unsigned int : 31;
}
```

Intrinsic Floating-Point Functions The Microsoft compiler supports inline generation of the **x86 Specific** → **atan**, **atan2**, **cos**, **exp**, **log**, **log10**, **sin**, **sqrt**, and **tan** functions **END x86 Specific** when the Generate Intrinsic Functions (/Oi) option is specified. For C, ANSI conformance is lost when these intrinsics are used, because they do not set the **errno** variable.

Enable Function-Level Linking

This option allows the compiler to package individual functions in the form of packaged functions (COMDATs). The linker requires that functions be packaged separately as COMDATs to exclude or order individual functions in a DLL or .EXE file. Command-line equivalent: /Gy

You can use the linker's /OPT:REF option to exclude unreferenced packaged functions from the .EXE file. For more information on /OPT:REF, see Chapter 26, "LINK Reference." You can use the linker's /ORDER option to place packaged functions in a specified order in the .EXE file. For more information on /ORDER, see Chapter 26, "LINK Reference."

Inline functions are always packaged if they are instantiated as calls (for example, if inlining is turned off, or you take a function address). In addition, C++ member functions defined within the class declaration are automatically packaged; other functions are not, and selecting the Enable Function-Level Linking option is required to compile them as packaged functions.

Eliminate Duplicate Strings

This option enables the compiler to place a single copy of identical strings into the .EXE file. Because identical strings are copied into a single memory location, programs compiled with this option can be smaller than those compiled without it. This space optimization is also called "string pooling." Using this option ensures that string pooling occurs in most cases. Command-line equivalent: /Gf

When using the Eliminate Duplicate Strings option, your program must not write over pooled strings. Also, if you use identical strings to allocate string buffers, the Eliminate Duplicate Strings option pools the strings. Thus, what was intended as multiple pointers to multiple buffers ends up as multiple pointers to a single buffer. For example, with Eliminate Duplicate Strings, the following code causes s and t to point to the same memory because they are initialized with the same string:

```
char *s = "This is a character buffer";
char *t = "This is a character buffer";
```

Enable Minimal Rebuild

The Enable Minimal Rebuild option controls minimal rebuild, which determines whether C++ source files that include changed C++ class definitions (stored in header (.H) files) need to be recompiled. The compiler stores dependency information between source files and class definitions (which source file is dependent on which class definition stored in which .H file) in the project's .IDB file during the first compile. Subsequent compiles use the information stored in the .IDB file to determine whether a source file needs to be compiled, even if it includes a modified .H file. Command-line equivalent: /Gm

Note Minimal rebuild relies on class definitions not changing between include files. Class definitions must be global for a project (there should be only one definition of a given class), because the dependency information in the .IDB file is created for the entire project. If you have more than one definition for a class in your project, disable minimal rebuild.

Enable Incremental Compilation

The Enable Incremental Compilation option controls the incremental compiler, which compiles only those functions that have changed since the last compile. The compiler saves state information from the first compile in the project's .IDB file (the default name is *project*.IDB or VC40.IDB for files compiled without a project). The compiler uses this state information to speed subsequent compiles. Command-line equivalent: /Gi

The following options prevent incremental compilation:

- Disabe Incremental Compilation (/Gi–)
- Place Debug Information in Object Modules (/Z7)
- Generate a Listing File (/FA)
- Generate Function Prototypes (/Zg)
- Preprocess the File (/E, /EP, or /P)

If the compiler cannot find the project's .PDB file or .IDB file (or either is read-only), it cannot incrementally compile.

Note   Object (.OBJ) files created with the Enable Incremental Compilation option are larger than those with incremental compilation disabled because of padding. Padding allows the compiler to add to the .OBJ file without recreating it. Because these .OBJ files are larger, you should disable incremental compilation when building a version of an .OBJ file (or library) for release.

Suppress Startup Banner and Information Messages

This option suppresses display of the sign-on banner (when the compiler starts up) and informational messages (during compiling). Command-line equivalent: /nologo

Listing Files

The Listing Files category options (see Figure 20.5) create browse information (.BSC) files and code listing files.

Figure 20.5 Listing Files Category on the C/C++ Tab

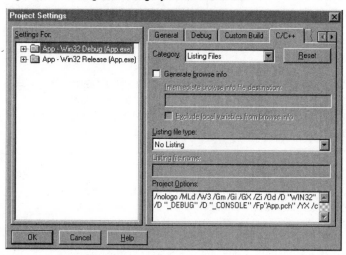

Generate Browse Info

This option creates .SBR files with complete symbolic information. During the build process, the Microsoft Browse Information File Maintenance Utility (BSCMAKE) uses the .SBR files to create a .BSC file that you can examine in browse windows. Command-line equivalent: /FR

For more information, see Chapter 16, "Browsing Through Symbols."

Intermediate Browse Info File Destination

Use the Intermediate Browse Info File Destination text box to specify a directory and/or filename for the .SBR and .BSC files created by using the Generate Browse Info option. Command-line equivalent: /FR*filename* or /Fr*filename*

Exclude Local Variables

This option creates .SBR files with complete symbolic information, excluding information about local variables. During the build process, BSCMAKE uses the .SBR files to create a .BSC file that you can examine in browse windows. Command-line equivalent: /Fr

For more information, see Chapter 16, "Browsing Through Symbols."

Listing File Type

These options specify the type of listing files to be created.

No Listing   Creates no listing file. This is the default setting.

Assembly-Only Listing   Creates files with assembly code only. The default listing-file extension is .ASM. Command-line equivalent: /FA

Assembly, Machine Code, and Source   Creates files containing source code, assembly code, and machine code. The default listing-file extension is .COD. Command-line equivalent: /FAcs

Assembly with Machine Code   Creates files containing assembly code and machine code. The default listing-file extension is .COD. Command-line equivalent: /FAc

Assembly with Source Code   Creates files containing assembly code and source code. The default listing-file extension is .ASM. Command-line equivalent: /FAs

Listing File Name

Use the Listing File Name text box to specify a directory and/or filename for the listing file selected from the Listing File Type list box. Command-line equivalent: /FA*filename*

Optimizations

The Optimizations category options (see Figure 20.6) determine how the compiler fine-tunes the performance of your program. Four of the five optimization categories (Default, Disable (Debug), Maximize Speed, and Minimize Size) in the Optimizations drop-down list box require no further optimization on your part. If you select the fifth optimization category, Customize, you can set specific optimizations using the selections in the Optimizations list box.

You can also use the **optimize** pragma to control optimization of your program. For more information on the **optimize** pragma, see "optimize" in Chapter 2 of the *Preprocessor Reference*.

Figure 20.6   Optimizations Category on the C/C++ Tab

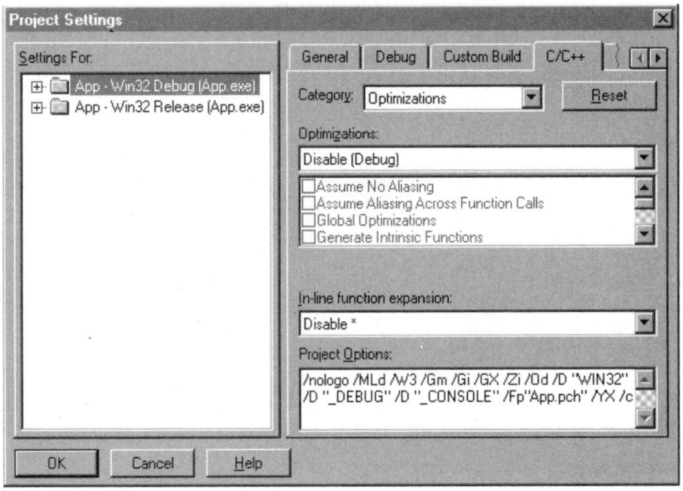

Types of Optimizations

You can select one of the following optimization categories:

Default Removes all optimization options from the command line. In this case, the compiler favors generation of faster, but possibly larger, machine code. If there is a choice between multiple possible machine-code sequences for an expression, the code generator chooses the fastest sequence. Command-line equivalent: /Ot

Disable (Debug) Turns off all optimizations in the program and speeds compilation. This option simplifies debugging because it suppresses code movement. Command-line equivalent: /Od

From the command line, this option is the default setting.

Maximize Speed Creates the fastest code in the majority of cases. Command-line equivalent: /O2

The effect of using this option is the same as specifying the following options in the Common/Project/Source File Options text box or on the command line:
```
/Og /Oi /Ot /Oy /Ob1 /Gs /Gf /Gy
```

x86 Specific →You can use other options to improve the speed of many applications. For example, this option doesn't use the /G5 option to produce code that is optimized for computers based on the Pentium processor.

The Maximize Speed option implies the use of the Frame Pointer Omission (/Oy) option. If your project requires EBP-based addressing, also specify the /Oy– option, or use the **optimize** pragma with the **y** and **off** arguments to gain maximum optimization with EBP-based addressing. The compiler detects most situations where EBP-based addressing is required (for instance, with the **_alloca** and **setjmp** functions, and with structured exception handling).**END x86 Specific**

Note The Maximize Speed option is set by default for release builds.

Minimize Size Creates the smallest code in the majority of cases. Command-line equivalent: /O1

The effect of using this option is the same as specifying the following options in the Common/Project/Source File Options text box or on the command line:
```
/Og /Os /Oy /Ob1 /Gs /Gf /Gy
```

x86 Specific →The Minimize Size option implies the use of the Frame Pointer Omission (/Oy) option. If your project requires EBP-based addressing, also specify the /Oy– option, or use the **optimize** pragma with the **y** and **off** arguments to gain maximum optimization with EBP-based addressing. The compiler detects most situations where EBP-based addressing is required (for instance, with the **_alloca** and **setjmp** functions, and with structured exception handling).**END x86 Specific**

Customize   Makes a multiple-selection list box available so that you can select a
custom set of optimizations.

Customize

If you select the Customize option from the Optimizations box in the Optimizations
category, you can select one or more of the following optimizations from the list box
that becomes available. However, if you select this option from the Optimizations box
in the General category, you must select the Optimizations category in order to select
any of the following optimizations:

Assume No Aliasing   Tells the compiler that your program does not use aliasing. An
alias is a name that refers to a memory location that is already referred to by a
different name. Using this option allows the compiler to apply optimizations it
couldn't otherwise use, such as storing variables in registers and performing loop
optimizations. Command-line equivalent: /Oa

The following rules must be followed for any variable not declared as **volatile**, or
else the /Oa and /Ow options are ignored. In these rules, a variable is referenced if
it is on either side of an assignment, or if a function uses it in an argument:

- No pointer references a variable that is used directly.
- No variable is used directly if a pointer to the variable is being used.
- No variable is used directly if the variable's address is taken within a function.
- No pointer is used to access a memory location if another pointer is used to
  modify the same memory location.

Aliasing bugs most frequently show up as corrupted data. If variables are assigned
seemingly random values, compile the program with the Disable (/Od) option. If
the program works when compiled with /Od, do not use /Oa or /Ow.

You can disable optimizations around code that uses aliasing (for individual
functions) by using the **optimize** pragma with the **a** or **w** option. For more
information on the **optimize** pragma, see "optimize" in Chapter 2 of the
Preprocessor Reference.

Assume Aliasing Across Function Calls   Tells the compiler that no aliasing
occurs within function bodies but might occur across function calls. After each
function call, pointer variables must be reloaded from memory. Command-line
equivalent: /Ow

The following rules must be followed for any variable not declared as **volatile**, or
else the /Oa and /Ow options are ignored. In these rules, a variable is referenced if
it is on either side of an assignment, or if a function uses it in an argument:

- No pointer references a variable that is used directly.
- No variable is used directly if a pointer to the variable is being used.
- No variable is used directly if the variable's address is taken within a function.

- No pointer is used to access a memory location if another pointer is used to modify the same memory location.

Aliasing bugs most frequently show up as corrupted data. If variables are assigned seemingly random values, compile the program with the Disable (/Od) option. If the program works when compiled with /Od, do not use /Oa or Ow.

You can disable optimizations around code that uses aliasing (for individual functions) by using the **optimize** pragma with the **a** or **w** option. For more information on the **optimize** pragma, see "optimize" in Chapter 2 of the *Preprocessor Reference*.

Global Optimizations   Provides local and global optimizations, automatic-register allocation, and loop optimization. Command-line equivalent: /Og

- *Local and global common subexpression elimination*   In this optimization, the value of a common subexpression is calculated once. In the following example, if the values of b and c do not change between the three expressions, the compiler can assign the calculation of b + c to a temporary variable and substitute the variable for b + c:

```
a = b + c;
d = b + c;
e = b + c;
```

  For local common subexpression optimization, the compiler examines short sections of code for common subexpressions. For global common subexpression optimization, the compiler searches entire functions for common subexpressions.

- *Automatic register allocation*   This optimization allows the compiler to store frequently used variables and subexpressions in registers; the **register** keyword is ignored.

- *Loop optimization*   This optimization removes invariant subexpressions from the body of a loop. An optimal loop contains only expressions whose values change through each execution of the loop. In the following example, the expression x + y does not change in the loop body:

```
i = -100;
while( i < 0 )
{
    i += x + y;
}
```

  After optimization, x + y is calculated once rather than every time the loop is executed:

```
i = -100;
t = x + y;
while( i < 0 )
{
```

```
        i += t;
}
```

Loop optimization is much more effective when the compiler can assume no aliasing, which you set with the /Oa or /Ow option.

The following code fragment could have an aliasing problem:

```
i = -100;
while( i < 0 )
{
    i += x + y;
    *p = i;
}
```

Without /Oa or /Ow, the compiler must assume that x or y could be modified by the assignment to *p and cannot assume that x + y is constant for each loop iteration. If you specify /Oa or /Ow, the compiler assumes that modifying *p cannot affect either x or y, and x + y can be removed from the loop.

You can enable or disable global optimization on a function-by-function basis using the **optimize** pragma with the **g** option. For more information on the **optimize** pragma, see "optimize" in Chapter 2 of the *Preprocessor Reference*.

Generate Intrinsic Functions   This option replaces some function calls with intrinsic or otherwise special forms of the function that help your application run faster. Programs that use intrinsic functions are faster because they do not have the overhead of function calls, but may be larger due to the additional code created. Command-line equivalent: /Oi

x86 Specific→If you use the Generate Intrinsic Functions option, the following function calls are replaced with their intrinsic (inline) forms:

_disable	**_outp**	**abs**	**memset**
_enable	**_outpw**	**fabs**	**strcat**
_inp	**_rotl**	**labs**	**strcmp**
_inpw	**_rotr**	**memcp**	**strcpy**
_lrotl	**_strset**	**memcpy**	**strlen**
_lrotr			

Note   The **_alloca** and **setjmp** functions are always created as intrinsics; this behavior is not affected by /Oi.

The floating-point functions listed below do not have true intrinsic forms. If you use the Generate Intrinsic Functions option, the listed functions are replaced with versions that pass arguments directly to the floating-point chip rather than pushing them onto the program stack.

acos	**cosh**	**pow**	**tanh**
asin	**fmod**	**sinh**	

The floating-point functions listed below have true intrinsic forms when you specify both /Oi and /Og (or any option that includes /Og: /Ox, /O1, and /O2):

atan	**exp**	**log10**	**sqrt**
atan2	**log**	**sin**	**tan**
cos			

The intrinsic floating-point functions do not perform any special checks on input values; as a result, they work in restricted ranges of input and have different exception handling and boundary conditions than the library routines with the same name. Using the true intrinsic forms implies loss of IEEE exception handling and the loss of **_matherr** and **errno** functionality; the latter implies the loss of ANSI conformance. However, the intrinsic forms can considerably speed up floating-point intensive programs, and for many programs, the conformance issues are of little practical value.

You can use the Improve Float Consistency (/Op) or the Disable Language Extensions (/Za) option to override the creation of true intrinsic floating-point functions. In this case, the functions are created as library routines that pass arguments directly to the floating-point chip instead of pushing them onto the program stack. **END x86 Specific**

You also use the **intrinsic** pragma to create intrinsic functions or the **function** pragma to explicitly force a function call. For more information on these pragmas, see Chapter 2 of the *Preprocessor Reference*.

Improve Float Consistency Improves the consistency of floating-point tests for equality and inequality by disabling optimizations that could change the precision of floating-point calculations. Command-line equivalent: /Op

By default, the compiler uses the coprocessor's 80-bit registers to hold the intermediate results of floating-point calculations. This increases program speed and decreases program size. However, because the calculation involves floating-point data types that are represented in memory by less than 80 bits, carrying the extra bits of precision (80 bits minus the number of bits in a smaller floating-point type) through a lengthy calculation can produce inconsistent results.

With the Improve Float Consistency option, the compiler loads data from memory prior to each floating-point operation and, if assignment occurs, writes the results back to memory upon completion. Loading the data before each operation guarantees that the data does not retain any significance greater than the capacity of its type.

A program compiled with this option may be slower and larger than one compiled without it.

Note This option disables inline generation of floating-point functions. The standard run-time library routines are used instead.

If you select the Disable Language Extensions (/Za) option from the Customize category in order to compile for ANSI compatibility, the use of the Improve Float Consistency (/Op) option is implied. The use of /Op improves the consistency of floating-point tests for equality and inequality. The nature of the improved consistency provides strict ANSI conformance and is the only situation under which /Op is selected by default. The /Op– option is provided to override the default selection of /Op with /Za. Specify /Op– in the Common/Project/Source File Options text box (or on the command line), after /Za, to disable /Op.

Favor Small Code   Minimizes the size of .EXE files and DLLs by instructing the compiler to favor size over speed. The compiler can reduce many C and C++ constructs to functionally similar sequences of machine code. Occasionally these differences offer trade-offs of size versus speed. If you do not select this option, code may be larger and may be faster. Command-line equivalent: /Os

Favor Fast Code   Maximizes the speed of .EXE files and DLLs by instructing the compiler to favor speed over size. The compiler can reduce many C and C++ constructs to functionally similar sequences of machine code. Occasionally these differences offer trade-offs of size versus speed. Command-line equivalent: /Ot

x86 Specific →The following example code demonstrates the difference between the Favor Small Code (/Os) option and the Favor Fast Code (/Ot) option:

```
/* differ.c
    This program implements a multiplication
    operator.
    Compile with /Os to implement
    multiply explicitly as multiply.
    Compile with /Ot to implement as a
    series of shift and LEA instructions.
 */
int differ(int x)
{
    return x * 71;
}
```

As shown in the fragment of machine code below, when differ.c is compiled using the Favor Small Code (/Os) option, the compiler implements the multiply expression in the return statement explicitly as a multiply to produce a short but slower sequence of code:

```
mov    eax, DWORD PTR _x$[ebp]
imul   eax, 71                   ; 00000047H
```

Alternatively, when differ.c is compiled using Favor Fast Code (/Ot), the compiler implements the multiply expression in the return statement as a series of shift and LEA instructions to produce a fast but longer sequence of code:

```
mov eax, DWORD PTR _x$[ebp]
mov ecx, eax
shl eax, 3
lea eax, DWORD PTR [eax+eax*8]
sub eax, ecx
```

END x86 Specific

Frame-Pointer Omission   Suppresses creation of frame pointers on the call stack. This option speeds function calls, because no frame pointers need to be set up and removed. It also frees one more register, **x86 Specific** →EBP on the Intel 386 (or later), **END x86 Specific** for storing frequently used variables and subexpressions. Command-line equivalent: /Oy

The Full Optimization (/Ox), Minimize Size (/O1), and Maximize Speed (/O2) options imply the use of the Frame-Pointer Omission (/Oy) option. Specifying /Oy– in the Common/Project/Source File Options text box (or on the command line) after the /Ox, /O1, or /O2 option disables /Oy, whether it is explicit or implied.

Full Optimization   Combines optimizing options to produce the fastest possible program. Command-line equivalent: /Ox

The effect of using this option is the same as typing the following options in the Common/Project/Source File Options text box or on the command line:

```
/Ob1 /Og /Oi /Ot /Oy /Gs
```

Note   The use of the Full Optimization (/Ox) option implies the use of the Frame-Pointer Omission (/Oy) option. **x86 Specific** → If your code requires EBP-based addressing, you can specify the /Oy– option after the /Ox option or use the **optimize** pragma with the **y** and **off** arguments to gain maximum optimization with EBP-based addressing. The compiler detects most situations where EBP-based addressing is required (for instance, with the **_alloca** and **setjmp** functions and with structured exception handling). **END x86 Specific**

In-line Function Expansion

Controls which functions become expanded. Expanding a function inline makes the program faster because it does not incur the overhead of calling the function.

Disable   Disables in-line expansion. This is the default. Command-line equivalent: /Ob0

Only __inline   Expands only functions marked as **inline** or **__inline** or, in a C++ member function, defined within a class declaration. Command-line equivalent: /Ob1

Any Suitable   Expands functions marked as **inline** or **__inline**, as well as any other function that the compiler chooses. Command-line equivalent: /Ob2

The compiler treats the inline expansion options and keywords as suggestions. There is no guarantee that functions will be inlined, and there is no control over the inlining of individual functions.

You can also use the **auto_inline** pragma to exclude functions from being considered as candidates for inline expansion. For more information on the **auto_inline** pragma, see "auto_inline" in Chapter 2 of the *Preprocessor Reference*.

Precompiled Headers

The Precompiled Headers category options (see Figure 20.7) speed compile time by allowing you to precompile any C or C++ code (including inline code).

Figure 20.7   Precompiled Headers Category on the C/C++ Tab

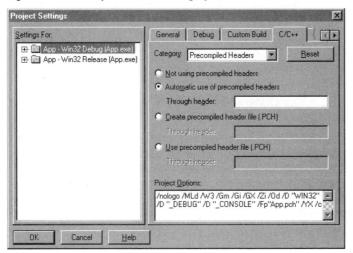

Programming projects typically use code that is stable (such as WINDOWS.H and AFXWIN.H) and code that is still under development. You can speed up your build times by precompiling the stable code, saving the precompiled state in a precompiled header (PCH) file, and then combining the PCH with uncompiled code in subsequent builds. This shortens the compile time for subsequent builds because the precompiled code is not recompiled, it is simply reused.

There are two different precompiled header systems (in order of efficiency):

- Per-File Use of Precompiled Headers (Create Precompiled Header File and Use Precompiled Header File options)

- Automatic Use of Precompiled Headers

The Automatic Use Of Precompiled Headers option is used by default except for projects that use the Microsoft Foundation Classes.

Not Using Precompiled Headers

This option disables the use of PCHs.

Automatic Use of Precompiled Headers

This option creates a file named *project*.PCH if it doesn't already exist, and compiles only header (.H) files into this .PCH file. If you have no project open, it creates a file named VC40.PCH. The inclusion of .H files stops when the compiler encounters the first declaration, definition, **hdrstop** pragma, or **#line** directive in the source file being compiled with the option, or after the .H file specified in the Through Header text box. In subsequent compilations, the PCH is used after the compiler makes its final consistency check. Command-line equivalent: /YX

For more information, see Consistency Rules for Automatic Use of Precompiled Headers later in this section. For more information on the **hdrstop** pragma, see "hdrstop" in Chapter 2 of the *Preprocessor Reference*.

Through Header When creating a PCH, the compiler compiles all code up to and including the .H file specified in the Through Header text box. When using a PCH, the compiler treats all code occurring before the specified .H file as precompiled. It skips to just beyond the **#include** directive associated with the .H file, uses the code contained in the .PCH file, and then compiles all code after *filename*. Command-line equivalent: /YX*filename*.

Consistency Rules for Automatic Use of Precompiled Headers

If a .PCH file exists, it is compared to the current compilation for consistency. The following requirements must be met; otherwise, a new .PCH file is created, and the new file replaces the old:

- The current compiler options must match those specified when the PCH was created. However, if a significant portion of the source code of the currently compiled module matches the module for which the PCH was created, the compiler can create a new PCH for the matching part. This subsetting action increases the number of modules for which a PCH can be used.

- The current working directory must match that specified when the PCH was created.

- The order and values of all **#include** and **#pragma** preprocessor directives must match those specified when the PCH was created. These, along with **#define** directives, are checked as they appear during subsequent compilations that use the PCH. The **#pragma** directives must be nearly identical—multiple spaces outside of strings are treated as a single space to allow for different programming styles.

- The values of **#define** directives must match. However, a group of **#define** directives in sequence need not occur in exactly the same order, because there are no semantic order dependencies for **#define** directives.

- The value and order of include paths specified on the command line with /I options must match those specified when the PCH was created.

- The timestamps of all the .H files (all files specified with **#include** directives) used to build the PCH must match those that existed when the PCH was created.

Create Precompiled Header File (.PCH)

This option creates a precompiled header (.PCH) file. Only header (.H) files are precompiled into the PCH. The creation of the PCH stops after the compiler compiles the .H file specified in the Through Header text box or when it encounters a **hdrstop** pragma. Command-line equivalent: /Yc

For more information on the **hdrstop** pragma, see "hdrstop" in Chapter 2 of the *Preprocessor Reference*.

Through Header   The compiler compiles all code up to and including the .H file specified in the Through Header text box. Command-line equivalent: /Yc*filename*.)

Use Precompiled Header File (.PCH)

This option specifies using a precompiled header (.PCH) file during builds. The PCH must have been created using the Create Precompiled Header File option. Command-line equivalent: /Yu

Through Header   Type the name of a header (.H) file in the Through Settings text box. The compiler treats all code occurring before the .H file as precompiled. It skips to just beyond the **#include** directive associated with the .H file, uses the code contained in the .PCH file, and then compiles all code after *filename*. Command-line equivalent: /Yu*filename*.

Consistency Rules for Per-File Use of Precompiled Headers

When you use a PCH, the compiler assumes the same compilation environment— using consistent compiler options, pragmas, and so on—that was in effect when you created the PCH, unless you specify otherwise. If the compiler detects an inconsistency, it issues a warning and identifies the inconsistency where possible. Such warnings do not necessarily indicate a problem with the PCH; they simply warn you of possible conflicts. The consistency requirements for PCHs are explained in the following list:

Compiler Option Consistency   The following compiler options can trigger an inconsistency warning when using a PCH:

- Macros created using the Preprocessor (/D) option must be the same between the compilation that created the PCH and the current compilation. The state of defined constants is not checked, but unpredictable results can occur if these change.

- PCHs do not work with the /E and /EP options.

- PCHs must be created using either the Generate Browse Info (/FR) option or the Exclude Local Variables (/Fr) option before subsequent compilations that use the PCH can use these options.

C7 Compatible (/Z7)   If this option is in effect when the PCH is created, subsequent compilations that use the PCH can use the debugging information.

If the C7 Compatible (/Z7) option is not in effect when the PCH is created, subsequent compilations that use the PCH and that option trigger a warning. The debugging information is placed in the current .OBJ file, and local symbols defined in the PCH are not available to the debugger.

Include Path Consistency   A PCH does not contain information about the include path that was in effect when it was created. When you use a .PCH file, the compiler always uses the include path specified in the current compilation.

Source File Consistency   When you specify the Use Precompiled Header File (/Yu) option, the compiler ignores all preprocessor directives (including pragmas) that appear in the source code that will be precompiled. The compilation specified by such preprocessor directives must be the same as the compilation used for the Create Precompiled Header File (/Yc) option.

Pragma Consistency   Pragmas processed during the creation of a PCH usually affect the file with which the PCH is subsequently used. The **comment** and **message** pragmas do not affect the remainder of the compilation.

The following pragmas are retained as part of a PCH. They do affect the remainder of a compilation that uses the PCH.

alloc_text	**include_alias**	**pack**
auto_inline	**inline_depth**	**pointers_to_members**
check_stack	**inline_recursion**	**setlocale**
code_seg	**init_seg**	**vtordisp**
data_seg	**intrinsic**	**warning**
function	**optimize**	

Preprocessor

The Preprocessor category options (see Figure 20.8) control symbols, macros, and include paths used by the C/C++ preprocessor.

Figure 20.8 Preprocessor Category on the C/C++ Tab

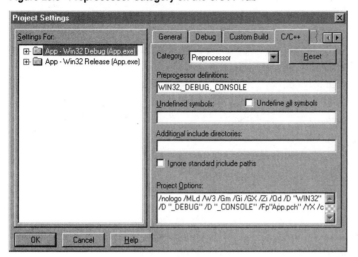

Preprocessor Definitions

Specify one or more macros in the Preprocessor Definitions text box. You create these named macros for your own purposes. Macros typed in this text box are visible only to the preprocessor; you can use the **#if** or **#ifdef** preprocessor directives to test their existence. The behavior of the Preprocessor Definitions text box differs from the behavior of the /D command-line option; you cannot use either an equal sign (=) or a number sign (#) to assign a value to symbols entered in the text box.

Undefined Symbols

Type the name of a previously defined macro in the Undefined Symbols text box to undefine it. To undefine additional macros, type additional ones, using a space to separate each. This option cannot be used to undefine symbols created with a **#define** directive. Command-line equivalent: /U *macro*

When used from the command line, a space between /U and *macro* is optional. To undefine additional symbols, repeat /U *macro*.

Undefine All Symbols

Select the Undefine All Symbols check box to undefine every previously defined macro. This option cannot be used to undefine macros created with a **#define** directive. Command-line equivalent: /u

Both the Undefined Symbols (U *macro*) and the Undefine All Symbols (/u) options turn off the Microsoft-specific macros shown in the following table.

Macro	Function
_CHAR_UNSIGNED	Default **char** type is unsigned. Defined when the /J option is specified.
_CPPRTTI	Defined for code compiled with the Enable Run-Time Type Information (/GR) option.
_CPPUNWIND	Defined for code compiled with the Enable Exception Handling (/GX) option.
_DLL	Defined when the Multithreaded DLL (/MD or /MDd) option is specified.
_M_IX86	Defined as 400 for Blend (/GB), 300 for 80386 (/G3), 400 for 80486 (/G4), and 500 for Pentium (/G5).*
_MSC_VER	Defines the compiler version. Defined as 1000 for Microsoft Visual C++ version 4.0. Always defined.
_WIN32	Defined for Win32 applications. Always defined.*
_MT	Defined when the Multithreaded DLL (/MD or /MDd) or Multithreaded (/MT or /MTd) option is specified.

*x86 Specific

Additional Include Directories

Add one or more directories to the list of directories searched for include files. Use a space to separate directories to be searched when entering more than one directory. Directories are searched only until the specified include file is found. You can use this option with the Ignore Standard Include Paths (/X) option. Command-line equivalent: /I *directory*

When used from the command line, a space between /I and *directory* is optional.

The compiler searches for directories in the following order:

1. Directories containing the source file.

2. Directories specified with the /I option, in the order that CL encounters them.

3. Directories specified in the INCLUDE environment variable.

Ignore Standard Include Paths

Prevents the compiler from searching for include files in directories specified in the PATH and INCLUDE environment variables. Command-line equivalent: /X

You can use this option with the Additional Include Directories (/I *directory*) option.

Setting Linker Options

You set linker options on the Link tab of the Project Settings dialog box. The settings that you select control the Microsoft 32-bit Incremental Linker (LINK.EXE).

This chapter describes the option categories that are available on the Link tab of the Project Settings dialog box.

▶ **To view the Project Settings dialog box**

- From the Build menu, choose Settings.

The linker option categories are described in the following sections:

- General Category Options
- Customize Category Options
- Debug Category Options
- Input Category Options
- Output Category Options

Note The linker options that are not available as controls within option categories on the Link tab of the Project Settings dialog box are described in Chapter 26, "LINK Reference." Chapter 26 describes how to use the linker from the command line. It also describes module-definition files.

General Category Options

- The General category (see Figure 21.1) summarizes the options that are most commonly used. Each General category option, with the exception of the Enable Profiling option, is also available in another option category. Enable Profiling, Common/Project options, and Reset are described in this section. Setting an option in the General category changes the same option in its other category, and vice versa.

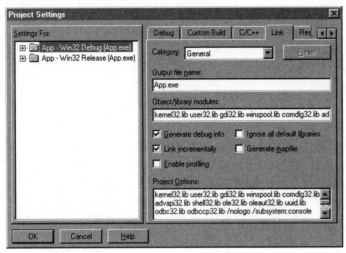

Figure 21.1   General Category on the Link Tab

Enable Profiling

The Enable Profiling option creates an output file that can be used with the profiler. This option is found only in the General category on the Link tab. Command-line equivalent: /PROFILE

A profiler-ready program has a map (.MAP) file. If it contains debugging information, the information must be stored in the output file instead of in a program database (.PDB) file and must be in Microsoft Format.

Selecting the Enable Profiling check box enables the Generate Mapfile option in the General and Debug categories. If you select the Generate Debug Info check box, be sure to select the Microsoft Format option button under Debug Info in the Debug category.

On the command line, /PROFILE has the same effect as setting the /MAP option; if the /DEBUG option is specified, then /PROFILE also implies the options /DEBUGTYPE:CV and /PDB:NONE. In either case, /PROFILE implies /INCREMENTAL:NO.

Common/Project Options

The Common/Project Options text box displays the linker options that are currently selected. The options are displayed using their command-line equivalents.

You can type in this text box when a single project is selected in the Settings For pane of the Project Settings dialog box. When one project is selected, the text box is named Project Options. Otherwise, the text box is named Common Options. You cannot type in the text box when it is named Common Options.

The Project Options text box accepts any option that is available from the Link tab. It also accepts those linker options that are otherwise available only from the command line. For details on these options, see Chapter 26, "LINK Reference."

You are responsible for the accuracy of any option you type in the Project Options text box. If an option is recognized as one that can be set using a dialog box control, the dialog box control is changed to reflect the option. However, if the option is not recognized, it is left in the options string and passed to the linker as is.

Reset

The Reset button resets the project settings of a project to the settings that existed when the project was created. This button is available if both of the following conditions are met:

- A single project is selected in the Settings For pane of the Project Settings dialog box.

- The settings of the selection have changed.

The Reset button is not available when multiple projects are selected.

Customize Category Options

- The Customize category options (see Figure 21.2) control the linking session and affect linker output.

Figure 21.2   Customize Category on the Link Tab

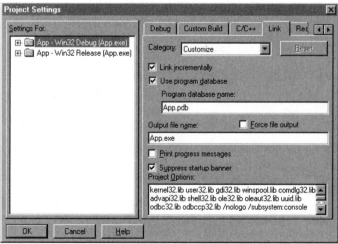

Link Incrementally

This option controls how the linker handles incremental linking. Command-line equivalent: /INCREMENTAL:{YES|NO}

By default, the linker runs in incremental mode. To override a default incremental link, clear the Link Incrementally check box (or specify /INCREMENTAL:NO on the command line).

An incrementally linked program is functionally equivalent to a program that is nonincrementally linked. However, because it is prepared for subsequent incremental links, an incrementally linked executable (.EXE) file or dynamic-link library (DLL):

- Is larger than a nonincrementally linked program due to padding of code and data. (Padding allows the linker to increase the size of functions and data without recreating the .EXE file.)
- May contain jump thunks to handle relocation of functions to new addresses.

Note To ensure that your final release build does not contain padding or thunks, link your program nonincrementally.

To link incrementally regardless of the default, select the Link Incrementally check box (or specify /INCREMENTAL:YES on the command line). When this option is selected, the linker issues a warning if it cannot link incrementally, and then links the program nonincrementally. Certain options and situations override the Link Incrementally (/INCREMENTAL:YES) option.

Most programs can be linked incrementally. However, some changes are too great, and some options are incompatible with incremental linking. LINK performs a full link if any of the following options are specified:

- Link Incrementally is not selected (/INCREMENTAL:NO).
- COFF Format (/DEBUGTYPE:COFF) is selected.
- Both Formats (/DEBUGTYPE:BOTH) is selected.
- /OPT:REF is selected.
- /ORDER is selected.
- Use Program Database is not selected (/PDB:NONE) when Generate Debug Info (/DEBUG) is selected.

Additionally, LINK performs a full link if any of the following situations occur:

- The incremental status (.ILK) file is missing. (LINK creates a new .ILK file in preparation for subsequent incremental linking.)
- There is no write permission for the .ILK file. (LINK ignores the .ILK file and links nonincrementally.)
- The .EXE or .DLL output file is missing.

- The timestamp of the .ILK, .EXE, or .DLL is changed.

- A LINK option is changed. Most LINK options, when changed between builds, cause a full link.

- An object (.OBJ) file is added or omitted.

- An object that was compiled with the /Yu /Z7 option is changed.

Use Program Database

This option controls how the linker produces debugging information. Command-line equivalent: /PDB:*filename*

By default, when the Generate Debug Info (/DEBUG) option is specified, the linker creates a program database (PDB), which holds debugging information. If Generate Debug Info (/DEBUG) is not specified, the Use Program Database (/PDB) option is ignored.

If the Use Program Database check box is not selected (or if /PDB:NONE is specified on the command line), the linker does not create a PDB, but instead puts old-style debugging information into the .EXE file or DLL. The linker then calls the CVPACK.EXE tool, which must be in the same directory as LINK.EXE or in a directory in the PATH environment variable.

Debugging information in a PDB must be in Microsoft Format (/DEBUGTYPE:CV). If either COFF Format (/DEBUGTYPE:COFF) or Both Formats (/DEBUGTYPE:BOTH) is selected, no PDB is created.

Incremental linking is suppressed if the Use Program Database check box is not selected (or if /PDB:NONE is specified on the command line).

For information on overriding the default name of the PDB, see the next section, Program Database Name.

Program Database Name

This option sets the filename for the program database (PDB). Command-line equivalent: /PDB:*filename*

The linker creates a PDB when the Generate Debug Info (/DEBUG) option is specified. The default filename for the PDB has the base name of the program and the extension .PDB. To override the default name, type a filename in the Program Database Name text box (or specify /PDB:*filename* on the command line).

Debugging information in a PDB must be in Microsoft Format (/DEBUGTYPE:CV). If either COFF Format (/DEBUGTYPE:COFF) or Both Formats (/DEBUGTYPE:BOTH) is selected, no PDB is created, and the Program Database Name (/PDB:*filename*) option is ignored.

For information on controlling how the linker produces debugging information, see the previous section, Use Program Database.

Output File Name

This option overrides the default name and location of the program that the linker creates. Command-line equivalent: /OUT:*filename*

By default, the linker forms the filename using the base name of the first .OBJ file specified and the appropriate extension (.EXE or .DLL).

The Output File Name option controls the default base name for a .MAP file or import library. For details, see "Generate MapFile" on page 419 in this chapter and the description of the /IMPLIB option in Chapter 26, "LINK Reference."

Force File Output

This option tells the linker to create a valid .EXE file or DLL even if a symbol is referenced but not defined or is multiply defined. Command-line equivalent: /FORCE

On the command line, the /FORCE option can take an optional argument:

- Use /FORCE:MULTIPLE to create an output file whether or not LINK finds more than one definition for a symbol.
- Use /FORCE:UNRESOLVED to create an output file whether or not LINK finds an undefined symbol.

A file created with this option may not run as expected. The linker will not link incrementally when the /FORCE option is specified.

Print Progress Messages

This option displays details about the linking process. Command-line equivalent: /VERBOSE

The linker sends information about the progress of the linking session to the Output window. On the command line, the information is sent to standard output and can be redirected to a file.

The displayed information includes the library search process and lists each library and object name (with full path), the symbol being resolved from the library, and a list of objects that reference the symbol.

Suppress Startup Banner

This option prevents display of the copyright message and version number. Command-line equivalent: /NOLOGO

The Suppress Startup Banner option also suppresses echoing of command files. For details, see "LINK Command Files" in Chapter 26, "LINK Reference."

By default, this information is sent by the linker to the Output window. On the command line, it is sent to standard output and can be redirected to a file.

Debug Category Options

The Debug category options (see Figure 21.3) control the creation of debugging information and mapfile output.

Figure 21.3 Debug Category on the Link Tab

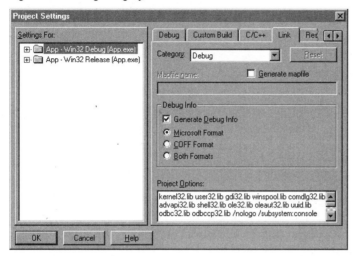

Mapfile Name

This option overrides the default name for a mapfile. Command-line equivalent: /MAP:*filename*

By default, when the Generate Mapfile (/MAP) option is specified, the linker names the mapfile with the base name of the program and the extension .MAP. To override the default name, type a filename in the Mapfile Name text box (or on the command line, type a colon (:) followed by *filename*).

Generate Mapfile

This option tells the linker to create a mapfile. Command-line equivalent: /MAP

The linker names the mapfile with the base name of the program and the extension .MAP. To override the default name, use the Mapfile Name (/MAP:*filename*) option.

A mapfile is a text file that contains the following information about the program being linked:

- The module name, which is the base name of the file
- The timestamp from the program file header (not from the file system)
- A list of groups in the program, with each group's start address (as *section:offset*), length, group name, and class

- A list of public symbols, with each address (as *section*:*offset*), symbol name, flat address, and .OBJ file where the symbol is defined
- The entry point (as *section*:*offset*)
- A list of fixups

Generate Debug Info

This option creates debugging information for the .EXE file or DLL. Command-line equivalent: /DEBUG

The linker puts the debugging information into a program database (PDB). It updates the PDB during subsequent builds of the program.

An .EXE file or DLL created for debugging contains the name and path of the corresponding PDB. The debugger reads the embedded name and uses the PDB when you debug the program. The linker uses the base name of the program and the extension .PDB to name the program database, and embeds the path where it was created. To override this default, use the Program Database Name (/PDB:*filename*) option.

The .OBJ files must contain debugging information. Use the compiler's Program Database (/Zi), Line Numbers Only (/Zd), or C7 Compatible (/Z7) option (described in Chapter 20, "Setting Compiler Options"). If an object, whether specified explicitly or supplied from a library, was compiled with the Use Program Database (/PDB:*filename*) option, its debugging information is stored in a PDB for the .OBJ file, and the name and location of the .PDB file are embedded in the object. The linker looks for the object's PDB first in the absolute path written in the .OBJ file, and then in the directory that contains the .OBJ file. You cannot specify a PDB's filename or location to the linker.

If the Use Program Database option is not selected (or if /PDB:NONE is specified on the command line), or if either COFF Format (/DEBUGTYPE:COFF) or Both Formats (/DEBUGTYPE:BOTH) is selected, the linker does not create a PDB, but instead puts the debugging information into the .EXE file or DLL.

The Generate Debug Info (/DEBUG) option changes the default for the /OPT option from REF to NOREF. For details on the /OPT option, see Chapter 26, "LINK Reference."

Microsoft Format

This option creates Microsoft Format debugging information. Command-line equivalent: /DEBUGTYPE:CV

To use Microsoft Format debugging information, select the Microsoft Format option button under Debug Info. If the Generate Debug Info check box is not selected, this choice is unavailable. On the command line, if /DEBUG is specified, the default type is /DEBUGTYPE:CV; if /DEBUG is not specified, /DEBUGTYPE is ignored.

COFF Format

This option creates Common Object File Format (COFF)-style debugging information. Command-line equivalent: /DEBUGTYPE:COFF

Some debuggers require COFF debugging information. To use COFF-format debugging information, select the COFF Format option button under Debug Info. If the Generate Debug Info check box is not selected, this choice is unavailable. On the command line, specify /DEBUGTYPE:COFF; if /DEBUG is not specified, /DEBUGTYPE is ignored.

When this option is set, the linker does not create a PDB; in addition, incremental linking is disabled.

Both Formats

This option creates both COFF debugging information and Microsoft Format debugging information. Command-line equivalent: /DEBUGTYPE:BOTH

To create a program with both Microsoft Format Symbolic Debugging Information and COFF debugging information, select the Both Formats option button under Debug Info. If the Generate Debug Info check box is not selected, this choice is unavailable. On the command line, specify /DEBUGTYPE:BOTH; if /DEBUG is not specified, /DEBUGTYPE is ignored.

When this option is set, the linker does not create a PDB; in addition, incremental linking is disabled. The linker must call the CVPACK.EXE tool to process the Microsoft Format debugging information. CVPACK must be in the same directory as LINK or in a directory in the PATH environment variable.

Input Category Options

The Input category options (see Figure 21.4) control how the linker uses libraries and stub files.

Figure 21.4 Input Category on the Link Tab

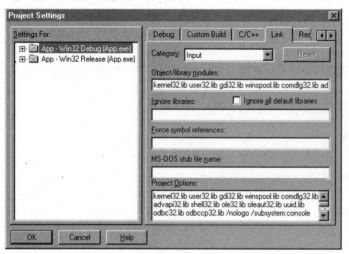

Object/Library Modules

This option passes an object file or standard library (either static or import) to the linker. Command-line equivalent: *filename*

To pass a file to the linker, specify the filename in the Object/Library Modules text box. You can specify an absolute or relative path with the filename, and you can use wildcards in the filename. If you omit the dot (.) and filename extension, the linker assumes .OBJ for the purpose of finding the file. The linker does not use filename extensions or the lack of them to make assumptions about the contents of files; it determines the type of file by examining it and processes it accordingly.

Ignore Libraries

This option tells the linker to remove one or more default libraries from the list of libraries it searches when resolving external references. Command-line equivalent: /NODEFAULTLIB:*library*

The linker resolves references to external definitions by searching first in libraries specified in the Object/Library Modules text box (or on the command line), then in default libraries specified with the /DEFAULTLIB option, then in default libraries named in .OBJ files.

To specify multiple *libraries*, type a comma (,) between the library names.

To suppress the search in all default libraries, select the Ignore All Default Libraries check box (or specify /NODEFAULTLIB with no arguments on the command line).

The Ignore Libraries (/NODEFAULTLIB:*library*) option overrides /DEFAULTLIB:*library* when the same *library* name is specified in both.

Ignore All Default Libraries

This option tells the linker to remove all default libraries from the list of libraries it searches when resolving external references. Command-line equivalent: /NODEFAULTLIB

The linker resolves references to external definitions by searching first in libraries specified in the Object/Library Modules text box (or on the command line), then in default libraries specified with the /DEFAULTLIB option, then in default libraries named in .OBJ files.

To suppress the search in a specific library, use the Ignore Libraries (/NODEFAULTLIB:*library*) option (or specify a colon (:) and the library name on the command line).

The Ignore All Default Libraries (/NODEFAULTLIB) option overrides /DEFAULTLIB:*library*.

Force Symbol References

This option tells the linker to add a specified symbol to the symbol table. Command-line equivalent: /INCLUDE:*symbol*

Type a *symbol* name in the Force Symbol References text box. To specify multiple symbols, type a comma (,), a semicolon (;), or a space between the symbol names. On the command line, specify /INCLUDE:*symbol* once for each symbol.

The linker resolves *symbol* by adding the object that contains the symbol definition to the program. This feature is useful for including a library object that otherwise would not be linked to the program.

Specifying a symbol with the Force Symbol References (/INCLUDE:*symbol*) option overrides the removal of that symbol by /OPT:REF. For details on the /OPT:REF option, see Chapter 26, "LINK Reference."

MS-DOS Stub File Name

This option attaches an MS-DOS stub program to a Win32 program. Command-line equivalent: /STUB:*filename*

A stub program is invoked if the file is executed in MS-DOS. It usually displays an appropriate message; however, any valid MS-DOS application can be a stub program.

Specify a *filename* for the stub program in the MS-DOS Stub File Name text box (or after a colon (:) on the command line). The linker checks *filename* to be sure that it is a valid MS-DOS executable file, and issues an error message if the file is not valid. The program must be an .EXE file; a .COM file is invalid for a stub program.

If the MS-DOS Stub File Name (/STUB:*filename*) option is not used, the linker attaches a default stub program that issues the following message:

```
This program cannot be run in MS-DOS mode.
```

Output Category Options

The Output category options (see Figure 21.5) control the linker when producing a Win32 project.

Figure 21.5 Output Category on the Link Tab

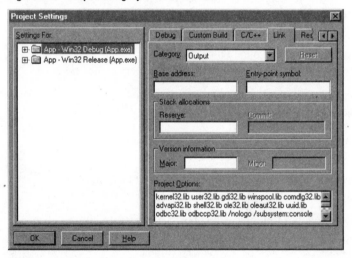

Base Address

This option sets a base address for the program, overriding the default location for an .EXE file (at 0x400000) or a DLL (at 0x10000000). The operating system first attempts to load a program at its specified or default base address. If sufficient space is not available there, the system relocates the program. To prevent relocation, use the /FIXED option. For details on the /FIXED option, see Chapter 26, "LINK Reference." Command-line equivalent: /BASE:{*address* | @*filename,key*}

Type the preferred base address in the Base Address text box (or in the *address* argument on the command line). The linker rounds the specified number up to the nearest multiple of 64K.

On the command line, another way to specify the base address is by using the *filename* preceded by an at sign (@), and a *key* into the file. The *filename* is a text file that contains the locations and sizes of all the DLLs your program will use. The linker looks for *filename* in either the specified path or, if no path is specified, in directories specified in the LIB environment variable. Each line in *filename* represents one DLL and has the following syntax:

key address size ;*comment*

The *key* is a string of alphanumeric characters and is not case sensitive. It is usually the name of a DLL, but it need not be. The *key* is followed by a base *address* in C-language, hexadecimal, or decimal notation and a maximum *size*. All three arguments are separated by spaces or tabs. The linker issues a warning if the specified *size* is less than the virtual address space required by the program. A *comment* is specified by a semicolon (;) and can be on the same or a separate line. The linker ignores all text from the semicolon to the end of the line. This example shows part of such a file:

```
main    0x00010000    0x08000000    ; for PROJECT.EXE
one     0x28000000    0x00100000    ; for DLLONE.DLL
two     0x28100000    0x00300000    ; for DLLTWO.DLL
```

If the file that contains these lines is called DLLS.TXT, the following example command applies this information:

```
link dlltwo.obj /dll /base:dlls.txt,two
```

You can reduce paging and improve performance of your program by assigning base addresses so that DLLs do not overlap in the address space.

An alternate way to set the base address is with the *BASE* argument in a **NAME** or **LIBRARY** statement. The /BASE and /DLL options together are equivalent to the **LIBRARY** statement. For details on /DLL, **NAME**, and **LIBRARY**, see Chapter 26, "LINK Reference."

Entry-Point Symbol

This option sets the starting address for an .EXE file or DLL. Command-line equivalent: /ENTRY:*function*

Type a function name in the Entry-Point Symbol text box (or in the *function* argument on the command line). The function must be defined with the **__stdcall** calling convention. The parameters and return value must be defined as documented in the Win32 API for **WinMain** (for an .EXE file) or **DllEntryPoint** (for a DLL). It is recommended that you let the linker set the entry point so that the C run-time library is initialized correctly, and C++ constructors for static objects are executed.

By default, the starting address is a function name from the C run-time library. The linker selects it according to the attributes of the program, as shown in the following table.

Function name	Default for
mainCRTStartup (or **wmainCRTStartup**)	An application using /SUBSYSTEM:**CONSOLE**; calls **main** (or **wmain**)
WinMainCRTStartup (or **wWinMainCRTStartup**)	An application using /SUBSYSTEM:**WINDOWS**; calls **WinMain** (or **wWinMain**), which must be defined with **__stdcall**
_DllMainCRTStartup	A DLL; calls **DllMain**, which must be defined with **__stdcall**, if it exists

If the /DLL or /SUBSYSTEM option is not specified, the linker selects a subsystem and entry point depending on whether **main** or **WinMain** is defined. For details on the /DLL and /SUBSYSTEM options, see Chapter 26, "LINK Reference."

The functions **main**, **WinMain**, and **DllMain** are the three forms of the user-defined entry point.

Stack Allocations

This option sets the size of the stack in bytes. Command-line equivalent: /STACK:*reserve*[,*commit*]

The Reserve text box (or the *reserve* argument on the command line) specifies the total stack allocation in virtual memory. The default stack size is 1 MB. The linker rounds up the specified value to the nearest 4 bytes.

The optional value specified in the Commit text box (or in the *commit* argument on the command line) is subject to interpretation by the operating system. In Windows NT, it specifies the amount of physical memory to allocate at a time. Committed virtual memory causes space to be reserved in the paging file. A higher *commit* value saves time when the application needs more stack space, but increases the memory requirements and possibly the startup time.

Specify the *reserve* and *commit* values in decimal or C-language notation.

An alternate way to set the size of the stack is with the **STACKSIZE** statement in a module-definition (.DEF) file. For details on **STACKSIZE**, see Chapter 26, "LINK Reference." **STACKSIZE** overrides the Stack Allocations (/STACK) option if both are specified. You can change the stack after the .EXE file is built by using the EDITBIN tool. For details on EDITBIN, see Chapter 32, "EDITBIN Reference."

Version Information

This option tells the linker to put a version number in the header of the .EXE file or DLL. Command-line equivalent: /VERSION:*major*[.*minor*]

The *major* and *minor* arguments are decimal numbers in the range 0 through 65,535. The default is version 0.0.

An alternate way to insert a version number is with the **VERSION** module-definition statement. For details on **VERSION**, see Chapter 26, "LINK Reference."

Customizing Visual C++

CHAPTER 22

Customizing Microsoft Developer Studio

With Microsoft Developer Studio, you can customize various aspects of its layout and operation by:

- Arranging the layout of windows and toolbars.
- Adding your favorite toolbar buttons to the toolbar.
- Assigning shortcut keys to commands.
- Adding your tools to the Tools menu.
- Specifying directories for build utilities, include files and libraries.

With Developer Studio, you can arrange the display area in the way that best suits your preferences and work habits. Some arrangements are maintained with each project. In a project, for instance, you can size editor windows, move them to convenient locations, and automatically save these locations with your project.

Other arrangements are maintained globally. For instance, you can display some windows in one layout while you are editing your files or building your project, and another layout when you are debugging.

Some windows can either be fixed along the application window border or moved anywhere on your screen. These windows are called docking tool windows.

Some of the commands in Developer Studio are assigned shortcut keys by default. Other commands do not have any default shortcut key assigned to them. In Developer Studio, you can:

- Delete existing assignments for shortcut keys.
- Replace default shortcut keys with different ones.
- Assign shortcut keys to commands that have none by default.
- Assign multiple shortcut keys to a command.

Using these assignments, you can choose your own set of shortcut keys—ones that are familiar and natural for you to use, or that have some easily remembered value.

Microsoft Developer Studio provides F1 source-file help for language keywords and function calls. In some cases, language elements may have entries in multiple topics or information titles (an information title is an .MVB file such as Books Online or Microsoft Development Library). If you press F1 on a source-file keyword, say GetArcDirection, Developer Studio looks for information on the keyword in the current title. If multiple topics exist for the keyword, Developer Studio displays the Select Reference dialog box. The Select Reference dialog box lists not only the topics but also other titles with topics for the keyword. You can select another title if you wish. For further information, see Finding Information.

Note   You can also customize other aspects of Developer Studio. To find out about customizing text editor windows and their use of fonts or colors, see Chapter 3, "Using the Text Editor." To find out about customizing settings for debugging, see Chapter 17, "Using the Debugger."

Working with Window Types

Microsoft Developer Studio has two types of windows, which it treats in different ways, as shown in the following table.

Type	Attributes	Layout Associated With
Document windows	Position and size can be changed only within the application window. Can be maximized and minimized.	Project
Docking tool windows and toolbars	Attach to *docks* along the borders of the application window, or float anywhere on your screen. A toolbar is a type of docking tool window. All docking tool windows except toolbars can convert to document windows.	Editing or debugging
Full-screen mode	Editing window expands to the size of the entire screen.	Editing or debugging

The layout for window types—that is, their visibility, position, and size—is associated either with a project, in the case of document windows, or with editing or debugging operations, in the case of docking tool windows and toolbars. Once you have chosen a layout, that layout is persistent. If you close a project and later open it again, the document windows have the last layout that you used: The same windows are open, and they have the same sizes and positions. When you create layouts of docking tool windows or toolbars, either for editing, debugging, or full-screen mode, those layouts are used for all subsequent sessions until you change them again.

All window types can display pop-up menus with commands appropriate for the window in its current state. For example, the pop-up menu for an editor window, which is a type of document window, displays the Cut, Copy, and Paste commands while editing, but displays the Toggle Breakpoint and QuickWatch commands while debugging. Click the right mouse button in the window to display the pop-up menu.

There is also a pop-up menu associated with the dock along the border of the application window. If you click the right mouse button in the dock area or on a toolbar, the menu displays commands to show or hide all of the docking tool windows, and to customize the toolbars. The various pop-up menus are shown in Figure 22.1.

Figure 22.1   Pop-up Menus Displayed with the Right Mouse Button

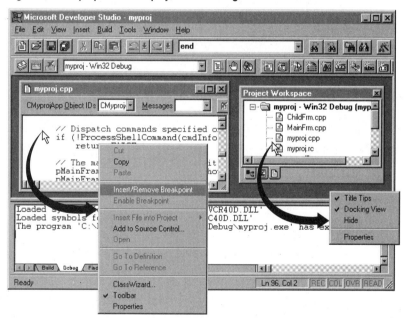

Working with Document Windows

The following windows are document windows:

- Editor windows, either for text or resources
- Resource browser window

Document windows are associated with the project workspace. Developer Studio records their positions, sizes, any selections made in them, window splits, and so on when you close a project. When you open the project again, these characteristics are restored.

Document windows also can display pop-up menus with commands appropriate for the window in its current state. Click the right mouse button in the document window to display the pop-up menu.

See Also Positioning Document Windows, Selecting Document Windows to Display When Opening a Project, Working with Docking Tool Windows

Positioning Document Windows

You can position the document windows for a project to suit your preferences. These positions are then retained when you close the project. When you open the project again, Developer Studio restores these window positions, opens the necessary files, and displays their contents in the windows, with any window splits and selections that you have made.

▶ **To move a document window**

- Point to the title bar, and drag the window to the location you want.

▶ **To size a document window**

- Point to the window border, and drag the window border to the size yu want.

▶ **To display the pop-up menu for a document window**

- Click the right mouse button in the window.

▶ **To tile document windows**

- From the Window menu, choose Tile Horizontally.

    −or−

    From the Window menu, choose Tile Vertically.

▶ **To overlap document windows**

- From the Window menu, choose Cascade.

▶ **To split document windows**

  1 From the Window menu, choose Split.

  2 Drag the splitter bars in the window to the location you want, and click the mouse to set the location of the splitter bars.

Selecting Document Windows to Display When Opening a Project

You can specify whether to display project documents when you open a project.

▶ **To display project documents when you open a project**

  1 From the Tools menu, choose Options.

The Options dialog box appears.

2 Select the Workspace tab.

3 Select the Reload Documents When Opening Project check box.

4 Choose the OK button.

▶ **To not display project documents when you open a project**

1 From the Tools menu, choose Options.

The Options dialog box appears.

2 Select the Workspace tab.

3 Clear the Reload Documents When Opening Project check box.

4 Choose the OK button.

Working with Docking Tool Windows

With docking tool windows, you can customize the workspace by

- Showing or hiding the docking tool window.
- Changing the display mode from docked to floating.
- Resizing any floating docking tool window.
- Giving docking tool windows the display characteristics of a document.

The choice and layout of docking tool windows are always associated with either editing or debugging, even if you have selected the characteristics of document windows. The debugging docking tool windows are available only during the debug process.

The following windows are docking tool windows:

- Output window
- Watch window
- Variables window
- Registers window
- Memory window
- Call Stack window
- Disassembly window
- Project Workspace window
- InfoViewer Topic window

 Tip Docking tool windows can display pop-up menus with commands appropriate for the window in its current state. Click the right mouse button in the window to display the pop-up menu.

Showing and Hiding Docking Tool Windows

You can show or hide the Output, Project Workspace, and InfoViewer Topic windows at any time. You can show or hide the debugging windows only during the debug process.

▶ **To show a docking tool window**

• From the View menu, choose the docking tool window that you want to show.

   –or–

1 With the right mouse button, click the border of a docking tool window (see "Working with Window Types" on page 430).

   The pop-up menu appears. The window names with checks appearing next to them are currently displayed.

2 Select the unchecked docking tool window that you want to show.

   The window appears in its default location, or in the last location that you assigned it.

▶ **To hide a docking tool window**

1 Click in the window to make it active.

2 From the Window menu, choose Hide.

   –or–

   With the right mouse button, click inside the window, from the pop-up menu, choose Hide.

   –or–

   If the docking tool window is currently displayed as a document window, double-click the control box in the upper-left corner of the window.

Positioning Docking Tool Windows

The window positions for docking tool windows are not associated with the current project; they remain the same no matter which project you open. However, the locations of the docking tool windows can be different depending on whether you are editing or debugging. You can create one layout with your choice of docking tool windows for editing, and another layout with a different choice of docking tool windows for debugging. When you switch from editing to debugging, the layout automatically changes.

Docking tool windows can have either of two display modes: floating or docked.

Floating Mode

In floating mode, a docking tool window has a thin title bar and can appear anywhere on your screen. A floating window is always on top of all other windows.

Figure 22.2   Floating Variables Window

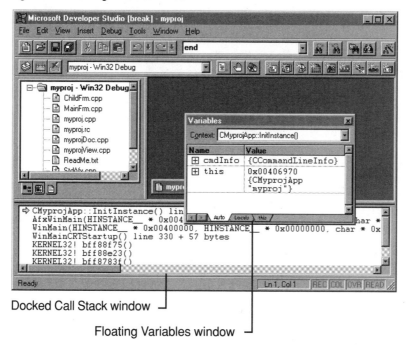

Docked Call Stack window ⌐

Floating Variables window ⌐

Docked Mode

In docked mode, a docking tool window is fixed to a dock along any of the four borders of the main Microsoft Developer Studio window.

Figure 22.3   Docked Variables Window

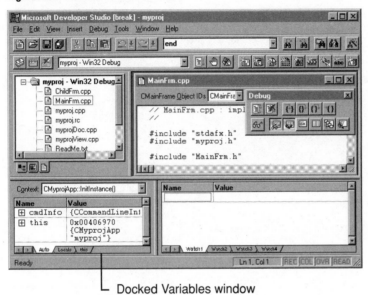

└─ Docked Variables window

You can specify whether tool windows appear as docked windows or as floating windows.

▶ **To change a docked window to a floating window**

1 Point to a blank area on the window border.

2 Drag the window away from the dock to the position that you want.

–or–

Double-click in the window border.

▶ **To dock a floating window**

1 Point to the title bar of the docking tool window.

2 Drag the window to any of the four borders of the application window.

–or–

Double-click the window title bar to return the window to its previous docked location.

A docking tool window stretches to fill the entire border to which you drag it, as shown in Figure 22.4. A toolbar changes to a single row or column and takes the space required by its tool buttons.

Figure 22.4   Window in Floating and Docked Modes

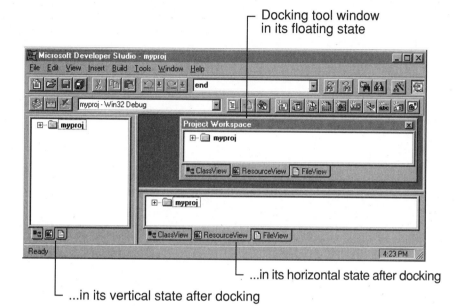

Docking tool window in its floating state

...in its horizontal state after docking

...in its vertical state after docking

▶ **To position a floating window over a dock**

1 Point to the title bar of the window.

2 Hold down the CTRL key, and drag the window over any dock area of the application window.

The window moves into position over the dock, but remains a floating window.

Sizing Docking Tool Windows

You can resize any floating docking tool window in any direction. You can also size docked docking tool windows by moving their splitter bar or bars. If two or more tool windows are in the same dock, you can size them by moving the splitter bar between them.

▶ **To resize a docking tool window**

1 Point to the border of a docked or floating window.

The mouse pointer turns into a sizing arrow.

2 Drag the splitter bar or border to resize the window.

Changing Docking Tool Window Characteristics

You can use the Options dialog box of the Tools menu to give docking tool windows the display characteristics of document windows. Even though toolbars are docking tool windows, you cannot give them document window characteristics.

Note A docking tool window can appear as a docked window, a floating window, or a document window. Although a docking tool window can appear with any of these characteristics, it remains a docking tool window.

▶ **To enable or disable the document characteristics of a docking tool window**

1 From the Tools menu, choose Options.

   The Options dialog box appears.

2 Select the Workspace tab.

3 In the Docking Views list box, select the check box for a window to enable its docking characteristics. Clear the check box for a window to disable its docking characteristics.

   An unselected window behaves like a document window.

   Note By default, the Disassembly and InfoViewer Topic windows have the characteristics of document windows.

4 Choose the OK button.

Alternatively, clear the check box for docking tool windows that you want to have the characteristics of document windows.

▶ **To quickly switch between docking and document characteristics in a docking tool window**

1 Click the right mouse button inside the window.

2 From the pop-up menu, choose Docking View.

If the docking tool window has the display characteristics of a document window, it changes to the display characteristics of a docked window. If the docking tool window has the display characteristics of a docked window, it changes to the display characteristics of a document window.

Working with Toolbars

Toolbars can contain buttons that correspond to menu commands in Developer Studio. A toolbar provides a quick and convenient method for carrying out commands that you use often.

When Developer Studio starts up in its standard configuration after installation, it displays the Standard toolbar and command choices. If you are not satisfied with the standard choices, you can choose to display other toolbars, as well as which command buttons to display on any toolbar.

Note The toolbar categories that appear for the first time depend on the packages that you have installed on your system.

Because toolbars are docking tool windows, you can either fix a toolbar along a border of the application window, or you can turn it into a floating window that can move anywhere on your screen.

In addition to the Standard toolbar, Developer Studio displays toolbars that reflect the editors that are currently open. For example, if you open the resource file for your project, and then open a bitmap resource, the toolbars associated with the Image editor are displayed. The current state of the program determines whether the tools on any given toolbar are enabled or disabled.

Toolbar positions are not associated with the current project, but depend on which editors are open and whether you are editing, debugging, or using full-screen mode. For example, you can create one layout with your choice of toolbars for editing, another layout with a different choice of toolbars for debugging, and another layout with different toolbars for full-screen mode. When you switch between editing, debugging, and full-screen mode, the layout automatically changes.

Showing and Hiding Toolbars

When Microsoft Developer Studio starts up in its standard configuration after installations, it displays the predefined toolbars on its dock. The toolbar categories that appear depend on the software that you have installed on your system. You can choose, however, which toolbars you want to show at any time.

▶ To show or hide a toolbar using the main menu

1 From the View menu, choose Toolbars.

The Toolbars dialog box appears.

2 Select the check boxes for the toolbars that you want to show.

3 Clear the check boxes for the toolbars that you want to hide.

Each selected toolbar appears immediately, in its default location, or in the last location that you assigned to it. Each hidden toolbar disappears immediately.

4 Choose the Close button.

▶ To show or hide a toolbar using the pop-up menu

1 Click the right mouse button on a toolbar, either floating or docked.

The pop-up menu appears. The toolbar names with checks appearing next to them are currently displayed.

2 Select the unchecked toolbars that you want to show.

3 Select the checked toolbars that you want to hide.

Each selected toolbar appears immediately. It appears in its default location, or in the last location that you assigned it, if you assigned it one. Each hidden toolbar disappears immediately.

4 Choose the Close button.

▶ **To hide a floating toolbar**

- Click the close box in the upper-right corner of the window.

Showing ToolTips

You can display the name of a tool when you place the cursor on the tool button. You can also display the shortcut keys associated with the tool button.

▶ **To show ToolTips**

1 From the View menu, choose Toolbars.

The Toolbars dialog box appears.

2 Select Show ToolTips if you want to display the name of a tool when you place the cursor on the toolbar button.

3 Select With Shortcut Keys if you want to display in the tooltip the shortcut keys associated with the tool button.

4 Choose the Close button.

See Also   Viewing and Changing the Shortcut Keys

Creating a Custom Toolbar

You can create a custom toolbar and add any tool button to it. You can either name the new toolbar with a title of your choice, or allow Developer Studio to give it the default title "Toolbar," followed by a number.

▶ **To create a named toolbar**

1 From the View menu, choose Toolbars.

The Toolbars dialog box appears.

2 Choose the New button.

The New Toolbar dialog box appears.

3 In the Toolbar Name text box, type the name of your custom toolbar.

4 Choose the OK button.

Two windows appear:

- In the upper-left corner of your application window, a new toolbar window with the name that you specified appears.

- The Customize dialog box appears.

5 Select the Toolbars tab.

The Toolbars tab gives you choices for categories of toolbar buttons. These categories are listed in the Categories list box. When you select a category, the Buttons frame displays all the buttons in the selected category. Each button represents a command.

6 In the Categories list box, select a category.

7 Drag the buttons that you want from the selected category onto the custom toolbar.

8 Repeat steps 6 and 7 until you have all the buttons that you want on your toolbar.

9 Choose the Close button.

▶ **To quickly create a toolbar with a default name**

1 From the Tools menu, choose Customize.

The Customize dialog box appears.

2 Select the Toolbars tab.

The Toolbars tab gives you choices for categories of toolbar buttons. These categories are listed in the Categories list box. When you select a category, the Buttons frame displays all the buttons in the selected category. Each button represents a command.

3 In the Categories list box, select a category.

4 Drag the first button from the selected category onto any area of your screen (except an existing toolbar).

The first button creates a toolbar named Toolbar*n*, where *n* is 1, 2, 3, 4, and so on.

5 Repeat steps 3 and 4 until you have all the buttons that you want on your toolbar, but for step 4 drag the button onto the toolbar that you have just created.

6 Choose the Close button.

Note   A toolbar with only a few buttons may be too short to fully display its name.

Modifying a Toolbar

You can easily add buttons to a toolbar, remove buttons from a toolbar, arrange buttons on a toolbar, copy toolbar buttons, or rename a custom toolbar.

▶ **To add buttons to a toolbar**

1 From the Tools menu, choose Customize.

The Customize dialog box appears.

2 Select the Toolbars tab.

The Toolbars tab gives you choices for categories of toolbar buttons. These categories are listed in the Categories list box. When you select a category, the Buttons frame displays all the buttons in the selected category. Each button represents a command.

3 In the Categories list box, select a category.

4 Drag a button from the Buttons frame onto the toolbar.

5 Repeat steps 3 and 4 until you have all the buttons you want on your toolbar.

6 Choose the Close button.

▶ **To remove buttons from a toolbar**

1 From the Tools menu, choose Customize.

The Customize dialog box appears.

2 Select the Toolbars tab.

3 Drag the button that you want to remove away from the toolbar.

4 Choose the Close button.

▶ **To move buttons on a toolbar**

1 From the Tools menu, choose Customize.

The Customize dialog box appears.

2 Select the Toolbars tab.

3 Drag the button that you want to move to a new location on the same toolbar or on another displayed toolbar.

4 Choose the Close button.

▶ **To quickly move buttons on a displayed toolbar**

- Hold down the ALT key, and drag the button that you want to move to a new location on the same toolbar or on another displayed toolbar.

▶ **To copy buttons from a toolbar**

1 From the Tools menu, choose Customize.

The Customize dialog box appears.

2 Select the Toolbars tab.

3 Hold down the CTRL key, and drag the button from the Buttons frame to its new location on the same toolbar or on another displayed toolbar.

4 Choose the Close button.

▶ **To quickly copy buttons on a toolbar**

● Hold down the ALT+CTRL key combination, and drag the button that you want to copy from another toolbar to a new location on the same toolbar or on another displayed toolbar.

Note If you hold down the CTRL key, or a CTRL key combination, and drag a button onto an area where there is no existing toolbar, Developer Studio creates a new toolbar with a default name.

▶ **To insert a space between buttons on a toolbar**

1 From the Tools menu, choose Customize.

The Customize dialog box appears.

2 Select the Toolbars tab.

3 Perform one or more of the following actions:

- To insert a space before a button that is not followed by a space, drag the button to the right or down until it overlaps the next button about halfway.

- To insert a space before a button that is followed by a space that you want to retain, drag the button until the right or bottom edge is just touching the next button or just overlaps it.

- To insert a space before a button that is followed by a space that you want to close, drag the button to the right or down until it overlaps the next button about halfway.

4 Choose the Close button.

▶ **To close up a space between buttons on a toolbar**

1 From the Tools menu, choose Customize.

The Customize dialog box appears.

2 Select the Toolbars tab.

3 Drag the button on one side of the space toward the button on the other side of the space until it overlaps the next button about halfway.

If there is no space on the side of the button that you are dragging away from, and you drag the button more than halfway past the adjacent button, a space is inserted on the opposite side of the button that you are dragging.

4 Choose the Close button.

▶ **To resize a combo box on a toolbar**

1 From the Tools menu, choose Customize.

The Customize dialog box appears.

2 Select the Toolbars tab.

3 On the toolbar, select the combo box that you want to resize.

4 Drag the right edge of the combo box to the size that you want.

5 Choose the Close button.

▶ **To rename a custom toolbar**

1 From the View menu, choose Toolbars.

The Toolbars dialog box appears.

2 In the Toolbars list, select the toolbar that you want to rename.

3 In the Toolbar Name text box, type the new name for the toolbar.

4 Choose the Close button.

Resetting a Toolbar

If you have modified a predefined toolbar, either by adding or removing buttons, you can easily restore its default settings.

▶ **To reset a toolbar**

1 From the View menu, choose Toolbars.

The Toolbars dialog box appears.

2 In the Toolbars list box, select the toolbar that you want to reset.

3 Choose the Reset button.

4 Choose the Close button.

Deleting a Toolbar

You can delete any custom toolbar that you have created.

▶ **To delete a custom toolbar**

1 From the View menu, choose Toolbars.

The Toolbars dialog box appears.

2 In the Toolbars list box, select the toolbar that you want to delete.

You cannot delete any of the predefined toolbars.

3 Choose the Delete button.

4 Choose the Close button.

Docking Toolbars

When Developer Studio starts up in its standard configuration after installation, it displays the Standard toolbar on the top dock of the main application window, as shown in Figure 22.5.

Figure 22.5 Standard Toolbar Layout

Toolbars can have either of two display modes: floating or docked.

Floating Mode

In floating mode, a toolbar has a thin title bar and can appear anywhere on your screen. A floating toolbar is always on top of all other windows. You can modify the size or position of a toolbar when it is floating.

Figure 22.6 Floating Toolbar

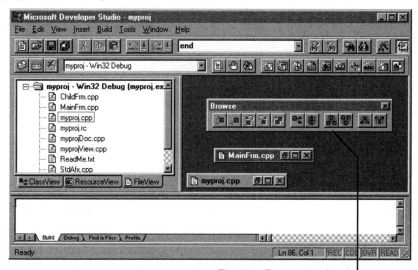

Floating Browse toolbar ⅃

Docked Mode

In docked mode, a toolbar is fixed to a dock along any of the four borders of the application window. You cannot modify the size of a toolbar when it is docked.

Figure 22.7   Docked Toolbar

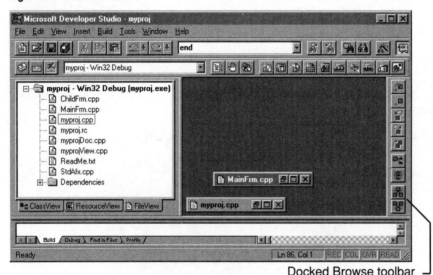

Docked Browse toolbar ─┘

You can dock any of the predefined toolbars that you choose to display, or any of the custom toolbars that you create. You can move any toolbar from its docked position, which automatically converts it into a floating toolbar.

▸ **To change a docked toolbar to a floating toolbar**

1 Point to a blank area in the toolbar.

2 Drag the toolbar away from the dock to the position that you want.

▸ **To dock a floating toolbar**

1 Point to the toolbar title bar or a blank area in the toolbar.

2 Drag the toolbar to any of the four borders of the application window.

   When the mouse pointer reaches the boundary of the docking area, the toolbar window assumes a shape appropriate for the docking location. Along the top and bottom borders, it becomes a single horizontal row of buttons; along the sides, it becomes a single vertical row.

▸ **To quickly move a toolbar onto or off of the toolbar dock**

• Double-click a blank area in a docked toolbar, or the title bar of a floating toolbar.

   If you double-click a docked toolbar, it moves to its previous floating position.

If you double-click the title bar of a floating toolbar, it moves to the last toolbar dock on which it was displayed. If the toolbar has not been docked before, it moves to a new row in the toolbar dock below the menu bar.

▸ **To position a floating toolbar over a dock**

1 Point to a blank area of the toolbar or its title bar.

2 Hold down the CTRL key, and drag the toolbar over any dock area of the application window.

The toolbar moves into position over the dock, but remains a floating toolbar.

 Tip   The orientation of a docked toolbar generally corresponds to the orientation of the dock. Toolbars dock vertically on vertical docks, and horizontally on horizontal docks. You can switch a toolbar's docked orientation between horizontal and vertical by pressing or releasing the SHIFT key as you drag and drop the toolbar.

Sizing Floating Toolbars

You can resize any floating toolbar. The toolbar changes the row and column arrangement of its buttons to accommodate whatever new orientation you give it. The toolbar takes the least amount of space necessary to display all of its buttons.

Note   You cannot change the size or orientation of a docked toolbar.

▸ **To resize a floating toolbar**

1 Move the mouse pointer over the toolbar window border.

The mouse pointer turns into a sizing arrow.

2 Drag the border to resize the toolbar.

Customizing the Keyboard

Keyboard shortcuts offer an alternative method of performing actions for users who prefer keyboard use over mouse use. With Microsoft Developer Studio, you can:

- Display the current keyboard shortcuts (this includes custom key settings and any selected editor emulation).
- Assign shortcut keys to available commands.

Displaying the Keyboard Shortcuts

You can display the current keyboard shortcuts, including custom key settings and editor emulations.

▸ **To display keyboard shortcuts**

1 From the Help menu, choose Keyboard.

The Help Keyboard dialog box appears, with a list of keyboard shortcuts.

2 Perform one or more of the following actions:

- Choose the Category, Command, Keys, or Description button to sort the list alphabetically in different ways.

- Choose the Print button to print out the contents of the dialog box.

- Choose the Copy button to copy the contents of the dialog box to the Clipboard so you can paste them into the word processor or the editor of your choice.

3 Double-click the Control-menu box in the upper-left corner to close the Help keyboard dialog box.

Assigning Shortcut Keys

You can use the Keyboard tab on the Customize dialog box to establish your choice of shortcut keys for any of the available commands. You can assign more than one shortcut key for any command. You can delete or change key assignments, and you can assign shortcut keys for each editor. You can also reset all shortcut keys to their default settings.

Note If you use any of the incremental search commands (IncrementalSearch, IncrementalSearchBack, IncrementalSearchRE, IncrementalSearchREBack), you can modify the search by toggling the word mode (CTRL+W), regular expression mode (CTRL+T), and case sensitive mode (CTRL+C). These keystrokes are not bindable and only affect the incremental search command.

▶ **To assign a shortcut key**

1 From the Tools menu, choose Customize.

The Customize dialog box appears.

2 Select the Keyboard tab.

3 In the Editor drop-down list box, select the editor in which you want the shortcut key to invoke the command.

4 In the Categories list box, select the category that contains the command to which you want to assign the shortcut key.

5 In the Commands list box, select the command to which you want to assign the shortcut key. A description of the command's effect appears in the Description box, and the currently assigned shortcut keys appear in the Current Keys box.

6 Click the Press New Shortcut Key box, and press the shortcut key or key combination that you want.

If you press a key or key combination that is invalid, no key is displayed, and the Assign button is unavailable. You cannot assign key combinations with TAB, ESC, F1, or combinations such as CTRL+ALT+DEL, which Windows NT uses.

If you press a key or key combination that is currently assigned to another command, that command appears under Currently Assigned To.

7 Choose the Assign button.

Any previous shortcut key assignment for the key or key combination that you specified is replaced by the new assignment.

You can repeat steps 3 through 7 until you have made all of the key assignments that you want.

8 Choose the Close button.

All of your shortcut key assignments are now in effect.

▶ **To delete a shortcut key**

1 From the Tools menu, choose Customize.

The Customize dialog box appears.

2 Select the Keyboard tab.

3 In the Editor drop-down list box, select the editor in which the shortcut key invokes the command.

4 In the Categories list box, select the category that contains the command for which you want to delete the shortcut key.

5 In the Commands list, select the command for which you want to delete the shortcut key.

A description of the command's effect appears in the Description box, and the currently assigned shortcut keys appear in the Current Keys list box.

6 In the Current Keys list box, select the shortcut key to delete.

7 Choose the Remove button.

You can repeat steps 3 through 7 until you have deleted all of the key assignments that you want.

8 Choose the Close button.

All of your shortcut key deletions are now in effect.

▶ **To reset all shortcut keys to their default values**

1 From the Tools menu, choose Customize.

The Customize dialog box appears.

2 Select the Keyboard tab.

3 Choose the Reset All button.

4 Choose the Close button.

All commands now have their original, default shortcut key assignments.

See Also   Displaying the Keyboard Shortcuts

Customizing the Tools Menu

You can use the Tools tab in the Customize dialog box to add, delete, and edit Tools menu items. You can add frequently used utilities to the Tools menu and run them from within Microsoft Developer Studio.

See Also   Tools Options, Using Argument Macros

Adding Commands to the Tools Menu

You can add up to 16 commands to the Tools menu. A tool can be any program that will run on your operating system.

As an example, the following procedure demonstrates how to add the Windows Notepad accessary to the Tools menu.

▶ **To add a command to the Tools menu**

1 From the Tools menu, choose Customize.

The Customize dialog box appears.

2 Select the Tools tab.

3 Choose Add.

The Add Tool dialog box appears.

4 In the Command text box, type `NOTEPAD.EXE`.

   −or−

   Choose the Browse button, select the appropriate drive and directory, and then select NOTEPAD.EXE from the list of filenames.

5 In the Arguments text box, type any arguments to be passed to the program.

   You can use the drop-down arrow next to the Arguments text box to display a menu of arguments. Select an argument from the list to insert argument syntax into the Arguments text box.

6 In the Initial Directory text box, type the file directory where the command is located.

   You can use the drop-down arrow next to the Initial Directory text box to display a menu of directories. Select a directory from the list to insert directory syntax into the Initial Directory text box.

7 Choose the OK button.

8 Choose the Close button.

The command now appears on the Tools menu. To run the program, choose it from the menu.

You can change the default menu name of the newly added tool by editing the Menu Text text box. You can also add arguments to be passed to the program by typing them in the Arguments text box (see "Using Argument Macros" on page 452 later in this chapter), or set the initial directory for your program by typing it in the Initial Directory text box.

Note   If the program you are adding to the Tools menu has a .PIF file, the startup directory specified by the .PIF file overrides the directory specified in the Initial Directory text box.

Editing a Tools Menu Command

▶ **To edit a Tools menu command**

1 From the Tools menu, choose Customize.

The Customize dialog box appears.

2 Select the Tools tab.

3 In the Menu Contents box, select the menu command you want to edit.

4 Perform one or more of the following actions:

- To move the selected command up one position in the menu, choose the Move Up button.

- To move the selected command down one position in the menu, choose the Move Down button.

- To change the menu text, command line (tool path and file name), command-line arguments, or the initial directory, type the new information in the appropriate text box.

- To specify a letter in the menu title as an access key, precede that letter in the Menu Text text box with an ampersand (&).

   The first letter in the title is the keyboard access key by default.

- To be prompted for command-line arguments each time you run the tool, select the Prompt For Arguments check box.

5 Choose the Close button.

▶ **To remove a command from the Tools menu**

1 From the Tools menu, choose Customize.

The Customize dialog box appears.

2 Select the Tools tab.

3 In the Menu Contents box, select the command you want to delete.

4 Choose the Remove button.

5 Choose the Close button.

Tools Options

The Tools tab in the Customize dialog box includes three check boxes with which you can customize options that apply to the tool that is selected in the Menu Contents box. These options are described in the following table.

Option	Result
Prompt For Arguments	When this check box is selected, the Tool Arguments dialog box appears when you run the tool. The arguments you type in the Arguments box are passed to the program.
Redirect To Output Window	When this check box is selected, the standard output from the tool appears in the Output window. A separate virtual Output window is maintained for each tool whose output has been redirected to the Output window. The names of these tools appear in a tab at the bottom of the Output window when you run them. You can switch between virtual Output windows by selecting the tabs at the bottom of the Output window. See "Using Error Syntax for Tools" on page 454 later in this chapter to learn about additional capabilities gained by redirecting tool output to the Output window.
Close Window On Exiting	When this check box is selected, the command window automatically closes when the tool has finished executing. This option applies to character-mode applications only.

Using Argument Macros

You can specify arguments for any command that you add to the Tools menu.

▸ **To specify arguments for a Tools menu command**

1 From the Tools menu, choose Customize.

The Customize dialog box appears.

2 Select the Tools tab.

3 In the Menu Contents box, select the command for which you want to specify arguments.

4 In the Arguments text box, type the arguments that you want.

–or–

Select the drop-down arrow to the right of the Arguments text box to display a list of arguments. When you select an argument from this list, the argument is substituted as text in the Arguments text box.

5 Choose the Close button.

To help you integrate your tools with the environment, Developer Studio provides the argument macros shown in the following table.

Table 22.1   Argument Macros

Macro Name	Expands to a String Containing
$(CurCol)	The current cursor column position within the active window.
$(CurDir)	The current working directory (defined as *drive+path*).
$(CurLine)	The current cursor line position within the active window.
$(CurText)	The current text (the word under the current cursor position, or a single-line selection, if there is one).
$(FileDir)	The directory of the current source (defined as *drive+path*); blank if a nonsource window is active.
$(FileExt)	The filename extension of the current source.
$(FileName)	The filename of the current source (defined as *filename*); blank if a nonsource window is active.
$(FilePath)	The complete filename of the current source (defined as *drive+path+filename*); blank if a nonsource window is active.
$(TargetArgs)	The command-line arguments that are passed to the application you are developing. To set these command-line arguments, type the argument in the Program Arguments text box on the Debug tab accessed by the Settings command on the Build menu.
$(TargetDir)	The directory of the current target (defined as *drive+path*).
$(TargetExt)	The filename extension of the current target.
$(TargetName)	The filename of the current target (defined as *filename*).
$(TargetPath)	The complete filename of the current target (defined as *drive+path+filename*).
$(WkspDir)	The directory of the current workspace (defined as *drive+path*) that contains the .MDP file; blank if no workspace is currently open.
$(WkspName)	The current workspace name (defined as *filename*) without the .MDP extension; blank if no workspace is currently open.

Macro recognition is not case sensitive. All path macros end in a backslash (\).

To use a macro as an argument, type the macro name in the Arguments text box. Or, for macros that expand to a directory, you can type the macro name in the Initial Directory box. As an example, the following procedure demonstrates how to add the **$(FilePath)** argument macro to the Windows Notepad accessory (installed in a previous procedure).

▶ **To add an argument macro to an installed tool and then run it**

1 From the Tools menu, choose Customize.

The Customize dialog box appears.

2 Select the Tools tab.

3 In the Menu Contents box, select the command that you want to edit.

In this case, select the Notepad accessory that you installed earlier.

4 In the arguments text box, type $(FilePath).

−or−

Select the drop-down arrow to the right of the Arguments text box to display a list of Arguments. When you select an argument from this list, the argument is substituted as text in the Arguments text box.

For example, use the drop-down arrow to the right of the Arguments text box and select the $(FilePath) macro.

5 Choose the Close button.

6 Open any source file, or make an open source file active by clicking it.

7 For example, from the Tools menu, choose Notepad.

The Windows Notepad accessory opens, with the active source file as its text file.

Using Error Syntax for Tools

When you select the Redirect To Output Window check box for a tool on the Tools tab of the Customize dialog box, you gain access to the Output window's error parser.

The error parser detects filenames, errors, and line-number information of output strings, and makes each line in the file a hot link to the specified file and line number. For example, you can double-click an error line in the Output window that contains the error number, filename, and line number where the error occurred, and jump directly to the referenced line in the correct source file.

The Find In Files dialog box also uses the error parser. For instance, you can double-click any output line from a Find In Files operation to jump to the referenced file and line.

Error Syntax Example

For example, you could install Microsoft Macro Assembler on the Tools menu to compile assembly code, and then jump to source-code syntax errors directly from its error list in the Output window. The error syntax is as follows (+ denotes one or more; * denotes zero or more):

Error Type	Description
error_string	file_spec error_spec (STRING I file_spec STRING)
file_spec	FILENAME '('line_spec')' ':'
line_spec	NUMBER I NUMBER '-' NUMBER
error_spec	ERRORKEYWORD ERRORNUMBER ':'

Error Type	Description
where:	
STRING	Null-terminated string
FILENAME	Valid file specification and text file
NUMBER	{1–9}{0–9}
ERRORNUMBER	{A–Z}+{0–9}{0–9}{0–9}{0–9}
ERRORKEYWORD	"error" | "warning" | "fatal error"

Note Although the error number is part of this syntax, it is optional and not really useful to any tool except internal build tools. The error number is used internally to link to Books Online.

Showing the Status Bar

The status bar at the bottom of the application window displays information about Developer Studio. Its leftmost text field, for instance, describes the currently selected menu command or the action of the button currently under the mouse pointer.

The status bar also displays progress information about the current operation. For a text editor window, it shows the line and column position of the insertion point, the state of the RECORD KEYSTROKES AND COLUMN MODE, whether the editor is in insertion mode or overstrike mode, and whether the file is set for read-only access. Optionally, the clock can also be displayed on the status bar. Figure 22.8 depicts the status bar as it might appear while using the text editor.

Figure 22.8   A Status Bar

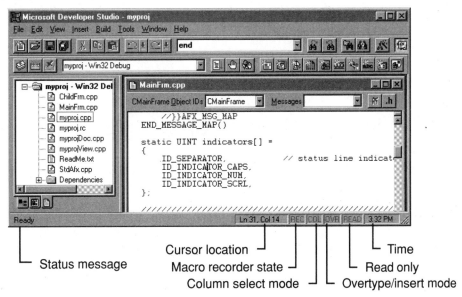

The default setting is to show the status bar.

▶ To show or hide the status bar

1 From the Tools menu, choose Options.

The Options dialog box appears.

2 Select the Workspace tab.

3 Select the Display Status Bar check box to show the status bar, or clear the Display Status Bar check box to hide the status bar.

4 Choose the OK button.

▶ To display the clock on the status bar

1 From the Tools menu, choose Options.

The Options dialog box appears.

2 Select the Workspace tab.

3 Select the Display Clock On Status Bar check box.

4 Choose the OK button.

Setting Directories

The Setup program determines the correct directory paths for several file types and updates the Directories dialog box with these paths. The file types are:

- Executable files (build utilities)
- Include files
- Library files
- Source files

On the Directories tab, accessed by choosing Options from the Tools menu, you can edit the directory paths where Developer Studio looks for the file types.

Directory information is stored in registry entries. The Show Directories For list box on the Directories tab displays the directories shown in the following table.

File Type	Path Contents
Executable files	Specifies where the build utilities, such as NMAKE, CL, LINK, and BSCMAKE, reside.
Include files	Specifies where the compiler should look for include files (files surrounded by angle brackets (< and >); for example, `#include <stdio.h>`).

File Type	Path Contents
Library files	Specifies where the linker should look for libraries to resolve external references.
Source files	Specifies where the debugger should look for default source files including Microsoft Foundation Class Library and Run-Time Library.

▶ **To add a directory to the Directories list**

1 From the Tools menu, choose Options.

The Options dialog box appears.

2 Select the Directories tab.

3 If necessary, select the platform from the Platform list box.

4 In the Show Directories For list box, select the category of directory.

5 In the Directories box, double-click the blank line at the bottom of the list (indicated by an empty rectangle), and type the directory name.

6 Choose the OK button.

Developer Studio searches directories in the order in which they appear in the list. After adding a directory, you can move it up or down in the list by dragging it up or down the list and dropping it in the new position.

▶ **To remove a directory from the Directories list**

1 From the Tools menu, choose Options.

The Options dialog box appears.

2 Select the Directories tab.

3 If necessary, select the platform from the Platform list box.

4 In the Show Directories For list box, select the category of directory.

5 In the Directories list box, double-click the directory that you want to remove.

6 Delete the text defining the directory.

7 Choose the OK button.

▶ **To prioritize a directory in the Directories list**

1 From the Tools menu, choose Options.

The Options dialog box appears.

2 Select the Directories tab.

3 If necessary, select the platform from the Platform list box.

4 In the Show Directories For list box, select the category of directory.

5 In the Directories box, select the directory that you want to prioritize.

6 Drag the selected directory to its new position.

7 Choose the OK button.

Using Full-Screen Mode

You can use the text editor and other resource editors in full-screen mode. When you initially select full-screen mode, a toolbar button with a small graphic of a computer screen is displayed. You can toggle full-screen mode on and off by clicking this button. If you close this toolbar button and want to restore it, follow the procedure below to redisplay the full-screen toolbar button.

▶ **To begin full-screen mode**

- From the View menu, choose Full Screen.

When you switch to full-screen mode for the first time, your current standard mode horizontal and vertical scroll bar settings are used for full-screen mode. However, you can have different window settings for full-screen mode and standard mode.

▶ **To change the full-screen mode window settings**

1 Begin full-screen mode.

2 From the Tools menu, choose Options.

When full-screen mode is active, you can display the Tools menu by pressing ALT+T.

3 Select the Editor tab.

4 Check the Window Settings that you want.

5 Choose the OK button.

▶ **To end full-screen mode**

- Press the ESC key.

  −or−

- Click the full-screen toolbar button.

  −or−

1 Press ALT+V to display the View menu.

2 Choose Full Screen to end full-screen mode.

▶ **To redisplay the full-screen toolbar button while in full-screen mode**

1 Begin full-screen mode.

2 From the Tools menu, choose Customize.

When full-screen mode is active, you can display the Tools menu by pressing ALT+T.

3 Select the Toolbars tab.

4 In the Categories list box, select View.

5 Drag the Toggle Full Screen button onto the full-screen application window.

6 Choose the Close button.

 Tip You should open a file for editing before beginning full-screen mode. If a file is not opened first, full-screen mode is displayed as a large, empty screen. If this happens, use the ESC key to restore the original screen mode.

Customizing with Other Options

You can choose other options to customize editing, debugging, working with projects, using components, and creating custom AppWizards.

See Also   Setting Editor Behavior, Debugger Windows, Working with Projects, Using Component Gallery, Creating Custom AppWizards

CHAPTER 23

Editor Emulations

The Microsoft Developer Studio text editor can emulate two popular text editors: BRIEF® and Epsilon™. With the emulation feature, the text editor can emulate the key bindings, text selection, caret display, window display, and most editing commands of the selected editor. Some editor behaviors are not available, notably those dealing with macros, shells, and other elements that have no substitute in the text editor.

The Epsilon emulation is based on the Lugaru Epsilon editor version 6.0, and the BRIEF emulation is based on the Borland BRIEF editor version 3.1.

Note Each editor emulation includes the use of native syntax for regular expressions during find and replace operations. For more information on regular expression syntax, see "Using Regular Expressions with Developer Studio," "Using Regular Expressions with BRIEF Emulation," and "Using Regular Expressions with Epsilon Emulation" in Chapter 3, "Using the Text Editor."

See Also Setting Editor Behavior, Using Epsilon Emulation, Using BRIEF Emulation, Viewing and Changing the Shortcut Keys

Setting Editor Behavior

You can use the Compatibility tab in the Options dialog box to set overall editor behavior. The Compatibility tab contains a drop-down list box of the available editors for emulation. The supported editor emulations are:

- Developer Studio
- Visual C++ version 2.0
- BRIEF
- Epsilon

The Options checklist contains the compatibility options and their default settings for the chosen editor. You can change these options to create a custom emulation model. When you create a custom emulation model, the word "Custom" appears in the list box with the name of the standard editor. For example, if you change some of the options for the BRIEF emulation, "Custom (BRIEF)" appears in the list.

For each emulation, the following default options are set:

- Developer Studio
  - Enable copy without selection
- Visual C++ version 2.0
  - Enable copy without selection
  - Enable virtual space
- BRIEF
  - Disable backspace at start of line
  - Enable copy without selection
  - Enable line-mode pastes
  - Enable virtual space
  - Include caret positioning in undo buffer
  - Use BRIEF's regular expression syntax
- Epsilon
  - Include caret positioning in undo buffer

▶ **To set an editor emulation**

1 From the Tools menu, choose Options.

The Options dialog box appears.

2 Select the Compatibility tab.

3 In the Recommended Options For list box, select the editor that you wish to emulate.

The default editor is Developer Studio.

The Options box lists the status of pre-defined editor options.

4 Choose the OK button.

▶ **To create a custom editor emulation**

1 From the Tools menu, choose Options.

The Options dialog box appears.

2 Select the Compatibility tab.

3 In the Recommended Options For list box, select a standard editor on which to base your custom editor.

The Options box lists the editor's current options.

4 Select the options you want to create the desired editor behavior.

The name of the custom editor reflects the name of the standard editor. For example, if you customize the BRIEF emulation, the custom editor is named "Custom (BRIEF)".

5 Choose the OK button.

See Also   Using Epsilon Emulation, Using BRIEF Emulation

Using Epsilon Emulation

The Epsilon emulation provides Epsilon default key bindings, caret display, text selection, and the following general editing commands.

 Tip   You can change individual shortcut keys with the Keyboard tab in the Customize dialog box.

Category	Epsilon Command	Developer Studio Command
Help	help	(Common help function.)
Bookmarks	set-bookmark	BookmarkDrop(Epsilon)
	jump-to-last-bookmark	BookmarkJumpToLast
	set-named-bookmark	Bookmark
	jump-to-named-bookmark	Bookmark
Buffer	select-buffer	WindowList
Files	find-file	FileOpen
	save-file	FileSave
	write-file	FileSaveAs
	insert-file	InsertFile
	save-all-buffers	FileSaveAs
Indenting	to-indentation	GoToIndentation
	indent-previous	(Use the TAB key.)
	indent-region	IndentSelectionToPrev
	center-line	WindowScrollToCenter
	tabify-region	TabifySelection
	untabify-region	UntabifySelection
	indent-under	IndentToPrev
Inserting and Deleting	quoted-insert	QuotedInsert
	open-line	LineOpenAbove
	backward-delete-character	(Use the BACKSPACE key.)
	delete-character	Delete
	delete-horizontal-space	DeleteHorizontalSpace

Category	Epsilon Command	Developer Studio Command
	delete-blank-lines	DeleteBlankLines
	overwrite-mode	(Use the INSERT key.)
Keyboard Macros	start-kbd-macro	ToolsRecordKeystrokes
	end-kbd-macro	ToolsStopRecording
	last-kbd-macro	ToolsPlaybackRecording
Killing and Yanking	set-mark	StreamSelectExclusive
	highlight-region	SelectHighlight
	exchange-point-and-mark	SelectSwapAnchor
	kill-line	LineCut
	kill-region	CutSelection
	copy-region	Copy
	yank	Paste
	append-next-kill	AppendNextCut
	rectangle-mode	SelectColumn
Miscellaneous	abort	Cancel
	exit	FileExit
	argument	SetRepeatCount
	goto-line	GoTo
Moving Around	beginning-of-line	Home
	end-of-line	LineEnd
	down-line	LineDown
	up-line	LineUp
	forward-character	CharRight
	backward-character	CharLeft
	center-window	WindowScrollToCenter
	next-page	PageDown
	previous-page	PageUp
	scroll-up	WindowScrollUp
	scroll-down	WindowScrollDown
	goto-beginning	DocumentStart
	goto-end	DocumentEnd
	beginning-of-window	WindowStart
	end-of-window	WindowEnd
Paragraphs	forward-paragraph	ParaDown
	backward-paragraph	ParaUp
	mark-paragraph	SelectPara

Category	Epsilon Command	Developer Studio Command
Parenthetic Expressions	find-delimiter	GoToMatchBrace
	forward-level	LevelDown
	backward-level	LevelUp
	kill-level	LevelCutToEnd
	backward-kill-level	LevelCutToStart
Running Programs	next-error	GoToNextErrorTag (A default key binding is not provided for this command.)
	previous-error	GoToPrevErrorTag (A default key binding is not provided for this command.)
Sentences	forward-sentence	SentenceRight
	backward-sentence	SentenceLeft
	kill-sentence	SentenceCut
Searching and Replacing	incremental-search	IncrementalSearch
	reverse-incremental-search	IncrementalSearchBack
	regex-search	IncrementalSearchRE
	reverse-regex-search	IncrementalSearchREBack
	grep	FileFindInFiles
	next-match	FindNext
	previous-match	FindPrev
	replace-string	FindReplace
	query-replace	FindReplace
	regex-replace	FindReplaceRE
	word-mode, regular-expression-mode, case-sensitive-mode, and incremental-mode	(These commands are available only in incremental search mode, not in dialog mode. The commands are not key bindable.)
Tags	goto-tag	Browse
	pluck-tag	BrowseGoToDefinition
Transposing	transpose-characters	CharTranspose
	transpose-words	WordTranspose
	transpose-lines	LineTranspose
Undo	undo	Undo
	redo	Redo

Category	Epsilon Command	Developer Studio Command
	undo-changes	UndoChanges
	redo-changes	RedoChanges
Windows	one-window	WindowSinglePane
	split-window	WindowSplitHorizontal
	split-window-vertically	WindowSplitVertical
	kill-window	WindowKillPane
	zoom-window	WindowMaximize
	move-to-window	WindowNextPane
	next-window	WindowCycle
	previous-window	WindowPrevious
Word Commands	forward-word	WordRight
	backward-word	WordLeft
	backward-kill-word	WordDeleteToStart
	kill-word	WordDeleteToEnd
	transpose-words	WordTranspose
	capitalize-word	WordCapitalize
	lowercase-word	WordLowerCase
	uppercase-word	WordUpperCase

Note The entire set of emulation commands is available to each editor. For more information, see "Viewing and Changing the Shortcut Keys" later in this chapter.

Using BRIEF Emulation

The BRIEF emulation provides BRIEF default key bindings, caret display, text selection, and the following general editing commands.

 Tip You can change individual shortcut keys with the Keyboard tab in the Customize dialog box.

Category	BRIEF Command	Developer Studio Command
Help	Help	(Common help function.)
Undo and Redo	Undo	Undo
	Redo	Redo
Saving and Exiting	Exit	FileExit
	Write	FileSave
	Write All and Exit	FileSaveAllExit

Category	BRIEF Command	Developer Studio Command
Editing Text	Backspace	(Use the BACKSPACE key.)
	Delete	(Use the DELETE key.)
	Delete Line	LineDelete
	Delete Next Word	WordDeleteToEnd
	Delete Previous Word	WordDeleteToStart
	Delete to Beginning of Line	LineDeleteToStart
	Delete to End of Line	LineDeleteToEnd
	Enter	(Use the ENTER key.)
	Insert Mode Toggle	EditToggleOvertype
	Open Line	LineOpenBelow
	Quote	QuotedInsert
Buffers	Delete Current Buffer	FileClose
	Edit File	FileOpen
	Next Buffer	WindowNext
	Previous Buffer	WindowPrevious
	Read File into Buffer	InsertFile
Search and Translate	Case Sensitivity Toggle	ToggleCaseSensitivity
	Incremental Search	IncrementalSearch
	Regular Expressions Toggle	EditToggleRE
	Search Again	FindRepeat
	Search Backward	FindPrev
	Search Forward	Find
	Translate Again	FindReplace
	Translate Forward	FindReplace
Windows	Center Line in Window	WindowScrollToCenter
	Change Window	WindowSwitchPaneUp, WindowSwitchPaneDown, WindowSwitchPaneLeft, WindowSwitchPaneRight. (A default key binding is not provided for this command.)
	Create Window	WindowSplitHorizontal, WindowSplitVertical
	Delete Window	WindowDeleteRowUp, WindowDeleteRowDown, WindowDeleteColLeft, WindowDeleteColRight
	Line to Bottom of Window	WindowScrollToBottom
	Line to Top of Window	WindowScrollToTop

Category	BRIEF Command	Developer Studio Command
	Quick Window Switch	WindowSwitchPaneUp, WindowSwitchPaneDown, WindowSwitchPaneLeft, WindowSwitchPaneRight
	Resize Window	WindowSplit
	Zoom Window Toggle	WindowMaximize
	Column Mark	SelectColumn
Blocks and Marks	Drop Bookmark	BookmarkDrop(BRIEF)
	Indent Block	IndentSelection
	Jump Bookmark	Bookmark
	Line Mark	SelectLine
	Lower Case Block	LowerCaseSelection
	Mark/Unmark	SelectChar
	Noninclusive Mark	SelectCharInclusive
	Outdent Block	UnindentSelection
	Print Block	FilePrint
	Swap Cursor and Mark	SelectSwapAnchor
	Upper Case Block	UpperCaseSelection
	Copy to Scrap	Copy
Scrap	Cut to Scrap	Cut
	Paste from Scrap	Paste
	Back Tab	(Use the SHIFT+TAB keys.)
Cursor Movement	Beginning of Line	Home(BRIEF)
	Cursor Movement	(Use the arrow keys.)
	End of Buffer	DocumentEnd
	End of Line	End(BRIEF)
	End of Window	WindowEnd
	Go to Line	GoTo
	Left Side of Window	WindowLeftEdge
	Next Character	(Use the right arrow key.)
	Next Word	WordRight
	Page Down	PageDown
	Page Up	PageUp
	Previous Character	(Use the left arrow key.)
	Previous Word	WordLeft
	Right Side of Window	WindowRightEdge
	Scroll Buffer Down in Window	WindowScrollUp

Category	BRIEF Command	Developer Studio Command
	Scroll Buffer Up in Window	WindowScrollDown
	Tab	(Use the TAB key.)
	Top of Buffer	Home(BRIEF)
	Top of Window	WindowStart
	Pause Recording Toggle	ToolsPauseRecording
Macros, Playback, and Remember	Playback	ToolsPlaybackRecording
	Remember	ToolsRecordKeystrokes
	Go To Routine	Browse
Special Commands	Next Error	GoToNextErrorTag
	Repeat	EditSetRepeatCount

Note   The entire set of emulation commands is available to each editor. For more information, see "Viewing and Changing the Shortcut Keys" below.

Viewing and Changing the Shortcut Keys

You can customize the keyboard for the selected editor and the editing commands. Customization is stored only for the current editor. If you change emulation, you will lose all of your custom key assignments.

Specific commands and their associated shortcut keys are available for the following categories:

- File
- Edit
- View
- Insert
- Build
- Debug
- Tools
- Image
- Layout
- Window
- Help

Each category contains a variety of commands that you can assign to individual keystrokes. For more information, see "Customizing the Keyboard" in Chapter 22, "Customizing Developer Studio."

Note You can display all of the current keyboard shortcuts, including custom key settings and editor emulations. For more information, see "Displaying the Keyboard Shortcuts" in Chapter 22, "Customizing Developer Studio."

▶ To find the current shortcut key

1 From the Tools menu, choose Customize.

The Customize dialog box appears.

2 Select the Keyboard tab.

3 In the Editor drop-down list box, select Text.

4 In the Categories list box, select the category.

5 In the Commands list box, select the command.

Epsilon-specific commands contain the text "Epsilon." BRIEF-specific commands contain the text "BRIEF."

The Current Keys box displays the current shortcut keys. Multiple assignments are listed on separate lines.

6 Choose the Close button.

▶ To change the current shortcut key

1 From the Tools menu, choose Customize.

The Customize dialog box appears.

2 Select the Keyboard tab.

3 In the Categories list box, select the category.

4 In the Commands list box, select the command.

The Current Keys box displays the current shortcut keys. Multiple assignments are listed on separate lines.

5 Change the focus to the Press New Shortcut Key box, then press the keystroke combination you want to assign. If you make a mistake, use the BACKSPACE key to correct it, not the DEL key.

If the key combination is currently assigned to another command, the command is displayed in the Currently Assigned To box.

6 Choose the Assign button.

The new keystroke combination is added to the Current Keys box.

7 Choose the Close button.

▶ **To remove a shortcut key assignment**

1 From the Tools menu, choose Customize.

The Customize dialog box appears.

2 Select the Keyboard tab.

3 In the Categories list box, select the category.

4 In the Commands list box, select the command.

The Current Keys box displays the current shortcut keys. Multiple assignments are listed on separate lines.

5 Select the current key assignment that you want to remove.

6 Choose the Remove button.

The keystroke combination is removed from the Current Keys box.

7 Choose the Close button.

▶ **To reset all keystroke assignments**

1 From the Tools menu, choose Customize.

The Customize dialog box appears.

2 Select the Keyboard tab.

3 In the Editor drop-down list box, select the editor.

4 Choose the Reset All button and confirm your choice.

All keystroke combinations for the selected editor revert to their default settings.

5 Choose the Close button.

Creating Custom AppWizards

With AppWizard you can create Custom AppWizards to create applications for your special needs. The topics listed below describe what custom AppWizards are, when they are useful, and how you create them:

- Understanding Custom AppWizards
- Overview of Creating a Custom AppWizard
- Debugging Custom AppWizards
- Creating a ClassWizard Information File Template
- Providing Context-Sensitive Help
- AppWizard Programming Reference

Understanding Custom AppWizards

AppWizard is the tool to use when you need to create a new application. It quickly generates the starter files you need for the most common application types. But what about those special applications that are unique to your work? What do you do if you or your clients need applications with features that the standard AppWizard can't provide? The answer is that you can create custom AppWizards.

Custom AppWizards are useful for creating generic application project types that can repetitively generate common functionality — application types that can be used over and over again. Custom AppWizards are not useful for creating one-off project types.

Like AppWizard, a custom AppWizard presents the user with choices, tracks the user's decisions, and uses those decisions to generate the code, resources, and project files that the Visual C++ build tools require to build a skeletal, working application.

For example, if you work for a company where people commonly need special views of database information, you can create a custom AppWizard to generate generic dialog-based front ends to a database. You can even ensure that the dialog box is always embellished with a company logo.

Possibilities for custom AppWizards are:

- Create a custom AppWizard that is based on the code and resources in an existing project.

- Modify code in existing AppWizard templates.

- Add one or more steps to the existing AppWizard's steps.

- Create a custom set of steps.

For more information on creating a custom AppWizard, see Overview of Creating a Custom AppWizard.

See Also   Using a Custom AppWizard, Overview of Creating a Custom AppWizard, Understanding the Files that AppWizard Creates, Adding Functionality to Your Custom AppWizard, Debugging Custom AppWizards, Creating a ClassWizard Information File Template, Providing Context-Sensitive Help, AppWizard Programming Reference

Using a Custom AppWizard

Once you have created a custom AppWizard, it is launched by its user from the New Project Workspace dialog box or the Insert Project dialog box. When the custom AppWizard user finishes using the custom AppWizard, the New Project Information dialog box displays the name and features of the chosen project. There is nothing new here. The custom AppWizard functions just like AppWizard with regard to the New Project Workspace dialog box, the Insert Project dialog box, and the New Project Information dialog boxes.

In fact, a custom AppWizard is just an extension of existing AppWizard technology. A running custom AppWizard uses many of the services of AppWizard to do its work. Users of a custom AppWizard that is based on an existing application or a custom AppWizard with no steps will not see any differences —only the New Project Workspace dialog box or the Insert Project dialog box and the New Project Information dialog box as usual. A user of a more complex custom AppWizard will proceed through a sequence of steps much like they would if using AppWizard.

Both AppWizard and a custom AppWizard are implemented as two dialog boxes: an outer one and an inner one. See Figure 24.1. The outer dialog box contains the title bar and the Help, Cancel, Back, Next, and Finish buttons. It serves as a master control panel and also frames the inner dialog box.

The inner dialog box can actually be one or more dialog boxes, each representing one step in the project generation process. See Figure 24.1.

Figure 24.1   AppWizard's Structure

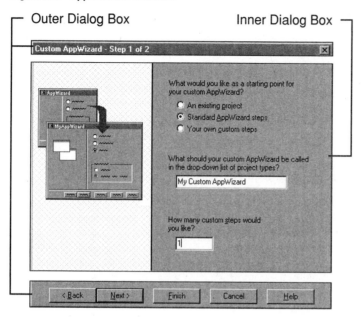

See Also   Understanding Custom AppWizards, Overview of Creating a Custom AppWizard, Debugging Custom AppWizards, Creating a ClassWizard Information File Template, Providing Context-Sensitive Help

Overview of Creating a Custom AppWizard

Creating a custom AppWizard requires the following steps:

1. Use the New Project Workspace dialog box or the Insert Project dialog box to create a Custom AppWizard project.

   For more information, see "How to Create a Custom AppWizard Project" on page 478.

2. Edit two text templates, CONFIRM.INF and NEWPROJ.INF. Your finished custom AppWizard uses these to create the custom AppWizard user's application.

   For more information, see "Understanding CONFIRM.INF and NEWPROJ.INF" on page 488.

3. Use the Microsoft Developer Studio to create any other templates that your custom AppWizard requires.

   For more information, see "Understanding Custom Resource Templates" on page 484.

4. Use the Visual C++ programming tools to add functionality to your custom AppWizard.

5. Use the AppWizard API to add calls into MFCAPWZ.DLL to create communication between the finished custom AppWizard and AppWizard (MFCAPWZ.DLL).

For more information, see "AppWizard Programming Reference" on page 495.

6. Use the Visual C++ programming tools to build your custom AppWizard. A custom AppWizard is given an extension of .AWX, rather than .DLL, and is automatically added to the MSDEV\TEMPLATE directory. Once in this directory, your custom AppWizard becomes a project type and can be selected from the Type drop-down list in the Insert Project dialog box and the New Project Workspace dialog box.

You'll have to learn some of the inner workings of AppWizard to perform steps 3 and 5. But first, you need an overview of the players and the tools. The players are described in Table 24.1; the tools in Table 24.2.

Table 24.1 The Players

Players	Description
You	You are the custom AppWizard writer. Your job is to design and implement a custom AppWizard. In this documentation, "you" refers to a custom AppWizard writer.
Custom AppWizard user	You, or any other developer, who uses a custom AppWizard with the purpose of creating an application for one or more end users.
User	The end user who uses the application created from the project generated by the custom AppWizard. In this documentation, "user" refers to the end user.

As you can see, creating a custom AppWizard is a layered interaction between you (the custom AppWizard writer), the custom AppWizard user, and the end user who ultimately uses the application.

Table 24.2 describes the tools that you use —in addition to the familiar Microsoft Developer Studio, compiler, linker, etc. — to create a custom AppWizard for a custom AppWizard user.

Table 24.2 The Tools

Tools	Description
AppWizard	A tool that you use to create an application that is based on the Microsoft Foundation Class Library (MFC).
	AppWizard is composed of MFCAPWZ.DLL and all of the dynamic-link libraries (DLLs) containing localized resources — those with names described by APPWZ*.DLL.
Custom AppWizard	A tool that you use to create custom applications. Your custom AppWizard is used to create an application. The custom AppWizard appears, to its user, as one or more steps that are embedded within a framework that looks like AppWizard.

Table 24.2   The Tools *(continued)*

Tools	Description
MFCAPWZ.DLL	The DLL that implements AppWizard. It also interacts with a finished custom AppWizard to lend it an AppWizard-like look and feel.
	MFCAPWZ.DLL has two different interfaces: an on-screen appearance that looks much like AppWizard (with a title bar and Help, Cancel, Back, Next, and Finish buttons), and an AppWizard API that you use to establish lines of communication and control between MFCAPWZ.DLL and your custom AppWizard.
CUSTMWZ.AWX	The dynamic-link library, which is itself a custom AppWizard, that implements the Custom AppWizard project type. You select this project type from the New Project Workspace dialog box or the Insert Project dialog box in order to choose the features of your custom AppWizard. The CUSTMWZ.AWX source code is included as a sample program in the MSDEV\SAMPLES\APPWIZ\CUSTOMWZ directory.
AppWizard API	The application programming interface that provides you with calls into MFCAPWZ.DLL. You use the API to specify custom AppWizard and MFCAPWZ.DLL behavior in reaction to a custom AppWizard user's on-screen manipulation of the Help, Cancel, Back, Next, and Finish buttons. For more information on the AppWizard API, see "AppWizard Programming Reference" on page 495.
Custom resource templates	There are two types of custom resource templates: binary and text. A finished custom AppWizard uses these templates to create a final application. For more information, see "Standard Custom Resource Templates" on page 534.
Binary templates	Binary templates are not parsed by MFCAPWZ.DLL during the application generation process. They are copied verbatim to a new application. Binary templates can include, but are not restricted to, files such as .BMP and .RTF. For more information, see "Understanding Binary Templates" on page 493.
Text templates	Text templates are parsed by MFCAPWZ.DLL during the application generation process. They can, for example, contain source code, macros, and directives that a custom AppWizard can use to generate a new project's source-code files. Typically, the new project's final application is built from these source files. Text templates can include, but are not restricted to, files such as .H, .CPP, .RC, .CLW, .ODL, .RTF, and .RC2. For more information, see "Understanding Text Templates" on page 456.

See Also   How to Create a Custom AppWizard Project, Understanding the Files that AppWizard Creates, Adding Functionality to Your Custom AppWizard,

Understanding Custom Resource Templates, Understanding Text Templates, How Macros Get Their Values, How to Specify Macros in Directives or Text, Understanding Binary Templates, Debugging Custom AppWizards, Creating a ClassWizard Information File Template, Providing Context-Sensitive Help, AppWizard Programming Reference

How to Create a Custom AppWizard Project

You use the New Project Workspace dialog box or the Insert Project dialog box, AppWizard, Microsoft Developer Studio, and the Visual C++ build tools to create a custom AppWizard. You can create custom AppWizards based on one of the three categories: an existing project, the standard AppWizard steps, or your own custom steps. These are described below.

An Existing Project

By choosing this category, you can leverage code from a workspace that contains a single existing project. The project's files must have originally been created by AppWizard, and the names of the existing project's files and classes (C*YourApp*View, C*YourApp*Doc, etc.) should be those generated by AppWizard.

The existing project's name must not contain nonalphanumeric characters, such as DBCS characters. The existing files, originally created from AppWizard, can include minor changes or additions, but major changes can introduce flaws into your new custom AppWizard.

If the base class's default, AppWizard-provided class, and/or filenames have been modified, Custom AppWizard cannot convert them to macro form as it adds them to the text templates that it generates. This is also true if you use ClassWizard to add classes to a default AppWizard project. Custom AppWizard will still parse the modified names and add them to the templates, and your custom AppWizard will generate an application, but your custom AppWizard will not be able to modify the names based on the project name provided by your custom AppWizard's user. You can work around this by adding the appropriate macros to the names in the text templates. For more information on text templates, see "Understanding Text Templates" on page 486. For more information on macros, see "How Macros Get Their Values" on page 491.

You may find it useful to examine the CUSTMWZ.AWX source code, found in the MSDEV\SAMPLES\APPWIZ\CUSTOMWZ directory, that is included as a sample program.

Standard AppWizard Steps

By choosing this category, you can use one of the existing sequences of AppWizard steps that create an executable file or a DLL. You can use the AppWizard steps by themselves, or add your own custom steps to them.

Note You can't connect your own custom AppWizard code with existing AppWizard dialog templates. For example, if your custom AppWizard uses the standard OLE options page,

AppWizard will use its own OLE options step dialog template and dialog class; you cannot modify the AppWizard dialog template or class.

Your Own Custom Steps

By choosing this category, you can create a custom AppWizard that presents a completely new set of custom steps to the user.

Creating a Custom AppWizard

The procedures below list the steps necessary to create a custom AppWizard based on any of the three categories —an existing project, the standard AppWizard steps, or your own custom steps — previously described in "How to Create a Custom AppWizard Project." The first procedure describes how to use the Custom AppWizard project type to create a custom AppWizard.

Note A custom AppWizard cannot run on any platform other than Win32 because Microsoft Developer Studio runs only on Win32. A custom AppWizard can, however, generate applications that target other platforms.

▶ **To create a custom AppWizard**

1 Start Visual C++.

2 From the File menu, choose New.

The New dialog box appears.

3 In the New box, select Project Workspace.

4 Choose OK.

The New Project Workspace dialog box appears.

5 In the Name text box, type a name.

The name that you specify in the Name text box is used to derive the default names for the **CCustomAppWiz** class and its files.

6 From the Type list, select Custom AppWizard.

7 Accept the Platform for this project.

Because your custom AppWizard will run only on a Win32 operating system, Win32 is selected by default.

8 In the Location text box, specify the path of the project workspace. A directory will be created if you specify one that does not exist.

−or−

Use the Browse button to select a drive and a directory.

9 Choose Create.

Custom AppWizard - Step 1 of 2, appears. Figure 24.2 shows this step and describes the three custom AppWizard types you can create.

Figure 24.2 Custom AppWizard Step 1

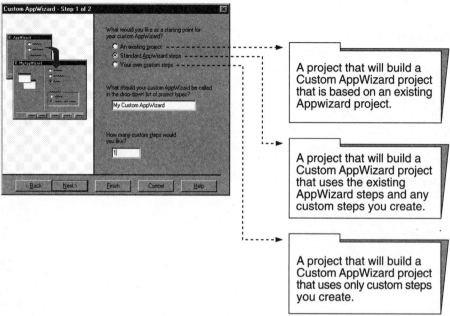

A project that will build a Custom AppWizard project that is based on an existing Appwizard project.

A project that will build a Custom AppWizard project that uses the existing AppWizard steps and any custom steps you create.

A project that will build a Custom AppWizard project that uses only custom steps you create.

▶ **To specify a custom AppWizard type, name, and number of steps**

From Step 1 of 2, you can select from three categories of custom AppWizards. You can also specify the name that your custom AppWizard will display in the Type list and the number of custom steps that it will need.

1 Select a custom AppWizard category:

- An existing project

  Select this option if you want your custom AppWizard to generate code, resource, and project files that are based on those found in a workspace that contains a single existing project. For more information on this option, see "How to Create a Custom AppWizard Project" on page 478.

  If you select this option, the AppWizard title bar displays "Step 1 of 2," and the Next button is activated. The text box for specifying the number of custom steps is grayed out because the features of the resulting custom AppWizard project are defined by the features of the existing project; you will not need to provide any custom AppWizard steps.

- Standard AppWizard steps

  Select this option if you want your custom AppWizard to use an existing sequence of AppWizard steps. For more information on this option, see "How to Create a Custom AppWizard Project" on page 478.

If you select this option, the title bar displays "Step 1 of 2," and the Next button is activated.

- Your own custom steps

  Choose this option if you want to create an entirely new custom AppWizard.

  If you select this option, the title bar changes to "Step 1 of 1" and the Next button is deactivated.

2 Type a name under the heading "What should your custom AppWizard be called in the drop-down list of project types?"

This name will appear in the New Project Workspace dialog box's Type list once your custom AppWizard's DLL is moved to the MSDEV\TEMPLATE directory.

3 If you have chosen to base your custom AppWizard on either the standard AppWizard steps or a completely custom set of steps, specify the required number of custom steps under the heading "How many custom steps would you like?"

Note If your project is based on the standard AppWizard steps, type a number only if you plan to create steps other than the standard ones.

For each step that you specify, MFCAPWZ.DLL will provide a resource template that you can edit in the dialog editor, and a **CAppWizStepDlg** class derived from the MFC library's **CDialog** class.

▶ To specify the location of an existing project

If you've chosen to base your custom AppWizard on an existing project, you must specify the location of the existing project:

1 From Step 1 of 2, choose the Next button.

AppWizard displays the second step.

2 In Step 2 of 2, type the location of the workspace that contains the existing project on which your custom AppWizard will be based. Alternatively, you can use the Browse button to navigate to the base project.

▶ To choose the type of standard AppWizard steps

If you've chosen, from Step 1 of 2, to use standard AppWizard steps:

1 In Step 2 of 2, under the title "Which AppWizard steps would you like to include in your custom AppWizard?" select either:

- AppWizard Executable

  This sequence of AppWizard steps creates projects that will build into executable files.

  –or–

- AppWizard Dynamic Link Library

  This AppWizard step creates projects that will build into DLLs.

▶ **To specify the language(s) that your custom AppWizard will support**

If you've chosen to use standard AppWizard steps:

- In the list box under the title "Which languages will your custom AppWizard support?" select the languages that your custom AppWizard will support.

  The list box contains a language name for each language DLL in your \MSDEV\BIN\IDE directory. The names of these DLLs take the form APPWZ*.DLL. For example, if \MSDEV\BIN\IDE contains APPWZENU.DLL and APPWZDEU.DLL, the list box will list both English and German.

  For each language you select from the list box, AppWizard will copy language-specific versions of the standard AppWizard resource templates from the associated language DLL to your custom AppWizard project's template directory. Then, after your finished custom AppWizard is copied to a custom AppWizard user's \MSDEV\TEMPLATE directory, the custom AppWizard user can use your custom AppWizard to generate projects that support any of the languages you select.

  Note The language DLLs (such as APPWZENU.DLL and APPWZDEU.DLL) contain only standard AppWizard resource templates. You must supply any nonstandard resource templates required by applications that your custom AppWizard creates. For a complete list of the standard AppWizard resource templates, see "Standard Custom Resource Templates" on page 534.

▶ **To complete the process of specifying your custom AppWizard project**

1 Once you are satisfied with the features you have selected for your custom AppWizard, choose the Finish button.

  The New Project Information dialog box appears and lists the features that you have selected.

2 Choose the OK button.

  AppWizard will generate code files, resource files, and project files based on the features listed in the New Project Information dialog box. It then automatically opens your new custom AppWizard project in a project window.

See Also Overview of Creating a Custom AppWizard, Understanding the Files that AppWizard Creates, Adding Functionality to Your Custom AppWizard, Understanding Custom Resource Templates, Debugging Custom AppWizards, Creating a ClassWizard Information File Template, Providing Context-Sensitive Help, AppWizard Programming Reference

Understanding the Files that AppWizard Creates

AppWizard uses the name that you specify in the Name box of the New Project Workspace dialog box to derive names for some of its files and classes.

You'll undoubtedly want to examine the source-code files you create. If you chose to have AppWizard add comments to the files it creates for your project, AppWizard will also create a text file, README.TXT, in your new application directory. This file explains the contents and uses of the other new files created by AppWizard.

See Also Understanding Custom AppWizards, Using a Custom AppWizard, Overview of Creating a Custom AppWizard, Adding Functionality to Your Custom AppWizard

Adding Functionality to Your Custom AppWizard

You add functionality to your custom AppWizard in the same manner that you add functionality to any other AppWizard project. That is, you use the resource editors to edit your project's resources and use the WizardBar, ClassWizard, and the text editor to edit your code. Figure 24.3 graphically illustrates these steps.

The only difference between adding functionality to an AppWizard project and to a custom AppWizard project is dealing with custom resource templates. After examining your project's structure, you'll note that it contains a TEMPLATE directory. The files in this directory contain custom resource templates. MFCAPWZ.DLL and your finished custom AppWizard will use these to create the custom AppWizard user's application.

Figure 24.3   Adding Functionality to Your Custom AppWizard

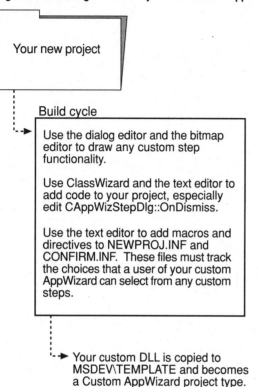

Your new project

Build cycle

Use the dialog editor and the bitmap editor to draw any custom step functionality.

Use ClassWizard and the text editor to add code to your project, especially edit CAppWizStepDlg::OnDismiss.

Use the text editor to add macros and directives to NEWPROJ.INF and CONFIRM.INF. These files must track the choices that a user of your custom AppWizard can select from any custom steps.

Your custom DLL is copied to MSDEV\TEMPLATE and becomes a Custom AppWizard project type.

See Also   Understanding the Files that AppWizard Creates, Understanding Custom Resource Templates, Understanding CONFIRM.INF and NEWPROJ.INF, Understanding Text Templates, How Macros Get Their Values, How to Specify Macros in Directives or Text, Understanding Binary Templates, Debugging Custom AppWizards, Creating a ClassWizard Information File Template, Providing Context-Sensitive Help, AppWizard Programming Reference

Understanding Custom Resource Templates

AppWizard obtains the building blocks for the code, resource, and project files it creates from special files called custom resource templates. There are two types of custom resource templates: text templates and binary templates. Text templates are used to create the source files for a project, and binary templates usually contain bitmaps for user-interface components, such as toolbars.

AppWizard always provides you with a copy of the CONFIRM.INF and NEWPROJ.INF templates and, if you use existing sequences of AppWizard steps, AppWizard copies its own custom resource templates into your custom AppWizard project for you to use and/or modify. You can also use Microsoft Developer Studio to create your own templates and add them to your custom AppWizard project.

Custom resource templates are resources of type "TEMPLATE". You can see these if you double-click your project's resource script file (.RC) in the Project Workspace window. All custom resource templates are in the folder called "TEMPLATE". Because these are custom resources, Microsoft Developer Studio makes no assumptions about their content, and treats it as binary data. If you double-click a custom resource type in the Project Workspace window, Microsoft Developer Studio opens the associated file in a binary editor. If you want to edit a custom resource, you must know the actual type it represents and choose that type from the Open As list in the Open dialog box.

▶ To open a custom resource type in the appropriate editor

1 From the File menu, choose Open.

   The Open dialog box appears.

2 Select the drive and directories where the template is stored.

3 In the List Files Of Type box, set the types of files to display.

   Files with the chosen extension are displayed in the File Name box.

   This box serves as a filter to display all files with a given extension. For example, selecting Image Files in the List Files Of Type box displays all files with *.BMP, *.DIB, *.ICO, and *.CUR extensions in the File Name box.

4 In the File Name box, select a filename.

5 From the Open As list, select the type of file that describes the template you wish to open.

   The Auto type will correctly recognize custom resource template file extensions such as .BMP, .H, and .CPP and open an associated file in the correct editor. Select the Text type from the Open As list to edit custom resource templates that represent resource scripts (.RC files).

▶ To create a custom resource template

1 Copy the file you wish to import as a custom resource template to your project's TEMPLATE directory.

2 From the Insert menu, choose the Resource command.

   The Insert Resource dialog box appears.

3 From the Resource Type pane, select the type of the custom resource template.

4 Choose the Import button.

   The Import Resource dialog box appears.

5 Using the Drives and Directories lists, select your project's TEMPLATE directory.

6 In the List Files Of Type box, set the types of files to display. Files with the chosen extension are displayed in the File Name box.

This box serves as a filter to display all files with a given extension. For example, selecting Bitmaps in the List Files Of Type box displays all files with *.BMP and *.DIB extensions in the File Name box.

7 In the File Name box, select a filename.

8 From the Open As list, select Custom.

9 Choose the Import button.

The Custom Resource Type dialog box appears.

10 From the Resource Type list, choose "TEMPLATE".

11 Choose OK.

The file is imported into your project as a custom resource type and opened in the binary data editor.

The custom resource type is added to your project under your projects "TEMPLATE" folder, which is available by selecting the ResourceView pane in the Project Workspace window. The custom resource template type is given an ID of IDR_TEMPLATE*, where * is a number that is unique within the "TEMPLATE" folder. You can use the Properties command on the pop-up menu to change the ID. To activate the ID's pop-up menu, place the mouse cursor on the new custom resource template's ID in the "TEMPLATE" window and press the right mouse button.

See Also Overview of Creating a Custom AppWizard, Understanding the Files that AppWizard Creates, Adding Functionality to Your Custom AppWizard, Understanding Text Templates, How Macros Get Their Values, How to Specify Macros in Directives or Text, Understanding Binary Templates, Creating a ClassWizard Information File Template, AppWizard Programming Reference

Understanding Text Templates

A text template is a type of custom resource template. AppWizard uses the content of text templates to create the source files of a new project. Text templates typically contain lines of source code, such as C++ code or resource-script directives. Text templates also contain macros and directives that AppWizard uses to determine the final content of template-generated source files.

AppWizard puts templates into the TEMPLATE directory of a generated project. Once templates are part of a project, you can either use them without modification or edit them to add custom functionality to your custom AppWizard. You can also add your own text templates to a project.

The following code-template fragment shows C++ code with embedded macros and directives. The values of macros such as **$$ROOT$$** and **$$APP_CLASS$$** control the names of files and classes. The existence of macros such as **VERBOSE** controls whether flow-of-control directives, such as **$$IF**, evaluate to true.

For more information on macros, see "How Macros Get Their Values" on page 491. For more information on directives, see "Standard AppWizard Directives" on page 516.

```
// $$root$$.h : main header file for the $$ROOT$$ application

#include "resource.h"    // main symbols

/////////////////////////////////////////////////////////////////////////////
// $$APP_CLASS$$:
// See $$root$$.cpp for the implementation of this class

class $$APP_CLASS$$ : public $$APP_BASE_CLASS$$
{
public:
    $$APP_CLASS$$();

// Overrides
    // ClassWizard generated virtual function
    // overrides
    //{{AFX_VIRTUAL($$APP_CLASS$$)
    public:
    virtual BOOL InitInstance();
    //}}AFX_VIRTUAL

// Implementation

    //{{AFX_MSG($$APP_CLASS$$)
$$IF(VERBOSE)
    // NOTE - the ClassWizard will add and
    //     remove member functions here.
    //     DO NOT EDIT what you see in these
    //     blocks of generated code!
$$ENDIF
    //}}AFX_MSG
    DECLARE_MESSAGE_MAP()
};
```

See Also   Overview of Creating a Custom AppWizard, Understanding the Files that AppWizard Creates, Adding Functionality to Your Custom AppWizard, Understanding Custom Resource Templates, Understanding CONFIRM.INF and NEWPROJ.INF, How Macros Get Their Values, How to Specify Macros in Directives or Text, Creating a ClassWizard Information File Template, Providing Context-Sensitive Help, AppWizard Programming Reference.

Understanding CONFIRM.INF and NEWPROJ.INF

CONFIRM.INF and NEWPROJ.INF are special text templates that MFCAPWZ.DLL (AppWizard) inserts into every custom AppWizard project. They are the blueprints that a custom AppWizard uses to construct the project files from which a final, end-user application can be built. The content of CONFIRM.INF becomes the content of the New Project Information dialog box. This presentation of information in the New Project Information dialog box allows a user to examine their chosen project features. NEWPROJ.INF contains the instructions that AppWizard uses to construct a user's project.

AppWizard will provide CONFIRM.INF and NEWPROJ.INF templates in varying states of readiness, depending on whether you choose to base your custom AppWizard project on:

- An existing project

  In this case, the content of NEWPROJ.INF is based on the content of the existing project. CONFIRM.INF is left empty; you will need to add text, macros, and directives to CONFIRM.INF that describe, in human-readable form, each feature a user can choose from each of your custom AppWizard's steps.

- Standard AppWizard steps

  In this case, the content of both templates is based on the existing AppWizard steps. If you add your own custom steps to the standard AppWizard steps, you'll need to add text, macros, and directives to CONFIRM.INF that reflect each feature a custom AppWizard user can choose in each custom step. You will also need to add statements, macros, and directives to NEWPROJ.INF that can build a project for any combination of features a custom AppWizard user can select from the custom steps.

- Your own custom steps

  In this case, both templates are empty. You must add text, macros, and directives to CONFIRM.INF that reflect each feature a user can choose in each custom step. You will also need to add statements, macros, and directives to NEWPROJ.INF so that it can build a project for any combination of features a user can select from the custom steps.

For more information, see CONFIRM.INF and NEWPROJ.INF.

See Also   Overview of Creating a Custom AppWizard, Understanding the Files that AppWizard Creates, Adding Functionality to Your Custom AppWizard, CONFIRM.INF, NEWPROJ.INF, Understanding Text Templates, How Macros Get Their Values, How to Specify Macros in Directives or Text, Creating a ClassWizard Information File Template, Providing Context-Sensitive Help, AppWizard Programming Reference

CONFIRM.INF

CONFIRM.INF contains a human-readable description of each project component (such as the project name and the names of its primary classes). It also contains a description of each feature that a custom AppWizard user can select from each step. The following code shows how macros and flow-of-control directives are used to generalize the content of a CONFIRM.INF:

```
$$// confirm.inf = the text sent to the New Project
$$// Information dialog box
Application type of $$ROOT$$:
    Dialog-Based Application targeting:
        Win32

Classes to be created:
    Application: $$APP_CLASS$$ in $$ROOT$$.h and $$ROOT$$.cpp
    Dialog: $$DLG_CLASS$$ in $$DLG_HFILE$$.h and $$DLG_IFILE$$.cpp

Features:
    + About box on system menu
$$IF(INDENTED_BRACES)
    + Curly braces indented from previous level
$$ELSE // !INDENTED_BRACES
    + Curly braces flush with previous level
$$ENDIF // NOT_INDENTED_BRACES
$$IF(COMPANY_LOGO)
    + A company logo
$$ENDIF //COMPANY_LOGO
$$IF(3-D)
    + 3D Controls
$$ENDIF //3-D
```

This example of CONFIRM.INF contains lines of text (such as `Classes to be created:`), macros (such as `$$APP_CLASS$$` and `$$ROOT$$`), and flow-of-control directives (such as `$$IF` and `$$ENDIF`). Once a user chooses the Finish button of a custom AppWizard, MFCAPWZ.DLL parses CONFIRM.INF as follows:

- Each line of text is gathered into a **CString** object, and each encountered macro is expanded.

- Any line beginning with **$$//** is a comment and is ignored.

- Any line of text between an **$$IF** and an **$$ENDIF** is converted to a **CString** if the associated macro, such as INDENTED_BRACES and COMPANY_LOGO, exists and thus evaluates to true.

- The resulting CStrings reflect the custom AppWizard user's choices and are written to the New Project Information dialog box. Thus, they can view the features of their proposed project.

For more information on how MFCAPWZ.DLL parses templates, see "Understanding Text Template Parsing" on page 491.

See Also Overview of Creating a Custom AppWizard, How to Create a Custom AppWizard Project, Understanding the Files that AppWizard Creates, Adding Functionality to Your Custom AppWizard, Understanding CONFIRM.INF and NEWPROJ.INF, NEWPROJ.INF, Understanding Text Templates, How Macros Get Their Values, How to Specify Macros in Directives or Text, Creating a ClassWizard Information File Template, Providing Context-Sensitive Help, AppWizard Programming Reference

NEWPROJ.INF

NEWPROJ.INF contains the instructions that MFCAPWZ.DLL uses to construct a custom AppWizard user's project. The instructions are statements, directives, and macros that work together to describe the structure of a project. The following code shows how statements and macros are used to generalize the instructions of a NEWPROJ.INF file:

```
+dlgroot.rc    .\$$ROOT$$.rc
+dlgroot.clw   .\$$ROOT$$.clw
dlgroot.h .\$$ROOT$$.h
+dlgroot.cpp   .\$$ROOT$$.cpp
dialog.h    .\$$ROOT$$dlg.h
+dialog.cpp    .\$$ROOT$$dlg.cpp
readme.txt .\readme.txt
resource.h .\resource.h
stdafx.h    .\stdafx.h
+stdafx.cpp    .\stdafx.cpp
/RES
=root.ico  .\res\$$ROOT$$.ico
root.rc2   .\res\$$ROOT$$.rc2
```

In general, there are two kinds of NEWPROJ.INF statements: those that create directories, and those that fill the directories with files. In the previous example, the /RES statement causes MFCAPWZ.DLL to create a project subdirectory named RES. The +dlgroot.rc   .\$$ROOT$$.rc statement causes MFCAPWZ.DLL to look for a custom resource template named DLGROOT.RC, give it a name determined by the value of the **$$ROOT$$** macro, and place the resulting file in the new project's root directory. The plus sign (+) is a flag that marks this template for inclusion in the project file (.MAK). For more information on the NEWPROJ.INF statements, see "NEWPROJ.INF Statements" on page 497.

For brevity, directives (such as **$$IF**, **$$ELSE**, and **$$ENDIF**) are not shown in the previous example, but they can be used as shown in the CONFIRM.INF example. For more information on directives, see "Standard AppWizard Directives" on page 516. For more information on macros, see "How Macros Get Their Values" on page 491.

See Also Overview of Creating a Custom AppWizard, How to Create a Custom AppWizard Project, Understanding the Files that AppWizard Creates, Adding Functionality to Your Custom AppWizard, Understanding CONFIRM.INF and NEWPROJ.INF, CONFIRM.INF, Understanding Text Templates, Understanding Text

Template Parsing, How Macros Get Their Values, How to Specify Macros in Directives or Text, Creating a ClassWizard Information File Template, Programming Reference

Understanding Text Template Parsing

The function **CCustomAppWiz::ProcessTemplate** parses a template line by line and passes everything that is not a macro or directive directly to an output stream. If a line contains a macro, which is not an argument to a directive, **ProcessTemplate** replaces the macro with its associated value, retrieved from the dictionary, and passes the altered line to the output stream. For example, given a project named MyProject and an output stream named ROOT.CPP, the following line in a text template:

```
#include "$$root$$.h"
```

becomes

```
#include "MyProject.h"
```

in a project file named MYPROJECT.CPP. For more information on macros, see "How Macros Get Their Values" on page 491.

If a line is a directive, **ProcessTemplate** obeys the rules set down by the directive. For more information on directives, see "Standard AppWizard Directives" on page 516.

ProcessTemplate passes the parsed string to MFCAPWZ.DLL. If the output stream is directed to CONFIRM.INF or NEWPROJ.INF, MFCAPWZ.DLL will use the files during the project generation process. For more information on these files, see "Understanding CONFIRM.INF and NEWPROJ.INF" on page 488.

If the output stream represents a source file, MFCAPWZ.DLL does no further processing of the file. Instead, MFCAPWZ.DLL inserts the file into a new project structure following rules set out in NEWPROJ.INF.

See Also   Overview of Creating a Custom AppWizard, Understanding the Files that AppWizard Creates, Adding Functionality to Your Custom AppWizard, Understanding Custom Resource Templates, Understanding CONFIRM.INF and NEWPROJ.INF, Understanding Text Templates, How Macros Get Their Values, How to Specify Macros in Directives or Text, Creating a ClassWizard Information File Template, AppWizard Programming Reference

How Macros Get Their Values

There are two kinds of macros: standard AppWizard macros and those you create. Macros are created by adding them to a **CMapStringToString** dictionary named *project*aw.m_Dictionary that is declared in *project*AW.H.

AppWizard gathers the values for some of its standard macros from the New Project Workspace dialog box. It then uses these values to name a user's project, files, and classes. AppWizard also uses macros that represent project features, such as **3D**, **TOOLBAR**, and **STATUSBAR**. For more information on the standard AppWizard

macros, see "Standard AppWizard Macros" on page 523 and
"**CCustomAppWiz::m_Dictionary**" on page 509.

See Also   Overview of Creating a Custom AppWizard, Adding Functionality to Your
Custom AppWizard, Understanding Custom Resource Templates, Understanding
CONFIRM.INF and NEWPROJ.INF, Understanding Text Templates, Understanding
Text Template Parsing, How to Specify Macros in Directives or Text, AppWizard
Programming Reference, **CCustomAppWiz::m_Dictionary**

How to Specify Macros in Directives or Text

A macro name that is used as an argument to a directive, such as **$$IF**, does not need
dollar signs ($$) to mark its beginning and end; any dollar signs found are
interpreted as part of the macro's name. For instance, the
CCustomAppWiz::ProcessTemplate function's parser treats both AMACRO and
$$AMACRO$$ as macro names in the following two directive statements:

```
$$IF(AMACRO);
$$IF($$AMACRO$$);
```

A macro name in text, however, requires dollar signs ($$) to mark its beginning and
end, as shown in the following fragment extracted from one of AppWizard's custom
resource templates:

```
/////////////////////////////////////////////////////
// $$APP_CLASS$$

BEGIN_MESSAGE_MAP($$APP_CLASS$$, $$APP_BASE_CLASS$$)
    //{{AFX_MSG_MAP($$APP_CLASS$$)
$$IF(VERBOSE)
        // NOTE - the ClassWizard will add and
        //      remove mapping macros here.
        //      DO NOT EDIT what you see in these
        //      blocks of generated code!
$$ENDIF
    //}}AFX_MSG
    ON_COMMAND(ID_HELP, CWinApp::OnHelp)
END_MESSAGE_MAP()
```

For more information on macros, see "How Macros Get Their Values" on page 491.

See Also   Adding Functionality to Your Custom AppWizard, Understanding Custom
Resource Templates, Understanding CONFIRM.INF and NEWPROJ.INF,
Understanding Text Templates, Understanding Text Template Parsing, How Macros
Get Their Values, Understanding Binary Templates, AppWizard Programming
Reference.

Understanding Binary Templates

A binary template is a type of custom resource template. Binary templates usually contain bitmaps. These bitmaps are the user-interface components, such as toolbar buttons and icons, that AppWizard and a custom AppWizard use when generating a project. Binary templates do not contain macros or directives and are not parsed. They are, instead, copied verbatim into the end user's project.

See Also   Adding Functionality to Your Custom AppWizard, Understanding Custom Resource Templates, AppWizard Programming Reference

Debugging Custom AppWizards

When MFCAPWZ.DLL generates your skeleton custom AppWizard project, it provides you with both Release and Pseudo Debug projects. The Pseudo Debug project is a Release project that disables optimizations and generates debugging information using the compiler's Program Database (/Zi) option and the linker's Generate Debug Information (/DEBUG) option. These option settings allow you to use the debugger while you are developing your custom AppWizard.

You must use the Pseudo Debug project to debug your custom AppWizard. Release projects (including Pseudo Debug projects) and Debug projects use two different and incompatible memory allocators. You do not have access to the Debug versions of the Visual C++ binarys. Using the Pseudo Debug project allows your custom AppWizard and the Release version of the Visual C++ binarys to use the same memory allocator.

A Pseudo Debug project defines the **_PSEUDO_DEBUG** preprocessor symbol, rather than the **_DEBUG** preprocessor symbol that signals a normal debug project, and uses its own local copies of the **ASSERT**, **TRACE**, and **VERIFY** debugging macros. You can find these macros in the generated files DEBUG.H and DEBUG.CPP.

The **ASSERT**, **ASSERT_VALID**, **TRACE**, and **VERIFY** macros that exist in the MFC code are not available to you because your custom AppWizard must use the Release version of MFC. This means that these macros are not available if you inadvertently write code that would trigger them.

▶ **To debug your custom AppWizard**

1 With your custom AppWizard's project open, choose the Settings command from the Build menu.

   The Project Settings dialog box appears.

2 Select the Debug tab.

3 In the Executable For Debug Session box, type the location of MSDEV.EXE. For example, `C:\MSDEV\BIN\MSDEV.EXE`.

4 Choose OK.

The next time you start the debugger, Microsoft Developer Studio will launch a new instance of Microsoft Developer Studio.

5 Use the original instance of Microsoft Developer Studio to set breakpoints in your custom AppWizard code and to examine its data using the Watch window and other debugging tools as needed.

6 Use the second instance of Microsoft Developer Studio to launch your custom AppWizard for debugging.

See Also Overview of Creating a Custom AppWizard, Adding Functionality to Your Custom AppWizard, Creating a ClassWizard Information File Template, AppWizard Programming Reference

Creating a ClassWizard Information File Template

The Custom AppWizard project adds a custom resource template for generating a ClassWizard Information (.CLW) file to the following types of new custom AppWizard projects:

- Those based on an existing project, if the existing project contained a .CLW file (which it should).

- Those based on an existing sequence of standard AppWizard steps.

If your custom AppWizard generates a .CLW file and you alter your custom AppWizard so that it generates projects that contain more classes than CUSTMWZ.AWX originally generated, then those additional classes will not automatically appear in the .CLW file your custom AppWizard generates. The custom AppWizard user will notice upon opening ClassWizard for the project your custom AppWizard generated that the additional classes are not available.

To avoid this problem, edit your custom AppWizard's NEWPROJ.INF file so that it no longer generates a default .CLW. Then, when the custom AppWizard user attempts to use ClassWizard, ClassWizard presents a dialog box that notes that no .CLW file exists and offers to build one. The .CLW file is built after the user chooses Yes.

See Also Working With Classes, Rebuilding the ClassWizard (.CLW) File, Understanding Custom Resource Templates.

Providing Context-Sensitive Help

The Custom AppWizard project type provides you with the tools you need to create a help file that describes your custom steps:

- A starter rich-text (.RTF) file, HLP*project*.RTF, containing a topic for each custom step that the Custom AppWizard project type generated for you. You can use any rich-text format word processor, such as Microsoft Word for Windows, to add information to each custom-step topic in your *project*.RTF file.

- A help project (.HPJ) file to control compiling your *project*.RTF file into a WinHelp help file.

- A batch file, MAKEHELP.BAT, that compiles your *project*.RTF file into a help (.HLP) file. Type MAKEHELP.BAT as a command from a console command line, and MAKEHELP.BAT will use *project*.HPJ to create a help file from your *project*.RTF file.

Note   You cannot integrate your custom AppWizard's help with the Microsoft Developer Studio help system. But if you build a custom AppWizard that uses an existing sequence of AppWizard steps, your custom AppWizard will automatically use the Microsoft Developer Studio help file that was created for the standard AppWizard steps. Your custom AppWizard will use your own WinHelp help file for the custom steps. The effect is seamless to the user.

Your custom AppWizard, which has an extension of .AWX, and its help file must use the same base filename, and both must reside in MSDEV\TEMPLATE. When the end user clicks a custom step's Help button, MFCAPWZ.DLL invokes WinHelp and passes it the current step's help ID and the name of your custom AppWizard's help file.

See Also   Adding Context-Sensitive Help, Help: Authoring Help Topics, Understanding Custom AppWizards, Using a Custom AppWizard, Overview of Creating a Custom AppWizard, Understanding the Files that AppWizard Creates, Adding Functionality to Your Custom AppWizard, Understanding Custom Resource Templates, AppWizard Programming Reference

AppWizard Programming Reference

MFCAPWZ.DLL contains the code that controls the default behavior of AppWizard. It also contains the code that controls the interactions between AppWizard and your custom AppWizard. This reference describes the programming interface to MFCAPWZ.DLL. You can use the interface to add funtionality to the default behavior of your custom AppWizard. For more information, see the descriptions of the items in the following table.

Statements	Description
NEWPROJ.INF Statements	The syntax for and behavior of the statements that MFCAPWZ.DLL uses to generate a project.

AppWizard C++ Classes	Description
CAppWizStepDlg	The class from which custom AppWizard steps are derived.
CCustomAppWiz	The class that provides communication services between MFCAPWZ.DLL and your custom AppWizard.
OutputStream	The class that wraps two member functions used to write custom resource templates to an output stream.

AppWizard C Functions	Description
C Functions Exported by MFCAPWZ.DLL	MFCAPWZ.DLL and your custom AppWizard use these C functions to communicate.

AppWizard Macros	Description
The Dictionary	Storage location for both your macros and the standard AppWizard macros.
Standard AppWizard Macros	Macros that track the choices an AppWizard user makes from the New Project Workspace dialog box, from the Insert Project dialog box, and from AppWizard's steps. MFCAPWZ.DLL uses many of the same macros to track the choices that a custom AppWizard user makes from the New Project Workspace or Insert Project dialog box.

Custom Resource Templates	Description
Custom Resource Templates	The building blocks that MFCAPWZ.DLL and a finished custom AppWizard use to create a final application. Developer Studio allows you to create and add your own custom resource templates to your custom AppWizard project.
Standard Custom Resource Templates	The templates that MFCAPWZ.DLL and the DLLs containing localized resources — those with names that take the form APPWZ*.DLL — use to build the files and user-interface components that compose a project.

AppWizard Directives	Description
Standard AppWizard Directives	Directives, such as **$$IF, $$ELIF, $$ELSE, $$ENDIF, $$INCLUDE, $$BEGINLOOP, $$ENDLOOP**, and **$$SET_DEFAULT_LANG** used by MFCAPWZ.DLL to generalize its custom resource templates so that the templates can be used for multiple project types. You will probably need to use these directives when you write a custom AppWizard.

See Also   Overview of Creating a Custom AppWizard, Adding Functionality to Your Custom AppWizard, **CAppWizStepDlg**, **CCustomAppWiz**, **OutputStream**, C Functions Exported by MFCAPWZ.DLL, The Dictionary, Standard AppWizard Macros, Understanding Custom Resource Templates, Standard Custom Resource Templates, Understanding CONFIRM.INF and NEWPROJ.INF

NEWPROJ.INF Statements

NEWPROJ.INF contains statements that MFCAPWZ.DLL reads to determine a project structure. A statement in NEWPROJ.INF can use either of the following two forms of syntax:

/directory   This statement directs MFCAPWZ.DLL to create a subdirectory of the project directory. Note that the slash is a forward slash, not a backslash. This is how, for example, AppWizard creates a separate RES subdirectory under the project directory, and how the Custom AppWizard project type creates its TEMPLATE subdirectory.

−or−

[*flags*]*template-name* tab-character *destination-filename*   This statement directs MFCAPWZ.DLL to use a custom resource template named *template-name* to generate a file named by *destination-filename*. If *destination-filename* includes a path, all directories on the path must exist. Remember that you can use the */directory* statement to create a directory. You generate the tab-character by pressing the TAB key.

flags   A flag is any of three optional characters defined in Table 24.3. They can appear in any order and any combination, but must appear immediately before *template-name*. No characters (not even whitespace) can separate the flags from each other or from *template-name*.

Table 24.3   Template Name Flags

Flag	Description
=	Copies the template, verbatim, to *destination-filename*. This flag tells MFCAPWZ.DLL to use **CopyTemplate** rather than **ProcessTemplate**. **ProcessTemplate** is the default.
	For example, the following line causes MFCAPWZ.DLL to call **CopyTemplate** to copy the project's icon directly to the project:
	`=ROOT.ICO    $$root$$.ico`
	Note that using the lowercase version of the **$$root$$** macro causes the generated filename to be lowercase. For more information on the **root** macro, see "New Project Workspace and Insert Project Dialog Box Options"on page 524.
+	Specifies that the generated file is a project file (such as .CPP and .ODL files) that MFCAPWZ.DLL must add to the project makefile. This is how an MFCAPWZ.DLL adds files to the generated project.
*	Forces **LoadTemplate** to use an AppWizard resource rather than a custom AppWizard resource. Use this flag when you want your custom AppWizard to bypass its own template in preference to AppWizard's copy. For example, when the Custom AppWizard project type (CUSTMWZ.AWX) generates a custom AppWizard that is based on an existing sequence of AppWizard steps, it needs AppWizard's NEWPROJ.INF, not its own. Using this flag is unnecessary in most situations because MFCAPWZ.DLL looks for a template in AppWizard's resources if it can't first find the template in the custom AppWizard's resources. This flag simply bypasses the initial check in the custom AppWizard's resources. For example, the following line causes **ProcessTemplate** to add the MFCAPWZ.DLL version of DLGROOT.CPP to the generated project's makefile:
	`*+DLGROOT.CPP    $$root$$.cpp`
	Note that using the lowercase version of the **$$root$$** macro causes the generated filename to be lowercase. For more information on the **root** macro, see "New Project Workspace and Insert Project Dialog Box Options" on page 524.

template-name   The resource ID of a custom resource template. When an end user presses the OK button from the New Project Information dialog box, MFCAPWZ.DLL begins parsing NEWPROJ.INF. For each *template-name* found in NEWPROJ.INF, MFCAPPWZ.DLL calls **LoadTemplate** with *template-name* to load the custom resource template for processing. If *template-name* is not found, the custom AppWizard displays an error in a message box, stops code generation, and returns to the dialog box from which template parsing began.

destination-filename   Names the file and directory in which MFCAPWZ.DLL generates the file associated with *template-name*. The named directory must already exist. If it doesn't, MFCAPWZ.DLL presents a message box to inform you that it can't generate the file and stops code generation.

See Also   Overview of Creating a Custom AppWizard, Understanding the Files That AppWizard Creates, Adding Functionality to Your Custom AppWizard, Understanding CONFIRM.INF and NEWPROJ.INF, CONFIRM.INF, NEWPROJ.INF, Understanding Text Templates, How Macros Get Their Values, How to Specify Macros in Directives or Text

CAppWizStepDlg

The **CAppWizStepDlg** class is the class from which custom AppWizard steps are derived. Recall that the AppWizard and custom AppWizard user interface is comprised of nested dialog boxes: an outer one and one or more inner ones. The outer dialog box contains the title bar and the Help, Cancel, Back, Next, and Finish buttons. It serves as a master control panel and also frames the inner dialog box.

The outer dialog box frames an area that can contain one or more dialog boxes called steps. These steps, derived from **CAppWizStepDlg**, contain controls that allow AppWizard or a custom AppWizard to gather information from a user.

Each custom AppWizard step is a combination of a dialog template and its associated **CAppWizStepDlg**-derived class. AppWizard automatically generates a dialog template and a **CAppWizStepDlg**-derived class for each custom step in your custom AppWizard.

Use the dialog editor to add controls to the dialog template, and then use ClassWizard to add class members representing the controls to the **CAppWizStepDlg**-derived class.

For more information on ClassWizard, see Chapter 14, "Working With Classes." **CAppWizStepDlg** is derived from the Microsoft Foundation Class Library (MFC) **CDialog** class. For more information on **CDialog**, see the *Microsoft Foundation Class Library Reference*.

Typically, in a custom AppWizard, instances of each **CAppWizStepDlg**-derived class are constructed when AppWizard (MFCAPWZ.DLL) calls **CCustomAppWiz::InitCustomAppWiz** and destroyed when AppWizard calls **CCustomAppWiz::ExitCustomAppWiz**.

#include <customaw.h>

See Also   Overview of Creating a Custom AppWizard, Adding Functionality to Your Custom AppWizard, **CAppWizStepDlg** Class Members, **CCustomAppWiz**, **OutputStream**, C Functions Exported by MFCAPWZ.DLL, The Dictionary, Standard AppWizard Macros, Understanding Custom Resource Templates, Standard Custom Resource Templates, Understanding CONFIRM.INF and NEWPROJ.INF.

CAppWizStepDlg Class Members
Construction

CAppWizStepDlg	Constructs a **CAppWizStepDlg** object.

Overridables

OnDismiss	Called whenever a custom AppWizard user chooses the Next, Back, or Finish button. Override in order to create, update, or remove macros from the dictionary through calls to **aw.m_Dictionary**.

See Also   Overview of Creating a Custom AppWizard, Adding Functionality to Your Custom AppWizard, **CAppWizStepDlg**, **OnDismiss**, **CCustomAppWiz**, **OutputStream**, C Functions Exported by MFCAPWZ.DLL, The Dictionary, Standard AppWizard Macros, Understanding Custom Resource Templates, Standard Custom Resource Templates, Understanding CONFIRM.INF and NEWPROJ.INF

CAppWizStepDlg::CAppWizStepDlg
CAppWizStepDlg(UINT *nIDTemplate* **);**

Parameters
nIDTemplate   Contains the ID number of a dialog box template resource.

Remarks
Accepts a template ID number, usually with an **IDD_** prefix (for example, IDD_CUSTOM1) and constructs a resource-based dialog box: a step, in the case of a custom AppWizard.

See Also   Overview of Creating a Custom AppWizard, Adding Functionality to Your Custom AppWizard, **CAppWizStepDlg::OnDismiss**, **CCustomAppWiz**, **OutputStream**, C Functions Exported by MFCAPWZ.DLL, The Dictionary, Standard AppWizard Macros, Understanding Custom Resource Templates, Standard Custom Resource Templates, Understanding CONFIRM.INF and NEWPROJ.INF

CAppWizStepDlg::OnDismiss
BOOL OnDismiss( );

Return Value
Nonzero if the dialog box can be dismissed; otherwise 0.

Remarks
A step's **OnDismiss** member function is called by MFCAPWZ.DLL whenever a custom AppWizard user performs any action that calls **CCustomAppWiz::Next** or **CCustomAppWiz::Back**. A step's **OnDismiss** member function is also called if the user chooses the Finish button.

Typically, you will call **UpdateData(TRUE)** from **OnDismiss** to transfer a step's control values to the appropriate **CAppWizStepDlg** member variables. You should then use the **CCustomAppWiz::m_Dictionary** member to transfer the values to the custom AppWizard's dictionary. The values in the dictionary are the values that the **CCustomAppWiz::ProcessTemplate** member function uses to map the macros it finds while parsing a custom resource template to their actual values.

If the data is invalid, your custom AppWizard can display a dialog box and return **FALSE**, in which case MFCAPWZ.DLL will not continue to the next step.

See Also   CCustomAppWiz::Back, CCustomAppWiz::Next, CCustomAppWiz::m_Dictionary, CAppWizStepDlg::CAppWizStepDlg, CCustomAppWiz::ProcessTemplate, CCustomAppWiz, OutputStream, C Functions Exported by MFCAPWZ.DLL

CCustomAppWiz

The **CCustomAppWiz** class provides communication services between MFCAPWZ.DLL and your custom AppWizard. MFCAPWZ.DLL calls these member functions. The base-class implementations of the **CCustomAppWiz** member functions reside in MFCAPWZ.DLL, but your custom AppWizard can override them.

#include <customaw.h>

See Also   CCustomAppWiz::Back, CCustomAppWiz::Next, CCustomAppWiz::m_Dictionary, CAppWizStepDlg::CAppWizStepDlg, CCustomAppWiz::CopyTemplate, CCustomAppWiz::ExitCustomAppWiz, CCustomAppWiz::InitCustomAppWiz, CCustomAppWiz::GetPlatforms, CCustomAppWiz::LoadTemplate, CCustomAppWiz::PostProcessTemplate, CCustomAppWiz::ProcessTemplate

CCustomAppWiz Class Members

Data Members

m_Dictionary	Provides a dictionary of macros. Some of the macros are supplied by MFCAPWZ.DLL and some by you. **ProcessTemplate** uses the dictionary to map macros that are embedded in custom resource templates to their actual values.

Overridables

Back	Moves to the previous step. Called whenever a custom AppWizard user chooses the Back button.
CopyTemplate	Called by MFCAPWZ.DLL to copy verbatim a binary template into the custom AppWizard user's project.
ExitCustomAppWiz	Called by MFCAPWZ.DLL just before it unloads the custom AppWizard. **ExitCustomAppWiz** is a convenient place to perform any cleanup required by the custom AppWizard.

Overridables

GetPlatforms	Called by MFCAPWZ.DLL immediately after it loads and initializes the custom AppWizard. Override to obtain the list of platforms currently installed for Visual C++ and choose those that your custom AppWizard will support.
InitCustomAppWiz	Called by MFCAPWZ.DLL immediately after it loads the custom AppWizard. **InitCustomAppWiz** is a convenient place to perform initialization required by the custom AppWizard.
LoadTemplate	Called by MFCAPWZ.DLL to load custom resource templates, such as NEWPROJ.INF and CONFIRM.INF, for further processing.
Next	Moves to the next step. Called whenever a custom AppWizard user chooses the Next button.
PostProcessTemplate	Called by MFCAPWZ.DLL after it finishes parsing a template. **PostProcessTemplate** is a convenient place for you to deallocate memory that you allocated for a custom resource template. Typically you will not need to override this function.
ProcessTemplate	Called by MFCAPWZ.DLL to process a custom resource template returned by **LoadTemplate**. **ProcessTemplate** expands embedded macros, obeys embedded directives, and directs the output to an output stream.

See Also   **CCustomAppWiz::Back**, **CCustomAppWiz::Next**, **CCustomAppWiz::m_Dictionary**, **CAppWizStepDlg::CAppWizStepDlg**, **CCustomAppWiz::CopyTemplate**, **CCustomAppWiz::ExitCustomAppWiz**, **CCustomAppWiz::GetPlatforms**, **CCustomAppWiz::InitCustomAppWiz**, **CCustomAppWiz::LoadTemplate**, **CCustomAppWiz::PostProcessTemplate**, **CCustomAppWiz::ProcessTemplate**

CCustomAppWiz::Back

virtual CAppWizStepDlg* Back(CAppWizStepDlg* *pDlg* **);**

Return Value
A pointer to the previous step. If *pDlg* points to the first step, **Back** returns NULL to indicate that MFCAPWZ.DLL should next display the New Project Workspace dialog box or the Insert Project dialog box. For more information on steps, see the class **CAppWizStepDlg** on page 499.

Parameters
pDlg   Pointer to the current step.

Remarks
Back moves to the previous step. AppWizard (MFCAPWZ.DLL) calls this function whenever a user chooses the Back button. The Back button is located on the main,

outer dialog box that MFCAPWZ.DLL displays. For more information on steps and a description of the two-dialog-box structure of AppWizard and custom AppWizards, see **CAppWizStepDlg** on page 499.

Before **Back** is called, MFCAPWZ.DLL calls the **CAppWizStepDlg::OnDismiss** member function of the currently displayed step. You override **CAppWizStepDlg::OnDismiss** to transfer data from the step's controls to the appropriate variables and to update the appropriate dictionary values. If your custom AppWizard returns **FALSE** from the call to the overridden **CAppWizStepDlg::OnDismiss**, then the current step remains active, and **Back** is not called.

See Also CCustomAppWiz::Next, CAppWizStepDlg::OnDismiss, CAppWizStepDlg::CAppWizStepDlg

CCustomAppWiz::CopyTemplate

virtual void CopyTemplate(LPCTSTR *lpszInput*, **DWORD** *dwSize*, **OutputStream*** *pOutput* **);**

Parameters

lpszInput A pointer, returned by **CCustomAppWiz::LoadTemplate**, to a custom resource template.

dwSize The size of the custom resource template. Provided by the **LoadTemplate** function's *rdwSize* argument.

pOutput A pointer to the stream that represents the destination of the output from **CCustomAppWiz::CopyTemplate**.

Remarks

CopyTemplate copies a binary template (a type of custom resource template) verbatim into the end user's project. For more information on binary templates, see "Understanding Binary Templates" on page 493.

See Also CCustomAppWiz::LoadTemplate, CCustomAppWiz::ProcessTemplate, CCustomAppWiz::PostProcessTemplate, Understanding Custom Resource Templates, Understanding Binary Templates

CCustomAppWiz::ExitCustomAppWiz

virtual void ExitCustomAppWiz( );

Remarks

AppWizard (MFCAPWZ.DLL) calls **ExitCustomAppWiz** just before it unloads your custom AppWizard from memory. Use **ExitCustomAppWiz** to perform any cleanup necessary, such as deallocating instances of each of your custom AppWizard's **CAppWizStepDlg**-derived steps. The base-class version of **ExitCustomAppWiz** does nothing.

See Also CCustomAppWiz::InitCustomAppwiz

CCustomAppWiz::GetPlatforms

virtual void GetPlatforms(CStringList& *rPlatforms* **);**

Parameters

rPlatforms   A reference to a **CStringList** of each platform currently installed on
Microsoft Visual C++. Platform names that *rPlatforms* can contain are shown in
the following table.

Platform Name	Comes With
Win32 (x86)	Visual C++
Win32 (MIPS)	Visual C++ RISC edition
Win32 (ALPHA)	Visual C++ RISC edition
Win32 (PowerPC)	Visual C++ RISC edition
Macintosh	Visual C++ Cross Development edition for Macintosh
Power Macintosh	Visual C++ Cross Development edition for Macintosh

Remarks

The **GetPlatforms** member function allows you to specify which operating-system
and hardware platforms your custom AppWizard will support. MFCAPWZ.DLL calls
this function with a list containing an entry for each platform currently installed on
Microsoft Visual C++. You override **GetPlatforms** to parse and modify this list.
Typically, you will remove those platform names from the list that your custom
AppWizard does not support.

AppWizard calls **GetPlatforms** after loading and initializing a custom AppWizard. It
uses the platform names in *rPlatforms*, which are always in English, to determine
which platform names will appear in your custom AppWizard's Platforms checklist.
For each English name in *rPlatforms*, AppWizard places a locale-specific platform
name into your custom AppWizard's Platforms checklist.

For each platform selected by the custom AppWizard user, MFCAPWZ.DLL sets a
corresponding target macro in the dictionary and removes those for the nonselected
platforms.

The following example shows how to traverse a platforms list and remove all strings
that don't start with "Win32", thus keeping the Intel® Win32, MIPS® Win32, and
ALPHA™ Win32 as target platforms and removing the Macintosh® target platforms.

```
// This custom AppWizard only targets Win32 platforms,
void CSampleAppWiz::GetPlatforms(CStringList& rPlatforms)
{
    POSITION pos = rPlatforms->GetHeadPosition();
    while (pos != NULL)
```

```
    {
        POSITION posCurr = pos;
        CString strPlatform=rPlatforms->GetNext(pos);
        if (strPlatform.Left(5) != _T("Win32"))
            rPlatforms->RemoveAt(posCurr);
    }
}
```

If you do not override **GetPlatforms**, MFCAPWZ.DLL will display the names of all of the currently loaded platforms in the Platforms checklist.

Unlike the Win32 or Power Macintosh™ platforms, the 680x0 Macintosh does not support DLLs. Even if *rPlatforms* contains "Macintosh", this platform name will not show up in the Platforms checklist when a custom AppWizard creates a DLL.

A custom AppWizard creates an executable file by default. If your custom AppWizard creates a DLL, set the standard AppWizard macro "**PROJTYPE_DLL**" in the **InitCustomAppWiz** function as follows:

```
YourProjectNameaw.m_Dictionary["PROJTYPE_DLL"] = "1";
```

This code informs MFCAPWZ.DLL to not display the 680x0 Macintosh platform name in the Platforms checklist, and to create a project makefile that builds a DLL rather than an executable file. AppWizard (MFCAPWZ.DLL) automatically generates this code if you create a custom AppWizard based on the standard AppWizard steps for creating a DLL. Note that MFCAPWZ.DLL only checks that "PROJTYPE_DLL" exists and has a value —the actual macro value is not important unless your custom AppWizard requires that it have meaning.

See Also   target macro, The Dictionary

CCustomAppWiz::InitCustomAppWiz
virtual void InitCustomAppWiz( );

Remarks
AppWizard (MFCAPWZ.DLL) calls the **InitCustomAppWiz** member function just after loading a custom AppWizard. This occurs immediately after a custom AppWizard user has selected your custom AppWizard in the Type list in either the New Project Workspace or the Insert Project dialog boxes.

This function provides a place for you to perform any initialization required by the custom AppWizard, such as setting internal structures to default values and allocating an instance of each **CAppWizStepDlg** class. These instances will later be returned to AppWizard when it calls your custom AppWizard's **Next** and **Back** functions.

You can also override default AppWizard settings in **InitCustomAppWiz** by modifying the contents of the dictionary. For example, if your company or customer requires that context-sensitive help be a default feature, you can add "HELP" to the dictionary, from within **InitCustomAppWiz**, and cause AppWizard's Context-

Sensitive Help check box to be selected by default. This example, of course, assumes that your custom AppWizard uses the relevant standard AppWizard step and associated templates.

The base-class version of **InitCustomAppWiz** does nothing.

See Also   CCustomAppWiz::ExitCustomAppwiz, CCustomAppWiz::Back, CCustomAppWiz::Next, The Dictionary, CAppWizStepDlg::CAppWizStepDlg

CCustomAppWiz::LoadTemplate

virtual LPCTSTR LoadTemplate(LPCTSTR *lpszTemplateName***, DWORD&** *rdwSize***, HINSTANCE** *hInstance* **= NULL);**

Return Value
A pointer to the loaded custom resource template for use by **CCustomAppWiz::CopyTemplate** or **CCustomAppWiz::ProcessTemplate**.

Parameters

lpszTemplateName   A pointer to a string that contains the name (such as "NEWPROJ.INF" or "RESOURCE.H") of a custom resource template. The custom resource has a type of "TEMPLATE".

rdwSize   The size of the custom resource template is returned in this parameter. **LoadTemplate** provides this value for use by **CCustomAppWiz::CopyTemplate** and **CCustomAppWiz::ProcessTemplate**.

hInstance   A pointer that can either be **NULL** or be the handle of a Win32 module (a DLL or executable file) that you specify. In either case, *hInstance* informs **LoadTemplate** where it can find the custom resource template named by *lpszTemplateName*.

Remarks
After the user chooses the OK button in the custom AppWizard's New Project Information dialog box, **LoadTemplate** finds, locks, and loads into memory the custom resource of type "TEMPLATE" that is named by *lpszTemplateName*.

If *hInstance* is **NULL**, the base-class implementation of **LoadTemplate** first looks in your custom AppWizard's DLL for the custom resource template named by *lpszTemplateName*, and then, if the template is not there, among AppWizard's custom resource templates. If *hInstance* is not **NULL**, the base-class implementation of **LoadTemplate** looks in the Win32 module *hInstance*.

You can override **LoadTemplate** to load templates from sources other than your custom AppWizard's DLL or the AppWizard DLLs. For more information on this process, see the implementation of **LoadTemplate** in the sample code for CUSTMWZ.AWX in the MSDEV\SAMPLES\APPWIZ\CUSTOMWZ directory.

See Also   CCustomAppWiz::CopyTemplate,
CCustomAppWiz::ProcessTemplate, **CCustomAppWiz::PostProcessTemplate**, Understanding Custom Resource Templates, Understanding Text Templates

CCustomAppWiz::Next
virtual CAppWizStepDlg* Next(CAppWizStepDlg* *pDlg* **);**

Return Value
A pointer to the next step.

If *pDlg* is **NULL**, your custom AppWizard should return a pointer to Step 1. This default action, provided by CUSTMWZ.AWX, occurs when the user chooses the Create button from either the New Project Workspace dialog box or the Insert Project dialog box.

If *pDlg* is the last step, your custom AppWizard should return **NULL**. This default action, provided by CUSTMWZ.AWX, occurs if **SetNumberOfSteps** is called incorrectly or if your project is based on an existing project. In the first case, MFCAPWZ.DLL assumes that there are no more steps and displays the New Project Information dialog box. In the second case, no steps are required, and the code provided by CUSTMWZ.AWX for **Next** adds project- and class-name macros to the dictionary.

For more information on steps, see **CAppWizStepDlg**.

Parameters
pDlg   Pointer to the current step, or **NULL** if the custom AppWizard user has chosen the Create button from either the New Project Workspace or Insert Project dialog box.

Remarks
Next moves to the next step. AppWizard (MFCAPWZ.DLL) calls this function whenever a user chooses either the Next button or the Create button. The Next button is located on the main, outer dialog box that MFCAPWZ.DLL displays. The Create button is located on both the New Project Workspace and the Insert Project dialog boxes. If there is no next step, the Next button is inactive. For more information on steps and a description of the two-dialog-box structure of AppWizard and custom AppWizards, see **CAppWizStepDlg** on page 499.

Before **Next** is called, MFCAPWZ.DLL calls the **CAppWizStepDlg::OnDismiss** member function of the currently displayed step. You override **OnDismiss** to transfer data from the step's controls to the appropriate variables and to update the appropriate dictionary values. If your custom AppWizard's call to **OnDismiss** returns FALSE, then the step remains active, and **Next** is not called.

See Also   The Dictionary, **SetNumberOfSteps**, **CCustomAppWiz::Back**, **CAppWizStepDlg::OnDismiss**

CCustomAppWiz::PostProcessTemplate

virtual void PostProcessTemplate(LPCTSTR *szTemplate* **);**

Parameters
szTemplate   A pointer to a template.

Remarks
If you override **CCustomAppWiz::LoadTemplate** to load a custom resource template into memory (one that isn't stored in AppWizard's DLLs or your custom AppWizard's DLL), **PostProcessTemplate** provides a convenient place for you to deallocate the custom resource template's memory. MFCAPWZ.DLL calls **PostProcessTemplate** after it finishes parsing a custom resource template.

See Also   Understanding Custom Resource Templates, **CCustomAppWiz::LoadTemplate**, **CCustomAppWiz::CopyTemplate**, **CCustomAppWiz::ProcessTemplate**

CCustomAppWiz::ProcessTemplate

virtual void ProcessTemplate(LPCTSTR *lpszInput***, DWORD** *dwSize***, OutputStream*** *pOutput* **);**

Parameters
lpszInput   A pointer, returned by **CCustomAppWiz::LoadTemplate**, to a custom resource template.

dwSize   The size of the custom resource template. Provided by the **LoadTemplate** function's *rdwSize* argument.

pOutput   A pointer to the stream that represents the destination of the output from **ProcessTemplate**.

Remarks
ProcessTemplate accepts a string, which is a custom resource template returned by **LoadTemplate**, parses the string, and passes the string back to MFCAPWZ.DLL through an output stream (*pOutput*).

When **ProcessTemplate** parses the string, it expands macros and obeys AppWizard directives. The result is usually a source file (such as an .H, .CPP, or .RC file) that can be placed directly into the structure of a new project or is a CONFIRM.INF file or a NEWPROJ.INF file. For more information on template parsing, see "NEWPROJ.INF Statements" on page 497.

The default, base-class version of **ProcessTemplate** uses the dictionary to expand macros.

You can implement new directives by overriding the default behavior of **ProcessTemplate** to parse them. For information on the standard AppWizard directives, see "Standard AppWizard Directives" on page 516.

See Also   Understanding Custom Resource Templates, The Dictionary, Standard AppWizard Directives, Understanding CONFIRM.INF and NEWPROJ.INF, NEWPROJ.INF Statements, **CCustomAppWiz::LoadTemplate**, **CCustomAppWiz::CopyTemplate**, **CCustomAppWiz::PostProcessTemplate**

CCustomAppWiz::m_Dictionary

*project***aw.m_Dictionary[**"*macroname*"**] =** "*value*"**;**
*project***aw.m_Dictionary.RemoveKey(**"*macroname*"**);**

Parameters

project   The name of your project as specified in the New Project Workspace dialog box or the Insert Project dialog box.

"macroname"   Pointer to the current step. The quotations marks are required.

"value"   Any value that makes sense for your application. The macro exists if it has a value assigned to it. The quotations marks are required.

Remarks

Use the **m_Dictionary** data member (the dictionary), which is of the type **CMapStringToString**, to create macros, remove macros, or update the value of macros. Some macros are supplied by MFCAPWZ.DLL and some by you. The **CCustomAppWiz::ProcessTemplate** member function uses the dictionary to map macros that it encounters while parsing custom resource templates to their actual values. For more information on the macros supplied by MFCAPWZ.DLL, see "Standard AppWizard Macros" on page 516.

Typically, you will call the dictionary's member functions (which are provided by **CMapStringToString**) in a custom step's **OnDismiss** function as follows:

Each of your custom AppWizard's custom steps is a dialog box that is represented by a class. Each step's class has an **OnDismiss** member function that is called whenever the user of a custom AppWizard chooses the Back, Next, or Finish button. After you use the dialog resource editor to add controls to your custom steps, use ClassWizard to add variables to each step's class. In this way, you can take advantage of the dialog data exchange (DDX) code that ClassWizard adds to your class.

Typically, you will add code in each **OnDismiss** function that defines, provides values for, or removes macros as follows:

```
BOOL CStep1Dlg::OnDismiss()
{
    if (!UpdateData(TRUE))
        return FALSE;

    else
    {
        if (!m_Indented)
        {
            myaw.m_Dictionary["INDENTED_BRACES"]="";
            myaw.m_Dictionary["NOT_INDENTED_BRACES"]="";
        }
        else
        {
            myaw.m_Dictionary["INDENTED_BRACES"]="\t";
            myaw.m_Dictionary.RemoveKey("NOT_INDENTED_BRACES");
        }
        if (m_CompanyLogo)
            myaw.m_Dictionary["COMPANY_LOGO"]="Yes";
        else
            myaw.m_Dictionary.RemoveKey("COMPANY_LOGO");

        if (m_3DControls)
            myaw.m_Dictionary["3-D"]="Yes";
        else
            myaw.m_Dictionary.RemoveKey("3-D");

        return TRUE;  // return FALSE if the dialog
                      //   shouldn't be dismissed
    }
}
```

See Also   **CMapStringToString**, **CAppWizStepDlg::OnDismiss**,
CustomAppWiz::ProcessTemplate, Standard AppWizard Macros

OutputStream

The **OutputStream** class wraps two member functions that are used by
CCustomAppWiz::CopyTemplate and **CCustomAppWiz::ProcessTemplate** when
they process custom resource templates. You will only need to override the
OutputStream member functions if you override **CopyTemplate** and/or
ProcessTemplate.

#include <customaw.h>

See Also   **CCustomAppWiz::CopyTemplate**, **CustomAppWiz::ProcessTemplate**,
Understanding Custom Resource Templates

Class Members

Overridables

WriteLine	Called in **CCustomAppWiz::ProcessTemplate** to write lines from a custom resource template to an output stream.
WriteBlock	Called in **CCustomAppWiz::CopyTemplate** to write a custom resource template, usually a bitmap, to an output stream.

OutputStream::WriteBlock

WriteBlock(LPCTSTR *pBlock*, **DWORD** *dwSize* **)**;

Parameters

pBlock Points to a block of memory that usually contains a custom resource template.

dwSize Size of the block of memory. This must be smaller than or equal to the *dwSize* returned through the **CCustomAppWiz::LoadTemplate** argument list.

Remarks

Writes a block of memory to an output stream—usually an open file. The base-class implementation of the **CopyTemplate** function calls **WriteBlock** to write a binary template to the output stream specified in the argument list of **CopyTemplate**.

See Also CCustomAppWiz::LoadTemplate, CCustomAppWiz::CopyTemplate, OutputStream::WriteLine, CCustomAppWiz::ProcessTemplate

OutputStream::WriteLine

WriteLine(LPCTSTR *lpsz* **)**;

Parameters

lpsz Points to a null-termintated string that is a custom resource template.

Remarks

Writes the text pointed to by *lpsz*, up to and including the first newline character (\n), to an output stream—usually an open file or, in the case of CONFIRM.INF, the display window of the New Project Information dialog box.

CCustomAppWiz::ProcessTemplate parses custom resource templates line by line and calls **WriteLine** to write each processed line (which can appear as text, source code, or resource script statements) to the output stream specified in the argument list of **ProcessTemplate**.

See Also CCustomAppWiz::LoadTemplate, CCustomAppWiz::ProcessTemplate, CCustomAppWiz::CopyTemplate, OutputStream::WriteBlock

C Functions Exported by MFCAPWZ.DLL

These functions, implemented in MFCAPWZ.DLL, provide communication services between your custom AppWizard and MFCAPWZ.DLL.

#include <customaw.h>

Exported C Functions

GetDialog	Gets a pointer to the specified standard AppWizard step. This function is called by a custom AppWizard that uses one of the standard sequences of AppWizard steps.
SetCustomAppWizClass	Provides a pointer to your custom AppWizard's **CCustomAppWiz** class.
SetNumberOfSteps	Sets the number of steps in your custom AppWizard.
ScanForAvailableLanguages	Scans for all of the localized resource DLLs — those with names described by APPWZ*.DLL — found in the MSDEV\BIN\IDE directory.
SetSupportedLanguages	Sets the languages that a custom AppWizard supports, which may be different from the localized resource DLLs found in the MSDEV\BIN\IDE directory.

See Also **GetDialog**, **SetCustomAppWizClass**, **CCustomAppWiz**, **SetNumberOfSteps**, **ScanForAvailableLanguages**, **SetSupportedLanguages**

GetDialog

CAppWizStepDlg* GetDialog(AppWizDlgID *nID* **);**

Return Value
A pointer to the standard AppWizard step specified in the *nID* argument.

Parameters
nID   The enumerated value of a standard AppWizard step.

Remarks
CUSTMWZ.AWX generates calls to **GetDialog** in the **CCustomAppWiz::InitCustomAppWiz** function of every custom AppWizard that uses one of the two standard sequences of AppWizard steps—one call for each of the standard AppWizard steps that a custom AppWizard needs. The returned pointers are automatically stored by the custom AppWizard and are returned in response to an MFCAPWZ.DLL call to **CCustomAppWiz::Next** or **CCustomAppWiz::Back**.

The actual calls to **GetDialog** and storage of the returned pointers occurs in the constructor of a CUSTMWZ.AWX-generated class named **CDialogChooser**. The pointers are stored, sequentially, in an order determined by the original order of the standard AppWizard steps. Pointers to any custom steps you specify are automatically added to the end of the sequence of pointers returned by the calls to **GetDialog**.

You will probably not add your own call to **GetDialog** or modify the existing calls to **GetDialog** unless you want to change the default order in which your custom AppWizard presents steps to its users.

The standard AppWizard offers two different sequences of steps to the AppWizard user: AppWizard Executable and AppWizard Dynamic Link Library. Each step in each sequence is represented by an enumerated value, as shown in Table 24.4.

Table 24.4   Enumerated Values of Standard AppWizard Steps

Value	Description
APWZDLG_APPTYPE	Step 1, MFC AppWizard (exe)
	Allows the user to choose a type of application (single document (SDI), multiple documents (MDI), or dialog based) and the languages into which their application's resource strings will be translated.
APWZDLG_DATABASE	Step 2, MFC AppWizard (exe)
	Allows the user to specify the type of database support for SDI and MDI applications. Possible choices are None, Header files only, Database view without file support, or Database view with file support.
APWZDLG_DLGAPPOPTIONS	Step 2, MFC AppWizard (exe)
	Allows the user to choose standard application features for dialog-based applications (About box, Context-sensitive help, and 3D controls) and to name the application's dialog box. Also allows the user to choose Windows sockets.
APWZDLG_OLE	Step 3, MFC AppWizard (exe)
	Allows the user to specify the level of OLE compound document support for SDI and MDI applications (None, Container, Mini-server, Full-server, Both container and server). Also allows the user to choose support for OLE compound files and OLE automation.
APWZDLG_DOCAPPOPTIONS	Step 4, MFC AppWizard (exe)
	Allows the user to choose standard application features for MDI and SDI applications (Dockable toolbar, Initial status bar, Printing and print preview, Context-sensitive help, and 3D controls). Allows the user to choose MAPI (Messaging API) and Windows sockets and to specify the number of files remembered in their application's most recently used list.

Table 24.4 Enumerated Values of Standard AppWizard Steps *(continued)*

Value	Description
APWZDLG_PROJOPTIONS	Step 5, MFC AppWizard (exe)
	Allows the user to choose whether AppWizard generates commented or uncommented MFC code in their project and whether they want their project linked with the static MFC library or the shared MFC DLL.
APWZDLG_CLASSES	Step 6, MFC AppWizard (exe)
	Allows the user to modify the default class and file names that AppWizard will generate.
APWZDLG_DLLPROJOPTIONS	Step 1, MFC AppWizard (dll)
	Allows the user to choose whether AppWizard generates commented or uncommented MFC code in their project and whether they want their project linked with the static MFC library or the shared MFC DLL. Also allows the user to choose OLE automation and Windows sockets support.

See Also **CCustomAppWiz::InitCustomAppWiz**, **CCustomAppWiz::Next**, **CCustomAppWiz::Back**

SetCustomAppWizClass

void SetCustomAppWizClass(CCustomAppWiz *pAW* **);**

Parameters
pAW Points to your **CCustomAppWiz** class.

Remarks
Called in the **DLLMain** function of your custom AppWizard to provide MFCAPWZ.DLL with a pointer to your custom AppWizard's **CCustomAppWiz** class. The communication services between MFCAPWZ.DLL and your custom AppWizard that are provided by the **CCustomAppWiz** member functions occur through *pAW*. The code that calls **SetCustomAppWizClass** is automatically generated when you use the Custom AppWizard project type to generate your custom AppWizard.

See Also **CCustomAppWiz**

SetNumberOfSteps

void SetNumberOfSteps(int *nSteps* **);**

Parameters
nSteps The total number of steps that your custom AppWizard presents to its users. Set *nSteps* to–1 to communicate to MFCAPWZ.DLL that you want your custom AppWizard's title bar to display only the current step number (for example,

"Step 1" rather than "Step 1 of 6"). Set *nSteps* to 0 to communicate to MFCAPWZ.DLL that your custom AppWizard has no steps and only wants to use the New Project Workspace or the Insert Project dialog boxes (for example, when your custom AppWizard is based on an existing project, and there are no options for the custom AppWizard user to select.)

Remarks

Your custom AppWizard calls **SetNumberOfSteps** in **CCustomAppWiz::InitCustomAppWiz** to communicate the total number of steps to MFCAPWZ.DLL. The resulting information allows MFCAPWZ.DLL to accurately number the steps in your custom AppWizard's title bar and to correctly activate or gray the Next button.

Although the initial call to **SetNumberOfSteps** in **InitCustomAppWiz** is generated for you, you should also call it when an end user's choice will change the number of steps the user will see.

See Also   **CCustomAppWiz::InitCustomAppWiz**

ScanForAvailableLanguages

BOOL ScanForAvailableLanguages(CStringList& *rLanguages* **);**

Return Value

TRUE if one or more localized resource DLLs are found in the MSDEV\BIN\IDE directory, otherwise FALSE.

Parameters

rLanguages   Stores strings describing each localized resource DLL —those with names described by APPWZ*.DLL —found in the MSVDEV\BIN\IDE directory.

Remarks

The **ScanForAvailableLanguages** function requests that MFCAPWZ.DLL scan the MSVDEV\BIN\IDE directory and store, in *rLanguages*, a descriptive string for each localized resource DLL found. Each entry in the list takes the following form:

"*language-name (APPWZ*.DLL-name);translation-identifier*"

For example:

```
"U.S. English (appwzenu.dll);0x040904e4"
```

The *translation-identifier* is identical to the value of the block header of the "StringFileInfo" block in a Version resource. It's a **DWORD** represented in hexadecimal format, with a high word representing the language and a low word representing the character set (code page).

If **ScanForAvailableLanguages** returns FALSE, MFCAPWZ.DLL displays an error message in a message box. Retry and Cancel buttons allow flexible recovery from this error.

Your custom AppWizard will probably never call **ScanForAvailableLanguages**. CUSTMWZ.AWX does call **ScanForAvailableLanguages** to determine which languages AppWizard currently supports. CUSTMWZ.AWX uses the result to fill the language list for step 2.

See Also   **$$SET_DEFAULT_LANG**, **SetSupportedLanguages**, **CCustomAppWiz::GetPlatforms**

SetSupportedLanguages

SetSupportedLanguages(LPCTSTR *szSupportedLangs* **);**

Parameters
szSupportedLangs   Stores a string of the form:

"*language-name#1 (APPWZ*.DLL-name#1);translation-identifier#1*\n

language-name#2 (APPWZ*.DLL-name#2);translation-identifier#2\n...

...*language-name#i (APPWZ*.DLL-name#i);translation-identifier#i*\n"

The string is a series of substrings, each separated by the newline character (\n). Each substring has the same format as each entry in the **CStringList** parameter in **ScanForAvailableLanguages**.

Remarks
The **SetSupportedLanguages** function reports to MFCAPWZ.DLL the languages that are supported by your custom AppWizard. This function is only used if your custom AppWizard uses the AppWizard Executable standard sequences of AppWizard steps and is called in **CCustomAppWiz::InitCustomAppWiz** to fill the languages checklist in AppWizard's Step 1. The code that calls **SetSupportedLanguages** is automatically generated when you use the Custom AppWizard project type to generate your custom AppWizard

See Also   **$$SET_DEFAULT_LANG**, **ScanForAvailableLanguages**, **CCustomAppWiz::GetPlatforms**

Standard AppWizard Directives

AppWizard directives, such as **$$IF** and **$$ENDIF**, are used to generalize custom resource templates so that the content of the templates can be used for multiple project types. Directives in a template guide the MFCAPWZ.DLL API **ProcessTemplate** function as it processes a template to produce a project file or the content of the New Project Information dialog box. For example, based on the value of a macro, a sequence of **$$IF**, **$$ELIF**, **$$ELSE**, and **$$ENDIF** directives can force **ProcessTemplate** to selectively insert lines of C++ code into a header or an implementation file (.H or .CPP, respectively) used by a project generated by your custom AppWizard.

ProcessTemplate recognizes the following directives:

$$IF	**$$BEGINLOOP**
$$ELIF	**$$ENDLOOP**
$$ELSE	**$$SET_DEFAULT_LANG**
$$ENDIF	**$$//**
$$INCLUDE	

These directives must appear at the beginning of a line with no preceding white space, and, other than any arguments and one optional comment, there can be nothing else on the line.

If you wish the parser to emit "$$" literally (and not to signify that a macro or directive will follow), use "$$$$". Occurrences of "$$$$" are translated as "$$".

See Also   **$$IF**, **$$ELIF**, **$$ELSE**, **$$ENDIF**, **$$INCLUDE**, **$$BEGINLOOP**, **$$ENDLOOP**, **$$SET_DEFAULT_LANG**, **$$SET_DEFAULT_LANG**, **$$//**

$$IF, $$ELIF, $$ELSE, and $$ENDIF

$$IF(*macro-list*)

   textA

$$ELIF(*macro-list*)

   textB

$$ELSE

   textC

$$ENDIF

Parameters

macro-list   One or more macro names. A macro name can be preceded by the logical NOT operator (!). Multiple macro names are separated by the logical OR (||) operator. A macro name can be one of the standard AppWizard macros or one that you create by adding it to the dictionary.

Remarks

The **$$IF** directive, with the **$$ELIF**, **$$ELSE**, and **$$ENDIF** directives, controls the flow of control that the **ProcessTemplate** function follows while parsing a custom resource template.

When the parser encounters an **$$IF** directive, it searches the dictionary for each macro name it finds in *macro-list*, in sequential order. The parser checks only for a macro name's existence in the dictionary, not its value. Once a macro name is found in the dictionary, the parser stops checking the other macro names, the **$$IF** evaluates to TRUE, and *textA* is parsed. If the parser finds none of the macro names in the dictionary, the **$$IF** evaluates to FALSE and the parser processes any subsequent **$$ELIF** directive's *macro-list* as it did the **$$IF** *macro-list*. If an **$$ELIF** evaluates to TRUE, *textB* is parsed. If no **$$ELIF** directive evaluates to TRUE, the **$$ELSE** body (*textC*) is parsed. The **$$ENDIF** directive marks the end of the **$$IF** construct, and normal parsing resumes with the next line.

In the **$$IF** and **$$ELIF** arguments, any macro name can be preceded by the logical NOT operator (**!**) to force the parser to check for non-existence in the dictionary. For example, the following code fragment evaluates to true if MACRO1 is not in the dictionary:

```
$$IF(!MACRO1)
```

Each **$$IF** directive in a custom resource template must be matched by a closing **$$ENDIF** directive. Multiple **$$ELIF** directives can appear between the **$$IF** and **$$ENDIF** directives, but at most one **$$ELSE** directive is allowed. That **$$ELSE** directive, if present, must follow all the **$$ELIF**s (if any) in that **$$IF-$$ENDIF** block. If a custom resource template contains an **$$IF**, any following **$$ELIF** and/or **$$ELSE** is optional. An ending **$$ENDIF** is mandatory. **$$IF** constructs can be nested up to five levels deep.

There is no logical AND (**&&**) operator. If you wish to have text parsed only when MACRO1 and MACRO2 are defined, you can accomplish this as follows:

```
$$IF(MACRO1)
$$IF(MACRO2)
text
$$ENDIF //MACRO2
$$ENDIF //MACRO1
```

See Also The Dictionary, **CCustomAppWiz::ProcessTemplate**, Standard AppWizard Directives, Standard AppWizard Macros

$$INCLUDE

$$INCLUDE(*template-name-macro* **);**

Parameters
template-name-macro A macro name with a value that must be the name of a custom resource template. A macro name can be one of the standard AppWizard macros or one that you create by adding it to the dictionary.

Remarks
The parser searches for an **$$INCLUDE** directive's *template-name-macro* in the dictionary. If *template-name-macro* is in the dictionary, the associated custom resource template is loaded and parsed. Once the associated template is parsed, parsing of the original template resumes.

Note The template associated with *template-name-macro* must be a text template and must be parsed using **ProcessTemplate**. The base-class version of **ProcessTemplate** will not parse binary templates.

If *template-name-macro* is not in the dictionary, MFCAPWZ.DLL displays an error message and stops the file generation process. If the template associated with *filename-macro* is not found, again a message is displayed and an exception is thrown.

You can nest **$$INCLUDE** directives arbitrarily deep. That is, if one template includes a second template via **$$INCLUDE**, that second template may include a third via **$$INCLUDE**, and so on. However, templates cannot be recursively included. That is, if template A includes template B, which includes template C, and so on, then template A cannot be included in the include chain. MFCAPWZ.DLL detects recursive includes, prints an error message, and stops the file generation process.

See Also   The Dictionary, **CCustomAppWiz::ProcessTemplate**, Standard AppWizard Directives, Standard AppWizard Macros

$$BEGINLOOP and $$ENDLOOP

$$BEGINLOOP(*macro-name*);

   text

$$ENDLOOP;

Parameters

macro-name   A macro name that you have added to the dictionary with a value that must be a numeric string in decimal format (for example, "12"). The *macro-name* argument must be the name of a macro, not a constant value.

text   One or more lines of text that may include C++ code, resource script statements, macros, directives, or whatever you parsed.

Remarks

Custom resource templates can use a **$$BEGINLOOP** and **$$ENDLOOP** construct to force the **CCustomAppWiz::ProcessTemplate** function's parser to process *text* the number of times specified by the value of *macro-name*.

The parser treats every macro that it encounters between a **$$BEGINLOOP** and an **$$ENDLOOP**, including *macro-name*, in the following manner:

1. If, for example, the parser encounters a macro named **VAR**, it looks in the dictionary for a macro named **VAR_**n, where n is an integer that corresponds to the number of times that the parser has iterated through *text*. The iterations are numbered 0, 1, ..., n-1, so that the parser looks for macros named **VAR_0**, **VAR_1**, and so on.

2. If the parser does not find **VAR_**n in the dictionary, it looks just for **VAR**.

Loops cannot be nested. A second **$$BEGINLOOP** before the first **$$ENDLOOP** is illegal.

See Also The Dictionary, **CCustomAppWiz::ProcessTemplate**, Standard AppWizard Directives, How Macros Get Their Values

$$SET_DEFAULT_LANG

$$SET_DEFAULT_LANG(*macro-name*);

Parameters

macro-name A macro name you add to the dictionary. The value of *macro-name* must be a three-letter string that corresponds to a language previously selected by an AppWizard or custom AppWizard user. Table 24.5 provides a partial list of possible values for *macro-name*.

Table 24.5 Language Identifiers

Value	Language
DEU	German
ENU	English
ESP	Spanish
FRA	French
ITA	Italian
SVE	Swedish

Remarks

You use the **$$SET_DEFAULT_LANG** directive to specify a language-identifer for the **CCustomAppWiz::LoadTemplate** function to use when it searches for a custom resource template to load for use by **CCustomAppWiz::CopyTemplate** or **CCustomAppWiz::ProcessTemplate**.

Note Code to perform the following procedure is automatically generated if your custom AppWizard uses the existing set of AppWizard steps for generating an executable file and if you select more than one language from the Custom AppWizard project type's language list.

If you use the **$$SET_DEFAULT_LANG** directive in a loop defined by the **$$BEGINLOOP** and **$$ENDLOOP** directives, you can use **$$BEGINLOOP** and **$$ENDLOOP** to modify macros to write code that finds, extracts, and processes multiple language versions of a language-specific template. For information on how **$$BEGINLOOP** and **$$ENDLOOP** modify macros, see **$$BEGINLOOP** and **$$ENDLOOP** on page 519.

The language identifier, which is the value of *macro-name*, also specifies the search order that **LoadTemplate** uses to search for a DLL.

Say that **$$SET_DEFAULT_LANG** is called with a *macro-name* that expands to "DEU". **LoadTemplate** will go through the following algorithm to locate a template named TEMPLATE.RC:

1. Try locating TEMPLATE_DEU.RC in the custom AppWizard's resources.

2. If not there, try locating TEMPLATE.RC in the custom AppWizard's resources.

3. If not there, try locating TEMPLATE.RC in MFCAPWZ.DLL

4. If not there, try locating TEMPLATE.RC in APPWZDEU.DLL

5. If not there, try locating TEMPLATE.RC in all the other APPWZ*.DLLs selected by the custom AppWizard user.

6. If not there, display an error and stop file generation.

Notice that in step 1, **LoadTemplate** looks for the template under the localized name (TEMPLATE_DEU.RC). If it can't find a template named TEMPLATE_DEU.RC in the custom AppWizard's resources, it reverts back to searching for the actual name (TEMPLATE.RC).

Note   If AppWizard itself is being run rather than a custom AppWizard, MFCAPWZ.DLL starts the search process at step 3, and thus never tries to locate the template under the localized name.

Example

Imagine that a user of your custom AppWizard generates a project that will generate an application for use by English-, French-, and Japanese-speaking people. To create the user's project, your custom AppWizard must find the templates containing strings translated into these languages. It must seach in DLLs that include, at least, your custom AppWizard's DLL, MFCAPWZ.DLL, and possibly APPWZENU.DLL, APPWZFRA.DLL, and APPWZJPN.DLL. For simplicity, we will examine finding and loading one template, FILE.TXT.

Because FILE.TXT is a text file, it will probably be translated into English, French, and Japanese. Your custom AppWizard's DLL must contain three versions of this file named FILE_ENU.TXT, FILE_FRA.TXT, and FILE_JPN.TXT. Also, your custom AppWizard must make the following addition to the dictionary:

```
myprojectaw.m_Dictionary["FILE"] = "FILE.TXT";
```

To track the three languages specified by the user, you add macros to the dictionary as follows:

```
myprojectaw.m_Dictionary["LANG_SUFFIX_0"] = "ENU";
myprojectaw.m_Dictionary["LANG_SUFFIX_1"] = "FRA";
myprojectaw.m_Dictionary["LANG_SUFFIX_2"] = "JPN";
```

Then, when your customAppWizard must find and load language-specific templates, it does so in a loop as follows:

```
$$BEGINLOOP(NUM_LANGS)
$$SET_DEFAULT_LANG(LANG_SUFFIX)
$$// Include text from the
$$// properly localized template:
$$INCLUDE(FILE)
$$ENDLOOP
```

If NUM_LANGS has the value of "3", then this loop will iterate three times. During each iteration, MFCAPWZ.DLL will modify its lookup procedure for the LANG_SUFFIX macro and **CCustomAppwiz::LoadTemplate** will modify its template-loading procedure as follows:

- First iteration: LANG_SUFFIX first becomes LANG_SUFFIX_0. The value of FILE is extracted from the dictionary and, when **$$INCLUDE** causes **LoadTemplate** to be called, the value of FILE is combined with the value of LANG_SUFFIX_0 to produce FILE_ENU.TXT.

- Second iteration: LANG_SUFFIX first becomes LANG_SUFFIX_1. The value of FILE is extracted from the dictionary and, when **$$INCLUDE** causes **LoadTemplate** to be called, the value of FILE is combined with the value of LANG_SUFFIX_1 to produce FILE_FRA.TXT.

- Third interation: LANG_SUFFIX first becomes LANG_SUFFIX_2. The value of FILE is extracted from the dictionary and, when **$$INCLUDE** causes **LoadTemplate** to be called, the value of FILE is combined with the value of LANG_SUFFIX_2 to produce FILE_JPN.TXT.

Thus, the value of LANG_SUFFIX is transformed to "ENU", "FRA", and "JPN" and **LoadTemplate** will know to first load APWZENU.DLL, then APWZFRA.DLL, and finally APWZJPN.DLL if any of the templates it seeks are not in the custom AppWizard's DLL. For more information on the transformation of macro names, see **$$BEGINLOOP** and **$$ENDLOOP** on page 519.

Note The argument to the **$$SET_DEFAULT_LANG** directive must correspond to an APPWZ*.DLL already chosen by the AppWizard or custom AppWizard user. Otherwise, MFCAPWZ.DLL will display an error message and stop file generation immediately after parsing the **$$SET_DEFAULT_LANG** directive.

See Also The Dictionary, **CCustomAppwiz::LoadTemplate**, **CCustomAppwiz::ProcessTemplate**, **CCustomAppwiz::CopyTemplate**, **CCustomAppwiz::PostProcessTemplate**, **$$BEGINLOOP**, **$$ENDLOOP**, Standard AppWizard Directives, How Macros Get Their Values.

$$//

Remarks

The **ProcessTemplate** function's parser treats a line beginning with **$$//** as a comment. A comment can be preceded by just // when it appears after a directive on the same line. The following line is a comment:

```
$$// This line is a comment
```

The following line begins with an **$$ENDIF** directive and ends with a comment:

```
$$ENDIF //MACRO1
```

See Also   **CCustomAppwiz::ProcessTemplate**, Standard AppWizard Directives, Standard AppWizard Macros

Standard AppWizard Macros

This reference describes the macros that AppWizard uses to generalize its custom resource templates. These macros correspond to, or are related to, controls in AppWizard's steps. You have access to these macros if your custom AppWizard uses one of the standard sequences of AppWizard steps: AppWizard Executable (exe) or AppWizard Dynamic-Link Library (dll).

The following macros are organized by the step (for MDI and SDI applications) where they are used. Some of the described macros also appear on analogous steps for dialog-based and DLL applications (for example, 3D is described with the other MDI/SDI step 4 macros, but it is also used by the dialog-based application's step 2).

New Project Workspace and Insert Project Dialog Box Options

Step 1, Project Type Options

Step 2, Database Options

Step 3, OLE Options

Step 4, Application Options

Step 4, Advanced Options, Document Template Strings Tab

Step 4, Advanced Options, Frame Styles Tab

Step 4, Advanced Options, Macintosh-Specific Tab

Step 5, Project Options

Step 6, Class and File Names

The following catagories also exist:

Miscellaneous Macros

Language Loop Macros

New Project Workspace and Insert Project Dialog Box Options

Macro	Type	Description
FULL_DIR_PATH	text	The full path of the directory in which the generated project will be placed (including the new subdirectory), with a trailing backslash.
ROOT	text	The project name, no extension (all uppercase).
Root **root**	text	The project name, no extension (cases as entered by user).
SAFE_ROOT	text	The project name, entered from the New Project Workspace dialog box or the Insert Project dialog box, stripped of any characters that are not alphanumeric characters (a-z, A-Z, and 0-9) or the underscore (_). The resulting value is safe to use in the name of a preprocessor and/or a C/C++ symbol.
TARGET_INTEL	BOOL	The project targets the Intel Win32 operating system.
TARGET_MIPS	BOOL	The project targets the MIPS Win32 operating system.
TARGET_ALPHA	BOOL	The project targets the ALPHA Win32 operating system.
TARGET_MAC	BOOL	The project targets the Macintosh (set if either 680x0 Macintosh or Power Macintosh is chosen).
TARGET_68KMAC	BOOL	The project targets the 680x0 Macintosh.
TARGET_POWERMAC	BOOL	The project targets the Power Macintosh.

See Also The Dictionary, **CCustomAppwiz::ProcessTemplate**, **CCustomAppwiz::PostProcessTemplate**, How Macros Get Their Values

Step 1, Project Type Options

Only one of the Project Type macros can be in the dictionary.

Macro	Type	Description
PROJTYPE_MDI	BOOL	Whether the AppWizard user or custom AppWizard user has selected a multiple document interface.
PROJTYPE_SDI	BOOL	Whether the AppWizard user or custom AppWizard user has selected a single document interface.
PROJTYPE_DLG	BOOL	Whether the AppWizard user or custom AppWizard user has selected a dialog-based application.

Macro	Type	Description
PROJTYPE_DLL	BOOL	Whether the AppWizard user or custom AppWizard user has specified that the project be a DLL. If this macro is set, the 680x0 Macintosh platform is not listed in the New Project Workspace or the Insert Project's Platforms checklist, and the project makefile builds a DLL rather than an executable file.
PROJTYPE_CUSTOMAW	BOOL	Whether the AppWizard user or custom AppWizard user has selected a Custom AppWizard project type. Note that this macro will rarely be used in a custom AppWizard. It is only used when CUSTMWZ.AWX is launched.

See Also   The Dictionary, **CCustomAppwiz::ProcessTemplate**, **CCustomAppwiz::PostProcessTemplate**, How Macros Get Their Values

Step 2, Database Options

One or more database macros may be defined.

Macro	Type	Description
DAO	BOOL	Whether the selected data source is DAO; otherwise, it is ODBC.
DB	BOOL	Whether the AppWizard user or custom AppWizard user has selected, at least, minimal database support. In other words, a radio button other than None is chosen by the user.
DB_NO_DETECT	BOOL	Whether MFC should automatically detect when columns have been modified. TRUE means do not auto detect.
DB_TABLE_TYPE	text	Type of recordset class being created. For DAO, **DB_TABLE_TYPE** can be one of the following: • dbOpenDynaset • dbOpenSnapshot • dbOpenTable For ODBC, **DB_TABLE_TYPE** can be one of the following: • Snapshot • Dynaset

Macro	Type	Description
DB_NO_FILE	BOOL	Whether the AppWizard user or custom AppWizard user has specified a database application that allows document serialization. The **CRecordView** macro, documented with the Step 6 macros, determines whether an application includes database support.
RECSET_VARS	text	A string containing the declarations of a recordset's column member variables. Used in the recordset's header (.H) file.
RECSET_VAR_BINDINGS	text	A string containing the initialization of a recordset's column member variables. Used in the recordset's constructor, which is in the implementation (.CPP) file for the recordset.
RECSET_RFX	text	A string containing the RFX statements for a recordset's column member variables. Used in the recordset's **DoFieldExchange** member function, which is found in the recordset's .CPP file.
PARAM_VARS	text	A string containing the declarations of a recordset's parameter member variables. Used in the recordset's header (.H) file.
PARAM_VAR_BINDINGS	text	A string containing the initialization of a recordset's parameter member variables. Used in the recordset's constructor, which is in the implementation (.CPP) file for the recordset.
PARAM_RFX	text	A string containing the RFX statements for a recordset's parameter member variables. Used in the recordset's **DoFieldExchange** member function, which is found in the recordset's .CPP file.
RECSET_VARIABLE	text	The application's main document class needs to refer to this recordset. This macro expands to the required data member variable of the document class.

See Also   The Dictionary, **CCustomAppwiz::ProcessTemplate**, **CCustomAppwiz::PostProcessTemplate**, How Macros Get Their Values.

Step 3, OLE Options

Only one of the OLE macros can be in the dictionary.

Macro	Type	Description
CONTAINER	BOOL	Whether the AppWizard user or custom AppWizard user has specified that the application is only an OLE container.
FULL_SERVER	BOOL	Whether the AppWizard user or custom AppWizard user has specified that the application is an OLE full-server.
MINI_SERVER	BOOL	Whether the AppWizard user or custom AppWizard user has specified that the application is an OLE mini-server.
CONTAINER_SERVER	BOOL	Whether the AppWizard user or custom AppWizard user has specified that the application is an OLE container-server.

More than one of the following OLE macros may be set.

Macro	Type	Description
APP_CLSID	text	Struct form of the application's globally unique identifier (GUID). Only used if the user has chosen OLE support.
APP_CLSID_REG	text	Registration form of the application's GUID. Only used if the user has chosen OLE support.
AUTOMATION	BOOL	Whether the AppWizard user or custom AppWizard user has chosen OLE Automation.
COMPFILE	BOOL	Whether the AppWizard user has chosen OLE compound file support.
DISPIID_CLSID_ODL	text	ODL form of the dispinterface GUID. Only used if the user has chosen OLE Automation support.
LIB_CLSID_ODL	text	ODL form of the library's GUID. Only used if the user has chosen OLE Automation support.
OLECTL	BOOL	Whether the application supports using OLE Controls.

See Also   The Dictionary, **CCustomAppwiz::ProcessTemplate**, **CCustomAppwiz::PostProcessTemplate**, How Macros Get Their Values.

Step 4, Application Options

The following options are set from the Step 4 Application Options dialog box.

Macro	Type	Description
TOOLBAR	BOOL	Whether the AppWizard user or custom AppWizard user has specified that the application have a toolbar.
STATUSBAR	BOOL	Whether the AppWizard user or custom AppWizard user has specified that the application have a status bar.
PRINT	BOOL	Whether the AppWizard user or custom AppWizard user has specified that the application have printing support.
HELP	BOOL	Whether the AppWizard user or custom AppWizard user has specified that the application have context-sensitive help.
3D	BOOL	Whether the AppWizard user or custom AppWizard user has specified that the application use 3D controls.
ABOUT	BOOL	Whether the AppWizard user or custom AppWizard user has specified that the dialog-based application include an About box.
MAPI	BOOL	Whether the AppWizard user or custom AppWizard user has specified that the application include MAPI support.
SOCKETS	BOOL	Whether the AppWizard user or custom AppWizard user has specified that the project have sockets support.
HAS_MRU	BOOL	Whether the AppWizard user or custom AppWizard user has specified a nonzero value in the most recently used (MRU) text box.
SIZE_MRU	text	The value in the MRU text box.

See Also   The Dictionary, **CCustomAppwiz::ProcessTemplate**, **CCustomAppwiz::PostProcessTemplate**, How Macros Get Their Values

Step 4, Advanced Options, Document Template Strings Tab

The following macros are set from the Document Template Strings tab of the Step 4 Advanced Options dialog box.

Macro	Type	Description
DOC	text	The value in the Doc Type Name text box.
DOC_FILENEW	text	The document's File New string.
DOC_FILTER	text	The document's (Win32) filter string.
DOC_REGID	text	The value entered in the File Type Name text box.
DOC_REGNAME	text	The document's registration database name.
HAS_SUFFIX	BOOL	Whether the application has a document suffix (extension) specified.

Macro	Type	Description
TITLE	text	The caption string for an application's main title bar or, in a dialog-based application, the dialog's title.
SUFFIX	text	If **HAS_SUFFIX** is defined, **SUFFIX** is the user-specified document suffix for the application.

See Also   The Dictionary, **CCustomAppwiz::ProcessTemplate**, **CCustomAppwiz::PostProcessTemplate**, How Macros Get Their Values

Step 4, Advanced Options, Window Styles Tab

The following macros are set from the Window Styles tab of the Step 4 Advanced Options dialog box.

Macro	Type	Description
FRAME_STYLES	BOOL	Whether the AppWizard user or custom AppWizard user has specified nondefault main frame styles.
SW_ARG	text	Argument to the **ShowWindow** function. Normally this is "**m_nCmdShow**", but if the user has chosen "maximized" or "minimized" for the main frame, this value is "**SW_SHOWMAXIMIZED**" or "**SW_SHOWMINIMIZED**", respectively.
FRAME_STYLE_FLAGS	text	If nondefault main frame styles are selected by the AppWizard user, this macro's value represents the selected main frame styles and is added to the style data member of the **CREATESTRUCT** passed to **PreCreateWindow**.
MDICHILD	BOOL	Whether the AppWizard user or custom AppWizard user has specified splitter windows in an MDI application and/or chosen nondefault child frame styles. AppWizard must generate a class derived from **CMDIChildWnd**.
CHILD_FRAME_STYLES	BOOL	TRUE, if the user has chosen nondefault child frame styles.
CHILD_FRAME_STYLE_FLAGS	text	If nondefault child frame styles are selected by the AppWizard user, the value of this macro is the text that represents the selected child frame styles, and is added to the style data member of the **CREATESTRUCT** passed to **PreCreateWindow**.

Macro	Type	Description
SPLITTER_MDI	BOOL	TRUE, if the AppWizard user has chosen splitter windows in an MDI application.
SPLITTER_SDI	BOOL	TRUE, if the AppWizard user has chosen splitter windows in an SDI application.

See Also   The Dictionary, **CCustomAppwiz::ProcessTemplate**, **CCustomAppwiz::PostProcessTemplate**, How Macros Get Their Values

Step 4, Advanced Options, Macintosh-Specific Tab

The following macros are set from the Macintosh-Specific tab of the Step 4 Advanced Options dialog box.

Macro	Type	Description
CREATOR	text	The document's file creator specified in the Application Signature text box.
FILE_TYPE	text	The document's Macintosh file type specified in the Document File Type text box.
MAC_FILTER	text	The document's Macintosh filter string specified in the Document File Name text box.
R_FILE	text	The name of the Macintosh resource (.R) file.

See Also   The Dictionary, **CCustomAppwiz::ProcessTemplate**, **CCustomAppwiz::PostProcessTemplate**, How Macros Get Their Values

Step 5, Project Options

Macro	Type	Description
VERBOSE	BOOL	TRUE, if the user chooses to include source comments and README.TXT.
MFCDLL	BOOL	TRUE, if the project uses MFC in a DLL.

See Also   The Dictionary, **CCustomAppwiz::ProcessTemplate**, **CCustomAppwiz::PostProcessTemplate**, How Macros Get Their Values

Step 6, Class and File Names

AppWizard creates macros to name classes and files by combining the macro prefixes listed in Table 24.6 with any of the macro components listed in Table 24.7. For example, the value of a combined macro **DOC_CLASS** will be the name of the application's document class —typically, something like "CProjectDoc." No single application will use all combinations.

Table 24.6   Macro Prefixes

Macro Prefix	Description
DOC	Refers to the application's document class.
APP	Refers to the application's **CWinApp**-derived class.
FRAME	Refers to the application's main frame class (derived from **CFrameWnd** or **CMDIFrameWnd**).
CHILD_FRAME	Refers to the application's MDI child frame class (**CMDIChildFrameWnd**).
VIEW	Refers to the application's view class.
DLG	Refers to the application's main dialog class. Only used for a dialog-based application.
RECSET	Refers to the application's main recordset class.
SRVRITEM	Refers to the application's main server-item class (derived from **CServerItem**).
CNTRITEM	Refers to the application's main container-item class (derived from **CContainerItem**).
IPFRAME	Refers to the application's in-place frame class (derived from **CIPFrameWnd**).

Table 24.7   Macro Components

Macro Component	Description
_CLASS	Class name.
_BASE_CLASS	Base class name.
_IFILE	Class implementation filename (without the extension). Both uppercase and lowercase versions of these macros are defined. If the macro name is uppercase (for example, APP_IFILE), its value will be uppercase (for example, PROJECT). If the macro name is lowercase (for example, app_ifile), its value will be lowercase (for example, project).
_HFILE	Class header filename (without the extension). Both uppercase and lowercase versions of these macros are defined. If the macro name is uppercase (for example, APP_HFILE), its value will be uppercase (for example, PROJECT). If the macro name is lowercase (for example, app_hfile), its value will be lowercase (for example, project).

Only one of the following macros is defined to indicate the main view's base class.

Macro	Type	Description
CView	BOOL	If and only if the view derives from **CView**.
CFormView	BOOL	If and only if the view derives from **CFormView**.
CScrollView	BOOL	If and only if the view derives from **CScrollView**.
CEditView	BOOL	If and only if the view derives from **CEditView**.
CRecordView	BOOL	If and only if the view derives from **CRecordView**. Set if user has selected a database view with or without file support.

See Also The Dictionary, **CCustomAppwiz::ProcessTemplate**, **CCustomAppwiz::PostProcessTemplate**, How Macros Get Their Values

Miscellaneous Macros

Macro	Type	Description
DLGLOC_RC	text	This is always "DLGLOC.RC", and is used in an **$$INCLUDE** directive in the DLGALL.RC custom resource template.
HLPARG_MAC	text	Help-file macro used in the MAKEHELP.BAT custom resource template. Always "1".
HLPARG_MACPATH	text	Help-file macro used in the MAKEHELP.BAT custom resource template. Always "2".
HM_FILE	text	Help-file macro used in the MAKEHELP.BAT custom resource template. Base name of the .HM file.
LANG_LIST_SUFFIXES	text	Comma-separated string containing a list of the three-letter abbreviations of all languages selected by the AppWizard user (for example, "ENU, FRA"). If an application supports only one language, the list is "".
LOC_RC	text	This is always "LOC.RC", and is used in an **$$INCLUDE** directive in the ALL.RC custom resource template.
MACLOC_RC	text	This is always "MACLOC.RC", and is used in an **$$INCLUDE** directive in the ALL.RC custom resource template.
mac_hpj	text	Help-file macro used in the MAKEHELP.BAT custom resource template. Base name of the Macintosh .HPJ file.
MFCPath	text	Path on the AppWizard user's computer where the MFC library resides.
YEAR	text	The current year.

See Also   The Dictionary, **CCustomAppwiz::ProcessTemplate**,
CCustomAppwiz::PostProcessTemplate, How Macros Get Their Values

Language Loop Macros

The following macros are used in a language loop, which is a block of text delimited
by the **$$BEGINLOOP(NUM_LANGS)** and **$$ENDLOOP** directives.

Macro	Type	Description
LANGUAGE	text	Name of language (for example, "U.S. English").
LANG_SUFFIX	text	Three-letter abbreviation of language (for example, "ENU").
HLP_DIR_LOC	text	Name of directory to be created in the generated project, which will contain the localized elements of the application's context-sensitive help (for example, "HLP\ENU"; in an application with only one language, this is always "HLP").
RES_DIR_LOC	text	Name of directory to be created in the generated project, which will contain those files included by the application's .RC file that are localized (for example, "RES\ENU"; in an application with only one language, this is always "RES").
RES_DIR_LOC_DBLSLASH	text	Same as RES_DIR_LOC, except any backslashes are doubled (for example, "RES\\ENU"; again, this is always "RES" in an application with only one language).
MFC_DIR_LOC	text	Name of directory that contains the localizable resources the application will include from MFC. All backslashes are doubled. (For example, "L.FRA\\"; all English resources from MFC are in the main include directory. This macro expands to "" in the case of English.)
LANG_PREAMBLE	text	Code that is inserted in the application's .RC file, which precedes a localized resource.

For example:
```
#if !defined(AFX_RESOURCE_DLL) ||
defined(AFX_TARG_ENU)
#ifdef _WIN32
LANGUAGE 9, 1
#pragma code_page(1252)
#endif
```

(In an application with only one language,
this is "".)

Macro	Type	Description
LANG_PREAMBLE_INQUOTES	text	Same as **LANG_PREAMBLE**, except each line is tabbed and enclosed in quotes:
		For example:
| | | ```
"#if !defined(AFX_RESOURCE_DLL) |
defined(AFX_TARG_ENU)"
    "#ifdef _WIN32"
    "LANGUAGE 9, 1"
    "#pragma code_page(1252)"
    "#endif"
``` |
| **LANG_POSTAMBLE** | text | Code that's inserted in the application's .RC file, which follows a localized resource. |
| | | For example: |
| | | ```
#endif
``` |
		(In an application with only one language, this is "".)
LANG_POSTAMBLE_INQUOTES	text	Same as **LANG_POSTAMBLE**, except each line is tabbed and enclosed in quotes:
		For example:
| | | ```
    "#endif"
``` |
		(In an application with only one language, this is "".)
NUM_LANGS	text	The number of languages the user has chosen. (Commonly used as the argument to **$$BEGINLOOP**.)
MULTIPLE_LANGS	BOOL	Whether the user chose more than one language. Currently, never defined. Reserved for future use.

See Also The Dictionary, **CCustomAppwiz::ProcessTemplate**, **CCustomAppwiz::PostProcessTemplate**, How Macros Get Their Values

Standard Custom Resource Templates

AppWizard uses a standard set of custom resource templates to build the projects it generates. It also copies some subset of these templates to custom AppWizard projects that are based on the standard AppWizard steps. These templates allow custom AppWizards to generate projects just as AppWizard does.

These standard templates provide a common look and feel to applications created from AppWizard projects and include templates from which .H, .CPP, .RC, .CLW, .ODL, and .RC2 files are built. They also include bitmaps of standard user-interface components and templates that simplify generating help files.
```

Localization of Standard Templates

The standard templates are separated into two main categories: localized and nonlocalized. Localized templates contain strings that have been translated into languages other than English. These strings are stored in the language DLLs — DLLs with names described by APPWZ*.DLL, where * is a language code such as ENU or JPN. The nonlocalized templates are stored in MFCAPWZ.DLL. When a localized template is generated for a custom AppWizard project, the template's filename will contain an embedded language code. Thus, for a custom AppWizard that supports Japanese, the templates named DLGLOC.RC and ROOT.HPJ will be renamed as DLGLOC_JPN.RC and ROOT_JPN.HPJ. The names of nonlocalized templates remain the same.

AppWizard provides a set of templates that are common to all project types and some that are unique to each major project type. Major project types are dynamic-link library, dialog-based, single document interface (SDI), and multiple document interface (MDI). In addition, AppWizard provides resource templates for help files, as well as database, OLE, and Macintosh applications. The following sections provide details about the individual templates:

All AppWizard Projects

Dialog-Based Applications

Dynamic-Link Libraries

MDI and SDI Applications

OLE Applications

Help File Support

Custom AppWizard Help File Support

Database Applications

Macintosh Applications

All AppWizard Projects

AppWizard copies the following resource templates into every AppWizard project:

README.TXT   Two of these templates are generated: one in a custom AppWizard project's root directory and one in the custom AppWizard project's TEMPLATE directory. The first describes the files that AppWizard generated for your custom AppWizard project. The second is a template that the custom AppWizard writer uses to create a README.TXT file for the custom AppWizard user. This file is one of the templates provided by MFCAPWZ.DLL.

ROOT.RC2   This secondary resource script file is copied to your custom AppWizard project's TEMPLATE directory. Its purpose is to contain those resources that are not edited in Microsoft Developer Studio. Resources that are edited in Microsoft

Developer Studio are kept in the main .RC file. This file is one of the templates provided by MFCAPWZ.DLL.

STDAFX.CPP   This implementation file is copied to your custom AppWizard project's TEMPLATE directory. It is used to build a precompiled header (.PCH) file and a precompiled types file named STDAFX.OBJ. This file is one of the templates provided by MFCAPWZ.DLL.

STDAFX.H   This header file is copied to your custom AppWizard project's TEMPLATE directory. It is used to build a .PCH file and a precompiled types file named STDAFX.OBJ. This file is one of the templates provided by MFCAPWZ.DLL.

See Also   Standard Custom Resource Templates, Dialog-Based Applications, Dynamic-Link Libraries, MDI and SDI Applications, OLE Applications, Help File Support, Custom AppWizard Help File Support, Database Applications, Macintosh Applications

Dialog-Based Applications

DIALOG.CPP   The primary implementation file for the project's main dialog box and About dialog box. This file is one of the templates provided by MFCAPWZ.DLL.

DIALOG.H   The primary header file for the project's main dialog box and About dialog box. This file is one of the templates provided by MFCAPWZ.DLL.

DLGALL.RC   The primary resource script file that contains all resources that are not localized (translated into languages such as French or Japanese). DLGALL.RC includes (via **$$INCLUDE** directives) a resource script file, DLGLOC.RC, that contains all of the localized templates. DLGALL.RC is one of the templates provided by MFCAPWZ.DLL.

DLGLOC.RC   The localized resource script file. A localized version of this template resides in each of the localized-resource DLLs, those with names described by APPWZ*.DLL, such as APPWZDEU.DLL. This template is also used for DLL projects. There is no Macintosh version of DLGLOC.RC because dialog-based applications and DLL projects have no need for separate Macintosh resources.

DLGRES.H   The primary header file for resources. This template is also used for dynamic-link libraries. This file is one of the templates provided by MFCAPWZ.DLL.

DLGROOT.CLW   ClassWizard information file for dialog-based applications generated by AppWizard. This file is one of the templates provided by MFCAPWZ.DLL.

DLGROOT.CPP   The primary implementation file, *project*.CPP, where *project* is the project name entered by the end user of the custom AppWizard. This file is one of the templates provided by MFCAPWZ.DLL.

DLGROOT.H   The primary header file, *project*.H, where *project* is the project name entered by the end user of the custom AppWizard. This file is one of the templates provided by MFCAPWZ.DLL.

ROOT.ICO   The application icon. This template is also used by MDI and SDI applications. It is one of the templates provided by MFCAPWZ.DLL.

See Also   Standard Custom Resource Templates, All AppWizard Projects, Dynamic-Link Libraries, MDI and SDI Applications, OLE Applications, Help File Support, Custom AppWizard Help File Support, Database Applications, Macintosh Applications

Dynamic-Link Libraries

DLGRES.H   The primary header file for resources. This template is also used for dialog-based applications. It is one of the templates provided by MFCAPWZ.DLL.

DLLROOT.CLW   The ClassWizard information file for DLLs generated by AppWizard. This file is one of the templates provided by MFCAPWZ.DLL.

DLLROOT.CPP   The primary implementation file, *project*.CPP, where *project* is the project name entered by the end user of the custom AppWizard. This file is one of the templates provided by MFCAPWZ.DLL.

DLLROOT.H   The primary header file, *project*.H, where *project* is the project name entered by the end user of the custom AppWizard. This file is one of the templates provided by MFCAPWZ.DLL.

ROOT.DEF   The module-definition file, *project*.H, where *project* is the project name entered by the end user of the custom AppWizard. The module-definition file contains the list of functions to be exported from the end user's DLL. This file is one of the templates provided by MFCAPWZ.DLL.

See Also   Standard Custom Resource Templates, All AppWizard Projects, Dialog-Based Applications, MDI and SDI Applications, OLE Applications, Help File Support, Custom AppWizard Help File Support, Database Applications, Macintosh Applications

MDI and SDI Applications

AFXCORE.RTF   A rich-text file for generating a help (.HLP) file. This file is one of the resource templates provided by the localized language DLLs, such as APPWZJPN.DLL.

ALL.RC   The primary resource script file that resides in MFCAPWZ.DLL and contains all resources that are not localized (translated into languages such as French or Japanese). ALL.RC includes, via **$$INCLUDE** directives, two localized templates that contain all of the localized resources: LOC.RC and MACLOC.RC. Localized versions of these templates reside in each of the localized-resource DLLs, those with names described by APPWZ*.DLL, such as APPWZDEU.DLL.

CHILDFRM.CPP   The child-frame implementation file. This file is one of the templates provided by MFCAPWZ.DLL.

CHILDFRM.H   The child-frame header file. This file is one of the templates provided by MFCAPWZ.DLL.

DOC.CPP   The document implementation file. This file is one of the templates provided by MFCAPWZ.DLL.

DOC.H   The document header file. This file is one of the templates provided by MFCAPWZ.DLL.

DOC.ICO   The document icon. This file is one of the resource templates provided by the localized language DLLs, such as APPWZJPN.DLL.

FRAME.CPP   The main-frame implementation file. This file is one of the templates provided by MFCAPWZ.DLL.

FRAME.H   The main-frame header file. This file is one of the templates provided by MFCAPWZ.DLL.

LOC.RC   The localized resource script file that contains all the localizable lines of the .RC file except for the Macintosh menus and accelerators. This file is one of the resource templates provided by the localized language DLLs, such as APPWZJPN.DLL.

RESOURCE.H   The primary header file for resources. It is one of the templates provided by MFCAPWZ.DLL.

ROOT.CPP   The primary implementation file, *project*.CPP, where *project* is the project name entered by the end user of the custom AppWizard. This file is one of the templates provided by MFCAPWZ.DLL.

ROOT.H   The primary header file, *project*.H, where *project* is the project name entered by the end user of the custom AppWizard. This file is one of the templates provided by MFCAPWZ.DLL.

ROOT.CLW   The ClassWizard information file for SDI and MDI applications generated by AppWizard. This file is one of the templates provided by MFCAPWZ.DLL.

ROOT.ICO The application icon. This template is also used by dialog-based applications. It is one of the templates provided by MFCAPWZ.DLL.

VIEW.CPP   The view implementation file. This file is one of the templates provided by MFCAPWZ.DLL.

VIEW.H   The view header file. This file is one of the templates provided by MFCAPWZ.DLL.

APPEXIT.BMP   A bitmap, for use in help files, that creates the user interface for closing the application. This file is one of the resource templates provided by the localized language DLLs, such as APPWZJPN.DLL.

BULLET.BMP   A bitmap, for use in help files, that creates a bullet for items in a bulleted list. This file is one of the resource templates provided by MFCAPWZ.DLL.

CURARW2.BMP   A bitmap, for use in help files, that creates the horizontal-sizing cursor. This file is one of the resource templates provided by MFCAPWZ.DLL.

CURARW4.BMP   A bitmap, for use in help files, that creates the move cursor. This file is one of the resource templates provided by MFCAPWZ.DLL.

CURHELP.BMP   A bitmap, for use in help files, that creates the toolbar button for SHIFT+F1 help. This file is one of the resource templates provided by MFCAPWZ.DLL.

EDITCOPY.BMP   A bitmap, for use in help files, that creates the toolbar button for the Edit menu's Copy command. This file is one of the resource templates provided by MFCAPWZ.DLL.

EDITCUT.BMP   A bitmap, for use in help files, that creates the toolbar button for the Edit menu's Cut command. This file is one of the resource templates provided by MFCAPWZ.DLL.

EDITPAST.BMP   A bitmap, for use in help files, that creates the toolbar button for the Edit menu's Paste command. This file is one of the resource templates provided by MFCAPWZ.DLL.

EDITUNDO.BMP   A bitmap, for use in help files, that creates the toolbar button for the Edit menu's Undo command. This file is one of the resource templates provided by MFCAPWZ.DLL.

FILENEW.BMP   A bitmap, for use in help files, that creates the toolbar button for the File menu's New command. This file is one of the resource templates provided by MFCAPWZ.DLL.

FILEOPEN.BMP   A bitmap, for use in help files, that creates the toolbar button for the File menu's Open command. This file is one of the resource templates provided by MFCAPWZ.DLL.

FILEPRNT.BMP   A bitmap, for use in help files, that creates the toolbar button for the File menu's Print command. This file is one of the resource templates provided by MFCAPWZ.DLL.

FILESAVE.BMP   A bitmap, for use in help files, that creates the toolbar button for the File menu's Save command. This file is one of the resource templates provided by MFCAPWZ.DLL.

HLPSBAR.BMP   A bitmap, for use in help files, that creates the status bar. This file is one of the resource templates provided by the localized language DLLs, such as APPWZJPN.DLL.

HLPTBAR.BMP   A bitmap, for use in help files, that creates a cutaway view of the toolbar. This file is one of the resource templates provided by MFCAPWZ.DLL.

RECFIRST.BMP   A bitmap, for use in help files, that creates the toolbar button for the Record menu's First command. This file is one of the resource templates provided by MFCAPWZ.DLL.

RECLAST.BMP   A bitmap, for use in help files, that creates the toolbar button for the Record menu's Last command. This file is one of the resource templates provided by MFCAPWZ.DLL.

RECNEXT.BMP   A bitmap, for use in help files, that creates the toolbar button for the Record menu's Next command. This file is one of the resource templates provided by MFCAPWZ.DLL.

RECPREV.BMP   A bitmap, for use in help files, that creates the toolbar button for the Record menu's Previous command. This file is one of the resource templates provided by MFCAPWZ.DLL.

SCMAX.BMP   A bitmap, for use in help files, that creates the frame's maximize button. This file is one of the resource templates provided by MFCAPWZ.DLL.

SCMENU.BMP   A bitmap, for use in help files, that creates a cutaway view of the System and File menus. This file is one of the resource templates provided by the localized language DLLs, such as APPWZJPN.DLL.

SCMIN.BMP   A bitmap, for use in help files, that creates the frame's minimize button. This file is one of the resource templates provided by MFCAPWZ.DLL.

TBA___.BMP   A bitmap that creates the default toolbar. The toolbar does not include a Help button. This file is one of the resource templates provided by MFCAPWZ.DLL.

TBAH__.BMP   A bitmap that creates the default toolbar and includes a Help button. This file is one of the resource templates provided by MFCAPWZ.DLL.

TBD__.BMP   A bitmap that creates the default toolbar and includes a database view without file support. The toolbar does not include a Help button. This file is one of the resource templates provided by MFCAPWZ.DLL.

TBDH_.BMP   A bitmap that creates the default toolbar and includes a database view with no file support. The toolbar includes a Help button. This file is one of the resource templates provided by MFCAPWZ.DLL.

TBR__.BMP   A bitmap that creates the default toolbar and includes a database view and file support. The toolbar does not include Help button. This file is one of the resource templates provided by MFCAPWZ.DLL.

TBRH_.BMP   A bitmap that creates the default toolbar and includes a database view and file support. The toolbar includes a Help button. This file is one of the resource templates provided by MFCAPWZ.DLL.

See Also   Standard Custom Resource Templates, Dialog-Based Applications, Dynamic-Link Libraries, OLE Applications, Help File Support, Custom AppWizard Help File Support, Database Applications, Macintosh Applications

OLE Applications

AFXOLECL.RTF   A rich-text file for generating a help (.HLP) file containing information on MDI and SDI OLE containers. This file is one of the resource templates provided by the localized language DLLs, such as APPWZJPN.DLL.

AFXOLESV.RTF   A rich-text file for generating an MDI and SDI OLE server application's help file. This file is one of the resource templates provided by the localized language DLLs, such as APPWZJPN.DLL.

CNTRITEM.CPP   The container-item implementation file for MDI and SDI OLE container applications.

CNTRITEM.H   The container-item header file for MDI and SDI OLE container applications.

IPFRAME.CPP   The in-place frame implementation file for MDI and SDI OLE server applications.

IPFRAME.H   The in-place frame header file for MDI and SDI OLE server applications.

ROOT.REG   The registry information file to contain the globally unique identifier (GUID) that an application must expose to the registry, along with all other information needed to register the generated application as an OLE server or the default editor of a particular document type. All references to a GUID in this file are through AppWizard macros whose values are set when the end user chooses OLE server or OLE automation from the OLE Options dialog box.

ROOT.ODL   The Object Description Language file to contain a GUID for each OLE object that an application must expose through OLE automation. All references to a GUID in this file are through AppWizard macros whose values are set when the end user chooses OLE automation from the OLE Options dialog box.

SRVRITEM.CPP   The server-item implementation file for MDI and SDI OLE server applications.

SRVRITEM.H   The server-item header file for MDI and SDI OLE server applications.

TBA_I.BMP   A bitmap file that creates an in-place frame toolbar for default OLE server and mini-server applications. The toolbar does not include a Help button. An OLE server application displays TBA_I.BMP, rather than TBA__.BMP, upon activation as an in-place server from within an OLE container application. Mini-servers only use the in-place toolbar because mini-servers can't be launched as stand-alone applications. This file is one of the resource templates provided by MFCAPWZ.DLL.

TBAHI.BMP   A bitmap file that creates an in-place frame toolbar for default OLE server and mini-server applications. The toolbar includes a Help button. An OLE server application displays TBAHI.BMP, rather than TBAH_.BMP, upon activation as an in-place server from within an OLE container application. Mini-servers only use the in-place toolbar because mini-servers can't be launched as stand-alone applications. This file is one of the resource templates provided by MFCAPWZ.DLL.

TBRHI.BMP   A bitmap file that creates a floating, dockable toolbar for the in-place frame toolbar, which includes database view and file support. The toolbar includes a Help button. An OLE server application with a database view displays TBRHI.BMP, rather than TBRH_.BMP, upon activation as an in-place server from within an OLE container application. Mini-servers only use the in-place toolbar because mini-servers can't be launched as stand-alone applications. This file is one of the resource templates provided by MFCAPWZ.DLL.

TBR_I.BMP   A bitmap file that creates a floating, dockable toolbar for the in-place frame toolbar, which includes database view and file support. The toolbar does not include a Help button. An OLE server application with a database view displays TBR_I.BMP, rather than TBR__.BMP, upon activation as an in-place server from within an OLE container application. Mini-servers only use the in-place toolbar because mini-servers can't be launched as stand-alone applications. This file is one of the resource templates provided by MFCAPWZ.DLL.

See Also   Standard Custom Resource Templates, All AppWizard Projects, Dialog-Based Applications, Dynamic-Link Libraries, MDI and SDI Applications, Help File Support, Custom AppWizard Help File Support, Database Applications, Macintosh Applications

Help File Support

AFXDLG.RTF   This rich-text file is copied to your custom AppWizard project's TEMPLATE directory. It is used to generate a help (.HLP) file for dialog-based applications. This file is one of the resource templates provided by the localized language DLLs, such as APPWZJPN.DLL.

AFXPRINT.RTF   This rich-text file is copied to your custom AppWizard project's TEMPLATE directory. It contains only print and print preview topics and is used to generate a help file for MDI and SDI applications that use printing and print preview. This file is one of the resource templates provided by the localized language DLLs, such as APPWZJPN.DLL.

DLGROOT.CNT   Windows 95 WinHelp contents file for dialog-based applications. This text file creates the hierarchy of help topics that is displayed on the Contents tab of your custom AppWizard's help file.The nodes of the hierarchy are links into the actual help file. This file is one of the templates provided by MFCAPWZ.DLL.

ROOT.CNT   Windows 95 WinHelp contents file for SDI and MDI applications. This text file creates the hierarchy of help topics that is displayed on the Contents tab of your custom AppWizard's help file.The nodes of the hierarchy are links into the actual help file. This file is one of the templates provided by MFCAPWZ.DLL.

ROOT.HPJ   This help project file is copied to your custom AppWizard project's TEMPLATE directory. It is used to generate Win32 application help files and lists all of the .RTF files that MAKEHELP.BAT must process to produce an .HLP file.

This file is one of the resource templates provided by the localized language DLLs, such as APPWZJPN.DLL.

See Also   Standard Custom Resource Templates, All AppWizard Projects, Dialog-Based Applications, Dynamic-Link Libraries, MDI and SDI Applications, OLE Applications, Custom AppWizard Help File Support, Database Applications, Macintosh Applications

Custom AppWizard Help File Support

AppWizard gives you the tools you need to create context-sensitive help for the custom steps in your custom AppWizard:

- A starter file in rich-text format (.RTF) that contains a topic for each custom step AppWizard generates. You need only use an .RTF editor (such as Microsoft Word) to supply the text for the ready-made topics.

- A MAKEHELP.BAT that generates a header map (.HM) file and compiles the custom AppWizard's help (.HLP) file. The .HM file defines (**#define**) the help IDs of your custom custom AppWizard steps to numeric values that are readable by the help compiler (HC30.EXE and HC31.EXE). It also invokes the help compiler to generate the help file.

- A help project (.HPJ) file that controls compiling the .RTF file into an .HLP file.

Your custom AppWizard file, which has an extension of .AWX, and its help file must use the same base filename, and both must reside in MSDEV\TEMPLATE. When the custom AppWizard user clicks a custom step's Help button, MFCAPWZ.DLL invokes WinHelp and passes it the current step's help ID and the name of your custom AppWizard's help file.

Note   You cannot integrate your custom AppWizard's help with the Microsoft Developer Studio help system. However, if you build a custom AppWizard that uses an existing sequence of AppWizard steps, your custom AppWizard will automatically use the Microsoft Developer Studio help file that was created for the standard AppWizard steps. Your custom AppWizard will use your own WinHelp help file for the custom steps. The effect is seamless to the user.

See Also   Standard Custom Resource Templates, All AppWizard Projects, Dialog-Based Applications, Dynamic-Link Libraries, MDI and SDI Applications, OLE Applications, Help File Support, Database Applications, Macintosh Applications

Database Applications

The following resources support the database features that AppWizard offers.

AFXDB.RTF   Rich text file. for generating a database-application help (.HLP) file. This file is one of the resource templates provided by the localized language DLLs, such as APPWZJPN.DLL.

RECSET.CPP   Recordset implementation file for MDI and SDI applications. This file is one of the templates provided by MFCAPWZ.DLL.

RECSET.H Recordset header file for MDI and SDI applications. This file is one of the templates provided by MFCAPWZ.DLL.

TBDH_.BMP Bitmap file that creates a toolbar for database view applications without file support. This file is one of the resource templates provided by MFCAPWZ.DLL.

See Also Standard Custom Resource Templates, All AppWizard Projects, Dialog-Based Applications, Dynamic-Link Libraries, MDI and SDI Applications, OLE Applications, Help File Support, Custom AppWizard Help File Support, Macintosh Applications

Macintosh Applications

AFXCRMAC.RTF This rich-text file is copied to your custom AppWizard project's TEMPLATE directory. It is used to generate a Macintosh help file for MDI and SDI applications. This file is one of the resource templates provided by the localized language DLLs, such as APPWZJPN.DLL.

AFXPTMAC.RTF This rich-text file is copied to your custom AppWizard project's TEMPLATE directory. It contains only print and print preview topics and is used to generate a help (.HLP) file for Macintosh MDI and SDI applications that use printing and print preview. This file is one of the resource templates provided by the localized language DLLs, such as APPWZJPN.DLL.

MACCMD.BMP A bitmap, for use in help files, that creates the Macintosh command-key symbol. This file is one of the resource templates provided by MFCAPWZ.DLL.

MACLOC.RC A localized resource script file that contains all of the Macintosh menus and accelerators. This file is one of the resource templates provided by the localized language DLLs, such as APPWZJPN.DLL.

MACROOT.HPJ This help project file is copied to your custom AppWizard project's TEMPLATE directory. It is used to generate a Macintosh help file and lists all of the .RTF files that MAKEHELP.BAT must process to produce an .HLP file. This file is one of the resource templates provided by the localized language DLLs, such as APPWZJPN.DLL.

ROOT.R Resource script containing all of the Macintosh-specific resources. This file is one of the resource templates provided by MFCAPWZ.DLL.

See Also Standard Custom Resource Templates, All AppWizard Projects, Dialog-Based Applications, Dynamic-Link Libraries, MDI and SDI Applications, OLE Applications, Help File Support, Custom AppWizard Help File Support, Database Applications

Command-Line Tools

CL Reference

CL is a 32-bit tool that controls the Microsoft C and C++ compilers and linker. The compilers produce Common Object File Format (COFF) object (.OBJ) files. The linker produces executable (.EXE) files or dynamic-link libraries (DLLs).

Most compiler options are available on the C/C++ tab of the Project Settings dialog box. Each of the options on the C/C++ tab is described in Chapter 20, "Setting Compiler Options." The description of each option includes the name of the equivalent command-line option.

An alphabetic reference to the CL options not available as options on the C/C++ tab of the Project Settings dialog box begins on page 552 in this chapter. Other topics covered include:

- Description of CL syntax
- Using CL

Description of CL Syntax

The CL command line uses the following syntax:

CL [*option...*] *file...* [*option* | *file*]... [*lib...*] [@*command-file*] [/link *link-opt...*]

The following table describes input to the CL command.

Entry	Meaning
option	One or more CL options. See Chapter 20, "Setting Compiler Options," and "Reference to Command-Line Only Options," later in this chapter, for more information.
	Note that all options apply to all specified source files.
file	The name of one or more source files, .OBJ files, or libraries. CL compiles source files and passes the names of the .OBJ files and libraries to the linker.
lib	One or more library names. CL passes these names to the linker.

Entry	Meaning
command-file	A file that contains multiple options and filenames. See "CL Command Files," later in this chapter, for more information.
link-opt	One or more of the linker options described in Chapter 21, "Setting Linker Options," and Chapter 26, "LINK Reference." CL passes these options to the linker.

You can specify any number of options, filenames, and library names, as long as the number of characters on the command line does not exceed 1024, the limit dictated by the operating system.

Note The command-line input limit of 1024 characters is not guaranteed to remain the same in future releases of Windows NT.

Filename Syntax

CL accepts files with names that follow FAT, HPFS, or NTFS naming conventions. Any filename can include a full or partial path. A full path includes a drive name and one or more directory names. CL accepts filenames separated either by backslashes (\) or forward slashes (/). A partial path omits the drive name, which CL assumes to be the current drive. If you don't specify a path, CL assumes the file is in the current directory.

The filename extension determines how files are processed. C and C++ files, which have the extension .C, .CXX, or .CPP, are compiled. Other files, including .OBJ files, libraries (.LIB), and module-definition (.DEF) files, are passed to the linker without being processed.

Specifying CL Options

You can specify CL options on the command line, in command files, and in the CL environment variable. Options specified in the CL environment variable are used every time you invoke CL. If a command file is named in the CL environment variable or on the command line, the options specified in the command file are used. Unlike either the command line or the CL environment variable, a command file allows you to use multiple lines of options and filenames. See "CL Command Files" and "CL Environment Variable" later in this chapter for more information.

Options are specified by either a forward slash (/) or a dash (–). If an option takes an argument, the option's description documents whether a space is allowed between the option and the arguments. Option names (except for the /HELP option) are case sensitive.

Order of Options

Options can appear anywhere on the CL command line, except for the /link option, which must occur last. The compiler begins with options specified in the CL

environment variable and then reads the command line from left to right—
processing command files in the order it encounters them. Each option applies to all
files on the command line. If CL encounters conflicting options, it uses the rightmost
option.

CL Command Files

A command file is a text file that contains options and filenames you would otherwise
type on the command line or specify using the CL environment variable. CL accepts
a compiler command file as an argument in the CL environment variable or on the
command line. Unlike either the command line or the CL environment variable, a
command file allows you to use multiple lines of options and filenames.

Options and filenames in a command file are processed according to the location of a
command filename within the CL environment variable or on the command line.
However, if the /link option appears in the command file, all options on the rest of the
line are passed to the linker. Options in subsequent lines in the command file and
options on the command line after the command file invocation are still accepted as
compiler options. For more information on how the order of options affects their
interpretation, see the previous section, Order of Options.

A command file must not contain the CL command. Each option must begin and end
on the same line; you cannot use the backslash (\) to combine an option across two
lines.

A command file is specified by an at sign (@) followed by a filename; the filename
can specify an absolute or relative path.

Example
If the following command is in a file named RESP:

```
/Og /link LIBC.LIB
```

and you specify the following CL command:

```
CL /Ob2 @RESP MYAPP.C
```

the command to CL is as follows:

```
CL /Ob2 /Og MYAPP.C /link LIBC.LIB
```

Note that the command line and the command-file commands are effectively
combined.

CL Environment Variable

Use the CL environment variable to specify files and options without giving them on
the command line. The CL environment variable has the following syntax:

SET CL=[[*option*] ... [*file*] ...] [/link *link-opt* ...]

The CL environment variable is useful if you often specify a large number of *files* and *options* when you compile. You can define the *files* and *options* you use most often with the CL variable and give only the *files* and *options* you need for specific purposes on the command line. The CL environment variable is currently limited to 1024 characters—the command-line input limit in Windows NT.

You cannot use the /D option to define a symbol that uses an equal sign (=). You can substitute the number sign (#) for an equal sign. In this way, you can use the CL environment variable to define preprocessor constants with explicit values (for example, /DDEBUG#1).

Example

The following example of a CL environment variable setting:

```
SET CL=/Zp2 /Ox /I\INCLUDE\MYINCLS \LIB\BINMODE.OBJ
```

is equivalent to the following CL command:

```
CL /Zp2 /Ox /I\INCLUDE\MYINCLS \LIB\BINMODE.OBJ INPUT.C
```

The following example causes CL to compile the source files FILE1.C and FILE2.C, and then link the object files FILE1.OBJ, FILE2.OBJ, and FILE3.OBJ:

```
SET CL=FILE1.C FILE2.C
CL FILE3.OBJ
```

This has the same effect as the following command line:

```
CL FILE1.C FILE2.C FILE3.OBJ
```

Using CL

You can use CL to compile specified source files into COFF .OBJ files, or to compile and link source files, .OBJ files, and libraries into an .EXE file or a DLL. To compile without linking, use the /c option.

Fast Compilation

One way to speed compilation is to use minimal rebuild and incremental compilation. With minimal rebuild, a feature specific to C++, the compiler can recompile a source file only if it is dependent on changes to a class in a header file. With incremental compilation, the compiler only recompiles those functions that have changed since the last compile time.

For more information on minimal rebuild, see "Enable Minimal Rebuild" in Chapter 20. For more information on incremental compilation, see "Incremental Compilation" in Chapter 20.

You can also use the precompiled header options to speed compilation. For more information on the precompiled header options, see "Precompiled Headers" in Chapter 20.

Linking

CL automatically invokes the linker after compiling unless the /c option is used. CL passes to the linker the names of .OBJ files created during compiling and the names of any other files specified on the command line. The linker uses the options listed in the LINK environment variable. You can use the /link option to specify linker options on the CL command line. Options that follow the /link option override those in the LINK environment variable. The options in the following table suppress linking.

Option	Description
/c	Compile without linking
/E, /EP, /P	Preprocess without compiling or linking
/Zg	Generate function prototypes
/Zs	Check syntax

For further details about linking, see Chapter 21, "Setting Linker Options," and Chapter 26, "LINK Reference."

Example

Assume that you are compiling three C source files: MAIN.C, MOD1.C, and MOD2.C. Each file includes a call to a function defined in a different file:

- MAIN.C calls the function func1 in MOD1.C and the function func2 in MOD2.C.

- MOD1.C calls the standard library functions **printf** and **scanf**.

- MOD2.C calls graphics functions named myline and mycircle, which are defined in a library named MYGRAPH.LIB.

To build this program, compile with the following command line:

```
CL MAIN.C MOD1.C MOD2.C MYGRAPH.LIB
```

CL first compiles the C source files and creates the object files MAIN.OBJ, MOD1.OBJ, and MOD2.OBJ. The compiler places the name of the standard library in each .OBJ file. For more details, see "Use Run-Time Library" in Chapter 21.

CL passes the names of the .OBJ files, along with the name MYGRAPH.LIB, to the linker. The linker resolves the external references as follows:

1. In MAIN.OBJ, the reference to func1 is resolved using the definition in MOD1.OBJ; the reference to func2 is resolved using the definition in MOD2.OBJ.

2. In MOD1.OBJ, the references to **printf** and **scanf** are resolved using the definitions in the library that the linker finds named within MOD1.OBJ.

3. In MOD2.OBJ, the references to myline and mycircle are resolved using the definitions in MYGRAPH.LIB.

Reference to Command-Line Only Options

The remainder of this chapter is an alphabetic reference to the CL command-line options that are not available in the categories on the C/C++ tab of the Project Settings dialog box. These options are listed in Table 25.1.

If a command-line option can take one or more arguments, its syntax is shown under a Syntax heading before its description. For more information on these options, see Chapter 20, "Setting Compiler Options."

Table 25.1   CL Options Set from the Command Line

/C	/Ge	/P
/c	/GF	
	/Gh	
/D	/Gs	/Tc
		/Tp
/E	/H	/V
/EP	/HELP	
		/Yd
/F	/J	
/Fd		/Zg
/FI	/LD	/Zl
/Fm	/LDd	/Zs
/Fo	/link	
/Fp		

Table 25.2 shows all options that are available in the categories on the C/C++ tab of the Project Settings dialog box. These options can also be used from the command line. For more information on these options, see Chapter 20, "Setting Compiler Options."

Table 25.2   CL Options Set from the Project Settings Dialog Box

/D	/Gy	/Od	/vmv
	/Gz	/Og	
/FA		/Oi	/w
/Fa	/I	/Op, /Op–	/W
/FR		/Os	/WX
/Fr	/MD	/Ot	
	/MDd	/Ow	/X
/G3	/ML	/Ox	
/G4	/MLd	/Oy, /Oy–	/Yc
/G5	/MT		/Yu

Table 25.2   CL Options Set from the Project Settings Dialog Box *(continued)*

/GB	/MTd	/U	/YX
/Gd		/u	
/Gf	/nologo		/Z7
/Gi, /Gi–		/vd	/Za
/Gm, /Gm–	/O1	/vmb	/Zd
/Gr	/O2	/vmg	/Ze
/GR, /GR–	/Oa	/vmm	/Zi
/GX, /GX–	/Ob	/vms	/Zp

/C

This option preserves comments during preprocessing when used with the /E, /P, or /EP option, and is not valid if /E, /P, or /EP is not used. If you do not specify the /C option, the preprocessor does not pass source-file comments to its output file.

/c

This option suppresses linking; only .OBJ files are created. No .EXE file or DLL is produced.

Example
The following example creates the object files FIRST.OBJ and SECOND.OBJ. The file THIRD.OBJ is ignored.

```
CL /c FIRST.C SECOND.C THIRD.OBJ
```

/D

Syntax
/Dname[= | # [{*string* | *number*}]]

This option defines symbols or constants for your source file.

The *name* is the name of the symbol or constant. It can be defined as a string or as a number. No space can separate /D and *name*. Enclose the *string* in double quotation marks (") if it includes spaces. If you omit both the equal sign (=) and the *string* or *number*, the *name* is assumed to be defined, and its value is set to 1. Note that the *name* argument is case sensitive.

Defining symbols and constants with the /D option has the same effect as using a **#define** preprocessor directive at the beginning of your source file. The constant is defined until either an **#undef** directive in the source file removes the definition, or the compiler reaches the end of the file.

You cannot set the CL environment variable to a string that contains an equal sign (=). To use /D with the CL environment variable, specify a number sign (#) instead of an equal sign (=):

```
SET CL "/DTEST#0"
```

Note The action of /D differs from the Preprocessor Definitions option available in both the General category and the Preprocessor category. These categories are on the C/C++ tab of the Project Settings dialog box. With the /D option, you can define a symbol and use an equal sign (=) or a number sign (#) to assign the symbol a value.

Use the constants created by the compiler and the /D option in combination with either the **#if** or **#ifdef** directive to compile source files conditionally.

You can redefine a keyword, identifier, or numeric constant that has been defined in a source file. If a constant defined in a /D option is also defined within the source file, CL uses the definition on the command line until it encounters a redefinition in the source file.

You can undefine a previous definition. To do so, use the /D option with a keyword, identifier, or numeric constant, and append an equal sign (=) followed by a space.

Examples

The following command removes all occurrences of the keyword **__far** in TEST.C:

```
CL /D__far=  TEST.C
```

The following command defines the symbol DEBUG in TEST.C:

```
CL /DDEBUG  TEST.C
```

/E

This option preprocesses C and C++ source files and copies the preprocessed file to the standard output device. The output is identical to the original source file, except that all preprocessor directives are carried out, macro expansions are performed, and comments are removed. You can use the /C option with /E to preserve comments in the preprocessed output.

Unlike the /EP option, /E adds **#line** directives to the output. The **#line** directives are placed at the beginning and end of each included file and around lines removed by preprocessor directives that specify conditional compilation. Use the /E option when you want to resubmit the preprocessed listing for compilation. The **#line** directives renumber the lines of the preprocessed file so that errors generated during later stages of processing refer to the line numbers of the original source file rather than to the preprocessed file. You can use the /EP option to suppress **#line** directives.

The /E option suppresses compilation. It also suppresses the output files from the /FA, /Fa, and /Fm options.

Note You cannot use precompiled headers with the /E option.

The following table summarizes the actions of the /E, /EP, and /P options.

Option	Result
/E	Sends preprocessor output, including **#line** directives, to **stdout**.
/P	Sends preprocessor output, including **#line** directives, to a file (.I).
/EP	Sends preprocessor output, without **#line** directives, to **stdout**.
/E /EP	Sends preprocessor output, without **#line** directives, to **stdout**.
/P /EP	Sends preprocessor output, without **#line** directives, to a file (.I).

Example

The following command creates a preprocessed file from the source file ADD.C. It preserves comments and adds **#line** directives. The output is displayed:

```
CL /E /C ADD.C
```

/EP

The /EP option is similar to the /E option. It preprocesses C and C++ source files and copies the preprocessed file to the standard output device. The output is identical to the original source file, except that all preprocessor directives are carried out, macro expansions are performed, and comments are removed. You can use the /C option with /EP to preserve comments in the preprocessed output. Unlike /E, however, /EP does not add **#line** directives to the output.

The /EP option suppresses compilation. It also suppresses the output files from the /FA, /Fa, and /Fm options.

The following table summarizes the actions of the /E, /EP, and /P options.

Option	Result
/E	Sends preprocessor output, including **#line** directives, to **stdout**.
/P	Sends preprocessor output, including **#line** directives, to a file (.I).
/EP	Sends preprocessor output, without **#line** directives, to **stdout**.
/E /EP	Sends preprocessor output, without **#line** directives, to **stdout**.
/P /EP	Sends preprocessor output, without **#line** directives, to a file (.I).

Example

The following command creates a preprocessed file from the source file ADD.C. It preserves comments, but does not insert **#line** directives. The output is displayed:

```
CL /EP /C ADD.C
```

/F

Syntax

/F *number*

This option sets the program stack size to a specified number of bytes. If you don't specify this option, a stack size of 1 MB is used by default. The *number* argument can be in decimal or C notation. The argument can range from a lower limit of one to the maximum stack size accepted by your linker. A space is optional between /F and *number*.

You can also set stack size by using the linker's /STACK option or by running EDITBIN on an .EXE file.

You may want to increase the stack size if your program gets stack-overflow diagnostic messages.

Output-File Options

These output-file options create or rename output files. They affect all C or C++ source files specified in the CL environment variable, on the command line, or in any command file. They include:

- /Fd (Name the Program Database and Incremental Compilation State File)
- /Fe (Name the Executable File)
- /Fm (Generate a Map File)
- /Fo (Name the Object File)
- /Fp (Name or Use a Precompiled Header File)

Other output-file options are available in the Listing Files category on the C/C++ tab of the Project Settings dialog box. They include:

- Generate Browse Info (/FR)
- Exclude Local Variables (/Fr)
- Intermediate Browse Info File Destination (/FR[*filename*] or /Fr[*filename*])
- Listing File Type (/FA[cls])
- Listing File Name (/Fa[*filename*])

For more information on the Generate Browse Info, Exclude Local Variables, Intermediate Browse Info File Destination, Listing File Type, and Listing File Name options, see "Listing Files" in Chapter 20.

Drive, Path, and File Specifications

Each output-file option accepts a *filename* argument, with which you can specify a location and a name for the output file. The argument can include a drive name, a path specification, and/or a filename. No space is allowed between the option and the argument.

If *filename* is a path without a filename (that is, a directory), end the path with a backslash (\) to differentiate it from a filename. If a filename is specified without an extension, the output file is given a default extension. If no argument is specified, the output file is given the base name of the source file and an extension determined by the type of output file.

Device Names for Windows

You can append the device names AUX, CON, PRN, and NUL to the output-file options to direct the output file to the named device. No space is allowed between the option and the device name. Do not append a colon (:) to the device name. The device names and their behavior are shown in the following table.

Device name	Result
AUX	The listing file is sent to an auxiliary device.
CON	The listing file is sent to the console.
PRN	The listing file is sent to a printer.
NUL	No file is created.

Example
In the following example, appending PRN to /Fm sends a map file to the printer:

```
CL /FmPRN HELLO.CPP
```

/Fd

Syntax
/Fd*filename*

This option specifies a filename for a program database (PDB) other than the default name, VC40.PDB, created by /Zi. No space is allowed between /Fd and *filename*. If you do not specify an extension to *filename*, the extension .PDB is used. If *filename* ends in a backslash (to specify the name of a directory), the default filename, VC40.PDB, is used. For information on PDBs, see "Debug Info" in Chapter 20.

Note This option also names the compiler's state or .IDB file (used by minimal rebuild and incremental compilation).

Example

The following command creates a .PDB file called PROG.PDB that contains debugging information and an .IDB file called PROG.IDB that contains incremental compilation and minimal rebuild information.

```
CL /DDEBUG /Zi /FdPROG.PDB PROG.CPP
```

/Fe

Syntax

/Fefilename

This option names an .EXE file or DLL or creates it in a different directory. No space is allowed between /Fe and *filename*. By default, CL names the file with the base name of the first file (source or object) on the command line plus the extension .EXE (or .DLL if you use the /LD option to create a dynamic-link library).

If you specify the /c option to suppress linking, /Fe has no effect.

Examples

The following example compiles and links all C source files in the current directory. The resulting executable file is named PROCESS.EXE and is created in the directory C:\BIN.

```
CL /FeC:\BIN\PROCESS *.C
```

The following example is similar to the first example, except that the executable file is given the same base name as the first file compiled instead of being named PROCESS.EXE. The .EXE file is created in the directory C:\BIN.

```
CL /FeC:\BIN\ *.C
```

/FI

Syntax

/FI filename

The /FI option causes the preprocessor to process the header file specified by *filename*. Each *filename* is included as if it were specified with double quotation marks (") in an **#include** directive on line 0 of every C or C++ source file specified in the CL environment variable, on the command line, or in any command file. If multiple /FI options are used, the files are included in the order they are processed by CL. The space between /FI and *filename* is optional.

/Fm

Syntax
/Fm[*filename*]

This option instructs the linker to produce a map file. No space is allowed between
/Fm and *filename*. The map file contains a list of segments in the order of their
appearance within the corresponding .EXE file or DLL. By default, the map file is
given the base name of the corresponding C or C++ source file with a .MAP
extension. If you specify the /c option to suppress linking, /Fm has no effect.

Global symbols in a map file usually have one or more leading underscores, because
the compiler adds an underscore to the beginning of variable names. Many of the
global symbols that appear in the map file are symbols used internally by the
compiler and the standard libraries.

/Fo

Syntax
/Fo*filename*

This option names an .OBJ file or creates it in a different directory. No space is
allowed between /Fo and *filename*. By default, CL names the object file with the base
name of the source file plus the extension .OBJ. You can give any name and
extension you want for *filename*. However, it is recommended that you use the
conventional .OBJ extension.

Example
The following command line compiles the source file THIS.C and gives the resulting
object file the name THIS.OBJ by default. The directory specification B:\OBJECT\
tells CL to create THIS.OBJ in an existing directory named \OBJECT on drive B.

```
CL /FoB:\OBJECT\ THIS.C
```

/Fp

Syntax
/Fp*filename*

Use the /Fp option with the /YX, /Yc, and /Yu options to provide a name for a
precompiled header (.PCH) file (and path) that is different from the default. You can
also use /Fp to specify the use of a .PCH file that is different from the *filename*
argument to the /Yc option or the base name of the source file.

No space is allowed between /Fp and *filename*. If you do not specify an extension to
filename, an extension of .PCH is assumed. If *filename* ends in a backslash (to specify

the name of a directory), the default filename VC40.PCH is appended to *filename*. For more information, see the related options under "Precompiled Headers" in Chapter 20.

Examples

The following command renames the default VC40.PCH file created and used by /YX:

```
CL /YX /FpMYPCH.PCH PROG.CPP
```

The following command creates a precompiled header file DPROG.PCH for a debugging version of a program:

```
CL /DDEBUG /Zi /Yc /FpDPROG.PCH PROG.CPP
```

The following command specifies the use of a precompiled header file named MYPCH.PCH. The compiler assumes that the source code in PROG.CPP has been precompiled through MYAPP.H, and that the precompiled code resides in MYPCH.PCH. It uses the content of MYPCH.PCH and compiles the rest of PROG.CPP to create an .OBJ file. Because none of these options suppresses the linker, the output of this example is a file named PROG.EXE.

```
CL /YuMYAPP.H /FpMYPCH.PCH PROG.CPP
```

/Ge

This option (and the /Gs option with a *size* of 0) activates stack probes for every function call that requires storage for local variables. This mechanism is useful only if you rewrite the functionality of the stack probe. It is recommended that you use the /Gh option rather than rewriting the stack probe.

/GF

This option causes the compiler to pool strings and place them in read-only memory. By placing the strings in read-only memory, the operating system does not need to swap that portion of memory. Instead, it can read the strings back from the image file.

Strings placed in read-only memory cannot be modified; if you try to modify them, you will see an Application Error dialog box.

The /GF option is comparable to the /Gf option, except that /Gf does not place the strings in read-only memory. For more information on the /Gf option, see "Eliminate Duplicate Strings" in Chapter 20.

/Gh

This option calls **__penter** at the start of every method or function. The **__penter** function is not part of any library. This call is a hook for your use. Use assembly language to write the function.

Unless you plan to explicitly call **__penter**, you do not need to provide a prototype. The function must appear as if it had the following prototype, and it must push the content of all registers on entry and pop the unchanged content on exit:

```
void __cdecl __penter( void );
```

/Gs

Syntax

/Gs*size*

This option is an advanced feature with which you can control stack probes. A stack probe is a sequence of code that the compiler inserts into every function call. When activated, a stack probe reaches benignly into memory by the amount of space required to store the associated function's local variables.

If a function requires more than *size* stack space for local variables, its stack probe is activated. The default value of *size* is the size of one page (4K for 80x86 processors). This value allows a carefully tuned interaction between an application for Win32 and the Windows NT virtual-memory manager to increase the amount of memory committed to the program stack at run time.

 Warning   The default value of *size* is carefully chosen to allow the program stack of applications for Win32 to grow at run time. Do not change the default setting of /Gs unless you know exactly why you need to change it.

Some programs, such as virtual device drivers, do not require this default stack-growth mechanism. In such cases, the stack probes are not necessary. You can stop the compiler from generating stack probes by setting *size* to a value that is larger than any function will require for local variable storage. No space is allowed between /Gs and *size*.

The /Gs option with a *size* of 0 has the same result as the /Ge option.

You can turn stack probes on or off by using the **check_stack** pragma. Note that the /Gs option and the **check_stack** pragma have no effect on standard C library routines; they affect only the functions you compile. For more information on the **check_stack** pragma, see Chapter 2 of the *Preprocessor Reference*.

/H

Syntax

/H *number*

This option restricts the length of external (public) names. The program can contain external names longer than *number* characters, but the extra characters are ignored. A space between /H and *number* is optional. The compiler imposes no limit on the length of external identifiers.

The limit on length includes any compiler-created leading underscore (_) or at sign (@). The compiler adds a leading underscore (_) to names modified by the __cdecl (default) and __stdcall calling conventions, and a leading at sign (@) to names modified by the __fastcall calling convention. It appends argument size information to names modified by the __fastcall and __stdcall calling conventions, and adds type information to C++ names.

You may find the /H option useful when creating mixed-language or portable programs, or when using tools that impose limits on the length of external identifiers.

/HELP

Syntax
/HELP
/help
/?

This option displays a listing of compiler options to standard output.

/J

This option changes the default **char** type from **signed char** to **unsigned char**, and the **char** type is zero-extended when widened to an **int** type. If a **char** value is explicitly declared **signed**, the /J option does not affect it, and the value is sign-extended when widened to an **int** type.

The /J option defines **_CHAR_UNSIGNED**, which is used with **#ifndef** in the LIMITS.H file to define the range of the default **char** type.

Neither ANSI C nor C++ requires a specific implementation of the **char** type. This option is useful when you are working with character data that will eventually be translated into a language other than English.

/LD

This option creates a dynamic-link library (DLL). The /LD option does the following:

- Passes the /DLL option to the linker. The linker looks for, but does not require, a **DllMain** function. If you do not write a **DllMain** function, the linker inserts a **DllMain** function that returns TRUE.

- Links the DLL startup code.

- Creates an import library (.LIB), if an export (.EXP) file is not specified on the command line; you link the import library to applications that call your DLL.

- Interprets /Fe as naming a DLL rather than an .EXE file; the default program name becomes *basename*.DLL instead of *basename*.EXE. See page 558 in this chapter for more information on /Fe.

- Changes default run-time library support to /MT if you have not explicitly specified /MD, /ML, or /MT. For more information on these options, see "Use Run-Time Library" in Chapter 20.

Examples

The following command line:

```
CL /LD FILE1.CXX FILE2.CXX
```

tells the compiler to pass the following commands to the linker:

```
/OUT:FILE1.DLL
/DLL
/IMPLIB:FILE1.LIB
FILE1.OBJ FILE2.OBJ
```

The following command line creates both DLL\FILE1.DLL and DLL\FILE1.LIB:

```
CL /LD /FeDLL\ FILE1.C
```

If your source code contains no exported functions, the linker does not create an import library.

/LDd

Similar to the /LD option, this option creates a dynamic-link library (DLL), except that it:

- Defines _DEBUG.

- Uses the debug multithreaded library.

- Changes default run-time library support to /MTd if you have not explicitly specified /MDd, /MLd, or /MTd. For more information on these options, see "Use Run-Time Library" in Chapter 20.

Examples

The following command line:

```
CL /LDd FILE1.CXX FILE2.CXX
```

tells the compiler to pass the following commands to the linker:

```
/OUT:FILE1.DLL
/DLL
/IMPLIB:FILE1.LIB
FILE1.OBJ FILE2.OBJ
```

The following command line creates both DLL\FILE1.DLL and DLL\FILE1.LIB:

```
CL /LDd /FeDLL\ FILE1.C
```

If your source code contains no exported functions, the linker does not create an import library.

/link

Syntax

/link *option*

This option passes one or more linker options to LINK. The /link option and its linker options must appear after any filenames and CL options. A space is required between /link and *option*. For more information on the linker, see Chapter 21, "Setting Linker Options," and Chapter 26, "LINK Reference."

/P

This option writes preprocessor output to a file with the same base name as the source file, but with the .I extension. It adds **#line** directives to the output file at the beginning and end of each included file and around lines removed by preprocessor directives that specify conditional compilation. The preprocessed listing file is identical to the original source file, except that all preprocessor directives are carried out, and macro expansions are performed.

This option suppresses compilation; CL does not produce an .OBJ file, even if the /Fo option is specified. The /P option also suppresses production of the alternate output files created by the /FA, /Fa, or /Fm option.

The /P option is similar to the /E and /EP options, described earlier in this chapter. Using /EP with /P suppresses placement of **#line** directives in the output file.

The following table summarizes the actions of the /E, /EP, and /P options.

Option	Result
/E	Sends preprocessor output, including **#line** directives, to **stdout**.
/P	Sends preprocessor output, including **#line** directives, to a file (.I).
/EP	Sends preprocessor output, without **#line** directives, to **stdout**.
/E /EP	Sends preprocessor output, without **#line** directives, to **stdout**.
/P /EP	Sends preprocessor output, without **#line** directives, to a file (.I).

/Tc, /Tp

Syntax

/Tc *filename*
/Tp *filename*

The /Tc option specifies that *filename* is a C source file, even if it doesn't have a .C extension. The /Tp option specifies that *filename* is a C++ source file, even if it doesn't have a .CPP or .CXX extension. A·space between the option and *filename* is optional. Each option specifies one file; to specify additional files, repeat the option.

By default, CL assumes that files with the .C extension are C source files and files with the .CPP or the .CXX extension are C++ source files.

Example

The following CL command line specifies that MAIN.C, TEST.PRG, and COLLATE.PRG are all C source files. CL will not recognize PRINT.PRG.

```
CL MAIN.C /TcTEST.PRG /TcCOLLATE.PRG PRINT.PRG
```

/V

Syntax

/V *string*

This option embeds a text *string* in the .OBJ file. This *string* can label an .OBJ file with a version number or a copyright notice. Any space or tab characters must be enclosed in double quotation marks (") if they are a part of the *string*. A backslash (\) must precede any double quotation marks if they are a part of the *string*. A space between /V and *string* is optional.

You can also use the **comment** pragma with the **compiler** comment-type argument to place the name and version number of the compiler in the .OBJ file. For more information on the **comment** pragma, see comment in Chapter 2 of the *Preprocessor Reference*.

/Yd

This option, when used with the /Yc and /Z7 options, places complete debugging information in all object files created from a precompiled header (.PCH) file. Unless you need to distribute a library containing debugging information, use the /Zi option rather than /Z7 and /Yd. The /Yd option takes no argument. For more information on the debugging options, see "Debug Info" in Chapter 20.

Storing complete debugging information in every .OBJ file is necessary only to distribute libraries that contain debugging information. It slows compilation and requires considerable disk space. When /Yc and /Z7 are used without /Yd, the compiler stores common debugging information in the first .OBJ file created from the .PCH file. The compiler does not insert this information into .OBJ files subsequently created from the .PCH file; it inserts cross-references to the information. No matter how many .OBJ files use the .PCH file, only one .OBJ file contains the common debugging information.

Although this default behavior results in faster build times and reduces disk-space demands, it is undesirable if a small change requires rebuilding the .OBJ file containing the common debugging information. In this case, the compiler must rebuild all .OBJ files containing cross-references to the original .OBJ file. Also, if a common .PCH file is used by different projects, reliance on cross-references to a single .OBJ file is difficult.

Note The /Yd option is implied with use of the /YX option.

/Zg

This option creates a function prototype for each function defined in the source file, but does not compile the source file.

The function prototype includes the function return type and an argument type list. The argument type list is created from the types of the formal parameters of the function. Any function prototypes already present in the source file are ignored.

The list of prototypes is written to standard output. You may find this list helpful to verify that actual arguments and formal parameters of a function are compatible. You can save the list by redirecting standard output to a file. Then you can use **#include** to make the list of function prototypes a part of your source file. Doing so causes the compiler to perform argument type checking.

If you use the /Zg option and your program contains formal parameters that have **struct**, **enum**, or **union** type (or pointers to such types), the prototype for each **struct**, **enum**, or **union** type must have a tag.

/Zl

This option omits the default library name from the .OBJ file. By default, CL puts the name of the library in the .OBJ file to direct the linker to the correct library. For more information on the default library, see "Use Run-Time Library" in Chapter 21.

You can use /Zl to compile .OBJ files you plan to put into a library. Although omitting the library name saves only a small amount of space for a single .OBJ file, the total space saved is significant in a library that contains many object modules.

/Zs

This option tells the compiler to check only the syntax of the source files on the command line. No output files are created. Error messages are written to standard output. The /Zs option provides a quick way to find and correct syntax errors before you compile and link a source file.

LINK Reference

LINK is a 32-bit tool that links Common Object File Format (COFF) object files and libraries to create a 32-bit executable (.EXE) file or dynamic-link library (DLL).

The following tables, which summarize LINK options, are included in this reference:

- Alphabetic List of LINK Options
- Developer Studio LINK Options
- Compiler-Controlled LINK Options

The linker options available from the Link tab of the Project Settings dialog box are described in Chapter 21, "Setting Linker Options."

LINK Input Files

You provide the linker with files that contain objects, import and standard libraries, resources, module definitions, and command input. LINK does not use file extensions to make assumptions about the contents of a file. Instead, LINK examines each input file to determine what kind of file it is.

Note LINK no longer takes a semicolon (or any other character) as the start of a comment in response files and order files. Semicolons are only recognized as start of comments in module-definition files (.DEF).

LINK uses the following types of input files:

- .OBJ files
- .LIB files
- .EXP files
- .DEF files
- .PDB files
- .RES files

- .EXE files
- .TXT files
- .ILK files

.OBJ Files

LINK accepts .OBJ files that are either COFF or 32-bit Object Module Format (OMF). Microsoft's compiler creates COFF .OBJ files. LINK automatically converts 32-bit OMF objects to COFF.

.LIB Files

LINK accepts COFF standard libraries and COFF import libraries, both of which usually have the extension .LIB. Standard libraries contain objects and are created by the LIB tool. Import libraries contain information about exports in other programs and are created either by LINK when it builds a program that contains exports or by the LIB tool. For information on using LIB to create standard or import libraries, see Chapter 28, "LIB Reference." For details on using LINK to create an import library, see the /DLL option later in this chapter.

A library is specified to LINK as either a filename argument or a default library. LINK resolves external references by searching first in libraries specified on the command line, then in default libraries specified with the /DEFAULTLIB option, then in default libraries named in .OBJ files. If a path is specified with the library name, LINK looks for the library in that directory. If no path is specified, LINK looks first in the directory that LINK is running from, then in any directories specified in the LIB environment variable.

LINK cannot link a library of 32-bit OMF objects created by the 16-bit version of LIB. To use an OMF library, you must first use the 16-bit LIB (not provided in Visual C++ for Windows NT) to extract the objects. You can then either link the OMF objects or use the 32-bit LIB to convert them to COFF and put them in a library. You can also use the EDITBIN.EXE tool to convert an OMF object to COFF. For details on EDITBIN, see Chapter 31, "EDITBIN Reference."

.EXP Files

.EXP files contain information about exported functions and data items. When LIB creates an import library, it also creates an .EXP file. You use the .EXP file when you link a program that both exports to and imports from another program, either directly or indirectly. If you link with an .EXP file, LINK does not produce an import library, because it assumes that LIB already created one. For details about .EXP files and import libraries, see Working with Import Libraries and Export Files in Chapter 28, "LIB Reference."

.DEF Files

Module-definition (.DEF) files (described in further detail later in this chapter) provide the linker with information about exports, attributes, and other information about the program to be linked. Use the /DEF option to specify the .DEF filename. Because LINK provides options and other features that can be used instead of module-definition statements, .DEF files are generally not necessary.

.PDB Files

.OBJ files compiled using the /Zi option contain the name of a program database (PDB). You do not specify the object's PDB filename to the linker; LINK uses the embedded name to find the PDB if it is needed. This also applies to debuggable objects contained in a library; the PDB for a debuggable library must be available to the linker along with the library.

LINK also uses a PDB to hold debugging information for the .EXE file or .DLL file. The program's PDB is both an output file and an input file, because LINK updates the PDB when it rebuilds the program.

.RES Files

You can specify a .RES file when linking a program. The .RES file is created by the resource compiler (RC). LINK automatically converts .RES files to COFF. The CVTRES.EXE tool must be in the same directory as LINK.EXE or in a directory specified in the PATH environment variable.

.EXE Files

The MS-DOS Stub File Name (/STUB) option specifies the name of an .EXE file that runs with MS-DOS. LINK examines the specified file to be sure that it is a valid MS-DOS program.

.TXT Files

LINK expects various text files as additional input. The command-file specifier (@) and the Base Address (/BASE), /DEF, and /ORDER options all specify text files. These files can have any extension, not just .TXT.

.ILK Files

When linking incrementally, LINK updates the .ILK status file that it created during the first incremental link. This file has the same base name as the .EXE file or .DLL file, and it has the extension .ILK. During subsequent incremental links, LINK updates the .ILK file. If the .ILK file is missing, LINK performs a full link and creates a new .ILK file. If the .ILK file is unusable, LINK performs a nonincremental link. For details about incremental linking, see the Link Incrementally (/INCREMENTAL) option in Chapter 21, "Setting Linker Options."

LINK Output

Link output includes .EXE files, DLLs, map files, and messages.

Output Files

The default output file from LINK is an .EXE file. If the /DLL option is specified, LINK builds a .DLL file. You can control the output filename with the Output File Name (/OUT) option, described in Chapter 21, "Setting Linker Options."

In incremental mode, LINK creates an .ILK file to hold status information for later incremental builds of the program. For details about .ILK files, see .ILK Files earlier in this chapter. For more information about incremental linking, see the Link Incrementally (/INCREMENTAL) option in Chapter 21, "Setting Linker Options."

When LINK creates a program that contains exports (usually a DLL), it also builds a .LIB file, unless an .EXP file was used in the build. You can control the import library filename with the /IMPLIB option, described later in this chapter.

If the Generate Mapfile (/MAP) option is specified, LINK creates a map file.

If the Generate Debug Info (/DEBUG) and Microsoft Format (/DEBUGTYPE:CV) options are specified, LINK creates a PDB to contain debugging information for the program. For more information about these options, see Chapter 21, "Setting Linker Options."

Other Output

When you type link without any other command-line input, LINK displays a usage statement that summarizes its options.

LINK displays a copyright and version message and echoes command-file input, unless the Suppress Startup Banner (/NOLOGO) option is used.

You can use the Print Progress Messages (/VERBOSE) option to display additional details about the build.

LINK issues error and warning messages in the form LNK*nnnn*. This error prefix and range of numbers is also used by LIB, DUMPBIN, and EDITBIN. Consult Books Online for documentation on these errors. You can control the display of warnings with the /WARN option.

Running LINK on the Command Line

When you run LINK at a command prompt, you can specify input in one or more ways:

- On the command line
- Using command files
- In environment variables

LINK Command Line

To run LINK, use the following command syntax:

LINK *arguments*

The *arguments* include options and filenames and can be specified in any order. Options are processed first, then files. Use one or more spaces or tabs to separate arguments.

To pass a file to the linker, specify the filename on the command line after the LINK command. You can specify an absolute or relative path with the filename, and you can use wildcards in the filename. If you omit the dot (.) and filename extension, LINK assumes .OBJ for the purpose of finding the file. LINK does not use filename extensions or the lack of them to make assumptions about the contents of files; it determines the type of file by examining it, and processes it accordingly.

LINK Command Files

You can pass command-line arguments to LINK in the form of a command file. To specify a command file to the linker, use the following syntax:

LINK @*commandfile*

The *commandfile* is the name of a text file. No space or tab is allowed between the at sign (@) and the filename. There is no default extension; you must specify the full filename, including any extension. Wildcards cannot be used. You can specify an absolute or relative path with the filename. LINK does not use an environment variable to search for the file.

In the command file, arguments can be separated by spaces or tabs (as on the command line) and by newline characters.

You can specify all or part of the command line in a command file. You can use more than one command file in a LINK command. LINK accepts the command-file input as if it were specified in that location on the command line. Command files cannot be nested. LINK echoes the contents of command files, unless the /NOLOGO option is specified.

Example

The following command to build a DLL passes the names of object files and libraries in separate command files and uses a third command file for specification of the /EXPORTS option:

```
link /dll @objlist.txt @liblist.txt @exports.txt
```

LINK Environment Variables

LINK uses environment variables as follows:

- If the LINK variable is defined, LINK processes arguments defined in the variable before it processes the command line. The LINK environment variable can contain any arguments to the linker.

- If the LIB variable is defined, LINK uses the LIB path when it searches for a file (such as an object or library) specified on the LINK command line or with the /BASE option, or for a .PDB file named in an object. The LIB environment variable can contain one or more path specifications, separated by semicolons (;). You can set the LIB variable within Developer Studio by selecting the Directories tab in the Options dialog box (available from the Tools menu).

- If LINK needs to run CVPACK or CVTRES and cannot find it in the same directory as itself, LINK uses the PATH environment variable to look for the tool. CVPACK is required when creating Microsoft-format debugging information. CVTRES is required when linking a .RES file.

- LINK uses the directory specified in the TMP environment variable when linking OMF or .RES files.

LINK Options

You can specify options to LINK either within Developer Studio or on the LINK command line. Chapter 21, "Setting Linker Options," describes the option categories that are available from the Link tab in the Project Settings dialog box. The LINK options that are not available as controls on the Link tab are summarized in the following tables.

An option consists of an option specifier, either a dash (–) or a forward slash (/), followed by the name of the option. Option names cannot be abbreviated. Some options take an argument, specified after a colon (:). No spaces or tabs are allowed within an option specification, except within a quoted string in the /COMMENT option. Specify numeric arguments in decimal or C-language notation. Option names and their keyword or filename arguments are not case sensitive, but identifiers as arguments are case sensitive.

LINK first processes options specified in the LINK environment variable, followed by options in the order they are specified on the command line and in command files. If an option is repeated with different arguments, the last one processed takes precedence.

Options apply to the entire build; no options can be applied to specific input files.

Alphabetic List of LINK Options

Table 26.1 lists the LINK options, along with the equivalent Developer Studio option if available. Options listed as command-line only are described in this section. Developer Studio options are described in Chapter 21, "Setting Linker Options." Options marked as specific to a target are described in the appropriate documentation for that target.

Table 26.1   Alphabetic List of LINK Options

Command-line option	Developer Studio option
/ALIGN	—
/BASE	Output Category
/COMMENT	—
/DEBUG	Debug Category
/DEBUGTYPE	Debug Category
/DEF	—
/DEFAULTLIB	—
/DLL	—
/ENTRY	Output Category
/EXETYPE	—
/EXPORT	—
/FIXED	—
/FORCE	Customize Category
/HEAP	—
/IMPLIB	—
/INCLUDE	Input Category
/INCREMENTAL	Customize Category
/MACHINE	—
/MAP	Debug Category
/MERGE	—
/NODEFAULTLIB	Input Category
/NOENTRY	—
/NOLOGO	Customize Category
/OPT	—
/ORDER	—
/OUT	Customize Category

Table 26.1   Alphabetic List of LINK Options *(continued)*

Command-line option	Developer Studio option
/PDB	Customize Category
/PROFILE	General Category
/RELEASE	—
/SECTION	—
/STACK	Output Category
/STUB	Input Category
/SUBSYSTEM	—
/VERBOSE	Customize Category
/VERSION	Output Category
/VXD	—
/WARN	—

Developer Studio LINK Options

You can set LINK options in Developer Studio by using the Link tab in the Project Settings dialog box. Table 26.2 lists the options available in Developer Studio, along with the equivalent command-line options.

Table 26.2   Developer Studio LINK Options

Developer Studio	Command-line equivalent
General Category	
Output File Name	/OUT:*filename*
Object/Library Modules	*filename* on command line
Generate Debug Info	/DEBUG
Link Incrementally	/INCREMENTAL:{YES|NO}
Enable Profiling	/PROFILE
Ignore All Default Libraries	/NODEFAULTLIB
Generate Mapfile	/MAP
Customize Category	
Use Program Database	/PDB:*filename*
Link Incrementally	/INCREMENTAL:{YES|NO}
Program Database Name	/PDB:*filename*
Output File Name	/OUT:*filename*
Force File Output	/FORCE
Print Progress Messages	/VERBOSE
Suppress Startup Banner	/NOLOGO

Table 26.2   Developer Studio LINK Options *(continued)*

Developer Studio	Command-line equivalent
Debug Category	
Mapfile Name	/MAP:*filename*
Generate Mapfile	/MAP
Generate Debug Info	/DEBUG
Microsoft Format	/DEBUGTYPE:CV
COFF Format	/DEBUGTYPE:COFF
Both Formats	/DEBUGTYPE:BOTH
Input Category	
Object/Library Modules	*filename* on command line
Ignore Libraries	/NODEFAULTLIB:*library*
Ignore All Default Libraries	/NODEFAULTLIB
Force Symbol References	/INCLUDE:*symbol*
MS-DOS Stub File Name	/STUB:*filename*
Output Category	
Base Address	/BASE:*address*
Entry-Point Symbol	/ENTRY:*function*
Stack Allocations	/STACK:*reserve,commit*
Version Information	/VERSION:*major.minor*

Compiler-Controlled LINK Options

The CL compiler automatically calls LINK when you do not specify the /c option. CL provides some control over the linker through command-line options and arguments. Table 26.3 summarizes the features in CL that affect linking.

Table 26.3   Compiler-Controlled LINK Options

CL command-line specification	CL action that affects LINK
Any filename extension other than .C, .CXX, .CPP, or .DEF	Passes filename as input to LINK
filename.DEF	Passes /DEF:*filename*.DEF
/F*number*	Passes /STACK:*number*
/Fd *filename*	Passes /PDB:*filename*
/Fe *filename*	Passes /OUT:*filename*
/Fm *filename*	Passes /MAP:*filename*

Table 26.3   Compiler-Controlled LINK Options *(continued)*

CL command-line specification	CL action that affects LINK
/Gy	Creates packaged functions (COMDATs); enables function-level linking
/LD	Passes /DLL
/LDd	Passes /DLL
/link	Passes remainder of command line to LINK
/MD, /ML, or /MT	Places a default library name in the .OBJ file
/MDd, /MLd, or /MTd	Places a default library name in the .OBJ file
/nologo	Passes /NOLOGO
/Zd	Passes /DEBUG /DEBUGTYPE:COFF
/Zi or /Z7	Passes /DEBUG /DEBUGTYPE:CV
/Zl	Omits default library name from .OBJ file

For more information on CL, see Chapter 20, "Setting Compiler Options," and Chapter 25, "CL Reference."

LINK Command-Line Options

/ALIGN

Syntax
/ALIGN:*number*

This option specifies the alignment of each section within the linear address space of the program. The *number* argument is in bytes and must be a power of two. The default is 4K. The linker issues a warning if the alignment produces an invalid image.

/COMMENT

Syntax
/COMMENT:["]*comment*["]

This option inserts a *comment* string into the header of an .EXE file or DLL, after the array of section headers. The type of operating system determines whether the string is loaded into memory. This comment string, unlike the comment specified with the **DESCRIPTION** statement in a .DEF file, is not inserted into the data section. Comments are useful for embedding copyright and version information.

To specify a *comment* that contains spaces or tabs, enclose it in double quotation marks ("). LINK removes the quotation marks before inserting the string. If more than one /COMMENT option is specified, LINK concatenates the strings and places a null byte at the end of each string.

/DEF

Syntax
/DEF:*filename*

This option passes a module-definition (.DEF) file to the linker. Only one .DEF file can be specified to LINK. For details about .DEF files, see Module-Definition Files.

When a .DEF file is used in a build, no matter whether the main output file is an .EXE file or a DLL, LINK creates an import library (.LIB) and an export file (.EXP). These files are created regardless of whether the main output file contains exports.

Do not specify this option within Developer Studio; this option is for use only on the command line. To specify a .DEF file, add it to the project along with other files.

/DEFAULTLIB

Syntax
/DEFAULTLIB:*library*

This option adds one *library* to the list of libraries that LINK searches when resolving references. A library specified with /DEFAULTLIB is searched after libraries specified on the command line and before default libraries named in .OBJ files.

The Ignore All Default Libraries (/NODEFAULTLIB) option overrides /DEFAULTLIB:*library*. The Ignore Libraries (/NODEFAULTLIB:*library*) option overrides /DEFAULTLIB:*library* when the same *library* name is specified in both.

/DLL

Syntax
/DLL

This option builds a DLL as the main output file. A DLL usually contains exports that can be used by another program. There are three methods for specifying exports, listed in recommended order of use:

1. The **__declspec(dllexport)** keyword in the source code

2. An /EXPORT specification in a LINK command

3. An **EXPORTS** statement in a .DEF file

A program can use more than one method.

An alternate way to build a DLL is with the **LIBRARY** module-definition statement. The /BASE and /DLL options together are equivalent to the **LIBRARY** statement.

Do not specify this option within Developer Studio; this option is for use only on the command line. This option is set when you select either MFC AppWizard (dll) or Dynamic-Link Library under Type in the New Project Workspace dialog box.

/EXETYPE

Syntax
/EXETYPE:{DEV386|DYNAMIC}

This option is used when building a virtual device driver (VxD). A VxD is linked using the /VXD option.

Specify **DEV386** (the default) to create a VxD that is loaded by the operating system when it loads the program that uses it. Specify **DYNAMIC** to create a dynamically loaded VxD.

/EXPORT

Syntax
/EXPORT:*entryname*[=*internalname*][,@*ordinal*[,NONAME]][,DATA]

With this option, you can export a function from your program so that other programs can call the function. You can also export data. Exports are usually defined in a DLL.

The *entryname* is the name of the function or data item as it is to be used by the calling program. You can optionally specify the *internalname* as the function known in the defining program; by default, *internalname* is the same as *entryname*. The *ordinal* specifies an index into the exports table in the range 1 through 65,535; if you do not specify *ordinal*, LINK assigns one. The **NONAME** keyword exports the function only as an ordinal, without an *entryname*.

The **DATA** keyword specifies that the exported item is a data item. The data item in the client program must be declared using **extern __declspec(dllimport)**.

There are three methods for exporting a definition, listed in recommended order of use:

1. The **__declspec(dllexport)** keyword in the source code

2. An /EXPORT specification in a LINK command

3. An **EXPORTS** statement in a .DEF file

All three methods can be used in the same program. When LINK builds a program that contains exports, it also creates an import library, unless an .EXP file is used in the build.

LINK uses decorated forms of identifiers. The compiler decorates an identifier when it creates the .OBJ file. If *entryname* or *internalname* is specified to the linker in its undecorated form (as it appears in the source code), LINK attempts to match the name. If it cannot find a unique match, LINK issues an error message. Use the DUMPBIN tool described in Chapter 30, "DUMPBIN Reference" to get the decorated form of an identifier when you need to specify it to the linker. For more information on decorated names, see Appendix A, "Decorated Names."

Note   Do not specify the decorated form of C identifiers that are declared **__cdecl** or **__stdcall**.

/FIXED

Syntax
/FIXED

This option tells the operating system to load the program only at its preferred base address. If the preferred base address is unavailable, the operating system will not load the file. For more information, see "Base Address" in Chapter 21.

When /FIXED is specified, LINK does not generate a relocation section in the program. At run time, if the operating system is unable to load the program at that address, it issues an error message and does not load the program.

Some Win32 operating systems, especially those that coexist with MS-DOS®, must frequently relocate a program. A program created with the /FIXED option will not run on Win32s operating systems.

Do not use /FIXED when building device drivers for Windows NT.

/HEAP

Syntax
/HEAP:*reserve*[,*commit*]

This option sets the size of the heap in bytes.

The *reserve* argument specifies the total heap allocation in virtual memory. The default heap size is 1 MB. The linker rounds up the specified value to the nearest 4 bytes.

The optional *commit* argument is subject to interpretation by the operating system. In Windows NT, it specifies the amount of physical memory to allocate at a time. Committed virtual memory causes space to be reserved in the paging file. A higher *commit* value saves time when the application needs more heap space but increases the memory requirements and possibly the startup time.

Specify the *reserve* and *commit* values in decimal or C-language notation.

/IMPLIB

Syntax
/IMPLIB:*filename*

This option overrides the default name for the import library that LINK creates when it builds a program that contains exports. The default name is formed from the base name of the main output file and the extension .LIB. A program contains exports if one or more of the following are specified:

- The __declspec(dllexport) keyword in the source code
- An /EXPORT specification in a LINK command
- An EXPORTS statement in a .DEF file

LINK ignores /IMPLIB when an import library is not being created. If no exports are specified, LINK does not create an import library. If an export file is used in the build, LINK assumes that an import library already exists and does not create one. For information on import libraries and export files, see Chapter 28, "LIB Reference."

/MACHINE

Syntax
/MACHINE:{IX86|MIPS|MIPSR10|ALPHA|PPC|M68K|MPPC}

This option specifies the target platform for the program.

Usually, you do not need to specify the /MACHINE option. LINK infers the machine type from the .OBJ files. However, in some circumstances LINK cannot determine the machine type and issues an error message. If such an error occurs, specify /MACHINE.

/MERGE

Syntax
/MERGE:*from=to*

This option combines the first section (*from*) with the second section (*to*), naming the resulting section *to*. If the second section does not exist, LINK renames the section *from* as *to*.

The /MERGE option is useful for creating VxDs and overriding the compiler-generated section names.

/NOENTRY

Syntax
/NOENTRY

This option is required for creating a resource-only DLL.

Use this option to prevent LINK from linking a reference to **_main** into the DLL.

/OPT

Syntax
/OPT:{REF|NOREF}

This option controls the optimizations that LINK performs during a build. Optimizations generally decrease the image size and increase the program speed, at a cost of increased link time.

By default, LINK removes unreferenced packaged functions. An object contains packaged functions (COMDATs) if it has been compiled with the /Gy option. This optimization is called transitive COMDAT elimination. To override this default and keep unreferenced COMDATs in the program, specify /OPT:**NOREF**. You can use the /INCLUDE option to override the removal of a specific symbol.

If the /DEBUG option is specified, the default for /OPT changes from **REF** to **NOREF**, and all functions are preserved in the image. To override this default and optimize a debugging build, specify /OPT:**REF**. The /OPT:**REF** option disables incremental linking.

/ORDER

Syntax
/ORDER:@*filename*

This option tells LINK to optimize your program by placing certain COMDATs into the image in a predetermined order. LINK places the functions in the specified order within each section in the image.

Specify the order in *filename*, which is a text file that lists the COMDATs in the order you want to link them. Each line in *filename* contains the name of one COMDAT. An object contains COMDATs if it has been compiled with the /Gy option. Function names are case sensitive.

LINK uses decorated forms of identifiers. The compiler decorates an identifier when it creates the .OBJ file. If the name of the COMDAT is specified to the linker in its undecorated form (as it appears in the source code), LINK attempts to match the name. If it cannot find a unique match, LINK issues an error message. Use the DUMPBIN tool described in Chapter 30, "DUMPBIN Reference," to get the decorated form of an identifier when you need to specify it to the linker. For more information on decorated names, see Appendix A, "Decorated Names."

Note Do not specify the decorated form of C identifiers that are declared **__cdecl** or **__stdcall**.

If more than one /ORDER specification is used, the last one specified takes effect.

Ordering allows you to optimize your program's paging behavior through swap tuning by grouping a function with the functions it calls. You can also group frequently called functions together. These techniques increase the probability that a called function is in memory when it is needed and will not have to be paged from disk.

The /ORDER option disables incremental linking.

/RELEASE

Syntax
/RELEASE

This option sets the checksum in the header of an .EXE file.

The operating system requires the checksum for certain files, such as device drivers. It is recommended that you set the checksum for release versions of your programs to ensure compatibility with future operating systems.

The /RELEASE option is set by default when the /SUBSYSTEM:NATIVE option is specified.

/SECTION

Syntax
/SECTION:*name,attributes*

This option changes the *attributes* of a section, overriding the *attributes* set when the .OBJ file for the section was compiled.

Specify a colon (:) and a section *name*. The *name* is case sensitive.

Specify one or more *attributes* for the section. The attribute characters (E, R, W, and S) are not case sensitive. You must specify all *attributes* that you want the section to have; an omitted attribute character causes that attribute bit to be turned off. The meanings of the attribute characters are shown below.

Character	Attribute	Meaning
E	Execute	Allows code to be executed
R	Read	Allows read operations on data
W	Write	Allows write operations on data
S	Shared	Shares the section among all processes that load the image

Note that Win32s operating systems load all DLL data sections as "shared" even if that attribute is not set.

A section that does not have E, R, or W set is probably invalid.

/SUBSYSTEM

Syntax

/SUBSYSTEM:{CONSOLE|WINDOWS|NATIVE|POSIX}[,*major*[.*minor*]]

This option tells the operating system how to run the .EXE file. The subsystem is specified as follows:

- The CONSOLE subsystem is for a Win32 character-mode application. Console applications are given a console by the operating system. If **main** or **wmain** is defined, CONSOLE is the default.

- The WINDOWS subsystem applies to an application that does not require a console, probably because it creates its own windows for interaction with the user. Win32s operating systems can only run WINDOWS applications. If **WinMain** or **wWinMain** is defined, WINDOWS is the default.

- The NATIVE subsystem applies device drivers for Windows NT.

- The POSIX subsystem creates an application that runs with the POSIX subsystem in Windows NT.

The optional *major* and *minor* version numbers specify the minimum required version of the subsystem. The arguments are decimal numbers in the range 0 through 65,535. The default is version 4.00 for CONSOLE, WINDOWS, and NATIVE; and version 19.90 for POSIX.

The choice of subsystem affects the default starting address for the program. For more information, see the "Entry-Point Symbol" (/ENTRY:*function*) option in Chapter 21.

/VERBOSE:LIB

Syntax
/VERBOSE:LIB

Adding :LIB to the /VERBOSE option displays only progress messages indicating the libraries searched.

For more information on the /VERBOSE option, see "Print Progress Messages" in Chapter 21.

/VXD

Syntax
/VXD

This option creates a virtual device driver (VxD). When this option is specified, the default filename extension changes to .VXD. For details on VxDs, see the Microsoft Windows NT Device Driver Kit.

A .VXD file is not in Common Object File Format, and it cannot be used with DUMPBIN or EDITBIN. It does not contain debugging information. However, you can create a map file when you link a .VXD file.

A .VXD file cannot be incrementally linked.

/WARN

Syntax
/WARN[:*level*]

With this option, you can determine the output of LINK warning messages. The *level* parameter takes the value 0, 1, 2, or 3. Currently, this option controls a limited subset of LINK warning messages.

Note Setting *level* to 0 does not disable warning messages.

Module-Definition (.DEF) Files

A module-definition (.DEF) file is a text file that contains statements for defining an .EXE file or DLL. The following sections describe the statements in a .DEF file.

Because LINK provides equivalent command-line options for most module-definition statements, a typical program for Win32 does not usually require a .DEF file. The descriptions of the module-definition statements give the command-line equivalent for each statement.

Rules for Module-Definition Statements

The following syntax rules apply to all statements in a .DEF file. Other rules that apply to specific statements are described with each statement.

- Statements and attribute keywords are not case sensitive. User-specified identifiers are case sensitive.

- Long filenames containing spaces or semicolons (;) must be enclosed in quotation marks (").

- Use one or more spaces, tabs, or newline characters to separate a statement keyword from its arguments and to separate statements from each other. A colon (:) or equal sign (=) that designates an argument is surrounded by zero or more spaces, tabs, or newline characters.

- A **NAME** or **LIBRARY** statement, if used, must precede all other statements.

- Most statements appear at most once in the .DEF file and accept one specification of arguments. The specification follows the statement keyword on the same or subsequent line(s). If the statement is repeated with different arguments later in the file, the later statement overrides the earlier one.

- The **SECTIONS**, **EXPORTS**, and **IMPORTS** statements can appear more than once in the .DEF file. Each statement can take multiple specifications, which must be separated by one or more spaces, tabs, or newline characters. The statement keyword must appear once before the first specification and can be repeated before each additional specification.

- Many statements have an equivalent LINK command-line option. See the description of the corresponding LINK option for additional details.

- Comments in the .DEF file are designated by a semicolon (;) at the beginning of each comment line. A comment cannot share a line with a statement, but it can appear between specifications in a multiline statement. (**SECTIONS** and **EXPORTS** are multiline statements.)

- Numeric arguments are specified in decimal or C-language notation.

- If a string argument matches a reserved word, it must be enclosed in double quotation marks (").

NAME

Syntax
NAME [*application*][BASE=*address*]

This statement specifies a name for the main output file. An equivalent way to specify an output filename is with the /OUT option, and an equivalent way to set the base address is with the /BASE option. If both are specified, /OUT overrides **NAME**. See the "Base Address (/BASE)" and "Output File Name (/OUT)" options in Chapter 21, for details about output filenames and base addresses.

LIBRARY

Syntax
LIBRARY [*library*][BASE=*address*]

This statement tells LINK to create a DLL. At the same time, LINK creates an import library, unless an .EXP file is used in the build.

The *library* argument specifies the internal name of the DLL. (Use the Output File Name (/OUT) option to specify the DLL's output name.)

The **BASE=***address* argument sets the base address that the operating system uses to load the DLL. This argument overrides the default DLL location of 0x10000000. See the description of the "Base Address (/BASE)" option in Chapter 21 for details about base addresses.

An equivalent way to specify a DLL build is with the /DLL option, and an equivalent way to set the base address is with the /BASE option.

DESCRIPTION

Syntax
DESCRIPTION "*text*"

This statement writes a string into an **.rdata** section. Enclose the specified *text* in single or double quotation marks (' or "). To use a literal quotation mark (either single or double) in the string, enclose the string with the other type of mark.

This feature differs from the comment specified with the /COMMENT option.

STACKSIZE

Syntax
STACKSIZE *reserve*[,*commit*]

This statement sets the size of the stack in bytes. An equivalent way to set the stack is with the /STACK option. See the "Stack Allocations" option in Chapter 21 for details about the *reserve* and *commit* arguments.

SECTIONS

Syntax
SECTIONS *definitions*

This statement sets attributes for one or more sections in the image file. It can be used to override the default attributes for each type of section.

SECTIONS marks the beginning of a list of section *definitions*. Each *definition* must be on a separate line. The **SECTIONS** keyword can be on the same line as the first *definition* or on a preceding line. The .DEF file can contain one or more **SECTIONS** statements. The **SEGMENTS** keyword is supported as a synonym for **SECTIONS**.

The syntax for a section definition is:

section [**CLASS** '*classname*'] *attributes*

The *section* name is case sensitive. The **CLASS** keyword is supported for compatibility, but is ignored. The *attributes* are one or more of the following: **EXECUTE, READ, SHARED,** and **WRITE.**

An equivalent way to specify section attributes is with the /SECTION option.

EXPORTS

Syntax
EXPORTS *definitions*

This statement makes one or more *definitions* available as exports to other programs.

EXPORTS marks the beginning of a list of export *definitions*. Each *definition* must be on a separate line. The **EXPORTS** keyword can be on the same line as the first *definition* or on a preceding line. The .DEF file can contain one or more **EXPORTS** statements.

The syntax for an export definition is:

entryname[=*internalname*] [@*ordinal*[**NONAME**]] [**DATA**] [**PRIVATE**]

For information on the *entryname*, *internalname*, *ordinal*, **NONAME**, and **DATA** arguments, see the /EXPORT option.

The optional keyword **PRIVATE** tells IMPLIB to ignore the definition. **PRIVATE** prevents *entryname* from being placed in the import library. The keyword has no effect on LINK.

There are three methods for exporting a definition, listed in recommended order of use:

1. The **__declspec(dllexport)** keyword in the source code

2. An /EXPORT specification in a LINK command

3. An **EXPORTS** statement in a .DEF file

All three methods can be used in the same program. When LINK builds a program that contains exports, it also creates an import library, unless an .EXP file is used in the build.

VERSION

Syntax
VERSION *major*[*.minor*]

This statement tells LINK to put a number in the header of the .EXE file or DLL. The *major* and *minor* arguments are decimal numbers in the range 0 through 65,535. The default is version 0.0.

An equivalent way to specify a version number is with the "Version Information (/VERSION)" option described in Chapter 21.

Reserved Words

The following words are reserved by the linker. These names can be used as arguments in module-definition statements only if the name is enclosed in double quotation marks (").

APPLOADER	INITINSTANCE	PRELOAD
BASE	IOPL	PRIVATE
CODE	LIBRARY	PROTMODE
CONFORMING	LOADONCALL	PURE
DATA	LONGNAMES	READONLY
DESCRIPTION	MOVABLE	READWRITE
DEV386	MOVEABLE	REALMODE
DISCARDABLE	MULTIPLE	RESIDENT
DYNAMIC	NAME	RESIDENTNAME
EXECUTE-ONLY	NEWFILES	SECTIONS
EXECUTEONLY	NODATA	SEGMENTS
EXECUTEREAD	NOIOPL	SHARED
EXETYPE	NONAME	SINGLE
EXPORTS	NONCONFORMING	STACKSIZE
FIXED	NONDISCARDABLE	STUB
FUNCTIONS	NONE	VERSION
HEAPSIZE	NONSHARED	WINDOWAPI
IMPORTS	NOTWINDOWCOMPAT	WINDOWCOMPAT
IMPURE	OBJECTS	WINDOWS
INCLUDE	OLD	

Profiler Reference

This section provides reference information for using the components of the profiler from the command line and analyzing profiler statistics. The following topics are covered:

- Profiler batch processing
- Syntax and command-line options for PREP, PROFILE, and PLIST
- Exporting data from the profiler

Figure 27.1 illustrates how the profiler components interact.

For information on running the profiler in Microsoft Developer Studio, see Chapter 18, "Profiling Code."

Profiler Batch Processing

Profiling requires three separate programs: PREP, PROFILE, and PLIST. If you choose a standard option (other than Custom) from the Profile dialog box, Microsoft Developer Studio executes these programs for you automatically, passing arguments to the PREP program.

If you want maximum profiling flexibility, including the ability to format your output and to specify function and line-count profiling, you must write your own batch files that invoke PREP, PROFILE, and PLIST. You can run these batch files from either the Profile dialog box or from the command prompt. If you run the batch file from the dialog box, the PLIST output will, by default, be routed to the Developer Studio output window. Command-line batch output can also be routed to a file.

Figure 27.1 illustrates the profiler batch processing flow.

Figure 27.1 Profiler Batch Processing Flow

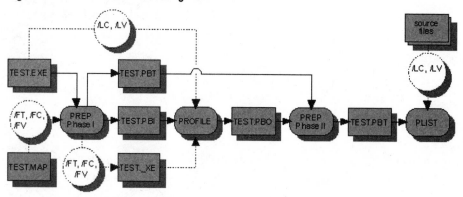

Notice that the PREP program is called twice—before and after the actual profiling. The command-line arguments govern PREP's behavior.

The .PBI, .PBO, and .PBT files are intermediate files that are used to transfer information between profiling steps. The broken lines indicate connections that depend on the PREP (Phase I) command-line options.

A typical profiler batch file might look like this:

```
PREP /OM /FT /EXC nafxcwd.lib %1
if errorlevel == 1 goto done
PROFILE %1 %2 %3 %4 %5 %6 %7 %8 %9
if errorlevel == 1 goto done
PREP /M %1
if errorlevel == 1 goto done
PLIST /SC %1 >%1.1st
:done
```

Note When you run a profiler batch file from the Profile dialog box using the Custom option, the PLIST standard output is routed to the Profile tab in the Output window. In the preceding batch file, the PLIST output is redirected to a file, as it would usually be in a batch file run from the command line.

The command-line parameters for PREP, PROFILE, and PLIST are described in "Profiler Command-Line Options" on page 594. When the batch file is run using the Custom option in the Profile dialog box, Developer Studio substitutes the project's program name for the %1 parameter. You can specify your program's command-line arguments on the Debug tab in the Project Settings dialog box.

If the preceding batch file was named FTIME.BAT, and you wanted to profile the program TEST from the Profile dialog box, you would select the Custom option, and then specify FTIME.BAT in the Custom Settings box. If you wanted to profile the TEST program from the command prompt, you would type:

```
FTIME TEST.EXE
```

Note If you are running a profiler batch file from Developer Studio, you can use Developer Studio to edit your batch file. Remember to save your batch files after editing, because Developer Studio does not save them automatically.

Profiler Batch Response Files

Similar to the linker, all three profiler programs accept response files. As a result, the command line:

```
PREP /OM /FT /EXC nafxcwd.lib %1
```

can be replaced by the line:

```
PREP @opts.rsp %1
```

if you create a file OPTS.RSP that contains this text:

```
/OM /FT /EXC nafxcwd.lib    # this is a comment
```

The number sign (#) in a response file defines a comment that runs through the end of the line.

Standard Batch Files

Six standard batch files are included with the profiler:

Filename	Description
FTIME.BAT	Function timing
FCOUNT.BAT	Function counting
FCOVER.BAT	Function coverage
LCOUNT.BAT	Line counting
LCOVER.BAT	Line coverage

These batch files contain only the minimum parameters for PREP Phase I. Use them as prototypes for your own batch files, which should contain selection parameters. If you ran an unmodified LCOVER batch file for a Microsoft Foundation Class Library application, for example, the output file could be thousands of lines long.

Profiler Command-Line Options

The next three sections describe the command-line options for the three components of the profiler:

- PREP
- PROFILE
- PLIST

PREP

The PREP program runs twice during a normal profiling operation. In Phase I, it reads an executable (.EXE) file and then creates .PBI and .PBT files. In Phase II, it reads .PBT and .PBO files and then writes a new .PBT file for PLIST.

Syntax

PREP [*options*] [*programname1*] [*programname2...programname8*]

PREP reads the command line from left to right, so the rightmost options override contradictory options to the left. None of the options are case sensitive. You must prefix options with a forward slash (/) or a dash (–), and options must be separated by spaces.

Parameter	Description
options	See "Options" below.
programname1	Filename of primary program to profile (.DBG, .EXE, or .DLL). PROFILE adds the .EXE extension if no extension is given. This parameter must be specified for PREP Phase I, but not for Phase II.
programname2... *programname8*	Additional programs to profile. These parameters can be specified for PREP Phase I only.

An 'X' in the following Options table indicates that a PREP command-line option applies to a particular phase.

Options

Option	I	II	Description
/EXC	X		Excludes a specified module from the profile (see "Remarks" on page 595).
/EXCALL	X		Excludes all modules from the profile (see "Remarks" on page 595).
/FC	X		Selects function count profiling.
/FT	X		Selects function timing profiling. This option causes the profiler to generate count information as well.
/FV	X		Selects function coverage profiling.

Option	I	II	Description
/INC	X		Includes in profile (see "Remarks" below).
/H[ELP]	X	X	Provides a short summary of PREP options.
/IO *filename*		X	Merges an existing .PBO file. Up to eight .PBO files can be merged at a time. The default extension is .PBO.
/IT *filename*		X	Merges an existing .PBT file. Up to eight .PBT files can be merged at a time. You cannot merge .PBT files from different profiling methods. The default extension is .PBT.
/LC	X		Selects line count profiling.
/LV	X		Selects line coverage profiling.
/M *filename*		X	Substitutes for the /IT, /IO, and /OT options.
/NOLOGO	X	X	Suppresses the PREP copyright message.
/OI *filename*	X		Creates a .PBI file. The default extension is .PBI. If /OI is not specified, the output .PBI file is *programname1*.PBI.
/OM	X		Creates a self-profiling file with an _XE or _LL extension for function timing, function counting, and function coverage. Without this option, the executable code is stored in the .PBI file. This option speeds up profiling and is used by Developer Studio.
/OT *filename*	X	X	Specifies the output .PBT file. The default extension is .PBT. If /OT is not specified, the output .PBT file is *programname1*.PBT.
/SF *function*	X		Starts profiling with *function*. The *function* name must correspond to an entry in the .MAP file.
/?	X	X	Provides a short summary of PREP options.

Environment Variable

PREP   Specifies default command-line options.

If a value for the PREP environment variable is not specified, the default options for PREP are:

```
/FT /OI filename /OT filename
```

where *filename* is set to the *programname1* parameter value.

Remarks

The /INC and /EXC options specify individual library (.LIB), object (.OBJ), and application source (.C, .CPP, or .CXX) files. For line counting and line coverage, you can specify line numbers with source files as:

```
/EXCALL /INC test.cpp(3-41,50-67)
```

This example includes only lines 3 through 41 and lines 50 through 67 from the source file TEST.CPP. Note the absence of spaces in the source specification.

To specify all source lines in a particular module, specify the .OBJ file as:

```
/EXCALL /INC test.obj
```

or by using the source filename with zero line numbers like this:

```
/EXCALL /INC test.cpp(0-0)
```

The following statement profiles from line 50 to the end of the file:

```
/EXCALL /INC test.cpp(50-0)
```

PROFILE

PROFILE profiles an application and creates a .PBO file of the results. Use PROFILE after creating a .PBI file with PREP.

Syntax

PROFILE [*options*] *programname* [*programargs*]

PROFILE reads the command line from left to right, so the rightmost options override contradictory options to the left. None of the options are case sensitive. You must prefix options with a forward slash (/) or a dash (–), and options must be separated by spaces.

If you do not specify a .PBO filename on the command line, PROFILE uses the base name of the .PBI file with a .PBO extension. If you do not specify a .PBI or a .PBO file, PROFILE uses the base name of *programname* with the .PBI and .PBO extensions.

Parameter	Description
options	See "Options" below.
programname	Filename of the program to profile. PROFILE adds the .EXE extension if no extension is given. See "Remarks" on page 597.
programargs	Optional command-line arguments for *programname*. See "Remarks" on page 597.

Options

Option	Description
/A	Appends any redirected error messages to an existing file. If the /E command-line option is used without the /A option, the file is overwritten. This option is valid only with the /E option.
/E *filename*	Sends profiler error messages to *filename*.
/H[ELP]	Provides a short summary of PROFILE options.
/I *filename*	Specifies a .PBI file to be read. This file is created by PREP.
/NOLOGO	Suppresses the PROFILE copyright message.

Option	Description
/O *filename*	Specifies a .PBO file to be created. Use the PREP utility to merge with other .PBO files, or to create a .PBT file for use with PLIST.
/X	Returns the exit code of the program being profiled.
/?	Provides a short summary of PROFILE options.

Remarks

You must specify the filename of the program to profile on the PROFILE command line. PROFILE assumes the .EXE extension if no extension is given.

You can follow the program name with command-line arguments; these arguments are passed to the profiled program unchanged.

If you are profiling code in a dynamic-link library (.DLL) file, give the name of an .EXE file that calls it. For example, if you want to profile SAMPLE.DLL, which is called by CALLER.EXE, you can type:

```
PROFILE CALLER.EXE
```

assuming that CALLER.PBI has SAMPLE.DLL selected for profiling. For more information, see "Profiling Dynamic-Link Libraries" in Chapter 12 of *Programming Techniques*.

Environment Variable

PROFILE   Specifies default command-line options.

If the PROFILE environment variable is not specified, there are no other default options.

PLIST

PLIST converts results from a .PBT file into a formatted text file.

Syntax

PLIST [*options*] *inputfile*

PLIST reads the command line from left to right, so the rightmost options override contradictory options to the left. None of the options are case sensitive. You must prefix options with a forward slash (/) or a dash (–), and options must be separated by spaces.

PLIST results are sent to STDOUT by default. Use the greater-than (>) redirection character to send these results to a file or device.

PLIST must be run from the directory in which the profiled program was compiled.

Parameter	Description
options	See Options below.
inputfile	The .PBT file to be converted by PLIST.

Options

Option	Description
/C *count*	Specifies the minimum hit count to appear in the listing.
/D *directory*	Specifies an additional directory for PLIST to search for source files. Use multiple /D command-line options to specify multiple directories. Use this option when PLIST cannot find a source file.
/F	Lists full paths in a tab-delimited file.
/H[ELP]	Provides a short summary of PLIST options.
/NOLOGO	Suppresses the PLIST copyright message.
/PL *length*	Sets page length (in lines) of output. The *length* must be 0 or in the range 15 through 255. A *length* of 0 suppresses page breaks. The default length is 0.
/PW *width*	Sets page width (in characters) of output. The *width* must be in the range 1 through 511. The default width is 511.
/SC	Sorts output by counts, highest first.
/SL	Sorts output in the order that the lines appear in the file. This is the default setting. This option is available only for line profiling.
/SLS	Forces line count profile output to be printed in coverage format.
/SN	Sorts output in alphabetical order by function name. This option is available only for function profiling.
/SNS	Displays function timing or function counting information in function coverage format. Sorts output in alphabetical order by function name.
/ST	Sorts output by time, highest first.
/T	Tab-separated output. Creates a tab-delimited database from the .PBT file for export to other applications. All other options, including sort specifications, are ignored when using this option. For more information, see "Exporting Data from the Profiler" on page 599.
/?	Provides a summary of PLIST options.

Environment Variable

PLIST   Specifies default command-line options.

If the PLIST environment variable is not specified, the default options for PLIST depend on the profile type, as shown in the following table.

Profile type	Sort option	Hit count option
Function timing	/ST	/C 1
Function counting	/SC	/C 1
Function coverage	/SN	/C 0
Line counting	/SL	/C 0
Line coverage	/SLS	/C 0

Analyzing Data from the Profiler

In addition to formatted reports, the PLIST report-generation utility can produce a tab-delimited file of profiler output. The following sections describe the data format of the file, steps for analyzing statistics in the file, and a Microsoft Excel macro that uses this file format.

Exporting Data from the Profiler

The PLIST /T command-line option causes PLIST to dump the contents of a .PBT file into a tab-delimited format suitable for import into a spreadsheet or database. This format can also be used by user-written programs.

For example, to create a tab-delimited file called MYPROG.TXT from MYPROG.PBT, type:

```
PLIST /T MYPROG > MYPROG.TXT
```

Note The ASCII tab-delimited format was designed to be read by other programs; it is not intended for general reporting.

Tab-Delimited File Format

Every piece of data stored by the profiler is available through the tab-delimited file. Because not all aspects of the database are recorded by every profiling method, unused fields within a record may be zero. For example, the total time of the program will be zero if the program is profiled for counts only. Also, all included functions are listed for function counting and timing profiles, even if those functions were not executed.

The tab-delimited format is arranged with one record per line and two to eight fields per record. Figure 27.2 shows how a database looks when it is loaded into Microsoft Excel. This database was produced using the PLIST /T command-line option.

Figure 27.2   Tab-Delimited File in Microsoft Excel

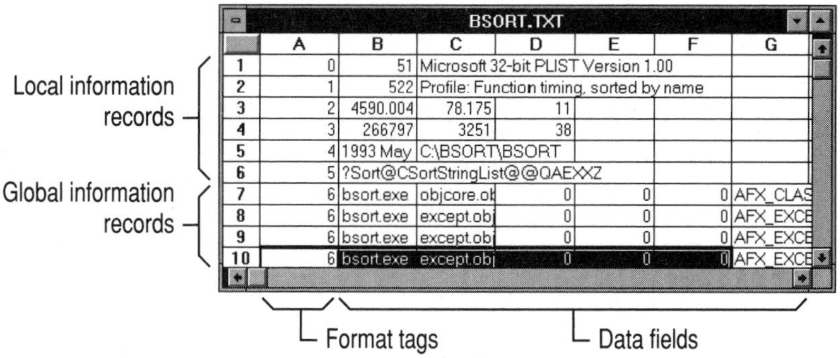

The first item in each record is a format tag number. These tags range from 0 through 7 and indicate the kind of data given in the other fields of the record. The fields in each record are described in the following sections:

- Global information records
- Local information records

Tab-delimited files are created with global information records first, organized in numerical order by format tag. The local information records, containing information about specific lines or functions, are created last. Local information records are organized by line number.

If the .PBT file contains information from more than one .EXE or .DLL file, the global information records will cover them all. Local information records include the Exe field, which specifies the name of the executable file that each record pertains to.

Global Information Records

The global information records contain information about the entire .EXE file. The format tag numbers for global information records are 0 through 5. The record formats, which are illustrated in the following sections, are as follows:

Profiler Banner

0	Version	Banner

Field	Explanation
0	Format tag number
Version	PLIST version number
Banner	PLIST banner

Profiling Method

1	Method	Description

Field	Explanation
1	Format tag number
Method	Numeric value that indicates the profiling type (see Table 27.1)
Description	ASCII description of the profiling type given by the Method field

The profiling types are listed in Table 27.1.

Table 27.1   Profiling Types

Method	Description
321	Profile: Line counting, sorted by line
324	Profile: Line coverage, sorted by line
521	Profile: Function counting, sorted by function name
522	Profile: Function timing, sorted by function name
524	Profile: Function coverage, sorted by function name

Profiling Time and Depth

2	Total Time	Outside Time	Call Depth

Field	Explanation
2	Format tag number.
Total Time	Total amount of time used by the program being profiled. This field is zero for counting and coverage profiles.
Outside Time	Amount of time spent before the first profiled function (with function profiling) or line (with line profiling) was executed. This field is zero for counting and coverage profiles.
Call Depth	Maximum number of nested functions found while profiling. Only profiled functions are counted. This field is zero for line profiling.

Hit Counts

3	Total Hits	Lines/Funcs	Lines/Funcs Hit

Field	Explanation
3	Format tag number
Total Hits	Total number of times the profiler detected a profiled line or function being executed
Lines/Funcs	Total number of lines or functions marked for profiling
Lines/Funcs Hit	Number of marked lines or functions executed at least once while profiling

Date/Command Line

4	Date	Command Line

Field	Explanation
4	Format tag number
Date	Date and time that the profile was run (ASCII format)
Command Line	PLIST command-line arguments

Starting Function Name

5	Starting Function Name

Field	Explanation
5	Format tag number
Starting Function Name	Decorated name of the starting function identified by the PREP /SF parameter

Local Information Records

The local information records contain information about specific functions or lines that were profiled. The format tag numbers for local information records are 6 and 7. A file can have only one type of local information record. The file formats, which are illustrated in the following sections, are as follows:

Function Information

6	Exe	Source	Count	Time	Child	Func

Field	Explanation
6	Format tag number.
Exe	ASCII name of the executable file that contains the function.
Source	ASCII name of the object module (including the .OBJ extension) that contains the function.
Count	Number of times the function has been executed.
Time	Amount of time spent executing the function in milliseconds. This field is zero for counting or coverage profiles.
Child	Amount of time spent executing the function and any child functions it calls. This field is zero for counting or coverage profiles.
Func	ASCII name of the function.

Line Information

7	Exe	Source	Line	Count

Field	Explanation
7	Format tag number.
Exe	ASCII name of the executable file that contains the first line of this function.
Source	ASCII name of the source file that contains the first line of this function.
Line	Line number.
Count	Number of times the line has been executed. For coverage profiles, this field is 1 if the line has been executed and 0 otherwise.

Analyzing Profiler Statistics

The profiler tab-delimited file format can contain a considerable amount of information. You can process this data in a spreadsheet, database, or user-written program.

Below are some steps for analyzing profiler statistics.

1. Collect the cumulative data from the global information records.

   These lines begin with the numbers 0 through 5. Each of these lines appears only once, and always in ascending order.

2. Determine the type of database by finding the value of the Method field. This field is the second field of the first record in the tab-delimited file.

   If the value in the Method field is greater than 400, the file comes from function profiling. If it is less than 400, the file comes from line profiling. The type of information in the local information records given later is directly related to this value.

   In any one file, the local information records are always of the same type, either line information or function information.

3. Process data from the local information records.

   For example, to calculate the percentage of hits on a given function, divide the value of the Count field in the sixth record in the file by the total number of hits from the Total Hits field in the third record.

4. Send the results to a file or STDOUT.

   Note Remember that there can be only one type of local information record (either line or function information) in a file.

Processing Profiler Output with Microsoft Excel

PROFILER.XLM is a sample Microsoft Excel version 4.0 macro that processes the tab-delimited file and graphs the results. The macro is in the \MSDEV\BIN directory.

Note The profiler sample code is installed when you set up Developer Studio. If the Microsoft Excel macro and other sample code are not on your disk, run Setup again to reinstall the Developer Studio sample code.

The PROFILER.XLM macro is composed of four submacros. The first two macros, in columns A and B, are helper macros that copy and preprocess the data for use by the second pair of macros, in columns C and D. The macro in column C, labeled CreateColumnChart, creates a graph showing the number of times that each function or line was executed. The macro in column D is CreateColumnTimeChart; it works like CreateColumnChart, but operates on timing information.

Using the PROFILER.XLM Macro

▶ **To run the PROFILER.XLM macro from within Microsoft Excel**

1 From the File menu, choose Open to open PROFILER.XLM.

2 From the File menu, choose Open to open the tab-delimited file that was created by PLIST.

3 If you have several open worksheets, activate the one containing the profiler data by selecting it with the mouse or by choosing its title from the Window menu.

4 Run the macro:

- Press CTRL+C for a chart based on hit counts.

- Press CTRL+T for a chart based on timing.

  You cannot get a timing chart if the file contains only counting or coverage information.

The macro typically takes only a few seconds to run. When it is complete, Microsoft Excel displays a three-dimensional bar chart based on the results in the file (see Figure 27.3). You can change the chart type by using the Gallery menu.

Figure 27.3 Graph Created with CreateColumnChart Macro

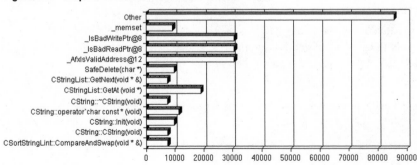

Note   This macro copies the data in the file to another worksheet before processing it. The original tab-delimited file is left untouched.

Changing the PROFILER.XLM Selection Criteria

The standard PROFILER.XLM macro displays hit counts greater than zero (for CTRL+C) and times greater than .01 millisecond (for CTRL+T). If you need to narrow these selections without analyzing the macro, edit the formulas in cells C10 and D10.

LIB Reference

- The Microsoft® 32-Bit Library Manager (LIB.EXE) creates and manages a library of Common Object File Format (COFF) object files. LIB can also be used to create export files and import libraries to reference exported definitions.

Overview of LIB

LIB creates standard libraries, import libraries, and export files that you can use with LINK when building a 32-bit program. (LINK is described in Chapter 21, "Setting Linker Options," and Chapter 26, "LINK Reference.") LIB runs from a command prompt.

You can use LIB in the following modes:

- Building or modifying a COFF library (described on page 610)
- Extracting a member object to a file (described on page 611)
- Creating an export file and an import library (described on page 611)

These modes are mutually exclusive; you can use LIB in only one mode at a time.

LIB Input Files

The input files expected by LIB depend on the mode in which it is being used, as shown in the following table.

Mode	Input
Default (building or modifying a library)	COFF object (.OBJ) files, COFF libraries (.LIB), 32-bit Object Model Format (OMF) object (.OBJ) files
Extracting a member with /EXTRACT	COFF library (.LIB)
Building an export file and import library with /DEF	Module-definition (.DEF) file, COFF object (.OBJ) files, COFF libraries (.LIB), 32-bit OMF object (.OBJ) files

Note OMF libraries created by the 16-bit version of LIB cannot be used as input to the 32-bit version of LIB.

LIB Output Files

The output files produced by LIB depend on the mode in which it is being used, as shown in the following table.

Mode	Output
Default (building or modifying a library)	COFF library (.LIB)
Extracting a member with /EXTRACT	Object (.OBJ) file
Building an export file and import library with /DEF	Import library (.LIB) and export (.EXP) file

Other LIB Output

In the default mode, you can use the /LIST option to display information about the resulting library. You can redirect this output to a file.

LIB displays a copyright and version message and echoes command files unless the /NOLOGO option is used.

When you type lib with no other input, LIB displays a usage statement that summarizes its options.

Error and warning messages issued by LIB have the form LNK*nnnn*. The LINK, DUMPBIN, and EDITBIN tools also use this range of errors. Documentation on these errors is available in Beyond Errors Microsoft Developer Studio Books Online (accessed from the InfoView pane of the Project Workspace window).

Structure of a Library

A library contains COFF objects. Objects in a library contain functions and data that can be referenced externally by other objects in a program. An object in a library is sometimes referred to as a library member.

You can get additional information about the contents of a library by running the DUMPBIN tool with the /LINKERMEMBER option. For more information about this option, see Chapter 30, "DUMPBIN Reference."

Running LIB

Various command-line options can be used to control LIB.

LIB Command Line

To run LIB, type the command lib followed by the options and filenames for the task you are using LIB to perform. LIB also accepts command-line input in command files, which are described in the following section. LIB does not use an environment variable.

Note If you are accustomed to the LINK32.EXE and LIB32.EXE tools provided with the Microsoft Win32 Software Development Kit for Windows NT, you may have been using either the command `link32 -lib` or the command `lib32` for managing libraries and creating import libraries. Be sure to change your makefiles and batch files to use the `lib` command instead.

LIB Command Files

You can pass command-line arguments to LIB in a command file by using the following syntax:

LIB @*commandfile*

The file *commandfile* is a text file. No space or tab is allowed between the at sign (@) and the filename. There is no default extension; you must specify the full filename, including any extension. Wildcards cannot be used. You can specify an absolute or relative path with the filename.

In the command file, arguments can be separated by spaces or tabs, as they can on the command line; they can also be separated by newline characters. Use a semicolon (;) to mark a comment. LIB ignores all text from the semicolon to the end of the line.

You can specify either all or part of the command line in a command file, and you can use more than one command file in a LIB command. LIB accepts the command-file input as if it were specified in that location on the command line. Command files cannot be nested. LIB echoes the contents of command files unless the /NOLOGO option is used.

Using LIB Options

An option consists of an option specifier, which is either a dash (−) or a forward slash (/), followed by the name of the option. Option names cannot be abbreviated. Some options take an argument, specified after a colon (:). No spaces or tabs are allowed within an option specification. Use one or more spaces or tabs to separate option specifications on the command line. Option names and their keyword or filename arguments are not case sensitive, but identifiers used as arguments are case sensitive. LIB processes options in the order specified on the command line and in command files. If an option is repeated with different arguments, the last one to be processed takes precedence.

The following options apply to all modes of LIB:

/MACHINE:{IX86|MIPS|M68K}   Specifies the target platform for the program. Usually, you do not need to specify /MACHINE. LIB infers the machine type from the .OBJ files. However, in some circumstances, LIB cannot determine the machine type and issues an error message. If such an error occurs, specify /MACHINE. In /EXTRACT mode, this option is for verification only.

/NOLOGO Suppresses display of the LIB copyright message and version number and prevents echoing of command files.

/VERBOSE Displays details about the progress of the session. The information is sent to standard output and can be redirected to a file.

Other options apply only to specific modes of LIB. These options are discussed in the sections describing each mode.

Managing a Library

The default mode for LIB is to build or modify a library of COFF objects. LIB runs in this mode when you do not specify /EXTRACT (to copy an object to a file) or /DEF (to build an import library).

To build a library from objects and/or libraries, use the following syntax:

LIB [*options...*] *files...*

This command creates a library from one or more input *files*. The *files* can be COFF object files, 32-bit OMF object files, or existing COFF libraries. LIB creates one library that contains all objects in the specified files. If an input file is a 32-bit OMF object file, LIB converts it to COFF before building the library. LIB cannot accept a 32-bit OMF object that is in a library created by the 16-bit version of LIB. You must first use the 16-bit LIB to extract the object; then you can use the extracted object file as input to the 32-bit LIB.

By default, LIB names the output file using the base name of the first object or library file and the extension .LIB. If a file already exists with the same name, the output file replaces the existing file. To preserve an existing library, use the /OUT option to specify a name for the output file.

The following options apply to building and modifying a library:

/LIST Displays information about the output library to standard output. The output can be redirected to a file. You can use /LIST to determine the contents of an existing library without modifying it.

/OUT:*filename* Overrides the default output filename. By default, the output library has the base name of the first library or object file on the command line and the extension .LIB.

/REMOVE:*object* Omits the specified *object* from the output library. LIB creates an output library by first combining all objects (whether in object files or libraries), and then deleting any objects specified with /REMOVE.

/SUBSYSTEM Tells the operating system how to run a program created by linking to the output library. For more information, see the description of the "LINK /SUBSYSTEM" option in Chapter 26 on page 585.

You can use LIB to perform the following library-management tasks:

- To add objects to a library, specify the filename for the existing library and the filenames for the new objects.

- To combine libraries, specify the library filenames. You can add objects and combine libraries with a single LIB command.

- To replace a library member with a new object, specify the library containing the member object to be replaced and the filename for the new object (or the library that contains it). When an object that has the same name exists in more than one input file, LIB puts the last object specified in the LIB command into the output library. When you replace a library member, be sure to specify the new object or library after the library that contains the old object.

- To delete a member from a library, use the /REMOVE option. LIB processes any specifications of /REMOVE after combining all input objects, regardless of command-line order.

Note   You cannot both delete a member and extract it to a file in the same step. You must first extract the member object using /EXTRACT, then run LIB again using /REMOVE. This behavior differs from that of the 16-bit LIB (for OMF libraries) provided in other Microsoft products.

Extracting a Library Member

You can use LIB to create an object (.OBJ) file that contains a copy of a member of an existing library. To extract a copy of a member, use the following syntax:

LIB *library* /EXTRACT:*member* /OUT:*objectfile*

This command creates an .OBJ file called *objectfile* that contains a copy of a *member* of a *library*. The *member* name is case sensitive. You can extract only one member in a single command. The /OUT option is required; there is no default output name. If a file called *objectfile* already exists in the specified directory (or the current directory, if no directory is specified with *objectfile*), the extracted *objectfile* replaces the existing file.

Working with Import Libraries and Export Files

You can use LIB with the /DEF option to create an import library and an export file. LINK uses the export file to build a program that contains exports (usually a dynamic-link library (DLL)), and it uses the import library to resolve references to those exports in other programs.

In most situations, you do not need to use LIB to create your import library. When you link a program (either an executable file or a DLL) that contains exports, LINK automatically creates an import library that describes the exports. Later, when you link a program that references those exports, you specify the import library.

However, when a DLL exports to a program that it also imports from, whether directly or indirectly, you must use LIB to create one of the import libraries. When LIB creates an import library, it also creates an export file. You must use the export file when linking one of the DLLs.

Building an Import Library and Export File

To build an import library and export file, use the following syntax:

LIB /DEF[:*deffile*] [*options*] [*objfiles*] [*libraries*]

When /DEF is specified, LIB creates the output files from export specifications that are passed in the LIB command. There are three methods for specifying exports, listed in recommended order of use:

1. A **__declspec(dllexport)** definition in one of the *objfiles* or *libraries*

2. A specification of /EXPORT:*name* on the LIB command line

3. A definition in an **EXPORTS** statement in a *deffile*

These are the same methods you use to specify exports when linking an exporting program. A program can use more than one method. You can specify parts of the LIB command (such as multiple *objfiles* or /EXPORT specifications) in a command file in the LIB command, just as you can in a LINK command.

The following options apply to building an import library and export file:

/DEBUGTYPE:{CV|COFF|BOTH}   Sets the format of debugging information. Specify CV for Microsoft Symbolic Debugging Information, required by Microsoft Developer Studio. Specify COFF for Common Object File Format debugging information. Specify BOTH for both COFF debugging information and Microsoft format debugging information.

/OUT:*import*   Overrides the default output filename for the *import* library being created. When /OUT is not specified, the default name is the base name of the first object file or library in the LIB command and the extension .LIB. The export file is given the same base name as the import library and the extension .EXP.

/EXPORT:*entryname*[=*internalname*][,@*ordinal*[,**NONAME**]][,**DATA**]   Exports a function from your program to allow other programs to call the function. You can also export data (using the **DATA** keyword). Exports are usually defined in a DLL.

The *entryname* is the name of the function or data item as it is to be used by the calling program. Optionally, you can specify the *internalname* as the function known in the defining program; by default, *internalname* is the same as *entryname*. The *ordinal* specifies an index into the export table in the range 1 through 65,535; if you do not specify *ordinal*, LIB assigns one. The **NONAME** keyword exports the function only as an ordinal, without an *entryname*. The **DATA** keyword is used to export data-only objects.

/INCLUDE:*symbol*   Adds the specified symbol to the symbol table. This option is useful for forcing the use of a library object that otherwise would not be included.

Using an Import Library and Export File

When a program (either an executable file or a DLL) exports to another program that it also imports from, or if more than two programs both export to and import from each other, the commands to link these programs must accommodate circular exports.

In a situation without circular exports, when you link a program that uses exports from another program, you must specify the import library for the exporting program. The import library for the exporting program is created when you link that exporting program. Therefore, you must link the exporting program before the importing program. For example, if TWO.DLL imports from ONE.DLL, you must first link ONE.DLL and get the import library ONE.LIB. You then specify ONE.LIB when you link TWO.DLL. When the linker creates TWO.DLL, it also creates its import library, TWO.LIB. You use TWO.LIB when linking programs that import from TWO.DLL.

However, in a circular export situation, it is not possible to link all of the interdependent programs using import libraries from the other programs. In the example discussed earlier, if TWO.DLL also exports to ONE.DLL, the import library for TWO.DLL won't exist yet when ONE.DLL is linked. When circular exports exist, you must use LIB to create an import library and export file for one of the programs.

To begin, choose one of the programs on which to run LIB. In the LIB command, list all objects and libraries for the program and specify /DEF. If the program uses a .DEF file or /EXPORT specifications, specify these as well.

After you create the import library (.LIB) and the export file (.EXP) for the program, you use the import library when linking the other program or programs. LINK creates an import library for each exporting program it builds. For example, if you run LIB on the objects and exports for ONE.DLL, you create ONE.LIB and ONE.EXP. You can now use ONE.LIB when linking TWO.DLL; this step also creates the import library TWO.LIB.

Finally, link the program you began with. In the LINK command, specify the objects and libraries for the program, the .EXP file that LIB created for the program, and the import library or libraries for the exports used by the program. To continue the example, the LINK command for ONE.DLL contains ONE.EXP and TWO.LIB, as well as the objects and libraries that go into ONE.DLL. Do not specify the .DEF file or /EXPORT specifications in the LINK command; these are not needed, because the export definitions are contained in the .EXP file. When you link using an .EXP file, LINK does not create an import library, because it assumes that one was created when the .EXP file was created.

BSCMAKE Reference

The Microsoft Browse Information Maintenance Utility (BSCMAKE.EXE) builds a browse information file (.BSC) from .SBR files created during compilation. You view a browse information file in a browse window. For information about browse windows, see Chapter 16, "Browsing Through Symbols."

When you build your program, you can create a browse information file for your program automatically, using BSCMAKE to build the file. You do not need to know how to run BSCMAKE if you create your browse information file in Microsoft Developer Studio. However, you may want to read this topic to understand the choices available.

If you build your program outside of Developer Studio, you can still create a custom .BSC that you can examine in Microsoft Developer Studio. Run BSCMAKE on the .SBR files that you created during compilation.

Building a .BSC File

BSCMAKE can build a new browse information file from newly created .SBR files. It can also maintain an existing .BSC file using .SBR files for object files that have changed since the last build.

Creating an .SBR File

The input files for BSCMAKE are .SBR files. The compiler creates an .SBR file for each object (.OBJ) file it compiles. When you build or update your browse information file, all .SBR files for your project must be available on disk.

To create an .SBR file with all possible information, specify Generate Browse Info in the Compiler Settings dialog box (or specify the /FR option).

To create an .SBR file that doesn't contain local symbols, specify Generate Browse Info, and then check Exclude Local Variables from Browse Info (or specify /Fr on the compiler command line). If the .SBR files contain local symbols, you can still omit them from the .BSC file by using BSCMAKE's /El option.

You can create an .SBR file without performing a full compile. For example, you can specify the /Zs option to the compiler to perform a syntax check and still generate an .SBR file if you specify /FR or /Fr.

The build process can be more efficient if the .SBR files are first packed to remove unreferenced definitions. The compiler automatically packs .SBR files. An unpacked .SBR file is required if you want to use the /Iu option with BSCMAKE to include unreferenced symbols in the .BSC file. If you want to prevent packing, specify /Zn on the compiler command line.

How BSCMAKE Builds a .BSC File

BSCMAKE builds or rebuilds a .BSC file in the most efficient way it can. To avoid potential problems, it is important to understand the build process.

When BSCMAKE builds a browse information file, it truncates the .SBR files to zero length. During a subsequent build of the same file, a zero-length (or empty) .SBR file tells BSCMAKE that the .SBR file has no new contribution to make. It lets BSCMAKE know that an update of that part of the file is not required and an incremental build will be sufficient. During every build (unless the /n option is specified), BSCMAKE first attempts to update the file incrementally by using only those .SBR files that have changed.

BSCMAKE looks for a .BSC file that has the name specified with the /o option. If /o is not specified, BSCMAKE looks for a file that has the base name of the first .SBR file and a .BSC extension. If the file exists, BSCMAKE performs an incremental build of the browse information file using only the contributing .SBR files. If the file does not exist, BSCMAKE performs a full build using all .SBR files. The rules for builds are as follows:

- For a full build to succeed, all specified .SBR files must exist and must not be truncated. If an .SBR file is truncated, you must rebuild it (by recompiling or assembling) before running BSCMAKE.

- For an incremental build to succeed, the .BSC file must exist. All contributing .SBR files, even empty files, must exist and must be specified on the BSCMAKE command line. If you omit an .SBR file from the command line, BSCMAKE removes its contribution from the file.

Increasing Efficiency with BSCMAKE

The building process can require large amounts of time, memory, and disk space. However, you can reduce these requirements by creating a smaller .BSC file and by avoiding unreferenced definitions.

Making a Smaller Browse Information File

Smaller browse information files take less time to build, use less disk space, reduce the risk of BSCMAKE running out of memory, and run faster in the Browse window. You can use one or more of the following methods to create a smaller file:

- Use BSCMAKE options to exclude information from the browse information file. These options are described on page 618.

- Omit local symbols in one or more .SBR files when compiling or assembling.

- If an object file does not contain information that you need for your current stage of debugging, omit its .SBR file from the BSCMAKE command when rebuilding the browse information file.

Saving Build Time and Disk Space

Unreferenced definitions cause .SBR files to take up more disk space and cause BSCMAKE to run less efficiently. The compiler automatically packs .SBR files to remove unreferenced definitions. The /Zn (Don't Pack Info) option prevents this packing. You can increase efficiency of disk space and BSCMAKE speed by not using /Zn and allowing the compiler to pack the .SBR files.

BSCMAKE Command Line

To run BSCMAKE, use the following command line syntax:

BSCMAKE [*options*] *sbrfiles*

Options can appear only in the *options* field on the command line.

The *sbrfiles* field specifies one or more .SBR files created by a compiler or assembler. Separate the names of .SBR files with spaces or tabs. You must specify the extension; there is no default. You can specify a path with the filename, and you can use operating-system wildcards (* and ?).

During an incremental build, you can specify new .SBR files that were not part of the original build. If you want all contributions to remain in the browse information file, you must specify all .SBR files (including truncated files) that were originally used to create the .BSC file. If you omit an .SBR file, that file's contribution to the browse information file is removed.

Do not specify a truncated .SBR file for a full build. A full build requires contributions from all specified .SBR files. Before you perform a full build, recompile the project and create a new .SBR file for each empty file.

The following command runs BSCMAKE to build a file called MAIN.BSC from three .SBR files:

```
BSCMAKE main.sbr file1.sbr file2.sbr
```

BSCMAKE Command File

You can provide part or all of the command-line input in a command file. Specify the command file using the following syntax:

BSCMAKE @*filename*

Only one command file is allowed. You can specify a path with *filename*. Precede *filename* with an at sign (@). BSCMAKE does not assume an extension. You can specify additional *sbrfiles* on the command line after *filename*. The command file is a text file that contains the input to BSCMAKE in the same order as you would specify it on the command line. Separate the command-line arguments with one or more spaces, tabs, or newline characters.

The following command calls BSCMAKE using a command file:

```
BSCMAKE @prog1.txt
```

The following is a sample command file:

```
/n /v /o main.bsc /El
/S (
toolbox.h
verdate.h c:\src\inc\screen.h
)
file1.sbr file2.sbr file3.sbr file4.sbr
```

BSCMAKE Options

This section describes the options available for controlling BSCMAKE. Several options control the content of the browse information file by excluding or including certain information. The exclusion options can allow BSCMAKE to run faster and may result in a smaller .BSC file. Option names are case sensitive (except for /HELP and /NOLOGO).

/Ei (*filename*...) Excludes the contents of the specified include files from the browse information file. To specify multiple files, separate the names with a space and enclose the list in parentheses. Parentheses are not necessary if you specify only one *filename*. Use /Ei along with the /Es option to exclude files not excluded by /Es.

/El Excludes local symbols. The default is to include local symbols. For more information about local symbols, see Creating an .SBR File.

/Em Excludes symbols in the body of macros. Use /Em to include only the names of macros in the browse information file. The default is to include both the macro names and the result of the macro expansions.

/Er (*symbol*...) Excludes the specified symbols from the browse information file. To specify multiple symbol names, separate the names with a space and enclose the list in parentheses. Parentheses are not necessary if you specify only one *symbol*.

/Es Excludes from the browse information file every include file specified with an absolute path or found in an absolute path specified in the INCLUDE environment variable. (Usually, these are the system include files, which contain a lot of information that you may not need in your browse information file.) This option does not exclude files specified without a path or with relative paths or files found in a relative path in INCLUDE. You can use the /Ei option along with /Es to exclude files that /Es does not exclude. If you want to exclude only some of the files that /Es excludes, use /Ei instead of /Es and list the files you want to exclude.

/HELP Displays a summary of the BSCMAKE command-line syntax.

/Iu Includes unreferenced symbols. By default, BSCMAKE does not record any symbols that are defined but not referenced. If an .SBR file has been packed, this option has no effect for that input file because the compiler has already removed the unreferenced symbols.

/n Forces a nonincremental build. Use /n to force a full build of the browse information file whether or not a .BSC file exists and to prevent .SBR files from being truncated. See How BSCMAKE Builds a .BSC File.

/NOLOGO Suppresses the BSCMAKE copyright message.

/o *filename* Specifies a name for the browse information file. By default, BSCMAKE gives the browse information file the base name of the first .SBR file and a .BSC extension.

/S (*filename*...) Tells BSCMAKE to process the specified include file the first time it is encountered and to exclude it otherwise. Use this option to save processing time when a file (such as a header, or .H, file for a .C or .CPP source file) is included in several source files but is unchanged by preprocessing directives each time. You may also want to use this option if a file is changed in ways that are unimportant for the browse information file you are creating. To specify multiple files, separate the names with a space and enclose the list in parentheses. Parentheses are not necessary if you specify only one *filename*. If you want to exclude the file every time it is included, use the /Ei or /Es option.

/v Provides verbose output, which includes the name of each .SBR file being processed and information about the complete BSCMAKE run.

/? Displays a brief summary of BSCMAKE command-line syntax.

The following command line tells BSCMAKE to do a full build of MAIN.BSC from three .SBR files. It also tells BSCMAKE to exclude duplicate instances of TOOLBOX.H:

```
BSCMAKE /n /S toolbox.h /o main.bsc file1.sbr file2.sbr file3.sbr
```

BSCMAKE Exit Codes

BSCMAKE returns an exit code (also called a return code or error code) to the operating system or the calling program.

Code	Meaning
0	No error
1	Command-line error
4	Fatal error during build

DUMPBIN Reference

The Microsoft COFF Binary File Dumper (DUMPBIN.EXE) displays information about 32-bit Common Object File Format (COFF) binary files. You can use DUMPBIN to examine COFF object files, standard libraries of COFF objects, executable files, and dynamic-link libraries (DLLs).

Note DUMPBIN runs only from the command line.

DUMPBIN Command Line

To run DUMPBIN, use the following syntax:

DUMPBIN [*options*] *files...*

Specify one or more binary files, along with any options required to control the information. DUMPBIN displays the information to standard output. You can either redirect it to a file or use the /OUT option to specify a filename for the output.

When you run DUMPBIN on a file without specifying an option, DUMPBIN displays the /SUMMARY output.

When you type the command dumpbin without any other command-line input, DUMPBIN displays a usage statement that summarizes its options.

DUMPBIN Options

An option consists of an option specifier, which is either a dash (–) or a forward slash (/), followed by the name of the option. Option names cannot be abbreviated. Some options take arguments, specified after a colon (:). No spaces or tabs are allowed within an option specification. Use one or more spaces or tabs to separate option specifications on the command line. Option names and their keyword or filename arguments are not case sensitive. Most options apply to all binary files; a few apply only to certain types of files.

DUMPBIN has the following options:

/ALL   Displays all available information except code disassembly. Use /DISASM to display disassembly. You can use /RAWDATA:NONE with /ALL to omit the raw binary details of the file.

/ARCHIVEMEMBERS   Displays minimal information about member objects in a library.

/DISASM   Displays disassembly of code sections, using symbols if present in the file.

/EXPORTS   Displays all definitions exported from an executable file or DLL.

/FPO   Displays frame pointer optimization (FPO) records.

/HEADERS   Displays the file header and the header for each section. When used with a library, it displays the header for each member object.

/IMPORTS   Displays all definitions imported to an executable file or DLL.

/LINENUMBERS   Displays COFF line numbers. Line numbers exist in an object file if it was compiled with Program Database (/Zi), C7 Compatible (/Z7), or Line Numbers Only (/Zd). An executable file or DLL contains COFF line numbers if it was linked with Generate Debug Info (/DEBUG) and COFF Format (/DEBUGTYPE:COFF).

/LINKERMEMBER[:{1|2}]   Displays public symbols defined in a library. Specify the 1 argument to display symbols in object order, along with their offsets. Specify the 2 argument to display offsets and index numbers of objects, and then list the symbols in alphabetical order, along with the object index for each. To get both outputs, specify /LINKERMEMBER without the number argument.

/OUT:*filename*   Specifies a *filename* for the output. By default, DUMPBIN displays the information to standard output.

/RAWDATA[:{BYTES|SHORTS|LONGS|NONE}[,*number*]]   Displays the raw contents of each section in the file. The arguments control the format of the display, as shown below:

Argument	Result
BYTES	The default. Contents are displayed in hexadecimal bytes, and also as ASCII characters if they have a printed representation.
SHORTS	Contents are displayed in hexadecimal words.
LONGS	Contents are displayed in hexadecimal longwords.
NONE	Raw data is suppressed. This argument is useful to control the output of /ALL.
number	Displayed lines are set to a width that holds *number* values per line.

/RELOCATIONS   Displays any relocations in the object or image.

/SECTION:*section*   Restricts the output to information on the specified *section*.

/SUMMARY   Displays minimal information about sections, including total size. This option is the default if no other option is specified.

/SYMBOLS   Displays the COFF symbol table. Symbol tables exist in all object files. A COFF symbol table appears in an image file only if it is linked with the Generate Debug Info and COFF Format options under Debug Info on the Debug category for the linker (or the /DEBUG and /DEBUGTYPE:COFF options on the command line).

EDITBIN Reference

The Microsoft COFF Binary File Editor (EDITBIN.EXE) modifies 32-bit Common Object File Format (COFF) binary files. You can use EDITBIN to modify object files, executable files, and dynamic-link libraries (DLLs).

Note EDITBIN runs only from the command line.

EDITBIN converts the format of an Object Module Format (OMF) input file to COFF before making other changes to the file. You can use EDITBIN to convert the format of a file to COFF by running EDITBIN with no options.

EDITBIN Command Line

To run EDITBIN, use the following syntax:

EDITBIN [*options*] *files...*

Specify one or more files for the objects or images to be changed, and one or more options for changing the files.

When you type the command editbin without any other command-line input, EDITBIN displays a usage statement that summarizes its options.

EDITBIN Options

An option consists of an option specifier, which is either a dash (–) or a forward slash (/), followed by the name of the option. Option names cannot be abbreviated. Some options take arguments, specified after a colon (:). No spaces or tabs are allowed within an option specification. Use one or more spaces or tabs to separate option specifications on the command line. Option names and their keyword or filename arguments are not case sensitive.

/BIND

This option sets the addresses of the entry points in the import address table for an executable file or DLL. Use this option to reduce load time of a program.

/BIND[:PATH=*path*]

Specify the program's executable file and DLLs in the *files* argument on the EDITBIN command line. The optional *path* argument to /BIND specifies the location of the DLLs used by the specified files. Separate multiple directories with a semicolon (;). If *path* is not specified, EDITBIN searches the directories specified in the PATH environment variable. If *path* is specified, EDITBIN ignores the PATH variable.

By default, the program loader sets the addresses of entry points when it loads a program. The amount of time this process takes varies, depending on the number of DLLs and the number of entry points referenced in the program. If a program has been modified with /BIND, and if the base addresses for the executable file and its DLLs do not conflict with DLLs that are already loaded, the operating system does not need to set these addresses. In a situation where the files are incorrectly based, the operating system relocates the program's DLLs and recalculates the entry-point addresses, which adds to the program's load time.

/HEAP

This option sets the size of the heap in bytes.

/HEAP:*reserve*[,*commit*]

The *reserve* argument specifies the total heap allocation in virtual memory. The default heap size is 1 MB. The linker rounds up the specified value to the nearest 4 bytes.

The optional *commit* argument is subject to interpretation by the operating system. In Windows NT and Windows 95, it specifies the amount of physical memory to allocate at a time. Committed virtual memory causes space to be reserved in the paging file. A higher *commit* value saves time when the application needs more heap space but increases the memory requirements and possibly the startup time.

Specify the *reserve* and *commit* values in decimal or C-language notation.

/NOLOGO

This option suppresses display of the EDITBIN copyright message and version number.

/NOLOGO

/REBASE

This option sets the base addresses for the specified files. EDITBIN assigns new base addresses in a contiguous address space according to the size of each file rounded up to the nearest 64K. For details about base addresses, see "Base Address" in Chapter 21.

/REBASE[:*modifiers*]

Specify the program's executable files and DLLs in the *files* argument on the EDITBIN command line in the order in which they are to be based. You can optionally specify one or more *modifiers*, each separated by a comma (,):

Modifier	Action
BASE=*address*	Provides a beginning address for reassigning base addresses to the files. Specify *address* in decimal or C-language notation. If BASE is not specified, the default starting base address is 0x400000. If DOWN is used, BASE must be specified, and *address* sets the end of the range of base addresses.
BASEFILE	Creates a file named COFFBASE.TXT, which is a text file in the format expected by LINK's /BASE option.
DOWN	Tells EDITBIN to reassign base addresses downward from an ending address. The files are reassigned in the order specified, with the first file located in the highest possible address below the end of the address range. BASE must be used with DOWN to ensure sufficient address space for basing the files. To determine the address space needed by the specified files, run EDITBIN with /REBASE on the files and add 64K to the displayed total size.

/RELEASE

This option sets the checksum in the header of an executable file.

/RELEASE

The operating system requires the checksum for certain files, such as device drivers. It is recommended that you set the checksum for release versions of your programs to ensure compatibility with future operating systems.

/SECTION

This option changes the attributes of a section, overriding the attributes that were set when the object file for the section was compiled or linked.

/SECTION:*name*[=*newname*][,*attributes*][,*alignment*]

After the colon (:), specify the *name* of the section. To change the section name, follow *name* with an equal sign (=) and a *newname* for the section.

To set or change the section's *attributes*, specify a comma (,) followed by one or more attributes characters. To negate an attribute, precede its character with an exclamation point (!). The following characters specify memory attributes:

Attribute	Setting
c	code
d	discardable
e	executable
i	initialized data
k	cached virtual memory
m	link remove
o	link info
p	paged virtual memory
r	read
s	shared
u	uninitialized data
w	write

To control *alignment*, specify the character a followed by a character to set the size of alignment in bytes, as follows:

Character	Alignment size in bytes
1	1
2	2
4	4
8	8
p	16
t	32
s	64
x	no alignment

Specify the *attributes* and *alignment* characters as a string with no white space. The characters are not case sensitive.

/STACK

This option sets the size of the stack in bytes and takes arguments in decimal or C-language notation. The /STACK option applies only to an executable file.

/STACK:*reserve*[,*commit*]

The *reserve* argument specifies the total stack allocation in virtual memory. EDITBIN rounds up the specified value to the nearest 4 bytes.

The optional *commit* argument is subject to interpretation by the operating system. In Windows NT and Windows 95, *commit* specifies the amount of physical memory to allocate at a time. Committed virtual memory causes space to be reserved in the paging file. A higher *commit* value saves time when the application needs more stack space but increases the memory requirements and possibly startup time.

NMAKE Reference

The Microsoft Program Maintenance Utility (NMAKE.EXE) is a 32-bit tool that builds projects based on commands contained in a description file.

Running NMAKE

The syntax for NMAKE is:

NMAKE [*option*...] [*macros*...] [*targets*...] [@*commandfile*...]

NMAKE builds only specified *targets* or, if none are specified, the first target in the makefile. The first makefile target can be a pseudotarget that builds other targets. NMAKE uses makefiles specified with /F; if /F is not specified, it uses the MAKEFILE file in the current directory. If no makefile is specified, it uses inference rules to build command-line *targets*.

The *commandfile* text file contains command-line input. Other input can precede or follow @*commandfile*. A path is permitted. In *commandfile*, line breaks are treated as spaces. Enclose macro definitions in quotation marks if they contain spaces.

NMAKE Options

NMAKE options are described in the following table. Options are preceded by either a slash (/) or a dash (–) and are not case sensitive. Use **!CMDSWITCHES** to change option settings in a makefile or in TOOLS.INI.

Option	Action
/A	Forces build of all evaluated targets, even if not out-of-date with respect to dependents. Does not force build of unrelated targets.
/B	Forces build even if timestamps are equal. Recommended only for very fast systems (resolution of two seconds or less).
/C	Suppresses default output, including nonfatal NMAKE errors or warnings, timestamps, and NMAKE copyright message. Suppresses warnings issued by /K.

Option	Action
/D	Displays timestamps of each evaluated target and dependent and a message when a target does not exist. Useful with /P for debugging a makefile. Use **!CMDSWITCHES** to set or clear /D for part of a makefile.
/E	Causes environment variables to override makefile macro definitions.
/F *filename*	Specifies *filename* as a makefile. Spaces or tabs can precede *filename*. Specify /F once for each makefile. To supply a makefile from standard input, specify a dash (–) for *filename*, and end keyboard input with either F6 or CTRL+Z.
/HELP, /?	Displays a brief summary of NMAKE command-line syntax.
/I	Ignores exit codes from all commands. To set or clear /I for part of a makefile, use **!CMDSWITCHES**. To ignore exit codes for part of a makefile, use a dash (–) command modifier or **.IGNORE**. Overrides /K if both are specified.
/K	Continues building unrelated dependencies, if a command returns an error. Also issues a warning and returns an exit code of 1. By default, NMAKE halts if any command returns a nonzero exit code. Warnings from /K are suppressed by /C; /I overrides /K if both are specified.
/N	Displays but does not execute commands; preprocessing commands are executed. Does not display commands in recursive NMAKE calls. Useful for debugging makefiles and checking timestamps. To set or clear /N for part of a makefile, use **!CMDSWITCHES**.
/NOLOGO	Suppresses the NMAKE copyright message.
/P	Displays information (macro definitions, inference rules, targets, **.SUFFIXES** list) to standard output, and then runs the build. If no makefile or command-line target exists, it displays information only. Use with /D to debug a makefile.
/Q	Checks timestamps of targets; does not run the build. Returns a zero exit code if all targets are up to date and a nonzero exit code if any target is not. Preprocessing commands are executed. Useful when running NMAKE from a batch file.
/R	Clears the **.SUFFIXES** list and ignores inference rules and macros that are defined in the TOOLS.INI file or that are predefined.
/S	Suppresses display of executed commands. To suppress display in part of a makefile, use the @ command modifier or **.SILENT**. To set or clear /S for part of a makefile, use **!CMDSWITCHES**.
/T	Updates timestamps of command-line targets (or first makefile target) and executes preprocessing commands but does not run the build.
/X *filename*	Sends NMAKE error output to *filename* instead of standard error. Spaces or tabs can precede *filename*. To send error output to standard output, specify a dash (–) for *filename*. Does not affect output from commands to standard error.

TOOLS.INI and NMAKE

NMAKE reads TOOLS.INI before it reads makefiles, unless /R is used. It looks for TOOLS.INI first in the current directory and then in the directory specified by the INIT environment variable. The section for NMAKE settings in the initialization file begins with [NMAKE] and can contain any makefile information. Specify a comment on a separate line beginning with a number sign (#).

Exit Codes from NMAKE

NMAKE returns the following exit codes.

Code	Meaning
0	No error (possibly a warning)
1	Incomplete build (issued only when /K is used)
2	Program error, possibly due to one of the following:
	▪ A syntax error in the makefile
	▪ An error or exit code from a command
	▪ An interruption by the user
4	System error— out of memory
255	Target is not up-to-date (issued only when /Q is used)

Contents of a Makefile

A makefile contains:

- Description blocks
- Commands
- Macros
- Inference rules
- Dot directives
- Preprocessing directives

Other features of a makefile include wildcards, long filenames, comments, and special characters.

Wildcards and NMAKE

NMAKE expands filename wildcards (* and ?) in dependency lines. A wildcard specified in a command is passed to the command; NMAKE does not expand it.

Long Filenames in a Makefile

Enclose long filenames in double quotation marks, as follows:

```
all : "VeryLongFileName.exe"
```

Comments in a Makefile

Precede a comment with a number sign (#). NMAKE ignores text from the number sign to the next newline character. The following are examples of comments:

```
# Comment on line by itself
OPTIONS = /MAP  # Comment on macro definition line

all.exe : one.obj two.obj  # Comment on dependency line
    link one.obj two.obj
# Comment in commands block
#   copy *.obj \objects  # Command turned into comment
    copy one.exe \release

.obj.exe:  # Comment on inference rule line
    link $<

my.exe : my.obj ; link my.obj  # Err: cannot comment this
 # Error: # must be the first character
.obj.exe: ; link $<  # Error: cannot comment this
```

To specify a literal number sign, precede it with a caret (^), as follows:

```
DEF = ^#define  #Macro for a C preprocessing directive
```

Special Characters in a Makefile

To use an NMAKE special character as a literal character, place a caret (^) in front of it. NMAKE ignores carets that precede other characters. The special characters are:

```
: ; # ( ) $ ^ \ { } ! @ —
```

A caret (^) within a quoted string is treated as a literal caret character. A caret at the end of a line inserts a literal newline character in a string or macro.

In macros, a backslash (\) followed by a newline character is replaced by a space.

In commands, a percent symbol (%) is a file specifier. To represent % literally in a command, specify a double percent sign (%%) in place of a single one. In other situations, NMAKE interprets a single % literally, but it always interprets a double %% as a single %. Therefore, to represent a literal %%, specify either three percent signs, %%%, or four percent signs, %%%%.

To use the dollar sign ($) as a literal character in a command, specify two dollar signs ($$). This method can also be used in other situations where ^$ works.

Description Blocks

A description block is a dependency line optionally followed by a commands block:

```
targets... : dependents...
   commands...
```

A dependency line specifies one or more targets and zero or more dependents. A target must be at the start of the line. Separate targets from dependents by a colon (:); spaces or tabs are allowed. To split the line, use a backslash (\) after a target or dependent. If a target does not exist, has an earlier timestamp than a dependent, or is a pseudotarget, NMAKE executes the commands. If a dependent is a target elsewhere and does not exist or is out-of-date with respect to its own dependents, NMAKE updates the dependent before updating the current dependency.

Targets

In a dependency line, specify one or more targets, using any valid filename, directory name, or pseudotarget. Separate multiple targets with one or more spaces or tabs. Targets are not case sensitive. Paths are permitted with filenames. A target cannot exceed 256 characters. If the target preceding the colon is a single character, use a separating space; otherwise, NMAKE interprets the letter-colon combination as a drive specifier.

Pseudotargets

A pseudotarget is a label used in place of a filename in a dependency line. It is interpreted as a file that does not exist and so is out of date. NMAKE assumes a pseudotarget's timestamp is the most recent of all its dependents; if it has no dependents, the current time is assumed. If a pseudotarget is used as a target, its commands are always executed. A pseudotarget used as a dependent must also appear as a target in another dependency; however, that dependency does not need to have a commands block.

Pseudotarget names follow the filename syntax rules for targets. However, if the name does not have an extension (that is, does not contain a period), it can exceed the 8-character limit for filenames and can be up to 256 characters long.

Multiple Targets

NMAKE evaluates multiple targets in a single dependency as if each were specified in a separate description block.

This...	...is evaluated as this

`bounce.exe leap.exe :`
`jump.obj`
`  echo Building...`
	`bounce.exe : jump.obj`
	`   echo Building...`
	`leap.exe : jump.obj`
	`   echo Building...`

Cumulative Dependencies

Dependencies are cumulative in a description block if a target is repeated.

This...	...is evaluated as this
| ```
bounce.exe : jump.obj
bounce.exe : up.obj
   echo Building
bounce.exe...
``` | ```
bounce.exe : jump.obj
up.obj
   echo Building
bounce.exe...
``` |

Multiple targets in multiple dependency lines in a single description block are evaluated as if each were specified in a separate description block, but targets that are not in the last dependency line do not use the commands block.

This...	...is evaluated as this
| ```
bounce.exe leap.exe :
jump.obj
bounce.exe climb.exe :
up.obj
   echo Building...
``` | ```
bounce.exe : jump.obj
up.obj
   echo Building
bounce.exe...
climb.exe : up.obj
   echo Building
climb.exe...
leap.exe : jump.obj
# invokes an inference rule
``` |

Targets in Multiple Description Blocks

To update a target in more than one description block using different commands, specify two consecutive colons (::) between targets and dependents.

```
target.lib :: one.asm two.asm three.asm
    ml one.asm two.asm three.asm
    lib target one.obj two.obj three.obj
target.lib :: four.c five.c
    cl /c four.c five.c
    lib target four.obj five.obj
```

A Side Effect

If a target is specified with a colon (:) in two dependency lines in different locations, and if commands appear after only one of the lines, NMAKE interprets the dependencies as if adjacent or combined. It does not invoke an inference rule for the dependency that has no commands, but instead assumes that the dependencies belong to one description block and executes the commands specified with the other dependency.

This...	...is evaluated as this

```bounce.exe : jump.obj```
 ``` echo Building```
 ```bounce.exe...```
 	
 ```bounce.exe : up.obj```
	```bounce.exe : jump.obj```
	 ```up.obj```
	 ``` echo Building```
	 ``` bounce.exe...```

This effect does not occur if a double colon (::) is used.

This...	...is evaluated as this

```bounce.exe :: jump.obj```
 ``` echo Building```
 ```bounce.exe...```
 	
 ```bounce.exe :: up.obj```
	```bounce.exe : jump.obj```
	 ``` echo Building```
	 ``` bounce.exe...```
	
	 ```bounce.exe : up.obj```
	 ```# invokes an inference rule```

Dependents

In a dependency line, specify zero or more dependents after the colon (:) or double colon (::), using any valid filename or pseudotarget. Separate multiple dependents with one or more spaces or tabs. Dependents are not case sensitive. Paths are permitted with filenames.

Inferred Dependents

An inferred dependent is derived from an inference rule and is evaluated before explicit dependents. If an inferred dependent is out of date with respect to its target, NMAKE invokes the commands block for the dependency. If an inferred dependent does not exist or is out-of-date with respect to its own dependents, NMAKE first updates the inferred dependent. For more information about inferred dependents, see Inference Rules.

Search Paths for Dependents

Each dependent has an optional search path, specified as follows:

{*directory*[;*directory...*]}*dependent*

NMAKE looks for a dependent first in the current directory, and then in directories in the order specified. A macro can specify part or all of a search path. Enclose directory names in braces ({ }); separate multiple directories with a semicolon (;). No spaces or tabs are allowed.

Commands in a Makefile

A description block or inference rule specifies a block of commands to run if the dependency is out of date. NMAKE displays each command before running it, unless /S, .SILENT, !CMDSWITCHES, or @ is used. NMAKE looks for a matching inference rule if a description block is not followed by a commands block.

A commands block contains one or more commands, each on its own line. No blank line can appear between the dependency or rule and the commands block. However, a line containing only spaces or tabs can appear; this line is interpreted as a null command, and no error occurs. Blank lines are permitted between command lines.

A command line begins with one or more spaces or tabs. A backslash (\) followed by a newline character is interpreted as a space in the command; use a backslash at the end of a line to continue a command onto the next line. NMAKE interprets the backslash literally if any other character, including a space or tab, follows the backslash.

A command preceded by a semicolon (;) can appear on a dependency line or inference rule, whether or not a commands block follows:

```
project.obj : project.c project.h ; cl /c project.c
```

Command Modifiers

You can specify one or more command modifiers preceding a command, optionally separated by spaces or tabs. As with commands, modifiers must be indented.

Modifier	Action
@*command*	Prevents display of the command. Display by commands is not suppressed. By default, NMAKE echoes all executed commands. Use /S to suppress display for the entire makefile; use .SILENT to suppress display for part of the makefile.
–[*number*]*command*	Turns off error checking for *command*. By default, NMAKE halts when a command returns a nonzero exit code. If *–number* is used, NMAKE stops if the exit code exceeds *number*. Spaces or tabs cannot appear between the dash and *number*; at least one space or tab must appear between *number* and *command*. Use /I to turn off error checking for the entire makefile; use .IGNORE to turn off error checking for part of the makefile.
!*command*	Executes *command* for each dependent file if *command* uses $** (all dependent files in the dependency) or $? (all dependent files in the dependency with a later timestamp than the target).

Filename-Parts Syntax

Filename-parts syntax in commands represents components of the first dependent filename (which may be an implied dependent). Filename components are the file's drive, path, base name, and extension as specified, not as it exists on disk. Use **%s** to represent the complete filename. Use **%|**[*parts*]**F** (a vertical bar character follows the percent symbol) to represent parts of the filename, where *parts* can be zero or more of the following letters, in any order:

Letter	Description
No letter	Complete name (same as **%s**)
d	Drive
p	Path
f	File base name
e	File extension

For example, if the filename is c:\prog.exe:

%s will be c:\prog.exe

%:F will be c:\prog.exe

%:dF will be c

%:pF will be c:\

%:fF will be prog

%:eF will be exe

Inline Files in a Makefile

An inline file contains text you specify in the makefile. Its name can be used in commands as input (for example, a LINK command file), or it can pass commands to the operating system. The file is created on disk when a command that creates the file is run.

Specifying an Inline File

The syntax for specifying an inline file in a command is:

<<[*filename*]

Specify two angle brackets (<<) in the command where the filename is to appear. The angle brackets cannot be a macro expansion. When the command is run, the angle brackets are replaced by *filename*, if specified, or by a unique NMAKE-generated name. If specified, *filename* must follow angle brackets without a space or tab. A path is permitted. No extension is required or assumed. If *filename* is specified, the file is created in the current or specified directory, overwriting any existing file by that name; otherwise, it is created in the TMP directory (or the current directory, if the

TMP environment variable is not defined). If a previous *filename* is reused, NMAKE replaces the previous file.

Creating Inline File Text

The syntax to create the content of an inline file is:

inlinetext

.

.

.

<<[KEEP | NOKEEP]

Specify *inlinetext* on the first line after the command. Mark the end with double angle brackets (<<) at the beginning of a separate line. The file contains all *inlinetext* before the delimiting brackets. The *inlinetext* can have macro expansions and substitutions, but not directives or makefile comments. Spaces, tabs, and newline characters are treated literally.

Inline files are temporary or permanent. A temporary file exists for the duration of the session and can be reused by other commands. Specify **KEEP** after the closing angle brackets to retain the file after the NMAKE session; an unnamed file is preserved on disk with the generated filename. Specify **NOKEEP** or nothing for a temporary file. **KEEP** and **NOKEEP** are not case sensitive.

Reusing Inline Files

To reuse an inline file, specify <<*filename* where the file is defined and first used, then reuse *filename* without << later in the same or another command. The command to create the inline file must run before all commands that use the file.

Multiple Inline Files

A command can create more than one inline file. The syntax to do this is:

   command << <<
inlinetext
<<[KEEP | NOKEEP]
inlinetext
<<[KEEP | NOKEEP]

For each file, specify one or more lines of inline text followed by a closing line containing the delimiter. Begin the second file's text on the line following the delimiting line for the first file.

Macros and NMAKE

Macros replace a particular string in the makefile with another string. Using macros, you can create a makefile that can build different projects, specify options for commands, or set environment variables. You can define your own macros or use NMAKE's predefined macros.

Defining an NMAKE Macro

Use the following syntax to define a macro:

macroname=string

The *macroname* is a combination of letters, digits, and underscores (_) up to 1024 characters, and is case sensitive. The *macroname* can contain an invoked macro. If *macroname* consists entirely of an invoked macro, the macro being invoked cannot be null or undefined.

The *string* can be any sequence of zero or more characters. A null string contains zero characters or only spaces or tabs. The *string* can contain a macro invocation.

Special Characters in Macros

A number sign (#) after a definition specifies a comment. To specify a literal number sign in a macro, use a caret (^), as in ^#.

A dollar sign ($) specifies a macro invocation. To specify a literal $, use $$.

To extend a definition to a new line, end the line with a backslash (\ ). When the macro is invoked, the backslash plus newline character is replaced with a space. To specify a literal backslash at the end of the line, precede it with a caret (^), or follow it with a comment specifier (#).

To specify a literal newline character, end the line with a caret (^), as in:

```
CMDS = cls^
dir
```

Null and Undefined Macros

Both null and undefined macros expand to null strings, but a macro defined as a null string is considered defined in preprocessing expressions. To define a macro as a null string, specify no characters except spaces or tabs after the equal sign (=) in a command line or command file, and enclose the null string or definition in double quotation marks (" "). To undefine a macro, use **!UNDEF.** For information, see "Makefile Preprocessing Directives" on page 648.

Where to Define Macros

Define macros in a command line, command file, makefile, or the TOOLS.INI file.

In a makefile or the TOOLS.INI file, each macro definition must appear on a separate line and cannot start with a space or tab. Spaces or tabs around the equal sign are ignored. All string characters are literal, including surrounding quotation marks and embedded spaces.

In a command line or command file, spaces and tabs delimit arguments and cannot surround the equal sign. If *string* has embedded spaces or tabs, enclose either the string itself or the entire macro in double quotation marks (" ").

Precedence in Macro Definitions

If a macro has multiple definitions, NMAKE uses the highest-precedence definition. The following list shows the order of precedence, from highest to lowest:

1. A macro defined on the command line

2. A macro defined in a makefile or include file

3. An inherited environment-variable macro

4. A macro defined in the TOOLS.INI file

5. A predefined macro, such as **CC** and **AS**

Use /E to cause macros inherited from environment variables to override makefile macros with the same name. Use **!UNDEF** to override a command line.

Using an NMAKE Macro

To use a macro, enclose its name in parentheses preceded by a dollar sign ($):

$(*macroname*)

No spaces are allowed. The parentheses are optional if *macroname* is a single character. The definition string replaces $(*macroname*); an undefined macro is replaced by a null string.

Macro Substitution

To substitute text within a macro, use the following syntax:

$(*macroname*:*string1*=*string2*)

When *macroname* is invoked, each occurrence of *string1* in its definition string is replaced by *string2*. Macro substitution is case sensitive and is literal; *string1* and *string2* cannot invoke macros. Substitution does not modify the original definition. You can substitute text in any predefined macro except **$$@**.

No spaces or tabs precede the colon; any after the colon are interpreted as literal. If *string2* is null, all occurrences of *string1* are deleted from the macro's definition string.

Special NMAKE Macros

NMAKE provides several special macros to represent various filenames and commands. One use for some of these macros is in the predefined inference rules. Like all macros, the macros provided by NMAKE are case sensitive.

- Filename macros

- Recursion macros
- Command macros and options macros
- Environment-variable macros

Filename Macros

Filename macros are predefined as filenames specified in the dependency (not full filename specifications on disk). These macros do not need to be enclosed in parentheses when invoked; specify only a $ as shown.

Macro	Meaning
$@	Current target's full name (path, base name, extension), as currently specified.
$$@	Current target's full name (path, base name, extension), as currently specified. Valid only as a dependent in a dependency.
$*	Current target's path and base name minus file extension.
$**	All dependents of the current target.
$?	All dependents with a later timestamp than the current target.
$<	Dependent file with a later timestamp than the current target. Valid only in commands in inference rules.

To specify part of a predefined filename macro, append a macro modifier and enclose the modified macro in parentheses.

Modifier	Resulting Filename Part
D	Drive plus directory
B	Base name
F	Base name plus extension
R	Drive plus directory plus base name

Recursion Macros

Use recursion macros to call NMAKE recursively. Recursive sessions inherit command-line and environment-variable macros and TOOLS.INI information. They do not inherit makefile-defined inference rules or **.SUFFIXES** and **.PRECIOUS** specifications. To pass macros to a recursive NMAKE session, either set an environment variable with SET before the recursive call, or define a macro in the command for the recursive call, or define a macro in TOOLS.INI.

Macro	Definition
MAKE	Command used originally to invoke NMAKE.
MAKEDIR	Current directory when NMAKE was invoked.
MAKEFLAGS	Options currently in effect. Use as /$(MAKEFLAGS).

Command Macros and Options Macros

Command macros are predefined for Microsoft products. Options macros represent options to these products and are undefined by default. Both are used in predefined inference rules and can be used in description blocks or user-defined inference rules. Command macros can be redefined to represent part or all of a command line, including options. Options macros generate a null string if left undefined.

Microsoft Product	Command Macro	Defined As	Options Macro
Macro Assembler	**AS**	ml	**AFLAGS**
Basic Compiler	**BC**	bc	**BFLAGS**
C Compiler	**CC**	cl	**CFLAGS**
COBOL Compiler	**COBOL**	cobol	**COBFLAGS**
C++ Compiler	**CPP**	cl	**CPPFLAGS**
C++ Compiler	**CXX**	cl	**CXXFLAGS**
FORTRAN Compiler	**FOR**	fl	**FFLAGS**
Pascal Compiler	**PASCAL**	pl	**PFLAGS**
Resource Compiler	**RC**	rc	**RFLAGS**

Environment-Variable Macros

NMAKE inherits macro definitions for environment variables that exist before the start of the session. If a variable was set in the operating-system environment, it is available as an NMAKE macro. The inherited names are converted to uppercase. Inheritance occurs before preprocessing. Use the /E option to cause macros inherited from environment variables to override any macros with the same name in the makefile.

Environment-variable macros can be redefined in the session, and this changes the corresponding environment variable. You can also change environment variables with the SET command. Using the SET command to change an environment variable in a session does not change the corresponding macro, however.

For example:

```
PATH=$(PATH);\nonesuch

all:
    echo %PATH%
```

In this example, changing PATH changes the corresponding environment variable PATH; it appends \nonesuch to your path.

If an environment variable is defined as a string that would be syntactically incorrect in a makefile, no macro is created and no warning is generated. If a variable's value contains a dollar sign ($), NMAKE interprets it as the beginning of a macro invocation. Using the macro can cause unexpected behavior.

Inference Rules

Inference rules supply commands to update targets and to infer dependents for targets. Extensions in an inference rule match a single target and dependent that have the same base name. Inference rules are user-defined or predefined; predefined rules can be redefined.

If an out-of-date dependency has no commands, and if **.SUFFIXES** contains the dependent's extension, NMAKE uses a rule whose extensions match the target and an existing file in the current or specified directory. If more than one rule matches existing files, the **.SUFFIXES** list determines which to use; list priority descends from left to right. If a dependent file does not exist and is not listed as a target in another description block, an inference rule can create the missing dependent from another file with the same base name. If a description block's target has no dependents or commands, an inference rule can update the target. Inference rules can build a command-line target even if no description block exists. NMAKE may invoke a rule for an inferred dependent even if an explicit dependent is specified.

Defining a Rule

To define an inference rule, use the following syntax:

.fromext.toext:
    commands

The *fromext* represents the extension of a dependent file, and *toext* represents the extension of a target file. Extensions are not case sensitive. Macros can be invoked to represent *fromext* and *toext*; the macros are expanded during preprocessing. The period (.) preceding *fromext* must appear at the beginning of the line. The colon (:) is preceded by zero or more spaces or tabs. It can be followed only by spaces or tabs, a semicolon (;) to specify a command, a number sign (#) to specify a comment, or a newline character. No other spaces are allowed. Commands are specified as in description blocks.

Search Paths in Rules

An inference rule that specifies paths has the following syntax:

{*frompath*}*.fromext*{*topath*}*.toext*:
    commands

An inference rule applies to a dependency only if paths specified in the dependency exactly match the inference-rule paths. Specify the dependent's directory in *frompath* and the target's directory in *topath*; no spaces are allowed. Specify only one path for each extension. A path on one extension requires a path on the other. To specify the current directory, use either a period (.) or empty braces ({ }). Macros can represent *frompath* and *topath*; they are invoked during preprocessing.

Predefined Rules

Predefined inference rules use NMAKE-supplied command and option macros.

Rule	Command	Default Action
.asm.exe	$(AS) $(AFLAGS) $*.asm	ml $*.asm
.asm.obj	$(AS) $(AFLAGS) /c $*.asm	ml /c $*.asm
.c.exe	$(CC) $(CFLAGS) $*.c	cl $*.c
.c.obj	$(CC) $(CFLAGS) /c $*.c	cl /c $*.c
.cpp.exe	$(CPP) $(CPPFLAGS) $*.cpp	cl $*.cpp
.cpp.obj	$(CPP) $(CPPFLAGS) /c $*.cpp	cl /c $*.cpp
.cxx.exe	$(CXX) $(CXXFLAGS) $*.cxx	cl $*.cxx
.cxx.obj	$(CXX) $(CXXFLAGS) /c $*.cxx	cl /c $*.cxx
.bas.obj	$(BC) $(BFLAGS) $*.bas;	bc $*.bas;
.cbl.exe	$(COBOL) $(COBFLAGS) $*.cbl, $*.exe;	cobol $*.cbl, $*.exe;
.cbl.obj	$(COBOL) $(COBFLAGS) $*.cbl;	cobol $*.cbl;
.f.exe	$(FOR) $(FFLAGS) $*.f	fl $*.f
.f.obj	$(FOR) /c $(FFLAGS) $*.f	fl /c $*.f
.f90.exe	$(FOR) $(FFLAGS) $*.f90	fl $*.f90
.f90.obj	$(FOR) /c $(FFLAGS) $*.f90	fl /c $*.f90
.for.exe	$(FOR) $(FFLAGS) $*.for	fl $*.for
.for.obj	$(FOR) /c $(FFLAGS) $*.for	fl /c $*.for
.pas.exe	$(PASCAL) $(PFLAGS) $*.pas	pl $*.pas
.pas.obj	$(PASCAL) /c $(PFLAGS) $*.pas	pl /c $*.pas
.rc.res	$(RC) $(RFLAGS) /r $*	rc /r $*

Inferred Dependents and Rules

NMAKE assumes an inferred dependent for a target if an applicable inference rule exists. A rule applies if:

- *toext* matches the target's extension.
- *fromext* matches the extension of a file that has the target's base name and that exists in the current or specified directory.
- *fromext* is in **.SUFFIXES**; no other *fromext* in a matching rule has a higher **.SUFFIXES** priority.
- No explicit dependent has a higher **.SUFFIXES** priority.

Inferred dependents can cause unexpected side effects. If the target's description block contains commands, NMAKE executes those commands instead of the commands in the rule.

Precedence in Inference Rules

If an inference rule is multiply defined, NMAKE uses the highest-precedence definition. The following list shows the order of precedence from highest to lowest:

1. An inference rule defined in a makefile; later definitions have precedence.

2. An inference rule defined in TOOLS.INI; later definitions have precedence.

3. A predefined inference rule.

Dot Directives

Specify dot directives outside a description block, at the start of a line. Dot directives begin with a period (.) and are followed by a colon (:). Spaces and tabs are allowed. Dot directive names are case sensitive and are uppercase.

Directive	Action
.IGNORE :	Ignores nonzero exit codes returned by commands, from the place it is specified to the end of the makefile. By default, NMAKE halts if a command returns a nonzero exit code. To restore error checking, use **!CMDSWITCHES**. To ignore the exit code for a single command, use the dash (–) modifier. To ignore exit codes for an entire file, use /I.
.PRECIOUS : *targets*	Preserves *targets* on disk if the commands to update them are halted; has no effect if a command handles an interrupt by deleting the file. Separate the target names with one or more spaces or tabs. By default, NMAKE deletes a target if a build is interrupted by CTRL+C or CTRL+BREAK. Each use of **.PRECIOUS** applies to the entire makefile; multiple specifications are cumulative.
.SILENT :	Suppresses display of executed commands, from the place it is specified to the end of the makefile. By default, NMAKE displays the commands it invokes. To restore echoing, use **!CMDSWITCHES**. To suppress echoing of a single command, use the **@** modifier. To suppress echoing for an entire file, use /S.
.SUFFIXES : *list*	Lists extensions for inference-rule matching; predefined as: .exe .obj .asm .c .cpp .cxx .bas .cbl .for .pas .res .rc

To change the **.SUFFIXES** list order or to specify a new list, clear the list and specify a new setting. To clear the list, specify no extensions after the colon:

```
.SUFFIXES :
```

To add additional suffixes to the end of the list, specify

```
.SUFFIXES : suffixlist
```

where *suffixlist* is a list of the additional suffixes, separated by one or more spaces or tabs. To see the current setting of **.SUFFIXES**, run NMAKE with /P.

Makefile Preprocessing

You can control the NMAKE session by using preprocessing directives and expressions. Preprocessing instructions can be placed in the makefile or in TOOLS.INI. Using directives, you can conditionally process your makefile, display error messages, include other makefiles, undefine a macro, and turn certain options on or off.

Makefile Preprocessing Directives

Preprocessing directives are not case sensitive. The initial exclamation point (!) must appear at the beginning of the line. Zero or more spaces or tabs can appear after the exclamation point, for indentation.

!CMDSWITCHES {+|−}*option*... Turns each *option* listed on or off. Spaces or tabs must appear before the + or − operator; none can appear between the operator and the option letters. Letters are not case sensitive and are specified without a slash (/). To turn some options on and others off, use separate specifications of **!CMDSWITCHES**.

Only /D, /I, /N, and /S can be used in a makefile. In TOOLS.INI, all options are allowed except /F, /HELP, /NOLOGO, /X, and /?. Changes specified in a description block do not take effect until the next description block. This directive updates **MAKEFLAGS**; changes are inherited during recursion if **MAKEFLAGS** is specified.

!ERROR *text* Displays *text* in error U1050, then halts NMAKE, even if /K, /I, **.IGNORE**, **!CMDSWITCHES**, or the dash (−) command modifier is used. Spaces or tabs before *text* are ignored.

!MESSAGE *text* Displays *text* to standard output. Spaces or tabs before *text* are ignored.

!INCLUDE [<]*filename*[>] Reads *filename* as a makefile, then continues with the current makefile. NMAKE searches for *filename* first in the specified or current directory, then recursively through directories of any parent makefiles, then, if *filename* is enclosed by angle brackets (< >), in directories specified by the **INCLUDE** macro, which is initially set to the INCLUDE environment variable. Useful to pass **.SUFFIXES** settings, **.PRECIOUS**, and inference rules to recursive makefiles.

!IF *constantexpression* Processes statements between **!IF** and the next **!ELSE** or **!ENDIF** if *constantexpression* evaluates to a nonzero value.

!IFDEF *macroname* Processes statements between **!IFDEF** and the next **!ELSE** or **!ENDIF** if *macroname* is defined. A null macro is considered to be defined.

!IFNDEF *macroname* Processes statements between **!IFNDEF** and the next **!ELSE** or **!ENDIF** if *macroname* is not defined.

!ELSE[IF *constantexpression*|**IFDEF** *macroname*|**IFNDEF** *macroname*] Processes statements between **!ELSE** and the next **!ENDIF** if the prior **!IF**, **!IFDEF**, or **!IFNDEF** statement evaluated to zero. The optional keywords give further control of preprocessing.

!ELSEIF Synonym for **!ELSE IF**.

!ELSEIFDEF Synonym for **!ELSE IFDEF**.

!ELSEIFNDEF Synonym for **!ELSE IFNDEF**.

!ENDIF Marks the end of an **!IF**, **!IFDEF**, or **!IFNDEF** block. Any text after **!ENDIF** on the same line is ignored.

!UNDEF *macroname* Undefines *macroname*.

Expressions in Makefile Preprocessing

The **!IF** or **!ELSE IF** *constantexpression* consists of integer constants (in decimal or C-language notation), string constants, or commands. Use parentheses to group expressions. Expressions use C-style signed long integer arithmetic; numbers are in 32-bit two's-complement form in the range −2147483648 to 2147483647.

Expressions can use operators that act on constant values, exit codes from commands, strings, macros, and file-system paths.

Makefile Preprocessing Operators

The **DEFINED** operator is a logical operator that acts on a macro name. The expression **DEFINED** (*macroname*) is true if *macroname* is defined. **DEFINED** in combination with **!IF** or **!ELSE IF** is equivalent to **!IFDEF** or **!ELSE IFDEF**. However, unlike these directives, **DEFINED** can be used in complex expressions using binary logical operators.

The **EXIST** operator is a logical operator that acts on a file-system path. **EXIST** (*path*) is true if *path* exists. The result from **EXIST** can be used in binary expressions. If *path* contains spaces, enclose it in double quotation marks.

Integer constants can use the unary operators for numerical negation (−), one's complement (~), and logical negation (!).

Constant expressions can use the following binary operators

Operator	Description	Operator	Description
+	Addition	||	Logical OR
–	Subtraction	<<	Left shift
*	Multiplication	>>	Right shift
/	Division	==	Equality
%	Modulus	!=	Inequality
&	Bitwise AND	<	Less than
|	Bitwise OR	>	Greater than
^	Bitwise XOR	<=	Less than or equal to
&&	Logical AND	>=	Greater than or equal to

To compare two strings, use the equality (==) operator and the inequality (!=) operator. Enclose strings in double quotation marks.

Executing a Program in Preprocessing

To use a command's exit code during preprocessing, specify the command, with any arguments, within brackets ([ ]). Any macros are expanded before the command is executed. NMAKE replaces the command specification with the command's exit code, which can be used in an expression to control preprocessing.

Appendixes

Decorated Names

Functions in C and C++ programs are known internally by their decorated names. A decorated name is a string created by the compiler during compilation of the function definition or prototype.

A decorated name is sometimes required when you specify a function name to LINK or other tools. For details about the situations that require decorated names, consult the documentation for the tool you are using.

Note The decorated naming convention for pointers to member functions changed in Visual C++ version 4.0. C++ libraries created with Visual C++ version 2.0 should be recompiled to link properly with source files compiled with Visual C++ version 4.0.

Using Decorated Names

In most circumstances, you do not need to know the decorated name of a function. LINK and other tools can usually handle the name in its undecorated form.

However, certain situations require that you specify the name in its decorated form. You must specify the decorated name of C++ functions that are overloaded and special member functions, such as constructor and destructor functions, in order for LINK and other tools to be able to match the name. You must also use decorated names in assembly source files that reference a C or C++ function name.

Warning If you change the function name, class, calling convention, return type, or any parameter, the decorated name is no longer valid. You must get the new version of the function name and use it everywhere the decorated name is specified.

Format of a C++ Decorated Name

A decorated name for a C++ function contains the following information:

- The function name.
- The class that the function is a member of, if it is a member function. This may include the class that encloses the function's class, and so on.

- The namespace the function belongs to (if it is part of a namespace).
- The types of the function's parameters.
- The calling convention.
- The return type of the function.

The function and class names are encoded in the decorated name. The rest of the decorated name is a code that has internal meaning only for the compiler and the linker. The following are examples of undecorated and decorated C++ names.

Undecorated Name	Decorated Name
`int a(char){int i=3;return i;};`	`?a@@YAHD@Z`
`void __stdcall b::c(float){};`	`?c@b@@AAGXM@Z`

Format of a C Decorated Name

The form of decoration for a C function depends on the calling convention used in its declaration, as shown below.

Calling Convention	Decoration
__cdecl (the default)	Leading underscore (_)
__stdcall	Leading underscore (_) and a trailing at sign (@) followed by a number representing the number of bytes in the parameter list
__fastcall	Same as __stdcall, but prepended by an at sign instead of an underscore

Viewing Decorated Names

You can get the decorated form of a function name after you compile the source file that contains the function definition or prototype. To examine decorated names in your program, you can do one of the following:

- Use a listing
- Use the DUMPBIN tool

Using a Listing to View Decorated Names

To get the decorated form of a function using a compiler listing, do the following:

1. Generate a listing by compiling the source file that contains the function definition or prototype with the Listing File Type (/FA[cls]) compiler option (described in Chapter 20) set to one of the following: Assembly with Machine Code; Assembly with Source Code; Assembly, Machine Code, or Source.

2. Find the line that contains the undecorated function definition in the resulting listing.

3. Examine the previous line. The label for the PROC NEAR command is the decorated form of the function name.

Using DUMPBIN to View Decorated Names

To get the decorated form of a function using DUMPBIN (see Chapter 30, "DUMPBIN Reference"), run DUMPBIN on the .OBJ or .LIB file using the /SYMBOLS option. Find the undecorated function definition in the output. The undecorated name is followed by the decorated name, each enclosed in parentheses.

Initializing and Configuring Microsoft Developer Studio

Microsoft Developer Studio stores information about initialization and configuration within the Registry. Most of the settings in the Registry are read-write: Developer Studio reads them at startup and writes them at the end of the session if they have changed. Other settings are read-only: Developer Studio reads them at startup but never writes them. The only way that you can change this read-only information is to use the Registry editor. For Windows NT, the Registry editor is REGEDT32.EXE, and for Windows 95, the Registry editor is REGEDIT.EXE.

The Registry is divided into "keys," which are represented as folders in the Registry editor. Each key contains one or more entries, consisting of a value and a string or number, which are shown in the right pane of the Registry editor. For example, the Dialog Editor key in the Registry contains information about the startup settings for Grid and GridSize.

Caution Microsoft Developer Studio and other applications use Registry information to control each application's behavior. If the expected Registry information is missing or incorrect, the application's behavior may be unpredictable. When you modify or add Registry keys, be sure to enter the key and its values correctly.

You can customize Developer Studio by modifying existing Registry information and adding various device descriptions and default settings.

▶ **To modify Registry information**

1 From the MS-DOS prompt, run REGEDIT.EXE (for Windows 95) or REGEDT32.EXE (for Windows NT).

–or–

Double-click the Registry icon in the system tools program group.

The Registry editor appears.

Note You may need to add the Registry icon to your system tools program group.

2 Select the folder with the Registry information you want to modify.

3 To open a Registry key for editing, double-click the Registry key.

−or−

From the Edit menu, choose Modify, Delete, or New.

If you select New, you also select the type of new key: Key, String Value, Binary Value, or DWORD Value.

4 Type the Value Name, Value Data, and Base (either hexadecimal or decimal).

5 Choose OK.

For more information on defining Registry keys, see the following examples:

- Setting Default Dialog Box Buttons
- Setting User Interface Fonts
- Setting the Default Magnification Factor
- Describing Mouse Pointer Devices
- Describing Icon Devices

Setting Default Dialog Box Buttons

Key Name: HKEY_CURRENT_USER\Software\Microsoft\Developer\Dialog Editor

Value Name: InitialButtons

Data Type: **REG_DWORD**

Data: *integer*

This key determines if a new dialog box template is created with the OK and Cancel buttons, where:

- If *integer* is 0, the dialog box templates are blank.
- If *integer* is 1, the dialog box templates are created with the OK and Cancel buttons.

Setting User Interface Fonts

Key Name: HKEY_CURRENT_USER\Software\Microsoft\Developer\Fonts

Value Name: [Normal][Small][Fixed]

Data Type: **REG_STRING**

Data: *font-name,size*[pt]

This key determines the fonts used by various user interface elements of the system, where:

- *font-name* specifies the actual font name.

- *size* defines the font size in pixels or points.
- [**pt**] indicates point values. If this field is blank, pixel values are assumed.

The Normal font is used by the status bar, dialog boxes, and browse windows. The Small font is used by toolbars and other docking windows for their captions. The Fixed font is used by the hexadecimal (raw data) editor.

The default fonts listed below are for the U.S. product running on a single-byte character-set system. They are built into the product and do not normally appear in the Registry.

```
Normal:REG_STRING:MS Sans Serif,8pt
Small:REG_STRING:SmallFonts,-9
Fixed:REG_STRING:Courier,14
```

Negative numbers specify the character height, and positive numbers specify the cell height. A font's character height is the cell height minus any internal leading.

Setting the Default Magnification Factor

Key Name: HKEY_CURRENT_USER\Software\Microsoft\Developer\Graphics Editor

Value Name: DefaultZoom

Data Type: **REG_DWORD**

Data: *range*

Sets the default value for the ratio of magnified and actual-size views in the graphic editor window, where:

- *range* is 2 through 10 (if this entry does not appear in the Registry, the default value of 6 is used).

Describing Mouse Pointer Devices

Key Name: HKEY_CURRENT_USER\Software\Microsoft\Developer\Mouse Pointer Devices

Value Name: *device-name*

Data Type: **REG_SZ**

Data: *number-of-colors,width,height*

Specifies the names of display devices and the attributes of their corresponding mouse pointer images, where:

- *device-name* is the name of the new mouse pointer device that appears in the New Device Image dialog box when you add a mouse pointer image.

- *number-of-colors* specifies the number of colors supported by the device. The number of colors entry must be 2 or 16.

- *width* is the image width in pixels.

- *height* is the image height in pixels.

Describing Icon Devices

Key Name: HKEY_CURRENT_USER\Software\Microsoft\Developer\Icon Devices

Value Name: *device-name*

Data Type: **REG_SZ**

Data: *number-of-colors,width,height*

Specifies the names of display devices and the attributes of their corresponding icon images, where:

- *device-name* is the name of the new icon device that appears in the New Device Image dialog box when you add an icon image.

- *number-of-colors* specifies the number of colors supported by the device. The number of colors entry must be 2 or 16.

- *width* is the image width in pixels.

- *height* is the image height in pixels.

DDESpy Reference

You can use DDESpy (DDESPY.EXE) to monitor dynamic data exchange (DDE) activity in the Microsoft Windows NT operating system. To start DDESpy, double-click its icon in the Microsoft Visual C++ 4.0 program group.

Note You may need to add the DDESpy icon to the Microsoft Visual C++ 4.0 program group.

Because DDE is a cooperative activity, DDE-monitoring applications must follow certain guidelines for your system to operate properly while it is in use.

The following topics are covered:

- Selecting the Output
- Using the Monitor Menu
- Tracking Options

Selecting the Output

DDESpy can display DDE information in a window or on your debugging terminal, or it can save the displayed information in a file for later use.

You use the Output menu to select where DDESpy sends output. If you choose the File command, you can specify the name of an output file, or choose the No File button. After you have chosen the File command, DDESpy asks you for an output filename every time you restart it. This prompt can be turned off by reopening the File dialog box and choosing the No File button.

From the Output menu, you can also choose to send your output to either a debug terminal or to the DDESpy window. If you choose a window, you can clear the display window using the Clear Screen command. You can use the Mark command to add marker text to the display—for example, before a DDE event to make it easier to find the event in the output file.

Output Menu Command	Description
File	Specifies the name of an output file.
Debug Terminal	Sends your output to a debug terminal.
Screen	Sends your output to a DDESpy window.
Clear Screen	Clears the display window.
Mark	Marks the text.

Using the Monitor Menu

You use the Monitor menu to specify one or more types of DDE information that DDESpy displays. The following information can be displayed:

- String-Handle Data
- Sent DDE Messages
- Posted DDE Messages
- Callbacks
- Errors
- Filters

The DDE protocol passes information by using shared memory. The contents of the shared memory depend on the type of DDE transaction. Several structures have been defined to allow applications using DDE to access the information in shared memory. DDESpy displays the contents of the appropriate structure for the DDE activity being monitored.

String-Handle Data

The DDE protocol uses the **MONHSZSTRUCT** structure to pass string-handle data. DDESpy displays the following information from this structure:

- Task (application instance)
- Time, in milliseconds, since you started Windows
- Activity type (create, destroy, or increment)
- String handle
- String contents

The following example shows a typical DDESpy display of string-handle data:

```
Task:0x94f, Time:519700, String Handle Created: c4a4(this is a test)
Task:0x94f, Time:526126, String Handle Created: c4aa(another test)
```

Sent DDE Messages

The DDE protocol uses the **MONMSGSTRUCT** structure to post DDE messages. DDESpy displays the following information from this structure:

- Task
- Time
- Handle of receiving window
- Transaction type (sent)
- Message type
- Handle of sending application
- Other message-specific information

The following example shows a typical DDESpy display of DDE message activity:

```
Task:0x8df Time:642402 hwndTo=0x38dc Message(Sent)=Initiate:
        hwndFrom=9224, App=0xc35d("Server")
        Topic=*
Task:0x94f Time:642457 hwndTo=0x2408 Message(Sent)=Ack:
        hwndFrom=9396, App=0xc35d("Server")status=c35d(fAck
        fBusy )
        Topic=Item=0xc361("System")
```

Posted DDE Messages

The DDE protocol uses the **MONMSGSTRUCT** structure to post DDE messages. The information displayed for posted DDE messages is similar to the information displayed for sent DDE messages. DDESpy displays the following information from this structure:

- Task
- Time
- Handle of receiving window
- Transaction type (posted)
- Message type
- Handle of sending application
- Other message-specific information

Callbacks

The DDE protocol uses the **MONCBSTRUCT** structure to pass information to application callback functions. DDESpy displays the following information from this structure:

- Task

- Time
- Transaction type
- Exchanged-data format (if any)
- Conversation handle
- String handles and their referenced strings
- Transaction-specific data

The following example shows a typical DDESpy display of callback activity:

```
Task:0x8df Time:2882628 Callback:
        Type=Advstart, fmt=0x1("CF_TEXT"), hConv=0xc24b4,
        hsz1=0xc361("System") hsz2=0xc4df("xxcall"), hData=0x0,
        lData1=0x83f0000, lData2=0x0
        return=0x0
```

Errors

When an error occurs during a DDE transaction, the DDE protocol places the error value and associated information in a **MONERRSTRUCT** structure. DDESpy uses this structure to display the following information about the error:

- Task (the handle of the application that caused the error)
- Time
- Error value and name

Filters

You can use the Message Filters and Callback Filters options to choose the types of DDE messages and callbacks to monitor.

Tracking Options

DDESpy can also display information about aspects of DDE communication in your Windows system:

- String handles
- Conversations
- Links
- Services

You can use the Track menu to specify which DDE activity DDESpy tracks. When you choose a command from the Track menu, DDESpy creates a separate window for the display of information in conjunction with the DDE functions. For each window created, DDESpy updates the displayed information as DDE activity occurs. Events that occurred prior to creation of the tracking window are not displayed in the tracking window.

DDESpy can sort the displayed information in the tracking window. If you select the heading for a particular column in the tracking window, DDESpy sorts the displayed information based on the column you select. This feature can be useful if you are searching for a particular event or handle.

Tracking String Handles

Windows maintains a system-wide string table containing the string, string handle, and string usage count that applications use in DDE transactions.

▶ **To display the system string table**

- From the Track menu, choose the String Handles command.

Tracking Conversations

The Conversations window shows the service name, current topic, and server and client handles for each active conversation.

▶ **To display all active DDE conversations in your Windows system**

- From the Track menu, choose the Conversations command.

Tracking Links

The Links window shows the server name, topic, item format, transaction type, client handle, and server handle for every active advise loop in your Windows system.

▶ **To display all active DDE advise loops**

- From the Track menu, choose the Links command.

Tracking Services

Server applications use the **DdeNameService** function to register with the DDE protocol. When the DDE protocol receives the **DdeNameService** function call, it adds the server name and an instance-specific name to a list of registered servers.

▶ **To display a list of registered servers**

- From the Track menu, choose the Services command.

PView Reference

With the PView process viewer (PVIEW.EXE), you can examine and modify many characteristics of the processes and threads running on your system. PView can help you answer questions such as these:

- How much memory does the program allocate at various points in its execution, and how much memory is being paged out?

- Which processes and threads are using the most CPU time?

- How does the program run at different system priorities?

- What happens if a thread or process stops responding to Dynamic Data Exchange (DDE), OLE, or pipe input/output (I/O)?

- What percentage of time is spent running application program interface (API) calls?

 Warning   With PView, you can modify the status of processes running on your system. As a result, by using PView, you can stop processes and potentially halt the entire system. Make sure you save edited files before running PView.

The following topics are covered:

- Opening PView
- Process Selection
- Process Memory Used
- Priority (base process)
- Thread Priority
- Thread Selection
- Thread Information
- Memory Details Dialog Box

Opening PView

To start PView, double-click its icon in the Microsoft Visual C++ 4.0 program group. PView opens by displaying the main Process Viewer dialog box.

Note You may need to add the PView icon to the Microsoft Visual C++ 4.0 program group.

The following buttons control PView actions.

Button	Description
Exit	Closes PView.
Memory Details	Opens the Memory Details dialog box.
Kill Process	Removes the highlighted process from the system. This is different from choosing Close from the System menu, because the process is not informed of the shutdown (with **WM_DESTROY**) before it is stopped.
Refresh	Updates information in the Process Viewer dialog box and the Memory Details dialog box.
Connect	Displays information about the computer specified in the Computer text box. The Computer text box should contain the network name of the computer you wish to view. Your ability to connect to a remote system may be affected by security on the target machine.

The Process Viewer dialog box displays information on active processes and threads. You can select, modify, and view the behavior of processes and threads with the following PView features:

- Process Selection
- Process Memory Used
- Priority
- Thread Priority
- Thread Selection
- Thread Information

Process Selection

The Process selection list box displays information on the accessible processes running on the system. From this list, you can select a process for viewing. All subsequent PView information and controls derive from the process selected in this list.

Note Because Windows NT is a secure operating system, you may not be able to view or alter attributes of some programs running on the system. See your Windows NT user's guide for more information on security.

The Process selection list box contains the following fields.

Field	Description
Process	Name of the process on this line (usually an .EXE filename).
Processor Time	Amount of CPU time that this process has used.
Privileged	Percentage of CPU time that was spent executing privileged code (code in the Windows NT Executive).
User	Percentage of CPU time that was spent executing user code. This time includes time running protected subsystem code.

Process Memory Used

The Process Memory Used box displays information on the memory usage of the process selected in the Process selection list box.

Field	Description
Working Set	Average amount of physical memory used by the process. The longer a process has been running, the more accurate this value is.
Heap Usage	Current total heap being used by the process. Heap space is taken by dynamically allocated data, including memory reserved by **malloc**, **new**, **LocalAlloc**, **HeapAlloc**, **VirtualAlloc**, and **GlobalAlloc**.

Priority

With the Priority options box, you can change the base priority of the process highlighted in the Process selection list box. This priority determines the activity of all threads of the selected process.

Field	Description
Very High	Maximum priority. CPU time is split between this and other Very High priority processes. Lower priority processes execute only when all Very High priority processes are blocked.
Normal	Standard priority group, also known as foreground. Most applications run with normal priority.
Idle	Lowest priority group, also known as background. Processes with this priority execute only when the system has no higher-priority processes that need CPU time. Screen savers run at this priority.

Thread Priority

The Thread Priority box shows the base priority of the thread selected in the Thread selection list box. This is not an absolute priority, but is a range of priorities that can be assigned by the operating system to the selected thread.

Priority	Description
Highest	Highest priority level allowed by the process priority.
Above Normal	Slightly elevated priority.
Normal	Standard priority level for the given process priority.
Below Normal	Reduced priority.
Idle	No CPU time will be spent on this thread unless all other threads are blocked.

Thread Selection

The Thread selection list box displays statistics for threads of the process selected in the Process selection list box so you can select a thread for further operations.

Field	Description
Thread(s)	Thread ID number. This is the handle returned by **CreateThread**.
Processor Time	Amount of time that this instance of the thread has been running.
Privileged	Percentage of CPU time that was spent executing privileged code (code in the Windows NT Executive).
User	Percentage of CPU time that was spent executing user code. This time includes time running protected subsystem code.

Thread Information

The Thread Information box displays execution information about the thread selected in the Thread selection list box.

Field	Description
User PC Value	Value of the instruction pointer for this thread.
Start Address	Address of the entry point of this thread. This information is useful for debugging.
Context Switches	Number of times that this thread has received CPU attention.
Dynamic Priority	Current dynamic thread priority. This number is determined by many factors, including user activity.

Memory Details Dialog Box

The Memory Details dialog box gives information on the process selected in the Process selection list box.

▶ **To view the Memory Details dialog box**

- Choose Memory Details.

  −or−

  Double-click on a process in the Process selection list box.

▶ **To update the information in the Memory Details dialog box**

- Return to the Process Viewer dialog box and choose Refresh.

The Memory Details dialog box consists of the following buttons and groups.

Buttons and Groups	Description	
OK	Returns to the Process Viewer dialog box.	
Process	Displays name and process ID of the process selected in the Process selection box of the Process Viewer dialog box.	
User Address Space for	Select a specific .EXE or .DLL file or select Total Image Commit to display the following statistics for all components of the selected process:	
	Total	Sum of all user address space.
	Inaccessible	Address space that cannot be accessed. This includes memory reserved by **VirtualAlloc**.
	Read Only	Read-only data and code.
	Writeable	Total data address space that can be written to.
	Writeable (Not Written)	Data address space that can be written to, but has not been.
	Executable	Code in selected .EXEs and .DLLs.
Mapped Commit	Displays the following statistics for Mapped Commit memory:	
	Total	Sum of all mapped address space.
	Inaccessible	Address space that cannot be accessed. This includes memory reserved by **VirtualAlloc**.
	Read Only	Read-only data and code.
	Writeable	Total data address space that can be written to.
	Writeable (Not Written)	Data address space that can be written to, but has not been.
	Executable	Code in selected .EXEs and .DLLs.

Buttons and Groups	Description	
Private Commit	Displays the following statistics for Private Commit memory:	
	Total	Sum of all private address space.
	Inaccessible	Address space that cannot be accessed. This includes memory reserved by **VirtualAlloc**.
	Read Only	Read-only data and code.
	Writeable	Total data address space that can be written to.
	Writeable (Not Written)	Data address space that can be written to, but has not been.
	Executable	Code in selected .EXEs and .DLLs.
Virtual Memory Counts	Displays the following statistics on Virtual Memory usage:	
	Working Set	Average amount of virtual memory used by the process. The longer a process has been running, the more accurate this value is.
	Peak Working Set	Maximum value attained by the Working Set described above.
	Private Pages	Number of pages marked as private.
	Virtual Size	Current size of virtual memory for this process.
	Peak Virtual Size	Maximum size of virtual memory for this process.
	Fault Count	Number of page faults. Each page fault represents an attempt to access memory at an address that was not in physical memory.

ZoomIn Reference

You can use the ZoomIn utility (ZOOMIN.EXE) to capture and enlarge an area of the Windows desktop.

▶ **To use ZoomIn**

1 Double-click the ZoomIn icon in the Microsoft Visual C++ 4.0 program group.

Note You may need to add the ZoomIn icon to the Microsoft Visual C++ 4.0 program group.

2 Click within the ZoomIn window's client area and drag the rectangle over the target area you want to enlarge.

This target area can be anywhere in the Windows graphical desktop area. The area over which you center the ZoomIn rectangle appears in the ZoomIn window's client area.

3 Release the mouse button when the desired target area is visible in the ZoomIn window.

To enlarge the image, use the scroll bar to scroll down. To reduce the image to its original size, use the scroll bar to scroll up. Each successive click on the scroll bar enlarges or shrinks the image.

ZoomIn Menus

Edit Menu

You can use the Edit menu to copy to the clipboard and update the ZoomIn window image.

Menu Command	Description
Copy	Copies the contents of the ZoomIn window to the Clipboard.
Refresh	Updates the image in the ZoomIn window. This update is visible only if the Windows desktop target area has changed since it was last captured by ZoomIn.

Options Menu

You can use the Options menu to specify the update interval.

Menu Command	Description
Refresh Rate	Enables the automatic update of the ZoomIn window. This dialog box also allows you to specify, in increments of one-tenth of a second, the automatic update interval.

Help Menu

You can use the Help menu to display information about ZoomIn.

Menu Command	Description
About	Displays copyright and version information about ZoomIn.

WinDiff Reference

The WinDiff utility (WINDIFF.EXE) graphically compares the contents of two files or two directories. With WinDiff, you can compare and modify the contents of files and directories using a graphical Windows interface.

▶ **To start WinDiff**

Double-click the WinDiff icon in the Microsoft Visual C++ 4.0 program group.

−or−

Use the WinDiff command line.

Note   You may need to add the WinDiff icon to the Microsoft Visual C++ 4.0 program group.

WinDiff Command Line

The full WinDiff command-line syntax is:

WINDIFF *path1* [*path2*] [-s [*options*] *savefile*]

Parameters

path1   Compares files in *path1* with files in current directory.

path1 path2   Compares files in *path1* with files in *path2*.

options   Can be any combination of the following options:

- /*s*: Compares files that are the same in both paths.
- /*l*: Compares only files in the first (left) path.
- /*r*: Compares only files in the second (right) path.
- /*d:* Compares two different files in both paths.

savefile   Name of text file to which comparison results are written.

Using the Expand/Outline Button

You can display the filenames or the expanded contents of the selected files. When you choose the Expand button, the contents of the files are expanded and the button label then changes to Outline. When you choose the Outline button, only the filenames are displayed. Files with the same name but different contents are displayed in red text. Identical files are displayed in black text.

▶ To display the expanded contents of the files

1 Select the files you want to compare.

2 From the Expand menu, choose Both Files.

3 From the View menu, choose Expand.

–or–

Choose the Expand button.

WinDiff Colors

File contents are displayed in three background colors.

Background Color	Description
Red	Indicates different text from the first (left) file.
Yellow	Indicates different text from the second (right) file.
White	Indicates identical text from both files.

WinDiff Menus

File Menu

You can use the File menu to define selection, naming, and printing options.

Menu Command	Description
Compare Files	Displays the File Open dialog box, in which you can enter the names of two files to compare.
Compare Directories	Displays the Select Directories dialog box, in which you can enter the names of two directories to compare.
Abort	Terminates a file-scanning operation. This menu selection is unavailable until a scanning operation is initiated.
Save File List	Displays the Save File List dialog box, in which you can specify the output file where the comparison results are to be written.
Copy Files	Displays the Copy Files dialog box, in which you can specify files to be copied from one directory to another.

Menu Command	Description
Print	Prints the comparison results.
Exit	Terminates WinDiff.

Edit Menu

You can use the Edit menu to designate the text editor you want to use and to specify which files to display for editing.

Menu Command	Description
Edit Left File	Displays the contents of the first (left) file using the default Notepad editor.
Edit Right File	Displays the contents of the second (right) file using the default Notepad editor.
Edit Composite File	Displays both files using the default Notepad editor.
Set Editor	Displays a WinDiff dialog box, in which you can specify the editor to be used for the preceding operations. By default, Notepad is used.

View Menu

You can use the View menu to compare both the content and graphical representation of two files.

Menu Command	Description
Outline	Displays only the list of filenames (equivalent to the Outline button).
Expand	Displays comparison of the contents of selected files (equivalent to the Expand button).
Picture	Displays a graphical representation of the contents of the two files.
Previous Change	Goes directly to previous area of the file that was changed (if any).
Next Change	Goes directly to next area of the file that was changed (if any).

Expand Menu

You can use the Expand menu to display changed lines in the selected file. You can also turn off the display of line numbers.

Menu Command	Description
Left File Only	Expands only the first (left) file, with changed lines colored appropriately.
Right File Only	Expands only the second (right) file, with changed lines colored appropriately.

Menu Command	Description
Both Files	Expands both files, with changed lines colored appropriately.
Left Line Numbers	Displays line numbers for the first (left) file.
Right Line Numbers	Displays line numbers for the second (right) file.
No Line Numbers	Turns off the line number display.

Options Menu

You can use the Options menu to specify file comparison criteria.

Menu Command	Description
Ignore Blanks	Ignores blank spaces in the expanded view, so that lines differing only in the amount of white space are shown as identical.
Mono Colors	Displays differences in black and white only.
Show Identical Files	In outline view, displays files that are identical.
Show Left-Only Files	In outline view, displays files that appear only in the first (left) path.
Show Right-Only Files	In outline view, displays files that appear only in the second (right) path.
Show Different Files	In outline view, displays files that are in both paths, but are different.

Mark Menu

You can use the Mark menu to mark comparison results.

Menu Command	Description
Mark File	Marks selected comparison results.
Mark Pattern	Displays the Mark Files dialog box, in which you can specify the file marking pattern.
Hide Marked Files	Hides all marked files.
Toggle Marked State	Reverses the marked status of marked and unmarked files.

Help Menu

You can use the Help menu to display information about WinDiff.

Menu Command	Description
About	Displays copyright and version information about WinDiff.

Index

X

Y

Z

Contributors to *Visual C++ User's Guide*

Robert Ackerman, Writer
Diane Berkeley, Writer
Pat Bezzio, Editor
Chris Burt, Writer
Richard Carlson, Index Editor
John Chaffins, Writer
David Adam Edelstein, Art Director
Pat Fenn, Production
Cathy Fisher, Proofreader
Barbara Haerer, Editor
Larry Happ, Proofreader
Erik Larsen, Writer
Robert Reynolds, Illustrator
Linda Robinson, Production
Terri Sharkey, Editor
Melba Wallace, Editor
Terry Ward, Writer
Edward Wright, Writer